Studia Fennica
Linguistica 11

The Finnish Literature Society (SKS) was founded in 1831 and has, from the very beginning, engaged in publishing operations. It nowadays publishes literature in the fields of ethnology and folkloristics, linguistics, literary research and cultural history.

The first volume of the Studia Fennica series appeared in 1933. Since 1992, the series has been divided into three thematic subseries: Ethnologica, Folkloristica and Linguistica. Two additional subseries were formed in 2002, Historica and Litteraria. The subseries Anthropologica was formed in 2007.

In addition to its publishing activities, the Finnish Literature Society maintains research activities and infrastructures, an archive containing folklore and literary collections, a research library and promotes Finnish literature abroad.

Minna Saarelma-Maunumaa

Edhina Ekogidho – Names as Links

The Encounter between African and European Anthroponymic Systems among the Ambo People in Namibia

Finnish Literature Society • Helsinki

Studia Fennica Linguistica 11

The publication has undergone a peer review.

VERTAISARVIOITU
KOLLEGIALT GRANSKAD
PEER-REVIEWED
www.tsv.fi/tunnus

The open access publication of this volume has received part funding via
a Jane and Aatos Erkko Foundation grant.

A digital edition of a printed book first published in 2003 by the Finnish Literature Society.
Cover Design: Timo Numminen
EPUB: Tero Salmén

ISBN 978-951-746-529-8 (Print)
ISBN 978-952-222-816-1 (PDF)
ISBN 978-952-222-820-8 (EPUB)

ISSN 0085-6835 (Studia Fennica)
ISSN 1235-1938 (Studia Fennica Linguistica)

DOI: http://dx.doi.org/10.21435/sflin.11

A free open access version of the book is available at http://dx.doi.
org/10.21435/sflin.11 or by scanning this QR code with your mobile device.

BoD – Books on Demand, Nordersted, Germany

Acknowledgements

"Edhina ekogidho", the title of this book, is a common saying among the Ambos in Namibia. The noun *edhina* means 'name' and *ekogidho* 'joining, connecting permanently together'. Hence, this expression means that personal names serve as links between people; they connect people together.

This book on Ambo personal names, which is based on my Ph.D. thesis, also connects many people together. First of all, I would like to thank the supervisor of my thesis, Professor Emeritus Eero Kiviniemi, whose inspiring lectures on Finnish onomastics made me choose anthroponymy as my field of research. It was his encouragement that made me an onomastician. My special thanks also go to my other fellow-onomasticians in Finland – Dr. Terhi Ainiala, Professor Ritva Liisa Pitkänen, and many others – for their warm support during the various stages of my studies.

I also want to express my gratitude to the Finnish Evangelical Lutheran Mission and the many Finnish missionaries who have worked in Namibia for their contribution to the development of my research interests. I would especially like to thank my Ndonga teacher Ms. Lahja Lehtonen, who checked all the translations of Ambo names presented in this thesis, as well as the other Finnish missionaries whom I interviewed for my research.

My special thanks also go to Ms. Riikka Halme at the University of Helsinki (Finland), Professor Adrian Koopman at the University of Natal in Pietermaritzburg (South Africa), and Professor Emeritus Anthony Davey in Pietermaritzburg, who all read the manuscript and gave many valuable comments on both language and content. In addition, I thank Professor Karsten Legère at Göteborg University (Sweden) and Professor S.J. (Bertie) Neethling at the University of the Western Cape (South Africa), who acted as pre-examiners of this thesis and gave constructive criticism. Professor Henry Fullenwider at the Language Centre of the University of Helsinki made the final revision of my English. The blame for any faults of fact or language remain mine, however. I also thank Mr. Timo Jokivartio who prepared the maps in this book.

Of the various institutions and people in Namibia, I must first and foremost thank the Evangelical Lutheran Church in Namibia (ELCIN) for allowing me to utilise its parish records for this research. I also wish to thank all the Namibians whom I interviewed for this study. In particular, I would like to mention the late Hans Namuhuja, who was an excellent informant on Ndonga history and culture. I also thank Mr. Petrus Mbenzi at the University of Namibia for his co-operation, as well as the Finnish missionaries in Namibia for their assistance in many practical matters during my field work.

Thanks are also due to the staff of various libraries and archives in Finland, Germany, Namibia and South Africa, e.g. the Archives of the Finnish Evangelical Lutheran Mission in Helsinki (Finland), the Archives of the United Evangelical Mission in Wuppertal (Germany), the Federal Archives in Berlin (Germany), the National Library of Namibia in Windhoek, the Auala ELCIN Library in Oniipa (Namibia) and the libraries of the UNISA (University of South Africa) and the HSRC (Human Sciences Research Centre) in Pretoria (South Africa). I am also grateful to many of my fellow-onomasticians in South Africa for their assistance in finding relevant articles and studies on African anthroponymy. Similarly, I owe thanks to the historians at the University of Joensuu (Finland) for helping me with the ELCIN parish register material.

I would also like to express my sincere gratitude to the Finnish Cultural Foundation for the financial support which made long-term research work possible, as well as the Department of Finnish at the University of Helsinki for financing one of my research trips to Namibia and for assisting me financially with the final revision of my thesis. I am also very grateful to the Finnish Literature Society for publishing my thesis.

Finally, I wish to thank my parents, Rev. Timo Saarelma and Mrs. Katri Saarelma, as well as my sister Hanna and my two brothers Tuomas and Antti, for their encouragement. Last but not least, I thank my husband Matti Maunumaa, who also helped me with all the computer problems that I faced in the course of this work.

Vantaa, 14 September, 2003

Minna Saarelma-Maunumaa

Contents

Introduction

The Aims of the Study

The general aim of this study is to analyse the changes in the personal naming system of the Ambo people in Namibia (formerly South West Africa), caused by the Christianisation and Europeanisation of the traditional Ambo culture. The process started in 1870, when the first Europeans, a group of Lutheran missionaries from Finland, settled in the Ambo area. For decades, the Finnish missionaries were practically the only Europeans living and working in this remote area. As their activities covered most of the Ambo area, their role in this process was crucial. Later, German missionaries, both Lutheran and Catholic, as well as British missionaries sent by the Anglican church, also worked in some Ambo communities and thus introduced new elements to the Ambo culture.

Another important factor in this process was colonisation. In 1884, South West Africa became a German colony. In the beginning, the Germans showed little interest in the Ambo area, which was situated on the periphery of the vast colony. However, the situation changed rapidly after the Herero and Nama wars of 1904–1907, when the Germans faced a severe lack of labour in the southern parts of the country. It was above all the migrant labour system that spread the European mode of life to the Ambo communities, and this continued under the South African regime (1915–1990). Hence, the influence of the settlers of German, British and Afrikaner origin who had Ambo employees working in their households, farms, mines, etc., was also significant in the personal naming of the Ambo people.

The adoption of Christianity, together with the spread of European cultural patterns, has led to radical changes in the Ambo naming system. In this process, many traditional naming customs have been replaced by new European and Christian ones. However, this study will show that the result of this process was not a Europeanised naming system as such, but an entirely new and dynamic system which includes elements of both African and European origin.

As is the case with most anthroponymic research, this study is interdisciplinary in nature. The main approach will be sociolinguistic, more

9

precisely: socio-onomastic. Primarily, this study represents "general onomastics", as it deals with an encounter between two naming systems and changes within a naming system on a structural level. Thus, from a general onomastic viewpoint, the purpose of this study is to analyse the impact of intercultural contact on personal names. The main questions are: What happens to one naming system when it encounters another? Which elements of the new system are adopted, and which elements of the old system survive in the process? How do these elements affect each other, i.e. what happens to the European elements when they become part of an African naming system, and how are the African elements influenced by the European ones? Moreover, what are the underlying sociocultural and linguistic reasons for these changes, and what stages can be differentiated in the process? Finally, how does the new, dynamic naming system function in the society, and what changes can it be expected to undergo in the future?

Because of its general onomastic approach, this study should not be understood to represent primarily either Ambo linguistics or Finnish linguistics. Nevertheless, it also presents a linguistic analysis of a large number of individual names from the etymological as well as morphological and semantic point of view. As the writer of this study has a background in European (Finnish) onomastics, the main emphasis will be on the analysis of names adopted from European naming systems into the Ambo system. While the analysis of Ambo names will be more general in nature, it strives to be thorough enough for the purposes of this study.

In addition to being a study in linguistics, this study deals mainly with cultural history, church history and anthropology. The general perspective will be historical, as the main aim is to analyse historical developments in a naming system, together with the various sociocultural reasons behind these developments. As this thesis specifically deals with changes in an anthroponymic system, it can be said to represent historical onomastics, or even *dynamic onomastics*, a term suggested by Herbert (1997, p. 4).[1] It is interesting to note that this has not been a common approach within African onomastics. According to Herbert (1996, p. 1223),

> One of the less studied aspects of anthroponymy in sub-Saharan Africa concerns changes in naming practices. Almost all mentions of names and/or naming treat the repertoire and the process as static and fail to note the very close relationship between changes in sociocultural organization, most particularly as a result of culture contact, and changes in name types.

Anthropology is linked to this study by an analysis of the Ambo personal naming system as part of the Ambo culture. Beside examining names as linguistic elements, this study investigates the naming ceremonies of the Ambo people, their religious beliefs associated with personal naming, the use of names in the everyday lives of the people, etc. Changes in these customs will be described and analysed in their sociocultural context up to the present day. In this respect, this study also represents anthropological linguistics.[2]

Another important aspect of this study is that it examines the influence of Christianity on name-giving. Many creditable theses and publications have been written on this topic in various European countries. Many of them deal either with medieval name-giving or the influence of the Reformation on personal names in different parts of Europe.[3] However, the influence of Christian missionary activities – together with colonialism – on name-giving outside Europe has been a neglected field of research. It is clear that such research would offer valuable material for a comparative study of changes in naming systems caused by the adoption of Christianity, both in different parts of the world and at different times. Compared with the corresponding changes in many European naming systems, the process in the Ambo system – as well as in many other African naming systems – has been exceptionally rapid. It is also of great significance that there is precise written documentation of this change in the church records of the Evangelical Lutheran Church in Namibia (ELCIN), starting from the early years of Christian influence in the Ambo communities. As is well known, this is not the case in European countries.[4]

Relation to Other Research Projects

Thematically, even if not officially, this study can be seen as a continuation of a research project entitled "Cultural change of the Ovambos in Northern Namibia during the years 1870–1915" which was started in 1982 and was funded by the Academy of Finland (Eirola *et al.* 1983, p. 6).[5] This project produced three doctoral theses in Finland within the years 1990–1992: Martti Eirola's "The Ovambogefahr: The Ovamboland Reservation in the Making (Eirola 1992), Harri Siiskonen's "Trade and Socioeconomic Change in Ovamboland, 1850–1906" (Siiskonen 1990), and Frieda-Nela Williams's "Precolonial Communities of Southwestern Africa: A History of Owambo Kingdoms 1600–1920" (Williams 1994). Some Finnish anthropologists have also worked on topics concerning the traditional Ambo culture (e.g. Hiltunen 1986, 1993; Salokoski 1992; Tuupainen 1970). Hence, this study is closely linked to previous historical and anthropological research on the Ambo people in Finland, even if it represents linguistics (onomastics).

On the whole, onomastics has been a neglected branch of linguistic studies of most African countries. The main emphasis of African onomastics has also been on the study of place names, not of personal names. Nevertheless, many anthropologists have been interested in name-giving. In their studies, they often describe name-giving ceremonies and analyse the use of personal names in the society, etc. However, their point of view is anthropological, not onomastic, which means that they do not analyse naming systems as linguistic systems or names as linguistic elements.[6] It is clear, though, that the research done by anthropologists is of great importance to African onomastics, as it offers valuable material for onomastic studies.

Not surprisingly, onomastic studies concerning Namibia – and especially anthroponymic studies – have been limited in number. Aside from my own theses and articles (Saarelma-Maunumaa 1995, 1996a, 1996b, 1997a, 1997b, 1999a, 1999b, 2001), there are only a few academic publications on personal names in Namibia. Moreover, many of them are not written by linguists but by anthropologists. For example, Brenzinger (1999) has handled personal names of the Kxoe, Budack (1979, 1988) nicknames of the "Rehoboth Basters" and inter-ethnic names for white men in Namibia, Fisch (1979) the name-giving of the Kavango people, and Otto (1985) Herero name-giving. In 2001, the writer of this study was the only one to have written theses on personal names in Namibia or published articles on Ambo name-giving.

As Namibia was under South African rule until it gained its independence in 1990, onomastic research on Namibia was for a long time closely connected with South African onomastics. Of all African countries, onomastic research has undoubtedly been most active in South Africa, even though the main thrust there has been toponymic research. In 1970, the South African Centre of Onomastic Sciences (later the Onomastic Research Centre) of the Human Sciences Research Council was established in Pretoria to "stimulate, co-ordinate and undertake names research". Several research projects have been carried out in this centre, including one on German place names in South West Africa (Namibia).[7] The Names Society of Southern Africa (NSA) was founded in 1981 to promote onomastic research in southern Africa by organising congresses and symposia and by publishing the journal Nomina Africana. The third congress of this society was held in Windhoek, the capital city of Namibia, in 1985. (Raper 1995, p. 258.) In 2000, an Onomastic Studies Unit was established at the University of Natal, Pietermaritzburg, to further encourage onomastic activities in South Africa.

Raper (1995) presents an overview of the history and recent trends of onomastic studies in South Africa (and Namibia) in "Namenforschung – Name Studies – Les noms propres", the international handbook of onomastics (Eichler *et al.* 1995). It might be useful to mention some examples here of the studies on the personal naming of the different ethnic groups in South Africa. The personal naming of the Zulus has been researched by Dickens (1985), Koopman (1979a, 1979b, 1986, 1987a, 1987b, 1989), Ndimande (1998), Suzman (1994), Turner (1992, 1997) and Von Staden (1987); Xhosa personal naming by Neethling (1988, 1990, 1994, 1995, 1996), De Klerk and Bosch (1995, 1996), Coetser (1996) and Finlayson (1984); Tsonga naming by Golele (1991); Sotho and Tswana personal names by Herbert and Bogatsu (Herbert & Bogatsu 1990, Herbert 1995); and Sotho and Xhosa naming by Thipa (1986). Comparative articles with a more general viewpoint have been published especially by Herbert (1996, 1997, 1998, 1999a, 1999b). Some of the above-mentioned articles and theses deal with the influence of culture contact on personal naming as well. However, as the "New South Africa", i.e. the post-apartheid South Africa, is a multicultural society with a wide variety of ethnic groups communicating with each other more actively than before, this viewpoint will no doubt be increasingly relevant in South African anthroponymy in the future.

As this study also deals with names in the Ambo languages, it is related to the linguistic research done in this field both inside and outside Namibia. All in all, this research has not been very active, despite the fact that roughly half of the population of Namibia are Ambo speakers and the role of the Ambo languages is fairly strong in the society. Today, there are two written languages based on the different linguistic varieties of Ambo: Ndonga and Kwanyama. These varieties were developed as written languages originally by the Finnish and German missionaries who were active in linguistic work. The missionaries published grammars, dictionaries and textbooks, and some of them also wrote articles in linguistic journals.[8] Later, Ndonga and Kwanyama were developed and standardised under the control of the South African government. (Fourie 1992, p. 15–24.)

Before the independence of Namibia, there were altogether four M.A. or Ph.D. theses dealing with Ambo linguistics. The first M.A. thesis was written by Janse van Vuuren (1966), and the first Ph.D. thesis by Viljoen (1979).[9] Since 1990, a few more have been written, both in Namibia and outside the country.[10] Ndonga has also relatively modern grammatical descriptions (Fivaz 1986; Tirronen 1960), which is not the case with Kwanyama. A number of academic articles have also been published on various issues dealing with Ambo linguistics (Maho 1998, p. 31–32). As there is still a lot of basic research waiting to be done in this field, it is not surprising that onomastic research has not been active either.

Clearly, this study also touches on Finnish onomastics, as many of the European personal names adopted by the Ambo people are of Finnish origin. In fact, the Ambo area seems to be the only place in the world outside Finland where one can find significant Finnish influence on the personal nomenclature of the local people. Such being the case, this study hopes to be a valuable addition to Finnish anthroponymy as well.

Sources
Archive Sources and Name Data

For the most part, this study is based on old written material of the Ambo area, both archival sources and literature. The most important archives utilised for this study are the missionary archives in Finland (the Archives of the Finnish Missionary Society in the National Archives of Finland, Helsinki)[11] and in Germany (the United Evangelical Mission Archives, Wuppertal-Barmen), as well as the German colonial archives (in the Federal Archives, Berlin). The ethnographic collection of Emil Liljeblad (ELC) in the Helsinki University Library is also of special importance to this research, and the name data for this study were collected from the parish records of the Evangelical Lutheran Church in Namibia (ELCIN).

The Archives of the Finnish Missionary Society (FMSA), which today form part of the National Archives of Finland in Helsinki, contain a great deal of information about the traditional naming practices of the Ambo groups, the first baptisms in the Ambo area, the adoption of European and biblical names by the converts, discussions on African baptismal names, and so on. It is of great importance that this material also reveals the attitudes of both the Finnish missionaries and the local people to name-giving. The archives of the United Evangelical Mission at Wuppertal also contain such material, although not as much, as the Ambo area was never one of the main areas in which the Rhenish missionaries worked. The colonial archives in Berlin (in the Federal Archives) include useful material on name-giving practices in German South West Africa, as well as on the Ambo communities under German rule.

When utilising these missionary and colonial archives, one should remember that the point of view in this material is clearly European. The traditional Ambo culture, as well as the Christianisation process of the Ambo communities, is described in these documents in the way the Europeans saw these matters, not as the Ambo people experienced them. Of course, this is a problem which any researcher faces when dealing with the history of Africa.

The most important source dealing with the traditional naming practices of the Ambo people is the ethnographic collection of Emil Liljeblad (ELC) in the Helsinki University Library in Finland. This material, collected during a fieldwork period in 1930–32 from different parts of the Ambo area, contains 125 exercise books with 4,800 pages in different linguistic varieties of Ambo, and 2,016 folio sized pages of translations into Finnish.[12] The material includes examples of different aspects of traditional Ambo culture, such as wedding customs, witchcraft and sorcery, reflections on God and the creation of the world, death magic and burial rites, as well as oral tradition in the form of proverbs and riddles, songs and tales. In addition, the collection contains descriptions of name-giving practices among the different Ambo groups.

Altogether, Liljeblad had 195 informants representing different Ambo subgroups (Salokoski 1992, p. 10). A question which needs to be raised here is the reliability of these informants, many of whom were teachers and pastors of the Lutheran church and former students of Liljeblad.[13] Hiltunen (1993, p. 16) points out that many of these informants were former diviners and their children, and as they had abandoned the traditional religion, the taboo not to reveal tribal secrets no longer applied to them.[14] Salokoski (1992, p. 11) also states that "at the time the material was collected, only those who had abandoned traditional beliefs were likely to give away the more esoteric parts of local tradition". Aune Liljeblad, daughter of the collector, remarks that it was crucial for the results of the field work that Emil Liljeblad could interview people with whom he had a close and confidential relationship (Kokoelman selitykset, ELC).

All in all, Hiltunen (1993, p. 17) regards the material collected by Liljeblad as reliable and not biased in one way or another. On the other hand, Salokoski (1992, p. 11) points out that as many of the informants were from important families in the traditional society and had become powerful persons in the church , it is often "the voice of a power-holding stratum" that can be heard in the material. She also states that the influence of Christian thought sometimes merges into the description of pre-Christian tradition, and that the fact that the informants were predominantly male gives a clear bias to both topics and perspective (Salokoski 1992, p. 11–12). As far as name-giving is concerned, Salokoski's last point cannot be seen as a serious drawback, since in the traditional Ambo culture giving names to children was primarily the responsibility of men. The descriptions of name-giving practices do not reflect the influence of Christian thought, either.

The name material presented and analysed in this study is based on a corpus containing the baptismal names of a total of 10,920 members of the Evangelical Lutheran Church in Namibia (ELCIN). The names were taken from registers of baptisms of three congregations, Elim, Okahao and Oshigambo, representing three Ambo subgroups, from the period 1913–1993. As the parish records of the seven oldest congregations in the Ambo area were microfilmed in Namibia in 1993–94, they are available for researchers in Finland in the University of Joensuu (Siiskonen 1994, p. 25–26).[15]

A linguistic analysis of these baptismal names forms an important part of this study. With the use of this corpus, it is possible to present a careful analysis of the variety of names given to Lutheran Ambo Christians, as well as of the main trends in their name-giving, starting almost from the first Ambo converts. The analysis of these names was made with the assistance of various name books (concerning mainly European first names and surnames), dictionaries, translations of the Bible, and so on. As roughly 70 per cent of the people in the Ambo area are today members of the Evangelical Lutheran church (Notkola & Siiskonen 2000, p. 40), this material reflects well the general name-giving trends of the majority of the population. The developments in the name-giving of the Anglican and Catholic Ambos, as well as of the non-Christian minority, will be discussed as well. However, this analysis is not based on statistical material but on literary sources and interviews. This is also the case when discussing other types of names of the Ambo people: surnames, nicknames, etc.

Literature

As is the case with many other African countries, most of the written information on Namibia and the Ambo area has been published outside the country, mainly in Finland and Germany.[16] The literature used for this study can be divided into three groups:

1. Missionary and colonial literature concerning the Ambo people
2. Research literature on the traditional Ambo culture and the history of the Ambo communities and Namibia
3. Research literature on personal naming in other cultures, especially in African societies, and on the influence of Christianisation and Europeanisation on indigenous African cultures

The first two can be regarded as primary literature sources, whereas the third serves to offer comparative material from other cultures. Most of the literature utilised for this study is published either in English, German or Finnish. Some books and articles are also in Afrikaans, Ndonga, Swedish and Danish.

As the Ambo area was the first, and for a long time the main, mission field of the Finnish Evangelical Lutheran Mission (formerly the Finnish Missionary Society), publications on the Ambo area have been numerous in Finland. The Finns have published books in which various aspects of traditional Ambo culture are presented – and often commented on from a Christian perspective (e.g. Haahti 1913; Hopeasalmi 1946; Mustakallio 1903; Närhi 1929; Savola 1924). Many books also deal with the history of missionary work in the Ambo area, without representing academic historical research (e.g. Hänninen 1924; Pentti 1959; Perheentupa 1923; Suomalaista raivaustyötä Afrikan erämaassa 1945; Tarkkanen 1927). Some describe the life of individual missionaries or Ambo Christians (e.g. Aho 1933, 1941; Auala 1975; Hamutumua 1955; Helenius 1930; Holopainen 1993; Ihamäki 1985; Kivelä 1991; Levänen 1935, 1963, 1964; Perheentupa 1935; Ranttila 1935; Saari 1952; Weikkolin 1888). The Finnish missionary literature deals mainly with the southern parts of the Ambo area, in particular the Ndonga subgroup.

The main emphasis of the German missionary literature is on the northern parts of the Ambo area, i.e. Oukwanyama. These books also deal with traditional Ambo culture (e.g. Brincker 1900; Tönjes 1996), the history of Rhenish missionary work among the Ambo people (e.g. Aus den Anfangstagen der Ovambomission 1904; Himmelreich 1900) and the work and life of individual German missionaries and Ambo Christians (e.g. Erstlinge von den Arbeitsgebieten der rheinischen Mission 1899; Welsch 1923, 1925; Wulfhorst 1912). The German colonial literature on the Ambo area (e.g. Haussleiter 1906) turned out to be of minor importance for this study, as not much of it deals with cultural issues. Altogether, none of these Finnish or German books presents a profound analysis of the personal naming of the Ambo people, but several aspects of name-giving, both traditional and Christian, are taken up here and there.

How reliable is this literature then as a source for academic research? It is apparent that when the European missionaries made observations on Ambo culture, they did this from a narrow European and Christian viewpoint. Hence, even if these books do contain unique information that cannot be found elsewhere,[17] they do not meet the requirements of academic research. It is quite obvious that one of the main purposes for the existence of this literature was to motivate people in Finland and Germany to support missionary work financially. Thus, the descriptions of the missionaries were influenced by the need to "open the hearts" of European Christians to missionary work. In these books, the traditional Ambo culture is generally described as something primitive, sometimes even evil, whereas the work of the missionaries is often painted in rosy colours, as is apparent in comparing the more truthful archival material with this "missionary propaganda", as it has been called.[18] It is hard to believe that the missionaries misrepresented the truth deliberately in describing the naming practices of the Ambo people, but they were obviously not familiar with all the details of these customs. It is also most likely that they found some customs too "brutal" to be described in detail to their Christian audiences in Europe.

The research literature on the traditional Ambo culture and the history of the Ambo communities is, of course, much less problematic as a source. Academic research on Namibia has been most active in Finland, Germany, South Africa, Britain and the United States (Hillebrecht 1985, p. 121–126), and a lot of this vast corpus of material is available to researchers in the National Library of Namibia, as well as in various libraries in Finland. However, Eurocentrism is a problem that concerns all research done by Europeans on Africa, including this study. On the other hand, it has been noted that an outsider's perspective can also be fruitful: a stranger might see something that a researcher living within the culture cannot (Salokoski 1992, p. 12). One may also claim that in any research dealing with European influence on Africa, the European viewpoint is of equal importance to the African one.

For this study, the research literature dealing with personal naming in other African societies and with the Christianisation and Europeanisation of African cultures was of vital importance. Beside offering valuable comparative material, these studies show that the theoretical frameworks and questions behind these individual cases are often similar. The onomastic theories presented by some well-known scholars have also stimulated the analysis of the Ambo naming system.

However, despite the fact that linguistic contacts have long attracted the attention of linguists, the influence of culture contact on personal naming has been a neglected topic, especially from a theoretical point of view.[19] Even if one can find terse and critical comments on this topic in many articles and theses dealing with personal names, no general theory of the impact of culture contact on personal naming systems has been offered so far.[20]

Interviews

As was already pointed out, the archival material, as well as the missionary and research literature concerning the Ambo area, was mainly produced by Europeans and is thus unavoidably Eurocentric. There are also a number of books, articles and theses written by Namibians about the history of Namibia and the Ambo culture (e.g. Hishongwa 1992; Katjavivi 1989; Nambala 1987, 1994; Nampala 2000; Namuhuja 1996; Shejavali 1970; Williams 1994). However, as only some of these publications mention name-giving, they were not sufficient to include the Namibian viewpoint in this research. Hence, the need to interview Ambo people about their name-giving practices was obvious.

In the course of this research it became clear that the archive and literary sources contain a lot of valuable material on name-giving in the traditional Ambo culture, as well as on the names of the first Ambo Christians. However, it was surprisingly difficult to find written material on the name-giving of the Ambo people from the 1950s up to the present day. It seems that there are at least two reasons for this. Firstly, at the beginning of the missionary work in the Ambo area, the need to inform people in Finland and Germany about the Ambo culture was much more urgent than later, when the life of the Ambo people had already become familiar to them. Secondly, the name-giving of the Ambo converts seems to have been of special interest to the Europeans as long as it was a new phenomenon. The more baptisms there were, the less they were written about, and soon they became part of the everyday life of the Ambo congregations. Thus, interviews were also needed to fill this gap in the written research material.

The interviews for this study were carried out in Namibia in 1997 and 2000, as well as a few in South Africa in 2000 and in Finland over the years 1994–2001. There appeared to be two methods to choose between, of which the latter was chosen. First, one could have interviewed a large number of ordinary name-givers all over the Ambo area with the assistance of a well-planned questionnaire.[21] From this vast material, general conclusions could then have been drawn about the personal naming of the Ambo people. With this approach, the research would have been as close to the actual name-givers as possible. However, this method was not chosen, primarily because such interviews would have been too laborious to carry out. The interviews should also have been done in the Ambo languages with an interpreter.

The second method, which was eventually chosen, was to interview a limited number of people who were experts on name-giving in Ambo society, i.e. people who knew Ambo traditions.[22] These were pastors of Lutheran, Anglican and Catholic parishes who were key figures in Christian name-giving, midwives who gave names to babies in hospitals, and so on. All those interviewed were educated people who spoke English fluently. As many of them discuss name-giving regularly with the fathers – or parents – of the children, they can be regarded as having close contact with the actual name-givers in the Ambo area. However, these people were not interviewed as experts only, but also as ordinary name-givers, i.e. as people who have given names to their own children and who have chosen surnames for themselves, etc. Beside these Ambo informants, some Finnish missionaries were also interviewed for this study.

NOTES

1   Herbert's (1997, p. 4) exact definition of *dynamic onomastics* is "study of changes in names and naming systems".

2   Hoebel (1972, p. 594) describes the difference between a conventional linguist and an anthropological linguist in this way: "To the conventional linguist, the study of language and languages is often an end in itself. The anthropological linguist, however, while he may share these linguistic concerns, tends to add a somewhat different dimension. He is more interested in language as a phenomenon within cultures, to strive to understand the intricate problems of the ways in which language and culture relate to each other."

3   Just to mention one example of each in German onomastics: Volker Kohlheim's "Regensburger Rufnamen des 13. und 14. Jahrhunderts" (1977a) treats medieval name-giving, whereas Rudolf Kleinöder's "Konfessionelle Namengebung in der Oberpfalz von der Reformation bis zur Gegenwart" (1996) is concerned with name-giving after the Reformation.

4   In Europe, the practice of writing down the names of the baptised was started in the late Middle Ages. The oldest parish register, dating back to the late 14th century, was found in Gemona, Italy. In Finland, parishes were ordered to keep registers starting in 1686. (Lempiäinen 1965, p. 195, 197.)

5   The project was carried out by the Institute of History at the University of Joensuu, the Scandinavian Institute of African Studies and the Institute of History at the University of Oulu (Eirola *et al.* 1983, p. 7).

6   Herbert (1997, p. 4) also points out that the dynamic nature of anthroponymic systems has not received much attention by ethnographers dealing with African cultures. Typically, they have offered brief descriptions of naming systems at a given point in time, and presented rough typologies for names. As Herbert (1997, p. 4) puts it, they "neglect the workings of the larger system".

7   German toponyms in Namibia have especially been Möller's (1986, 1987, 1990) area of study. Research on Namibian place names has also been done by Moritz (1983), Nienaber and Raper (Nienaber & Raper 1977, 1980; Raper 1978), among others.

8   The life-work of the Finnish missionary Toivo Tirronen, who published a number of academic articles, textbooks and dictionaries on Ndonga, should especially be mentioned here (Dammann 1981, p. 12–15). For the role of the Germans in the linguistic research of Kwanyama, see Dammann 1984 (p. 80–84).

9   Janse van Vuuren's M.A. thesis (1966) deals with the orthography and phonology of Kwanyama and Ndonga, and Viljoen's Ph.D. thesis (1979) with the copulative in Ndonga and Kwanyama. Viljoen's M.A. thesis (1972), however, treats verbal conjugations in Ndonga. Zimmermann (1971) wrote an M.A. thesis on Kwanyama nouns. All these theses were written at South African universities, and in Afrikaans.

10 For example, an M.A. thesis was written in 1998 on the tone in Kwanyama nouns in the University of Helsinki, Finland (Halme 1998).

11 According to Hiltunen (1986, p. 18), the world's most valuable collection of research material on the Ambo area can be found in the Finnish missionary archives. Martti Eirola's "Namibiana in Finland" (1985), a guide to the Finnish archival sources concerning Namibia, has been most useful for this study. This guide was published as part of a documentation programme of the United Nations' Institute for Namibia (UNIN), which aimed to inventory and catalogue literary information concerning Namibia (Eirola 1985, p. 18).

12 Liljeblad collected his material by asking his informants to write down everything that they knew about Ambo customs, hence the notebooks are written in various Ambo linguistic varieties (Hiltunen 1986, p. 17). About half of the material was translated by Emil Liljeblad himself, and the other half by Mrs. Anna Glad after

Liljeblad's death in 1937. Some of the original manuscripts were also destroyed. (Eirola 1985, p. 305; Salokoski 1992, p. 10.) This study made use of the translations, not the original Ambo texts. As the collection includes an alphabetical subject index, it was relatively easy to find the relevant material on name-giving in this massive collection.

13   Rev. Liljeblad worked as a missionary in the Ambo area over the years 1900–08 and 1912–1919 (Peltola, 1958, p. 262).

14   Martti Rautanen (lecture on the religion and sacred places of Ondonga, 29.11.1903, Hp:110, FMSA) states that people generally consider their religion sacred and are therefore not willing to talk about it openly to outsiders. According to Rautanen, it took the Finns several years and a lot of effort to get to know the traditional religion of the Ambo people. Salokoski (1992, p. 11) also points out, when analysing the reliability of Emil Liljeblad's collection, that "not even a convert wanted indiscriminately to disclose secrets of the old tradition".

15   The microfilming of these parish records was part of a research project named "Population development in Northern Namibia" which was carried out by the Department of History at the University of Joensuu and the Department of Sociology at the University of Helsinki. In the African context, this material is claimed to be exceptional as it is so massive and covers such a long period of time. The parish records have also turned out to be pretty reliable. (Siiskonen 1994, p. 25–26.) In 2001, the parish records of these congregations over the years 1993–2000 were also microfilmed in Namibia. Unfortunately, it was impossible to utilise this more recent material for the name analysis in this study.

16   Suzman (1994, p. 254) points out how ironic it is that the records of traditional naming practices in Africa mainly come from the very agents of acculturation and change.

17   The uniqueness of missionary material is acknowledged by many scholars. Bitterli (1989, p. 47) says: "There can be no doubt that, thanks to what may be called their intimate relationship with other cultures, the missionaries became the professional group which, in every case of contact, possessed the fullest information about the alien culture."

18   Eirola et al. (1983, p. 26) put it in this way: "The goals of missionary literature were, however, often of a propaganda nature for the readers in the home country, which reduces its usefulness. Therefore also missionary literature needs rigorous source criticism."

19   Harald Haarmann (1983, p. 154) draws attention to this as well: "In der Namenforschung hat man sich zwar mit Personennamen befaßt, die entlehnt worden sind, meines Erachtens ist aber die Entlehnung und Verwendung fremder Namen in einer Sprache noch nicht systematisch im Hinblick auf ihre Rolle im Sprachkontaktprozess ... behandelt worden." Eichler (1989, p. 377) also points out that the vast literature on language contact very seldom deals with onomastic questions.

20   There have been some attempts at a theoretical analysis of the influence of culture contact on names, but the main emphasis in them is usually on toponyms (e.g. Eichler 1989; Šrámek 1978).

21   This is a method used by many onomasticians in South Africa (e.g. De Klerk & Bosch 1995; Dickens 1985; Herbert & Bogatsu 1990; Herbert 1995; Koopman 1986; Suzman 1994). Often these onomasticians use field-workers to conduct the actual interviews. In some cases, it seems to be important to have interviewers who are from the research area and are thus known to the local people (Suzman 1994, p. 257).

22   One should bear in mind what the famous anthropologist Bronislaw Malinowski (1945, p. 154) pointed out: "what the 'old men of the tribe' tell us about the past can never be scientific or historical truth, since it is always affected by sentiment, by retrospective regrets, and longings". According to Malinowski (1945, p. 154), such statements should rather be treated as mythology.

Personal Names and Cultural Change

Culture, Language and Names

The Concept of Culture

It is generally acknowledged that changes in personal nomenclature often reflect major changes in society. Because of this phenomenon, personal names have been described as a mirror of the culture of the people (Essien 1986, p. 87). However, before exploring the theories of cultural and onomastic change further, it is necessary to look at the concept of culture first. It seems that anthropological literature offers us a large number of definitions of culture.[23] It would be useless to analyse the historical development of these definitions here, but some basic ideas need to be taken up.

Firstly, the word *culture* may be used in two ways: either to refer to human culture as a whole – which is a mere abstraction – or to a specific culture, one of the numerous manifestations of "human culture". This is due to the fact that as cultures develop in many and varied environments, there are also many different cultures (Ayisi 1988, p. 2). Secondly, culture and society are always closely related. They are counterparts, just as the two faces of a sheet of paper (Kroeber 1948, p. 267). There can be no human culture without a society, and no human society without a culture. Hence, culture is a phenomenon which the human species has and other social species, e.g. ants and bees, lack. Thus, culture can be defined as "all the activities and nonphysiological products of human personalities that are not automatically reflex or instinctive". (Kroeber 1987, p. 80–81.) It is "the unique aspect of man", and this uniqueness has been explained by man's ability to use symbols, which has also led to the development of language (Downs 1971, p. 29–30).

According to the classical definition of the 19th-century British anthropologist Edward Tylor (1974, p. 1), culture is "that complex whole which includes knowledge, belief, art, morals, law, custom, and any other capabilities and habits acquired by man as a member of society". It is important to note that culture is acquired by learning. It is what we learn

21

from other people and the past, and what we ourselves may add to. Because of this, anthropologists often talk about "social inheritance" or "tradition" when defining culture. This cross-generational aspect has led to the understanding of culture as a "superorganic" entity. It is organic, but at the same time more than organic, as it exists beyond its human carriers and continues to exist after they have died. (Kroeber 1987, p. 81–82; Bodley 1994, p. 8.) With respect to everyday life, culture has been seen as "the 'know-how' that a person must possess to get through the task of daily living" (Wardhaugh 1992, p. 217).

Many modern anthropologists emphasise the cognitive aspect of culture. They think of culture as a mental map which is shared by a number of people and which guides them in their relation to their surroundings and other people. (Downs 1971, p. 35.) On the other hand, several anthropologists state that both thought and behaviour are needed in an adequate definition of culture (Bodley 1994, p. 7).

Furthermore, culture is agreed to be systematic by nature. It has thus been described as a "system of symbols":

> We can say that culture is a system of symbols shared by a group of humans and transmitted by them to upcoming generations. ... The important word in the definition, however, is *system*. The symbols shared within any given group of humans are not random collections of customs, activities, etc. Rather, we discover that each culture tends to have a logic of its own that makes the various elements of the culture related and interdependent. (Downs 1971, p. 31.)

The systematic nature of culture was emphasised by the functionalist school of anthropology, which is identified with the names of A.R. Radcliffe-Brown and Bronislaw Malinowski. In the early 20th century, they started to analyse cultural traits with respect to their function. As they saw it, cultural elements persist because of their function in society, not because they are relics of ancient times. (Langness 1985, p. 68–82; Murphy 1989, p. 221.)

It is easy to see that the various definitions typically emphasise one aspect of human culture or another. In a sense, one might assume that most of them are at least partly true, even if their viewpoints may be limited. Bodley (1994, p. 9)[24] has presented eight categories for the definitions of culture:

Topical	Culture consists of everything on a list of topics, or categries, such as social organization, religion, or economy.
Historical	Culture is social heritage, or tradition, that is passed on to future generations.
Behavioral	Culture is shared, learned human behavior, a way of life.
Normative	Culture is ideals, values, or rules for living.
Functional	Culture is the way humans solve problems of adapting to the environment or living together.
Mental	Culture is a complex of ideas, or learned habits, that inhibit impulses and distinguish people from animals.

Structural   Culture consists of patterned and interrelated ideas, symbols, or behaviors.

Symbolic   Culture is based on arbitrarily assigned meanings that are shared by a society.

In this study, the structural and functional aspects of culture will be emphasised. The anthroponymic system of the Ambo people is seen as a subsystem of the Ambo culture, and the various functions of personal names will be analysed not only in their linguistic, but also in their sociocultural context.

Cultural Change and Culture Contact

Cultural change is a universal phenomenon. All cultures change in the course of time, more or less rapidly. There is no such thing as a stable society, even if the synchronic method used by many anthropologists – i.e. investigating a culture at a particular time – may lead one to think that way. As all life is constantly changing, the diachronic perspective is most relevant in all research dealing with human cultures. But why do cultures change? In trying to find answers to this question, anthropologists have stressed both internal and external factors in their theories.

In 1859 Charles Darwin presented his ideas on evolution in biology, and this became a central concept in anthropology. According to the cultural evolutionary theory of L.H. Morgan and Edward Tylor, who followed soon after Darwin, all cultures develop "unilinearily", through similar phases, from a primitive stage towards civilisation. This unilinear evolution was seen as a result of similar independent inventions[25] in different societies. Hence, the reasons for change were considered to be internal. Differences between cultures were explained by the varying speed of this development, caused for instance by natural impediments such as climate. These 19th century evolutionists found civilisation primarily in the EuroWestern societies, whereas the non-European, "primitive" societies fell into the categories of "savagery" or "barbarism" in their theories. (Friedl 1976, p. 373–374; Hiebert 1983, p. 415; Murphy 1989, p. 220; Steward 1963, p. 15.)

Toward the end of the 19th century the theory of unilinear evolution faced severe criticism. The main point raised was that it ignored the principal source for change, namely contact between cultures. It had also become evident that the development of cultures does not follow the same rules everywhere. Franz Boas in particular challenged the theory of universal evolution.[26] Together with his students, Boas investigated the origin and spread of various aspects of culture. Instead of constructing theories, these scholars concentrated on particular culture histories and strived to explain individual cases on the basis of empirical research. An important concept for them was *diffusion*, the passing of cultural items from one society to another. (Friedl 1976, p. 374–375; Hiebert 1983, p. 416–417; Murphy 1989, p. 222–223.) It has been pointed out that most cultural change, even more than 90 per cent, is due to diffusion, while independent invention explains only a small part of it. The importance of diffusion also explains why geographically isolated societies change more slowly than other societies. (Nanda 1987, p. 82; Murphy 1989, p. 223.)

In the early 20th century, a new school of anthropology was developed based on the idea of acculturation.[27] Leading figures in this school were Malinowski and Mead. (Hiebert 1983, p. 417.) The term *acculturation* has been defined as follows:

> Acculturation occurs when a society undergoes drastic culture change under the influence of a more dominant culture and society with which it has come in contact. The acculturating society alters its culture in the direction of adjustment and (greater or lesser) conformity to cultural ideology and patterns of the dominant society. (Hoebel 1972, p. 660.)

Scholars interested in acculturation have investigated reasons for the adoption of some cultural elements and the rejection of others. They have also tried to find out why some borrowed elements are modified, whereas others are left intact, and how the new elements are fitted into the receiving cultural system. They have found that elements that fill a conscious need are likely to be accepted, especially if they can be interpreted as modifications of some already existing elements.[28] Nonmaterial elements are also found to meet resistance more easily than objects of material culture. (Titiev 1959, p. 198–199.) As cultures are systematic by nature, an element of obvious benefit may also be rejected if it affects some other aspects of the culture (Downs 1971, p. 31–32). Indeed, as Murphy (1989, p. 233) has pointed out, cultures form systems, and any disturbance in one part of a system may influence the other parts: thus, in a process of acculturation, "more happens ... than diffusion and its consequences".[29]

In general, the result of an acculturation process is increased similarity of the two cultures in question (Kroeber 1948, p. 425). However, as cultures are dynamic by nature, the actual outcome is often impossible to predict. Bronislaw Malinowski (1945, p. 25), the well-known functionalist, especially stressed the dynamic nature of culture contact:

> The nature of culture change is determined by factors and circumstances which cannot be assessed by the study of either culture alone, or of both of them as lumber rooms of elements. The clash and interplay of the two cultures produce new things.

Some cultures are also found to be more "open" than others, i.e. they adopt new ideas more easily. These cultures are structurally more flexible in the sense that they allow more alternatives in their cultural system. (Hiebert 1983, p. 420.) Some elements are also adopted because the culture they come from is considered more prestigious (Murphy 1989,

p. 225). Typically, acculturation takes place in a situation in which a stronger group aims to impose its cultural values on a weaker one. This often results in a period of uncertainty during which the traditional values no longer apply, but the new values do not yet fit into the system either. (Titiev 1959, p. 200.) Several scholars have also presented typologies for different types of culture contact. For example, there are contacts between two entire cultures and contacts in which one part is a selected segment of a culture only, as is the case with European missionaries in many African societies (Friedl 1976, p. 376–377).

In the 1930s and 1940s, the evolutionary theory was revived in the form of neo-evolutionism. The new approach was introduced by Leslie White and Julian H. Steward, who stressed economic and technological factors in the development of human culture and thus represented cultural materialism (Murphy 1989, p. 229–230). As far as White saw it, cultures are means of harnessing and using energy, and they become more complex as they develop new techniques for that purpose.[30] As his model was intended to cover the evolution of all human culture, it has been called "universal evolution". (Hiebert 1983, p. 423; Steward 1963, p. 16.) Steward's theory, in contrast, represented "specific evolution", i.e. the study of development in particular cultures. He pointed out that in different environmental circumstances and with a different technology, cultures tend to develop into different directions. Hence he called his theory "multilinear". In general, specific evolutionists see culture as an adaptive process by which human beings adjust to their natural and sociocultural environments. Their approach has also been called "cultural ecology". (Hiebert 1983, p. 423–424; Langness 1985, p. 100; Murphy 1989, p. 231; Steward 1963, p. 18–19.)

The major field of interest in recent anthropology has been modernisation. This process, which has spread from Western societies all over the world, covers a number of separate processes, such as industrialisation, urbanisation and Westernisation. It has been noted that the changes in non-Western societies do not necessarily follow the patterns of modernisation in the West, mainly because of the difference in values and traditions. Besides their impact on technological and economic factors, these changes influence practically all aspects of traditional life. Some of the main consequences of modernisation have been the shift from the extended family to the nuclear family, the growing independence of young people and women, the change from localism to nationalism and from "folk culture" to "urban culture". A new conception of time has also been adopted along with other Western attitudes. The role of mass media has often been important in this process. (Friedl 1976, p. 394–402; Murphy 1989, p. 235.)

As we can see, the phenomenon of cultural change has inspired anthropologists. Some of them emphasise internal factors in this process, others external factors. However, no agreement on the "prime-mover" in cultural change has been achieved. As Service (1975, p. 96) remarks, cultural change is always a complex process:

Down with prime-movers! There is no single magical formula that will predict the evolution of every society. The actual evolution of the culture of particular societies is an adaptive process whereby the society solves problems with respect to the natural and to the human-competitive environment. These environments are so diverse, the problems so numerous, and the solutions potentially so various that no single determinant can be equally powerful for all cases.

Language and Culture

As has already been pointed out, culture can be seen as a system of symbols – and so can language. The ability to symbolise, to make one thing stand for something else, is what makes man unique. With the use of symbols, and especially human language, which can be seen as "a systematic arrangement of sounds and meanings", culture is also transmitted to coming generations. Language makes it possible to teach other people the results of experiences they might never undergo themselves.[31] (Downs 1971, p. 30–31.) Hence, it is clear that language and culture are inseparable: neither exists without the other. It is equally impossible to imagine a human culture without a language and a human language without a culture. These two are mutually dependent and also acquired simultaneously (Haslett 1989, p. 31).

Language and culture are interdependent, but how close is their relationship? Should they be understood as two separate entities or even as identical? According to Langacker (1994, p. 26), language and culture are neither separate nor identical entities, but they overlap extensively, and both are facets of cognition. The most common approach, however, is to see language simply as part of culture. For example, Landar (1966, p. 130) states that language is a set of habits concerning sign behaviour, whereas culture is the total set of man's habits. The picture might also look different when looking at it from different viewpoints:

> [I]n some respects, language and culture do exist as separate structured entities and should be identified as such while in other respects, language becomes embedded in culture acting as the link between cultural practices and the mental creativity of human society. In theory, the descriptive meaning of language and culture and the functional relationship that is being established between them will always be different depending on which aspects of human behaviour and mental creativity are under consideration. (Tengan 1994, p. 126.)

Lévi-Strauss, the famous structuralist, points out that the entities that are related to each other, are always *a* culture and *a* language, not culture and language in general (Tengan 1994, p. 126). If one agrees with this, a lot of data are required before it is possible to formulate any general theories about this relationship.

The question of dominance with respect to language and culture has been a much-discussed issue among the linguists and anthropologists in the 20th century. Is it so, as the Sapir-Whorf hypothesis suggests, that linguistic categories determine – or at least influence – the reality which the speakers of a language perceive, or the other way round: that linguistic structures merely reflect the reality these people live in? (Bodley 1994, p. 113–114; Wardhaugh 1992, p. 218.) Significant relationships have been shown between the general aspects of the grammar and those of the culture, and it seems that language and culture may both affect each other. For example, the physical and social environment may affect the vocabulary of a language. Thus Eskimo languages have several words for snow, whereas many other languages have one. On the other hand, different vocabularies may lead people to "view the world" differently. For example, the colour vocabulary of the Navahos divides the colour scale in a different way than the English one and hence calls attention to different aspects of it. (Henle 1969, p. 379–382.) It has even been stated that people who speak different languages practically live in different perceptual worlds (Bodley 1994, p. 113–114; Wardhaugh 1992, p. 220).

It was especially German romanticism in the late 18th and early 19th centuries that linked language with identity and nation. The German linguists stressed that one's world view ("Weltsicht"), carried by a specific language, is the basis for individual identity. (Edwards 1985, p. 23; Ehlich 1994, p. 107.) However, later scholars have pointed out that such identities can also survive the loss of the original group language, as a new adopted language may come to serve in the same role (Edwards 1985, p. 159). Hence, the link between *a* language and *a* culture may not be as close as it seems, even if language and culture as such are always inseparable. Altogether, the relationship between language and culture is a complex one, and no simple answers should be taken as satisfactory.

Cultural Change – Linguistic Change

The relationship between cultural change and linguistic change is a challenging topic as well, and one which should be discussed before further investigating the links between cultural and onomastic change. It has been noted that even if scholars have been interested in contact issues for long, there has not been much coordination between the studies of language contact and culture contact and their methods (Weinreich 1968, p. 5).[32] Nevertheless, the basic question one must ask here is: how and why do languages change – as they obviously all do – and what is the role of culture in this process?

Just as was the case with all cultural change, linguistic change has been explained by both internal and external factors (Wardhaugh 1992, p. 192–193).[33] It is generally agreed that language carries within it the seeds of its change: it is constantly changing, and the lack of uniformity in language provides the material for most linguistic changes. Even without any outside influence, such changes would still appear. However, external factors seem to be the usual cause for linguistic change. (Brandt 1972, p. 57.) Linguistic elements are frequently adopted by borrowing from other languages, and some languages tend to be more open in this respect (Wardhaugh 1992, p. 193). Beside individual words, elements of grammatical structure may also be adopted. Most commonly borrowed are elements attached to cultural items, whereas the fundamental vocabulary of the language, e.g. pronouns, tends to remain unchanged. (Hoebel 1972, p. 598, 615–616.)

Internal factors were emphasised especially by the 19th century school of historical linguistics, which brought the concept of evolution into the study of language. The method of this school was comparative: regularities in language change were discovered by isolating linguistic elements and analysing them diachronically. In doing so, historical linguists treated languages as autonomous systems, independent of their contexts and users. They also saw linguistic changes as self-motivating, that is, motivated by phonetic and other linguistic rules. (Blount & Sanches 1977a, p. 1–2.)

Despite the obvious benefits of the comparative method, this discipline was challenged by sociolinguists who stressed that languages should be studied in their sociocultural context. According to Weinreich (1968, p. 4), "the linguist who makes theories about language influence but neglects to account for the socio-cultural setting of the language contact leaves his study suspended, as it were, in mid-air".

The sociolinguists also emphasise that language is fundamentally social behaviour. Hence, they investigate linguistic elements in relation to their social importance, an aspect that was neglected by earlier linguists. (Blount & Sanches 1977a, p. 3.) In addition, while earlier linguists typically treated languages as uniform in structure, the sociolinguistic approach emphasises diversity and variation, which is understood to correlate with social factors (Brandt 1972, p. 53). This approach has also led to the interest in the links between cultural change and linguistic change:

> Essentially any radical social change, especially where contact between different cultures is involved, brings about a restructuring of the communication system(s), thereby producing language change (Blount & Sanches 1977a, p. 4).

As this quotation also shows, the general idea of the relationship between language change and cultural change has been that it is the changes in culture that cause linguistic changes, not vice versa. However, some linguists hold that changes in language may also have significant influence on cultural change. For example, changes in the semantic structure of the language may cause changes in the cognitive orientation of the person, which may then affect other cultural aspects (Brandt 1972, p. 59). As was noted earlier, the Sapir-Whorf hypothesis also claims that linguistic structures may affect human perception and thought.

It is clear that culture contact does not necessarily result in language contact: elements of another culture may be adopted without any influence on the language(s) in question.[34] It is also important to note that linguistic changes can be caused by both linguistic and non-linguistic elements of the other culture.[35] Often such situations are so complex that the original source for the change is impossible to trace, especially in multicultural and multilingual contexts. To sum up, one may claim that there are four main sources for linguistic change, and in many cases, these factors seem to work together: 1. Internal linguistic factors, 2. The influence of the surrounding culture, 3. The influence of another language, and 4. The influence of other cultural elements of another culture.

Personal Names and Culture

Personal names are often said to be cultural universals, by which it is meant that in all human societies, people are given names and the bestowal of names follows conventionalised rules (Alford 1988, p. 1). In all cultures, the basic purpose of personal naming is "to provide a symbolic system of individual identification" (Akinnaso 1980, p. 277). Just as the act of naming is universal, names are also universally classified as nouns in different languages (Van Langendonck 1997, p. 39), which means that their role in the linguistic system is the same everywhere.

The Concept of Name. The concept of name has puzzled linguists and philosophers for centuries – or for millennia. However, it seems that there is little agreement about what a name is. A large number of definitions have been presented by various scholars, and usually they have been met with more or less severe criticism.[36] For example, Algeo (1973, p. 12–13) has listed four criteria used for classifying and defining proper names in English: orthographic, morphosyntactic, referential, and semantic. On the orthographic level, there are capitalised words and uncapitalised ones; on the morphosyntactic level, there are proper nouns and common nouns; on the referential level, singular terms and general terms, and on the semantic level, proper names (names) and common names (appellatives). Eventually, he concludes that what names are depends on which level of language one deals with, and whether one is concerned with the universals of naming or naming within a specific language.[37] Apparently, the definitions also seem to depend on whether the scholar has place names or personal names in mind.[38]

Some linguists (e.g. Laur 1989) have followed Ludwig Wittgenstein's advice and tried to define the word *name* by looking at the ways it is used in the language.[39] Nevertheless, the result of such a method cannot be a short definition of a name but a detailed analysis of the various uses of this word in various languages. A number of scholars have also come to the conclusion that there is, after all, no essential difference between proper names and appellatives, or that the difference is only gradual (Van Langendonck 1997, p. 37).

Despite the numerous approaches to this question, it is generally agreed that proper names[40], contrary to common names, function to denote particulars, such as individuals, entities and members of classes (Bean 1980, p. 305). More than two thousand years ago, Aristotle separated individuals, e.g. *Callias*, from universals, e.g. *man*, and the divisions between proper name (*nomen proprium*) and common name (*nomen appellativum*), as well as meaning (*significatio*) and reference (*nominatio*) were further developed in the Middle Ages (Summerell 1995, p. 370). Traditionally, proper names are understood to be monoreferential: their function is to individualise their objects (Ainiala 1997, p. 15). In addition, they are considered to refer to individuals without having to specify their characteristics.

The idea that proper names simply stand for their bearers and do not indicate their attributes is especially attributed to J.S. Mill.[41] (Bean 1980, p. 306; Schneider 1994, p. 69.) For Mill (1906, p. 20), proper names are denotative, not connotative, i.e. they are words which denote objects without signification. Therefore, the application of a name to a person is purely arbitrary: any name would be just as appropriate as any other. (Algeo 1973, p. 53, 55.) As Mill says in his "A System of Logic" (1906, p. 20),

> Proper names are not connotative: they denote the individuals who are called by them; but they do not indicate or imply any attributes as belonging to those individuals. When we name a child by the name of Paul, or a dog by the name Caesar, these names are simply marks used to enable those individuals to be made subjects of discourse. It may be said, indeed, that we must have had some reason for giving them those names rather than any others; and this is true; but the name, once given, is independent of the reason.

Mill's view has been developed by other philosophers of language, especially Kripke (Schneider 1994, p. 69). On the other hand, it has also been challenged by several scholars. Some of them have remarked that in many naming systems, name-giving is by no means arbitrary but very carefully patterned (Algeo 1973, p. 57).[42] It has also been suggested that as proper names are more specific in reference than common nouns, they must be the most meaningful of all words and hence not meaningless (Algeo 1973, p. 63–64; Jespersen 1924, p. 65–66). In his early philosophy, Wittgenstein (1922, 3.203) even identified the meaning of the name with its referent.[43] At the opposite extreme, it has also been claimed that basically all proper names have the same meaning, which could be identified with the function of the name (Pollock 1982, p. 99). Some onomasticians (e.g. Laur 1989, p. 103) have also pointed out, rather practically, that the semantic content of a name must be relevant, since it seems to be of central interest in onomastic research.[44]

Even if one agrees that most naming has some motivation, one may still hold the idea that this is not necessary. A name can function as a name without any lexical meaning. In other words, even if names often have a lexical meaning, this meaning is irrelevant in regard to their functioning as names in society.[45] Basically, a name stands for its object because of the act of naming which creates a connection between the name and its bearer (Bean 1980, p. 307), not because the name "tells something" about the bearer. The act of naming has been seen as a speech act which includes a performative utterance: the person does not only say something but is actually doing something with his or her words, if specific conditions in the real world are met. Hence, to say "I name this ship Liberty Bell" is, under certain circumstances, to name a ship. (Wardhaugh 1992, p. 283.)[46]

Many onomasticians also agree that appellatives must have *meaning* in order to function properly, while names must have *content*, and these functions are to connote and to denote respectively. The distinction between *onomastic meaning* (i.e. that names are significant on the onomastic level) and *lexical meaning* (i.e. that names are significant on the lexical level) has also been found helpful in onomastics. (Nicolaisen 1995, p. 388, 391.) However, even if names can and do function without lexical meaning, some societies tend to put a strong emphasis on the semantic transparency of names, and various social functions may be attached to these meanings. Therefore, the lexical meaning of the name is an aspect which needs to be taken into account in the socio-onomastic analysis of many anthroponymic systems, especially African ones, as we shall see in this study.

Names as Part of Naming Systems. Names should not be seen as individual elements of a language only, but as elements of naming systems. Volker Kohlheim has analysed the systematic nature of names in a way which is also useful for this study, and we shall use his ideas as a starting-point here.[47] In V. Kohlheim's opinion (1998, p. 173), a naming system – or an *onymic system*, as he calls it – is a system,

> because it consists of a set of elements which are bound together by specific structural relationships ... thereby forming a boundary which separates the system from its environment.

According to Volker Kohlheim (1998, p. 173), these elements, and the relationships between them, form the *structure* of the system, while the *organisation* of the system refers to its function in its environment. The primary function of a naming system is "to identify a certain individuality". The naming system, as he sees it, is always a subsystem of the language, which in turn is part of the social system of the society. The social system is the extralinguistic environment for the naming system. Kohlheim points out that there are different naming systems in different languages, and several naming systems within a language; anthroponyms, toponyms, and so on. These naming systems, he remarks, should not be understood to form a fictitious single entity or be put into any hierarchical order, but they may each consist of a number of subsystems. (V. Kohlheim 1998, p. 173–175.) What these subsystems are exactly, obviously depends on the culture in question, as in different societies different kinds of names are used for different kinds of objects, and they may also be structured differently. In all anthroponymic systems, however, personal names can be divided into two main classes: 1. Individual names that designate individual people (in the European context: first names and bynames), and 2. Collective names that refer to groups of people, e.g. a family (Van Langendonck 1995, p. 487–488; 1996, p. 1228).[48]

Based on V. Kohlheim's ideas, we could state that an anthroponymic system consists of different types of personal names – which are all linguistic elements – and of the ways in which they are structured in this system. An anthroponymic system is also connected to its extralinguistic environment in many ways, as personal naming typically has a variety of secondary sociocultural functions beside its primary function to identify people. While the function of identification is characteristic of all anthroponymic systems, these secondary functions may be different in different societies.

Personal names are considered especially important in the formation of individual and social identity, and this secondary function seems to be common to all anthroponymic systems. Hanks and Hodges (1990, p. vii), for example, point out that a person's name is "a badge of cultural identity" and that religious affiliation and native language are often key factors in the choice of a given name. According to Alford (1988, p. 51), personal names symbolise individual identity in two ways: they tell the members of the society who the individual is, and they tell the individual who he or she is or is expected to be. Naming an individual may also indicate that he or she is a legitimate member of a group. Hence, alongside the function of differentiating people, personal naming serves the function of categorising people. In general, personal naming makes the child part of the social world and gives him or her a social identity. (Alford 1988, p. 29–30, 69.) Thus, a name is seldom, if ever, "just a name". It has also been pointed out that personal names carry a great deal of information about the culture in question: about people's values, cultural practices, ethnic and religious backgrounds, and so on. Raper (1983, p. 4) remarks that "personal names reflect, better than any other language form, various social and other attitudes and relationships, social barriers, the way in which social groups behave towards languages and other aspects of society".

Hence, even if personal names do not need to carry information about a culture in order to function as names, they carry a lot of cultural significance, as they are used for various sociocultural functions. As Herbert (1998, p. 187) puts it, "names are products and reflections of the intimate links between language and sociocultural organization". Because of this, the relationship between personal names and culture is of vital importance when analysing anthroponymic systems and their functioning in the society.

Cultural Change – Onomastic Change

As has already been pointed out, anthroponymic change has not been examined thoroughly from a systematic point of view. In this study, we assume that since anthroponymic systems are units in the same way as other linguistic and cultural systems are, they can be expected to follow similar patterns when undergoing changes. All naming systems obviously undergo changes and these changes can be explained by both internal and external factors.

Again, let us take V. Kohlheim's (1998) analysis of the naming system as a starting-point for our discussion. Kohlheim points out that as the naming system is a subsystem of the language, changes in the language – for example in the sound system – may influence the structure of the naming system. These changes may then affect the internal functioning of the naming system, but they do not affect the organisation of the system, which means that its external function remains intact. Kohlheim points out that elements of one naming system may also be transferred to another: a place name may become a surname, for example. Changes in the social system may also cause changes in the structure of the naming system, e.g. by adding new elements to it or eliminating others. However, they also tend to influence the organisation of the naming system, thus changing its identity and eventually developing a new one. V. Kohlheim's example of this phenomenon is the replacement of a single name system by a system of first name and surname in Medieval Europe, which is typically explained by changes in the extralinguistic environment, such as the growth of the population in cities. Hence, the German anthroponymic system in the 10th century is not the same as that of the 15th century, because the organisation of the system has changed over that time, not only its elements. On the other hand, the German anthroponymic system in the 12th century and in the 15th century can be seen as one system, even if they share very few common elements, because the system has retained its organisation. (Kohlheim 1998, p. 174–175, 177.) V. Kohlheim (1998, p. 177) explains this phenomenon as follows:

> Because it is the organisation of a system, and not its structure, which defines its identity, a system may become completely unrecognisable between one phase of its history and another with respect to its structure, but it is still the same system if its organisation remains intact.

In his article, V. Kohlheim (1998) does not say anything about culture contact as a possible source for onomastic change, even if one suspects that the changes in the extralinguistic environment that he refers to may well be caused by the encounter between different cultures.[49] If we add this viewpoint to the analysis of onomastic change, we could state that the original impulse for a change in an anthroponymic system may have six possible sources:

1. The anthroponymic system itself[50]
2. Its linguistic environment, i.e. the language system that it is part of
3. Its extralinguistic environment, i.e. the social system – or culture – that it is part of
4. Another anthroponymic system[51]
5. Another language
6. Another social system or culture

In practice, it is often impossible to define the original source of the change, as onomastic change is typically caused by several internal and external factors working together. Sometimes the influence is direct, sometimes indirect. For example, a foreign language may first cause changes in the language system, which in turn cause changes in the naming system. In many cases, it is also difficult to say if a particular change in an anthroponymic system is due to local sociocultural developments or to the influence of another naming system, as similar sociocultural developments tend to cause similar changes in personal naming in different societies (Kiviniemi 1982b, p. 30). However, it is important to note that these changes are typically not predictable. V. Kohlheim (1998, p. 177) stresses that the perturbations which the extralinguistic environment exerts on the naming system cannot determine any changes within it, it can only set them in motion. Indeed, onomastic change is a dynamic process which may produce new things – as is the case with all cultural change (Malinowski 1945, p. 25).

It has often been stated that compared to other linguistic elements, personal names are very easily adopted from other languages (Kiviniemi 1982b, p. 33).[52] Raper (1983, p. 4) points out that personal names are situated on the level of language which is most susceptible to variations and innovations. According to Šrámek (1978, p. 390), this may be due to the fact that names of foreign origin do not usually cause significant changes in the language system, and hence they are less "threatening" to it than many other linguistic elements. In its new environment, a borrowed name is seen as a mere lexical element which may undergo formal changes when adopted, or remain unchanged.

In this study, we aim to apply anthropological acculturation theories to the analysis of the change in the Ambo anthroponymic system. This change is seen primarily as a result of the acculturation process in the Ambo culture caused by European cultural influence and the adoption of Christianity. From a linguistic viewpoint, the Ambo naming system is understood to be part of the Ambo language, which in turn is part of the Ambo culture. This naming system consists of individual elements (personal names) and the relationships between them which form its structure. However, changes in the structure of the system may cause changes in its organisation and eventually lead to the formation of a new naming system. In this study, we shall look at the various ways in which elements of European naming systems have been adopted – or rejected – in the Ambo system, and how they have been modified – or left intact – in the process. We shall also see how some elements of the traditional system have disappeared in the process, and how the functions of the remaining elements and the borrowed ones may have changed. In addition, we shall focus on the diffusion of the borrowed elements in the Ambo society, i.e. how the new names and naming customs were spread historically, geographically and in the social hierarchy of the Ambo society.

In addition, we shall analyse the various sociocultural and linguistic reasons for this process. It is also important to point out that even if this study concerns acculturation, which is always a two-way process, the focus will be on the European influence on the Ambo naming system, not vice versa, even if there has been minor influence in the opposite direction as well.[53]

Developments in European Personal Naming Systems

European Naming Systems in the Pre-Christian Era

In order to compare the changes in the Ambo naming system with the changes in European anthroponymic systems, we shall have a closer look at the history of some European naming systems in this section. As the European influence on traditional Ambo culture has been mainly of Finnish and German origin, it is reasonable to concentrate on these two anthroponymic systems here. Altogether, the changes in the Finnish and German personal naming systems in the Middle Ages were caused by many factors similar to the process in Ambo society in the 20th century, the most important of them being the adoption of Christianity.[54]

Let us start with an overview of these two naming systems, Finnish and German, in the pre-Christian era. First, it should be noted that they were not stable before the advent of Christianity, for they had been affected by contacts with other peoples and by various internal developments within these cultures. Unfortunately, the sources dealing with pre-Christian naming in Europe are very limited. The scholars' reconstructions of these old naming systems are not – and can never be – perfect, even if they may succeed in revealing their most characteristic features. German, however, is much better off than Finnish in this respect, as there are mentions of traditional German personal names since the time of the writings of ancient Greek and Roman historians (Seibicke 1982, p. 131).

It is a general assumption in onomastics that in many, if not all cultures, people originally had one individual name only. As people lived in small societies, one name was enough to differentiate them from each other. (Kiviniemi 1982a, p. 29.) This seems to have been the case with the Germanic naming system as well (Van Langendonck 1995, p. 488). Germanic names are also supposed to have been unique in the earliest times, which means that they were not repeated in the society and thus there was a wide variety of them. Most of these names were composed of two elements, and in a minority of cases of one element only. (Wilson 1998, p. 70.)[55] Such compound names can be found in many other European languages as well, e.g. in Greek and Russian, due to common Indo-European linguistic roots (Seibicke 1982, p. 122; Withycombe 1977, p. xiv–xv).

The old German compound names consisted primarily of nouns and adjectives. In men's names, the latter part of the name was a masculine lexeme, in women's names a feminine lexeme, while the grammatical gender of the first part had no such reference. Hence, *Siegfried* and *Hildeger* were men's names, *Sieghild* and *Hildegar* women's names. There were also specific lexemes which were more common as the first elements of men's names (e.g. *Eber-*), or as women's names (e.g. *Swan-*). With the feminine suffix *-a*, male names could also be modified into female names, e.g. *Adalbert > Adalberta*. The number of elements which could be used for the latter part was smaller than those suitable for the first part. These compound names also had abbreviated forms, e.g. *Wolfgang > Wolf* and *Gertrud > Gerta*. Names consisting of a single element were also used: *Bruno, Karl, Wigant*, etc. (Seibicke 1982, p. 122–123, 126–128.)

Siebs (1970, p. 15–17) has presented a semantic analysis of the elements in old German names. His classification consists of sixteen semantic classes, such as mythological figures, animals and plants, the forces of nature, friendly and hostile attitudes, masculine qualities, etc.[56] However, many scholars have advised caution when analysing the meanings of compound names. Their meanings should not be understood as combinations of the lexical meanings of their elements, e.g. *Bernhard* does not necessarily mean 'strong as a bear', even if its elements contain the meanings of 'bear' and 'strong'. (Seibicke 1982, p. 124– 125; Siebs 1970, p. 17.)

Even if Germanic names were originally individual, various features were later introduced to indicate attachment to family (Wilson 1998, p. 70). A major change in the motives for name-giving occurred when the Germans started to name children after their grandparents. Hence, from the name of the person, other people could often tell which family he or she belonged to. It also became common practice to form names for children out of the parents' names. If the father was *Hildebrand* and the mother *Gertrud*, the sons could bear names such as *Gerbrand, Trudbrand, Brandger* and *Trudger*, and the daughters names such as *Hildtrud, Brandtrud, Brandhild* and *Trudhild*.[57] (Seibicke 1982, p. 125–126; Wilson 1998, p. 70.)

Obviously, naming children after other people led to a situation in which several people had similar names. However, one may assume that as people lived in small communities, this did not cause insurmountable problems. As different kinds of bynames seem to belong to all anthroponymic systems (Kiviniemi 1982a, p. 49), they were most probably used in these societies too, even if not systematically. It is also clear that naming after other people, together with the common practice of abbreviating and modifying names, meant that the original meaning of the name often lost its significance. Morgan (1995, p. 121), who has investigated Welsh names, remarks that "each name was originally coined with intentional lexical meaning, but that with repetition and familiarity, a name becomes a mere pointer or indicator".[58]

What was the traditional Finnish naming system like, then? As there is not much written information available on the life of the Finns before they embraced Christianity, not much is known about this subject either. Nevertheless, many old Finnish personal names have been preserved in Finnish surnames and place names, as well as in oral literature. (Maliniemi 1947, p. 41–42.) In written sources, old Finnish personal names begin to appear in the 14th century only, and even then, the material is very limited. On the other hand, comparison with old names of other Baltic-Finnish languages, which all belong to the Finno-Ugric language family, has turned out to be most helpful in this research. (Kiviniemi 1982b, p. 33–35.)

The traditional Finnish naming system seems to have resembled the Germanic one in many respects. It was a system based on one individual name, occasionally accompanied by a byname (Forsman 1894, p. 64;

Kiviniemi 1982a, p. 50; 1982b, p. 35). These old Finnish – or more precisely, Proto-Finnic – individual names were often compound names as well. A number of words were used as basic name elements, such as *Hyvä* ('good'), *Iha* ('glad, good spirit'), *Mieli* ('pleasant'), *Päivä* ('sun, day'), *Toivo* ('hope, promise') and *Valta* ('power'). New names were formed from them either by derivation (*Hyvä-ri, Hyvä-tty, Mieli-kkä, Mieli-tty*) or by compounding (*Ihamieli, Hyvätoivo, Mielipäivä*). Altogether, scholars have found about twenty basic name elements which were used in the Baltic-Finnish languages.[59] Many of them were also used separately as single names (*Hyvä, Iha, Toivo*). (Kiviniemi 1982a, p. 38; Stoebke 1964, p. 109–111, 147.)

According to Stoebke (1964, p. 147), the compound name system is non-derived in the Baltic-Finnish languages, even if it resembles the Germanic system in many respects. He points out that many of these names cannot be direct borrowings from the Germanic languages and that Germanic names are much more warlike than the peaceful Proto-Finnic names. (Kiviniemi 1982a, p. 41.) As Stoebke (1964, p. 148) sees it, Proto-Finnic names mainly reflect love, goodness, joy, pleasantness, beauty, hope, etc. Later scholars, however, see that this compound system must have developed during the later Proto-Finnic era, and probably under Germanic influence (Nissilä 1965, p. 84–87; Kiviniemi 1982a, p. 42; 1982b, p. 36).

It seems that the Proto-Finns also had other kinds of single-element names, for example mythological names such as *Ahti, Kaleva, Tapio* and *Väinö*, and many others: *Ilo* 'joy', *Laulaja* 'singer', *Parantaja* 'healer', etc. Names referring to nature, such as *Etana* 'snail', *Hirvi* 'elk', *Honka* 'pine', *Myrsky* 'storm', *Susi* 'wolf', and *Talvi* 'winter', were used as personal names too. However, it is possible that these were originally bynames, not "real" names. (Kiviniemi 1982a, p. 41–43.) Onomasticians have also pointed out that just as in many other European naming systems, the lexical meanings of old Finnish personal names often lost their significance in the course of time. Maliniemi (1947, p. 43) presumes that many of them were already obscure to the people who used them.

Even if there is almost no written material available on the traditional name-giving ceremonies of the Finns, one can find a few descriptions of these customs among other Baltic-Finnish groups. It seems that among the Baltic-Finnish peoples, names were conferred upon children by a special priest or diviner (*arpoja*). The name was chosen from among several alternatives, and it was attached to family and kin. That children were given names of deceased relatives, was supposedly done in order to revive the souls of these people. (Forsman 1894, p. 27–29; Kiviniemi 1982a, p. 45–46.)[60]

Christianity and Personal Naming

Christianity has undoubtedly been the most important single factor in the development of European naming systems during the last thousand years. The adoption of this new religion not only brought new names to the personal nomenclatures of the people, but also affected traditional naming patterns. The departure from the old naming systems was so radical that the whole process has been called a revolution (Wilson 1998, p. 99). But what is, basically, the relationship between Christianity and personal naming? It seems to be a common assumption, even among some names researchers, that Christianity and "Christian names" have always gone hand in hand. A good example of this can be found in Madubuike's "A Handbook of African Names" (1976, p. 11):

> Of course, Christianity has, from its very beginning, insisted that each con- vert should bear a new name, symbol of new life, following the baptismal ceremony. A typical example is that of Saul, enemy of the Christians, who later changed his way of life when he joined the Christians, and symbolized his new life by answering Paul.

However, there is no evidence to support this view. Many scholars have pointed out that there was no specific Christian nomenclature anywhere, at least not before the 4th century. The early Christians had ordinary Jewish, Greek and Latin names, including names of pagan gods and other names referring to heathen cults: *Apollos, Mercurius, Saturninus, Venus,* etc. Even some bishops were called *Dionysius, Eros* and *Hero* at that time. (V. Kohlheim 1996a, p. 1049; Lehmann 1969, p. 173; Wilson 1998, p. 58–59.)[61] The idea that Saul changed his name into *Paul* after becoming a Christian seems to be a misunderstanding as well. At that time, many Jews living in diaspora had two names, and it is assumed that apostle Paul already had two names before his conversion: the Hebrew name *Saul(us)* and the Greek/Latin name *Paulos/Paulus* (Iso Raamatun tietosanakirja 1973, p. 4073; Palva 1974, p. 190).[62] Thus, it seems that among the early Christians, conversion did not usually result in a name change. As Wilson (1998, p. 59) points out,

> It was not thought appropriate to change one's name on conversion or at baptism. Baptism never implies a change of name in the New Testament or for many centuries afterwards.

It has been suggested that with the introduction of infant baptism, some Christian parents may have associated this ritual with conferring of names which had religious significance, and hence some adults started to assume extra or alternative Christian names at baptism as well. The first reliable information of adults adopting new Christian names at baptism dates from the 6th and 7th centuries. (Wilson 1998, p. 59–60.) V. Kohlheim (1996a, p. 1049–1050) has divided these early Christian names into five groups:

1. Names expressing Christian ideas and virtues (*Agapeius, Anastasius/-ia, Felix, Victor*)
2. Names of Christian festivals (*Natalis, Epiphanius/-ia, Paschasius/-ia*)
3. Theophoric names (*Dominicus, Theodorus, Theodosius, Theodulus*)
4. Names of biblical characters (*Andreas, Johannes, Paulus, Petrus, Susanna*)
5. Names of martyrs (*Cyprianus, Laurentius, Stephanus, Thekla*).

Some of these names were entirely new, but many of them were also used by pagans. However, by the end of the Roman Empire, specifically Christian names were still rare in Europe, and they continued to be uncommon in the early medieval period (Wilson 1998, p. 60–61, 86). Thus Christian names were long an exception, not a rule.

In principal, the connection between baptism and name-giving is understood to be casual in the Christian doctrine. As we have seen, baptism was not a naming ritual originally (Wilson 1998, p. 99), and theologically, name-giving has not been seen as an essential part of it. According to Martin Luther, for example, the one power, work, use, fruit and end of baptism is salvation; baptism is what makes people Christians (Trigg 1994, p. 75–76). In his most important writings dealing with baptism, Luther (1983a, p. 543–553; 1983b, p. 428–448) does not even mention name-giving. In the late 16th century, however, the Roman Catholic church decided to require the use of saints' names in baptism (Withycombe 1977, p. xxvi), and similarly, the Eastern Orthodox church has required the use of Orthodox saints' names as baptismal names (Kasanko 1982, p. 7–8). Altogether, it has been noted that even if name-giving does not belong to the "core of the baptismal *ordo*", it has been attached to this ritual in many churches, though in varying degrees of importance (Chupungco 1998, p. 55).

There are many reasons for this attachment. It is a well-known fact that most societies have a special ceremony for naming the child and introducing him or her to the society (Alford 1988, p. 45–46, 50). As the adoption of Christianity has led to the abandonment of traditional naming ceremonies in many cultures, it is not surprising that the ritual of baptism came to serve this purpose. The relationship between baptism and naming is also strengthened by the fact that in many societies, the name becomes official after the child is baptised and his or her name is recorded in the church registers. All over the world, it is also common that a change in identity is reflected in a name change (Alford 1988, p. 85), and this seems to explain, at least partly, the willingness of many converts to assume new names, which they regard as Christian, at baptism.[63]

The term *Christian name* is widely used, but it is not unproblematic. Some researchers (e.g. Meldgaard 1994, p. 203) define it broadly as a name which has relevance to Christianity in one way or other. V. Kohlheim (1996a, p. 1048) feels that Christian names are not merely names given by Christians but names that are, or originally were, given primarily for a Christian reason. According to him, there are two main principles for religious name-giving: 1. A name can be given on semantic grounds, i.e. it is semantically transparent and given because of its religious connotations, and 2. A name can be given because it refers to a person who holds an important position in the religion: the founder of the religion, his followers and other holy or respected characters. Within Christianity, Kohlheim (1996a, p. 1048) claims, the latter principle has played a more important role.

In this study, we shall see many examples of these two naming types, both in European and African naming systems. Names of biblical characters have been extremely popular all over the Christian world. It should be noted, however, that even if these names are generally assumed because of their reference to biblical characters, they have been semantically transparent names in their original languages. For example, the Hebrew name *Haggai* means 'born during a feast', *Debora* 'bee', *Natanaël* 'God has given', and so on. (Jenni 1996, p. 1854).[64] Later, when these names were adopted as "Christian names" by other cultures, their lexical meanings lost their significance and the reference to the biblical character became relevant. Because of this, the original meanings of these names are usually not known to their European or African bearers. This holds true of the saints' names as well, whose origins cover almost the whole world known to the Europeans in the Middle Ages (Meldgaard 1994, p. 202).[65] In this study, we shall also see how several ordinary European names received the status of "Christian names" in Africa, as they were adopted because of their reference to European missionaries.[66]

The Christianisation of Personal Names in Europe

Thus far, it has become clear that the spread of so-called Christian names has not run parallel to the spread of Christianity and Christian baptisms (V. Kohlheim 1996b, p. 1204). Among many European peoples, the Christianisation of personal names took place several centuries after the new faith was adopted. For example, Christianity started to spread to Germany in the 8th century, but it was only at the end of the 12th century that it had any significant effect on personal naming, and another two centuries were needed before the new foreign names had become common among the Germans. Similarly, Christianity arrived in Scandinavia in the 9th century, and the actual change in personal names began in the 13th century. In Finland the process started much later, as the Christianisation of Finland did not begin until the 11th century, and the change in personal naming took approximately two or three centuries.[67] (Kiviniemi 1982a, p. 60–61; 1982b, p. 37.)

The actual revolution in European personal naming thus occurred during the medieval period.[68] The main reason for this development was the new practice of naming people after saints. The calendar of the saints was the main source for these new names (Kiviniemi 1993, p. 119; Meldgaard 1994, p. 210). Children were typically named after a saint whose feast was on or near their birthday or who was regarded as a special patron of the family. The most popular names were those of "universal" saints, especially the central characters of the New Testament. (Wilson 1998, p. 86, 100–101.) The names of local saints were less popular (V. Kohlheim 1996a, p. 1053).[69] In many countries, e.g. in Scandinavia, these foreign names were initially introduced by the kings and other powerful people, whose families assumed them first (Blomqvist 1993, p. 28; Utterström 1994, p. 287).[70]

The saint cult was not a new phenomenon in the Church at that time, as it had already developed around the year 400. Why did it take so long before it had any significant effect on personal naming? It has been pointed out that it was not until the central medieval period that the Germanic groups were Christianised and hence ready to assume a new naming pattern. By that time, the saint cult had also become extremely powerful and the Germanic anthroponymic system had been impoverished, and more and more names lost their semantic transparency.[71] Hence, there seems to have been a latent need for a new type of names. The new naming principle also stressed individual name choice and thus reflected the new individualistic trends of the time. (V. Kohlheim 1996a, p. 1051.) Obviously, the traditional practice of naming children after family members offered fewer alternatives for the name-givers than the new system. However, it was not always easy for the people to abandon their old naming practices, which also reflected their belief in the transmigration of souls. This also seems to explain why it took so long in many countries before "Christian" names became common. (Kiviniemi 1982a, p. 61–62.) The use of saints' names, on the other hand, reflected the growing power of the Church, which influenced every aspect of a person's life at that time (Withycombe 1977, p. xxvi).

The new custom of naming people after saints was brought to Germany via France from its origins in Italy. This innovation was first spread from city to city, and the rural population and the nobility adopted it somewhat later. It was especially the burghers in the cities who were willing to accept this innovation. Saints' names also settled in women's names more rapidly than in men's names. (V. Kohlheim 1996a, p. 1052.) The change in the German anthroponymic system was so drastic that Seibicke (1982, p. 134) has called it a "Paradigmenwechsel", a change of paradigm.

As the saints' names were mainly of foreign origin – Hebrew, Greek and Latin – and were not understandable to the people, their lexical meaning could not play any role in the new system. Even so, these foreign names became increasingly popular in Germany, and in the 15th and 16th centuries they form a clear majority, 90 per cent and even more, of the names of the people in many places.[72] Among the most popular names were *Johannes, Nikolaus, Petrus, Michael, Martin* and *Georg* for the men, and *Margarethe, Elisabeth, Katharina, Anna, Agnes* and *Sophia* for the women. (Seibicke 1982, p. 135.) These foreign names were also adapted phonologically to their new environment, and many of them got hypocoristic name forms: *Johannes* became *Hans, Nicolaus Chlaus* or *Niclas, Martinus Mertein, Katharina Katrey,* etc. (V. Kohlheim 1996b, p. 1203). Many German names also remained in use, primarily because they were also saints' names (Seibicke 1982, p. 135). Examples of these are *Heinrich, Konrad, Lienhart* and *Wolfgang* (V. Kohlheim 1996a, p. 1053).[73]

In Finland, the Christianisation of personal names was even more thoroughgoing than in Germany: the old Finnish personal names disappeared totally from use. One reason for this was that they were not preserved as saints' names. The only saint who was canonised on the Finns' initiative is the first bishop of Finland, Bishop Henry (Henrik), who was English by birth. It is also important to note that the Finns had already borrowed a number of foreign personal names before the saints' names became popular in the country.[74] The powerful people in Finland did not have traditional names either, as was the case in many other countries. Hence, there were no strong traditions in the society which could have protected the use of old Finnish names. (Kiviniemi 1982a, p. 61, 66.) Maliniemi (1947, p. 47) refers to the lack of national resistance in Finland, which at that time was occupied by the Swedes.[75] The language of administration was Swedish (often beside Latin), which meant that names were usually recorded in their Swedish forms in documents (Kiviniemi 1993, p. 121; Maliniemi 1947, p. 47).

Saints' names also had domesticated forms in Finland: *Andreas* became *Antti, Benedictus Pentti, Henrik Heikki, Jacobus Jaakko, Laurentius Lauri, Martinus Martti, Matias Matti, Mikael Mikko*, etc., just as *Birgitta* became *Pirkko, Cecilia Silja, Christina Kirsti, Katarina Katri, Margareta Marketta*, etc. (Maliniemi 1947, p. 47–52, 56). Such alternative forms were also needed to differentiate people with similar names (Kiviniemi 1993, p. 121).

The most common names for Finnish and Swedish men in the Middle Ages were (Finnish/Swedish forms) *Jussi/Johannes, Olli/Olof, Niilo/Nils, Lauri/Lars, Pekka/Per, Antti/Anders* and *Jaakko/Jakob*. In the 16th century, the number of different mens' names within one parish was typically between 30 and 40, and the most popular five names could cover 50 per cent of all men. The popularity of a name usually depended on the role of that particular saint in the calendar of the saints. (Kiviniemi 1982a, p. 70; 1982b, p. 37–38.) The Church had thousands of canonised saints, but the calendars of different dioceses included about two hundred names only (Maliniemi 1947, p. 49). Hence, some differences between the most popular names in Finland and in Sweden can be explained by the differences in their saint calendars. There were also regional differences in Finland, as the patron saints of Finnish medieval churches were important in local name-giving. (Kiviniemi 1982b, p. 38.)

To sum up, this "revolution" in German and Finnish anthroponymic systems meant that indigenous names were replaced by a limited number of saints' names which were mainly of foreign origin.

From Bynames to Hereditary Surnames

The decline in the name stock was a phenomenon which characterised all European naming systems in the Middle Ages and resulted in the growing frequency of certain names. The most popular name for men, *John,* became so common that across Europe, up to one man in three had this name. One of the consequences of this process was the use of hypocoristic name forms, which helped to differentiate people from each other, e.g. sons from their fathers. Hence in Italy, the son of *Malatesta* could be called *Malatestino* and the son of *Grifone Grifoneto*. (Wilson 1998, p. 104, 109–113.)[76]

It soon became clear that the single name system could not serve the function to individualise people in medieval society. This was a problem especially in the cities, which grew rapidly at that time. (Fleischer 1968, p. 83.) Therefore, a new process started which eventually led to the present-day surname system. The first stage of this process was that bynames[77] became part of the naming system, i.e. specific byname types were formed and they became used systematically.[78] The second stage was that they became hereditary. (Kiviniemi 1982b, p. 31.) From a systematic point of view, this process meant that the old single name system was replaced by a double name system which consisted of two elements: the first name and the surname (Neumann 1973, p. 194).[79] The whole development was relatively slow and irregular throughout all of Europe (Wilson 1998, p. 115). It started in Italy in the 9th century, and spread from there to France and other parts of Europe (R. Kohlheim 1996a, p. 1280).[80] Let us have a closer look at Germany and Finland again.

This process began in Germany in the 12th century, and it took several centuries to complete (R. Kohlheim 1996a, p. 1280). Just as in many other countries, there were also several extraonomastic reasons for this development. Hereditary surnames were needed to mark hereditary political and juridical rights. Public administration also required names by which people could be identified in tax lists and other written documents. In a society where the son typically inherited the occupation of his father, it was also practical to show this with a common name. In addition, the surname served to emphasise family consciousness. An important factor in the acceptance of this innovation was also that it was considered fashionable. Surnames were first assumed among the nobility, from whom the fashion was spread to the upper classes of the cities and finally to the lower classes of the society. (Neumann 1973, p. 193–194; Seibicke 1982, p. 180–181.) Geographically, this innovation was spread from the south and west to the north and east; from big cities to smaller towns and eventually to the countryside as well (Fleischer 1968, p. 85; R. Kohlheim 1996a, p. 1280). By the end of the 12th century, surnames were already common in Cologne and Mainz, for example. However, there were still Germans in the 19th century who did not have surnames. (Pulgram 1993, p. 333.)

The primary source for German surnames was bynames, and German onomasticians have presented several typologies for them. The main groups are (Neumann 1973, p. 196; Seibicke 1982, p. 182–194):[81]

1. Surnames derived from personal names (*Althans, Heinzmann, Jürgens, Klauser*)
2. Surnames referring to place of residence (*Eckmann, Lindner, Steinhaus, von Goethe*)
3. Surnames referring to descent (*Beyer, Hesse, Niederländer, Schwabe*)
4. Surnames referring to occupations (*Huber, Lehmann, Schmidt, Wagner*)
5. Surnames derived from nicknames (*Fuchs, Lange, Röting, Schneidewind*)

The development of the surname system in Finland followed the Central European pattern, especially in the western parts of the country (Mikkonen & Paikkala 1992, p. 13).[82] In the Middle Ages, surnames were still uncommon in Sweden and Finland. Some hereditary surnames occurred at that time among the nobility and burghers of foreign, usually German, origin. From the 16th century on, many priests and other educated people adopted bynames which were often in Latin or Greek, e.g.

Agricola or *Melartopaeus*. (Blomqvist 1988, p. 30–31.) In 1626, the nobility of Sweden and Finland was ordered to adopt surnames (Mikkonen & Paikkala 1992, p. 13). Soon, people in towns began to assume surnames as well, and the last group to adopt this innovation was the rural population, who did so in the 19th century (Blomqvist 1988, p. 31–32). However, it was not until 1921 that a law was enacted in Finland which made it compulsory for all Finns to have a surname (Kangas 1991, p. 19).

Just as elsewhere in Europe, the Finnish surname system was developed from a systematic use of bynames (Mikkonen & Paikkala 1992, 13). In the Middle Ages, the most common practice to identify people in written documents was the use of a first name and a patronym: *Henrik Matsson* (in the Swedish form) or *Heikki Matinpoika* (in the Finnish form), often together with the place of residence: *Hanns Olsson Lusist* ('from Lusi'). For ordinary people, the patronym was often the only official name beside the individual name(s) until they finally adopted surnames. Many bynames which referred to the occupation or personal characteristics of the person, e.g. *Peer Seppä* ('smith') or *Nicki Rapareisi* ('mud thigh'), also became hereditary surnames. (Kiviniemi 1982a, p. 50–54.)

There are many types of surnames in Finland (Mikkonen & Paikkala 1992, p. 19–28):

1. Surnames based on personal names, e.g. *Hermunen* (< *Herman*), *Janatuinen* (< *Janottu*)
2. Surnames based on bynames, e.g. *Partanen* (< parta 'beard'), *Suutari* ('shoemaker')
3. Surnames based on names of houses, e.g. *Sammallahti* ('moss bay'), *Vuorela* (< *vuori* 'mountain, hill')
4. Names of noble families, e.g. *Tandefelt, Yrjö-Koskinen*
5. Surnames based on old names of the educated, e.g. *Alopaeus, Rautelin*
6. Surnames based on old burgher names, e.g. *Lundberg, Rosendal*
7. Surnames based on old soldier names, e.g. *Kuula, Tapper*
8. Young western Finnish *nen*-names referring to nature, e.g. *Järvinen* (< *järvi* 'lake'), *Saarinen* (< *saari* 'island')
9. Names inspired by the Finnish nationalist movement (names translated from Swedish), e.g. *Koskinen* (< *Forsman, koski* 'rapids'), *Vihervaara* (< *Grönberg,* 'green hill')

Later Developments in European Naming Systems

At the same time when surnames were adopted all over Europe, first names were also affected by new trends. In many places, secular motives came to replace religious motives in the choice of name. Wilson (1998, p. 103) describes the situation as follows:

> Once saints' names had been adopted for whatever reasons, they then became part of the established name system and were transmitted within it. Secular patronage, imitation and fashion would build on what was initially a religious impulse.[83]

The influence of court poetry on name-giving was considerable in the Middle Ages, and names such as *Arthur, Lancelot, Olivier* and *Roland* became popular in many countries. Thus, many Germanic names survived in the Middle Ages also because popular literature made them fashionable, not only because they were saints' names. These epic names were first borne by the nobility, and later they were spread among the peasants. It has been suggested that naming after epic heroes was regarded in the same way as naming after saints. Indeed, many of these heroes represented ideal types of Christian knights. (Wilson 1998, p. 107–108; V. Kohlheim 1996b, p. 1205.) Similarly, the influence of Dante and Petrarch was reflected in the popularity of *Beatrice* and *Laura,* and many other names from popular literature became fashionable (Hanks & Hodges 1990, p. xx). Philosophical trends also affected personal naming. For example, the 15th century humanism made classical Greek and Latin names popular all over Europe: *Achilles, Cicero, Cornelia, Diana,* etc. (Bach 1953, p. 40–41; V. Kohlheim 1996b, p. 1205; Seibicke 1982, p. 137–138.)

Despite this secularisation, Christianity continued to have an important role in name-giving. The Reformation led to significant differences in Catholic and Protestant name-giving.[84] Among the Catholics, naming after the saints continued to have a specific religious meaning: the saints acted as models, special protectors and advocates before God. After the Council of Trent, the Catholic church also required that children be given names of canonised saints. It has been pointed out, however, that in doing so the Church merely confirmed a prevailing practice. (Wilson 1998, p. 191.) After the Counter-Reformation, new saints also brought new names into the Catholic nomenclature, e.g. *Aloysius, Xaverius* and *Ignatius.* Names referring to the Catholic liturgy also became popular: *Avemaria, Paternoster, Pronobis.* (Bach 1953, p. 43, 49.) In the 16th century, *Joseph* and *Maria* also gained popularity in Germany. The former became a typical Catholic name, whereas the latter has been used by both Catholics and Protestants. (V. Kohlheim 1996a, p. 1054.)

Among the Protestants, saints' names were rejected and biblical names preferred (Wilson 1998, p. 193). In 16th century Germany, Protestant families particularly gave their children names from the Old Testament, such as *Abraham, Benjamin, Martha* and *Rebekka* (Seibicke 1982, p. 136). The turn to biblical names has been explained by the influence of Martin Luther's Bible translation and the Protestant custom of reading the Bible. Protestantism also emphasised the importance of the mother tongue, and new German names with religious meanings were created in the old style: *Christfried, Gottlob, Ehregott,* etc. (Bach 1953, p. 41, 47–48.) Foreign Christian names were also translated into German, e.g. *Amadeus* became *Gottlieb* and *Timotheus* became *Fürchtegott* (Schwarz 1949, p. 53). The use of old German names was propagated as well (Seibicke 1982, p. 136). In England, many names of non-biblical saints almost disappeared in the 16th century, whereas Old Testament names enjoyed a vogue. The Puritans also invented new English names with religious meanings, such as *Praise-God, Reformation, Renewed* and *Sorry-for-Sin*. (Withycombe 1977, p. xxxvi–xxxix).

The Reformation did not cause any immediate or major changes in the personal naming of the Finns. Even if hagiolatry was no longer practised in the Church of Finland, the most common names continued to be those of the central saints in the saint calendar (Kiviniemi 1982a, p. 71; Maliniemi 1947, p. 51). This may be explained by the fact that contrary to the religious situation in Germany, the whole of the Finnish church became Lutheran. As there was no Catholic counter-force in the country, there was no need to mark denominational differences with name-giving either.[85] In Sweden and Finland, the medieval calendar of the saints was gradually changed into a secular "name-day calendar" which commemorates ordinary names.[86] The first name-day calendars were published in the 17th century, and the first new names in them were mainly biblical. (Kiviniemi 1998, p. 213; 1993, p. 120.)

In Europe personal naming has often been attached to politics as well. The vogue for naming children after members of royal families has been strong in many countries, and this, for example, explains the popularity of *Carl, Fredrik, Gustaf* and *Lovisa* in Sweden (Utterström 1994, p. 290) and that of *Edward, Elizabeth, William* and *Robert* in England (Hanks & Hodges 1990, p. xv–xvi). In the 17th and 18th centuries when French culture was fashionable in Europe, many French names were adopted in other countries, e.g. *Louis, Charlotte* and *Henriette* in Germany (V. Kohlheim 1996b, p. 1205). The French Revolution also generated "revolutionary names", such as *Egalité* ('equality') and *Vérité* ('truth'), but their popularity did not last long (Wilson 1998, p. 209). The national awakening in the 19th century Finland led to a creation of hundreds of new Finnish names, many of which found their way to the Finnish name-day calendar and became very popular. Examples of these are *Impi* 'maiden', *Onni* 'luck', *Toivo* 'hope' and *Veikko* 'brother'. (Kiviniemi 1998, p. 212–213.)

An important development in the European naming systems was the spread of multiple first names. In the late 13th century, there were already people carrying two first names in Italy, from where, as it seems, this innovation was spread to Spain and France, and elsewhere in Europe (Wilson 1998, p. 215–217).[87] The bearing of double names was fairly common in 16th century Germany, especially among the nobility and in the cities, but it took some time before this practice spread to the countryside (Bach 1953, p. 36–38; Schwarz 1949, p. 54). It has been suggested that the use of more than one first name was a sign of a heightened self-awareness in the upper classes of the society. Multiple first names were also useful in differentiating people from each other: *Hans Jacob* from *Hans Konrad*, etc. Having more than one name also meant that children could have several patron saints. The number of names was often limited by the Church, but there were also people who had twenty, or even more than fifty first names. (Seibicke 1982, p. 147.)

This naming fashion spread to Finland in the 18th century from Sweden,[88] and it soon became common among the upper classes of the society and in the western parts of the country. In the beginning, it was also more typical for girls to have more than one name. In everyday speech, combinations of two names were often abbreviated into compound names, thus *Anna Kristiina* became *Annastiina,* and so on. Since the end of the 19th century, such compound names have also been given as official names, often written with a hyphen: *Anna-Liisa, Eeva-Stiina,* etc. In Germany, these name forms began to appear as official names at approximately the same time. (Kiviniemi 1993, p. 14–15, 22.) Examples of them are *Karlheinz, Hans-Jürgen, Annemarie* and *Eva-Maria* (Seibicke 1982, p. 141).

The influence of films, television and other popular culture became significant in European personal naming practices in the 20th century. Among many other names it explains the popularity of *Rhett* and *Scarlett* (from the popular novel and film "Gone with the Wind"), *Humphrey* and *Marilyn* (film stars Humphrey Bogart and Marilyn Monroe) or *Elvis* (musician Elvis Presley), as personal names. (Hanks & Hodges 1990, p. xx–xxi.)[89] Many scholars have also pointed out that the euphony of names has become more important as a motive for name-giving than any religious or cultural grounds in Europe today (V. Kohlheim 1996b, p. 1205). In many countries, names are chosen primarily because they are considered to be pleasant-sounding and beautiful (Gerritzen 1998, p. 146). However, choosing a name for a child is always a complex process in which many factors work together (Kiviniemi 1982a, p. 165–166).

Developments in African Personal Naming Systems

The African Concept of Name

In this section, we shall look at the most important developments in the anthroponymic systems of sub-Saharan Africa in the 20th century.[90] It should be noted that these naming systems do not necessarily have much in common. Just as there are many and varied cultures in Africa, so are there also many and varied naming systems.[91] Therefore, one ought to be careful when making generalisations about personal naming in Africa. Nevertheless, it has been stated that there are a number of significant differences between African and European personal naming patterns, especially in the understanding of the concept of name. Two aspects seem to be of special significance here: the relationship between the name and the person, and name meaningfulness. Let us investigate these first.

Name and Person. It is often claimed that the main difference between the European and African concept of name is that in Africa, the name and the person are inseparable. In traditional African thinking, the name *is* the person, whereas the European concept is that the name is a mere label which *refers* to the person. Hence in Africa, one is not only called X, one *is* X. (Herbert 1999a, p. 215–216; Koopman 1986, p. 14–15; Mbiti 1969, p. 119; Obeng 1998, p. 165.) Ojoade (1980, p. 198) puts this clearly too when he says:

> In a word, the traditional African name is much more than a means of identification. It is an essential part of the bearer.

The close connection between the name and the person is reflected in the common idea in African naming systems that the child is not a person until he or she is properly named. Should an infant die before naming, it is thought of as if it had never been born. This attitude has been explained by the high rates of infantile mortality in Africa: it helps the parents to overcome their sorrow after the death of the child. (Parrinder 1981, p. 94; Turnbull 1966, p. 53.) The dead are also regarded as having a personality only as long as there are people who recognise them by name. After that, the name disappears and these "living-dead" lose their humanness and become mere spirits.[92] (Mbiti 1969, p. 79, 134, 163.) Therefore, "keeping somebody's name alive" is a major concern for many Africans (Dahl 1998, p. 325).

In many African societies, children are traditionally named after departed relatives, which indicates the belief that the dead person has come back to the family through the birth of the baby (Mbiti 1991, p. 93; Parrinder 1969, p. 84–85).[93] Beidelman (1974, p. 287) points out that names are thus "ageless":

> [T]he names of the dead and the living are the same and, indeed, a name is therefore ageless, standing for an endless number of persons so that when one intones a name of a dead person, or even of the living, one could be invoking a large number of spirits, even ones about whom one has no clear knowledge or recollection.

African children are often named after living relatives as well and are thus identified with them. An example from Tanzania illustrates this well. Among the Sukuma-Nyamwezi people, who name the first son after his grandfather, the grandfather may say to his daughter-in-law: "You have given birth to me". Indeed, in societies in which children are systematically named after their grandparents, these two generations are often considered to be the same. They are, in a sense, merged into each other. (Brandström 1998, p. 144–145.)

It is also a common idea in Africa, e.g. among the Basotho, the Ibibio and the Yoruba peoples, that the name may have a psychological effect on the character and personality of the name-bearer (Essien 1986, p. 79; Hallgren 1988, p. 159; Mohome 1972, p. 171; Ojoade 1980, p. 196). Because of this, names of people with doubtful reputations are not adopted (Ayisi 1988, p. 26). Often people are expected to behave in such a manner as to uphold their name. Therefore if a person bears a name meaning 'the brave one', he is expected to be brave (Obeng 1998, p. 165).

In many African societies, people sharing the same name are considered to have a special relationship. Because of this special bond, namesakes may be expected to give presents to each other or help one another in times of difficulty. (Turnbull 1966, p. 56; Visser & Visser 1998, p. 230; Wieschhoff 1941, p. 212.) One may say that in these societies, the namesake relationship is an important part of the "social security system" of the people. Turnbull (1976, p. 181–182) analyses the namesake relationship among the Bushmen (San) as follows:

> It is not merely an economic bond-friendship; there is an almost religious quality to it, a sense of identification, of the inextricability of the fates of those sharing the same name, as though by virtue of that fact alone they have some power over each other. ... This name sharing is not necessarily invoked all the time, but it is one mechanism by which temporary alliances and bonds can be formed when there is need, either to secure support in a dispute, or shelter or food in times of shortage.

Because of the close connection between the name and the person, names are also used widely in witchcraft. It is a general belief in African cultures that there is hidden power in personal names: to know the names of a person means to control him or her (Hallgren 1988, p. 159). Thus, it is believed that calling out the name may for example cause the person to become ill or die (Krige 1988, p. 322–323). Personal names are also used for achieving positive goals. For example, a wrestler may invoke the name of a famous wrestler or a strong ancestor for inspiration during a match (Essien 1986, p. 85).

As names are viewed as components of the self in Africa, it is generally believed that they should not be used carelessly or in abuse (Beidelman 1974, p. 282). Therefore, name avoidance is a widespread custom among many African peoples. Often such practices are very carefully patterned. According to the Zulu and Xhosa custom of *hlonipha*, for example, a woman is not allowed to mention the names of her husband or her relatives-in-law, nor any word which is derived from the same word as these names. As a result, the speech of the women has come to differ considerably from that of the men. (Finlayson 1984, p. 138; Krige 1988, p. 30.) Among the Hausa people, a man avoids mentioning the name of his father, his first wife and his eldest child, even when he refers to other people who bear the same names. Instead of these names, he uses phrases such as "your namesake". In many societies, the names of the dead are not mentioned either. (Gregersen 1977, p. 161–162.)

Teknonymy, i.e. the practice of calling the person "mother-of -X", "father-of-X", etc., also serves the function of avoiding the mentioning of the "real" or "true" name of the person in many societies (Beidelman 1974, p. 284; Essien 1986, p. 85; Gregersen 1977, p. 162; Kidd 1906, p. 33–34; Mohome 1972, p. 180–181).[94] So does the custom of having a "secret" or "hidden" name, which is considered to be the real name of the person but is almost never mentioned for the fear of evil powers.

Instead of it, a public name, or a nickname, is used. Secret names are especially common in West Africa. (Gregersen 1977, p. 162; Ryan 1981, p. 139–140.)

The close link between the name and the person also explains the common custom of giving the child a "derogatory-protective" or a "death-prevention" name, which indicates its worthlessness, to protect the child from death. These names, with meanings such as 'dung-heap', 'tail of a dog' or 'let it be thrown away', are given in order to trick or confuse evil spirits so that the child may not appear of importance to them. This is especially done if the mother has previously lost other children. (Alford 1988, p. 63; Gregersen 1977, p. 161; Kidd 1906, p. 36; Mbiti 1991, p. 93; Obeng 1998, p. 165–166; Parrinder 1981, p. 93; Turnbull 1966, p. 53.) The Akan people believe that the funnier the name is, the better it works, as the child will be ashamed to go back to the world of the spirits bearing a funny name. It has been pointed out that even if such names ridicule the child and may suggest that he or she is not wanted, they actually show that the child is really wanted and loved. (Obeng 1998, p. 166, 169.)[95]

Name Meaningfulness. Another criterion frequently offered for distinguishing African and European personal naming is that of name meaningfulness. It is often stressed that African names carry semantic import, i.e. they "have meaning", and that this meaning is also identified by the people who bear them. (De Klerk & Bosch 1995, p. 69–70; Herbert & Bogatsu 1990, p. 3; Herbert 1996, p. 1222; 1997, p. 6; 1999a, p. 216; 1999b, p. 109; Moyo 1996, p. 12; Suzman 1994, p. 253.)[96] All over Africa, personal names are taken seriously and chosen with special care and consideration (Mbiti 1991, p. 92–93). They are often formed using rather complex linguistic patterns as well (Akinnaso 1980, p. 276).

Many traditional naming systems in Africa are characterised by name uniqueness. Even when children are named after relatives, there is usually only one living bearer for each name in these societies.[97] Altogether, personal naming shows great creativity in Africa, and names may often be formed of almost any linguistic elements. (Brenzinger 1999, p. 9; Herbert 1996, p. 1222, 1225; 1999a, p. 218.)[98] It has also been emphasised that the various meanings of African names throw light upon the whole traditional culture, and thus they may serve in reaching a deeper understanding of the people, their ideas and their way of life (Hallgren 1988, p. 168; Okere 1996a, p. 133).[99] Madubuike (1976, p. 13–14) sums this up as follows:

> Names given to people have definite meanings, and parents, relatives, and well wishers are very conscious when choosing the names of their children or of an individual. Thus names are not merely labels or simply tags which the individual carries along with him. They have a deep social significance and many names studied collectively express a world view, the *Weltanschauung* of the people.

It is important to note that the lexical meaning of the name does not usually reveal the whole significance of the name. Therefore, it is necessary to make a distinction between meaning and significance in African names (Herbert 1999a, p. 216). According to Herbert (1997, p. 6), significance is related to the reason for choosing a name, i.e. "what it means within the sociocultural fabric". Ebeogu (1993, p. 137) also remarks that African names always have a context: "each of them is the product of some experience, which produces a creative exercise that gives rise to the name ... Each of them therefore narrates a story." It has also been pointed out that the meanings of African names are often interpreted differently by different people. Even fathers and mothers may not "understand" the name of their child in a similar way. (Herbert 1996, p. 1222.) Akinnaso (1980, p. 279) also remarks that the information which is "symbolically stored and retrieved" in a personal name may not be known to every member of the community.

Why is it then that traditional African naming systems seem to emphasise the meaning of the name, contrary to European naming systems? First, one should note that all over the world, smaller-scale and less complex societies tend to use names with semantic meaning (Alford 1988, p. 60). One reason for this might be that in nonliterate cultures, where information is stored and transmitted orally, personal names often serve a "diary-keeping function" (Akinnaso 1980, p. 279). As was noted earlier, names were meaningful in traditional Germanic and Proto-Finnic naming systems as well. However, in the course of time, and because of various sociocultural and linguistic developments, name meaningfulness lost its significance, and personal names became mere pointers. In traditional European naming systems, the relationship between the name and the person was also considered to be close, and names were used for purposes of magic (Forsman 1894, p. 11–12; Kiviniemi 1982a, p. 30–32).

It is evident that the traditional European naming systems resembled the traditional African ones in many respects. However, it seems reasonable to assume that the contemporary differences between African and European personal naming do not originate from fundamental differences between "African" and "European" ways of thinking or philosophy, but from different sociocultural developments in these societies. A historical analysis of these naming systems also confirms that the major difference is not between "Africa" and "Europe" in the first place but, as we shall see later in this thesis, between traditional and modern naming in these societies.

On the other hand, it has been noted that not all Africans hold strong views about the meanings of their names, and the name is often seen as a mere label in Africa as well (Herbert 1996, p. 1225). One explanation for this may be that in Africa, the meaning of the name seems to tell much more about the name-giver than the name-bearer (Herbert 1999a, p. 220), and hence it is not as important to the latter as it is to the former. It is also clear that in those African societies in which children are named after other people, reference to the namesake is crucial, not the meaning of the name. For example, Ennis (1945, p. 7–8) points out that among the Ovimbundu people in Angola, the namesake custom "tends to destroy the meaning of names". Hessel and Cobi Visser (1998, p. 230) say about Naro names that "the meaning of a name is not of primary importance, it is much more the relationship it indicates that is important". Madubuike (1976, p. 96) remarks that because of the custom of inheriting relatives' names, many Gikuyus believe that their names have no special meaning. Based on all this, it is justified to claim that name meaningfulness is not equally important in all African societies.

Traditional African Naming Systems

The oldest written documents on African naming systems date back to the early contact period between Africans and Europeans. Based on available material, such as descriptions of naming practices by linguists, anthropologists and missionaries, church and government registers, and so on, onomasticians have striven to reconstruct traditional patterns of personal naming. (Herbert 1999b, p. 109–110.) It is important to note that these reconstructions often describe African naming systems as stable, typically as they were just before the European influence began to change them.[100] It is possible, though, that these naming systems underwent radical changes in earlier times as well, even if there are no historical documents on such processes. Most likely, African naming systems have affected each other in various ways over the centuries, as a result of various types of culture contact.

In this subsection, we shall take up a number of common features, as well as differences, in traditional African naming systems. This presentation is based mainly on academic articles published on African personal names in linguistic and anthropological journals, and on miscellaneous literature dealing with African cultures.

Name-giving Ceremonies and Name-givers. In many African societies, a baby is given a name soon after birth. Often this name is temporary, and the real name is bestowed later.[101] In some societies, the birth name refers to the day of the week the baby was born.[102] In others, it may indicate special circumstances of the birth, e.g. that the baby was born feet first, with extra fingers or with the mother dying at birth, or to the child's place in the family, e.g. that he or she was born after twins. (Parrinder 1981, p. 92–93.) Derogatory-protective names, which aim to protect the child from death, are often given as temporary names as well. These names typically have negative meanings such as 'I am dead' or 'I am ugly'. (Turnbull 1966, p. 53.) Sometimes the birth name is a name of endearment given by the mother or some other intimate relative (Magesa 1998, p. 90).

In many societies, the actual name-giving ceremony in which the child receives its "real" or "true" name, takes place about a week after the birth, when the mother and the child leave the room of birth for the first time.[103] This "outdooring" ceremony also serves to introduce the child to the community.[104] (Amin 1993, p. 1–2; Ayisi 1988, p. 25; Mbiti 1969, p.

119; Parrinder 1981, p. 93.) Yoruba girls are named on the seventh day and boys on the ninth day after birth, because of the Yoruba belief that females have seven ribs while males have nine (Akinnaso 1980, p. 277). In some societies, the real name is given much later. Among the Ibo people, for example, name-giving takes place twenty-eight days after birth. Until then, the child is called *omo ofu* 'new child'. The name is given on the same day that the mother visits the market for the first time after delivery. (Wieschhoff 1941, p. 212.) Among the Zulus, the name is usually bestowed when the child is a few weeks old, but it may be given at any other time as well (Krige 1988, p. 73). In many societies, the name is given at a great feast attended by family members, relatives, neighbours and friends, sometimes by the chief as well. However, some peoples are reported to have no special ceremony for naming their children. (Evans-Pritchard 1948, p. 166; Kidd 1906, p. 32; Krige 1988, p. 73; Mbiti 1969, p. 119; 1991, p. 92.)

There are also differences with regard to name-givers. In some cultures, the real name is bestowed traditionally by the father or grandfather, in others by the parents or grandparents, elders of the family jointly, or by an uncle. Sometimes the name is given by a friend, a person who is in a special joking-relationship with the parents, by women who have had children, or by someone who is popular in the community or has given the child a valuable present. (Ayisi 1988, p. 25; Kidd 1906, p. 34; Mbiti 1969, p. 119–120; Moyo 1996, p. 12; Okere 1996a, p. 134; Omari 1970, p. 68; Sumbwa 1997, p. 49; Turnbull 1966, p. 53.) The name may also be given by a diviner who has helped the mother with her pregnancy (Brandström 1998, p. 147).

Motives for the Choice of Name. The motives behind the choice of name seem to be various in traditional African naming systems, and the onomastic literature presents several typologies for them.[105] Names referring to events occurring at the time of birth are very common in many cultures. This may be due to the history-keeping function of personal names in Africa: the name locates the birth of a child within a specific historical context (Herbert 1997, p. 7). Hence, many Africans bear names which tell something about the time they were born. Such names often refer to the state of the weather or seasons of the year: thunder, rain, drought, famine, harvest, weeding, hunting, etc. Names may also refer to striking events in the community, such as quarrels in the family and cases of death.[106] Political events, e.g. a war or an enthronement of a chief, are often reflected in names as well. Some names also describe the physical appearance of the baby. (Kidd 1906, p. 34–35; Mbiti 1991, p. 93; Omari 1970, p. 66.)

Many African names show the feelings of the parents: joy, gratitude, etc. Names expressing religious feelings are also common. Frequently, the name of God is made part of the name. (Hallgren 1988, p. 161–162; Mbiti 1991, p. 93–94.) Negative feelings are also reflected in personal names, such as disappointment regarding the birth of the child or the parents' concern for the child's future. Often names include messages to other people, and as such, they serve to minimise social friction. (Wieschhoff 1941, p. 219–221.) All over Africa, it is typical that personal names are used for making comments and expressing attitudes and opinions about life (Iwundu 1973, p. 46). Names may also be derived from proverbs which reflect the African philosophy of life (Ennis 1945, p. 2–5; Musere 1998; Nsimbi 1950, p. 205; Ojoade 1980, p. 196).[107] Proverbial names are common among the Yoruba people. For example, the name *Aghorunse* is derived from the proverb "A ka gho urun ji a ri se", meaning 'examine closely a thing before you do it'. (Ojoade 1980, p. 199–200.)

In certain cases, name-giving is carefully patterned, and there is a special list of names for children born in particular circumstances. Such "systematic" names are given, for example, to twins and children succeeding them, to children born with legs first, or to a son born after many daughters.[108] (Brandström 1998, p. 147; Daeleman 1977, p. 189–192; Evans-Pritchard 1948, p. 167–168; Mohome 1972, p. 179–180; Ndoma 1977, p. 89.)

In many societies, e.g. among the Gikuyu, the Ovimbundu and the Sotho-Tswana peoples, children are systematically named after their relatives (Ennis 1945, p. 1; Herbert 1998, p. 190; Herbert & Bogatsu 1990, p. 6; Madubuike 1976, p. 95; Mohome 1972, p. 171–172). Among the Agni people of the Ivory Coast, the first-born son receives the name of his paternal grandfather and the first-born daughter that of her maternal grandmother. Other sons receive the names of the paternal grandfather's brothers and the daughters those of the grandfather's or the father's sisters. (Magesa 1998, p. 87–88.) This is practised to express the belief that the community which is living today is a reflection of the past and shall continue living in the future as well (Turnbull 1966, p. 55). Sometimes children are named after other people as well, especially after close friends of the name-giver or some prominent or famous people who are believed to have desirable characteristics. Often an intimate relationship develops between the two namesakes. (Essien 1986, p. 84; Mohome 1972, p. 172–173.)

Number of Names and Name Changes. The number of names given to an individual varies in different societies, and there seems to be no general rule in Africa for this. Generally, children are given more than one name: the first one(s) soon after birth and the rest later in life (Mbiti 1991, p. 94).[109] For example, a Bobo child receives three names. The first one is given seven days after birth, the second one when he or she starts walking, and the third one during the initiation ceremony. (Madubuike 1976, p. 127.) The Barotse people receive three names: the first one at the time of birth, the second one at puberty (in the case of girls) or at adolescence (in the case of boys), and the third one when the person becomes a parent (Sumbwa 1997, p. 49).

Some societies have a dual system for personal naming. The child may be given a secret name and an ordinary name at birth, and later he or she might receive other names which mark important stages in his or her life (Aguessy 1979, p. 116). In some cultures, the child receives one name from the father's family and another one from the mother's family, but only one remains in use (Beidelman 1974, p. 287; Wieschhoff 1941, p. 212). The Nuer people commonly have two names. One is used among the paternal kin and the other among the maternal kin. (Evans-Pritchard 1948, p. 167.) Even if the person receives several names during his or her lifetime, the name that was given first is often the most important one, as it is the name with which the child is introduced to the community (Brandström 1998, p. 142).

Names are also frequently changed in Africa, especially after some significant event in the person's life (Gregersen 1977, p. 162). For example, among the Ovimbundu people, a person may take a new name, "a name of despair", when facing troubles in life (Ennis 1945, p. 5). A new name may also be assumed after a serious illness (Ndoma 1977, p. 90). A change of name may also be attached to a new social role. The new ruler often receives a new name at the coronation ceremony, and the same may happen to people who become religious mediums. (Mbiti 1969, p. 174–175, 184.)

In many societies, the name of the person is abandoned after initiation (Mbiti 1991, p. 94), but initiate names may also be used during the initiation period only (Mohome 1972, p. 183). Teknonyms are also used to indicate that the person has gained a new social status by becoming a mother or a father (Beidelman 1974, p. 284–285; Evans-Pritchard 1948, p. 171). In some societies, slaves were given special names, and these names were often abandoned when they were freed (Ryan 1981, p. 152–153).

Praise Names and Other Nicknames. Nicknames, by which we mean unofficial names that are bestowed on individuals in addition to their given names (Alford 1988, p. 82)[110], are widely used in African societies. There are many types of them as well. Descriptive nicknames often make social comments about the behaviour of the person, and as such, they are a useful means for the society to express its opinion and to encourage people to change their way of life (Turnbull 1966, p. 56). Many nicknames are also given to show affection. Mothers and grandparents, for example, give pet names to their children, and such names may become their most commonly used ones (Essien 1986, p. 80–81; Krige 1988, p. 74).

Different kinds of "praise names" are also common in African societies, especially for men. Such praises are used to show respect and admiration in various situations, and they are typically created by the person himself or by his peers (Koopman 1987a, p. 42; Magesa 1998, p. 90). Royal praise names are common all over Africa. Kavango chiefs, for example, have had praise names meaning 'fire/light', 'python' or 'God' (Fisch 1979, p. 38–40). The Hausa people are reported to have special praise names for holders of particular occupations, as well as names which describe the way the person fulfils his office (Ryan 1981, p. 159). In some cultures, people inherit the praise name of their clan (Evans-

Pritchard 1948, p. 168). Special "war names" are often given for acts of bravery in battle, with meanings such as 'he who killed many in war' (Gregersen 1977, p. 162). The Sukuma-Nyamwezi people also have "wandering-names", i.e. names which are adopted by men who have been working in far-away places and which tell about their adventures (Brandström 1998, p. 148).

"Ox names" are also common in Africa. Nuer boys and girls, for example, have ox names which refer to the characteristics of their special oxen, and these names are used by age-mates especially at dances, with many embellishments and elaborations. The boys are named after their favourite oxen and the girls after bulls calved by the cows they milk. (Evans-Pritchard 1948, p. 168–169.)[111]

Names Referring to Family and Other Groups. In traditional African societies, every individual typically had his or her own names, and there were no "family names" shared by all people in a particular family (Mbiti 1969, p. 119). People with the same name were often distinguished by the use of descriptive bynames, occupational bynames or bynames referring to their workplaces or home villages (Madubuike 1976, p. 17–18).[112] However, there were some names which indicated attachment to family or wider kin-group. Patronyms – "son-of-X" or "daughter-of-X" – are especially common in many parts of Africa (Madubuike 1976, p. 16). According to the Ibibio custom, for instance, the person's official name consists of the individual name of the person and of that of the father and/or the grandfather, e.g. *Okon Etim Akpan* (Essien 1986, p. 82).

Clan names are also widely used. For example, Kaguru children automatically have one name referring to the father's clan. As this clan name is shared by all paternal siblings of the child, it sets the members of a household apart from other matrilineal kin. Usually this name is directly derived from the clan's name: a boy whose father belongs to the Welimbo ('birdlime') clan is called *Mulimbo* and his sister *Mamlimbo*. (Beidelman 1974, p. 282–283.)

There are also other kinds of names referring to groups in Africa. "Dance names" and "society names" which are assumed by members of dancing groups and religious societies practising esoteric cults, etc., are typical for example among the Sukuma-Nyamwezi people (Brandström 1998, p. 147–148). Ashanti children also belong to specific "spirit groups" after their fathers, and each group has a number of "surnames" which are commonly borne by their members (Busia 1970, p. 197, 199). Regimental names are also widespread. Zulu men who belong to the same regiment may all be called individually by the name of the regiment, which is chosen by the king. (Krige 1988, p. 112–113.) Names given to different age groups attending initiation rites are typical in many societies (Madubuike 1976, p. 97).

Altogether, there is a wide variety of name types in Africa, and not all of them are mentioned here. Giving names, and also playing with names, seems to be an important part of African cultures. As Mbiti (1991, p. 95) puts it, "there is no end to giving names to people in African societies".

In everyday life, many kinds of names are used, even if kinship terms are often used more frequently when addressing people (Brandström 1998, p. 149).

The Influence of Christianity and Colonialism on Personal Naming in Africa

European influence, and the influence of Christianity, started to change African cultures on a large scale when the colonisers and missionaries from various European countries settled in different parts of Africa in the 19th century.[113] In little more than a hundred years, the number of Christians in Africa increased to over 160 million, and this massive conversion corresponded with a rapid sociocultural change in African societies (Ikenga-Metuh 1987, p. 11). Beside Christianity, Islam also spread to Africa, particularly to the northern and western parts of the continent.[114] It has been noted that religious movements tend to spread most quickly in times of rapid social change when people search for answers to new problems (Peil & Oyeneye 1998, p. 163–164), and this is how the "African conversion" has been explained too.[115] Akinnaso (1983, p. 155) describes the sociocultural changes among the Yoruba people in Nigeria as follows:

> Basic changes in kinship, economic, and political organization, in the modes of communication, in the diagnosis and treatment of diseases, and indeed in the entire social structure and "worldview" of the Yoruba are due largely to the spread of literacy, the concomitant diffusion of Western cultures and technologies, and the conversion of most Yoruba to Christianity or Islam. Though these processes began more than a century ago, their effects have never been so seriously felt as in the last three decades.
>   Seriously affected are attitudes toward indigenous cultural traditions, especially toward traditional ritual performances.

When the Europeans came to the African continent, they were generally filled with the spirit of cultural and racial superiority, which encouraged them to condemn indigenous cultural practices. All over Africa, Christianity became identified with European culture, and conversion into this new religion typically meant abandoning the African identity. (Boahen 1990, p. 222, 336.) However, this did not lead to a total abandonment of traditional beliefs and practices. Among many other things, ancestor worship and polygyny continued to persist in many parts of Africa, even if they were usually opposed by the missionaries (Peil & Oyeneye 1998, p. 165). On the other hand, many African traditions were accepted by the missions (Hastings 1976, p. 38).

What happened to African personal naming in this process? Meeting with European naming systems and Christian name-giving practices led to exceptionally rapid and thoroughgoing changes in African naming systems. Together with many other African cultural practices, indigenous names were often condemned by the Europeans. To become a Christian usually meant that one had to be baptised and assume a new name (Boahen

57

1990, p. 336). It has been pointed out that this was done not only because African names were regarded as "pagan", but also because of the
missionaries' ignorance of indigenous names. As foreigners, they often
had serious difficulties trying to pronounce African names.[116] Hence,
meaningful African names were replaced by European and biblical names
such as *George*, *Peter* and *Esther*, which had no meaning to their bearers. (Mtuze 1994, p. 95.) It was also a new custom for many Africans to
choose names from a limited stock, e.g. the Bible, and this struck at the
core of traditional name-giving (Dickens 1985, p. 68).

The adoption of European culture, including European names, was
regarded as "an outward sign of the inward transformation from the 'pagan' to the Christian state" (Ayandele 1979, p. 243). Gradually, European and biblical names also became fashionable, and often non-Christians adopted them as well (Beidelman 1974, p. 291; Ndoma 1977, p.
90). As Moyo (1996, p. 13) puts it, "it was considered old-fashioned and
educationally unprogressive to have an African name only". Altogether,
it seems that foreign names were adopted eagerly by many colonised
Africans in the late 19th and early 20th centuries:

> To have a new and foreign name ... was a sign of changes from primitive to
> modern world. And the new and foreign name signified this process. This
> attitude was implanted into people's mind to the extent that even the people
> (Africans) themselves were not willing to be baptized into the new religions
> without having new and foreign names accompanied by the act of conver-
> sion. (Omari 1970, p. 68–69.)[117]

In general, the Protestants in Africa favoured biblical names, whereas
the Catholics named their children after saints.[118] Specifically Catholic
names are for example *Cosmos, Ignatius* and *Pius* for men, and *Agnes,
Francisca* and *Monica* for women (Dickens 1985, p. 63; Ekpo 1978, p.
280).[119] The popularity of biblical names among African Christians is
not surprising, considering that the Bible is the most widely translated
and read book in tropical Africa (Mugambi 1995, p. 142). The vogue for
naming children after biblical characters may also be due to the traditional belief that children will adopt the good qualities of the persons
they are named after (Mohome 1972, p. 173).

Many Africans were also named after European missionaries and immigrants. This led to the adoption of ordinary European names such as
Albert or *Alice*. Many names adopted by the Africans during the colonial
period also referred to various aspects of Western civilisation, e.g. *Busi-
nessman, Caesar, Doctor, Napoleon, Philadelphia* and *Shakespeare*.
(Dickens 1985, p. 71–75, 87–89, 92.)[120] European influence was notable
in indigenous names as well, as these examples from Rwanda show:
Mubirigi 'Belgian', *Ngomanzungu* 'European government', and *Kadage*
'little German' (Kimenyi 1989, p. 45). Sometimes African names were
made to resemble European ones in spelling too. For example, the Ibibio
name *'Ndi* 'I am coming' has been anglicised as *Andy*, *Àmá* has become
Amah and *Àkàn Akanson*. (Essien 1986, p. 75–76.)

In Africa, European and biblical names also have domesticated forms, as they were adapted phonologically to the local languages. Among the Kaguru people, *Moses* has thus become *Musa*, *Noah Nuhu* and *Pius Pusi* (Beidelman 1974, p. 291), and the Zulus have made *Albert Alibheti* and *Alfred Alufuledi* (Dickens 1985, p. 75). A Naro child named after Dr. Guenther in Botswana became *Ganda* (Visser & Visser 1998, p. 230). Sometimes the original name is very difficult to trace. Among the Bakongo people, the Portuguese name *Dom Fransisco* has become *Ndofula*, *Dom Sebastiao Ndombasi* and *Eduardo Ndualu* (Ndoma 1977, p. 93–94). In Rwanda, *Père Blanc* 'white father', which refers to the early missionaries of that area, became *Terebura* and *Père Busch* 'father Busch' *Terebushi* (Kimenyi 1989, p. 44). Even if foreign names usually have Africanised forms, the foreign form of the name was often retained when the person wanted to stress his or her religious affiliation (Ryan 1981, p. 162) or impress outsiders with a sophisticated name (Beidelman 1974, p. 291). Educated Africans have thus favoured names such as *Joseph Pythagoras* (Ayandele 1979, p. 257).

Some Christian missions, however, encouraged the use of indigenous African names with Christian meanings since the very beginning of their missionary activities in Africa (Omari 1970, p. 69). This is the case with the Leipzig Mission (die Leipziger Mission), for example, which started to work among the Chagga people in Tanzania in 1893. African names became popular in that region. Of the 4,070 people baptised in the Mamba congregation during the years 1898–1929, more than half (2,402) received African names, the first one of them being bestowed in 1899. These names were typically new formations which reflected Christian beliefs, e.g. *Ndeamtso* 'I am awaken' or *Ndeenengomoo* 'I was given life'. (Fritze 1930, p. 3, 23, 26, 42–43.)[121]

In traditional African societies, names including the element 'God' were quite common in pre-colonial times, but after the advent of Christianity they became even more popular in many places (Mbiti 1991, p. 94). For example, names such as *Nsengimana* 'I pray to God' and *Nduwimana* 'I belong to God' became common in Rwanda and Burundi when people embraced Christianity, together with clearly Christian names such as *Mujawayezu* 'the servant of Jesus' (Kimenyi 1989, p. 47–48). Also in South Africa, Bishop Colenso suggested African names for Zulu converts in the mid-19th century (Dickens 1985, p. 69), and many more examples can be found. Usually these early missionaries were willing to accept indigenous names provided that they had no heathenish connotations (Ayandele 1979, p. 244; Lehmann 1969, p. 180).

However, as European names were generally considered modern and fashionable by the colonised Africans, the idea of African baptismal names did not usually appeal to the converts. A good example of this can be found in Nigeria, where the decision of the Anglican Mission (Church Missionary Society) in 1883 to favour African names for converts created a sensation. Some families left the Anglican community when the local pastor refused to baptise children with other than African names, and many threw off these African names immediately after the baptism.

Some Nigerian Christians also worried that African baptismal names would make them lose their new-won prestige among the "pagans". The missionaries also had different opinions on the matter. Some of them defended foreign names because they could protect the converts from being enslaved, and because they created national unity among Christians coming from different tribes. (Ayandele 1979, p. 244.) The general idea among the missionaries seems to have been that an African could not be a Christian without a European "Christian" name. Therefore, the priests typically insisted on the use of biblical or saints' names at baptism. (Dickens 1985, p. 69, 120.)

Many Africans who did not convert to Christianity received European names at school or from their employers. Often the name was chosen without any consultation with the person in question. (Herbert 1996, p. 1224.) Thus, Africans were given names such as *Jim, Joe, Brandy Bottle, September, Tin-can* and *Jackets* – almost any name coming to mind seems to have been suitable (Kidd 1906, p. 36).[122]

All over Africa, the adoption of European names has led to the use of indigenous names at home and in traditional contexts, and European names in official contexts such as school, church, the workplace, government offices and mission hospitals. The distinction between European and African names thus reflects the distinction between the public and private sectors in the individual's life. (Herbert 1999a, p. 223; Moyo 1996, p. 13; Neethling 1995, p. 958.) Amin (1993, p. 38) describes this phenomenon in Ghana:

> Thus here we have a pupil who was obviously given a "Christian" name by the church, and his father's name was added on as a surname to fit the school requirements. He then bore the combined names of "Patrick Owusu Benefo" only one of which was recognized in his home environment! The other are school or church imposed names, which made him lose his own identity in the bizarre environment of the school and the church. At the western dominated school and church he had one set of names, while in his own cultural and traditional setting, he had a completely different set of names.

Many urbanised and educated Africans also chose to give exclusively European names to their children.[123] This practice was common after the Second World War and before the advent of the African nationalist movements in the late 1950s. (Herbert 1999a, p. 223–224; Kimenyi 1989, p. 48.)

All in all, it seems that there are big differences in Africa with regard to the depth of the influence of Christianity and Europeanisation on personal naming. Okere (1996a, p. 141) has characterised the influence of Christianity on Igbo personal names as follows:

> In fact, the only noticeable impact of Christianity on names is the systematic imposition of the names of foreign saints at baptism. But the baptismal name was always an additional name, coming some time later, at times years after the naming ceremony. Moreover, this ceremony was an out-of-church affair of the extended family, well beyond the influence of the missionary church.

The Revival of African Names and the Adoption of Surnames

The revival of African names is a trend which has characterised personal naming all over Africa especially since the 1960s, following the advent of African nationalist movements. In this process, European names have increasingly lost favour, and churches have come to accept African baptismal names as well.[124] (Herbert 1999a, p. 224.) However, there are also much earlier examples of this phenomenon in Africa. In Nigeria, the cultural nationalists achieved their first successes at the end of the 19th century, and some educated Africans assumed African names at that time. One of the leading figures in the nationalist movement, for example, changed his name *Joseph Pythagoras Haastrup* to *Ademuyiwa Haastrup*. (Ayandele 1979, p. 256–258.) Ayandele (1979, p. 258) has noted some of the reasons behind this phenomenon:

> Most of those who cast off alien names did so because these names reminded them of the days of slavery when their fathers were given the names, a history they wanted to forget. Others did so because alien names separated them in feeling from their own countrymen, encouraging to make them 'strangers in our own country'.
>
> The most important factor that made them decide to assume African names was that they saw themselves bearing meaningless names in a society that attached a great deal of importance to names.

Despite these early name changes, European names became increasingly popular in Nigeria at the beginning of the 20th century, and it was only in the 1940s that there was a tendency to use African names again (Wieschhoff 1941, p. 221–222). In Tanzania, where the cultural renaissance took place much later, mainly in the 1960s and 1970s, the reasons for name changes seem to have been more or less similar. African names were adopted to get rid of "one aspect of colonial mentality and heritage" and to show other people that the name-bearers were true Tanzanians or Africans. (Omari 1970, p. 69.) It has also been pointed out that African names could become popular again because they were no longer attached to traditional beliefs (Koopman 1987b, p. 156).

In some newly independent African countries, indigenous names were even made compulsory by their African leaders. Probably the most striking example comes from Zaïre, where President Mobutu Sese Seko insisted on the Africanisation of personal names and threatened to prosecute Catholic priests who refused to baptise people with African names in 1972. As a result, millions of Africans in Zaïre abandoned their baptismal names.[125] (Gregersen 1977, p. 163; Hastings 1976, p. 37.)

Even if African names were adopted eagerly in many places, this did not mean that people necessarily returned completely to their traditional naming patterns. Many European elements were retained and new ones adopted into African naming systems. In particular, European-type surnames became common all over Africa.[126] Just as in Medieval Europe, the adoption of surnames in African societies was due to the demands of administration, i.e. colonial bureaucracy (De Klerk & Bosch 1995, p. 71; Herbert 1997, p. 4). In different parts of Africa, different kinds of traditional names were used for this purpose. Sometimes customs vary within one ethnic group as well. Of the Kaguru people, for example, some use their father's personal name as a surname, some use their *welekwa* (paternal kin) name, some have their African personal name as a surname and a European name as a first name (Beidelman 1974, p. 291–292).[127] Many groups in Africa also use clan names as surnames. This is the case with the Zulus, for example (Koopman 1986, p. 54–55). Xhosa surnames, on the other hand, seem to have four main sources: ancestors' names, names referring to places, names referring to occupations, and nicknames (Neethling 1996, p. 33–36). Herbert (1997, p. 5) lists clan names, praise names, patronyms, eponyms, place names and colonial surnames as possible sources for the surnames of Africans.[128] Elsewhere he also makes a distinction between cases in which the surname system was based on an indigenous system of "second names" and those in which it was created *ex nihilo* (Herbert 1996, p. 1223).

Among the Hereros, the name of the father or an illustrious ancestor serves as a surname (Otto 1985, p. 126, 131). This is a general practice in many other African cultures as well (Madubuike 1976, p. 16). In Nigeria, the father's name was adopted as a surname, even if traditionally the name of the father was held so sacred that younger people could not mention it, not even after his death (Ayandele 1979, p. 259). Women in Nigeria also started to abandon their maiden names and adopt the husband's name after marriage, which is contrary to the local traditions (Essien 1986, p. 83). The same has happened in many other countries. The surname system has often been considered alien to African cultures, and it has also been criticised strongly (e.g. Kimenyi 1989, p. 48). On the other hand, surnames, and especially those based on ancestors' names, have preserved many traditional African names for coming generations (Hallgren 1988, p. 159). Ayandele argues that the people who adopted the surname system in Nigeria actually made a cultural synthesis which includes both African and European elements. His analysis could well be applied to other peoples in Africa:

> They retained parts of indigenous culture that were deemed valuable and borrowed judiciously from the European civilization they so much execrated. Realizing that complete cultural independence was impossible, they evolved a new synthesis which was neither reactionary traditionalism nor European-imitative but sufficiently African in appearance to satisfy their race-pride and sentiment. Moreover their new synthesis was a product of their own interest. Adoption of surnames was compatible with British law of property and inheritance in the Lagos colony which they had accepted without questioning. It fitted in well with the individualism towards which each Christian family was groping – the idea of a man, his wife and children in place of the extended family. (Ayandele 1979, p. 259.)

Contemporary Trends in African Name-Giving

As we have seen, some traditional naming customs have survived in Africa, some have disappeared, and some have new forms.[129] All over Africa, the contact between European and African naming systems has resulted in a dynamic synthesis, and this process is still going on and creating new forms. Let us look at this development from a systematic viewpoint.

Dickens (1985, p. 4; see also Herbert 1996, p. 1224) has divided the development of the Zulu anthroponymic system into four stages, which may well be applied to other African naming systems, even if the dates given below obviously differ in different systems. Roughly speaking, the first stage is characterised by traditional naming and name uniqueness, the second by the popularity of biblical names, the third by the increased use of other European names, and the fourth by the revival of African names:

1. The period before the arrival of the White man (pre-1840)
2. The period of intensive missionary activity (1840–1899)
3. The period of increased Westernization (influence of education, industrialization, urbanization, etc.) (1900–1949)
4. The period of "Black Consciousness" (1950–1982)

As Dickens wrote her thesis in 1985, her presentation naturally ends in the 1980s. Because of this, a fifth stage needs to be added to her list: the post-apartheid period in South Africa, which started in 1994.

Herbert (1999a, p. 223–224) looks at the same development from a structural viewpoint. According to him, the development from a system of a single name to that of two given names in anglophone southern Africa, i.e. in Botswana, Lesotho, South Africa, Swaziland and Zimbabwe, has gone through four stages:

1. AN	African name (often unique)
2. AN + EN	African name + English name
3. (EN + EN)[130]	English name + English name
4. AN + AN	African name + African name

In southern Africa, the rejection of English names has been stronger among urban residents in recent years, whereas the rural population more typically maintains the pattern of bearing both African and English names. Herbert (1999a, p. 224) also rightly points out that the last stage (4.) does not mean returning to the traditional naming pattern, even if its elements are completely African. Even if colonial names are today rejected, the Western pattern of two given names and a surname is retained.

South African onomasticians have also found other interesting trends in urban name-giving. Firstly, there is a clear shift from negative to positive naming in indigenous names, which means that traditional names which include negative social comments are disappearing, whereas names reflecting positive emotions have become more popular.[131] Secondly, there is a decrease in name uniqueness, as names are more often chosen from a repertoire of fashionable African names.[132] Many popular names are also related to Christian beliefs. Hence, names such as *uBongani* 'thanks', *uLindiwe* 'awaited', *uSibusiswe* 'blessed', *uSipho* 'gift' and *uThembani* 'hope' have become common among urban Zulus. These changes have been explained by the nuclearisation of the family in the urban context and the important role of the church in the social life of many people. (Suzman 1994, p. 266–268, 270.) In a study of six ethnic groups in southern Africa (Northern Sotho, Swati, Tsonga, Tswana, Venda, Zulu) it was noted that the dominant name type in urban centres was that type which was linked to Christianity by a praise, thanks or some other message (Herbert 1996, p. 1226).

There are also signs of the weakening of ethnic boundaries in personal naming: a Zulu child may receive a Sotho name, for example (Suzman 1994, p. 270). It seems that more and more people also choose names which they find pleasant-sounding, which is a new phenomenon in African personal naming (De Klerk & Bosch 1995, p. 79; 1996, p. 185). Clearly, the changes in South African name-giving are rapid, and Suzman (1994, p. 271) states that in a generation, traditional naming practices among different cultural groups may even become insignificant. It is reasonable to suggest that similar developments do and will characterise name-giving in other African societies, which are experiencing rapid urbanisation as well, even if they have not been researched as systematically as those in the South(ern) African context.

All in all, it seems that African personal naming has come to resemble modern European naming in many respects, despite the fact that the names themselves are increasingly African. On the other hand, the criterion of name meaningfulness continues to distinguish these two systems (Herbert & Bogatsu 1990, p. 14), even if there are also signs that the importance attached to the lexical meaning of the name is decreasing.

NOTES

23 In the 1950s, two American anthropologists, Kroeber and Kluckhohn (1952), published a list of 160 definitions of culture, and many more have been introduced since that. Vermeersch (1977) presents an analysis of the definitions Kroeber and Kluckhohn took up, as well as of some later publications on this subject. On the other hand, many anthropologists have given up formulating such definitions. In order to show what culture is, they simply refer to examples of cultural behaviour. (Downs 1971, p. 34.)

24 His typology is modified from the one developed by Kroeber and Kluckhohn (1952).

25 Usually, anthropologists see that cultures change internally by two main processes: *innovation* and *invention*. According to Nanda (1987, p. 80–81), an innovation is "a variation of an existing cultural pattern that is then accepted or learned by the other members of the society", whereas an invention is "the combination of existing cultural elements into something altogether new".

26   Boas (1963, p. 180) especially criticised the concept of primitiveness. He pointed out that inventions, social order and intellectual life are not always equally developed in a society: there are people whose material culture is rather poor, but who have a highly complex social organisation, etc. As the steps of invention do not always follow in the same order and there are often important gaps in this development, Boas (op. cit., p. 165) states that the theory of parallel development cannot be considered as correct.

27   The term *acculturation* has been used by American anthropologists, whereas the British have traditionally preferred the term *culture contact*. Herskovits, in his "Acculturation: The Study of Culture Contact" (1958, p. 2–15), presents a number of definitions of acculturation and discusses the relationships between the close but not synonymous terms *acculturation*, *diffusion* and *assimilation*.

28   For example, material objects whose use will save time and human energy are easily adopted. Therefore, manufactured clothes tend to replace home-made ones everywhere, and metal tools and weapons seldom fail to replace articles made of stone or wood. (Titiev 1959, p. 198.)

29   For example, Bitterli (1989, p. 39), with regard to the culture of Black Americans, says that "collision therefore did not result in the disappearance of the traditional culture, but led to a new form of culture, in which remnants of tradition entered into a remarkable synthesis with new materials to produce a unique outcome".

30   According to White (1969, p. 410), the purpose of culture is to serve the needs of man, both the ones that can be served only by exploiting the resources of the external world (food, clothing, etc.) and those that can be served by drawing upon the resources of the human organism only (psychic, social and spiritual needs).

31   It has been pointed out that a human language is always "super-individual". It is something much bigger and more significant than the speech of any individual person; it is a cumulative product of millions of individuals representing preceding generations. (Kroeber 1987, p. 83.)

32   Brandt (1972, p. 49) also remarks that linguistics has not added much to the study of social change, except to that of linguistic change.

33   Weinreich (1968, p. 5) calls these "structural" and "non-structural" factors: the former originate in the linguistic system, whereas the latter are derived from the contact of the system with the outside world.

34   As Titiev (1959, p. 199) sees it, language holds a strong resistance to acculturation: even when people are acculturated in other respects, they usually continue to speak their mother tongue.

35   Several scholars (e.g. Ehlich 1994, p. 109–111; Haarmann 1983, p. 157–159) have presented typologies for language contact. Usually these typologies list the possible consequences of such contacts, varying from minor effects on the vocabulary to the formation of new types of language, e.g. pidgins and creoles.

36   For the long history of philosophical interest in names, see Summerell's article "Philosophy of Proper Names" (1995). Schneider (1994, p. 6–12) gives a brief introduction to 20th century philosophical reflections on the concept of name by presenting the central ideas of Frege, Russell, Wittgenstein, Strawson and Searle on this topic. Pollock (1982, p. 40–54), in turn, presents four historical and current theories on proper names: 1. The connotation theory, 2. Searle's theory, 3. The denotation theory, and 4. The historical connection theory. It is important to note that philosophers often look at personal names from a different viewpoint than linguists or onomasticians, and there has not been much coordination between these theories.

37   Nicolaisen (1995) sees Algeo's attempt as an attractive but unsatisfactory way out of the dilemma. He points out that an onomastic item could well be called a name under most or all of these circumstances. Therefore, to quote Nicolaisen (1995, p. 387–388), "why not assume that there is a 'linguistic fact', called *name*, which

looks like a capitalized word in English orthography (but not in German ...), is often formed and behaves in many respects syntactically like a noun, is usually definite, particular, or singular in its reference (though not unique), and has onomastic meaning (or content) rather than lexical meaning. On all these levels, and normally on several or even all of them simultaneously, the name functions in the speech act of identification which is the prerequisite for the speech act of recognition."

38 The difference between an anthroponym and a toponym is traditionally understood to lie in their referentiality: anthroponyms are not monoreferential in the way toponyms are. For example, the Finnish lexicon is considered to contain only one personal name *Heikki*, even if there are thousands of men in Finland who have this name. On the other hand, the lexicon contains as many place names as there are places named, even if some of these names are similar in form. For this reason, it has been impossible to form a definition of a name which would cover both toponyms and anthroponyms. (Ainiala 1997, p. 15.)

39 Laur (1989, p. 26) looks at the use of the German word *Name* in everyday language, in linguistics, and in philosophy and logic.

40 The term *proper name* is traditionally used as the opposite of *common name*. However, according to present understanding, there are no names that are not proper. (Nicolaisen 1995, p. 386.) In this study, *name* and *proper name* are thus used as synonyms.

41 This view was already presented in the Middle Ages by William of Conches, who stated that the proper name refers without qualitative meaning to an individual substance (Summerell 1995, p. 370).

42 Algeo (1973, p. 57) gives as an example societies in which personal names are required to refer to the totem of the person's clan.

43 In his "Tractatus Logico-Philosophicus", Wittgenstein (1922, 3.203) says: "Der Name bedeutet den Gegenstand. Der Gegenstand ist seine Bedeutung." Wittgenstein (1922, 3.26) also sees the name as a "primitive sign" which cannot be analysed further by any definition.

44 Laur (1989, p. 103) refers to the common interest in etymologising names: "Die Deutung eines Eigennamens, das heißt, seine Etymologisierung und die Herausstellung der Bedeutung des so etymologisierten als ein Wort, scheint zunächst das Hauptziel der Namenkunde zu bilden." On the other hand, many onomasticians (e.g. Nicolaisen 1995, p. 388) doubt whether the search for meaningfulness on the lexical level is helpful at all in onomastic research, as it merely reduces a name to the word it originally was.

45 Many scholars (e.g. Kripke 1980, p. 96, 135) seem to agree that a name is originally based on a description of the object, but that it becomes irrelevant as soon as the reference is fixed.

46 J.L. Austin (1962, p. 150, 154) who presented the idea of performatives, divides them into five categories: verdictives, exercitives, commissives, behabitives, and expositives. The verb *name* is an exercitive, which means that "it is a decision that something is to be so". Beside *name*, Allan (1986, p. 167) has both *baptize* and *christen* in his list of performative verbs.

47 There have been a number of other attempts to describe the systematic nature of naming systems (e.g. Blanár 1996; Seibicke 1996; Van Langendonck 1995), but these turned out to be less helpful for this study.

48 Van Langendonck (1996, p. 1228) points out that in most European naming systems, a family name can function both as a collective name and a byname. As he sees it, a byname – in European naming systems – denotes all individual personal names that are not forenames (first names, Christian names).

49 In an earlier article, V. Kohlheim (1977b) applies the innovation theory to the study of the diffusion of onomastic innovations, such as the practice of naming children after saints in Medieval Europe. He analyses the stages of the onomastic diffusion process and the roles of social status and fashion in the acceptance of new personal names and name-giving practices.

50 What Brandt (1972, p. 57) says about linguistic elements in general may be applied to names as well: they carry within themselves seeds of change, and even without any outside influence one might expect that changes would occur. V. Kohlheim (1998, p. 176) also points out that there is a tendency towards systematisation on the structural level of most naming systems. For example, gender is marked morphologically in the Romance personal naming systems. These "system-like features" strengthen the relationships between the elements of the system and thereby stabilise its boundaries.

51 It is important to note that one naming system may also be influenced by another in cases where there are no deeper linguistic contacts between the two languages in question. For example, the influence of English on personal names in Brasil is significant, even if the English language has not had much influence on the Portuguese language (Thonus 1991, p. 27).

52 Kiviniemi (1982b, p. 33) gives as an example the Finnish name-day calendar, which did not contain a single name of Finnish origin before the 1880s. Even later, the majority of names in it were of foreign origin.

53 As Bitterli (1989, p. 50) has pointed out, acculturation is a process which affects everyone involved, also in cases where the technically superiour culture seems to be dominant and its influence on the other culture is more obvious. In this study, we shall for example see how some Finnish missionaries have given their children Ambo names.

54 Kiviniemi (1982b, p. 30) points out that altogether, the developments in European naming systems have been very similar, due to similar sociocultural developments in these societies.

55 Wilson (1998, p. 71–80) analyses in more detail the naming systems of two Germanic peoples: the Franks and the Anglo-Saxons.

56 Siebs' list (1970, p. 15–17) runs as follows: 1. mythologische Gestalten, 2. Tiere und Pflanzen, 3. sonstige Naturkörper und Naturkräfte, 4. Tageszeiten, 5. Himmelsrichtungen, 6. Kultmittel, 7. Volksstämme, 8. gesellschaftliche Stellung, 9. freundliches und feindliches Verhalten, 10. menschliche Tätigkeit, 11. Mannestugenden und sonstige menschliche Eigenschaften, 12. Farben, 13. Schutz u. Trutz, 14. öffentliche Ordnung, 15. Erfolg, 16. Wert und Besitz. It is interesting to compare this list with the semantic categories of traditional Welsh names presented by Morgan (1995, p. 122–123): 1. animals, 2. war and heroism, 3. office or rank, 4. wealth, 5. relationship, 6. beauty, 7. affection, 8. colour, 9. praise, 10. craft or skill, 11. liveliness, 12. metals, 13. trees, and 14. verb-roots with specific meanings.

57 According to Seibicke (1982, p. 126), it would be useless to derive the meanings of such names from the meanings of the parents' names: "Wahrscheinlicher ist, daß solche Bildungen symbolisieren sollen, daß etwas vom Vater und etwas von der Mutter auf das Kind übergeht und in ihm weiterlebt."

58 This seems to have been the case with Anglo-Saxon personal names as well: "Most authorities agree that the names and their elements did have lexical meaning in the earliest times. ... Later on, however, as the names became established as names, and as they were repeated, their original meaning was no longer taken literally. ... It also seems that the original meaning of names was sometimes not obvious and had to be pointed out by scholars as it does today." (Wilson 1998, p. 78–79.)

59 A list of common name elements, and the names in which they were used, in Baltic-Finnish languages can be found in Stoebke's "Die alten ostseefinnischen Personennamen im Rahmen eines urfinnischen Namensystems" (1964, p. 83–107). On the other hand, it has been noted that Stoebke's list is not faultless (Nissilä 1965, p. 81–82).

60 In his pioneering study on pre-Christian personal names in Finland, Forsman (1894, p. 19–23, 27–40) describes the name-giving practices of many Finno-Ugric peoples, e.g. the Lapps (the Saami) and the Mordvinians.

61　Before the year 1000, all popes except one used their original names in their new position. Hence there was a wide variety of Persian, Greek, Latin, Lombard, etc. papal names. In more modern times it has become customary for popes to adopt new names after their election. (Nau 1993, p. 59.)

62　Vilkuna (1947, p. 58) also gives the supposed change of *Saulus* into *Paulus* as an example of a name change caused by a radical change in a person's life. Warneck (1900, p. 276), however, points out that the fact that Paulus was known as Saulus since the beginning of his first mission triphad nothing to do with baptism.

63　According to Alford (1988, p. 85), names are typically changed at initiation into adulthood, at marriage, after the birth of a child, after the death of a relative or during a serious illness.

64　Jenni (1996, p. 1854) divides the Hebrew names in the Old Testament semantically into profane and religious names. The latter group consists of names which include a confession or reflect trust, hope or gratitude.

65　Meldgaard (1994, p. 202) divides the names which became popular in the Nordic countries after the adoption of Christianity into three groups: 1. Greek or Graecised names from the New Testament, 2. Hebrew names from the Old Testament and 3. Saints' names from various origins. However, there are also many personal names in the Old Testament other than Hebrew ones, and the names in the New Testament are not exclusively of Greek origin either (Jenni 1996, p. 1853).

66　In this study, the term *Christian name* is primarily used for biblical names and names of saints and other religious figures. In some cases, it is also used to refer to semantically transparent names which have religious meanings. In general, however, the use of this problematic term is avoided in this thesis.

67　It is impossible to give exact information about the spread of Christian personal names in Finland because of the lack of historical documents. The names of the rural population began to appear systematically in written documents in the 16th century only. (Kiviniemi 1982b, p. 33, 37.)

68　Wilson (1998, p. 86–92) presents an overview of the Christianisation of personal names in Italy, France and Britain.

69　National patron saints have also had a strong influence on personal naming in many countries: St. George in England, St. Andrew in Scotland, St. Patrick in Ireland, St. Birgit in Sweden, and so on. Altogether, the calendars of the saints included names of Church fathers, martyrs, mystics, ascetics, founders of religious orders, local saints, etc. (Hanks & Hodges 1990, p. xiii–xiv.) There were also special patron saints for different occupations. In Germany, Nikolaus was the patron saint of seamen and tradesmen, Hubertus that of hunters, Lukas of painters, etc. (Seibicke 1982, p. 134.)

70　Meldgaard (1994, p. 207) remarks that the first "Christian" names in Scandinavia were given in the royal families to the daughters, younger legitimate sons and the sons of the king's mistresses. The eldest sons, who were the potential heirs to the throne, received Scandinavian names.

71　Schwarz (1949, p. 46) points out that the adoption of saints' names did not cause the decline of old German names: "Diese bröckeln ja schon vorher ab. Schon seit 800 erlischt ihre Produktionskraft, im 12. Jh. wird der Einschrumpfungsprozeß deutlich."

72　At the end of the 15th century, the most popular ten names for men in Münsterland were *Johan, Heinrich, Herman, Bernt, Gert, Dirick, Evert, Albert, Arnt* and *Lambert*, and they were carried by 80 per cent of all men. The most popular names for women were *Else, Gese, Alke, Margareta, Styne, Mette, Katharina, Gerdrut, Kunne* and *Fenne*, and they were carried by 76 per cent of all women. (Kremer 1986, p. 279, 281.) It was typical that certain names, such as *Johann*, became extremely popular. At the end of the 16th century, 22 per cent of all men in Lippstadt were named *Johann*, and in the mid 18th century, 48 per cent of them had this name. (Fedders 1995, p. 765.)

73　For the same reason, vernacular names such as *Richard*, *Robert* and *William* were preserved in England (Dunkling 1977, p. 51). Many Germanic personal names survived in the Middle Ages also because they were used by noble families (Wilson 1998, p. 106).

74　For example, old German and Scandinavian personal names were borrowed by the Finns in the early Middle Ages from traders and craftsmen. Germanic and Baltic personal names were also adopted in the pre-Christian era. (Kiviniemi 1982a, p. 44–45; 1993, p. 117.)

75　Finland was part of Sweden until 1808, after which it was an autonomous grand duchy of the Russian Empire until it gained its independence in 1917.

76　These hypocoristic name forms indicated family relationships in the same way as repetition of name elements in the old Germanic naming systems had done (Wilson 1998, p. 112). Wilson (1998, p. 109–114) particularly analyses the reduction of the name stock and the use of hypocoristic forms in Italy, France and England.

77　A byname can be understood as a name which is added to another name already borne by the name-bearer (Neethling 1994, p. 89). Or, as Alford (1988, p. 70) puts it: "By-names are names of various sorts that are appended to given names, in order to clearly distinguish individuals." In this study, we use this term to refer to any name which a person may bear in addition to his or her "real name", be that a European-type forename or an African "real name" of the person. A byname may be used together with the person's name or instead of it. It may also be purely individual or refer to a group to which the person belongs. Thus, we divide bynames into 1. Individual bynames (various kinds of nicknames) and 2. Collective bynames (patronyms, surnames, etc.). Altogether, there are many terms for different kinds of bynames in European languages. Often terms which look similar in meaning, may also cover different concepts in different languages. In English, for example, one can find the terms *nickname, call name, hypocorism, petname, patronymic, surname, family name* and *last name*, in German *Beiname, Rufname, Spottname, Kosename, Spitzname, Zuname, Familienname* and *Geschlechtsname*, in Afrikaans *bynaam, noemnaam, roepnaam, familienaam* and *van*, in Swedish *tillnamn, binamn, smeknamn, öknamn, vedernamn, patronym* and *släktnamn*, and in Finnish *lisänimi, lempinimi, kutsumanimi, patronyymi* and *sukunimi*. Similarly, African languages have various terms for these names, which are often difficult to translate into European languages.

78　In written documents, it is often difficult to draw a line between a "real" byname and an occasional note of the recorder which aimed to individualise the person (Fleischer 1968, p. 77). Van Langendonck (1990, p. 437) rightly remarks that one should distinguish between onomastic systems in written sources on the one hand, and onomastic systems in spoken language on the other.

79　Usually, onomasticians talk about surnames only after they have been in use in two or three generations (Seibicke 1982, p. 195; Mikkonen & Paikkala 1992, p. 18). However, it might be justified to use this term also in cases where a person has consciously adopted for him/herself a surname, even if it has not yet been in use for two or more generations. In this study, the term *surname* is thus understood in the way suggested by Paikkala (1995, p. 124): "the surname (...) is an additional name (...), which is meant to be permanent and inherited within the family (...) or a name which aims to show a relation to the family (...)". It is interesting to note that there are also broader definitions of a surname in the onomastic literature. Van Langendonck (1995, p. 488; 1996, p. 1228) uses this term for a byname or a collective name that is added to, i.e. modifies an individual personal name. Hence, he sees that *the Baptist* in *John the Baptist* is a byname that functions as a surname. In this study, we regard *the Baptist* as an individual byname.

80　The results of this process were slightly different in different parts of Europe. R. Kohlheim (1996b, p. 1256) describes some European surname systems – e.g. the

Russian, the Hungarian and the Spanish – in her article. The development of the Slavic surname system has been examined by Kaleta (1990).

81   Wilson (1998, p. 118), who analyses the origins of surnames especially in Italy, France and Britain, divides them into four classes: 1. Names deriving from bynames or nicknames, 2. Names deriving from first names, often with patronymic prefixes or suffixes, 3. Names deriving from places or topographical features, and 4. Names deriving from occupations and offices.

82   The process was different in Eastern Finland where all people, including farmers, had hereditary surnames already in the 16th century. These names typically ended with -(i)nen. (Paikkala 1988, p. 27.)

83   According to Seibicke (1982, p. 152), it is reasonable to talk about naming fashions only after free name choice has become common. In Finland, fashion became an important aspect of personal naming in the 15th and 16th centuries, and in the late 20th century, naming fashions began to change rapidly (Kiviniemi 1993, p. 120, 122).

84   In Germany, this division is still reflected in contemporary personal naming (Seibicke 1982, p. 137).

85   The name-giving of the Orthodox minority in Finland, though, is traditionally based on the Orthodox saint calendar (Kiviniemi 1982a, p. 75).

86   Almost every day in the Finnish name-day calendar is designated as a name day for one or more names, and it is a general custom among the Finns to celebrate these name days. The celebration of name days most probably spread from the Catholic Germany to Sweden and Finland already before the Reformation (Blomqvist 1998, p. 59). For more on the history of the Finnish name-day calendar see Blomqvist 1998.

87   In England, this custom became common in the 17th century, mainly due to French influence. In the 18th century, multiple first names were very popular among the girls. (Withycombe 1977, p. xliii.)

88   Multiple first names arrived in Sweden from Germany in the late 16th century. The new naming pattern was adopted first in the royal family and among the nobility. (Benson 1990, p. 194–195.)

89   Vandebosch (1998, p. 243) describes the role of the media in name-giving: "The media are providing a pool of potential names, associating them with particular social characteristics and presenting some names as more desirable as others." Vandebosch (1998, p. 243) also points out that the media can create both positive and negative name stereotypes and thus increase or decrease the popularity of certain names.

90   There is not much literature published on African names and naming systems in general, and the books available mainly contain lists of African names without a deeper analysis of their backgrounds. Examples of these are: Abell 1992, Asante 1991, Chuks-Orji 1972, Madubuike 1976, and Osuntoki 1970.

91   Koopman (1986, p. 19) has even stated that the only common factor of African peoples with regard to names is that they all have a variety of names. Some African researchers, however, emphasise the cultural unity of Africa and accuse Western intellectuals of seeing the cultural diversity of Africa only. According to Asante, for example, African culture is "determined by a unity of origin as well as a common struggle". (Asante 1985, p. 3–4, 6.)

92   The Kaguru people believe that convicted witches and people who have died of serious diseases are non-persons and hence lose their names (Beidelman 1974, p. 286).

93   Magesa (1998, p. 87) notes that in African societies, personal names are used to keep alive in memory not only the people but certain of their characteristics as well: "Naming involves the incarnation or actualisation of a person (an ancestor), a certain desired moral quality or value, a physical trait or power, or an occasion or event."

94   According to Alford (1988, p. 90–91), the term *teknonymy* usually refers to the custom of designating parents according to the names of their children ("father-of-X", "mother-of-X"), but occasionally it may also refer to the practice of designating individuals according to any kin relationship, e.g. "grandparent-of-X", "son-of-X", "aunt-of-X", etc. In this study, this term is used in the former sense only.

95   Obeng (1998, p. 171–179) divides Akan death-prevention names into seven classes: 1. Names based on strangers' or migrants' names, 2. Names referring to destructive or dangerous animals, 3. Names referring to low status jobs, 4. Names referring to filthy places or objects, 5. Names referring to tabooed objects, 6. Names expressing emotions, and 7. Names expressing requests.

96   Herbert and Bogatsu (1990, p. 3) also point out that even if some Western names are semantically transparent, e.g. *Petunia* and *Ruby*, the relationship of these names to their sources is different from that of meaningful African names.

97   In some African societies, typically among small groups, names are still unique for the vast majority of people. This is the case with the Kxoe in Namibia; for examples see Brenzinger 1999.

98   However, it has been noted that even if the linguistic rules of the language suggest an infinite inventory of personal names, there are often sociocultural principles which restrict the formation of new names in African societies (Akinnaso 1980, p. 299).

99   Okere (1996a, p. 133) describes traditional Igbo names in this way: "Igbo names always bear a message, a meaning, a history, a record or a prayer. ... they embody a rich mine of information on the people's reflection and considered comment on life and reality. They provide a window into the Igbo world of values as well as their peculiar conceptual apparatus for dealing with life." On the other hand, Obeng (1998, p. 184) states that it is impossible to fully understand Akan names without a thorough knowledge of Akan society. Akinnaso (1983, p. 158), who has investigated Yoruba names, also points out that names are "conventionalized communicative acts" which cannot be understood by analysing names on the linguistic level only.

100   Unfortunately, several sources also describe traditional African naming systems without defining what point of time they actually refer to.

101   In some African societies, the name is chosen before the arrival of the baby (Mbiti 1991, p. 92). In most societies, no preparations, including choice of name, are made before the arrival of a new child (Ayisi 1988, p. 22).

102   Many African societies adopted this Arab custom together with Islam. However, day-names are also used among peoples that are not Islamic. (Turnbull 1966, p. 55–56.) Day-names are especially common in West Africa (Gregersen 1977, p. 162; Mbiti 1991, p. 93). An Akan child, for example, receives two names as soon as he or she is born: the name of the day of the birth and an associated byname that goes together with the day-name. Later the child is given a "proper" name when he or she is named after some important person. (Obeng 1998, p. 165.)

103   The peoples of western Kenya refer to the true name of the person as "the name of the stomach", "the name of the umbilical cord", "the inner name" or "the spirit name" (Magesa 1998, p. 90).

104   Descriptions of naming ceremonies in different African cultures are numerous in the literature. Some examples are: the Akan (Amin 1993, p. 2–4), the Boraana (Dahl 1998, p. 317–323), the Herero (Otto 1985, p. 127–128), the Kavango (Fisch 1979, p. 28–29), the Masai (Turnbull 1966, p. 53–54), the Meru (Nyaga 1997, p. 29), the Sukuma-Nyamwezi (Brandström 1998, p. 142–144), the Yoruba (Akinnaso 1980, p. 278), the Wolof and the Akamba (Mbiti 1969, p. 114, 119–120).

105   Amin (1993, p. 10–13) presents a typology for given names among a number of tribes in Ghana: 1. Death-related names, 2. Birth-related names, 3. God-related names, 4. Names related to the gift of life, 5. War-related names, 6. Extended family-related names, and 7. Advisory names. Wieschhoff (1941, p. 219–220)

divides names among the Ibo people of Nigeria into seven classes: 1. Names expressing circumstances related to the birth of the child, 2. Names expressing the hope that the child may live, 3. Names indicating disappointment regarding the birth of the child, 4. Names indicating that the child is given into the protection of spirits, 5. Names referring to circumstances pertaining to the life of the mother, 6. Names indicating that the mother feels more secure in her marriage after the birth of the child, and 7. Names intended to admonishingly address other people to minimize social friction. Kidd (1906, p. 34–36), on his part, mentions five main methods for choosing a name for an African child: 1. The child may be named after another person, 2. The name may refer to some current event, 3. The name may describe the baby's appearance, 4. The name may express a hoped-for character, and 5. The name may be chosen to break some evil spell which has caused the death of previous children (derogatory-protective names).

106 Magesa (1998, p. 89) notes that names referring to difficult times are given to recall the historical situation so that the people in the community would do everything they can to prevent a similar event from happening again.

107 Musere (1998, p. 78) says about the proverbial names of the Baganda people that they are not only derived from proverbs but are also used to recall entire proverbs and their meanings. In this way, personal names serve to preserve African oral literature.

108 In Africa, twins are often regarded as a sign of misfortune. In many societies, one or both of them, or the mother, were systematically killed. (Mbiti 1991, p. 95.) These customs have been explained by the similarity of twin-birth to an animals' litter, which suggested that they were not human. In some societies, twins have been regarded as sacred, however. (Parrinder 1969, p. 79; 1981, p. 93.) This is the case among the Kavangos in Namibia: twins were regarded as a gift from heaven (Fisch 1979, p. 30). The Hereros also regarded twin birth as a fortunate event (Hiltunen 1993, p. 215).

109 In many cases, the sources do not define which names are regarded as the "real" names of the person and which are nicknames or bynames of some sort. African languages also have their own terminologies for different kinds of names, which are not easily translatable into European languages. A good example of this is the Ndebele term *isibongo* (plural *izibongo*), which has been translated into English in different sources as *surname*, *clan name*, *totem name* and *praise name* (Lindgren 1998, p. 53).

110 This is how Alford (1988, p. 82) defines a nickname: "Nicknames are meaningful, usually descriptive, names, which are bestowed on individuals in addition to their given names, often at a later date. They may be appended to or used in place of given names or surnames. Nicknames are not formal or regularized name components, but rather are informal and unofficial names."

111 Gulliver (1952, p. 73) describes the use of ox names among the Jie: "According to the colour of its hide, shape of its horns and other features, an ox gives a name to its owner. ... Throughout the years a man has several ox-names in succession as his favourites change. ... As between clansmen and others who see each other daily, they are most commonly used the whole time."

112 Madubuike (1976, p. 17) mentions that sometimes these descriptive names also became hereditary and served as family names.

113 One can find much earlier Christian influence in Africa as well. Already during the first centuries of the Church, Christianity spread to northern Africa, Egypt, the Sudan and Ethiopia. Hence, Christianity arrived in Africa earlier than Islam, which started to spread there in the 7th century. (Mbiti 1969, p. 229.)

114 As this study deals with the influence of Christianity and Europeanisation on African name-giving, we shall not analyse the impact of Islam on personal names in detail here. However, it should be noted that just as the Christians have adopted biblical and saints' names in Africa, the Muslims have adopted names of the holy

persons of Islam: prophets, relatives of Mohammed, etc. (Gregersen 1977, p. 163). The influence of Christianity on sub-Saharan Africa as a whole has also been much greater than that of Islam since the colonial period (Herskovits 1967, p. 197).

115 Various explanations have been offered for this phenomenon, such as the collapse of the structures of traditional African societies and world-views caused by Western influence, and the development of African cosmology responding to both the modern situation and the activities of the missionaries (Ikenga-Metuh 1987, p. 12–13). Usually conversion is a long-term process in which new ideas are gradually mixed with the old (Peil & Oyeneye 1998, p. 164). In any conversion, there must also be a fair amount of continuity between the old and new beliefs (Kirby 1994, p. 67). Decisions about religious life are often linked to politics as well (Saunders 1988a, p. 179). From a practical viewpoint, it has been stated that the greatest contribution to the spread of Christianity was made by the introduction of education by the missionaries: many Africans came into contact with Christianity in schools. Many converts were also made through contact with Christian medical practices. (Boahen 1990, p. 221.) All in all, this phenomenon is a complex one and has various sociocultural and religious causes.

116 This seems to have been the case especially with languages using click sounds. Hence English names were adopted as a compromise for example among the Xhosa speakers in South Africa (Neethling 1995, p. 958). Moyo (1996, p. 13) also points out that European missionaries and colonisers in Malawi had considerable problems trying to pronounce Ngoni and Tumbuka names.

117 This is a typical phenomenon in many other parts of the world as well where Western missionaries gained new converts to Christianity. As Lehmann (1969, p. 175) points out, "es lag und liegt nicht nur an den bösen Missionaren: sehr viele Täuflinge haben große Lust und oft geradezu eine Sucht nach biblischen Namen".

118 Dickens's (1985, p. 63) discovery about the Zulus is that the Protestants used mainly Old Testament names, whereas the Catholics had predominantly New Testament and saints' names.

119 Interestingly, Ekpo's article on Ibibio names (1978) is for the most part identical with an earlier article published in the same journal, Names: Mohome's "Naming in Sesotho: Its Sociocultural and Linguistic Basis" (1972). However, as Ekpo – unlike Mohome – gives a number of examples of Roman Catholic names in his article, they are taken up here. Otherwise Ekpo's article is not used for this thesis.

120 In Cameroun, many boys received the name *Charles* or *de Gaulle* in the 1940s (Njock 2001, p. 13).

121 Fritze (1930, p. 18) points out that the converts themselves wanted to adopt new names at baptism, as a sign of their new life as Christians. Fritze's book "Der neue Name: Das neue Leben der Dschaggachristen im Lichte ihrer Taufnamen" (1930) presents a careful analysis of African baptismal names in one Chagga congregation, Mamba. This book may not be well-known among onomasticians, but it offers fascinating material on the semantics of African baptismal names.

122 Dickens (1985, p. 90–91) calls these *convenience names*, and gives *Butterfly*, *Fisch*, *Motor* and *Ostrich* as South African examples; houseboys and housegirls were typically called *Jim* and *Mary*. Europeans also gave nicknames to Africans working for them, such as *Haastig* 'fast' for a person who was not fast (Visser & Visser 1998, p. 230).

123 Among the Zulus, this seems to have been the case especially with people born into Christian families (Koopman 1987b, p. 156). According to Herbert (1997, p. 5), the custom of giving children only European names reflected the parents' acceptance of "colonial hegemony", and it is no longer practised in South Africa.

124 In many African countries, churches were affected by nationalist movements as well, and African names were seen as one means of preserving the character of a truly indigenous church, together with African music (Lucas 1950, p. 31–32).

125 Some European names, however, were preserved in Zaïre because they were phonologically adapted to the local language and hence were not easily recognisable, e.g. *Gusitu* < *Agostinho* (Ndoma 1977, p. 88, 94). Beside personal names, place names were also changed: *Leopoldville* became *Kinshasa* and *Stanleyville, Kinsangani* (Gregersen 1977, p. 156).

126 Interestingly, some early missionaries in Africa encouraged the use of European surnames among the converts – *Dos Santos, Johnson,* etc. –, but this practice faded away pretty soon (Hastings 1976, p. 38).

127 It seems that all of these names are not "real" surnames in the European sense, as they are not necessarily passed on to the next generation (Beidelman 1974, p. 292). Altogether, it is often impossible to find out if the African sources really mean hereditary surnames when they use the term *surname*.

128 In West Africa, surnames were sometimes formed by anglicising African names. In Ghana, *Qhene* 'chief' was translated as *King, Anti* was made *Anteson* 'son of Anti', *Dade* 'steel' *Steel-Dade, Kuntu* 'blanket' *Kuntu-Blankson,* and so on. However, this phenomenon was only temporary. (Amin 1993, p. 38–39.)

129 A good example of such new forms is to be found in Zulu praise names. Traditionally, Zulu praises were used in rural communities especially in courting, dancing and fighting contexts. In urban environments, modern forms were created, for example, football and boxing praises. (Koopman 1987a, p. 43.)

130 Herbert (1999a, p. 224) does not explain these brackets, but they may be understood to refer to the fact that only a small minority of the African population have had only European names in southern Africa.

131 These "negative" names have also been called "friction names" in the onomastic literature (Herbert 1999b, p. 116). Suzman (1994, p. 259) gives examples of such names among the Zulus, e.g. *uVelaphi* 'where does he come from?', a name given to an illegitimate child, and *uThulani* 'be quiet' given to a child by his mother who wanted her mother-in-law to stop complaining. It has also been noted that derogatory-protective names are extremely rare among urban residents in South Africa (De Klerk & Bosch 1995, p. 80; Herbert 1996, p. 1226). The same phenomenon has been noted in other African societies as well, e.g. among the Ngoni and Tumbuka peoples in Malawi where "accusatory names" have become rare and names reflecting hope, love, trust, etc. are popular in urban environments (Moyo 1996, p. 17–18). Obeng (1998, p. 185) also remarks that death-prevention names are not given to Akan children anymore. Among the Yoruba people, there is also a tendency to use positive names and avoid the derogatory connotations of traditional names (Akinnaso 1983, p. 155–156).

132 Herbert and Bogatsu (1990, p. 14) state that this phenomenon is found throughout urban African societies.

Cultural Change in the Ambo Area
of Namibia

Namibia, the Ambo Area and the Ambo People

Physical Environment and Population

Namibia (formerly South West Africa)[133] is located in the southwest corner of Africa, covering an area of 824,269 square kilometres, almost four times the size of the United Kingdom. The country is bordered by Angola to the north, Zambia and Zimbabwe to the northeast, Botswana to the east, and South Africa to the south. (Kiljunen 1981, p. 23.) The Namib Desert from which the name *Namibia* is derived, the Khoekhoegowab word *namib* possibly meaning 'shield' or 'enclosure' (Hishongwa 1992, p. 3; Maho 1998, p. 1), stretches down the western side of the country alongside the Atlantic Ocean.

Topographically, the land is divided into three regions: the Namib Desert, the Central Plateau, and the Kalahari Desert. The Namib Desert covers one-sixth of the country's total area. It is almost uninhabited, but its enormous riches have made Namibia one of the largest producers of gem diamonds in the world. The Central Plateau is a savannah and bush area, covering more than half of the country. The northern part of the plateau is suitable for cattle-grazing, and the southern part provides excellent pasture land for the Karakul sheep. Its mountain ranges also contain substantial mineral deposits as well as semi-precious stones. The Kalahari Desert is for the most part unsuitable for cultivation, except for the Ambo area and the Kavango area in the north. (Kiljunen 1981, p. 23–25.) Because of its deserts, Namibia's climate is the driest in sub-Saharan Africa (Nambala 1994, p. 8).

The Ambo area, i.e. the area traditionally inhabited by the Ambo communities, is located in the northernmost part of Namibia, between the Etosha Pan and the Kunene and Okavango rivers. Characteristic of this area are the so-called *oshanas*, flat flood channels which are filled with water coming from the Cuvelai River in Angola during the rainy season. The floods supply extra water, nutrients for the soil and fish, which provide a supplementary diet. The ground in the Ambo area is flat and sandy.

Map 1.

Namibia. Timo Jokivartio 2003.

In altitude, the plain varies between 1,100 and 1,200 metres. The rainy season usually lasts from November to March, but there are great variations in annual rainfall; floods and drought are both common. The weather is at its hottest in November (average + 25°C) and at its coolest in July (average + 16°C). Typical of the vegetation are mopane trees and especially fan palms, which do not grow elsewhere in Namibia. The region is categorised as part of the mixed and mopane savannah zone, but in the north and east there is also woodland savannah. (Eirola 1992, p. 29–30; Siiskonen 1990, p. 37–41; Williams 1994, p. 37.)

Namibia is one of the most sparsely populated countries in sub-Saharan Africa. According to the latest statistics (1998), the whole population is 1.7 million, and the average population density is 2.0 persons per square kilometre (World Bank Atlas 2000, p. 25, 35). Despite its small population, the country has a rich variety of peoples and cultures. From an anthropological perspective, there are four main groups in Namibia (Kiljunen 1981, p. 28):

1. The Khoesaan group includes several San (Bushman) groups, the earliest inhabitants of Namibia, as well as the Nama people, who all speak Khoesaan languages characterised by click sounds.

2. The Negroid group consists of the Ovambo (Ambo), Kavango, Herero, Himba and Tswana peoples, who all speak Bantu languages, as well as the Damara people and the various small groups living in the Caprivi area.

3. The so-called Coloureds include the "Rehoboth Basters": Boers' and Namas' descendants who moved to Namibia from the Cape Colony in the late 19th century, as well as other immigrants from the Cape Province.

4. The Europeans in Namibia are mainly of Afrikaner and German, but also of British origin.

In 1989, the population figures (%) were as follows (Malan 1995, p. 4):[134]

Ovambo	49.8
Kavango	9.3
Damara	7.5
Herero	7.5
Whites	6.4
Nama	4.8
Coloureds	4.1
Caprivians	3.7
San	2.9
Rehoboth Basters	2.5
Tswana	0.6
Other	0.9

The Ambo area has been densely populated from early times, and it is still the most densely populated rural area in Namibia today. The main sources of livelihood in this region are agriculture and cattle-raising. (Eirola 1992, p. 30, 32; Malan 1995, p. 14.) In 1994, the number of people, including non-Ambo, living in the Ambo area was estimated at 670,000, and the estimated number of the actual Ambo people in Namibia was 641,000 in 1989 (Grotpeter 1994, p. 397; Malan 1995, p. 14). It is difficult to determine how large the Ambo population was in the latter half of the 19th century when the first Europeans arrived in the area. The estimates of explorers and missionaries vary between 50,000 and 342,500. Most commonly it is believed to have been a little more than 100,000. (Siiskonen 1990, p. 42–43.)

The Ambo people are traditionally divided into seven or eight subgroups. According to Malan (1990, p. 3), the Ambo population is distributed among these groups as follows (%):[135]

Kwanyama	36.6
Ndonga	28.7
Kwambi	11.8
Ngandjera	7.7
Mbalantu	7.4
Kwaluudhi	5.0
Eunda and Nkolonkadhi	2.8

Terminology

The terminology concerning the Ambo area and the Ambo people is unclear and needs to be discussed here. Firstly, one can find several name
forms in the literature for the area inhabited by the Ambo communities.
The Germans have used both *Ovamboland* (e.g. Himmelreich 1900;
Welsch 1925) and *Amboland* (e.g. Hartmann 1903; Vedder 1973), and
the Finnish term has traditionally been *Ambomaa*[136] (e.g. Haahti 1913;
Pentti 1959; Saarelma-Maunumaa 1996a; Savola 1924) but later also
Ovambomaa (e.g. Kiljunen & Kiljunen 1980). In English, *Ovamboland*
seems to be the most common variant (e.g. First 1963; Eirola 1992; Lehtonen
1999; Nambala 1994; Salokoski 1992; Siiskonen 1990; Tuupainen 1970).
Estermann (1976, p. 52) speaks of *the Ambo country*. In some recent
studies written in English and published in Namibia, one can also find
Owamboland (e.g. Malan 1995; Williams 1994), *Wamboland* (Fourie
1992) and *Owambo* (Hishongwa 1992). In the Ambo linguistic varieties,
the forms *Owambo* (Ndonga) and *Ouwambo* (Kwanyama) are used.[137]
Grotpeter (1994, p. 392) remarks that this area "was generally referred
to as Ovamboland, but is today called Owambo". For this study, however, *the Ambo area* was chosen, as it goes back to the stem of the word
and is neutral with regard to different Ambo varieties.[138]

The main reason for this terminological variation is that the etymology of the word *Ovambo/Owambo* is not known to us.[139] According to a
generally accepted theory, this name was received from the Hereros when
the Ambo people went south to obtain copper (Bruwer 1966, p. 22;
Estermann 1976, p. 51). Schinz, who supported the theory of a Herero
origin for the name, stated that *Ovambo* is a shortened form of *Ovajamba*
'the rich'. Hahn's idea, in turn, was that *Ovambo* was derived from the
Ambo word *Ova-mbo* or *Oyoambo* meaning 'they over there'. Later Hahn
changed his view and saw that the root of the word, *mbo*, was connected
with the word *egumbo* meaning 'fixed abode or dwelling'. (Tötemeyer
1978, p. 4–5.) According to Estermann (1976, p. 51), the root *mbo* or
mpo could refer to the noun meaning 'ostrich'.[140] Brincker (1894, p. 208)
believes that the origin of this name can be found among the Ovimbundu
people in Angola where, according to him, the word *omwámbo* means
'copper Maltese cross'; the Ndonga people used to sell copper products
to other ethnic groups in the old days.[141]

Williams (1994, p. 56) presents five alternatives for the origin of
Ovambo: *Ovambo* 'they belong to that place', *Ovombo* 'there they are',
Ovawambo 'good people', *Ovawambu* 'people of Wambu' and *Aayamba*
'the rich people'. She herself holds to the *Ovawambu* theory and argues
this by referring to the long-existing relationship between the Ambo people and the Ovimbundu-related people who occupied the area of Wambu.
These groups, she states, wandered together in central and southern Angola before settling in their present areas. Altogether, it seems that the
etymology of *Ovambo* will remain a mystery.

Another problem with the term *Ovamboland*, and its related name
forms, is that it is not always clear which geographical area it refers to:

the whole area inhabited by the Ambo communities, or the Namibian (South West African) side of it only. When Namibia became a German colony in 1884, the border between German South West Africa and Portuguese Angola was drawn so as to leave the northernmost part of the Ambo communities, e.g. the biggest part of Oukwanyama, on the Portuguese side. In studies dealing with pre-colonial Ambo communities, the term *Ovamboland* is often used to refer to the whole area, whereas in those dealing with the Ambo area in the colonial times, it is typically the Namibian side of this area that is referred to.[142] In 1929, the Namibian side of the Ambo area was set aside as a territory for the Ambo people by the South African government, and in 1968 it became the first "homeland" in the country with a self-government, its official name being *Owambo* (Grotpeter 1994, p. 396–397; Väisälä 1980, p. 230). Hence, it is clear that the terms *Ovamboland* and *Owambo* carry political connotations.[143] For this study, however, the term *Ambo area* was also chosen in order to avoid such colonial connotations. With this term we refer to the area traditionally inhabited by the Ambo people in Namibia, in different stages of its history. When discussing traditional Ambo culture, it may sometimes refer to the whole area of the Ambo communities as well, as the sources do not always make this distinction.[144]

As this study gives preference to the term *Ambo area*, it also uses the form *Ambo* instead of *Ovambo*, *Owambo* or *Wambo*. Hence, we talk about *the Ambos, the Ambo naming system, Ambo customs*, etc. The common practice in other research literature, however, seems to be to use the terms *Ovamboland, the Ovambos*[145], *Ovambo customs*, etc. (e.g. Hiltunen 1993; Lehtonen 1999; Nambala 1994; Salokoski 1992; Siiskonen 1990; Tuupainen 1970).[146]

In English, the closely related linguistic varieties of the Ambo subgroups are usually referred to with the collective term *Oshiwambo* or *Ambo* (Legère 1998a, p. 40), sometimes also *Wambo* (Fivaz 1986, p. xvii). For this study, the form *Ambo* was chosen. Similarly, the forms *Ndonga, Kwanyama*, etc. are used to refer to the different varieties of Ambo. Thus, the *oshi-* prefix which is connected to languages in the Ambo linguistic varieties (*Oshindonga, Oshikwanyama*, etc.) is not retained. Ambo terms, place names, etc. are usually written according to the latest Ndonga or Kwanyama orthographies. The Ambo personal names analysed in this study, however, are presented as found in the original sources.

The Ambo Area in the Pre-Colonial Era

The Ambo Origins

The Ambo people belong to the southwestern Bantu group, but they are culturally close to the matrilineal agriculturalists in Central Africa (Malan 1995, p. 15). Because of the lack of written documents, not much is known about their origins. It is generally assumed that the Ambos arrived in the country as part of the Bantu movement from the northeast to the southwest of Africa, and that this happened some time between the 12th and 17th centuries. It is not known to us whether they came as a group, family by family or in individual clans, or from what direction they actually entered the country. (Nambala 1994, p. 28.) The proto-Bantu community is believed to have existed somewhere near today's Cameroun, from where the Bantus first moved to the Great Lakes of East Africa. From there, some groups continued their trek to southern Africa. (Fourie 1992, p. 1–4; Siiriäinen 1995, p. 74–77.)[147]

A popular theory is that the Ambo people came to Namibia from the north, from Angola, where many related people still live (Grotpeter 1994, p. 393). According to this hypothesis, they migrated together with the Kavangos and the Hereros past the headwaters of the Zambezi to the Okavango river. There the Kavangos left the main group, and the others moved on to southwestern Angola. (Fourie 1992, p. 4.) If these groups settled in Angola as early as around the year 1550, as has been suggested, they may be the oldest settled people in southern Africa (Fourie 1992, p. 4; Tötemeyer 1978, p. 4). In any case, it seems that these groups were the first Bantu-speaking people to enter the area of present Namibia (Bruwer 1966, p. 21; Maho 1998, p. 6). This theory of Ambo origins is supported by place names and personal names appearing in Ambo folktales, as well as by linguistic similarities between the Ambo languages and the languages of southern Angola, the Zambezi floodplains and that of the Kavangos.[148] There are also similarities in customs. (Fourie 1992, p. 4–7.)

The Ambo people have various legends about their origin that reflect these theories.[149] For example, according to the Kwanyama oral tradition, people lived "long long ago" by the big lakes in Central Africa (Sckär 1932, p. 3, UEMA). Some legends also tell about their common origins with other ethnic groups. Let us take one example here of a legend which explains the link to the Hereros, as well as the origin of Nangombe, the great ancestor of all Ambo people.[150] The story is repeated here as presented by Nambala (1994, p. 29):[151]

> It is about two brothers, Nangombe and Kadhu, the sons of Mangundu. Apparently the two brothers trekked southward from the north and journeyed south of the Zambezi until they reached the "Omumborombonga" tree somewhere in Ovamboland. It was at this tree they went their separate ways. Kadhu trekked further, first westward to the Kaokoveld and then southward to the central highlands of Namibia. Kadhu became the great ancestor of the Herero. Nangombe remained in Ovamboland and therefore was the Ovambo great ancestor.

Later the Ambos were divided into smaller groups, each with its own territory and political structure (Bruwer 1966, p. 22). A number of folktales report the order in which this happened and the reasons for the separation, even if there are also differences in these stories (Fourie 1992, p. 7–13; Tötemeyer 1978, p. 4). Ondonga is typically regarded as the "mother" or "grandmother" of all the other groups (Kuusi 1970, p. 5).[152]

Some of the names of these subgroups indicate occupations which are regarded as characteristic of those people: *Kwanyama* refers to game or meat, *Kwambi* to clay potters, and *Ngandjera* to iron traders (Bruwer 1966, p. 22). Many of them also include the name of the first leader of the group: *Ndonga, Kwambi, Ngandjera* (Fourie 1992, p. 8). Eventually, all these groups settled on the vast plains north of the Etosha Pan, where farming conditions were fairly good, i.e. in the area later known as Ovamboland. As sedentary agriculturalists, the Ambo people have mainly stayed in this region up to the present day. (Malan 1995, p. 16.)

Traditional Ambo Culture

What is meant with *traditional Ambo culture* in this study? Primarily, this phrase refers to the culture of the Ambo people as it was at the end of the 19th century (and at the beginning of the 20th century), as the oldest written documents on this topic date back to that time. At that time, the Ambo communities had not yet been influenced much by European missionary work either. However, the term *Ambo culture* should be understood as a theoretical generalisation, as the different Ambo groups also had various cultural specialities beside the common elements presented in this subsection. It should also be noted that the Ambo communities are not seen as pure ethnic units in this study. This is because not all members of these communities have been Ambo, even if the clear majority have.[153]

Family and Clans. The Ambo societies were matrilineal, which means that kinship was determined through the mother.[154] Thus, children were affiliated to the mother's clan and lineage only, not to the father's. Each Ambo community was composed of a number of clans, which were subdivided into lineages consisting of a number of families sharing a common ancestress. The number of clans in different Ambo groups varied between twenty and thirty, and they had names such as the Hyena clan, the Snake clan, the Elephant clan, the Lion clan and the Corn clan.[155] People belonging to the same clan were not allowed to marry one another. (Bruwer 1966, p. 22–23; Malan 1995, p. 18; Siiskonen 1990, p. 44; Williams 1994, p. 186.)

The basic unit of social organisation was the family, which consisted of a husband, his wife or wives, and their children. Polygamy was common, and usually men had at least two or three wives. As children belonged to the mother's family, the father was not regarded as a relative of his children. Hence, the mother's brother had an important role in the upbringing of children. In marriage, man and wife, who belonged to different clans, also had their own properties, including separate cattle and corn. In the case of a divorce, the wife left her husband's house with her children and property. The maternal family was important in cases of crime as well. If one of the family committed a crime, the rest were responsible for paying the fines for it. Inheritance followed the matrilineal line too. The wife and husband never inherited from each other, or the children from their father. (Hahn 1928, p. 25; Malan 1995, p. 19;

Ambo family. Emil Liljeblad / The Finnish Evangelical Lutheran Mission. 1900–1908.

Närhi 1929, p. 90–91; August Pettinen's diary 3.6.1889, Hp:91, FMSA; Savola 1924, p. 73, 76, 82–83, 102; Siiskonen 1990, p. 44.)

In the old days, full membership of the society was achieved through initiation ceremonies. By the end of the 19th century, circumcision of boys was no longer practised, but girls were allowed to marry only after special initiation ceremonies. In Ondonga, this *ohango* festival was arranged every second year, and it lasted from one to three months. (Eirola 1992, p. 39; Hahn 1928, p. 27–31.)

The Ambo Homestead. The Ambo families lived in separate homesteads surrounded by the fields of the family. Because of this settlement pattern, there were no true villages in the Ambo area. The father was the head of the homestead, and thus the social system of the Ambos was not only matrilineal but also patrilocal. In rare cases, e.g. if the father died, it was also possible for a woman to become head of a homestead. (Eirola 1992, p. 41; Malan 1995, p. 20; Siiskonen 1990, p. 45; Vedder 1973, p. 68; Williams 1994, p. 49.)

An Ambo homestead was composed of cattle kraals, several sleeping huts and other huts used for pounding corn, storing food and household utensils, etc. The different sections were separated from each other by a wooden palisade or a millet-stalk fence. A round wooden palisade around the whole homestead protected it from intruders. An important place in the homestead was the round, uncovered enclosure where tradition was transmitted and rituals performed. The homestead was moved to another place every two or three years. (Andersson 1967, p. 201–202; Malan 1995, p. 21–23; Savola 1924, p. 44–49; Siiskonen 1990, p. 44–45, 51; Vedder 1973, p. 68–69; Williams 1994, p. 49, 184–185.)[156]

Sources of Livelihood. The main source of livelihood in the Ambo communities was agriculture, in addition to animal husbandry. The wealth of an Ambo was measured by the number of his cattle. The main crops were millet and sorghum. Additional sources of food were beans and other vegetables, pumpkins, fruits, as well as fish and game. The annual cycle of social life was determined by the agricultural calendar, and it included various ritual ceremonies led by the king. For example, rainmaking rituals were common. The fields were not owned by the people, but were allocated to them by the king. Thus, land could not be inherited. A portion of each harvest had to be handed over to the court. Households were also responsible for cultivating the king's fields. (Eirola 1992, p. 32–34; Haahti 1913, p. 80–88; Peltola 1958, p. 20; Savola 1924, p. 130–138; Siiskonen 1990, p. 50–52, 55.)

Hunters. Emil Liljeblad / The Finnish Evangelical Lutheran Mission. 1900–1908.

Catching fish. Hannu Haahti / The Finnish Evangelical Lutheran Mission. 1911.

In Ambo societies, the practical cultivation work was the women's responsibility, whereas the men devoted themselves to herding and caring for the cattle. Beside, the men did the dairy work. Cattle functioned as the owner's capital, and they were used for renting land, as well as for compensation for damages. Goats, pigs, chickens and dogs were also kept. Handicrafts, such as weapons, tools, baskets and clay pots, were produced mainly for home use, but also for sale. The Ambo people were especially skilled in metalwork. Salt, which was fetched from the salt fields of Etosha Pan, was an important trade product as well. (Eirola 1992, p. 41; Haahti 1913, p. 84, 88; Savola 1924, p. 143–146; Siiskonen 1990, p. 52–55, 60–64.)

Political System. In most Ambo societies, the political system was based on a hereditary rulership. Only some small communities in the western Ambo area, Uukolonkadhi and Eunda, had no kings but a council of chiefs as the central authority. The king (*omukwaniilwa*) came from the royal clan and had the status of a divine king. He was an absolute monarch and in theory had unlimited power over his subjects. The king was also the high priest, judge of the society and commander-in-chief of the army. (Bruwer 1966, p. 23; Eirola 1992, p. 45–46; Nambala 1994, p. 30–32; Siiskonen 1990, p. 45–46.) Kingship was not inherited from father to son. Usually it was the king's brother or one of the sons of the king's sisters who became the new king.[157] (Hahn 1928, p. 8; Nambala 1994, p. 30; Yrjö Roiha to the mission director 10.11.1883, Eac:6, FMSA.)

The whole nation, ruled by the king, was divided into smaller administrative units, each governed by a chief, a headman, or the head of a family. The king was assisted by his advisors and the clergy. In some societies, the nation was at times divided between two kings. Except for the kingship, official positions were not hereditary in Ambo societies. All crimes and conflicts were handled at lower levels of the society, and only a few cases reached the king. Four types of punishment were used: death, exile, confiscation of property and fines. Wars between different Ambo communities were also common. (Eirola 1992, p. 48–50; Estermann 1976, p. 51; Hahn 1928, p. 19; Nambala 1994, p. 30–32; Siiskonen 1990, p. 46–48.)

Traditional Religion. The traditional religion of the Ambos was based on the idea of one God, called Kalunga.[158] Kalunga was the creator of the world and man, and the highest authority over the all of creation.[159] Kalunga was also believed to cause the rain and wind, to create a new sun every morning, to protect the cattle and fields, and so on. In case of emergency, he could also appear as a human and talk to people. Since Kalunga was regarded as a good character who did no harm to people, it was unnecessary to worship him. As Kalunga was neither feared nor honoured, the ties between him and his creatures were regarded as rather weak. Kalunga was understood to help people in their troubles, however, and the powers of the healers and witches were believed to come from him. (Haahti 1913, p. 108–109; Malan 1995, p. 28; Närhi 1929, p. 9–13; Savola 1907, p. 6–7; 1924, p. 166–170; Tönjes 1996, p. 179–180.)

The ancestral spirits (pl. *aathithi*) were much more important to the Ambos than Kalunga, and active religion was centred around them. The spirits of the dead were believed to affect the lives of their own families by causing illnesses, preventing the corn from growing, causing harm to the cattle, and so on. Thus, they were greatly feared and were given offerings, the most common type being a spittle offering. Porridge and blood offerings – chickens, dogs, oxen – were common too. The spirits were believed to be especially angered when traditional taboos were broken. (Hiltunen 1993, p. 34–35; Peltola 1958, p. 23; Savola 1907, p. 9–11; Savola 1924, p. 171–173, 178–179; Tönjes 1996, p. 180–184.)

Religious rites were abundant in the Ambo communities, being used for healing, rainmaking, securing luck in hunting, and various other purposes in everyday life. There were many kinds of healers and diviners who specialised in different matters. Basically, the power coming from Kalunga was considered to be good, but it could be used for evil purposes. Witchcraft was widespread, and many events in life, such as illnesses and deaths, were explained as caused by witches, who were then revealed by the diviners and punished. Beside people, material objects were believed to possess magical powers, and protective amulets were much used. (Haahti 1913, p. 114–118; Hiltunen 1993, p. 34–37; Malan 1995, p. 28–29; Peltola 1958, p. 23–24; Savola 1924, p. 176–178, 185–188; Tönjes 1996, p. 191–196.)

The Colonial Era

Early Contacts with Europeans and German Colonisation

The Europeans arrived in Namibia and the Ambo area later than in many other African countries. This was mainly due to the geographical isolation of the territory, which is bordered by a vast desert along the Atlantic coast. The first Europeans to leave a mark of their visit to Namibia were the Portuguese explorers who erected a stone cross on the Atlantic coast near today's Swakopmund in 1484. Two years later the famous Portuguese explorer Bartholomew Diaz landed at a narrow bay on the Namibian coast which was named Angra Pequena (later Lüderitz). Despite some occasional landings, the country remained untouched by the Europeans for centuries. The Namib Desert also protected the indigenous peoples of Namibia from the European slave trade. When the slave traders eventually found their way to Namibia in the 19th century, they came from the north, and many Ambos were taken as slaves at that time. (Dierks 1999, p. 3–4; First 1963, p. 61–62; Katjavivi 1989, p. 5; Kiljunen 1980, p. 28–29.)

In the 18th century, expeditions from South Africa were sent to explore the country and its riches, and several hunters and traders moved about in the area. The first European missionaries, sent by the London Missionary Society, started their work among the Nama people in 1805, and the Wesleyan Missionary Society followed in 1820. In 1842, the Rhenish Missionary Society from Germany came to work among the Namas and Hereros. In the latter half of the century, many immigrants arrived in the country from Europe, and also from South Africa. (Dierks 1999, p. 7–11; First 1963, p. 62–64; Kiljunen 1980, p. 29.)

The remote Ambo area was not of great interest to the Europeans. The vast savannah plain south of this area also isolated it from the rest of the country (Peltola 1994, p. 37). In 1851, the English explorer Frances Galton made a journey to the Ambo area together with the Swedish naturalist Charles John Andersson (First 1963, p. 63–64), and their descriptions (Andersson 1967; Galton 1853) are among the first written of the Ambo area.[160] From the mid-19th century, European traders started bringing items of European material culture to the Ambo area (Eirola *et al.* 1983, p. 49). In 1857, the Rhenish missionary Hugo Hahn visited the Ambo area investigating the possibility of starting missionary work there, but his visit ended with open conflict with the Ambos. Hahn's second trip in 1866 was more successful, and he promised the Ambo kings that he would send them missionaries. Due to a shortage of resources, however, the Germans suggested the Ambo area to the newly founded Finnish Missionary Society (FMS). In 1867, the FMS decided to start its work among the Ambo people, and the first Lutheran missionaries from Finland arrived in the area on July 8th, 1870.[161] (Dierks 1999, p. 17, 23–24; Kemppainen 1998, p. 43–44; Peltola 1958, p. 27–31, 40–41; Peltola 1994, p. 25, 48; Von Rohden 1874, p. 541–544; Tötemeyer 1978, p. 19.)

Ndonga men on their way to work in Swakopmund. August Pettinen / The Finnish Evangelical Lutheran Mission. 1901.

Beside preaching the Gospel, the German missionaries in Namibia set up businesses and thus gained economic power, which paved the way for the German occupation of South West Africa. Together with the traders, the missionaries also became involved in the politics and warfare between the indigenous peoples. Their influence on the wars between the Namas and the Hereros in the 19th century was particularly strong. Many missionaries served as advisers to the local chiefs and were often present when treaties were signed between them. (First 1963, p. 64–66; Kiljunen 1980, p. 29–30.)

In the late 19th century, Britain and Germany were both interested in having South West Africa as a colony. In 1876, Britain annexed the area around Walvis Bay, and in 1883 the German trader Adolf Lüderitz bought a tract of land on the Atlantic coast from the local chiefs. Eventually, the Berlin Conference recognised Germany's right to this territory in 1884, and the borders of the new colony were confirmed in 1890.[162] All over the colony, local chiefs were made to sign protection agreements giving the Germans land and cattle, as well as mining rights. It did not take long, however, before the local people realised that they had lost most of their land and property. In 1904 the Hereros, and a little later the Namas too, started a war against the colonisers, which resulted in a total defeat of both of these groups in 1907. (First 1963, p. 69–81; Katjavivi 1989, p. 7–10; Kiljunen 1980, p. 30–32.)

The German colonial administration was focused on the so-called Police Zone in the southern and central parts of the country. The Ambo area, which was situated on the periphery of the colony, succeeded in staying outside the colonial rule area until 1908, when the protection treaties were signed between the Ambo kings and the Germans. Even after that, the Ambo communities managed to retain their sovereignty to a great extent.[163] After the wars of 1904–1907, the Germans started to take more interest in the Ambos because of a severe lack of labour in the south. The Herero population had been reduced from over 80,000 to 15,000 in the war. More than half of the Namas had been killed as well. The famine experienced in the Ambo area at that time also forced Ambo men to find work in the south. (Eirola *et al.* 1983, p. 55; First 1963, p. 82; Kiljunen 1980, p. 33.)[164] By the year 1910, the number of Ambo contract workers had already reached 10,000. The Ambos worked mainly in the new Tsumeb copper mine, the diamond fields of Oranjemund, and in the construction of railways. (Hishongwa 1992, p. 52.)

It is clear that the German colonial regime, and particularly the migrant labour system, transmitted European cultural influence to the Ambo area. However, as Tötemeyer (1978, p. 19) has pointed out, the most significant single factor in this process was Lutheran missionary work, and especially that of the Finns. Tötemeyer (1978, p. 30) describes this influence in the following terms:

> The Finnish Mission Church in Ovamboland began its task without the direct protection of a colonial power that could assist it in the work of development. Not only did it replace traditional religious ideas with Christian values and a Western orientation, but it also acted as innovator and reformer in other spheres in the absence of – or perhaps because of the absence of – a colonizing nation. It strove for economic renewal and created new social codes of behaviour and new legal forms, thus inaugurating changes normally carried out by a secular authority.

The Christianisation of the Ambo People

In 1870, the first Finnish missionaries, a group of six men, started their work among the Ambo people. Mission stations were soon established in Ondonga, Uukwambi, Ongandjera and Oukwanyama. Within two years of their establishment, however, the latter three had to be abandoned, as the missionaries were expelled from the area. The work of the Finns was thus restricted to Ondonga until 1903. (Dierks 1999, p. 23–24; Martti Rautanen, Report for the year 1900, Brother Conference 24.1.1901, Hha:4, FMSA; Siiskonen 1990, p. 125–126.)

The difficulties that the missionaries faced at the beginning of their work were mainly caused by differences in expectations: the Finns wanted to preach the Gospel, whereas the Ambo kings were more interested in getting firearms, wagons and liquor. The kings also hoped that the missionaries would serve as their personal advisors and not as teachers of the whole community. Because the Finns were not familiar with Ambo customs, they also offended the people because of their disrespect for many of the Ambo traditions. In addition, they suffered from malaria and other tropical diseases. Some of them died in the Ambo area, and many left the country because of the difficulties. (Haahti 1913, p. 123–

Finnish missionaries and members of the Olukonda congregation outside the Olukonda church. The Finnish pioneer missionary Martti (Martin) Rautanen stands in the middle of the picture. August Pettinen / The Finnish Evangelical Lutheran Mission. 1899.

124; Siiskonen 1990, p. 125–126; Tarkkanen 1927, p. 5–6; Tötemeyer 1978, p. 19–20.) At times, the Finns were also so poor that they had to ask for food from the local people, who in turn thought that the Finns had come to the Ambo area to escape the poverty in their own country. The Ambos were also afraid that the Finns would steal their land. (Martti Rautanen, Report for the year 1882, Eac:5, FMSA.)

Despite these difficulties, the work of the Finns continued, and the attitudes of the local people changed gradually. The Finnish missionaries learned the local language and Ambo traditions, which made their work easier. The food supply organised by the missionaries during the famine of the late 1880s, as well as their medical work, also contributed to this development. (Peltola 1958, p. 64–65; Martti Rautanen, Report for the year 1900, Brother Conference 24.1.1901, Hha:4, FMSA; Savola 1924, p. 196.)

The first baptisms in the Ambo area took place at the Omulonga mission station in 1883 (Peltola 1994, p. 100–101; Pentti 1959, p. 109). During the following decades, and especially since the 1920s, Christianity spread rapidly among the Ambo people. New mission stations were established all over the Ambo area, and the number of missionaries grew as well. In 1890, the number of Christians was almost 500, and by 1910 more than 2000. By 1920 it was nearly 8000, and by 1930 more than 23 000.[165] In 1929, the work of the Finnish Missionary Society was expanded among the Kavangos as well. (Pentti 1959, p. 109–110; Savola 1924, p. 203–204; Shejavali 1970, p. 13, 19.)

The policy of the German colonial government concerning missionary activities in the Ambo area was that the whole area should belong to the Lutherans (Kemppainen 1998, p. 49). Beside the FMS, the Rhenish Missionary Society (RMS) worked in Oukwanyama from 1891 to 1916.[166] The Germans had four mission stations in this area, of which two were on the Portuguese side and two on the border. During the battles of the First World War, however, the Portuguese troops conquered the northern part of Oukwanyama. Most of the Christians moved to southern Oukwanyama, which was on the British side, and the German missionaries had to leave the country. In 1920, the work of the Rhenish Mission among the Kwanyamas was officially transferred to the Finns. (Hänninen 1924, p. 5, 8, 13; Høy 1995, p. 20; Menzel 1978, p. 233, 272; Nambala 1994, p. 73–74.)

In 1915, the whole of Namibia had been occupied by South African forces. After the war, the newly founded League of Nations made South Africa, on behalf of Britain, responsible for this territory under the terms of a League of Nations Mandate. The decision came into effect in 1921. (Katjavivi 1989, p. 13.) In 1924, the Union Mandatory decided that the Ambo area should be divided among three missions for missionary purposes: the Finnish Missionary Society, the Anglican Mission and the Catholics. The Anglicans were given permission to work among the Kwanyamas, whereas the Catholics chose Uukwambi and Ongandjera. (Nambala 1994, p. 96.) To the Finnish Mission, losing its monopoly for missionary work among the Ambo people came as a shock (Kemppainen 1998, p. 198).

The Anglicans (The Ovamboland Mission of the Province of South Africa) established their first mission in 1925 in Odibo, Oukwanyama, which was followed by many others. A hospital and several schools were also founded. The mission flourished, despite the fact that many British missionaries did not take the trouble to learn the local language. Later their work was extended to other parts of the Ambo area as well. The Roman Catholic Church founded its first mission in Oshikuku, Uukwambi, in 1924. Although the Catholics had initially chosen Ongandjera too, they went to Ombalantu instead and established a mission station there. The Catholic mission also founded many schools all over the Ambo area, as well as hospitals and clinics. Its personnel were mostly German. (Nambala 1994, p. 96–101; Tötemeyer 1978, p. 23–24.) The Finnish Mission was permitted to continue its work in Ondonga, but also at its other mission stations and schools in other Ambo communities. In the 1920s, the Finns had 163 mission stations in the Ambo area. (Kemppainen 1998, p. 84, 91.) The congregations grew rapidly, and in 1954 the Evangelical Lutheran Ovambo-Kavango Church (ELOC), later the Evangelical Lutheran Church in Namibia (ELCIN), was founded. In 1963, Leonard Auala became its first bishop.[167] (Nambala 1994, p. 89–90.) This church has been described as a "folk-church highly in line with the mood of the population" (Høy 1995, p. 21).[168]

Writing lesson at the Rehoboth mission station. Hannu Haahti / The Finnish Evangelical Lutheran Mission. 1911.

It is difficult to estimate the numbers of members of these churches in the Ambo area, as the statistics that are available are unreliable. The Evangelical Lutheran Church in Namibia (ELCIN) is clearly the biggest church in the whole country today with more than 560,000 members in 2000 (Suomen Lähetysseuran vuosikirja 2000, p. 62). It has been estimated that in the 1990s, roughly 70 per cent of the people in the Ambo area belonged to this church (Notkola & Siiskonen 2000, p. 40). In northern Namibia, one also hears larger estimates, e.g. 80–85 per cent (Nashihanga 18.4.1997). The number of Catholics in the Ambo area was about 40,000 in the 1990s (Grotpeter 1994, p. 444), and in 1972 there were 40,000 members in the Anglican parishes in the area (Tötemeyer 1978, p. 24). According to one estimate, 74.8 per cent of the Christians in the Ambo area were Lutherans, 12.9 per cent Catholics and 12.3 per cent Anglicans in 1973 (Notkola & Siiskonen 2000, p. 29).

Beside these churches, other denominations have also become active in northern Namibia recently, e.g. the Zionists, the Seventh Day Adventists and the Reformed Church. However, as their following is marginal, they have not exerted any significant influence on the development of the Ambo culture. It has been stated that in 1972, 20–22 per cent of the Ambo population did not belong to a Christian church. (Tötemeyer 1978, p. 25–26.) According to Hiltunen (1986, p. 103), the percentage of non-Christians for the whole population in the Ambo area was 5 per cent in the 1980s. Naturally the non-Christian population, of whom many are former church members, has been influenced by the Europeanisation of the Ambo culture in various ways as well.

The Impact of Missionary Work on Traditional Ambo Culture

Clearly, the Finnish missionary work affected every sphere of traditional Ambo life. Its influence was based on the new cultural system, which included the mission station network, clerical organisation, schooling system and medical work.[169] The traditional Ambo culture was Europeanised in many ways, even if this was not the primary goal of the missionaries. The traditional healing system was replaced by European medicine and traditional education by mission schools. The everyday life of the Ambos was changed because of practical instructions in agriculture and handcraft.[170] New social groups were formed: African clergy, teachers, etc. The transition from polygamy to monogamy also led to major changes in the division of labour and in the role of women in Ambo societies.[171] The pastoral power of the Finns, which was in the hands of male missionaries, seems to have strengthened the paternalistic side of the society. The missionaries also brought European influence to the political hierarchy by serving as counsellors for the kings and as mediators between them and the colonial authorities. (Eirola *et al.* 1983, p. 11, 50–51; Eirola 1992, p. 51–52.) It has been pointed out that the activities of the Finnish missionaries led to a victory over tribal particularism (Tötemeyer 1978, p. 21).[172] All in all, the "spiritual Europeanisation" of the life of the Ambo people, in the form of Finnish Lutheranism, led to the abandonment of many traditional beliefs and customs. For example, witchcraft became very rare in the Ambo area (Hiltunen 1986, p. 157).[173]

However, the new religion and European cultural elements were not accepted without resistance, which was very strong for quite a long time, particularly in remote areas (Eirola *et al.* 1983, p. 50). The Finns were confronted by the diviners and healers on the spiritual side, and on the political side they had to compete for the kings' favour with counsellors and other administrative officials. A new political group, which was called the "heathen party" by the missionaries, emerged in Ondonga at the end of the 19th century with the aim of expelling the missionaries from the country. The early practice of the Finns to gather all baptised Ambos close to the mission stations also caused disputes with the district chiefs. (Eirola 1992, p. 52; Peltola 1958, p. 93–94.) On the individual level, there were severe conflicts within Ambo families whose members had become Christians, as well as between such families and the missionaries (August Pettinen's diary 10.12.1889, 19.12.1889, Hp:91, FMSA; K.A. Weikkolin, Report for January, February and March 1883, Eac:6, FMSA).[174]

The acceptance of the new culture was not total either. Many traditional customs continued to live alongside the new ones. Baptised Ambos often practised these in secret, and some of these practices are still alive today. (Nambala 1994, p. 84; Nampala 2000, p. 10.) On the other hand, many traditional customs were supported by the missionaries. The Finns strove to make a difference between what could be considered as "national customs" and retained, and what should be regarded as "heathenism" and rejected (Valde Kivinen, Die Volksitten, manuscript 1936–1937, Hhb:2, FMSA; Martti Rautanen 22.1.1917, Hp:110, FMSA). However, they did not always agree about these matters. The wedding ox custom, for example, caused a lot of controversy among the missionaries (Martti Rautanen to Albin X. 4.1.1917, Hp:110, FMSA; Peltola 1994, p. 309–310).[175] It should be noted that many Finnish missionaries also collected Ambo folklore, e.g. songs, proverbs, riddles and folktales, and thus preserved it for coming generations (Kuusi 1970, p. 6–7; Mustakallio 1903, p. 65). The Finnish missionary archives (FMSA) contain valuable material on other Ambo customs as well, collected by the missionaries. The linguistic work of the Finnish Mission, i.e. the development of written languages, the publication of Bible translations and other literature and newspapers, was also culturally significant (Väisälä 1980, p. 233–234).

Compared to the Finnish missionary work, which had no colonial aspirations in the country, the work of the Rhenish Mission was more closely connected with colonial politics.[176] As the Germans worked in Oukwanyama for 25 years only, it is difficult to assess how strong their influence on the local culture was. In any case, it seems that the work of the Germans affected the Kwanyama culture in a similar way to that of the Finns in other Ambo communities, even if the form of European culture they represented was German.[177] The Germans also did linguistic work, publishing literature in the Kwanyama language, and writing reports on the traditional culture (e.g. Tönjes 1996; Sckär 1932, p. 3, UEMA).

Since the 1920s, German influence spread in the Ambo area with the advent of the Catholic missionaries as well. These German priests have been described as paternalistic in their approach. On the other hand, it has been pointed out that the Catholics incorporated aspects of traditional culture into their doctrines on a larger scale than any other mission in the Ambo area. This was because of their view that animism is not necessarily incompatible with Catholic ideas and values. (Grotpeter 1994, p. 443; Tötemeyer 1978, p. 23.) The Anglican missionaries from Britain also brought British influence to the Ambo area. According to Tötemeyer (1978, p. 24), however, their contribution to the modernisation of this area has been "mostly limited to the spiritual and medical care of the population".

The cultural change in the Ambo area can be attributed to a number of different factors, not only external, i.e. European missionary work and colonialism, but also internal. Malan (1978, p. 264–265) feels that the Ambo societies have experienced an internal social evolution which includes a transitional move from matrilineality to double descent, a changing mode of residence, and a decline of chieftaincy. This process, he claims, is primarily responsible for the discarding of traditional religious practices in the Ambo area, while Christianity and Western civilisation should be seen as secondary factors in it only:

Admittedly, the influence of teaching and evangelisation is so widely mani-
fest that it indeed appears to be the basic motivation for change. However, it
is also obvious that the general acceptance of Christianity could not have
been effected so rapidly, had the challenge met with the strong resistance
usually offered by rigid cultural institutions in a stable society. One must
therefore conclude that the disruptive influence of internal reorganisation
created conditions in which new institutions can ideally take root, hence the
high degree of acculturation in Ovambo society. (Malan 1978, p. 264.)

According to Malan (1990, p. 9), it was the loss of daily contact with
matrilineal kinsmen in particular that severed traditional religious ties
between kinsmen and made the Ambo people susceptible to Christianity. The Finnish historians researching the Ambo area (Eirola *et al.* 1983,
p. 45) also point out that it would be incorrect to state that the cultural
change in this area was caused by European influence only. They also
remark that in the encounter between two cultures, features may take
shape which have not formerly occurred in either of the cultures and
which cannot thus be explained by borrowing (Eirola *et al.* 1983, p. 45).

The South African Regime and the Years of
the Independence Struggle

As soon as South Africa was given the mandate to run Namibia it started
to incorporate this territory fully into the Union of South Africa, thus
violating the terms of the mandate. More white settlers arrived in the
country, especially Afrikaners from South Africa, and reserves were established for the African population. In the constitution approved by the
South African parliament in 1925, the black population, as well as the
so-called Coloureds, were left without political rights. However, the
League of Nations frequently criticised the actions of South Africa in
Namibia. (Katjavivi 1989, p. 13–14; Kiljunen 1980, p. 35–38.)

After the Second World War, South Africa refused to regard the United
Nations as the successor to the League of Nations and to make a trustee-
ship agreement with it concerning Namibia. This created an international
juridical and political debate which took several decades to resolve. Eventually, it resulted in the United Nations General Assembly resolution of
1966 to terminate South Africa's mandate over Namibia and to take over
the territory under the direct responsibility of the UN. In 1971, the International Court of Justice agreed that the termination of the mandate was
valid and that South Africa's occupation of Namibia should be regarded
as illegal. In the 1950s, the Nationalist Party, which had come into power
in South Africa, started to apply its apartheid policy in Namibia. The law
regarding the establishment of "homelands" for different ethnic groups
was enacted in 1968. (Green & Kiljunen 1981, p. 4; Kiljunen 1980, p.
38–41.)

South Africa was faced with resistance from the very beginning of its
presence in the territory. There were also confrontations between the
new regime and the Ambo communities. The Kwanyamas, led by King

Mandume, tried to retain their autonomy, but in the battles of 1917, the king and more than a hundred of his people were killed. In 1932, South African forces bombed Uukwambi and destroyed the house of King Iipumbu, who had showed reluctance to submit to their authority. The king was then banished to a remote part of the country. (Katjavivi 1989, p. 17–19.) After these events, both Oukwanyama and Uukwambi were governed by a council of chiefs (Nambala 1994, p. 36–37).

Contract workers also protested against bad working conditions and wages. Trade unions already were active in South West Africa in the 1920s, and in the next two decades there were a number of local strikes. In the 1950s, many Ambos studying in South Africa were influenced by the radical ideas emerging on the student campuses. The Ovamboland People's Organisation (OPO) was founded in Windhoek in 1959, with Sam Nujoma as its President.[178] The primary concern of this organisation was the conditions of the contract workers, but it also worked for national independence. OPO changed its name into SWAPO (the South West Africa People's Organisation) in 1960, and started an armed independence struggle in 1966. (Katjavivi 1989, p. 20–23, 60; Soggot 1986, p. 25–30.) In 1973, the United Nations recognised SWAPO as the only authentic representative of the Namibian people (Maho 1998, p. 9).

During the independence struggle, the Ambo area became a battlefield for SWAPO guerrillas and the South African Defence Force. From 1966 to 1989 it was a dangerous place for civilians. In the early 1970s, South Africa declared a state of war in the northern parts of the country, and the curfew and prohibition of public meetings made everyday life difficult in the Ambo area. Many people were also arrested and tortured, and thousands of Namibians chose to flee over the border to Angola or Zambia. (Grotpeter 1994, p. 397; Kiljunen 1980, p. 44.)

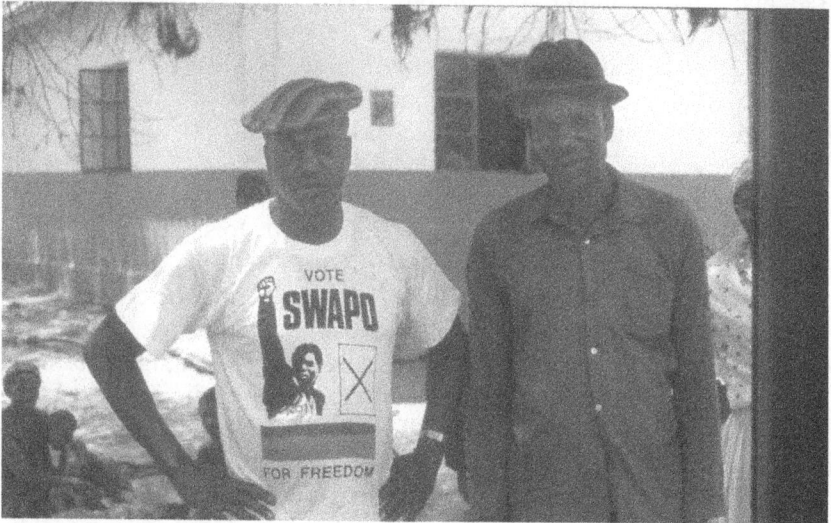

SWAPO (the South West Africa People's Organisation) started an armed independence struggle in 1966. Pirkko Lattunen / The Finnish Evangelical Lutheran Mission. 1989.

Beside political resistance, there was also cultural resistance in Namibia. From the 1920s, the Universal Negro Improvement Association (UNIA) was active in the urban centres of South West Africa, aiming to establish a "Universal Confraternity" among the black race and to promote the spirit of race pride. The slogan of this movement was "Africa for the Africans". However, the popularity of UNIA did not last long in Namibia. There was also a growing movement to reaffirm Herero culture, and an organisation called Otjiserandu ('the red band') was established among the Hereros in 1923. Many Hereros also left Christian churches and returned to their traditional beliefs. A number of independent African churches were also founded, such as the African Methodist Episcopal (AME) church in 1947, which became quite popular in the southern and central parts of the country. In 1955, the Oruaano church was established as an alternative to the Lutheran church, which had grown out of the Rhenish missionary work, and many Hereros joined it. Today it has a small following only. (Katjavivi 1989, p. 24–32.) Among the Ambos and Kavangos, however, religious separatism was almost non-existent.[179]

According to Soggot (1986, p. 33), the two Lutheran churches, which had their roots in the Finnish and German missionary work, represented the most powerful social organisations in Namibia and functioned as counter-forces to the ethnic division of apartheid:[180]

> It is the sheer mass of popular support in the two Lutheran Churches which provides, in the Southern African context, a unique feature of consolidation. ... The Churches, as a vast institutional common denominator, provide far-reaching immunity against the pernicious effects of ethnic division which have so often blemished the cause of liberation and democracy in Africa.

Gradually, these churches became outspoken opponents of apartheid and supporters of Namibian independence. In 1971 their leaders, Bishop Leonard Auala and Moderator Pastor Paulus Gowaseb, sent an Open Letter to South African Prime Minister Vorster, in which they expressed their wish that human rights be observed in the territory and that South West Africa be given its independence. This was the first of many such stands by the churches in Namibia. (Katjavivi 1989, p. 66–67; Väisälä 1980, p. 247–248.) The churches were also made to suffer for their political activity. The printing press of ELCIN in Oniipa was blown up three times in the 1970s and 1980s, probably to silence the church paper Omukwetu, which had dealt with political issues. (Grotpeter 1994, p. 133–134.) The Anglicans, who also spoke actively against apartheid, had their school in Odibo bombed in 1981. Many Anglican priests were also expelled from the country, among them Bishop Colin O'Brien Winter. (Nambala 1994, p. 102.) The Catholic Church in Namibia was rather neutral politically for quite a long time, but it adopted a more active role against apartheid later, together with the other churches (Grotpeter 1994, p. 443). In 1989, after a long political process, the United Nations General Assembly accepted the Namibian peace plan, and on March 21st, 1990, the Republic of Namibia was born (Dierks 1999, p. 178, 182).

Independent Namibia

Ethnicity and National Unity

In the first free and fair elections of the new Republic of Namibia in November 1989, SWAPO received 57.3 per cent of the votes, which made it the most powerful political party in the country. A new Constitution was adopted by the Constituent Assembly in February 1990, and Sam Nujoma, President of SWAPO, who had been in exile for thirty years, was elected the first president of Namibia. (Dierks 1999, p. 181–182.) Beside the President, many of SWAPO's leaders and top government officials were Ambos. As SWAPO membership is strongest among the Ambo people, they are also well represented in the National Assembly. Not surprisingly, it was feared that the role of SWAPO and the Ambos might become too strong in Namibia. (Grotpeter 1994, p. 141, 394, 397.) In the elections of 1999, SWAPO received 76 per cent of the votes, and Nujoma was elected President for his third term with a 77 per cent share of the votes (Suomen Lähetysseuran vuosikirja 2000, p. 62).

President Sam Nujoma in his home at Okahao. Minna Saarelma-Maunumaa. 2002.

Windhoek, the capital city of Namibia. Minna Saarelma-Maunumaa. 1997.

Since independence in 1990, major changes have taken place in the country. The biggest one, obviously, was that the apartheid system, which was based on the idea of separate development of ethnic groups, came to an end. As a consequence, the different ethnic groups in Namibia are in much more frequent contact with each other than before. The rapid urbanisation has also accelerated the process. Between the years 1981 and 1990, the population of the capital city of Windhoek grew by 46 per cent, and the growth in other cities was also significant (Maho 1998, p. 194). Today's Namibia is thus a multicultural society in which different cultures interact in various ways. On the other hand, the striving for national unity has led to the emphasis on Namibian identity for the people, while the ethnic identity is often regarded as a secondary aspect only. Nambala (1994, p. 9) sees the relationship between cultural diversity and national unity as follows:

> There is no country on the globe which can claim its people to be purely of one ethnic background. Ultimately, peace cannot be obtained on the basis of ethnic or racial lines of segregation. Diversities of ethnic backgrounds and cultures within a nation determined to shape its future are not to be reasons for schisms and enforced laws of segregations. A united nation is held together by a common spirit for freedom, self-determination and progress.

Despite the general aim to create a corporate Namibian identity, a number of ethnically based claims for kingships and land rights have occurred in the country since independence, one of them being the restoration of the Kwanyama monarchy. The role of ethnicity in nation building has also raised a lively public debate. On the one hand, ethnicity and traditional leadership have been seen as a severe threat to Namibian unity, and on the other hand, they have been supported as traditional African institutions that managed to survive the long colonial era. In a conference held in 1993, the Prime Minister of Namibia, Hage Geingob, while not underestimating the role of ethnicity, expressed the government's view that national identity should supersede other identities. (Malan 1995, p. 7–9.) However, Malan (1990, p. 9) claims that even if various new forms of secondary identity had emerged among the Ambo people by the end of the 1980s, such as black, Namibian or African identity, the primary form of ethnic identity among them was based on membership in a particular Ambo subgroup. Be that as it may, it is difficult to predict what kind of role ethnicity will play in Namibia in the future. In any event, it is an aspect which should not be underestimated.

In recent years, there has also been discussion on the revival of Ambo customs that were earlier banned by the missionaries, such as the initiation ceremony of the girls. The church leaders have been challenged to consider whether such traditions should be regarded as incompatible with Christianity or not. A growing number of Ambos are of the opinion that their traditional practices have often been destroyed unnecessarily and that the Ambo people should be liberated from the idea that their traditional culture represents "evil paganism". (Nampala 2000, p. 19–20.)

Africanisation seems to be a major cultural trend in Namibia today. After the long era of colonial rule, the indigenous peoples in Namibia seemingly wish to express with various cultural means that they are Africans. This is reflected in the popularity of African music, clothing, names, etc. The other major trend, however, is Westernisation, as globalisation and modernisation continue to spread the Western lifestyle, products and technology all over the country. Today, the Namibians are culturally and economically more closely connected to the rest of the world than ever before.

Politically, the first eleven years of Namibian independence were relatively peaceful. Some political disturbances did occur, e.g. in the Caprivi region, where the army and the police force suppressed a revolution in 1999 (Suomen Lähetysseuran vuosikirja 2000, p. 62). At times, fighting in neighbouring Angola also spilled over the border to northern Namibia (Grotpeter 1994, p. 397), and the war in the Congo, in which Namibia took part, threatened the peaceful development of the country (Suomen kehitysyhteistyö 2000, p. 77). Despite all this, life in the Ambo area has been rather peaceful. A serious threat to the life of all Namibians, however, is the rapid spread of HIV/AIDS. Alcoholism, unemployment and crime are serious social problems as well. (Suomen kehitysyhteistyö 2000, p. 77.) Culturally, the Ambo area is undergoing a modernisation process similar to that of the rest of Namibia, and Western cultural elements are increasingly being adopted as part of the local culture. The influence of the Finnish and other European missionaries on the life of the people in the Ambo area is minimal today, however. Since October 2000, all the Finnish missionaries in Namibia have been based in Windhoek (Suomen Lähetysseuran vuosikirja 2001, p. 56). After independence, a number of Finns have also come to Namibia to work in various development cooperation projects, some of which have been based in northern Namibia (Laamanen 1994, p. 12–13; Suomen kehitysyhteistyö 2000, p. 77–79).

Language and Cultural Identity

As a country of many ethnic groups, Namibia is also a country of many languages. The main linguistic groups (1991) are (Maho 1998, p. 13–14) as follows (%):

Bantu languages

Oshiwambo [181]	50.6
Otjiherero	8.0
Kavango	9.7
Caprivian	4.7
Setswana	0.4

Khoesaan languages

Khoekhoegowab (Nama/Damara)	12.5
Bushman	1.9

Indo-European languages

Afrikaans	9.5
English	0.8
German	0.9

Other/Not stated	1.0

Thus, Ambo speakers form the largest language group in Namibia, accounting for roughly half of the total population. The second largest group, with a proportion of 12.5 per cent are the speakers of Khoekhoegowab, i.e. the Namas and the Damaras, who share a lot of common history and culture. It should be noted that Afrikaans is spoken as a mother tongue not only by the Afrikaners but also by the so-called Coloureds and the

Namibia is a country of many ethnic groups and many languages. The choir of the university of Namibia (UNAM). Minna Saarelma-Maunumaa. 2000.

"Rehoboth Basters". The terms *Kavango* and *Caprivian* also cover several Bantu languages, and similarly, *Bushman* refers to several Khoesaan languages. (Maho 1998, p. 13–14.)

As regards language, the Ambo area is a highly uniform region. The Ambos speak seven different linguistic varieties of Ambo, which all belong to zone R (under 20) in the linguistic classification of Guthrie (Legère 1998, p. 40). The number of speakers of other languages in the area is minimal. Of the Ambo varieties, Kwanyama, Ndonga and Kwambi have the largest numbers of mother-tongue speakers. As the Finnish missionaries started their work in Ondonga, Ndonga was the first subject of their linguistic activities (Dammann 1984, p. 80). Over the years, the Finns have helped Ndonga to develop as a written language, as they published religious literature and school books and taught the Ambos to read (Tötemeyer 1978, p. 20). The first book in Ndonga, Pietari Kurvinen's "ABD Moshindonga", was published in 1877, the New Testament and Psalms in 1903, and the whole Bible in 1954. In 1901, the church paper Osondaha was established, and in 1936 it was succeeded by Omukwetu. Altogether, the contribution of the Finnish missionaries towards the development of Ndonga has been considerable. Beside Ondonga, Ndonga is used as a written language in schools and churches in the Uukwambi, Ombalantu, Ongandjera, Uukwaluudhi and Uukolonkadhi areas, where it is easily understood by the people. (Fourie 1992, p. 15–18; Malan 1995, p. 17; Tirronen 1976, p. 47; 1977, p. 11–12.) According to Fourie (1992, p. 24), Ndonga is "probably the best developed African language in Namibia as far as the availability of terminology, grammar, dictionaries and literature is concerned".

The Rhenish missionaries working in Oukwanyama also developed Kwanyama as a written language. The first book that they published in Kwanyama was a grammar in 1891. The Gospel according to Matthew appeared in print in 1896, and a Kwanyama-German dictionary in 1910. Later, the Finnish and Anglican missionaries contributed to the development of this language as well. The Finns in particular translated existing Ndonga material into Kwanyama.[182] These two Ambo languages are mutually intelligible, despite a number of phonological and lexical differences. The Catholics working in Uukwambi also published a few books, including the New Testament, in Kwambi, which is linguistically close to the Ndonga dialect. Because of positive changes in the ecumenical climate, Kwambi was not developed further. (Dammann 1984, p. 82–84; Fourie 1992, p. 15, 18.) Hence, the Ambos today have two written languages. It has been argued that had the Finns been the first to start missionary work in Oukwanyama too, the whole of the Ambo area would most probably have only one written language today (Peltola 1958, p. 126).

During the German regime, German was the language of the administration in the country. When South Africa came into power, English and Cape Dutch (later Afrikaans) were chosen as the official languages of the territory, whereas the status of German became semi-official. Of the two official languages, Afrikaans was more commonly used, as it was the language of administration and practically all secondary and most primary education. It also became the effective *lingua franca* throughout the country. Afrikaans was used in most communicative situations both between the whites and the indigenous peoples and between the different indigenous groups. The majority of the white population, more than 70 per cent, were also Afrikaans-speaking. (Duggal 1981, p. 5, 7; Pütz 1991, p. 457–458.) The Ambos who were employed as migrant workers, also had to learn Afrikaans. In the 1920s, the Finnish Mission chose Afrikaans, thus following the Rhenish Mission, as the medium of instruction in its schools, whereas the Catholics chose English.[183] (Fourie 1992, p. 15, 21.)

The apartheid policy of the ruling Nationalist Party of South Africa led to the active development of indigenous languages, especially after the late 1950s, when the Bantu Education Act (1953) went into effect in South West Africa. Language committees were established for Ndonga and Kwanyama too. These languages were standardised and their terminologies developed. They were also introduced as media of instruction in primary schools, and as subjects from grade 1 up to standard 10. School textbooks were published and several works of prose translated into both languages. These two Ambo languages were also increasingly used in the public media, e.g. in daily newspapers and the radio. However, it was not until 1989 that the University of Namibia offered Ndonga as a subject. (Fourie 1992, p. 21–24.) The "homeland" programmes of the apartheid regime, which separated the different ethnic groups geographically, also led to the localisation of indigenous languages. Hence, linguistic contacts between these groups were minimised. (Duggal 1981, p. 5.)

During the independence struggle, Afrikaans was considered as the language of the oppressor by many Namibians, while English was regarded as the language of liberation. English was also seen as an extraethnic language that could unite all Namibians into one national entity. People were thus motivated to learn and use English, and several school strikes were organised in the 1970s to replace Afrikaans with English. (Duggal 1981, p. 6–8; Pütz 1991, p. 458.) When Namibia became independent in 1990, English was chosen as the only official language of the country. The Constitution of the Republic of Namibia (1990, p. 3) says:

(1) The official language of Namibia shall be English.

(2) Nothing contained in this Constitution shall prohibit the use of any other language as a medium of instruction in private schools or in schools financed or subsidised by the State, subject to compliance with such requirements as may be imposed by law, to ensure proficiency in the official language, or for pedagogic reasons.

The use of languages other than English as the medium of instruction was confined to the primary school. In the secondary school and on the tertiary level, indigenous languages may be taken as subjects only. (Fourie

1992, p. 25.) With regard to indigenous languages, the language policy of today's Namibia is thus similar to that of the apartheid regime, even if the ideology behind it is different. Despite the new status of English, Afrikaans also continues to be the most widely used lingua franca in the country. (Maho 1998, p. 192, 196.)

The aim to build national unity and at the same time respect ethnic heterogeneity has been a difficult task for language planners in Namibia (Pütz 1991, p. 455). It has been noted that while in other countries ethnic minorities fight for their linguistic rights, Namibian peoples tend to reject them. This has been explained by a "colonial syndrome": for historical reasons, indigenous peoples in Namibia fear that ethnicity may be used for political manipulation.[184] On the other hand, there are clear signs that since independence, the Ambo languages have been more actively used in domains previously dominated by English or Afrikaans, such as banks and offices. (Fourie 1992, p. 26–27.)

NOTES

134 This is the last official estimate of the population in Namibia that has been made on an ethnic basis by the Central Statistics Office (CSO). Since independence in 1990, the ethnic identity of people has not been taken into account as a criterion of classification. (Malan 1995, p. 2.) However, it should be noted that such population figures were used for the purposes of the apartheid regime. Thus, they might have been manipulated for political reasons. Grotpeter (1994, p. 415) gives estimated population figures for these groups for several dates in Namibia's history, starting from the year 1877.

135 Tötemeyer (1978, p. 7) gives population estimates for these groups from the year 1879 to 1970.

136 The Finnish missionaries started to use the form *Ambomaa*, 'Amboland', because they saw that the prefix in the name *Ovambo* was a Herero prefix referring to the people, hence it should not occur in a name of a country (T.R., Muutama sana afrikalaisten nimien selitykseksi, Hhb:2, FMSA).

137 The Ndonga–English Dictionary translates *Owambo* as "Northern Namibia, Wamboland (Ovamboland)", and *Omuwambo* as "Wambo, inhabitant of Owambo (Northern Namibia)" (Tirronen 1986, p. 472–473).

138 This term was also recommended by Prof. Karsten Legère (Göteborg University, Sweden).

139 Some writers have also used the form *Ovampo* (Estermann 1976, p. 51; Seidel 1891, p. 37).

140 In Ndonga, the word for ostrich is *ompo* (English–Ndonga Dictionary 1996, p. 197).

141 This theory is not usually mentioned in later sources, however.

142 In his historical research covering the years 1850–1906, Siiskonen (1990, p. 41) uses the term *Ovamboland* for "the area inhabited by the Ovambo communities as well as the pasture and hunting lands belonging to their sphere of interest".

143 Because of this, many Ambo people use the term *northern Namibia* instead of *Ovamboland* or *Owambo* when speaking about this area in English. Often they simply refer to "the north" in everyday speech.

144 Some material utilised for this study also comes from the Angolan side of Oukwanyama, and examples will also be taken from there.

145 In the Ambo languages, the singular form for 'inhabitant of the Ambo area' or 'member of an Ambo community' is *omuwambo* and the plural form *aawambo* or *ovawambo* (Nambala 1994, p. 55). In English, the plural form ending with *s*, *Ovambos*, has been in general use. This form, however, has a double plural marking: the English -*s* and the Kwanyama *ova-*. Grotpeter (1994, p. 392), in turn, says: "While more properly called the Wambos today, these people have been most commonly known by Europeans as the Ovambos." The English–Ndonga dictionary (1996, p. 199) gives the plural form *Owambos* and translates it as *Aawambo*, and Kuusi (1970), Lehtonen (1999) and Tötemeyer (1978), for example, use the form *Ovambos*.

146 Some researchers also use *Owambo* (e.g. Williams 1994) or *Wambo* (e.g. Fourie 1992) in similar contexts.

147 There are also other theories about the geographical position of the nucleus of the Bantu languages; see e.g. Finlayson (1987, p. 51).

148 The Kavango people are so closely related to the Ambo people that they have often been regarded as belonging to the Ambo groups (Peltola 1958, p. 19; Kiljunen 1981, p. 28).

149 See Williams (1994, p. 60–67) for more details on Ambo traditions of origin and Ambo migrations.

150 Sckär (1932, p. 3, UEMA) presents a Kwanyama legend which explains the matriarchal order of the Ambo people: a woman named Janoni, daughter of Noni, became the mother of all chiefs. The same story can be found among the four legends of Ambo origin presented by Nambala (1994, p. 28–29).

151 Hahn (1928, p. 1–2) also refers to this legend when discussing Ambo origins.

152 That the Ndonga group was the "nucleus" of all Ambo groups is reflected in the practice that all the other kings received their power from the king of Ondonga until the 19th century (Bruwer 1966, p. 22).

153 For example, the San (Bushmen) have traditionally been close to the Ambo communities. The Ambos had these people serving as their bodyguards, executioners, spies, messengers and hunters. Many of them also settled down in Ambo-style houses, and intermarriage between these two groups has been fairly common. (Gordon 1992, p. 27–28.) There are also groups of Herero descendants living in the Kolonkadhi and Eunda communities (Tötemeyer 1978, p. 5).

154 In this presentation, we talk about the traditional Ambo culture in the past tense, even if many of these features and customs are still alive today.

155 Sckär (1932, p. 79–80, UEMA) gives a list of nineteen clans for the Kwanyamas, and so does Estermann (1976, p. 109). Närhi's (1929, p. 17) table includes twelve Ambo clans. Williams (1994, p. 186) gives a list of fifteen Ambo clans and compares them with the clans of the Kavangos and the Ovimbundu people in Angola. Tuupainen (1970, p. 140–141) presents an overview of the Ambo clans mentioned in earlier literature.

156 Tönjes (1996, p. 47–54) also gives a careful description of a Kwanyama homestead, as well as of the ceremonies attached to the moving of the house.

157 Nambala (1994, p. 35–38) gives a list of all the kings or chiefs in different Ambo subgroups from the 17th century up to the 1990s.

158 The word *Kalunga* is used for God among the Christian Ambos as well (Estermann 1976, p. 181; Haahti 1913, p. 109).

159 For the Ambo legends concerning the creation of man, see for example Närhi (1929, p. 14–16).

160 It was Andersson who first used the name *South West Africa*. Before that, the area was referred to as the *Trans-Gariep* meaning 'across the Oranje River'; *Gariep* is the Nama name for this river. However, the names referring to the traditional dwelling areas of the local ethnic groups, *Namaqualand*, *Damaraland* and *Ovamboland*, were more often used. (Katjavivi 1989, p. 5–6.)

161 It should be noted that Finland never had any colonial interests in Africa. At the time when the Finnish Missionary Society was founded, Finland was still part of

Russia and did not gain its independence until 1917. However, as the Ambo area (in Finnish: *Ambomaa*) was for long the only mission field of the Finnish Church, the relationship between the Finns and the Ambo people became particularly close.

162 This border, which left the northernmost part of the Ambo area on the Portuguese side, did not have any real effect on the life of the Ambos. As Hartmann (Bericht über das Amboland und seine Besitzergreifung (um 1904), p. 110, RKA 10.01:2159) puts it: "Die Ovambo selbst haben von dieser Grenzlinie natürlich keine Ahnung und leben so, als ob sie noch vollständig unabhängig wären."

163 In fact, many sources (e.g. Bruwer 1966, p. 73; Hishongwa 1992, p. 52–53) state that the Ambo area was never colonised by the Germans, as no direct rules of administration were imposed there. However, as Eirola (1992, p. 67) points out, the Germans did not neglect the development of affairs in this area, and they received information about the Ambo communities from local missionaries.

164 It has been stated that one of the reasons behind this massive migrant labour movement was also that the Finnish missionary work had created material needs which were then filled by earning money (Kouvalainen 1980, p. 108, 110).

165 The noticeable increase in the number of baptised Ambos in the 1920s has also been explained by the work of the first local pastors and evangelists who graduated in 1925 (Nambala 1994, p. 86).

166 The Roman Catholic Church was also interested in the Ambo area in the late 19th century. Because of the restrictions set up by the colonial government, they could not start missionary work there. Instead, they went to Okavango. However, many Ambos working in the south were baptised by the Catholics. The Anglicans showed an interest in the Ambo area as well, but the German government did not allow them to start a mission there either. (Nambala 1994, p. 95–96, 99–100; Tötemeyer 1978, p. 24.)

167 According to Tötemeyer (1978, p. 21), the attitude of the Finnish Mission right from the beginning was that an autonomous native church should be founded as soon as possible. This attitude was reflected, for example, in the fact that out of the 97 pastors of this church in 1972, only four were whites.

168 Tötemeyer (1978, p. 31) also emphasises the strength of group identity in this church: "Group identity on the strength of membership of the Ovambokavango Church is a fact, and it affords the institution the opportunity of being a strong regulating force in most spheres of life."

169 In 1913, training for teachers started in Oniipa, and several schools for both boys and girls were established in the Ambo area in the 1920s. Training for pastors and evangelists started in 1922, and the first Ambo pastors were ordained in 1925. The first European medical doctor in the Ambo area was Ms. Selma Rainio, who founded the Onandjokwe Lutheran Hospital in 1911. (Nambala 1994, p. 85–87.)

170 The most visible sign of European influence was probably the use of European clothes. When the Ambos were baptised, they were given white baptismal dresses which were often made in Finland. Over time, providing clothing for the people became a major concern to the Finns, even if the Ambos also got clothes from European traders. (Haakana 1960, p. 16–17, 32; Peltola 1994, p. 101, 131.)

171 Today, most Ambo families are monogamous (Malan 1978, p. 263).

172 Tötemeyer (1978, p. 21) argues that the Finnish missionaries "stimulated the political process of evolution towards unity and tribal community of interests, and thus a process of Ovamboland nation-building began". He also claims that the Ambo Christian identifies himself increasingly first as an Ambo and secondly as a member of a specific Ambo group.

173 Mustakallio (1903, p. 93) explains the fading away of traditional beliefs in Ondonga from the fact that the Ambo kings expelled the diviners from their country and sent them to the north in the late 19th century. The reason for this was that they had become too powerful in the society. Savola (1924, p. 204–205) also mentions that when king Martin Elifas (yaKadhikwa) of Ondonga was baptised in 1913, he prohibited the diviners from practising their occupation. Williams (1994, p. 187)

presents a list of traditional laws and social norms in Ambo kingdoms, according to which witchcraft and magic were prohibited.

174 The participation of Ambo girls in the traditional initiation ceremony especially caused a lot of controversy. At times, the missionaries were even in danger of losing their lives. (August Pettinen's diary 6.5. 1889, 24.7.1889, Hp:91, FMSA.)

175 Nampala (2000, p. 2) argues that many Ambo traditions were abandoned "not so much because of theologically based criticism, but rather because of the cultural imperialism of the early European missionaries".

176 It has been pointed out that colonial motives also explain the decision of the Rhenish Mission to send missionaries to the Ambo area: the Germans wanted to expand their control to the whole colony (Menzel 1978, p. 230). With the support of missionaries, they hoped to get the whole of the Ambo area peacefully under their control ("Aus dem Norden Deutsch-Südwest-Afrikas", p. 7, Deutsche Kolonialzeitung, 1.9. 1904).

177 One of the main differences between the Rhenish missionaries and their Finnish colleagues was that many of the Germans saw it as their task to spread German culture in the German colonies. Mirbt (1905, p. 22) represents this kind of thinking clearly: "... dann ist auch jeder Fortschritt der evangelischen Mission ein Fortschritt der Kultur, und jedes Fortschreiten der evangelischen Mission in unseren Kolonien eine Förderung deutsch-nationaler Kulturarbeit." It has also been claimed that the Rhenish missionaries did not believe in the capability of Africans to act as leaders in the church, whereas the Finns integrated Ambo Christians as teachers and pastors as early as possible (Høy 1995, p. 23–24; Perheentupa 1923, p. 6). The first black pastors of the Rhenish Mission in Namibia were ordained in 1949. In the Finnish Mission this happened in 1925, and since 1937 all its congregations have been run by black pastors. (Høy 1995, p. 21; Nambala 1994, p. 75, 86.)

178 Grotpeter (1994, p. 141) sees that the early training of pastors in the Finnish Mission created "a degree of self-confidence that has made the Ovambo people the leaders of Namibia in pushing for political autonomy".

179 Høy (1995, p. 24) explains this with the Finnish missionaries' sensitivity to the needs of the black people.

180 The domain of the ELCIN (the Evangelical Lutheran Church in Namibia) comprises primarily the Ambos and the Kavangos, while ELCRN (the Evangelical Lutheran Church in the Republic of Namibia) is to be found mainly among the Damaras, Namas and Hereros.

181 The prefixes in the names of different languages – oshi-, otji-, se-, chi-, etc. – are retained in this list, as this is how they were presented in the original source.

182 The Kwanyamas themselves demanded that their language should be used in their schools instead of Ndonga. "We do not want our nation to become Ondonga", they argued. (Ministers of Oukwanyama to August Hänninen 8.9.1936, Hp:10, FMSA.) The linguistic situation of the Ambo area was discussed at the missionary conference in 1937. The Finns agreed that the idea of creating one written language for the whole of the Ambo area was unrealistic, and that when developing Ndonga as a written language, elements of the western dialects should be incorporated into it too. (Missionary conference in Engela and Onandjokwe 26.8.–3.9.1937, 8 §, Dea:4, FMSA.) Previously, the Finns had seen it as their "holy duty" to retain Ndonga pure (Kielikomitean lausunto ošindongasta. 29.3.1917, Kirjekopiokirja 1916–1917, Hp:110, FMSA).

183 Afrikaans was not chosen by the Finnish Mission without discussions. Some of the Finnish missionaries thought that English would have been more useful because of its status as a world language. Others favoured Afrikaans, as it was widely used by the indigenous peoples in the country. (Lehtonen 1999, p. 78.)

184 Maho (1998, p. 193) also points out that there is widespread resentment of any kind of promotion of indigenous languages among the mother-tongue speakers of these languages in Namibia, due to the South African divide and rule policies.

Developments in the Ambo
Anthroponymic System

The Traditional Ambo Naming System

Name and Person

The analysis of the traditional Ambo naming system presented in this section is based mainly on old Finnish and German missionary literature and archival sources, and especially on the Emil Liljeblad Collection (ELC) in the Helsinki University Library. As these written sources deal with naming customs in different Ambo subgroups and at different points in time, the information that they give is often inconsistent.[185] Some inconsistencies may also be due to misleading or insufficient information given by Europeans who were not familiar with all the details of traditional Ambo culture.[186] Despite these shortcomings, the material seems to be sufficient to draw a relatively accurate overall picture of personal naming in Ambo societies in the late 19th and early 20th centuries. The interviews with Ambo informants carried out in 1997 and 2000 also gave additional information on many traditional naming customs.

Personal names had a very important role in the traditional Ambo culture and religion, as the name was seen as part of the personality of the individual. Hukka (1954, p. 102–103) divides the Ambo concept of man into three main spheres. In the centre there was *omwenyo*, i.e. the spirit or personality of man. Close to it was *ombepo*, the breathing. The third part consisted of four aspects: 1. *omuzizimba*, the shadow of man, 2. *olutu*, the body, 3. *edhina*, the name, and 4. *eha*, the place where the person is at a given time.[187] Other researchers have had slightly different ideas about the soul concept of the Ambos. This is not surprising, considering that there was obviously no uniform thinking about these matters among the Ambo subgroups. Aarni (1982, p. 65) also points out that there were a number of Ambo "philosophers" who had their own ideas, and thus the picture of soul may also have differed within one subgroup. In any case, it seems that in all subgroups the personal name was seen as an essential part of the person and his soul.

Because of the close connection between the name and the person, the real name of an Ambo was practically *oshidhila*, taboo.[188] The Ambo people thus often used different names on different occasions. (Aarni 1982, p. 68.) Various forms of address were also used instead of personal names, such as *tate* 'father', *meme* 'mother', *tatekulu* 'grandfather' and *kuku* 'grandmother'. The real names of the royal family were not used either. In general, the Ambos were reluctant to reveal their real names to strangers, and it was considered impolite to ask a person's name. Just as elsewhere in Africa, it was believed that as the name and the soul are interconnected, it would be possible to gain power over the soul of the person and to control his life by knowing his name. (Hopeasalmi 1946, p. 27–28.) Hence, when the Finnish missionary Hilma Koivu once asked for the name of an Ambo girl, the child was advised: "Do not tell, or you will die" (Hilma Koivu's diary I, October 1908, HKC).

In many Ambo ceremonies, mentioning the name of the person was also believed to have undesirable consequences. For example, in the Kwanyama rite of *oiyuo*, an annual festival of the youth, the girls were reported to say to the boys who tried to beat them: "Leave me alone, or I will say your name!" It was believed that if the girl mentioned the name, the boy would die. (Estermann 1976, p. 63–64.)[189] Obadja Iihuhua (ELC, p. 1580) also mentions that during the boys' circumcision ceremonies in Uukolonkadhi, the initiates' names were avoided, as it was feared that the one whose name was mentioned would die. Instead, the boys were simply called *omangololi* 'clatterers'. The name to be given to a new-born child was also kept secret by the Ambo people because of the fear of witchcraft (Hiltunen 1986, p. 68).

Indeed, because of the power attached to names, personal names were an essential part of Ambo witchcraft and sorcery.[190] Hiltunen (1986, p. 122–123) tells about the use of names in the custom of killing a person by stabbing a reflected image:

> The idea of killing by stabbing a reflected image is founded on the belief that in the reflected image as well as in the shadow there exists the soul-element of a person. In one case it is stated that it is the shadow of the person which appears upon the water in the pot. Now if one of these, the image or shade, is stabbed and killed by a person who knows the art, the person himself is destroyed. ... In the stabbing ceremony, uttering of the correct name of the person to be cursed is very important. Without it the whole act would be quite useless. The sorcerer has the magic power needed to make the use of the name effective.

Names were also used in search of witches. For example, if a sick man happened to mention the name of one of his wives during his ravings, it was concluded that this particular wife had bewitched him (A. Wulfhorst, Haschipala. Bilder aus dem Leben der Heiden in Ovamboland, p. 144–145. Vorträge und Aufsätze zur Ovambo-Mission 1910–1933. C/k:22, UEMA). Hahn (1928, p. 7) discusses the use of names in identifying possessors of evil spirits:

In Ovamboland the most favoured mode of "smelling out" (*eanekelo*) the possessors of evil spirits, wrong-doers or other culprits is with the aid of an ordinary Ovambo knife. This instrument is placed in the fire until it is red hot and then, with the edge downwards, drawn across the palm of his hand. While doing this the *onganga* utters the names of several suspects, and as long as the knife runs smoothly after a name has been mentioned and does not stick to or blister his hand, the person concerned is innocent. When, however, the progress of the knife across the palm is interrupted causing his hand to be burnt he jumps up with much ado and pointing the knife at the last-mentioned man, declares him guilty.

The relationship between people sharing the same name was considered especially close in the Ambo culture, as it was believed that sharing the same name (*uumbushe*), in a sense, also meant sharing the same personality. It has been argued that a namesake (*mbushandje* 'my namesake', *mbushoye* 'your namesake', *mbushe* 'his or her namesake') was seen as a closer relative than e.g. a cousin by the Ambo people (Aarni 1982, p. 68; English–Ndonga Dictionary 1996, p. 184). This was the case in particular when the father had asked for the permission of that person to name his child after him or her (Hukka 1954, p. 82–83). Occasionally, children were also named after deceased members of the community. Hukka (1954, p. 82) assumes that in the olden days, it may well have been the case that a child who was given a name of a dead person was actually regarded as being that person. According to Hiltunen (1993, p. 34), partial incarnation was considered possible in the Ambo culture, but only during the time the deceased was still remembered by others:

> The individual is not destroyed in death, but he turns into many spirits (*aathithi*), which continue their existence. This state continues as long as the deceased has someone who remembers him. Ordinary citizens may continue their existence in this way for a few (4–5) generations, royals for up to 20 generations. During this time a partial reincarnation is possible. A new born baby may bear the resemblance of a deceased member of the kin, which may give rise to the question: "Who has raised this or that person from the grave?". When the deceased are no longer remembered, their spirits fall in to a state of collective immortality.

Name sharing had an important role in many Ambo rituals as well. For example, in a ceremony that aimed to withdraw a curse that had prevented a woman from bearing children, the woman's relative, who uttered the curse, demanded that the future child should become her namesake, or if a boy, should be named after her sons.[191] (Ashipembe Eelu, ELC, p. 2004–2007.)

Temporary Names

The birth of a child was an important occasion in Ambo society. A pregnant woman was treated with great respect, and she was given special food during her pregnancy. About a month before the delivery, she went to her mother's or maternal aunt's house to give birth to her child.[192] This happened with the assistance of the woman's mother and other elderly women.[193] It seems that there were also special midwives in some Ambo communities.[194] In case of complications, a diviner (*onganga*) was sought for help. Usually the birth took place in a special hut which was used for this purpose only. Men were not allowed to enter the hut during the labour, but the husband could speak to his wife from a distance. When the delivery was over, the father was permitted to enter the hut. If the baby was a boy, the father was told that a frog-catcher was born; and in the case of a girl, that someone who would grind the meal for dinner had arrived.[195] (Estermann 1976, p. 58–59; Hahn 1928, p. 25; Närhi 1929, p. 18.)

Närhi (1929, p. 18–19) says that the body of the new-born baby was washed and anointed with almond oil, and the lips of the child and the breasts of the mother were greased to prevent the child from licking its lips later in life. This was regarded as bad manners. The child also got a leather strap around its neck to protect its father from death (Mustakallio 1903, p. 80). In addition, the infant was acquainted with the food of the world: it was given a taste of porridge (Mustakallio 1903, p. 80) or meal drink and tobacco (Närhi 1929, p. 19).

When the child was a few days old, an outdooring ceremony, called *epiitho*, took place.[196] In this ceremony, the baby was introduced to relatives and friends, and the mother became free to move outside the house again. (Hahn 1928, p. 25; Mustakallio 1903, p. 80.) There were several rituals attached to the outdooring. Some sources mention rites in which good crops and rains were predicted for the child's life (Mustakallio 1903, p. 80; Närhi 1929, p. 20–21; Nestori Väänänen, Hän tarvitsee parhaimman uskonnon: Esitys Amboneekerien uskonnosta, undated manuscript from the 1920s/1930s, p. 16, Hp:XXXIX, FMSA; Paulus Shijagaja, ELC, p. 910–911). Others indicate that in this ceremony, the child was introduced to his or her future jobs in the house (Sckär 1932, p. 58–59, UEMA; Vedder 1973, p. 69). Hahn (1928, p. 25–26), who tells about Ambo customs in general, describes this ceremony as follows:

> When the infant is four days old the *epitho* or the presentation of the child to relatives and intimate friends takes place. The latter are invited to come to the kraal and partake of a light breakfast outside the hut in which the mother is. During the meal the child is admired and fondled by all present and finally passed to an old male friend of the family who shaves off its crop of hair. If the infant is a boy the old man hands him to his wife who takes him to the front entrance of the kraal to show him to the world. She then returns past the cattle enclosure to introduce him to the cattle, his main care in after life. He is also taken and introduced to the milk calabashes and then returned to his mother.[197] As he is handed to the latter all present clap their hands and exclaim that it is a boy who will grow to a real man. This ends the *epitho*, much rejoicing and beer-drinking being indulged in subsequently.
>
> In the case of a girl a similar procedure is gone through with the exception that she is introduced to the threshing floor and the corn retainers instead of to the cattle kraal and milk calabashes.

110

According to several sources, an Ambo child received a temporary name first, and the real, permanent name was bestowed later. In Ondonga, the first name that the child got was traditionally called *edhina lyopomboga* 'name alongside spinach/cabbage' (*omboga* 'spinach, cabbage') (Amakali 10.10.2000; Nambala 14.4.1997; Namuhuja 14.4.1997). Most of the Ambos interviewed for this study did not know the origin of this term. Only Amakali (10.10.2000) explained it by saying that when the child was given a name, this vegetable had to be cooked and cakes made of it.

Some sources give the impression that the temporary name was given very soon after birth, before the *epiitho* ceremony, whereas other sources connect it specifically with this ceremony. It is also most confusing that some sources tell of one name-giving ceremony only. It is sometimes difficult to judge if it is the temporary name or the real name of the person that is referred to, or if it is possible that in some Ambo societies there really was only one name-giving. Because combining these stories would give a somewhat distorted picture of the matter, it is best to look at them separately.

Mustakallio (1903, p. 80), whose book deals with Ndonga customs, states that the child was given a temporary name very soon after birth. He also mentions the *epiitho* ceremony, but one gets the impression that the temporary name was given before that. According to Mustakallio, it was the mother of the child who gave the first name. Estermann (1976, p. 61) tells that among the Kwanyamas, the child was given a name before the mother left the hut, and that this was done by the father. Interestingly, this is the only naming ceremony that he mentions in his book. This is how he describes it:

> Four days after a birth, the mother can leave the hut. Before this, however, the father has proceeded to bestow a name on the newborn. This ceremony takes place in the big courtyard, while the mother and the other women utter shouts of joy inside the mother's hut. (Estermann 1976, p. 61.)

Hahn (1928, p. 26) says that the temporary name, which he describes as a nickname, was given at the *epiitho* ceremony. According to him, this name was given by the same old woman, the wife of an old friend of the family, whose duty it was at the ceremony to familiarise the child with his or her future jobs:

> Before the visitors depart the old woman gives the child a nickname by which it is known until formal naming by the father takes place about a month later (Hahn 1928, p. 26).

Närhi (1929, p. 19–21) claims that the child was given a temporary name on the sixth day after the birth if its navel was cured by then, or else on the eighth day, but never later. He also connects this name-giving with the *epiitho* ceremony, which he describes without actually using the term *epiitho*. According to Närhi, the father made a string which was wound around the baby's stomach, and the child was then given a temporary name. The child also got a string around its neck and its hair was shaved off. After this, the mother came out of the hut, and she and the midwife went to the fields, where good crops and rains were predicted. Eventually, the name-giving was celebrated by drinking beer. Unfortunately, Närhi does not say anything about who the giver of this temporary name was. Väänänen's (Nestori Väänänen, Hän tarvitsee parhaimman uskonnon: Esitys Amboneekerien uskonnosta, undated manuscript from the 1920s/1930s, p. 16, Hp:XXXIX, FMSA) descriptions of this name-giving ceremony resemble Närhi's. He also mentions that the child received another name when it grew a little older.

Savola (1924, p. 79–80), who deals mainly with traditional Ndonga culture, also connects name-giving with the *epiitho* ceremony. He says that the child was given a name about eight days after the birth. This was done by the father before the dawn of that day, and up until then the name was kept secret. When the father gave his son a name, he also gave him a bow and arrow. In addition, a string was put around the neck of the baby. The purification and outdooring of the mother took place at the same time as well. As this is the only naming ceremony that Savola describes in his book, one might get the impression that he is talking about the giving of the real name. However, this is not necessarily the case. Saari (1952, p. 59–60), who deals with traditional Mbalantu culture, also mentions one name-giving only. According to him, this took place roughly one week after the birth at a ceremony in which the baby boy was also taken to the cattle kraal and introduced as a warrior.

Tönjes (1996, p. 139) and Sckär (1932, p. 58–59, UEMA), who both deal with the Kwanyama culture, also connect name-giving with an outdooring ceremony which took place eight days after birth. However, they do not say if this name was temporary or not. Tönjes (1996, p. 139) mentions that the name was given by the father.[198] Wulfhorst (1912, p. 1), who also worked in Oukwanyama, says simply that Ambo children received their names from their fathers soon after birth.

To make all this even more confusing, Vedder (1973, p. 69) presents a distinction between an outdooring ceremony which took place three days after birth, and a name-giving ceremony which took place one week after birth. For the former, close relatives gathered to see the child, whereas for the latter, neighbours and friends were invited too, and they all brought beer and food to the celebration. When the child was named, the father took it from the mother, held it in his arms and mentioned the name, which was usually a name of one of his friends. This is the only naming ceremony of the Ambo people that Vedder mentions in his book.

The sources that list the most important Ambo ceremonies also draw a distinction between *epiitho*, i.e. the outdooring of the mother, and *eluko*, the name-giving ceremony (Mustakallio 1903, p. 95; Hopeasalmi 1946, p. 74).[199] This seems to support the idea that these really were separate occasions. Savola (Muutamia piirteitä muinais-israelilaisten ja nykyisten ondongalaisten olojen, lakien ja tapojen yhtäläisyyksistä, p. 9, Hp:125, FMSA) claims that in Ondonga, these ceremonies took place on the same day, usually on the eighth day after birth.

Many Ambos interviewed for this study in Ondonga supported the idea of two name-givings (e.g. Amkongo 14.4.1997; Nambala 14.4.1997; Namuhuja 14.4.1997). According to Namuhuja (14.4.1997), *edhina lyopomboga* was given as soon as the child was born, by an old woman who helped with the delivery. Later when the child had grown a little older, it received its real name from the father. Nambala (14.4.1997) said that the temporary name was bestowed by women who were present at the delivery, i.e. by the midwives, and that this name could be thought of as a nickname by which the child was known until it received its real name from the father. According to him, the bestowal of the real name took place on the outdooring day, a few days after birth.[200] The Ambo informants from Oukwanyama stressed that the first name was given by the father as soon as he heard whether the child was a "frog-catcher" or a "corn grinder", i.e. a son or a daughter. Only if the father was away at the time of birth could a temporary name be given by the mother or other relatives. According to these Kwanyama informants, the real name was bestowed later at the outdooring ceremony, and this was done by the father. (Kanana 19.9.2000; Malua 19.9.2000.)[201]

Altogether, it seems that many details of the traditional name-giving customs have been forgotten in the Ambo area, and the descriptions that one hears today are often inconsistent. Based on both old literature and interviews, it is impossible to say with certainty when and by whom the temporary name was given, whether the name given at the outdooring ceremony was temporary or not, or whether there was still another naming ceremony after that. It is most likely that there were different customs in different Ambo subgroups and at different times as well.

It seems that in some Ambo communities there were three namings altogether: 1. The one given by the midwives immediately after birth (a temporary name), 2. The one given by the father at the *epiitho* ceremony (another temporary name), and 3. The one given by the father at a later ceremony (the real name). However, it is possible that the other name-giving ceremony was abandoned later, which would explain the fact that it is not remembered anymore. Be that as it may, it seems justifiable to state that Ambo children traditionally received a temporary name first and a real, permanent name somewhat later.

The Bestowal of the Real Name and the Confirmation of the Namesake Relationship

Let us take a closer look at sources which mention another name-giving ceremony taking place after the outdooring ceremony, *epiitho*. It is clear that in all these sources, the real name of the person is referred to. According to these sources, this ceremony took place when the child was between one and three months old, and the namesake had an important role in these festivities. These sources also stress the role of the father in name-giving. As Pentti (1959, p. 35) remarks, giving the name was one of the few rights that an Ambo father had with regard to his child. On the other hand, Malua (19.9.2000) said that in Oukwanyama the grandfather, if he was alive, used to name the first-born child. After this the father named the other children. Munyika (16.10.2000) also said that traditionally, Kwanyama children were named by their fathers, but the name of the first-born child came from the elders, and preferably from the paternal grandfather.

According to Hahn (1928, p. 26), the formal naming of an Ambo child took place about a month after the *epiitho* ceremony. This is how he describes this *eluko* ceremony:

> Before the naming ceremony the father informs the mother to call together her relatives and friends. All those who attend bring beer and food. A special friend of the father brings some strands of bark from the *omugolo* bush and fashions it into a small necklace and belt. With these he proceeds to the mother's hut and places them on the child together with the customary leather belt made of ox-hide. Sitting on the ground close to his wife the father takes up the infant and passes it under his legs twice before handing it back to her with the remark "Here is your child, his or her name is, so and so." The relatives and friends are then called and the name, which has been kept secret up till then, is disclosed. The father then removes the bark belt and the necklace. This ceremony (*eluko*) is celebrated with much beer-drinking and feasting. (Hahn 1928, p. 26–27.)

Mustakallio (1903, p. 81–82) states that the child received its real name from the father at the age of a few weeks. In the morning of that day, the whole body of the child was anointed and pearls and wooden amulets were placed around the neck and arms in order to protect the child against diseases and to bring success in farming, cattle raising, hunting, and so on. After this, the father took the child, kneeled down and passed it under his right knee to show that he admitted that the child was his. Then he gave the child to the mother saying: "Heh, look, here is my child, So-and-so (mentioning the child's name), take it!". In the afternoon, the neighbours gathered in the house to hear what name the child had been given and to drink beer.

According to Närhi (1929, p. 22), the child received its real name at a time when the mother started to move about further away from the homestead. On this occasion, the father took the child into his arms and uttered its name, but he muttered this in order to prevent the mother from hearing it. Then he gave the baby to the mother as a sign that it was their mutual child. After this, the father went to see the person after whom he had named his child, and said to him or her: "I have talked about you in my home". The namesake answered him gratefully and sent the young namesake presents. After coming home, the father called his child by name loudly and clearly, so that everyone could hear it. The child was then clothed with a leather belt and a front strip, as well as a string of pearls.

Väänänen (Hän tarvitsee parhaimman uskonnon: Esitys Amboneekerien uskonnosta, undated manuscript from the 1920s/1930s, p. 16, Hp:XXXIX, FMSA) also mentions two name-giving ceremonies: the first connected to the outdooring ceremony and another one when the child grew a little older. According to Rautanen (Martti Rautasen Ambomaan kokoelma Suomen kansallismuseossa – Martti Rautanen's Ambo Collection at the National Museum of Finland 1983, p. 21–23, 30), the real name was bestowed at the age of approximately two months. On that day, the child was given a leather belt, which was then used as its ordinary clothing. After the name-giving, a boy was also given a little bow and arrows, which the person who took care of the child had to carry until the child was big enough to carry them for himself. Rautanen (Iizila j'Aandonga, Erstes Heft, 5., 57., Hp:122, FMSA) also says that the father was not allowed to go to war or over the river until his child had received a name. According to Paulus Shijagaja (ELC, p. 911), name-giving in Ondonga took place two or three months after the outdooring ceremony. He also mentions that on this occasion the child got a leather string and pearls around its neck.

Tuomas Uukunde (ELC, p. 81–82) says that in Ondonga, a child received its real name when it was one month old. The relatives of the father and the mother were invited to the name-giving ceremony, and they brought beer with them. No-one knew the name of the child until the party was over. After the party, the husband said to his wife: "Do you know what I will name him/her? I will tell this in secret to you only, but do not tell it to any other person before the name has been revealed to the namesake." The husband, together with a neighbour of his, then went to visit the namesake and invited him or her to greet the child. Chicken and porridge were cooked. When the visitors[202] had eaten enough, their bodies were anointed with grease so that when they walked in the fields, people knew that they had told the namesake of the name. The name of the child was announced to other people only after they had arrived home.

According to Jairus Uuanga (ELC, p. 1367–1368), the actual naming of the child in Ondonga took place privately between the parents in the hut where they slept.[203] Before sunrise, the father put his penis inside the mother. It was not supposed to go too deep or stay in too long, but had to be taken out quickly. It was believed that if the penis went too deep and the parents took fancy to it, the child would become idiotic. While the parents did this, the child was between them. Then the father took the child, passed it between his legs and gave it to the mother saying: "Take my So-and-so", mentioning the name that the mother did not yet know. If the mother did not hear the name that was uttered, she did not ask for it, but would wait until she heard it again. It was believed that if she asked for it, the child would become stupid and people would say that the parents had spoiled it during the naming. Unfortunately, Uuanga does not tell how old the infant was when this ceremony took place.

The report of naming in Ondonga by Gideon Iitula (ELC, p. 1402) describes the same scenario: the father and mother touching each other early in the morning without having sexual intercourse, passing of the child between the legs of the father who then uttered the name inaudibly, and the belief that the child would be idiotic if the mother asked for its name. In addition, Iitula (ELC, p. 1402–1403) says that when the ceremony was over, a special "naming porridge" was eaten in the hut. The sauce that was served with it, contained resin and a piece of the umbilical cord, which was supposed to make the father, who was unaware of it, fond of his child. After this, the father went to see the namesake together with a girl who carried meal and sorghum with her, and informed him or her of the child's name. Before the father left, the namesake anointed him with grease.[204]

After the naming ceremony (*eluko*), there were also special ceremonies to confirm the namesake relationship (*uumbushe*). It should be noted here that not anyone carrying the same name was considered as the namesake of the child, but only the person after whom he or she was named (Gideon Iitula, ELC, p. 1402). Tuomas Uukunde (ELC, p. 82–83) wrote the following about namesake ceremonies in Ondonga. A few days after *eluko*, a ceremony called *eyokolo*, 'taking out of the fire' (in order to prevent the child from burning), was performed.[205] This was done by the namesake who first sent a message to the parents telling them that he or she would come and *yokola* the child. Only a few people were invited to this ceremony: the namesake, two or four neighbours and two or four relatives of the parents. These people were gathered "to see how the namesake sees the face of his or her namesake". However, Uukunde tells that a ceremony called *ekwato*[206], 'catching', was an even bigger one than *eyokolo*. In this feast the child received presents from his or her namesake. A girl was given a dress made of ostrich eggshells, as well as black pearls. For a boy, the namesake was expected to make an *oonkutuwa* [207], a leather strip which the boy would wear on his back, and to carve a "namesake stick". It was feared that if a woman got married without *ekwato* being performed, she would either have weak children or no children at all. Hopeasalmi (1946, p. 74) also mentions *ekwato lyokanona* ('catching of the child') as one of the most important ceremonies of the Ambo people.

Reasons for Giving Names

Temporary Names. What were the names like that the Ambos used? Let us start with temporary names. According to many sources, these names typically referred to the time of the day the baby was born. A boy born in the morning could be called *Angula* and a girl *Nangula*, and a boy born during the night could become *Uusiku* and a girl *Nuusiku*.[208] Names were also given according to events taking place at the time of birth, e.g. *Mvula* 'rain' or *Uukongo* 'hunting'. (Närhi 1929, p. 20.) Amkongo (14.4.1997) mentioned four types of traditional temporary names and gave examples of them as well:

1. Names referring to the time of birth

Angula, Nangula	'morning'
Amutenya, Namutenya	'midday'
Uusiku, Nuusiku	'night'

2. Names referring to circumstances and events

Nandjala	'hunger, famine'
Akwenye	'spring' (hot, dry season)
Nathinge	'summer'(green season)
Namatembu	'moving, departure'
Angombe, Nangombe	'head of cattle' (the father had a lot of cattle at the time of birth)

3. Names of trees, rivers, important animals, etc.

Nembungu	'hyena'
Amunime	'big lion'
Mulunga	'fan palm'

4. Names referring to some characteristic behaviour of the child

Nandila	'ready to cry'

Nambala (14.4.1997) stated that the temporary names usually referred to the time of day of the birth or various circumstances around it: that the delivery had been difficult, that it was a twin birth, that the previous child had died at birth, that the child was crying when it was born, or that there was fighting going on at that time, etc.

It seems that in some cases, the bestowal of temporary names was highly systematic. This was especially the case with twins. In the Ambo culture, the birth of twins (*epaha*) was regarded as a great misfortune to the family and the whole community. Therefore, twins born to the royal family were killed, and if the wife of the king gave birth to twins, she was expelled from the court. Among ordinary people, twins were permitted to stay alive, but only after special purification rites. (Brincker 1900, p. 48; Hiltunen 1993, p. 201; Hopeasalmi 1946, p. 86; Savola 1924, p. 79.)[209] According to Hopeasalmi (1946, p. 91), twins were first given temporary names, which were *Uuanga* for a boy and *Nuuanga* for a girl, and the real names were bestowed after the purification ceremonies. Boys were named after their male cousins, girls after their female cousins, and a boy and a girl were named after some couple in the family. On the other hand, Närhi (1929, p. 82) states that twins were named once only, and the mother was not allowed to leave the homestead before that was done. Simson Shituua from Oukwanyama (ELC, p. 1631) reports that a boy twin was named after a man from the royal family and a girl twin after a woman from the same family.[210] Mateus Angolo from Ongandjera (ELC, p. 1383) mentions *Uuanga* and *Sekupe* as twins' names. However, it is not clear whether these two informants refer to the temporary names or the real names of the twins.

The birth of triplets, contrary to the birth of twins, was believed to bring good luck, and triplets were in the king's favour. Triplets were also named by the king. (Melander *et al.* 1942, p. 62.) Melander *et al.* (1942, p. 62) write of triplets in Ondonga who were named *Namapoha*, *Namzpungu* and *Tulumba* by the king. However, this source does not mention if these children were boys or girls.

Temporary names were "systematic" also if the mother had previously experienced a miscarriage or given birth to a dead child. Närhi (1929, p. 81–82) says that in such a case a boy was always named *Iimbondi* and a girl *Niimbondi*[211] often these names also remained as the real names of the children. Tuomas Uukunde (ELC, p. 69–70) tells that in such a situation a boy was named "God's *Iijambo*" and a girl "God's *Nelago*" in Ondonga, but if they had other namesakes, they did not retain these names. There were also many other kinds of "systematic" names. For example, Namuhuja (14.4.1997) said that if the father died before his son was born, the boy was given *Amakali* as his temporary name. Tuomas Uukunde (ELC, p. 80) also states that in Ondonga, the first child of the family was simply called "first-born" or "the first" in the beginning.

Savola (1924, p. 79–80) writes that many of the names given at the *epiitho* ceremony referred to the time of the day the baby was born, e.g. 'day', 'night', 'morning', but that there were also other kinds of names which referred to different actions or objects, or which had no linguistic meaning.[212] He also claims that similar names were used for boys and girls. Savola gives some examples of Ambo names in his undated manuscript "Muutamia piirteitä muinais-israelilaisten ja nykyisten ondongalaisten olojen, lakien ja tapojen yhtäläisyyksistä" (p. 9, Hp:125, FMSA), e.g. *Nandjala* 'hunger, famine', *Neloolo* 'good harvest', *Ndahambelela* 'I praise', *Nangombe* 'ox', and *Nembungu* 'hyena'. According to Sckär (1932, p. 59, UEMA), names bestowed at this ceremony often referred to the time of the day, e.g. *Haufiku* 'night', *Hamutenja* 'day', or were predictive by nature, e.g. *Pohamba* 'at the king's place' or *Ndilenga* 'I have a king's counsellor'.[213]

Real Names. As was already pointed out, an Ambo child usually received his or her real name from the father. According to Nambala (14.4.1997), the name that the father gave could be the same as the temporary name, or a different one. Most sources give the impression that an Ambo child received one real name only (e.g. Tönjes 1996, p. 139).[214] On the other hand, Namuhuja (14.4.1997) stated that at times, children could be given more than one name.

The real names of the Ambo people resembled temporary names to a great extent, even if the motives for the giving of these names were partly different. Many sources claim that an Ambo child was usually named after another person, who typically was a relative or a friend of the father. The namesake relationship carried a wealth of obligations, such as giving presents and looking after the child later in life. If the parents died, the namesake was often the one who took care of the orphan. The two namesakes were also practically identified with each other, and this was reflected in the way they were addressed. For example, a grown-up man was expected to call his father's young namesake "my father". (Pentti 1959, p. 36; Vedder 1973, p. 69.) This practice can be explained by the traditional belief that the person's name is an essential part of his personality (Hopeasalmi 1946, p. 27). Hahn (1928, p. 27) describes the Ambo namesake custom as follows:

The name chosen is generally that of the father's greatest friend, whether a relative or not, who is thereafter held in high esteem by the whole family. He also acts as a kind of god-father and after the naming presents the child with cattle or other presents, depending upon his wealth or standing.[215]

According to Väänänen (Hän tarvitsee parhaimman uskonnon: Esitys Amboneekerien uskonnosta, undated manuscript from the 1920s/1930s, p. 16, Hp:XXXIX, FMSA), a namesake relationship was sometimes regarded as more important than kinship, even if it did not include any hereditary rights.[216] Weikkolin (to the mission director 15.2.1883, Eac:6, FMSA) states that to be asked to become a namesake was the greatest honour and sign of friendship that one could experience in the Ambo community. Nampala (2000, p. 16) also emphasises the importance of the namesake relationship in Ndonga name-giving:

> Traditionally there would be an important name giving ceremony. The child would generally be named after a person who is responsible and trusted ... In most cases there was a link between a child and the person who they were named after. A common expression is 'edhina ekogidho' which means that if a child is named after a good person it is likely that that child will also grow up to be as good as their namesake (mbushe). The person whose name a child has taken would bring gifts to a ceremony (ezaleko/ekwato lyambushe).

Nambala (14.4.1997) said that in the old days Ambo fathers generally named their children after people who had desirable characteristics, as it was believed that the child would resemble his or her namesake. Namuhuja (14.4.1997) also reported that children were typically named after neighbours, friends and relatives, and hence a boy who was not born in the morning could also be called Angula 'morning'. It is clear that in such cases, the names did not say anything about their bearers or the conditions of their life, and thus their original meanings became insignificant. Their actual "meaning" was that they referred to the namesake.

It is important to note that the namesake relationship is not stressed equally strongly in all sources. This is what Tönjes (1996, p. 139) says about the motives for name-giving in Oukwanyama:[217]

> When deciding on the name, parents prefer to be guided by the circumstances and conditions in which the child was born. Children born during the night are often called Noufiku, or if it is a boy, Houfiku (oufiku means night). On occasion, children born during the floods (efundja) are named Nefundja.[218] Should the father be especially delighted at the birth of a new member of the family, the child may be given the name Ndahambelela, "I have thanked". One of my servants was called Shimweneneni which, translated literally, means "do not talk about it anymore". Perhaps his parents quarrelled before he was born. When the joyous occasion did take place, the quarrel was forgotten and it was said: "Shimweneneni, let us not speak about it any more."

Estermann (1976, p. 61) also does not mention namesakes in his description of Kwanyama name-giving, which according to him took place very soon after birth, when the mother was still in the sleeping hut:

> The Kwanyama go to no great trouble finding names. Anyone born during the night (*oufiku*) will be Haufiku, in the case of a boy, and Naufiku, if a girl. The same may be said of the word *ongula* ("morning"), which gives Hangula and Nangula. Or with the word *omutenya* ("day"), which forms the names Hamutenya and Namutenya respectively. It is clear though, that the time of birth is not of unique importance; other circumstances also contribute to furnishing names. Thus Nandyala will be some one who came into the world in a year of famine (*ondyala*); Haimbodi is the name of a boy whose mother has to take many remedies (*oimbodi*) during the period of pregnancy. A girl in this case will be called Naimbodi. Sometimes certain names are obligatory. Thus: Shihepo and Nehepo are a boy or girl whose father died before the birth of the child. They are children of misfortune (*ehepo*). ... Besides using these names there is no objection to resorting to some historical tale or using the first word of a proverb to form names, but this practice is rarer here than in the tribes west of the Kunene.

Mustakallio (1903, p. 82) writes that names were sometimes given according to some special characteristic of the child. Wulfhorst (1912, p. 1), on his part, gives Kwanyama examples of names which reflect the feelings of the father: *Nda hafa* 'I am glad', *Nda tila* 'I am afraid', *Shi kongu* 'I have searched for it', *Nda hambelela* 'I praise'.[219] Sometimes names contained whole stories. For example, Hamutumua (1955, p. 27–28) tells how she received the name *Kaunehafo*, 'there is no joy'. At the time when she was born, her uncle had to flee from Oukwanyama in fear of blood revenge, as he had accidentally shot his own child – whose mother was the king's sister – in a jealous rage. Because of this tragedy, the father of Hamutumua and his family had to run away into the bushes, where Hamutumua was born and given the name *Kaunehafo*.

Namuhuja (14.4.1997) said that the names given by the fathers often included messages to other people too. For example, a man could name his child *Mweyaokulya* 'you have come to eat' as a message to his wife.[220] Names could also be attached to the future jobs of the child. A boy could be named *Angombe*, which refers to cattle-raising, and a girl *Taatsu*, which refers to grinding corn. (Namuhuja 14.4.1997.)

Mustakallio (1903, p. 82) claims that similar names were used for boys and girls, i.e. that personal names did not differentiate between the sexes. As examples of such names he mentions *Elago* 'luck, happiness', *Ndakola* 'I am strong', and *Omvula* 'rain'. Väänänen (Hän tarvitsee parhaimman uskonnon: Esitys Amboneekerien uskonnosta, undated manuscript from the 1920s/ 1930s, p. 16, Hp:XXXIX, FMSA) also points out that as boys and girls mainly had similar names, it was difficult to judge by name if the person in question was a man or a woman.[221] However, it is clear that there were also differences in name forms, and we have already referred to some: *Angula* (boy) and *Nangula* (girl), *Uusiku* (boy) and *Nuusiku* (girl), etc. Typically, girls' names were formed with the name-deriving formative *na-/n-*: *Nangula* < *na + ongula*, *Nuusiku* <

na + uusiku. Väänänen (undated and untitled manuscript from the 1920s/ 1930s, p. 86, Hp:XXXIX, FMSA) says that there were special names for boys, e.g. *Kamati* 'little boy', and others for girls, e.g. *Nehoja*[222], but that mostly the same names were used for both sexes, often with a slight difference: *Uusiku* for a boy, *Nuusiku* for a girl.

Mateus Shehama (ELC, p. 1157–1158) from Oukwanyama gives examples of personal names with their meanings. The names with the initial letter *H* are boys' names and the ones with *N* girls' names:

Heita, Naita	Born while the father was on a plundering expedition
Haukongo, Naukongo	The father was hunting
Haihambo, Nahambo	The father was at *ohambo* ('cattle-post')
Haluendo, Naluendo	The father was travelling
Haimbondi, Naimbondi[223]	Born after a premature baby
Haipinge, Naupinge,	
Mingana	Born after someone had died
Shikomba, Nekomba,	
Shibute, Ndute	Born after twins
Haindongo, Naindongo,	
Shindongo, Nendongo	The father had syphilis[224]
Hamŭtenja, Namŭtenja	Midday
Hendjala, Nandjala	Famine[225]
Haufiku, Naufiku	Night
Helao, Nelao	Happiness, happy
Shisona, Nakašona	The father died before the child was born (the name means 'small, smallness')

The list given by Johannes Kaukungua (ELC, p. 1473–1474) from Oukwanyama resembles Shehama's list to a great extent. However, the name forms that he mentions are not Kwanyama forms:

Iita, Niita	Born while the father was on a plundering expedition
Uukongo, Nuukongo	Born while the father was hunting
Iijambo, Nahambo	Born when the father was at a cattle-post
Aluendo, Naluendo	Born when the father was travelling
Iimbondi, Niimbondi	Born after a child in the family had died soon after birth and the mother had been treated with herbs (*iimbondi* 'herbs')
Iipinge, Nuupinge,	
Mpingana	Born after someone in the family had died
Šikomba, Nekomba,	
Šivute, Mvute	Born after twins
Iindongo, Niindongo,	
Šindongo, Nendongo	Children of a father who had syphilis
Endjala, Nandjala	Born during a famine
Uusiku, Nuusiku	Born during the night
Elago, Nelago	Born after getting out of danger
Šisigona, Nakašona	Born after the death of the father

Mateus Angolo from Ongandjera (ELC, p. 1382–1383) lists typical names as well:

Iileka	Born when the father was carrying a cowlstaff while travelling
Iijambo, Naambo	Born while the father was at *ohambo* ('cattle-post')
Iipinge, Mpingana	Born after someone else had died
Amaẓila, Namaẓila	Born when there were frightening witches (*omaẓila*) moving around in the area
Hango, Nango	Born during *ohango* (girls' initiation ceremonies)
Sipingana	Someone had left or died
Uuanga, Sekupe	Twins
Sivute	Born backwards

Tirronen gives a lot of examples of traditional Ndonga names in his Ndonga–English Dictionary (1986). In most cases, he does not give the meaning of the name but mentions simply that it is either a personal name, or a man's name or a woman's name. However, there are explanations for some of the names in the dictionary:

Amakali	name of a son whose father has died before a name was given to the son
Amakaya	name of a smoker
Enkali	name of a boy whose father died before the boy was born
Muthela	name of a big and strong man
Nalwiho	name of a greedy person
Namakali	name of a daughter whose father died before name-giving
Nampiya	name of an anxious person
Namupolo	woman's name (one with beautiful features)
Namutse	personal name (of an outspoken person or of one having a big head); name of a hornless ox
Nandimbo	name of a poor woman (she has only one turn of string of pearls)
Nandjako	name of a rich woman
Nandjelo	name of a woman with beautiful features
Nankali	name of a daughter whose father died before the name-giving
Nehoya	the name of a single boy among his sisters or of a single girl among her brothers (> namupa)
Nepunda	name of a pot-bellied person
Niimbwila	name of a woman who cooked a very small portion of porridge
Niita	name of girl born in wartime
Nuushandjele	woman's name (meaning: with a small body)
Utyowa	man's name (meaning: with a small body)
Waningika	name of a well-shaped person

Judging from all these sources, there were two different tendencies in naming children among the Ambo people: 1. Naming after other people, and 2. Giving names which refer to the child and the conditions of his or her life: to events taking place at the time of birth, to the father's feelings, and so on. It is difficult to conclude which one of these was more important, as some sources – typically those dealing with Ondonga – stress the former, and others – especially those dealing with Oukwanyama – stress the latter. Obviously, the namesake relationship was not equally important in all Ambo subgroups. This idea is supported by the Ambo informants consulted for this study. Kanana (19.9.2000) said that in Ondonga, it has traditionally been very important to name the child after somebody. The namesake then has many responsibilities for the child, whereas in Oukwanyama children are often named after somebody only to retain the name of that person, and the namesake does not have any special responsibilities.

Ennis (1945), who studied the personal names of the Ovimbundu people in central Angola, a group closely related to the Ambo communities, also pays attention to similar opposite tendencies in name-giving. The Ovimbundu people have a namesake custom which closely resembles that of the Ambos: children are generally named after another person, who is then called *sando*, and a special relationship exists between the child and the namesake (Ennis 1945, p. 1).[226] Interestingly, Ennis (1945, p. 7–8) suggests that the namesake custom may be relatively new among the Ovimbundu people, and probably of foreign origin:

> It appears that the traditional idea of the Ovimbundu is that a name is bestowed upon or taken by a person for some definite reason pertaining to that person. ... On the other hand the custom of the *sando* tends to destroy the personal significance of names. A woman calls herself *Nanjamba* because she is the mother of twins. Then a baby is named after her and *Nanjamba* becomes a practically new and personally inappropriate name. This tends to destroy the meaning of names, and has already done so to a considerable extent. Comparatively few people can explain them ; others when asked the meaning of their names say they do not know, they were named after a certain person and that is as far as their curiosity extends. That the old names persist as much as they do goes to show that the namesake idea is comparatively new and probably of foreign origin.

Ennis's ideas are surely thought-provoking, and it would be intriguing to apply them to the development of the Ambo naming system as well. Hence, it may be possible that the namesake practice is a relatively new phenomenon – and of foreign origin – in Ambo society. The fact that this tradition is not equally strong in all Ambo subgroups could be seen as supportive evidence for this too.[227] However, it would not be fair to draw such conclusions based on the existing material. In any case, there were clearly two different trends in the Ambo name-giving in the late 19th and early 20th centuries, but it is impossible to say which earlier developments in the naming system had caused this.[228]

Herbert (1998, p. 188–190) points out that there are two types of anthroponymic systems in southern Africa. In the first type, which is typical for Zulu, Xhosa, Swati and Ndebele societies, names have a meaning. Usually these meanings refer to conditions or events surrounding the time of birth, physical features of the child, social conditions in the family or any subjective state of the name-giver. In the other type, which is in use among the Sotho-Tswana peoples, the same "commemorative" or family names are passed from one generation to the next. It seems evident that the traditional Ambo naming system was a mixture of these two "pure" types, with the exception that children in the Ambo communities were not systematically named after their relatives but also, and perhaps more often, after other people, typically the friends of the father.

Individual Bynames: Nicknames and Praise Names

The sources of this study give the impression that the real name given by the father was a permanent one, i.e. it was not changed later in life.[229] However, it seems that many kinds of individual bynames, e.g. nicknames and praise names, were used beside the real name of the person, even if the sources do not say much about them.

Ordinary Nicknames. Väänänen (undated and untitled manuscript from the 1920s/1930s, p. 86, Hp:XXXIX, FMSA) says that the Ambo people usually received a nickname after the actual name-giving, and that this happened at a time when the person's habits and traits of character had become visible. The "temporary name" which the child received soon after birth was sometimes retained as a type of nickname as well. According to Nambala (14.4.1997), many Ambos were known by three names in the old days: 1. The very first name (temporary name), 2. The real name given by the father, and 3. A nickname, or nicknames, which could be given by other people or invented by the person himself or herself. The practice of using nicknames can partly be explained by the name avoidance custom: the real name of the person was regarded as taboo, *oshidhila* (Aarni 1982, p. 68). Of course, giving individual bynames is also a universal phenomenon which can be found in all personal naming systems and which serves various social functions.

In Ndonga, the closest term for the English *nickname* is *edhina lyoponto* or *oshilukadhina* (Tirronen 1986, p. 22, 194).[230] Just as elsewhere in Africa, Ambo nicknames typically described the character of the individual, his or her behaviour or moral or physical qualities, or referred to his or her personal history. Indeed, what Madubuike (1976, p. 20) says about nicknames in Africa, can be said about traditional Ambo nicknames as well:

> Nicknames are spontaneous names given to an individual and relate to an aspect of his character, physique or quality. Nicknames are sometimes bestowed by friends, sometimes by enemies, and sometimes by admirers in appreciation of a feat performed, in derision, or even in anger. The type of name given to an individual depends largely on the circumstance, and the recipient usually has no power to stop people calling him by it. Thus nicknames are one of those names one cannot easily change, legally or otherwise.

Because of the lack of information concerning the nicknames of ordinary Ambo people in the old times, it may be useful to look at some Ambo names given to Europeans by the Ambos in the late 19th and early 20th centuries. It is reasonable to assume that they were given according to the same principles as the nicknames of the local people. For example, Väänänen (undated and untitled manuscript from the 1920s/1930s, p. 86, Hp:XXXIX, FMSA) tells of a Finnish missionary who often gave a deep sigh and was therefore given the name *Niifuro* 'breaths'.[231] Tirronen also mentions examples of such names in his Ndonga–English Dictionary (1986):

Ashipala	man's name; Birger Eriksson[232] (*oshipala* 'face')
Muthela gwaandjaIndongo	Captain Victor Francke
(*Muthela*	name of a big and strong man)
Nakale	personal name; name of H.L.P. Edes (1889–1975), native commissioner in Owambo (*uule* 'height')
Nakambalekanene	Martti Rautanen (1845–1926)
Nandago	personal name; August Pettinen (1857–1914) (*ondago* 'bulbous plant with small edible bulbs')
Nashimwele	Nestori Wäänänen (1882–1941) (*oshimwele* 'bad dagger')
Shongola	major C.H.L. Hahn (1886–1948) (*shongola* 'catch fish with a trap; limp, walk lame, hobble')

The fourth name in this list, which is the Ambo name of Martti Rautanen, the Finnish pioneer missionary among the Ambo people, is an illustrative example as such. Peltola (1994, p. 68) claims that Rautanen received his Ambo name because of the skullcap he used to wear while working in the daytime. As the Ambo people had never seen such a hat before, they gave Rautanen the name *Nakambale* (< *okambale* 'little palm basket'). Later Rautanen was also called *Nakambale Kanene* (or *Nakambalekanene*) 'big Nakambale', whereas his son Reinhold Rautanen was known as *Nakambalegona* 'little Nakambale'.[233] The motives for the other names mentioned by Tirronen are not as clear. According to Williams (1994, p. 22), *Nakale* referred to Edes's height, and Hahn was named *Shongola* "after the whip he used to beat the Mbalantu people".

It seems that several kinds of nicknames, e.g. ox names, were used in Ambo ceremonies in order to avoid the mentioning of the real name of the person. Hopeasalmi (1946, p. 79) says that during the girls' initiation ceremony, girls were praised because of their virginity and they were given names of oxen: a dark girl was called *Sindongo* and a light one *Kasese*.[234] Obadja Iihuhua (ELC, p. 1573–1574) writes that at the *ohango* ceremonies in Uukolonkadhi, the girl who was chosen to lead the girls' procession was given a new name, *Alukonga*, and the second girl got the name *Šilandula*.[235] Andreas Shafombabi (ELC p. 1044) in turn says, in connection with the breaking of "laws of iron" in a copper mine, that all the people working on the mine were given new names, including a new patronym. Most probably, all these alternative names used in Ambo ceremonies were temporary.

Praise Names. A special characteristic of southern African anthroponymy – and oral poetry – is the use of so-called *praise names*. It is sometimes difficult to make a distinction between an ordinary nickname and a praise name, as they often look similar. Many sources also talk about nicknames, when they should, more specifically, talk about praise names. Nevertheless, a praise name is a kind of a nickname which shows respect and admiration and which typically has a praise poem attached to it – or the whole poem, be it short or long, may be understood as the name. A praise name is often created by the person himself, but it may be given by other people as well. Gunner and Gwala (1994, p. 2–4) describe the Zulu praise names, *izibongo*[236], in a way which could be applied to Ambo praise names as well:

> In a way the term praise poetry or praise names is misleading because what izibongo are primarily concerned with is naming, identifying and therefore giving significance and substance to the named person or object. ... The act of praising focuses on identifying a person, embodying his or her personality through the process of naming and also in essence providing a link with his or her community, lineage and origins. Also the naming is a process of objectifying, so that once a name has been given, or self-given, it is in a way outside the power of the individual to remove it or contest it. It is a part of their identity, one which may be used even after their death when their praises are called out on ceremonial or public occasions. ... A single praise name is formed by nominalising either a single word, a phrase, a sentence, or a succession of sentences, so that the whole becomes a name ...

The word for *praise name* in Ndonga is *edhina eitango*. The verb *tanga* means 'praise, extol, glorify', the verb *itanga* 'recite one's presentation poem (speaking well of oneself, boast)', and the noun *eitango* is translated as 'self-presentation poem (telling boastingly of oneself)'. (Tirronen 1986, p. 110–111, 396.) Rautanen (to the mission director 23.4.1881, Eac:5, FMSA) says that beside their real names, people in Ondonga often had several bynames according to their qualities, and that these names had special praise poems attached to them, which at times could be very long. As an example, Rautanen mentions the praise names of King Kambonde[237], which among other things praised his beautiful body and his running speed. Unfortunately, he does not say what these names were. In a leaflet of the Rhenish Mission (Erstlinge von den Arbeitsgebieten der rheinischen Mission 1899, p. 39–40) there is a story of an Ambo king who gave the name *Kanunganiha* 'arsonist', "who runs faster than horses in order to destroy the region", to one of his men whom he often sent to steal cattle, burn villages and arrest people. The text in quotation marks, also in the original German text, most probably forms a praise poem, or a part of one, which was attached to this name.

It has been pointed out that praises of kings and chiefs are the most developed form of praise poetry in Africa (Koopman 1987b, p. 161). Mbenzi (Manuscript on Oshiwambo praise poetry, p. 11, 54) gives examples of praise names of Ambo kings. He states that the real name of the king was never mentioned in the praise poem, only his praise name:[238]

Onime ('lion'): Mandume gaNdemufayo (King of Oukwanyama 1911–1917)[239]

Ondilimani ('dynamite'): Iipumbu yaShilongo (King of Uukwambi 1908–32)

Okangwe ('small leopard'): Nehale lyaMpingana (King of Eastern Ondonga 1885–1908)

Olukaku halu tandula emusati ('a shoe that breaks mopani trees'): Tshaanika Natshilongo (King of Uukwaluudhi 1887–1930)[240]

Mbenzi (*op. cit.* p. 11) gives explanations for these names as well. King Mandume received the name with the meaning 'lion', because he was regarded to be as strong as a lion; he was also fearless when fighting against the Portuguese and South African armies. King Iipumbu was seen as dynamite, because he was willing to annihilate alien forces, and King Nehale was given the praise name meaning 'leopard' for he was as cruel as a leopard and ruled eastern Ondonga as a tyrant. The name of King Tshaanika (p. 54) shows that praise names could also consist of whole sentences. Beside kings' praises, traditional Ambo praise poetry included ritual praises, such as deity praises, praises of initiates, subclan praises, and non-ritual praises, such as self praises, animal praises (praises of domestic and wild animals), praises of ethnic groups, praises of warriors, praises of localities and praises of natural phenomena (Mbenzi, Manuscript on Oshiwambo praise poetry, p. 7–27). Nevertheless, it is mainly the kings' praises and self praises that are of interest here, as these two deal with the names of people.

Dammann and Tirronen (1975, p. 206–214) present seven self praises with translations into German in their Ndonga-Anthologie.[241] These poems for example contain names, or self descriptions, such as *Ndiwangu*, *Kaatondoka*, and *Shuumbwa*.[242] Dammann and Tirronen (1975, p. 206) also report that these poems were typically performed rapidly and in a high voice, and they often included references which were intelligible to the person in question only. They also tell that praise names were given by the parents to their children, who then lengthened them later in life. However, we shall say more about Ambo praise names when analysing the contemporary naming system of the Ambo people.

Collective Bynames: Patronyms and "Clan Names"; Other Forms of Address

As Ambo children were often named after other people, there were usually a number of people in the community, even within individual families living in the same homestead, who carried the same names. Naming people according to similar naming principles – e.g. giving names which referred to the time of the day the baby was born or to the circumstances surrounding the birth – also meant that certain names, such as *Angula* 'morning', *Mvula* 'rain' and *Nandjala* 'famine', became very popular. The tradition of giving children one real name only meant that people could not be distinguished from each other with additional real names either. The custom of using individual bynames, i.e. nicknames and praise names, obviously was one means to differentiate people in such a situation. Another means, and an important one, was the use of collective bynames, especially patronyms. Contrary to individual bynames, collective bynames do not refer to the individual only, but to the groups to which he or she belongs, such as family or clan.

Patronyms. It seems that patronyms were used systematically by the Ambo people in the late 19th and early 20th centuries (Savola 1924, p. 80; Tönjes 1996, p. 139). The name of the father was added as a kind of a surname[243] to the real name of the individual: if the father (in Oukwanyama) was *Hamuyela* and his child *Houfiku*, the child's full name was *Houfiku yaHamuyela*, i.e. *Houfiku* of *Hamuyela* (Tönjes 1996, p. 139). The name of the father was attached to the child's name with a possessive concord, its form depending on the class of the noun that the child's name was based on.[244] Hence, a man in Ondonga with the name *Amutenya* could have children whose full names were *Nangolo dhaAmutenya, Ndengu yaAmutenya, Nashikoto shaAmutenya, Namupala gwaAmutenya*, and *Nangombe yaAmutenya* (Namuhuja 1996, p. 10). It is important to note at this point that teknonymy, i.e. the practice of calling the person "mother-of-X" or "father-of-X", did not belong to the traditional Ambo naming system.[245] At least there is no mention of it in the sources.

It is difficult to say how old the custom of using patronyms really is among the Ambo people. In books dealing with the history of Ambo subgroups, patronyms are used for Ambo kings in as far as they are known by people living today, i.e. up to the 17th century (Nambala 1994, p. 35–38; Namuhuja 1996, p. 5). Their usefulness in retaining family history and the history of the community is evident, hence patronyms are frequently used in the Ambo praise poetry and other oral literature as well. However, judging from the written sources and oral tradition, one cannot say much about the use of patronyms in everyday speech during all these centuries. Interestingly, Hopeasalmi (1946, p. 28) says that patronyms were used with special care by the Ambo people because of the name avoidance custom. Especially if the father in question was dead, it was feared that ancestral spirits might attack the ones who carelessly mentioned his name. In any case, it is reasonable to suggest that as the Ambo communities grew larger, patronyms became increasingly important as a means of differentiating people from each other in the community.

In a way, it is interesting that the father's name was used as a person's additional byname, even if the traditional Ambo culture was matrilineal. As was already noted, clan and lineage affiliation ran through the mother in the Ambo communities, and inheritance and succession followed the matrilineal line as well. The maternal uncle was also much more important to the child than the father. (Bruwer 1966, p. 23; Malan 1995, p. 19; Peltola 1958, p. 22.) It has been reported that Ambo men did not usually refer to their offspring as their own children but as their mothers' children (Yrjö Roiha to the mission director 10.11.1883, Eac:6, FMSA). Hence, it may not be an overstatement to claim that the patronym, together with the bestowal of the real name, was one of the strongest ties between a father and his child in the Ambo culture. Nambala (14.4.1997) explained the central role of the father in personal naming by saying that with the name, the father admitted publicly that he was the father of the child and would take care of it.[246] In a sense, it is also logical that children who lived in the same homestead and had the same father, also carried the same "surname". Hence, instead of referring to the lineage or the clan of the child, the patronym referred to the family consisting of the father and his wife, or wives, and their children, who all lived in the same homestead and formed an important social and economic unit in the Ambo community.

Clan Names. In many African societies, addressing people by their clan names has been more common than the use of patronyms. This was not the case in the Ambo communities.[247] However, in certain cases names of clans were also used when addressing people. Estermann (1976, p. 84) tells how elderly women in Oukwanyama were addressed by their fathers' clan names:

> After the menopause a richer woman may install herself in a house of her own which an influential son has had built near his. She will go on living there, supported by him and looked after by a niece or granddaughter the rest of her life. ... It is curious to note that after establishing herself thus independently the old woman changes her name, or rather the name of her father's clan comes to be used instead of her former name. Thus people are heard to speak of *Mukwanangombe* ("The Woman of the Ox Clan"), *Mukwanime* ("The Woman of the Lion Clan"), etc.

Even if the old names were dropped from the daily usage, on some level the "real" name of the woman had to be retained as her only proper name. This would at least be in line with the general idea of personal names in the Ambo culture: the real name of the person, i.e. the name given by the father, was not changed later in life. It is also interesting to note that women were addressed by their fathers' clan names, not by their own ones. This may be seen as another proof of the important role of the father in the matrilineal Ambo culture.

It seems that all over the Ambo area, old women – never men – were at times addressed by their fathers' clan names as a sign of respect to the father (Amakali 10.10.2000; Mbenzi 24.3.1997; Nambala 14.4.1997; Namuhuja 14.4.1997). Such "clan names" were commonly used in Oukwanyama and in Uukwambi, whereas in Ondonga their usage has not been as systematic (Amaambo 3.4.1997; Nambala 14.4.1997; Namuhuja 14.4.1997). The fact that Estermann (1976, p. 84) wrote his examples *Mukwanangombe* and *Mukwanime* with capitals, indicates that he understood them as names. Nambala (14.4.1997), however, felt that these "clan names" should not be regarded as personal names, but as a form of address only. Kanana (19.9.2000), who comes from Oukwanyama, also stated that such a "clan name" is not a real "naming name" but "just a name of respect". In this study, we shall also consider them as such.

All in all, the traditional Ambo naming system included four kinds of names given to an individual. These names were all used for address and reference:

1. The temporary name given soon after birth
2. The real name given at the naming ceremony
3. Individual byname(s), e.g. praise names and other kinds of nicknames, which were either self-given or bestowed by other people
4. The patronym, i.e. the father's name which was attached to the real name of the person

Other Forms of Address. Beside personal names, kinship terms and other forms of address were commonly used by the Ambo people, as is the case with all personal naming systems. We already mentioned that such forms of address were used in everyday speech because of the name avoidance custom. Examples of these were *tate* 'father', *meme* 'mother', *tatekulu* 'grandfather' and *kuku* 'grandmother' (Hopeasalmi 1946, p. 28). It is important to note that the use of such kinship terms was not restricted to close relatives only. For example, *tate* 'father' could refer to all elderly male relatives of the person, including those who had received that status through a namesake relationship (Hukka 1954, p. 50–51). Hence, the head of the homestead was generally called *tate* by all his wives and children (Hahn 1928, p. 24). Malan (1995, p. 18) points out that the Ambo people have traditionally used kinship terms to demonstrate the bonds within a particular clan:

> They also demonstrate their kinship bond by using classificatory kinship terminology, according to which persons on the same generation level call each other *brother* and *sister*. Those on the first ascending generation are all referred to as *father* and *mother*, while the aged members of the clan are addressed as *grandfather* and *grandmother*.

The terms *tate* and *meme* were also generally used as a polite form of address for elderly people, and people belonging to the royal family could be addressed as *omuwa* 'my Lord' (Albin Savola, Muutamia piirteitä muinais-israelilaisten ja nykyisten ondongalaisten olojen, lakien ja tapojen yhtäläisyyksistä, undated manuscript, p. 14, Hp:125, FMSA). Hahn (1928, p. 8) says that an Ambo king, who was regarded as the father of his subjects, was generally referred to and addressed as *tate* 'father' or *Muenewita*, which according to Hahn means 'father of land' or 'Chief of war'.[248] The sisters of the king, who had an important role in society, were also addressed as *tate* (Melander *et al.* 1942, p. 32–33).

Ambo forms of address will be analysed in more detail when discussing the contemporary naming system of the Ambo people. Later, we shall also see that many of the special characteristics of the traditional Ambo naming system – naming traditions, name-giving motives, ideas attached to personal names, etc. – are still alive in the Ambo culture today.

130

The Encounter between African and European Naming Practices in the Ambo Area

The Spread of Biblical and European Names

The adoption of Christianity, and especially the practice of giving new names for converts at baptism, led to an exceptionally rapid and thoroughgoing change in the Ambo naming system. It is not known to us exactly when the first baptism of an Ambo took place. It seems that some Ambos were baptised by German missionaries in the Herero area in the early 1870s. In 1876, an Ambo woman named *Nanguroshi*, a servant of the missionary Pietari Kurvinen, was baptised in Finland with the name *Eva Maria*[249.] However, as these baptisms took place far away from the Ambo area, they did not have any significant effect on the spread of Christianity in the Ambo communities. (Nambala 1994, p. 82; Peltola 1958, p. 81.)

In the late 1870s, a few men who expressed their wish to be baptised turned up in the Ambo area (Martti Rautanen to the mission director 27.12.1878, Eac:5, FMSA). The missionaries started to teach them, and later others as well, and in 1881 there were dozens of people who had received baptismal instruction and wanted to be baptised. However, the Finns did not want to act precipitously in this matter, as they felt that the first people baptised should also serve as model Christians for other people. At that time in Ondonga, people were also afraid of the king's reaction to the baptism of his subjects: he might expel the missionaries and perhaps also kill the catechumens. (Tobias Reijonen to the mission director 24.1.1881, Eac:5, FMSA.)

As it was impossible to receive a baptism in the Ambo area at that time, four Ambo men went to Omaruru in the Herero area, where they were baptised in November 1881. These men, Martin Iipinge, Gustav Iithoko, Wilhelm Amutenya and Gabriel Nangolo, were baptised by the German missionary Gottlieb Viehe.[250] (Peltola 1958, p. 82–83.) It seems that the German missionaries followed the same practice when baptising these Ambos as they did with Hereros and other Namibians: the names given at baptism were biblical and European.[251] Of these four baptismal names[252], *Gabriel* is a biblical name and *Wilhelm* is German. *Martin* most probably refers to the Finnish missionary Martti (Martin) Rautanen and *Gustaf* to another Finnish missionary, Gustaf Mauritz Skoglund (Peltola 1958, p. 259–260). Undoubtedly, the name-giving practices of the Rhenish Mission had a strong influence on those of the newly established Finnish mission, which at that time, in a sense, was working under the protection of the Rhenish Mission in the Ambo area.

The news of the baptisms in the Herero area soon spread to the Ambo area, where the number of people requesting teaching and baptism started to increase (Peltola 1958, p. 83). On 6 January 1883, the first public baptism took place in the Ambo area, when six Ambo men were baptised by Tobias Reijonen at Omulonga.[253] The names of these men were *Moses Iimene, Elias Nangolo, Abraham Shikongo, Jakob Angula, Tobias*

The first Christians in the Ndonga royal family Albin (Kuedhi) yIitope and Martin (Nehale) gIitope. August Pettinen / The Finnish Evangelical Lutheran Mission. 1901–1905.

Negonya and *Johannes Nangombe.*[254] (Nambala 1994, p. 82; Peltola 1958, p. 83–84.) The names given at this baptism were biblical, and one of the converts was also Tobias Reijonen's namesake. Reijonen (1883, p. 71) states that these names were chosen by the men themselves. On 26 March, three more men were baptised in Ondonga by the missionary K.A. Weikkolin with the biblical names *Stefanus, Josef* and *Jonas* (K.A. Weikkolin to the mission director 26.3.1883, Eac:6, FMSA). The former names of these men were *Shelunga, Amutenya* and *Angula* (K.A. Weikkolin, Report for January, February and March 1883, Eac:6, FMSA).

The Ambo Christians who had been baptised in the Herero area also started to move back to the Ambo area at that time (Peltola 1958, p. 84).

King Kambonde (Eino Johannes) kaNgula of Ondonga was baptised on his death-bed in 1912 as the first Ambo king. Maria Wehanen / The Finnish Evangelical Lutheran Mission. 1912.

In the following year, more baptisms followed in Ondonga, in which the converts received names such as *David, Job, Johannes, Matheus, Simeon; Elisabeth, Emilia, Lydia, Maria, Marta, Sara* and *Sofia* (K. Hakala, Report for January, February and March 1884, Eac:6, FMSA), or *David, Elias, Paulus* and *Elisabet* (Martti Rautanen to the mission director 22.6.1884, Eac:6, FMSA). The attitude of the other people in the community towards these first Christians was often scornful, however (K.A. Weikkolin to the mission director 20.1.1885, Eac:6, FMSA; Martti Rautanen to the mission director 22.6.1884, Eac:6, FMSA).

It has been stated that in the beginning, King Kambonde kaMpingana of Ondonga was very sceptical about Christianity.[255] After the first pub-

133

King Nambala (Martin Elifas) yaKadhikwa of Ondonga. August Pettinen / The Finnish Evangelical Lutheran Mission. 1912.

lic baptisms, his attitude changed gradually, and he even expressed the wish that his subjects would become Christians (Peltola 1958, p. 84). The first baptisms in the Ndonga royal family took place in 1901, when two young men, Kuedhi and Nehale, who were both nephews to the king and thus possible heirs to the throne, were baptised. The former chose the name *Albin* after the Finnish missionary Albin Savola, and the latter became Martti (Martin) Rautanen's namesake, *Martin*. (Peltola 1958, p. 111; 1994, p. 243.) The first baptism of an Ambo king took place in 1912, when the King of Ondonga, Kambonde kaNgula, was baptised on his deathbed by the Finnish missionary Juho Wehanen. The king wanted to adopt the name *Eino Johannes*, which was the name of Wehanen's new-born son. His successor Nambala yaKadhikwa was baptised later that year by Martti (Martin) Rautanen, together with fifty-six of his subjects. As he chose the name *Martin Elifas*, he also became Rautanen's namesake. (Haahti 1913, p. 104; Nambala 1994, p. 36, 84; Peltola 1958, p. 143, 262; Savola 1924, p. 204.) According to Peltola (1994, p. 248), this baptism could be seen as a "Constantinian turn" in the kingdom of Ondonga. As the king was the highest authority in religious matters, his conversion to Christianity meant that the era of traditional religion ended in Ondonga, at least at some level. In 1918, the mother of the king, Amutaleni, was also baptised. She chose the name *Frida* and thus became the namesake of Martti Rautanen's wife Frieda Rautanen. (Peltola 1994, p. 251.)

In Oukwanyama, the first baptisms took place in 1895 when the German missionary August Wulfhorst baptised thirteen Kwanyama converts at the Omupanda mission station. In the following year eighteen people were baptised. (Aus den Anfangstagen der Ovambomission 1904, p. 29; Himmelreich 1900, p. 11–13; Aug. Wulfhorst, 25 Jahre unserer Missionsarbeit in Ovamboland, p. 34, C/i:20, UEMA.) In Ongandjera, the first baptisms took place in 1906 (Heikki Saari to the mission director 24.10.1906, Eac:12, FMSA), and in Uukwambi in 1912 (Nambala 1994, p. 85).

In the early 20th century, the number of Christians in Lutheran congregations grew rapidly in the Ambo area. In 1900, their number was 900, in 1920 7,695, and in 1930 23,126 (Nambala 1995, p. 12). Many Ambos who worked in the south were also baptised by the Catholics at that time. In the Ambo area, the first Catholic baptism took place in 1925 in Oshikuku, Uukwambi. The Anglican church also started to gain converts in Oukwanyama after the year 1925. (Nambala 1994, p. 96, 100–101.) All these baptisms meant that the new biblical and European names spread rapidly among the Ambo people. It is important to note that the baptism ceremony came to replace the traditional Ambo naming ceremonies. It also became a common custom among the Christians to have a small celebration at home after the baptism, to which friends and neighbours were invited to eat together and sing Christian songs. Sometimes traditional customs were reflected in these celebrations as well. (Ranttila 1935, p. 3; Väänänen 1935, p. 13.) Many unbaptised Ambos whose indigenous names were difficult for the Europeans to pronounce also received European names from their white employers in the south (Mwaetako 14.10.2000).

The new naming fashion spread both geographically and in the social hierarchy of the Ambo people. The mission stations, which were founded all over the Ambo area, served as centres for the geographical distribution of this innovation. Obviously, biblical and European names were at first more common near the mission stations than in the other areas. The Ambos who had received a European education in mission schools adopted these names first. The fact that this innovation was accepted relatively early by the highest level of the Ambo communities, i.e. in the royal families, accelerated this process as well. Hence, it was not only the European missionaries, but also some prominent people in the Ambo communities who acted as influential forces in the changing of the Ambo naming system.

Reasons for Giving Baptismal Names

How were the baptismal names chosen in the Ambo congregations? By whom and on what grounds? The Finnish and German missionaries often stress that the names were chosen by the converts themselves, and that this practice was encouraged by the missionaries (Aho 1941, p. 87; Aus den Anfangstagen der Ovambomission 1904, p. 29, 34; Büttner, o.J., p. 11; Erstlinge von den Arbeitsgebieten der rheinischen Mission 1899, p. 43; Hopeasalmi 1946, p. 100; Närhi 1929, p. 111; Väänänen 1935, p. 10; A. Wulfhorst, Vorträge und Aufsätze zur Ovambo-Mission 1910–1933, p. 227, C/k:22, UEMA; Welsch 1923, p. 12; 1925, p. 128).[256]

However, this was not always the case. At times, missionaries were also asked to choose these names. Helenius (1930, p. 48) writes about how she was allowed to choose a name for a two-week-old boy; she chose the name *Sem*. Levänen (1935, p. 21–22) tells how an Ambo man named *Stefanus* came to ask her for a suitable baptismal name for his daughter. Levänen made a list of twelve names, of which the man found *Ottiilia* and *Hellevi* the most beautiful. Eventually, the child was baptised *Helevi*, which is a domesticated Ambo form of the Finnish woman's name *Hellevi*.[257] At the time when the first Ambos were baptised, even some supporters of the Ambo mission in Finland would occasionally choose names for converts. In this way, one boy in Ondonga was named *Gabriel* (Tobias Reijonen to the mission director 31.10.1883, Eac:6, FMSA), and another one *Martin* (K.A. Weikkolin to the mission director 20.7.1885, Eac:6, FMSA).

The missionaries did not approve of all the names that the Ambo converts suggested either. For example, when K.A. Weikkolin's servant boy Uuanga wanted to be called *Sieppo* after Weikkolin's former dog, Weikkolin regarded this as primitive heathenism and refused to accept the name (K.A. Weikkolin, Report for July, August and September 1876, Eac:4, FMSA). Hopeasalmi (1946, p. 100) says that choosing a suitable name was often a difficult matter, which the missionary and the convert discussed in private; no third person was allowed to be present. In these situations, the missionaries undoubtedly used their power to eliminate names that they considered undesirable.[258] Many Ambo priests also favoured biblical and European names and thus had a strong influence on the choice of names (Amaambo 3.4.1997; Nambala 14.4.1997). Altogether, it seems that European and biblical names were taken for granted by the majority of missionaries and Ambo pastors for a long time, and also by the local people (Amkongo 14.4.1997).[259]

It is important to note that names of foreign origin were not always adopted as such, in particular when they were difficult for the Ambo people to pronounce. Many names were adapted to the phonology of the Ambo languages. Hence, the German woman's name *Adelheid* became

The catechumens baptised in the Ontananga church on 13 February, 1910. Maria Wehanen / The Finnish Evangelical Lutheran Mission. 1905.

Two recently baptised catechumens. Kalle Koivu / The Finnish Evangelical Lutheran Mission. 1925–1929.

137

Andele (Helenius 1930, p. 209) and the Finnish man's name *Vilho Viliho* (Mustakallio 1903, p. 70). Visapää (Lehtori Niilo Visapään matka Namibiaan 1937, Eurooppaa ja Afrikkaa, VI, p. 3, Hk:2, FMSA) also gives a number of examples: *Pitiliha < Fredrik, Petulusa < Petrus, Sifisa < Sakeus, Etuviha < Hedvig, Mahanama < Mahanaim, Petaja < Petäjä,* and *Penanena < Pennanen.*[260] Liljeblad's (to the mission director 5.8.1905, Eac:11, FMSA) examples are *Isopeta < Josafat, Alona < Aron* and *Makatalena < Magdalena.* Sometimes the original name is almost impossible to trace. For example, Levänen (1935, p. 5) mentions an Ambo man who was called *Halunaludu;* the original name turned out to be *Aron Ludvig.*

Since the first baptisms, it was also possible to have more than one baptismal name, which was a big change in the Ambo naming system as well. The 19th century sources mention names such as *Wilhelmina Maria* (K.A. Weikkolin, Report for December 1885 and January, February and March 1886, Eac:6, FMSA) or *Jairus Bartimäus* (Allerlei aus den Rheinischen Missionsgebieten: Ovamboland, 1897, p. 341).[261] However, such names were still rare at that time.

Let us have a closer look at the motives behind the choices of baptismal names. Six main motives are taken up here:

A New Name as a Sign of a New Life. Judging from both missionary and Ambo sources, it is clear that in the beginning many, if not most, Ambo converts wanted to take a new European or biblical name when they embraced Christianity. Varis (1988, p. 89) explains this by saying that, psychologically, a new "Christian" name was a symbol of a new life and of abandoning traditional beliefs. Büttner (o.J., p. 11) tells of an Ambo man who changed his name *Haimbodi* into *Henoch* when he was baptised. If people still addressed him with his old name after this, he used to say: "Haimbodi died at baptism and Henoch was resurrected." A new name was seen as a sign of a new Christian identity, whereas traditional Ambo names were generally regarded as unchristian or pagan by the Ambo Christians (Amaambo 3.4.1997; Ihambo 7.10.2000; Kanana 19.9.2000).

Varis (1988, p. 91) also points out that the new names emphasised the difference between an "Ambo pagan in his natural state" and a Christian Ambo, in a similar way to that of the new European-style clothing of the converts. Since everything European was regarded as Christian by the Ambo people at that time, also Finnish and German names were understood as "Christian" names, even if many of them originally had nothing to do with Christianity (e.g. *Wilhelm* or *Väinö*).[262] Obviously, these names were regarded as Christian also because they were carried by Finnish and German missionaries, who were the first Christians that the Ambo people got to know.

New Naming Fashion. The popularity of biblical and European names in the Ambo communities can also be explained by the fact that they became fashionable. At first, Ambo Christians were frequently ridiculed because of their new names, but soon this was changed into the opposite: people began to be ashamed of their traditional names and to favour new "Christian" names. Also some people in the Ambo area who had no intention of becoming Christians took a European or biblical name at that time.[263] (Suomalaista raivaustyötä Afrikan erämaassa 1945, p. 108; Walde Kivinen to the mission director 30.1.1937, Eac:38, FMSA.) On the other hand, many Ambos wanted to be baptised in order to get a new name, and with it, perhaps better opportunities in the labour market in the south (Tuure Vapaavuori, Mitä olisi tehtävä?, Missionary conference in Ombalantu 29.7. 1936, appendix 1, Hha:14, FMSA). Hence, it is clear that in the Ambo communities, biblical and European names were not adopted for religious reasons only. The new names also served as symbols of expected social progress in the colonial society. Just as elsewhere in Africa, European names were adopted eagerly by the colonised Ambo people as a sign of progress and the modern way of life. The transition from the "primitive" (African) to the "modern" (European) world was thus reflected clearly in personal naming.

Naming after Missionaries and Other Europeans. The popularity of biblical and European names has perhaps most often been explained by the traditional Ambo namesake custom (e.g. Pentti 1959, p. 36). Up to the present day, a large number of Ambo people have been named after European missionaries in the same way as many of the first Ambo Christians were named after Martti Rautanen and Albin Savola, for example. Thus, the Lutheran Ambos have adopted Finnish and German names[264], the Catholics mainly German ones[265], and the Anglicans primarily English names. Some Ambos who moved to the area from the Angolan side of the border, also have Portuguese names (Lehtonen 7.11.1994).

It is not surprising that European missionaries became popular as namesakes, because the Ambo Christians were of the opinion that a Christian should have a Christian namesake, as the namesake serves as a model for the child (Lehtonen 17.11.1994). Undoubtedly, the missionaries were respected as Christians. Often there was also a close friendship between the missionary and the name-giver (Amakali 10.10.2000). Namuhuja (14.4.1997) said that the Ambos who worked with the missionaries at the mission stations particularly wanted to name their children after these Europeans as a sign of respect. Missionaries who worked as teachers and nurses were also popular as namesakes (Amaambo 3.4.1997).[266] In some cases, there must have been expectations of financial support as well.[267]

Not only first names, but also surnames of missionaries, e.g. *Tylväs* (Nambala 1995, p. 76, 205), were adopted as baptismal names by the Ambo people.[268] Obviously, the difference between European first names and surnames was not of any special importance to the Ambo people, who did not have surnames.[269] Many Ambos have also been given the full name of his or her namesake. For example, Laina Kivelä (1991, p. 24) explains how she – once again – got an Ambo namesake, when a baby girl was named *Laina Kivelä* after her, and Namuhuja (14.4.1997) told about Ambos who had been given Finnish missionaries' names such as *Sylvi Kyllönen, Maija Kantele, Birger Eriksson* and *Erkki Lehto*.[270] Occasionally, if the child represented the opposite sex of the desired namesake, it could be named after some close relative of that person. In this way, one Ambo boy received the name *Hannu*, which is the name of missionary Kaino Kovanen's brother. Similarly, Bishop Leonard Auala named his son *Toivo* after missionary Laina Kivelä's father.[271] If the official name of the namesake was difficult to pronounce, a nickname could also be used instead of it. Thus, a little girl who was named after Sävy Vilkuna, became *Saija*. (Lehtonen 17.11.1994.)

Just as in the old days, a Christian namesake was expected to take care of the child during his or her lifetime. The custom of identifying namesakes with each other continued as well, and this was reflected in the ways people were addressed.[272] For example, the namesakes of Finnish missionaries were generally called "Finns" or "missionaries" by the Ambos (Ranttila 1935, p. 4).[273] The missionaries were also treated as family members in their namesakes' families.[274] Aarni (1982, p. 77), son of Finnish missionaries[275], describes the namesake relationship as follows:

> My mother's name was Aini. After a few years there was a score of girls in Ukwaludhi, where we lived, named 'Aini'. When the parents of these 'Ainis' came to visit relatives or sick friends, my mother was obliged to take care of her namesakes. Gifts were constantly presented to such 'relatives', and when this newly gained family came to visit, it was necessary to show them hospitality – at times for several days.

Some Ambos also named their children after the white employers for whom they worked on the farms and in towns in the south and with whom they were on good terms (Amaambo 3.4.1997; Amkongo 14.4.1997; Kanana 19.9.2000; Munyika 16.10.2000). This also explains many of the Afrikaans, German and English names of the Ambo people.[276]

Naming after Biblical Characters and Saints. It also seems to have been important for many Ambo Christians to have a biblical figure as a namesake and to identify with this Christian model (Ihambo 7.10.2000).[277] Väänänen (1935, p. 10), for example, tells of an Ambo boy who wanted to become Samuel "because it is a beautiful name and I would like to serve God the way Samuel did". Similarly, one Ambo man wanted to be named *Joseph* because, just like this biblical character, he was a carpenter (Allerlei aus den Rheinischen Missionsgebieten: Ovamboland 1897, p. 342). Another man chose the name *Johannes* after the disciple whom Jesus loved dearly, for he felt that he was also loved by Jesus (Hopeasalmi 1946, p. 100). Examples of such name choices are numerous in the early missionary literature.

The Ambos who have received a Catholic baptism have often been named after Catholic saints, based on the idea that there is a special relationship between the person and the saint he or she is named after. Hence, one can find names such as *Albinus, Bonifatius, Dominicus, Pelagia* and *Teresia* among the Catholic Ambo Christians (Amushila

11.10.2000). Because of the use of saints' names, it is often easy to recognise a Catholic Ambo by name, whereas the Lutheran and Anglican
Ambos have names which are more similar to each other (Mwaetako
14.10.2000).

Naming after Famous Characters. Some Ambos have also named their
children after famous people whom they did not know personally, e.g.
after historical and political characters. Holopainen (1993, p. 68) mentions an Ambo boy who was named *Lyndon Johnson* after the newly
elected president of the United States,[278] and Mbenzi (24.3.1997) gave
Martti Ahtisaari as a typical example of a well-known person after whom
many Ambo children were named around the time of Namibian independence.[279] However, since such famous people are not able to take
their responsibilities as a namesake, such as the wedding arrangements
for the one named after them, many people in the Ambo area have criticised this kind of name-giving (Mbenzi 24.3.1997).

Naming after Friends and Relatives. Beside naming children after
European missionaries, biblical characters, saints and well-known people, the custom of naming children after close friends and relatives has
continued among the Ambo people. It has remained extremely important as well. However, as the number of Christians grew rapidly in the
Ambo area in the 20th century, the names of ordinary people were more
and more often of European and biblical origin, not traditional Ambo
names. Because of this, the Ambo people started to adopt foreign names
from each other as well.

Hence, the same European and biblical names that were initially
adopted from the Europeans and the Bible were transferred from person
to person and from one generation to another in the Ambo area. At times,
such "namesake chains" could be very long, and it would not be unusual
for the original bearer of a name which is given today, actually to have
lived in the 19th century.[280] For example, the links that combine today's
Martins or Fridas to the family of the Finnish pioneer missionary Martti
(Martin) Rautanen are numerous.

All in all, it is interesting to note that the influence of Christianity and
Europeanisation did not destroy the traditional Ambo namesake custom
but rather gave it a new Christian slant. As ironic as it may sound, the
traditional namesake practice of the Ambos has been one of the major
forces in the Europeanisation of the Ambo personal nomenclature. However, there were also other reasons for the adoption of European and
biblical names: they were regarded as Christian by the Ambo people,
and they were seen as symbols of the new European way of life. It is
interesting to note that some sources explain the popularity of foreign
names in the Ambo area simply by claiming that the missionaries forced
the Ambo people to abandon their indigenous names (e.g. Iyambo 1970,
p. 84, 89). It seems that in most cases, such forcing, or persuasion, was
not necessary, as the Ambos themselves wanted to adopt new European
and biblical names for the various reasons mentioned above.

The Africanisation of Baptismal Names: Early 20th Century

In the early 20th century, and especially since the 1920s, the popularity of European and biblical names increased rapidly in the Ambo area. However, there was also resistance to the use of foreign names, both among the missionaries and the Ambo people. Gradually, this led to the adoption of African baptismal names.

As was noted earlier, the idea of accepting African baptismal names was discussed in many European missions in the late 19th and early 20th centuries. Some of them also decided to favour indigenous names. The German theologian Gustav Warneck suggested in his "Evangelische Missionslehre" (1900, p. 276) that if an adult convert wanted to adopt a new "Christian" name at baptism, it should rather be an indigenous one. These ideas evoked a response from the Finnish missionaries in the Ambo area too. Albin Savola (1903, p. 6–7) mentions how he said to a group of Ambo converts in 1901 that they could retain their old names at baptism if they so wished. Nevertheless, all of them chose new names, including Kuedhi and Nehale, the first Christians in the Ndonga royal family, who chose the names *Albin* and *Martin*. Nambala (14.4.1997) also pointed out that it is not well known among the Ambo people of today that in the old times some missionaries also encouraged the Ambo Christians to adopt African names.[281] According to him, people should not make sweeping generalisations and claim that the missionaries simply forced the Ambo people to adopt foreign names.

In 1905, two Finnish missionaries, Emil Liljeblad and Heikki Saari, decided to give Ambo names to their new-born daughters, which at that time was unheard of. Liljeblad named his daughter *Aune*[282] *Mtaleni Nahenda* 'look at Aune with mercy'. Liljeblad said that by doing this, he wanted to show that the Ambo people need not despise their beautiful indigenous names when embracing Christianity, and that the Christian spirit is not in the name but in the heart. (Emil Liljeblad to the mission director 5.8.1905, Eac:11, FMSA.) Saari gave his daughter the name *Kerttu*[283] *Nekulilo*, the latter being an Ambo name meaning '(with) redemption'. Saari said that he hoped that the Ambo people would follow his example by adopting beautiful indigenous names when becoming Christians, and stated that there was a wide variety of them. (Heikki Saari to the mission director 29.8.1905, Eac:11, FMSA.) Saari (to the mission director 30.9.1905, Eac:11, FMSA) also referred to the fact that indigenous names were used in Germany and Finland, and other countries as well, and pointed out that the name *Fredrik*, for example, was just as foreign to a Finn as any Ambo name.

Liljeblad's and Saari's name-giving created a stormy debate among the Finnish missionaries. The name *Nekulilo* was considered unchristian, or at least unsuitable for a Christian, and some missionaries even saw it as an example of blasphemy.[284] Saari was also accused of aiming to be different from other people. It seems that the Ambo names given by these Finns also caused astonishment among the local people. (Heikki Saari to the mission director 30.9.1905, Eac:11, FMSA.) Altogether,

Liljeblad and Saari were the most active missionaries in promoting the use of Ambo baptismal names at the beginning of the 20th century (Walde Kivinen to the mission director 30.1.1937, Eac:38, FMSA).

In Oukwanyama, the first African baptismal names were given in the baptisms of 1912/1913 by the missionary Sckär. This was done in an attempt to find out how the local people would react to such names. The reaction, not surprisingly, was rejection: the Ambo converts wanted to have names which showed that they were Christians.[285] (Hochstrate, Bericht der Station Namakunde vom Konferenzjahr 1912–13, p. 6, C/h:52, UEMA.) However, Ambo names continued to be given occasionally at baptisms. Levänen (1964, p. 86–88), for example, tells of a baptism ceremony in Engela, Oukwanyama, in 1927, in which many women took the name *Ndamonohenda* 'I have received mercy', and a rich woman who had renounced her possessions when she became a Christian was baptised as *Liefa* 'leave it'. Most of these 276 converts chose biblical names, however.[286]

It is clear that the practice of using European and biblical names caused a lot of problems in the Ambo communities. These names were not only difficult for the people to pronounce, but sometimes they even took on new meanings, if they happened to resemble Ambo words. For example, Saari (to the mission director 30.9.1905, Eac:11, FMSA) says that the name *Teofiilus*, as it was pronounced in Ongandjera, took on the meaning 'he will be grilled'. The missionaries also remarked that many domesticated name forms, e.g. *Isopeta* < *Josafat*, hardly resembled the original names, and that many European names were totally incomprehensible to the local people (Emil Liljeblad to the mission director 5.8.1905, Eac:11, FMSA).

A real problem for the Finnish mission was that many Ambos wanted to be baptised only in order to receive a new name. Therefore, many of them left the congregation soon after baptism. Being baptised and adopting a new name became a real fashion in the Ambo area, and the Finns wanted to prevent such people who had no deeper interest in Christianity from "destroying the congregations".[287] (Walde Kivinen, Raportti lähetysjohtaja Tohtori Uno Paunulle hänen saapuessaan tarkastusmatkalle Ambomaalle v. 1937, Hhb:2, FMSA.) The Finns also worried about the increasing popularity of certain names. Kivinen (to the mission director 30.1.1937, Eac:38, FMSA) tells that he had encouraged people to adopt African names at baptism, because "otherwise all men here will soon be called *Paulus, Petrus* and *Johannes*, and all women will have names such as *Martta* and *Johanna*".

The Ambo Name-Day Calendar 1938 and the Influence of the Independence Struggle on Personal Naming

In August 1937, there was an important discussion of African baptismal names at the conference of the Finnish missionaries in the Ambo area (Missionary conference in Engela and Onandjokwe 26.8.–3.9.1937, Hha:15, FMSA). At this meeting, missionary Walde Kivinen suggested that adult converts should be baptised with their original indigenous names, unless the name referred to traditional beliefs. Only in such a case would a name-change be accepted, and even then, the name should be changed into another indigenous name. Kivinen defended his suggestion by saying that this was the practice among the early Christians too and that it would prevent people from coming to the congregations only to get a new name. Heikki Saari also defended the use of Ambo names and argued that they could play a part in creating an Ambo people with a national spirit. However, he did not want to make them compulsory.

Missionary Viktor Alho, who represented the opposite view, pointed out that many Ambos had refused to adopt indigenous names at baptism: for them, a new name was a symbol of abandoning the past.[288] Missionary Hänninen, in turn, found it problematic that many Ambo names were used by both sexes. It was also suggested that those foreign names which the Ambo people could pronounce correctly should be retained. Eventually, it was decided at the conference that foreign baptismal names brought more problems than advantages, and the missionaries took the stand that indigenous names should be strongly promoted in the Ambo congregations.[289] Heikki Saari was also asked to collate a name-day calendar which would include Ambo names and thus serve as a name-guide for Ambo Christians. (Missionary conference in Engela and Onandjokwe 26.8.–3.9.1937, Hha:15, FMSA.)

What did the Ambos, who were not represented at this important meeting, think about this matter? It seems that there were two opposing schools among them too. As was pointed out, many Ambo Christians refused to adopt African names at baptism, both for religious and secular reasons. Many Ambo priests also refused to baptise children with indigenous names (Amkongo 14.4.1997; Nambala 14.4.1997).[290] On the other hand, some Ambo pastors championed the use of African baptismal names, e.g. Pinehas Kambonde in Olukonda (Walde Kivinen to the mission director 30.1.1937, Eac:38, FMSA).[291] Unfortunately, the missionary sources do not tell much about their ideas.

The Ambo name-day calendar, "Ondjalulamasiku Jomumvo 1938", was published the following year. Clearly, the model for this calendar was the Finnish name-day calendar, in which almost every day is designated as a name day for one or more names. In the 1938 Ambo calendar, there is one name for almost every day of the year, except for certain church festivals such as Good Friday, Easter and Christmas.

Most of these names are traditional Ambo names, such as *Amakali, Angula, Emvula, Endjala, Haufiku, Iipinge, Iipumbu, Iitope, Kambonde, Mandume, Mpingana, Nangombe, Nehoja, Niita* and *Uukongo*. Some Ambo names which reflect Christian ideas and values were also included, e.g. *Nahenda* 'mercy', *Nambili* 'peace' and *Nekulilo* 'redemption'. The Ambo name of the pioneer missionary Martti Rautanen, *Nakambale*, was also taken for the calendar. Whether the Ambo names in the calendar were meant for boys or girls, was not mentioned. Most probably some of them were meant for both sexes and some for boys or girls only, according to the Ambo tradition, e.g. *Elago* 'happiness, luck' for a boy

1938.		EPEMBAGONA.	III.
17 D	Joh. 11: 47—57		Ntinda
18 F	Joh. 12: 1—11		Nangaku
19 Sa	Joh. 12: 12—24		Nandjule

Ef. 5: I—9. — Luuk. 4: 3I—35.

20 S	Os. 3 jomeiẓiliko	Ngueẓa
21 M	Fil. 2: 1—10	Kanona
22 D	Joh. 12: 25—36	Iihuhua
23 W	Joh. 12: 37—50	Uuanga
24 D	Joh. 13: 1—20	Iitope
25 F	Joh. 13: 21—38	Kašušuka
26 Sa	Joh. 14: 1—11	Ntoni

Gal 4: 22—3I. Joh. 6: 52— 7I

27 S	Os. jopokati keiẓiliko	Muẓaki.
28 M	Fil. 2: 12—18	Nuujoma
29 D	Joh. 14: 12—20	Nuuanga
30 W	Joh. 14: 21—31	Mükonda
31 D	Joh. 15: 1—6	Tuuṣigilua

The Ambo name-day calendar, Ondjalulamasiku Omumvo 1938, contained suggestions for Ambo baptismal names.

and *Nelago* for a girl. Different Ambo varieties were also represented in this calendar. For example, beside the forms *Elago* and *Nelago*, the forms *Elao* and *Nelao* were included.

The calendar also contains a few biblical names: *Leevi, Noomi, Sakaria* and *Uria*. Some European names, in their Finnish forms, were also included: *Matti, Saku, Sesilia, Taavi*.[292] Of these, *Matti*'s name day is on the same day as it has been for centuries in the Finnish name-day calendar, on February 24th. The name *Monika* could be regarded both as an Ambo name meaning 'be visible, be seen, be found, appear' (Tirronen 1986, p. 229), or as a European name, which originally was the name of the mother of St. Augustine (Vilkuna 1993, p. 126).

The Finnish missionary sources do not say much about the intentions behind the Ambo name-day calendar, only that it was published to encourage the local people to adopt indigenous names. Whether the idea of celebrating name days was attached to it, is uncertain. In any case, it is interesting to note that the Finns wanted to promote the use of African names by publishing a name-day calendar, when a list of Ambo names could have served the same purpose. The sources of this study do not reveal how the calendar was welcomed by the Ambo people, either. In any case, it did not lead to a custom of celebrating name days in the Ambo communities. It also seems that the calendar of the year 1938 was the only one of its kind, as it was not repeated. The calendars published for the following years by the Finnish Mission in the Ambo area, at least the ones that have survived in the Finnish missionary archives, do not include any personal names.[293] Nevertheless, the analysis of the name data in this study will show that the 1938 calendar had a certain effect on the name-giving of the Ambo Christians, although it turned out to be a temporary one.

Later in this study, we shall also see that it was not until the 1950s and 1960s that African names were increasingly adopted as baptismal names in the Lutheran congregations. This happened together with the spread of the practice of giving children more than one name at baptism. In this process, the first baptismal names remained predominantly biblical and European, whereas the second and third names were almost exclusively African. A typical combination of names, for example, has been *Selma Magano* 'gift', in which the first name is a European and the second an Ambo name. In this way, African names gradually became part of the official nomenclature of the Lutheran Ambos.

This revival of African names can primarily be attributed to the rise of African nationalism and the struggle for independence that began to inspire people all over the Ambo area at that time. In a sense, it is not surprising that the earlier efforts of the Finnish missionaries and Ambo priests to promote the use of African names was met with little response: the time was not yet right for that. What was needed was a rise of African nationalism and political awareness, which was then reflected in personal naming as well.

Interestingly, the apartheid government of South West Africa also encouraged ethnic groups to use their indigenous names, as emphasising cultural and racial differences was in line with its apartheid policy. The government for example published a magazine called Bantu, which was distributed free of charge and in which the use of African names was promoted. Ironically, this also happened to fit well in the policy of the liberation movement. (Hukka 2.3.2000.)

Among the Anglican Ambos, the development of baptismal names was similar to that of the Lutherans: African names emerged again with the political revolt, i.e. the independence struggle. It also became a common custom in the Anglican parishes to give two baptismal names, of which one was "Christian", i.e. biblical or European, and the other African. (Mwaetako 14.10.2000.)

African names were accepted much later in the Catholic parishes of the Ambo area. In fact, indigenous baptismal names became possible in the whole Roman Catholic Church only after the Second Council of the Vatican (1963–1965), in which the Church made important decisions with regard to indigenous cultures (Amushila 11.10.2000). The documents of this council (Flannery 1980), emphasise that the Church does respect and foster the qualities and talents of the various races and nations. Anything in these people's way of life which is not indissolubly bound up with superstition and error she studies with sympathy, and, if possible, preserves intact. (The Second Council of the Vatican, *Sacro sanctum Concilium*, 4 December, 1963. In: Flannery 1980, p. 13.)

This new emphasis meant that indigenous names were accepted as baptismal names in the Catholic church, but only on the condition that they are not incompatible with Christianity. In the Ambo area, however, this took quite a long time. Even if the local priests understood the importance of using African baptismal names, the European missionaries were prejudiced. Therefore, it was only recently that the first African baptismal names were given to people at the Roman Catholic Mission in Oshikuku. The change came about when African priests started to promote this practice. Today, African names are considered fashionable among the Catholic Ambos, and they are preferred particularly by the young generation. (Amushila 11.10.2000.)

The Adoption of Surnames

A hereditary surname was an unknown phenomenon in the traditional Ambo naming system. As was noted, the Ambo people had the custom of using the father's name, a patronym, together with the real name of the person, e.g. *Nangombe yaAmutenya* or *Nelago lyaShikongo* (Namuhuja 1996, p. 92). However, a European-type surname system was developed gradually in Ambo society, especially since the 1950s, and it was based on old patronyms. The word for *surname* or *family name* in Ndonga is *ofani* (pl. *oofani*) (Tirronen 1986, p. 33), which is derived from the Afrikaans word *van* 'surname'.[294] There were many reasons for the adoption of surnames in the Ambo area: the demands of colonial administration, European influence, the influence of other ethnic groups in Africa who started to use surnames earlier than the Ambos, and the problems that the popularity of new foreign names had brought about in the Ambo naming system. Let us start with the last mentioned one.

In the Ambo naming system, the increasing popularity of European and biblical names led to a decline in the name stock. There were more and more people in the community who carried the same names, such as *Paulus, Petrus, Johanna* and *Martta*. As time went by and there were commonly Christians in two or more generations in a typical Ambo family, people could not be differentiated from each other with patronyms either. Namuhuja (14.4.1997), for example, reported that before surnames came into use, it was a real problem in Oniipa that so many people had similar names, such as *Ruusa Vilho, Selma Johannes* or *Selma Mateus*.[295] Because of this phenomenon, there was even a rule in one of the Ambo congregations that if the father was *Johannes*, he was not allowed to name his daughter *Maria* (Lehtonen 2.4.1997). The missionaries also found it problematic that there were several patronyms in use within one family. If the husband and wife already had children when they got married, the husband's children carried his name, but the wife's children could all carry different fathers' names. It also caused a lot of confusion among the missionaries that the first-generation Christians often gave different patronyms on different occasions, as their unbaptised fathers were often known by more than one name.[296] (Helenius 1930, p. 88–89.)

The German colonial government already had the idea that surnames should be taken into use in German South West Africa, and that they should be based on the fathers' names. In 1911, the governor of the colony, Theodor Seitz, referring to the difficulties in identifying the "natives", ordered that the fathers' names should be given in the "native registers" (*Eingeborenenregistern*) beside the actual name of the person, e.g. *Hans* (son of) *Kavizeri, Isaak* (son of) *Christian*. He also expressed his hope that the fathers' names would gradually become used as surnames.[297] (Seitz 29.3.1911, Kaiserlicher Gouverneur von Deutsch-Südwestafrika. J. Nr. 7381, p. 55, 10.01:2235, RKA.) The German missionaries also used the father's name beside the actual name of the person; only illegitimate children carried their mothers' names. They adopted this practice for the sake of uniformity, even if it was inconsistent with the traditional customs of many indigenous groups in the colony. For example, among the Namas a son traditionally received the "family name" of the mother and a daughter that of the father.[298] Another reason for favouring the fathers' names was that it was found problematic that some settlers had given their employees German "surnames" such as *Kognak*, *Schnaps*, *Schafskopf* ('blockhead') or *Kamel*. (Nochmals zur Namensgebung in den deutschen Schutzgebieten 1914, p. 4.) The practice of using fathers' names was continued by the administration of the South African regime. Hence, the contract form which was used for contracts of employment for migrant workers before the strikes of 1971 and 1972, contained separate columns for the name and the father's name of the person (Kane-Berman 1972, Appendix I).[299]

The Finnish missionaries also discussed the adoption of surnames in Ambo society, especially since the 1930s. The director of the Finnish Missionary Society, Matti Tarkkanen, expressed his opinion on the matter in a letter to a Finnish missionary: surnames should be taken into use, as otherwise it would be impossible to find a particular person among the thousands of Ambos carrying names such as *Johannes* or *Tuomas* (Matti Tarkkanen to August Hänninen 11.2.1931, Daa:30, FMSA).[300] The enthusiasm of Tarkkanen in this matter may partly be explained by the fact that at that time, surnames were a new phenomenon in Finland. They had become compulsory for all citizens in 1921 (Kangas 1991, p. 19). Surnames were also discussed at the missionary conference of 1937, in which the Finns decided to promote the use of African baptismal names. The minutes of this meeting mention briefly that it was stressed that surnames, together with indigenous baptismal names, should be strongly recommended in the Ambo congregations (Missionary conference in Engela and Onandjokwe 26.8.–3.9.1937, Hha:15, FMSA).

It seems that the South West African government in particular encouraged the Ambo people to adopt surnames (Auala 1975, p. 21; Ihamäki 1985, p. 14). According to Hukka (2.3.2000), surnames arrived in the Ambo area at a time when contacts with the "whites' world" had become closer, and surnames were favoured by the Lutheran church as well. It was of special importance that the official marriage registers of the government required that people have a surname. The church encouraged Ambo couples to register their marriages so that inheritance problems could be sorted out more easily and that children would inherit from their parents and parents from one another (Hukka 2.3.2000; Munyika 16.10.2000; Nashihanga 18.4.1997). Altogether, the church had an important role in this process, even if it did not insist on the use of surnames (Nashihanga 18.4.1997).

The process of adopting surnames in the Ambo naming system was a gradual one. For quite a long time, there were various customs with regard to patronyms and surnames. Some people used their fathers' names with the possessive concord, just as in the old times, e.g. *Nikodemus ja Kaluvi, Martta ga Tomas*.[301] Others dropped the possessive concord and used the father's name uninflected, either the Christian one or the Ambo one, as a kind of a surname, e.g. *Johannes Abraham* and *Johannes Kaukungua*.[302] Some used both the baptismal name and the original Ambo name of the father, e.g. *Sem ja Noa Kaukungua*. At times people also used one or other of their father's names on different occasions. (Aune Liljeblad 23.1.1952, Selityksiä painovirheisiin ja epäjohdonmukaisuuksiin (D), ELC.) This variation indicated that the naming system was going through a radical change.

It was only in the 1960s that hereditary surnames really came into use in the Ambo communities (Amaambo 3.4.1997; Munyika 16.10.2000; Nambala 14.4.1997; Namuhuja 14.4.1997). Hans Namuhuja (14.4.1997) claimed that he was the first one to adopt a surname in Ondonga. He got this idea when he was studying in South Africa in the late 1950s from other African students who had surnames. He chose the name *Namuhuja*[303], which was his great grandfather's name. Before that, he was known as *Hans Daniel Sakeus*. When Namuhuja came back home from South Africa, many people in the Ambo area followed his example. Nambala (14.4.1997) also stressed that the surname system of the Ambo people could not be ascribed solely to European influences, but also to the influence of other ethnic groups in Africa whose cultures were based on patrilineality.[304] It has also been pointed out that surnames were adopted by the Ambo people because they became fashionable (Namuhuja 14.4.1997).

One of the main agents in the spread of surnames in the Ambo area was the school institution (Munyika 16.10.2000; Nashihanga 18.4.1997). Many people had to adopt a surname when they went to school (Nambala 14.4.1997). In general, it seems that surnames were first adopted by pastors and teachers, i.e. by the educated people (Amaambo 3.4.1997; Nambala 14.4.1997). The innovation was then spread geographically from the schools and congregations all over the Ambo area, and in the social hierarchy from better educated Ambos to the less educated ones. Gradually, surnames also became hereditary, as they became used by the next generation as well. However, it was also possible for children to choose other surnames later in life (Auala 1975, p. 21; Nashihanga 18.4.1997). For quite a long time, it was customary for women to continue using their fathers' names rather than to adopt the surnames of their husbands (Amaambo 3.4.1997; Mbenzi 24.3.1997; Namuhuja 14.4.1997).

The fact that surnames became hereditary, obviously represented a big change in the Ambo anthroponymic system. Another major change took place when women started to adopt their husbands' surnames, and gradually this became a prevalent custom among the Ambo people (Amakali 10.10.2000; Nashihanga 18.4.1997; Namuhuja 14.4.1997;

149

Mbenzi 24.3.1997).[305] Many women who had not adopted their husbands' surnames when they married, also did that later.[306] In everyday life, women often continued to be called by their patronyms or their fathers' clan names, however. (Mbenzi 24.3.1997; Namuhuja 14.4.1997.)

Reasons for Choosing Surnames

The surname system of the Ambo people, which was developed in the latter half of the 20th century, was based entirely on fathers' and paternal forefathers' names. Instead of using patronyms that were changed every generation, the Ambos started to use their paternal ancestors' names as hereditary surnames. This kind of development has been common elsewhere in Africa as well:[307]

> In general the African tends to use his father's name as his surname. ... The practice of using the father's name as surname is gradually dying out in many parts of Africa. In its place is the growing tendency to use one family name (commonly that of the grandfather) as the surname for all members of the same family group. (Madubuike 1976, p. 16.)

Usually it was the name of the father, the grandfather or the grandfather's father that was adopted as a surname by an Ambo family (Nambala 14.4.1997; Namuhuja 14.4.1997). Typically, the Ambo people went back so far in their family history that they came across unbaptised ancestors who had indigenous Ambo names (Nashihanga 18.4.1997). Sometimes names of very distant forefathers were chosen as well (Munyika 16.10.2000), especially if that particular ancestor was a famous person whose memory the family wanted to keep alive (Mwaetako 14.10.2000). The Ambo names of Christian fathers and forefathers were also adopted as surnames. Let us look at some surname choices more carefully.

Petrus Amakali (10.10.2000) said that he adopted a surname when he was attending a boys' school in Olukonda in the early 1950s because he was told to do so by his teachers. He chose his grandfather's name *Amakali*, not his father's name, which was *Nambahu* or *Josef*. Later, the name *Amakali* also became his brothers' surname, and the wife of Amakali and his children also carry this name. Traditionally, *Amakali* is the name of a son whose father died before the name-giving (Tirronen 1986, p. 6).

Eino Amaambo (3.4.1997) chose his grandfather's Ambo name *Amaambo* as his surname; at baptism his grandfather had received the name *Abraham*. The Kwambi name *Amaambo* means that the child was born when the father was at a cattle-post. Amaambo said that he chose this name because he had himself spent a lot of time tending cattle as a young boy. Amaambo's brothers, as well as his father's children from his second marriage, also carry this surname. (Amaambo 3.4.1997.)

Sometimes surnames are based on Ambo nicknames (Namuhuja 14.4.1997). Petrus Mbenzi (24.3.1997) said that his father chose the name *Mbenzi* 'beard' as his surname. This was originally his grandfather's nickname. The brothers of his father chose the grandfather's real name

Uugwanga. As the surname system is relatively young in Ambo society, it is quite common for brothers and sisters to have different surnames (Auala 1975, p. 21; Lehtonen 2.4.1997; Nambala 14.4.1997; Nashihanga 18.4.1997). It has also been common to change one's surname several times during one's life. Especially during the war, many people adopted new names in order to hide their true identity. (Lehtonen 2.4.1997.)

Bishop Leonard Auala explains in his autobiography (Auala 1975, p. 21) why he chose his grandfather's name *Auala* as his surname.[308] First, he had thought of adopting his father's Ambo name *Nakanyala*. However, as his father was known as *Vilho Auala* and his Ambo name *Nakanyala* was forgotten, people would not have recognised whose son he was, if his name were *Leonard Nakanyala*. The surname *Auala*, on the other hand, made it clear that he was Vilho Auala's son. Auala also points out humbly that it was good to be "nothing", as the name *Auala* means 'nothingness'.[309] Before adopting this surname, Leonard Auala was known as *Leonard Vilho*, or with his Ambo name, *Nangolo Vilho*.

The Analysis of the Surname Corpus. In order to look at the surnames of the Ambo people from a broader perspective, a corpus which includes 240 surnames of Ambos was collected for this study. These names were taken from the register of theologians of the Evangelical Lutheran Church in Namibia (ELCIN) (Nambala 1995), and thus they represent the first people to adopt the surname innovation in Ambo society.[310] As Nambala's book also includes information on the paternal forefathers of these people, it was easy to trace the origins of these names. The names of this corpus are listed in Appendix 1.

The data show that 236 of these 240 Ambo theologians (98.3%) have an Ambo surname. Only 4 (1.7%) of them have either a biblical (*Abraham, Andreas, David*) or a European surname (*Leonard*).[311] Of these names 235 (97.9%) are clearly names of paternal forefathers: fathers, grandfathers, etc. The father's name is marked as a surname for 84 theologians (35%), and the grandfather's name or a name of a more distant forefather for 151 (62.9%). It is clear that many of the fathers' names in this register are actually patronyms, even if they are marked as surnames (*ofani*) in this book. In principal, it is impossible to make a difference between a patronym and a surname in cases where the person had deliberately chosen his or her father's name as a surname with the intention that it would become hereditary. Naturally, the fathers' names that are marked as surnames for Ambo theologians who lived in the first half of the 20th century cannot be anything but patronyms. The variation of the surname system is also reflected in this register. In some cases it also gives, beside the surnames, the patronyms that these theologians were formerly known by, e.g. *Abisai Aludhilu (Henok), Leonard Auala (Vilho)* and *Timoteus Shipanga (Andreas).*

The longest "name-chain" in the corpus reaches as far back as six generations. Jesaya Iipito's forefathers are: *Veijo yaSakaria yaAwene yaNalukaku lwaNantanda yIipito* (Nambala 1995, p. 97). In most cases,

151

the surname is the name of the grandfather or the great grandfather. It is clear that most of these Ambo theologians represent the first generation carrying surnames in their families. There are also a few cases represented in the material which show that a person had inherited his surname from his father, who was also an Ambo theologian, e.g. Eino Ekandjo (son) and Johannes Ekandjo (father); *Ekandjo* was the name of the grandfather of the latter (Nambala 1995, p. 65–66). Only one name in the corpus (0.4%) was adopted from the mother's father, most probably because the father was unknown (Nambala 1995, p. 181). Three names (1.3%) seem to be nicknames of forefathers, not their real names. For example, the name of Johannes Kashokulu's grandfather was *Nekundi*, but he was also known as *Kashokulu* (Nambala 1995, p. 112). For only one name in the corpus, *Gweendama*, no possible explanation was available in the register (Nambala 1995, p. 69).

Surnames and Ambo Culture. It has been very important to the Ambo people for their surnames to be African, and especially Ambo names (Mbenzi 24.3.1997; Nambala 14.4.1997; Namuhuja 14.4.1997). As the surnames of the Ambo theologians show, European and biblical names are extremely rare as surnames. It has been pointed out that by using Ambo surnames, the Ambo people wanted to express their African, as well as their Ambo identity (Amaambo 3.4.1997; Mbenzi 24.3.1997).[312] It has also been stated that the use of forefathers' names shows that the Ambo people want to stick to their cultural roots (Nashihanga 18.4.1997). Mwaetako (14.10.2000) pointed out that these names also reveal if the person in question is Kwanyama- or Ndonga-speaking, or speaks some other Ambo variant.

In a sense, it is interesting that the European-type surname system has been one of the major forces in the re-Africanisation of the personal nomenclature of the Ambo people. The surname system has undoubtedly been one of the means by which the Ambo people have managed to abandon names, such as *Selma Mateus*, which consist of European or biblical baptismal names and patronyms only. A good example of this development is the name of Shekutaamba Nambala. When Nambala went to school, he was still known as *Väinö Väinö*. He had the same Finnish man's name as a baptismal name and a patronym because he was named after his father. His other baptismal name is *Shekutaamba*. At school he adopted the surname *Nambala*, which was his grandfather's name, and later he also started to use his Ambo baptismal name instead of the Finnish one. Hence, Väinö Väinö became known as *Shekutaamba Nambala*, or *Shekutaamba V.V. Nambala*. (Nambala 14.4.1997.)

The adoption of the surname system has not been an easy process among the Ambos, and there are many opinions on the matter. Within the church, the surname system has mainly been welcomed, as it is considered a better system than the old patronymic system for differentiating people (Namuhuja 14.4.1997). It has also been found helpful in many respects that the whole nuclear family, i.e. the parents and their children, should carry the same name (Nashihanga 18.4.1997). Munyika

(16.10.2000) also pointed out that a surname connects a bigger family group than a father's name, for the children of brothers are also tied together by the same surname. For these reasons, many Ambos believe that adopting surnames was the right decision, even if it has caused a lot of confusion among the people (Amaambo 3.4.1997).

On the other hand, many people in the Ambo area have started to criticise the surname system (Amakali 10.10.2000; Nashihanga 18.4.1997). Shekutaamba Nambala (14.4.1997) pointed out that the Ambo people have lost a lot of their history by adopting surnames. According to him, surnames are highly problematic in a matrilineal culture. Nambala in particular sees the fact that Ambo women adopt their husbands' surnames as discrimination against women and that these women are "kidnapped from their roots".[313] The fact that the surnames of the Ambo people are almost exclusively of Ambo origin does not please Nambala either. He pointed out that in the patronymic system, the identification of the person was direct, as it showed clearly who the father of the person was, whereas in the surname system people carry names of ancestors whom they may not even know personally. All in all, Nambala's opinion is that the surname system is only "confusing our tradition", and therefore the patronymic system would be more suitable for the Ambo people. The ideas of Nambala represent those of a well-educated man who is familiar with Ambo traditions and whose opinions may influence others as well. Most people in the Ambo area, however, seem to think the way Nashihanga (18.4.1997) put it: "We inherited these things from the Europeans and accepted them as such. It just happened."

The Ambo surname system is based on names of paternal ancestors. Could there have been other alternatives as well? A surname system might also have been based on the matrilineal clans, as these are very important to the Ambo people. Williams (1994, p. 55) stresses the significance of the clans in the Ambo communities:

[I]n a matrilineal society like that of Owamboland, the clan is a more important social link than the surname, because a person's identity is traced through the clan lineage - and not through the surname, which leads to one's identity through the paternal line.

There are also many examples of African naming systems in which the surname system is based on clan names, even if these are typically patrilineal systems.[314] This is the case among the Zulus in South Africa, for example (Herbert 1996, p. 1223; Koopman 1986, p. 54).[315] However, it is important to note that in the Ambo culture, name-giving and personal names are so strongly attached to the father and his role in the child's life that such a development would not have been very likely. Besides, as the use of clan names has been relatively restricted in Ambo society, these names could not serve as a natural basis for a surname system. Since patronyms, on the other hand, were used systematically for all people, both men and women, it is not surprising that the surname system was based on them.

The Result of the Process: An "African-European"
Personal Naming System

Birth Names

In this section, we shall look at the new personal naming system which
has been developed in the Ambo area in the course of the 20th century as
a result of the encounter between European and African naming systems. It should be noted that this process is not yet complete, and one
can still find a lot of instability and opposing tendencies in the naming
practices of the Ambo people. On the other hand, as was remarked at the
beginning of this thesis, all personal naming systems are constantly changing, and a fully developed system can never be anything more than an
illusion. In any case, we shall look at the Ambo naming system during
the first ten years of Namibian independence, between the years 1990
and 2000.

The official naming system of the Ambo people consists of one or
more forenames, and a surname or a patronym which functions as a surname. As there is no legislation in the Republic of Namibia concerning
personal names, name-giving is basically free in the country (Mbenzi
24.3.1997; Mwaetako 14.10.2000; Nambala 14.4.1997). In practice,
however, it is regulated, especially by the local churches, which do not
accept all names as baptismal names (Amushila 11.10.2000; Mwaetako
14.10.2000; Nashihanga 18.4.1997). Naturally there are also many un-
written rules, social expectations and fashions, all of which affect personal naming in many ways. Beside official names, the Ambo people
also have many kinds of unofficial bynames – individual and collective
– which are analysed in this section as well. Let us start our analysis of
the contemporary Ambo naming system with the names that the Ambos
receive soon after birth, but before baptism.

Giving the child a name soon after birth is still a widespread custom
in the Ambo communities. In analysing the traditional Ambo naming
system, we called this name a *temporary name*. In this context, the term
birth name would be more appropriate, as this African name is often
retained as the most common – and the most intimate – call name of the
person in the home environment (Lehtonen 2.4.1997; Säynevirta
12.4.1997).[316] This name is referred to as *edhina lyopomboga*, 'name
alongside spinach/cabbage', even if the origin of this expression is unknown to most Ambos today (Nambala 14.4.1997; Namuhuja 14.4.1997).

Nowadays, when women commonly give birth to their children in
hospitals, new-born babies usually receive a birth name from the nurses
(Säynevirta 12.4.1997). Ester Enkono (14.10.2000), midwife in the
Onandjokwe Lutheran Hospital, where about 4,000 babies are born each
year, said that it is usually the assisting midwife who gives the birth
name to the child. Often other midwives, and occasionally the mother,
help with this as well. In the case of home deliveries, it is also the midwife who gives this name (Nambala 14.4.1997). This practice is explained

by the fact that the midwives need to address the baby somehow and, as there is no other name available at the time, they must create one (Malua 19.9.2000; Munyika 16.10.2000). According to the Ambo tradition, children are not named before they are born (Munyika 16.10.2000).

E. Enkono (14.10.2000) stressed the fact that according to tradition, the midwives should give the birth name. However, there is a lot of confusion surrounding this matter today. Not all fathers like the idea that their children are given names in hospital and not at home, and some of them have started to bestow birth names on their children by themselves (Amkongo 14.4.1997).[317] E. Enkono (14.10.2000) said that when the father comes to the hospital to see his child, the mother usually informs him of the name that the baby has been given, and the father either accepts it or not.[318] In cases where he disapproves, he names the child himself.[319] Nambala (14.4.1997) said that the father may also give a birth name to his child if he is present at the delivery. Nowadays many mothers also have a piece of paper with them in the hospital, on which the father has written down names for a boy and a girl (Nambala 14.4.1997). Sometimes the father may send another person to the hospital with information about the name, or wait until the baby arrives home and then name it (Amaambo 3.4.1997).

It seems that in most cases, the father has the final say in the giving of the birth name, and the names given by midwives are not taken very seriously. Such a name becomes important only if the father has accepted it, otherwise it remains a temporary name. Hence, it is not surprising that many of our Ambo informants stressed that it is the father who chooses the birth name today (e.g. Amushila 11.10.2000; Kanana 19.9.2000; Mbenzi 24.3.1997; Mwaetako 14.10.2000).[320] Nambala (14.4.1997) also mentioned that some parents give these names to their children in turn, and Kanana (19.9.2000) pointed out that couples who understand human rights give these names together, although they are not many yet.

What are these birth names like? E. Enkono (14.10.2000) said that many names bestowed by nurses express gratitude, especially those given after a difficult delivery, e.g. *Tangeni* 'let us thank' or *Hambelela* 'praise'. Some names refer to the way the baby was born. In cases of premature birth, for example, a baby girl may be given a Kwanyama name *Kaningholi* 'very little'. Many other events and circumstances are also reflected in these names. A baby whose mother left the hospital and baby soon after delivery, was given the name *Ndathigwapo* 'I was deserted'. Names which refer to the time of the birth are typical too: *Angula/Nangula* 'morning', *Amutenya/Namutenya* 'midday'. (E. Enkono 14.10.2000.) Some names also refer to weather conditions, e.g. *Nayiloke* 'may it rain' (Lehtonen 2.4.1997) or *Omvula* 'rain' (Säynevirta 12.4.1997). Special anniversaries and festivals are also reflected in birth names. Thus in 1995, when there was a special celebration of the 125 years of Finnish missionary work in the Ambo area, many babies received the name *Metumo* 'in mission' (Säynevirta 12.4.1997). Also, if the baby resembles someone else – is fat, for example – it might be given the name of that person.[321] Twins are without exception given specific names according to the Ambo tradition. If they are a girl and a boy, the girl is named *Shekupe* and the boy *Uuwanga*. If they are both girls, they are named *Shekupe* and *Nuuwanga*, and if both boys, their names would be *Uuwanga* and *Shekutaamba*. (E. Enkono 14.10.2000.)

Babies may also be named after European doctors. For example, many boys in the Onandjokwe Lutheran Hospital have been named *Veli-Pekka* after the Finnish doctor Veli-Pekka Jääskeläinen, who used to help women with fertility problems. A number of baby girls were named after his wife too. (E. Enkono 14.10.2000.) Säynevirta (12.4.1997) reported that in that hospital, many girls were also named *Selma* after the Finnish medical doctor Selma Rainio, the founder of the hospital. E. Enkono (14.10.2000) concluded that in hospitals, babies are given African names or named after doctors.

The birth names given by the fathers normally resemble those bestowed by the midwives. They are African names which usually refer to the time of the day of the birth, or events taking place at that time (Malua 19.9.2000; Mbenzi 24.3.1997; Munyika 16.10.2000). They may also express the father's feelings, such as joy, anger, frustration or doubt. (Malua 19.9.2000). Amaambo (3.4.1997) said that many birth names express gratitude, and the hopes of the father. For example, a father who hopes that there will be many girls in the family, may name his daughter *Taatsu* 'they grind', and a father who is thankful for having a boy in the house, may name his son *Nghilitha* 'I will not herd anymore'. The child may also receive the African name of the person whom the father has chosen as his child's namesake. For example, if the desired namesake is Abraham Hatuiikulipi Malua, the father may give the name *Hatuiikulipi*[322] as a birth name, and *Abraham* would be added to the child's name later at baptism. (Malua 19.9.2000.) Usually, however, the birth name is not a namesake name (Mbenzi 24.3.1997; Säynevirta 12.4.1997). Sometimes, if the father denies his paternity and refuses to give his child a name, the child may receive the name *Shilongo* (< *oshilongo* 'country, state, kingdom') from the mother, as a fatherless child is only a child of the country (Amaambo 3.4.1997).

E. Enkono (14.10.2000) stressed that as the names given by midwives are nicknames only, not official names, they are not registered anywhere. However, sometimes the name given by the midwife is also given as a baptismal name. In such a case, the midwife is usually invited to attend the baptism ceremony. (E. Enkono 14.10.2000.)

It seems that the traditional naming ceremonies are not practised in the Ambo area today. Amakali (10.10.2000) said that they were common for quite a long time after the advent of Christianity, as Christianity was not accepted by all people. Some baptised Ambos also kept to the old custom when naming their children: first they had the traditional naming ceremony, and after that the Christian baptism. The other Ambo informants also stated that the traditional naming ceremony is something that one does not see in the Ambo area anymore, and has not seen for decades (Kanana 19.9.2000; Munyika 16.10.2000). Nampala (2000,

p. 16) claims that "today that type of ceremony is no longer taking place because it has been replaced by the Christian baptism". Mwaetako (14.10.2000) also stated clearly that there is no outdooring ceremony anymore; nowadays people simply have to give birth names to their children by themselves. Amushila (11.10.2000), however, said that among the Catholic Ambos there is often a little celebration at home after the child is born, to which neighbours are invited to celebrate the new-born baby and to praise God. He stressed that this occasion has a Christian meaning today, and it is called *ehambelelo* 'praising'. Mwaetako (14.10.2000), in turn, said that if the father is working in the south and sends the name for his new-born child from there, the family often arranges a little celebration on the day the name arrives.

To sum up, the Westernisation of the health care system in the Ambo culture has brought about major changes in the traditional custom of giving children temporary names soon after birth. Today, the child often receives a name from the midwives in hospital. Nevertheless, the father is the one who ultimately decides if the name given will be used in the home environment. If the father does not like the name, he chooses another birth name for his child. Some parents have also begun to give these names together.

Baptismal Names

Today, the clear majority of Ambo children are baptised in a church, most of them in a Lutheran one. The Christian baptism has thus become the actual name-giving ceremony of the Ambo people (Munyika 16.10.2000; Mwaetako 14.10.2000; Nampala 2000, p. 16), and it is in this ceremony that an Ambo child receives his or her most important name, the "real" name (Pentti 1959, p. 35–36).[323] Together with the surname, or a patronym, the baptismal name – which is called *eshashwadhina* or *edhina lyuushashwa* in Ndonga (Tirronen 1986, p. 370; English–Ndonga Dictionary 1996, p. 104)[324] –becomes the official name of the person. The importance of this name is reflected, for example, in the fact that the Ambos have generally used the baptismal names of their fathers as patronyms, not their African names, e.g. *Leonard Vilho*, contrary to many other naming systems in Africa (Koopman 1986, p. 46). Altogether, it seems that the baptismal name is regarded as more important to the Ambo people than to many other peoples in Africa.[325] This may, among other reasons, be due to the fact that the traditional namesake custom is nowadays attached to the baptismal name, not to any other name of the person. On the other hand, Amakali (10.10.2000) pointed out that basically, the person's identity is linked to his or her Ambo name, not to the foreign name.

The Lutheran Population. In the Lutheran congregations in the Ambo area, baptisms usually take place once a month at the beginning of a Sunday service. Other kinds of baptisms, e.g. home baptisms, are very rare. (Nashihanga 18.4.1997.) The baptismal name is traditionally, and most commonly, chosen by the father, even for children born out of wed-lock.[326] Being named by the father is considered so important that during the pregnancy, unmarried women often go to the home of the father and stay there until the father acknowledges his paternity and agrees to give the baby a name. (Lehtonen 2.4.1997.) Sometimes the father may de-liberately delay with the name-giving, so that the child cannot be baptised as early as planned. This shames the mother. (Säynevirta 12.4.1997.)[327] In very difficult cases, people may turn to the tradi-tional court, which can force the father to accept the child. Some-times paternity tests are also needed in this process. (Mwaetako 14.10.2000.) Nambala (14.4.1997) said that some men also keep the name secret from the mother until the baptism day, which is in line with the Ambo tradition.

If the name cannot be given by the father, who may be far away or dead, the baptismal name is usually given by the grandfather, the fa-ther's brother or some other relative from the father's side (Amkongo 14.4.1997; Mbenzi 24.3.1997). The role of the father as a name-giver is still taken for granted by the majority of people in the Ambo area (Amaambo 3.4.1997; Amkongo 14.4.1997; Mbenzi 24.3.1997; Mwaetako 14.10.2000; Nashihanga 18.4.1997). Some parents have also started to choose baptismal names for their children together, or in turns (Amaambo 3.4.1997; Ihambo 7.10.2000).

In the Ambo area, children typically receive two or three names at baptism, of which the first one is European or biblical and the latter one(s) African. It is a general expectation that a person has both a Euro-pean and an Ambo name (Säynevirta 12.4.1997). However, African names have become more popular lately, and they are more often used in every-day life (Namuhuja 14.4.1997; Nashihanga 18.4.1997). According to Nambala (14.4.1997), it is more common among the educated Ambos to give African names to their children, whereas the less educated people prefer "traditional" European and biblical names.[328] The popularity of African names is most commonly explained by their meaningfulness to the Ambo people, contrary to European and biblical names, which are often obscure to them (e.g. Amakali 10.10.2000; Ihambo 7.10.2000; Namuhuja 14.4.1997; Nashihanga 18.4.1997). Nowadays African names are accepted as baptismal names in all Lutheran congregations, provided that their meanings are "good", i.e. not derogatory.[329] However, there are still some pastors who refuse to baptise children with Ambo names only. Altogether, there has not been much discussion about names in the Lu-theran church lately, and church law does not say anything about baptis-mal names either. (Nashihanga 18.4.1997.)

How does the church restrict name-giving in practice then? Nashihanga (18.4.1997) reported that some fathers in his congregation, Oniipa, want to discuss their name choices with the pastor, but many of them only bring the name to the pastor's office before the baptism. Nashihanga pointed out that discussions are necessary if there are names which he does not understand or which have a "bad meaning". Such names, he said, are typically given to children born out of wedlock. If the parents

Sunday service at the Lutheran church in Oniipa. Minna Saarelma-Maunumaa. 1997.

Children at the Anglican St. Thomas church in Oshakati. Minna Saarelma-Maunumaa. 2000.

159

were quarrelling at the time when the baby was born, the father can, for example, name his daughter *Mwalengwa* 'you are shamed', which carries a clear message to the mother.[330] Usually it is not a problem for the fathers, however, to change such derogatory names. Amaambo (3.4.1997) explained this type of names psychologically: when the Africans become angry, they prefer not to show it directly, in contrast to the Europeans.[331] Therefore, personal names are used for expressing emotions indirectly.[332] Other types of names may also have been rejected by the pastors. Ihambo (7.10.2000) told of a father who wanted to name his son *Christ*. Ihambo pointed out to him that the child could become a criminal, for instance, and refused to baptise the baby with this name.

The Non-Lutheran Population. The baptismal names of the Anglican Ambos resemble those of the Lutherans in many respects. Usually children receive two names, the one being a European or biblical name and the other one African. The only apparent difference is that among the Anglicans, foreign names are often given in their English form, e.g. *George, James, Peter, William; Elizabeth, Magdalene, Margaret* and *Ruth*. (Mwaetako 14.10.2000.)[333] Mwaetako (14.10.2000) pointed out that basically the church has no right to reject names given by the fathers. Only if the name is insulting is a negotiation needed. This does not happen often, however.

The Catholic Ambos have only recently started to bestow African names at baptism, and many babies still receive a biblical or European baptismal name only. For example, babies baptised in Oshikuku in 2000 have, as their only name names such as *Agnes, Cecilia, Eveline, Jakobina, Lucia, Maria, Natalia* and *Pauline*, or *Frans, Isak, Josef, Lazarus, Petrus, Placidus, Rufus* and *Stefanus*.[334] The foreign names of the Catholics are typically German and saints' names, but some Finnish names also appear in these lists, e.g. *Rauha, Saima* and *Vaino* (< *Väinö*).[335] In addition to single names, there are also combinations of a foreign name and an Ambo name, e.g. *Leonard Endjala* ('flood'), *Melania Hailinongwe* ('I eat with a leopard/enemy'), *Foibe Ndapandula* ('I thank'), *Oskar Tutaleni* ('let us look'), *Lovis-Ndinoshisho* ('I take care of it') and *Christof Natangwe* ('may He be praised'). Some children have also received Ambo names only, e.g. *Hafeni* 'be happy', *Penehupifo* 'there is salvation', *Taifanwa-Tuyenikelago* ('he is called', 'let us go to happiness') and *Ndinelago Naukelo* '(I have luck/happiness', 'the last born'). Father Stefanus Amushila (11.10.2000) said that African names are very fashionable among the Catholics today. The Ambo birth names of children may also be accepted as baptismal names, unless they are regarded as unsuitable for Christians. Amushila (11.10.2000) reported that he has for example rejected the name *Inamupopya* 'do not speak', as it showed that the people in question did not want to be reconciled. He also said that sometimes the African name of the person may be recorded in the list of baptisms, even if it is not an official baptismal name.[336]

People who do not belong to any Christian church form a small minority in the Ambo area.[337] Nashihanga (18.4.1997) said that many of

Schoolchildren at the Roman Catholic Mission in Oshikuku. Minna Saarelma-Maunumaa. 2000.

these people have European and biblical names, e.g. *Andreas*, even if they have not been baptised. Especially the ones who lived near towns and had been under the influence of the church, had adopted foreign names as a fashion. However, there are also some Ambo people living "in the bush", i.e. in the most remote parts of the Ambo area, who still have traditional Ambo names only.

Reasons for Giving Lutheran Baptismal Names. The baptismal name is chosen with special care by the Ambo people, and most commonly it is chosen by the father. As children usually receive more than one name at baptism, it is easy for the father to combine different name-giving motives when giving these names. European and biblical names are typically given after other people, as "namesake names", whereas many Ambo names reflect the father's feelings, express Christian ideas or refer to the circumstances surrounding the birth.[338] A careful analysis of these names will be presented later in this study, when analysing the baptismal names of three Lutheran congregations in the Ambo area. However, let us take up some points here which the name corpus will not reveal.

The most important motive for the giving of baptismal names is a namesake relationship, even if there are also Ambos who do not have a namesake (Amaambo 3.4.1997; Lehtonen 2.4.1997). Fathers typically name their children after their friends and relatives.[339] These names are given in the hope that the child will resemble his or her namesake.[340] Occasionally, the child may also be named after two people. In such a case, one of the namesakes becomes more important. Sometimes the child receives all the names of the namesake, sometimes only one of them. (Amkongo 14.4.1997.) Usually, it is not considered necessary to

161

inform the namesake of the fact in advance, but the father makes sure that this person attends the baptism ceremony. Often the namesake is also a godparent to the child, but this is not necessarily the case.[341] (Amaambo 3.4.1997.) Many children are also named after someone who died before the birth of the child (A. Enkono 18.10.2000).

In Ondonga, the namesake relationship carries special obligations today too: the namesake is expected to buy school clothes for the child and to assist him or her in various ways later in life. The namesake also has an important role at the wedding of the child.[342] (Amkongo 14.4.1997; Lehtonen 2.4.1997.) If the parents of the child happen to die, it is the namesake's duty to take care of the orphan. However, the child does not inherit from his or her namesake. Also when the parents are alive, the child often stays for a long time in the namesake's home. (Amaambo 3.4.1997.) Usually the child gives presents to the namesake as well. In everyday life, namesakes are also identified with each other in various ways, just as in the old times. For example, if the younger namesake gives birth to a baby, the older namesake is regarded as a mother as well. (Lehtonen 2.4.1997.) In Oukwanyama, the namesake relationship does not include any strong obligations. The Kwanyamas name their children after other people primarily because they want to retain their names (Kanana 19.9.2000). The idea that the child will inherit certain characteristics of his or her namesake is typically attached to it as well (Malua 19.9.2000).

The traditional namesake ceremonies, as they were in the old times, belong to the past now (Mwaetako 14.10.2000). Amaambo (3.4.1997), who was born in 1936, said that when he was a child there were such ceremonies, but that one does not see them anymore. Today, the namesake is often invited to a celebration which takes place in the child's home on its baptism day: an ox is slaughtered and the namesake brings clothes for the baby (Amaambo 3.4.1997). The special namesake gifts that were given in the old times at the namesake ceremony are today given any time between the baptism and the wedding. This is done at a little ceremony to which friends are invited and at which the namesake relationship is confirmed. (Mbenzi 24.3.1997.) These gifts may also be given when the child gets married, as a sign that the older namesake has accepted the younger one as a member of his or her family (Nampala 2000, p. 16).

As many of the namesake names of the Ambo people are of foreign origin today, i.e. European and biblical, their origins or meanings are usually not known to the Ambos (Amaambo 3.4.1997; Munyika 16.10.2000). Hence, a person might know that his or her name is originally the name of a Finnish missionary, but does not necessarily know what it means.[343] In principal, when naming children after other people, the connection between the name and the particular person is considered more important than the meaning of the name. (Munyika 16.10.2000.) In such cases, "a name is just a name", as Nambala (14.4.1997) put it. For this reason, many people do not care much about the meanings of these names (Mbenzi 24.3.1997). Today, however, foreign names are sometimes translated into the Ambo languages when they are bestowed as namesake names. This seems to be one way for the Ambos to Africanise their personal nomenclature, and to make their names meaningful.[344] Thus, the Finnish women's names *Lahja* 'gift' and *Päivi* (< *päivä* 'day') have become *Omagano* (< *omagano* 'gift') and *Namutenya* (< *omutenya* 'day') among the Ambos (Lehtonen 17.11.1994), and the biblical name *Petrus* is sometimes translated as *Manya* (< *emanya* 'stone, rock') (Kanana 19.9.2000). Lately, it has also become common to choose the African name of the namesake for the child, not his or her European name (Nambala 14.4.1997). Also, in such cases, the namesake relationship remains more important than the meaning of the name. Hence, a girl who was not born in the morning, may receive the name *Nangula* 'morning' from a namesake. (Lehtonen 2.4.1997.)

Nevertheless many, if not most, Ambo baptismal names are given because of their meanings, and they are carefully chosen – or created – by the father. The birth name of the child is often given as a baptismal name, but the baptismal name may be a totally new name as well (Amakali 10.10.2000; E. Enkono 14.10.2000; Nambala 14.4.1997). It is typical of Ambo baptismal names that the name itself is only the beginning, often the first word, of a longer sentence which may refer to various ideas or events in the father's life. Because of this, it is often difficult to grasp the "real" meaning of the name by looking at it only. (Mbenzi 24.3.1997.) Thus many names, even if their lexical meanings are perfectly clear, are not fully understood unless they are explained by the name-giver.[345] There can also be many different motives behind the same name given by different fathers (Malua 19.9.2000).

It is also a characteristic of Ambo baptismal names that many of them reflect Christian beliefs. The spiritual atmosphere is very strong in them. Often these names are fragments of Bible quotations. (Säynevirta 12.4.1997.) Many of the Ambo baptismal names given during the independence struggle also refer to the war, e.g. *Mekondjo* 'in the battle', *Niita* 'war', *Sindano* 'victory' (Amaambo 3.4.1997; Säynevirta 12.4.1997). Beside newly created names, many traditional Ambo names are also given as baptismal names today (Lehtonen 2.4.1997), however some of them are not semantically transparent anymore (Mbenzi 24.3.1997). Let us look at some examples of Lutheran baptismal names and the motives behind them.

Alpo Enkono (18.10.2000), who comes from Ongandjera, has two daughters. They both have a European name, which they assumed from a namesake, and an Ambo name which was given because of its meaning:

Hulda Talahole. This daughter was named *Hulda* after Enkono's mother. The full name of the mother was *Hulda Kashimbandjola*[346]. The Ambo name *Talahole* means 'look at love'.

Selma Etiigwana. This daughter was named *Selma* after Enkono's mother-in-law. The name *Etiigwana* 'bring the nations' refers to a mission hymn in the Lutheran hymn book which says "bring the nations to Christ". The daughter was born when the Namibian refugees came back home from many countries after independence.

Shekutaamba Nambala (14.4.1997), who comes from Ondonga, has three sons. They all have two African names, of which the first one was created by Nambala and the second one adopted from a namesake. Let us look at the names of one of his sons here:

Katwali Kampunda. Before this child was born, Nambala was studying in the United States. As Nambala and his wife did not want their child to be born in America, the family left the country before the delivery. The name *Katwali* 'we did not' refers to many things that Nambala's family did not do at that time. For example, they did not attend his mother's funeral, they did not have money, and they did not have their child born in the United States. The name *Kampunda* is the African name of this child's namesake, Nambala's uncle Jairus who was a SWAPO soldier. This uncle was on the battlefield with six of his comrades, and the others were all killed.

Veikko Munyika (16.10.2000), who comes from Oukwanyama, has three sons. Their biblical names are adopted from their namesakes, and their African names refer to Munyika's experiences at the time his sons were born:

Apollos Akutu. The son was named *Apollos* after Munyika's friend Apollos Kaulinge. The name *Akutu* 'oh shame, I am sorry that this is happening' has several explanations: 1. Munyika felt sorry because the first-born son was supposed to be named by his father, but as the father was in exile, he could not do that. 2. The son was born in the middle of very serious war circumstances when there were many raids into Angola by the South African army and lots of people were killed. 3. Munyika himself felt exiled, even if he was the only one of the family who was in the country.

David Aveshe. The son was named *David* after Munyika's father. The name *Aveshe* 'all, all of them' indicated that the whole of Munyika's family (which consisted of his parents and their nine children) went into exile except for him. At the same time, the name was a prayer for them all. "So all of them went and I was asking God to protect them."[347]

Tomas Amena. The son was named *Tomas* after Munyika's friend Tomas Shivute. The name *Amena* 'protect them' was a prayer asking for protection to Munyika's family and himself in the difficult times.

Aron Kanana (19.9.2000), who comes from Oukwanyama, has three sons, of which only one is named after somebody. Kanana tells that he chose these names together with his wife, and as a family they decided not to give foreign baptismal names to their children:

Mekondjo Inodhimbwa Taleke. The three names ('in a battle', 'do not forget', 'observe the hand') contain the idea: "In the battle do not forget that there is the hand of God that is giving."

Ndeitumba Tunatate Etuna. The three names ('I am brave', 'we have our father', 'he holds us') contain the idea: "I am brave, because we have a father who is holding us."

Manya Amkoshi Pendapala. This son was named *Manya Amkoshi* after a friend whose forenames are *Petrus Amkoshi. Manya* (< *emanya* 'rock, stone') is a translation of the biblical *Petrus. Amkoshi* is a Ndonga name, and Kanana does not know its meaning.[348] *Pendapala* 'be brave in an encouraging way' is the name that was given to this child before baptism, i.e. it was his birth name.

These examples may be sufficient to show how baptismal names are chosen – and created – among the Lutheran Ambos. To sum up, in the giving of baptismal names various elements are merged into each other: European and biblical names, Christian ideas, the Ambo namesake custom, and the traditional idea of names reflecting current events and feelings of the father. None of the Ambos interviewed for this study stressed the "beauty" of the name as an important reason behind the name choice.[349] As Säynevirta (12.4.1997) pointed out, the beauty of the name plays no significant role in the name-giving of the Ambos. Therefore, the motives for the giving of European and biblical names in Ambo society differ greatly from those in many European countries, where the euphony of names has become increasingly important in the choice of name (V. Kohlheim 1996b, p. 1205).

Individual Bynames: Nicknames and Praise Names

The nicknames of the Ambo people consist of "ordinary" nicknames and praise names. Birth names, which are given to babies soon after birth, can also be seen as nicknames – and indeed, they are often used as nicknames in the family circles later in life. Many birth names are also formed in the same way that ordinary nicknames are. However, as birth names have a special role in the Ambo naming system at the time when the child has not yet received his or her baptismal name, they are analysed separately in this study. In this subsection, we shall concentrate on names which are used in addition to or instead of the baptismal name of the person, typically in unofficial contexts.

Ordinary Nicknames. The Ambo people have various kinds of nicknames today – just as they had in the old days. In fact, it is characteristic of the Ambo culture that people enjoy playing with names and creating new names for each other (Nambala 14.4.1997).[350] Many people are also much better known by their nicknames than by their official names (Amaambo 3.4.1997; Amkongo 14.4.1997). At times, a nickname may also replace the baptismal name, or be used together with it, in official contexts.[351] For example, many young people add a nickname by which they are generally known to their official name when they go to the university (Mbenzi 24.3.1997). On the other hand, nicknames are often kept secret, and hence many people do not know their own nicknames.[352] It may be revealed at some stage of the person's life, however. (Munyika 16.10.2000.) Many nicknames are also used by a limited group only, e.g. by workmates, and thus they may remain unknown to the person's family, for example (Kanana 19.9.2000).

Ambos who have European names that are difficult to pronounce are often given nicknames for everyday usage (Amaambo 3.4.1997). Sometimes European names are also translated into the Ambo languages and used as nicknames. For example, Bishop Leonard Auala used to call his wife *Aluhe* 'always', because she had a Finnish name, *Aina,* which can be translated as 'always' (Auala 1975, p. 132–133).[353] Nicknaming has thus been one way for the Ambo people to avoid using their foreign names. On the other hand, there are also European nicknames, such as *Sister* for a woman who was active in the students' Christian movement and frequently addressed people as "brothers and sisters" (Munyika 16.10.2000).

Many "ordinary" nicknames of the Ambo people describe the physical qualities or personality of the individual, or refer to his or her personal history.[354] As Amkongo (14.4.1997) put it, "the way you look, speak, do your work, and so on, can earn you a name". Many names also reveal what the person likes, or refer to his or her most common expressions (Munyika 16.10.2000). Some nicknames are also insulting. However, the person in question has no option other than to accept the name that has been given.[355] (Amaambo 3.4.1997.) On the other hand, there are also nicknames which praise people (Amakali 10.10.2000). Let us look at some examples of Ambo nicknames (Amaambo 3.4.1997; Amakali 10.10.2000; Amkongo 14.4.1997; Lehtonen 7.11.1994; 2.4.1997; Mbenzi 24.3.1997; Munyika 16.10.2000; Säynevirta 12.4.1997):

Physical qualities

Nokathingo (< *okathingo* 'little neck')	a person with a long neck
Mbenzi (< *oombenzi* 'beard')	a bearded man
Nakale (< *-le* 'long, tall')	a tall person
Namwe, Kamwe (< *omwe* 'midge, mosquito')	a long and thin person

Personality

Amupopi (< *omupopi* 'speaker, talker')	a person who talks too much
Kaningilwa (< *ningila* 'do on behalf of')	a person who always needs other people to assist him or her
Kazamutumba (< *za* 'go, come', *omutumba* 'sitting position, sitting place')	a lazy, inefficient person
Mwenyomwaanawa ('good spirit')	a person who never gets angry, even if other people provoked him
Okangwe, Ongwe (< *ongwe* 'leopard')	a person who gets angry easily
Omukwaniilwa (< *omukwaniilwa* 'king')	a person who prefers being alone
Onkoshi, Nkoshi (< *onkoshi* 'lion')	a strong and lively person
Tuyoleni ('let us laugh')	a person who always laughs when other people come to him

Typical behaviour, personal history

Kahipi (< *ehipi* 'hippie, broad-legged trousers')	a person whose trousers were not as broadlegged as those of the others at a time when bell-bottom trousers were in fashion, i.e. he had a little *ehipi, okahipi,* only
Kahumba Kandola ('little harmonium')	a person who had a little harmonium which he used to play in the church[356]
Kashenye (< *okashenye* 'species of cicada')	a child who enjoys running after these insects and tries to get them out of the holes in the field
Mwiiyale ('in the palm bush' < *oshiyale* 'palm bush')	a person who was found drunk in the palm bush
Nadi (< *nadihokololwe* 'recite our text')	a pastor who used to start his baptismal classes by saying "recite our text", not with any kind of greeting
Nentoko (< *entoko* 'one round of a string of round of a string pearls around the waist; simpleton, shortwitted person')	a woman who used only one of pearls when she was a little girl (she herself finds this name insulting)
Yakula ('assist, help, look after')	a girl who often helped other people at home

The namesake custom is also applied to the use of nicknames: the namesakes share nicknames as well (Amaambo 3.4.1997). For example, as doctor Selma Rainio, the founder of the Onandjokwe Lutheran Hospital, was known as *Gwanandjokwe* 'of Onandjokwe' among the Ambo people, all Selmas in the Ambo area today may be called *Gwanandjokwe* after her. Similarly, as the Finnish missionary Johanna Rautanen was known as *Gwanaka*, all Johannas in the Ambo area today may be called *Gwanaka*. (Mbenzi 24.3.1997).[357] This practice also serves to show who the original namesake was, if there are many alternatives. Hence, the namesakes of the Finnish missionaries Lahja Lehtonen and Lahja Väänänen use different nicknames (Lehtonen 2.4.1997).[358] For the foreigners, nicknames are generally given on the same grounds as for the Ambos. Sometimes they may also receive Ambo names which resemble their own European names, e.g. the Finnish missionary Else Witting became *waIipinge*, 'of Iipinge', because her surname resembled the common Ambo name *Iipinge*. (Munyika 16.10.2000.)

The Ambo people also form nicknames from their European and biblical baptismal names, most commonly by abbreviation. English name forms are often used today. Here are some examples: *Abraham > Abe, Benjamin > Ben, Filippus > Philip, Jeremia > Jerry, Joel > Joe, Johannes > Johnny, John, Kristof > Chris, Mateus > Matthew, Nikodemus > Nick,*

Paulus > *Paul, Petrus* > *Peter, Robert* > *Rob, Sakeus* > *Saki, Samuel* > *Sam, Tomas* > *Tommy, Tom; Maria* > *Mary, Rakel* > *Rachel* (Amaambo 3.4.1997; Kanana 19.9.2000; Lehtonen 2.4.1997; Mbenzi 24.3.1997; Munyika 16.10.2000; Nambala 14.4.1997; Namuhuja 14.4.1997; Säynevirta 12.4.1997). English name forms are most common among the educated (Mwaetako 14.10.2000) and young people (Amaambo 3.4.1997). This practice is explained by the need to avoid long names, but more commonly by the fact that English, as the only official language of Namibia, has become very fashionable after independence. The television and other media also popularise many English names of famous actors and athletes. (Kanana 19.9.2000; Munyika 16.10.2000.)[359]

The popularity of the English language is reflected in Ambo baptismal names too, which many people today write in a way which makes them look more English, e.g. *Nangolo* > *Nangoloh* [360] (Mbenzi 24.3.1997). However, many people are against this practice, as they feel that African names should be kept as African names (Mbenzi 24.3.1997; Munyika 16.10.2000). Ambo names are also abbreviated, but this is not very common, as abbreviation means that these names would lose their meanings (Nambala 14.4.1997). However, there are examples of this phenomenon as well: *Andolaomumati* 'wish it had been a boy' > *Ando, Angula* 'morning' > *Angu, Katulipamwe* 'we were not together' > *Tuli, Ndeshimona* 'I found/got it' [361] > *Ndeshi, Okandeshi, Nuusiku* 'night' > *Nuusi, Pamwenatse* '(Lord is) with us' > *Natse* (Lehtonen 7.11.1994; Namuhuja 14.4.1997; Säynevirta 12.4.1997).[362] It has also become fashionable to form English-style nicknames from Ambo names, e.g. *Nangula* > *Nangy* (Mbenzi 24.3.1997). Basically, what Neethling (1994, p. 90) says about Xhosa nicknames can be applied to nicknames derived from Ambo names as well:

> Xhosa speakers, probably under the influence of Afrikaans and or English, feel the desire to diminuate first names and then partly according to the same system applicable to Afrikaans and English, i.e. through the suffixes -*i*, -*ie*, or -*y*. ... The phonological rule system of Xhosa is ignored.

Sometimes Ambo baptismal names are also translated into English and used as nicknames, e.g. *Ndahafa* 'I am happy' > *Happiness* (Kanana 19.9.2000).

Praise Names. Praise names and praise poetry are living traditions in the Ambo communities. It seems that many, but not all men, have a praise name (*edhina eitango*) today.[363] A praise name is typically given to a boy by his father (Amakali 10.10.2000; Nambala 14.4.1997). It is initially a short name, onto which the son adds new elements later in life (Mbenzi 24.3.1997; Nambala 14.4.1997). Sometimes praise names are given by other people as well, or created by the person himself. Women do not usually have praise names, except for some influential and famous women.[364] It seems that today, praise names are not so common among the intellectuals as they are among ordinary people. On the other hand, this tradition is alive among the children, who often recite these names at school, for example. (Munyika 16.10.2000.)

A personal praise consists of a short name and a longer poem that goes with it (Munyika 16.10.2000). A person who has a praise name must also be able to present his praise poem with style.[365] These praises are regarded as a special kind of poetry, as an "artistic thing" which requires special talent. Sometimes the presentation of a single poem could take hours. (Nambala 14.4.1997.) Praise names are often recited when people sit around the fire in the evening, or when they wrestle or play games. Sometimes the Ambo people arrange competitions for praise names too. It is generally thought that a good praise poem should be long, poetically well constructed and should flow nicely. (Munyika 16.10.2000.)

Often men also praise themselves when they are angry or in trouble, as they want to encourage themselves and gather their strength in this way. With praises men remind themselves and others whose sons they are and what kind of things they can do. They show that they are not afraid of the enemy. Some praises also exaggerate the achievements of the person, e.g. by claiming that he has killed many people, even if that were not the case. (Namuhuja 14.4.1997.) Praises are also used in war and in physical fights between two men (Munyika 16.10.2000). Occasionally, people may also be addressed by their praise names, even if this is not common (Mbenzi 24.3.1997). Mbenzi (Manuscript on Oshiwambo praise poetry, p. 31–32), describes the use of praise names in everyday life:

> Boys praise themselves when herding cattle especially when they participate in the throwing game known as "omakamunyole". ... Before a boy throws his stick he praises himself by reciting two or three lines of a praise poem. Boys also praise themselves for fun when they want to impress their peers. ... A boy who does not know his personal poem well is mocked at by other boys. Besides a man praises himself when he sneezes, coughs or when he stumbles over something.

Munyika (16.10.2000) pointed out that there are two ways of constructing a praise name by oneself. The first one is adopting the praise name of one's namesake. This is done especially by men who are named after famous people. Hence, the person learns the whole history of his namesake, which is combined in poetic form, which he must also be able to recite. Sometimes women also inherit praise names from their more famous namesakes. The other way is to construct one's own history by picking out highlights from one's life. For example, a cattle herder who once killed a lion alone when protecting his livestock will mention this event in his praise poem, and a freedom fighter may tell the whole history of his battles in his poem. These stories are then remembered. (Munyika 16.10.2000.)

Praise names typically refer to the good qualities of the person: his strength, his various achievements, life experiences, etc. (Namuhuja 14.4.1997). The Ambo informants used for this study gave a number of examples of these names, e.g. *Lyanampunda* 'big-bellied man', *Eshilikiti*[366] 'one in full armament, soldier' (Namuhuja 14.4.1997),

Kasindani 'winner', *Mutileni* 'be afraid of him' (Amakali 10.10.2000), *Kangwe Keenyala* 'little leopard with sharp nails' (Munyika 16.10.2000), *Kapenda* and *Pendapala* 'brave, be brave'[367] (Amaambo 4.3.1997). Mbenzi (Manuscript on Oshiwambo praise poetry, p. 3–4) gives several examples of whole personal praises. Let us take up one here:

Tatei, ongame omumati gwaShaalu	(O, Father, I am a boy of Shaalu
Nda nuka po nda fombuku	I am as nimble as a mouse
Omuntu olye nguno?	Who is this person?
Ongame Namutsegwaatilambudhi.	I am Namutsegwaatilambudhi.)

The name *Namutsegwaatilambudhi* means literally 'head that does not fear anything', and it is given to a dauntless person who always remains at the forefront in times of difficulties (Mbenzi, Manuscript on Oshiwambo praise poetry, p. 4).

The praise names of women are not usually associated with power and strength, but rather with beauty or cleverness, or with manipulative power (Munyika 16.10.2000).[368]

Collective Bynames: Patronyms and Surnames

Beside individual bynames, the Ambo people have collective bynames that indicate attachment to family or wider kin-group: patronyms and surnames.[369] Patronyms, which were also part of the traditional Ambo naming system, connect children with their fathers as well as children of the same father to each other. Surnames, on the other hand, typically connect the whole nuclear family, i.e. the parents and their children, together, and often the male relatives' families from the father's side as well, depending on how many generations ago the surname was adopted in the family and how many family members have decided to continue using it.

Although the first surnames were adopted in the 1950s, i.e. half a century ago, the surname system is not exclusive in Ambo society today. There are still old people, especially women, who carry their fathers' names as bynames and have never adopted hereditary surnames (Nashihanga 18.4.1997). In all official contexts, the patronyms of these people serve as surnames. The younger generation have surnames that they have almost exclusively inherited from their fathers. Hence, one may say that today there are two byname systems, the traditional patronymic system and a more recent surname system.

As was noted, the surname system has caused confusion among the Ambos, and some people have seen it as incompatible with the matrilineal Ambo culture. Above all, the surnames of married women have raised a lot of discussion. Today, the general custom is that women adopt their husbands' surnames (Amaambo 3.4.1997; Amakali 10.10.2000; Nashihanga 18.4.1997).[370] It has been pointed out that this system makes it difficult to recognise women by name, as they do not use the surnames of their own families after marriage (Munyika 16.10.2000).

For these reasons, many women today criticise the custom of adopting the husband's name in marriage (Nashihanga 18.4.1997). A number of liberated women have thus started to use hyphenated surnames, which consist of their original surname and the husband's surname, e.g. *Aune Shilongo-Hamunyela* (Amakali 10.10.2000; Mbenzi 24.3.1997; Namuhuja 14.4.1997), even if such names are sometimes regarded as problematic because of their length (Nambala 14.4.1997).[371] According to Lehtonen (2.4.1997), many of the Ambo women who use hyphenated surnames have been in exile abroad. Hence, this practice is obviously due to various foreign influences. Many professional women, e.g. doctors and nurses, have also chosen to use their maiden names only, in particular in Windhoek. Some women have also kept their own surnames because of the bureaucracy one faces in making changes in the Namibian identity card. Sometimes when the woman uses her maiden name, the husband's name is put in parenthesis after the woman's surname on official documents. For example, the name of Jefta Ihambo's wife is given as *Kristofina Ilonga (Ihambo)* on her identity card. (Ihambo 7.10.2000.)

Today, Ambo children also inherit their father's surname when the parents are not married. An unmarried woman may thus have several children who all have different surnames. Only if the father is unknown may the child receive the mother's surname.[372] (Mwaetako 14.10.2000.) This practice is obviously in line with the Ambo tradition that namegiving is normally done by the father. In the old times, the Ambo people had their fathers' real names as patronyms, and today they have their fathers' surnames.

Since independence, the Ambo people have not changed their surnames as frequently as they did during the war of independence, when a name change was often necessary for safety reasons. A change of name has also become subject to a fee in Namibia, which has prevented many people from changing their official names, even if they wished to do so (Amaambo 3.4.1997; Mwaetako 14.10.2000). Naturally, this has brought stability to the surname system. In everyday life, however, many people still use different names on different occasions (Kanana 19.9.2000).

Even if the surname system has become widespread in Ambo society, patronyms are still used in everyday life. A person who has a surname may occasionally be addressed by his or her patronym.[373] In such a case, the possessive concord is added to the name. Old women are commonly addressed by their patronyms, e.g. *gwaNangolo*. In general, being addressed by one's father's name is regarded as a special compliment among the Ambo people. Since independence, patronyms have also become increasingly popular in unofficial, or semi-official, contexts, for example in the newspapers. (Mbenzi 24.3.1997.) This phenomenon shows that the Ambos are not completely happy with the "foreign" surname system which they have, for various reasons, come to adopt.

The Usage of Names and Other Forms of Address

In an analysis of any anthroponymic system, it is important to look at the ways in which names and other forms of address are used in everyday life.[374] Which names are used in official contexts and which in unofficial contexts? In what kind of situations are names replaced by other forms of address, e.g. kinship terms? In African societies, as we have seen, many types of names are used by people in everyday life, but kinship terms are often used even more frequently (e.g. Brandström 1998, p. 149). Koopman (1987b, p. 136–140) gives an illustrative example of this by presenting an imaginary figure, Mr. Mkhize, a Zulu man who could be addressed in more than twenty different ways during a single day: with titles, kinship terms, his clan name, "Christian" name, his son's name, football name, etc.[375] In this subsection, we look at the Ambo naming system more closely from this perspective. This presentation concerns the usage of names and other forms of address particularly in Ondonga.

At home, Ndonga children call their parents *tate* 'father' and *meme* 'mother', not by their names. The parents also call each other, and also refer to each other, by these kinship terms.[376] (Amaambo 3.4.1997; Lehtonen 2.4.1997; Säynevirta 12.4.1997.) Occasionally, children may also address their mothers respectfully by their patronyms, e.g. *gwaNangolo*, or *Nangolonene* (*nene* 'big, great, older') (Mbenzi 24.3.1997).[377] Grandparents are called *kuku* 'grandmother' and *tatekulu* 'grandfather' by their grandchildren.[378] Also parents-in-law are addressed as *kuku* and *tatekulu* by their children-in-law. (Säynevirta 12.4.1997.) The mother's brother, who has an important role in the child's life, is also called *kuku* (Amaambo 3.4.1997; Tirronen 1986, p. 149; Säynevirta 12.4.1997). The father's brother may be called *tategona*, and the mother's sister *memegona* (Amaambo 3.4.1997). Other adults within the family are addressed by their kinship terms by the children, or simply as *tate* or *meme,* in the same way as adults outside the family. Old people are generally addressed as *kuku* and *tatekulu*, as well as many respected people, e.g. medical doctors.[379] The king, on the other hand, is always *tate*, not *tatekulu*. (Lehtonen 2.4.1997; Säynevirta 12.4.1997.) Tirronen (1986, p. 149, 226, 398) translates these basic kinship terms in his Ndonga–English Dictionary as follows:

meme	my/our mother[380]; form of addressing a married woman who is not very old
memegona	my mother's sister
tate	my/our father, mister
tategona	my/our father's brother or sister
kuku	my grandmother (previously also: my grandfather); my uncle (mother's brother); form of addressing to any old woman and one's mother's brother (an old man is usually addressed *tatekulu*)
mememweno	my mother-in-law
tatekulu	my mother's or my father's father; my paternal uncle; sir, mister
tatemweno	my father-in-law

Parents typically call their children by their African names. The African name which is used at home may be the birth name of the child or his or her Ambo baptismal name. Many kinds of nicknames are also used and frequently created, and they may change often too. (Amaambo 3.4.1997; Säynevirta 12.4.1997.) In practice, it is often the mother who decides which name is used at home: if she does not like the name the father has given, she may not use it. Often parents also call their children according to their order of birth: the first-born is called *osheeli*, the last-born *onkelo*,[381] and the ones between them are *omushakati* or *ontoyele/ ontowele*.[382] The birth order of children is very important in the Ambo culture, and often people ask about it, too. The grandparents may call their grandchildren by their Ambo names, but also as *omutekulu* or *okatekulu* 'grandchild'.[383] Children in the same family may call each other according to their birth order, but usually by their Ambo names or nicknames, in the same way as they call their friends. At school children use their official names given at baptism, which may be a European or biblical name or, more and more often, an Ambo name.[384] (Amaambo 3.4.1997; Lehtonen 2.4.1997; Säynevirta 12.4.1997.)

Namesakes almost never use each other's names. Instead, they call each other *mbushandje* 'my namesake'. The namesakes are also identified with each other in address: a person addresses the family members of his or her namesake in the same way as the namesake does, and he or she is addressed with the same kinship terms as the namesake by the relatives of the latter. Similarly, a child who is named after a grandparent, may be addressed as *kuku* or *tatekulu* by his or her brothers and sisters. (Mbenzi 24.3.1997; Säynevirta 12.4.1997.)

The practice of using kinship terms instead of personal names obviously has its roots in the traditional name avoidance custom of the Ambo people. Today, there are no religious ideas attached to this custom (Lehtonen 2.4.1997), but the old tradition is still reflected in the usage of personal names. The use of kinship terms also seems to serve an important social function. As Malan (1995, p. 18) stresses, the Ambo people use classificatory kinship terminology for address in order to demonstrate their kinship bond.

Adults who do not belong to the same family usually address each other as *tate/meme* + forename, or if the relationship is not very close or they want to show respect, as *tate/meme* + surname. The combination *tate/meme* + nickname is also possible, e.g. *meme Kanyeku*. It is also common to use titles with personal names, for example if the person in question is a doctor.[385] (Lehtonen 2.4.1997; Säynevirta 12.4.1997.) Men are typically addressed by their surnames, whereas with women this practice is not common (Namuhuja 14.4.1997).

Typically, it is the European name of the person that is used in official contexts, e.g. in the workplace, offices, schools, and in hospitals, whereas the African name is used primarily in the home environment. However, it depends on the person in question as to which name is most commonly used. Some people are known by their European names, some by their African ones, depending on what they want. (Mwaetako 11.10.2000.) Especially since independence, it has become increasingly popular to use African names in various "outside contexts" too, and many people have practically abandoned their European names.[386] A good example of this is Andimba Toivo ja Toivo, the leading SWAPO politician who was previously known as *Herman Toivo ja Toivo* (Munyika 16.10.2000); the name *Andimba* is based on the word *ondimba* 'hare' (Tirronen 1986, p. 258). The staff of the Onandjokwe hospital also use African names systematically when addressing each other. European names are especially used when in the company of Europeans who find the indigenous names difficult to pronounce.[387] (Säynevirta 12.4.1997.) Many types of nicknames are used among adults as well, and such names may become the most frequently used in normal communication. People are also addressed by the nicknames of their namesakes. (Lehtonen 2.4.1997; Mbenzi 24.3.1997.)

In Oukwanyama and Uukwambi, it is still a common custom to address women by their fathers' – i.e. not their own – clan names, e.g. *Mukwaanime < omukwaanime* 'member of the lion clan', and many women are better known by this name than by any other.[388] Among other Ambo groups, this practice is not so common, even if clans are still very important in the social life of the community. In Ondonga, their importance can particularly be seen at funerals and weddings, where clans are praised and people tell stories about them. Women, who have a central role in the clans of a matrilineal society, are experts in clan praises. (Mbenzi 24.3.1997; Namuhuja 14.4.1997; Säynevirta 12.4.1997.) In the church, collections are sometimes brought to the altar according to the clans of the people, and this is done imitating the sounds of the clan animals: lion, dog, sheep, ox, etc. (Lehtonen 2.4.1997). Today all Ambos, including young people, know which clan they belong to (Amaambo 3.4.1997).

Future Trends in Ambo Personal Naming

The personal nomenclature of the Ambo people has undergone a process which has led to fundamental changes in the Ambo naming system. The most significant of these are the adoption of biblical and European names, the practice of giving more than one "real" name to a person, the replacement of traditional name-giving ceremonies by the ceremony of baptism, and the adoption of surnames. In this process, many tendencies have been at work simultaneously, and often they have been competing with each other. On the one hand, there has been a strong tendency towards the Europeanisation of the naming system, and on the other hand, there has also been resistance to this development. The result, thus far, seems to be a naming system which consists of both African and European elements, with each of these elements having specific and separate functions. For example, the traditional Ambo namesake custom is retained, but it is often used for giving European and biblical baptismal names. Similarly, the European surname system has been adopted, but it is used for preserving traditional Ambo names. The practice of giving names according to the father's feelings and events which take place at the time of birth is retained, but it is used for giving baptismal names.

174

Rev. Teofilus Nelumbu baptises children in the Lutheran Emmanuel church in Windhoek. Pirre Saario / The Finnish Evangelical Lutheran Mission. 2003.

One can still find a number of different trends in this system, and it is difficult to predict which of them will be the major ones in the future. However, it may be useful to look at the naming practices of the Ambo people in the capital city of Windhoek if one wants to predict what could be expected to happen in the north too, where new trends and fashions typically arrive much later.[389] Let us look at three issues more carefully here: 1. The name-giver, 2. African, European and biblical names, and 3. Surnames and patronyms.

The Name-giver. All the Ambos interviewed for this study stressed that the father still has a central role in name-giving in Ambo society (e.g. Amaambo 3.4.1997; Amkongo 14.4.1997; Amushila 11.10.2000; Kanana 19.9.2000; Mbenzi 24.3.1997; Mwaetako 14.10.2000; Nashihanga 18.4.1997). However, this practice seems to be changing gradually. Since

Namibian independence, many parents have decided to choose names for their children together. This is especially the case among the Ambos living in Windhoek. The Ambos who are in favour of this practice, typically argue it as regards equality of men and women, which is emphasised in the constitution of the republic of Namibia. (Amaambo 3.4.1997; Ihambo 7.10.2000; Kanana 19.9.2000.) Ihambo (7.10.2000) said that often the husband chooses the name for the first-born, the wife for the second-born, and so on, or if the child is given two names, the husband may choose the one and the woman the other one. Kanana (19.9.2000) also pointed out that parents who understand human rights and are "liberated and free", name their children together, while the ones who are traditional, expect the father to name the child.

On the other hand, some Ambos do not see name-giving as an equality issue but as a social act that is very important to the child: by giving the name, the father announces publicly that he is responsible for his child (Nambala 14.4.1997). Naturally, these choices are always made at the individual level. Munyika (16.10.2000) stated that naming the child together with one's spouse is typical among the educated Ambos. According to him, the tradition of the grandfather naming the first-born child is also disappearing.

Amakali (10.10.2000) felt that the new practice of naming children together can also be explained by referring to the influence of other nations. Many Namibians who were in exile during the war or have studied abroad have been influenced by foreign naming practices. It may also be important that among other ethnic groups in Namibia, e.g. the Hereros and the Damaras, the mother can also give a name to the child (Mwaetako 14.10.2000; Otto 1985, p. 128). The fact that some Ambo men have started to give birth names to their children instead of the midwives (Amkongo 14.4.1997), also shows that the roles of men and women in name-giving are not clear in Ambo society today. In any case, there will most probably be more and more parents who want to name their children together. However, this change seems to be taking place fairly slowly in Ambo society (Amakali 10.10.2000).

African, European and Biblical Names. There are two current trends in the baptismal names of the Ambo people: the Africanisation of names on the one hand, and the increasing popularity of English names on the other. The first trend is reflected in the increasing number of parents, or fathers, who give only Ambo baptismal names to their children (Kanana 19.9.2000; Mbenzi 24.3.1997; Munyika 16.10.2000). As was noted, African names have been fashionable particularly since independence, and many Ambos who were previously known by their European or biblical names prefer to use their Ambo baptismal names in everyday life (Amkongo 14.4.1997; Mbenzi 24.3.1997; Munyika 16.10.2000; Nambala 14.4.1997; Nashihanga 18.4.1997). However, because of the namesake custom, which has remained important in the Ambo naming system, many Ambos think that the most popular European and biblical names will remain popular in the future too (e.g. Mbenzi 24.3.1997; Munyika 16.10.2000; Nambala 14.4.1997). Malua (19.9.2000) put this clearly:

It [the popularity of European and biblical names] will continue so long because some people want to give a name after somebody with a European name or biblical name. Just because of that. Not because he means that this is a Christian name, not because of that.[390]

On the other hand, the practice of choosing the African name of the namesake for the child (Nambala 14.4.1997), as well as that of translating the foreign name of a namesake into an Ambo name (Kanana 19.9.2000), would obviously decrease the number of European and biblical baptismal names. Interestingly, Munyika (16.10.2000) predicted that there may also come a stage when people would generally switch from the name *Selma* to *Gwanandjokwe*, for example, i.e. from the European name to the Ambo nickname that is generally attached to it. In general, Munyika (16.10.2000) believes that people in the Ambo area are moving away from European names to African names.[391]

The second trend, i.e. the popularity of English names, is reflected in many ways in daily name usage, even if English names are not yet popular as baptismal names in the Ambo area (Nashihanga 18.4.1997). According to Ihambo (7.10.2000), people in the north tend to stick to tradition, and therefore sometimes refuse to accept English names as baptismal names.[392] However, in everyday life many people frequently use English forms of biblical and European names, and it seems that this custom will continue. It is most probable that English names will become more popular as baptismal names too.[393] The baptismal registers of the Elim, Okahao and Oshigambo congregations over the years 1998–2000 indeed show that English names have become slightly more popular as baptismal names, even if they still form a clear minority among the names given at Lutheran baptisms. In these registers (1998–2000), one can find names such as:

> *Benson, Betty, Bobby, Brawe (< brave?), Charles, Colin, Daphne, Elton, Fellou (<fellow), Florence, George, Goodwill, Grace, Happy, Jackson, Janet, Johnson, Lucky, Marion, Memory, Morning, Peace-Maker, Pelican, Re Joyce (< rejoice), Remember, Rorlence (< Lawrence?), Robyson, Rose, Roseemary, Rosmarry, Smith, Stanley, Stanly, Sunday, Susan, Thank you, Tomson, Trevor, Vision.*

Name-giving trends of the Ambo people living in Windhoek also seem to indicate the increasing popularity of English names among the Ambos: English baptismal names have become very popular there in recent years (Ihambo 7.10.2000). Jefta Ihambo (7.10.2000), pastor of the Windhoek City Congregation of ELCIN, gave *Samuel Grace Hero* as a typical example of a contemporary baptismal name for an Ambo child.[394] According to him, Ambo children in Windhoek are usually given two or three names, of which one is an English name. Also, when children are named after those who have biblical names, these names are often bestowed in their English forms: if the namesake is *Markus,* the child is named *Mark*; if *Paulus, Paul,* and so on. Ihambo (7.10.2000) stated that at present Ambo names were popular, but that "English is coming fast" because of the popularity of the English language:

Finnish names such as Eino can be seen all over the Ambo area. Minna Saarelma-Maunumaa. 1997.

> The English language is very important in our society now. It is the official language. People want everything to be in English, they don't emphasise tradition anymore. People think that if you know English, you are a better person in the society. Westernisation plays more important role now, not Africanisation. ... Today's children will forget their mother tongue, but they speak fluent English. You can meet 18-year-old youngsters who cannot speak their mother tongue properly. ... Our mother tongue and culture will be forgotten.

Another trend, which can be seen in the name-giving of the Ambo people in Windhoek but not that clearly in the Ambo area in northern Namibia, is the borrowing of names from other indigenous groups, in particular the Hereros. Just as in South Africa (Suzman 1994, p. 270), there are signs of a weakening of ethnic boundaries in the personal naming of the Namibians living in urban environments. For example, the Herero name *Mbaparuka* 'I have been saved' has become popular among the Ambos in Windhoek (Ihambo 7.10.2000). Ihambo (7.10.2000) explained this by quoting the fact that today ethnic groups communicate with each other much more frequently than during the apartheid era. Mixed marriages are also common. Ihambo said that previously it was easy to judge by name if the person was a Herero, a Nama, an Ambo, etc., whereas today this is often impossible. The contacts between the Ambo area and Windhoek, as well as other places in the south, have also become more frequent since independence. Because of all this, one may assume that the personal nomenclature of the Ambo people living in the north will be more influenced by the names of other Namibian groups too.

What is going to happen to Finnish, German and Afrikaans names? Clearly, these non-English European names are not very fashionable among the Ambo people today, and their popularity can be expected to decline. However, these names will most probably remain in use as baptismal names for quite a long time, primarily because of the namesake custom. In any case, it seems very unlikely that there will come a time when the Ambo people have African names only. As Amaambo (3.4.1997) pointed out, there is also the "spirit of internationalism" in Namibia, which will influence personal naming in the Ambo area in the future too.[395]

Surnames and Patronyms. There are also two trends with regard to surnames in Ambo society. On the one hand, surnames have become acceptable, and most probably also will become more popular among the Ambo people (Namuhuja 14.4.1997). On the other hand, many people criticise the surname system as being incompatible with Ambo culture (Nambala 14.4.1997) and as a foreign system which was imposed on them by the Europeans (Namuhuja 14.4.1997). Some Ambos have also started to use patronyms again, at least in some contexts (Mbenzi 24.3.1997). However, it is difficult to predict what the future will look like in this respect. If Ambo baptismal names become more popular, it would be natural to use them for forming African patronyms too and thereby return to the traditional patronymic system.

It seems that there are many and varied opinions on this matter among the Ambo people, and it is most likely that the surname practice will be varied as well. Most probably, the majority of the Ambos will continue using surnames, as this is an international custom in modern societies today. However, some traditionalists may choose to use patronyms. Similarly, some married women might prefer to use their husbands' surnames, some may want to keep their maiden names, some may adopt hyphenated surnames, and some might turn back to patronyms. Nashihanga (18.4.1997) predicted that the number of women who will want to retain their maiden names will grow in the future. Munyika (16.10.2000) also pointed out that "these things are changing rapidly" because of the liberation of women, and that hyphenated names in particular have become common lately.

The popularity of the English language is also reflected in Ambo surnames, which many people today write in a way which makes them look more English, e.g. *Ndaitwa* > *Ndaithwah* or *Shamena* > *Shamenah* (Lehtonen 2.4.1997; Munyika 16.10.2000). If English continues to be fashionable in Namibia, as seems likely, this trend might also be significant in the future.

Altogether, what De Klerk and Bosch (1996, p. 167) say about naming trends in South Africa, could also be said about personal naming in Namibia:

> [I]n a post-apartheid South Africa, which offers increasing opportunity for interaction across cultures and languages, naming patterns are in a process of change, the directions of which are only beginning to be determined.

NOTES

185 Obviously, *the traditional Ambo naming system* is a theoretical generalisation in the same way as *the traditional Ambo culture* is. Thus, if one wants to be precise, one should talk about many Ambo naming systems instead of one: the Ndonga anthroponymic system, the Kwanyama anthroponymic system, etc. However, as these systems resemble each other to a great extent, they are analysed together in this study.

186 The missionaries often remind readers in their texts that not everything of the traditional culture was revealed to them by the Ambos (Martti Rautanen, lecture 29.11.1903, Kirjekopiokirja 25.11.1903–25.2.1904, Hp:110, FMSA; August Pettinen's diary 5.8.1889, Hp:91, FMSA).

187 The Ambo terms that Hukka (1954, p. 103) mentions are written here according to the latest Ndonga orthography. Thus *omuenjo* has become *omwenyo* and *ezina edhina*.

188 In this study, we use the term *real name* to refer to the permanent, "true" name of the person, which was given to an Ambo child by his or her father.

189 Name avoidance was also common with wild animals. For example, on the way to acquire iron, the Ambos were not allowed to call wild animals by their correct names. Thus, the lion was called "bush-pig", etc. If someone broke these rules, he was expected to be eaten by a lion or to get lost in the woods. This belief was based on the principle that cause is similar to effect. (Hiltunen 1993, p. 62, 72.)

190 The traditional distinction between witchcraft and sorcery is that witchcraft is inherent and operates directly, while sorcery is taught and often bought and it requires rites. Typically, witchcraft is also performed unconsciously, whereas the sorcerer works consciously. (Hiltunen 1986, p. 23.)

191 Hiltunen (1986, p. 139) tells that the cursers often softened towards those who had had misfortune and were thus willing to withdraw their curses.

192 Närhi (1929, p. 18) points out that if the birth took place at home and the mother or child happened to die during labour, the husband would be regarded as responsible for the death. If such a misfortune took place while the mother was amongst her own family, no one would be accused for that. Rautanen (in Dammann 1972/73, p. 44) also mentions that if the woman had no relatives, the birth could take place at the house of a close neighbour.

193 In the case of a first-born child, the grandmother or the great grand-aunt was expected to be present as well (Hahn 1928, p. 25).

194 Tönjes (1996, p. 138) tells that there were no midwives in Oukwanyama: the women simply helped each other or gave birth without any assistance. Estermann (1976, p. 58) states that Kwanyama women giving birth were assisted by "one or more old women, usually close relatives, who serve as midwives".

195 In the Ambo area, frogs were collected as supplementary food at the beginning of the rainy season. They were caught by males, and especially by young boys. (Siiskonen 1990, p. 57.)

196 Other forms for this term in the literature are *epiiso* (e.g. Hopeasalmi 1946, p. 74; Mustakallio 1903, p. 80) and *epitho* (e.g. Hahn 1928, p. 25). The Ndonga–English Dictionary (Tirronen 1986, p. 342) translates *epiitho* as 'passing, the first time to come out after a childbirth'. According to Vedder (1973, p. 69), this ceremony took place three days after the delivery, according to Mustakallio (1903, p. 80) on the fourth or fifth day. Hahn (1928, p. 25) mentions the fourth day, and Hopeasalmi (1946, p. 86–87) and Rautanen (in Dammann 1972/73, p. 46) agree on the sixth or eighth day.

197 Sckär (1932, p. 58–59, UEMA) tells that among the Kwanyamas, the father showed the future jobs to his son and the mother to her daughter.

198 Tönjes (1996, p. 139) describes the name-giving ceremony as follows: "Name-giving also involves the act of *okukulula*. The soft fluff on the infant's head is shaved off and its body is rubbed with the *olukula* ... On this occasion, the child

180

also receives its first adornment – a necklace of dark glass beads. Once these formalities have been completed, the mother is permitted to leave the homestead with the new-born child and may again move about outside."

199 The Ndonga–English Dictionary (Tirronen 1986, p. 194) translates *eluko* as 'naming; denomination', the verb *luka* means 'name, give a name, call; nominate' and *lukila* 'name after'; hence *elukilo* means 'naming after', but also 'setting a trap' or 'stretching a bowstring'.

200 Nambala (14.4.1997) used the English terms *lasting name* and *public name* for the real name given by the father.

201 On the other hand, Munyika (16.10.2000) assumes that the midwives also gave a name to the child in any case, even if the father happened to be present.

202 The description of Tuomas Uukunde (ELC, p. 81–81) is not perfectly clear, but it seems that he refers to the father and the neighbour with the word *visitors* here.

203 Savola (1924, p. 79) also points out that the actual name-giving took place very early in the morning, before sunrise. According to him, this happened about eight days after birth.

204 Dammann's and Tirronen's (1975, p. 143–144) report of *eluko* in Ondonga – which took place one month after birth – is consistent with Jairus Uuanga's and Gideon Iitula's stories: "Wenn die Sonne untergeht, geht der Mann, um in der Hütte der Frau, die das zu benennende Kind hat, zu schlafen. Wenn sie schlafen gehen, rühren sie einander nicht an, nein. Aber wenn die Morgenröte anbricht, geht der Mann zwischen die Beine der Frau, als ob sie Geschlechtsverkehr ausüben. Aber sie rühren sich nur an, begatten einander jedoch nicht. Wenn sie einander so berührt haben, stehen sie gleichzeitig auf. Der Mann reißt das Kind an sich, führt es durch seine Beine, wirft es der Mutter zu und sagt: "Nimm mein Kind!" Und die Mutter ergreift es. Das Bier der Namensgebung und den Brei essen sie in der Schlafhütte, der Mann mit seiner Frau. ... Wenn einige Tage verstrichen sind, geht der Mann zu demjenigen, nach dem er das Kind nannte, und sie gehen zu dem Salbgefäß aus Schildpatt. Sie bestreichen einander die Stirn mit der Salbe. Wenn er (der Vater) dann am Nachmittag nach Hause kommt, ruft er die Frau und sagt: "Bringe Nandago!" (Falls das Kind diesen Namen erhalten hat.)"

205 The Ndonga–English Dictionary (Tirronen 1986, p. 496) translates *eyokolo* as 'poking out of fire, removing from the kiln', and the verb *yokola* as 'take or poke out of the fire, remove from the kiln (clay pots after baking); give the first present to one's namesake; begin to move, get a move on, get going, run'.

206 Tirronen (1986, p. 167) translates *ekwato* as 'catching, grasping, seizing, arresting'.

207 Tirronen (1986, p. 295) explains *oonkutuwa* as 'two projecting leather strips on the back of the belt of a married man as a sign that he has erected his own homestead; wrinkles on the skin that have not been properly rubbed'.

208 Mustakallio (1903, p. 80) also mentions that a child born at midnight was often given a temporary name meaning midnight, a child born at dawn a name meaning dawn, and so on.

209 For more information on Ambo customs concerning twin birth see e.g. Dammann 1972/3, p. 46; Dammann & Tirronen 1975, p. 140–142; Estermann 1976, p. 59–60; Hahn 1928, p. 26; August Pettinen's diary 22.10.1889, Hp:91, FMSA; Martti Rautanen to the mission director 18.11.1889, Eac:7, FMSA; Tönjes 1996, p. 140–141.

210 Estermann (1976, p. 61) also says that in Oukwanyama, twins were "obligatorily given names of members of the royal family".

211 The Ndonga word *oshimbondi* (pl. *iimbondi*) means 'any herbaceous plant (not grass), herb, weed' (Tirronen 1986, p. 217). The mother had obviously been treated medically with herbs because of the problems in her previous pregnancies.

212 When Savola mentions names which have no linguistic meaning, he obviously refers to names which have lost their semantic transparency in the course of time.

213 These names are Kwanyama names; *Haufiku* 'night', for example, would be *Uusiku* in Ndonga.

181

214 See also Albin Savola's undated manuscript "Muutamia piirteitä muinais-israelilaisten ja nykyisten ondongalaisten olojen, lakien ja tapojen yhtäläisyyksistä" (p. 9, Hp:125, FMSA).

215 Vedder's (1973, p. 69) description of the namesake relationship among the Ambos is fairly similar: "Es wurde der Name eines Freundes vom Vater bevorzugt. Dieser Freund war damit in gewissem Sinn Pate geworden. Er hatte dem Kinde später kleine Geschenke zu machen und ein wachsames Auge über es zu halten."

216 Pentti (1959, p. 36) even says that the namesake relationship was "a holy matter" to the Ambo people, and practically more important than kinship.

217 Tönjes (1996, p. 139) writes about a naming ceremony which took place eight days after birth, and he does not mention any other name-giving ceremonies in his book. Contrary to all other sources, he mentions "parents", not the father, when talking about the choice of name.

218 The name meaning 'flood' was common all over the Ambo area. Here is one explanation for such a name in Uukwambi: "Den Namen Egelu, d. h. Sündflut, erhielt er bei seiner Geburt, weil zur Zeit derselben der Kunenefluß über seine Ufer getreten war und alles überschwemmt hatte, so daß die Krokodile und Seekühe auf dem Lande umhergingen und die Leute auf den Bäumen wohnten, bis sich das Wasser wieder verlaufen hatte." (Erstlinge von den Arbeitsgebieten der rheinischen Mission 1899, p. 39.)

219 Usually these names are written as one word: *Ndahafa, Ndatila,* etc. The book "Aus den Anfangstagen der Ovambomission" (1904, p. 32) also says that the Ambos typically gave names that expressed their present emotions: "Wenn den Ovambo Kinder geboren werden, so geben sie denselben wohl Namen, die aussprechen, was gerade um diese Zeit ihr Hertz bewegt. Sie nennen die Kinder etwa: Nda hafa, Ich freue mich, oder Ndi li po, Ich bin da, und ähnlich."

220 Maybe the husband thought that there were too many people sharing the food in his house.

221 Vedder (1973, p. 69) also claims that Ambo boys and girls had similar names: "Durch Klang oder Form voneinander unterscheidbare Namen für Knaben und Mädchen waren unbekannt."

222 According to Tirronen (1986, p. 270), *Nehoya* is the name of a single boy in a family of girls or of a single girl in a family of boys.

223 The correct Kwanyama forms for these names would be *Haimbodi* and *Naimbodi*.

224 Syphilis (*endongo*) was seen as an honourable disease among the Ambo people, and this was reflected in names as well. In Ondonga, both girls and boys could receive either *Nendongo* or *Iindongo* as their name in such a case. (A.G., ELC, p. 1117.)

225 Wulfhorst (25 Jahre unserer Ovambo-Arbeit, in: Rückblick auf 25 Jahre Ovambomission, 1917; 1966, p. 119, C/i:20, UEMA) says that after the severe famine of 1915, there were people all over the Ambo area who had the name *Endjala* 'famine'.

226 Ennis (1945, p. 1) suggests that the word *sando* may be of Portuguese origin, but that if so, "the word entered the language so long ago that no one now recognises its derivation".

227 On the other hand, there is also a strong namesake custom among the Kavangos, who are closely connected with the Ambo groups as well. Fisch (1979, p. 28–30) describes this custom as follows: "Das erstgeborene Kind wird in der Regel nach den Großeltern väterlicherseits benannt, für nachfolgende Kinder wählt man den Namen einer Person, welche der Vater des Kindes als "kleiner Vater" oder "kleine Mutter" anredet. ... Sofort nach der Namensgebung wird die Person, nach welcher das Kind benannt wurde, benachrichtigt, daß sie einen Namensvetter (*mbusa* in Kw, *mbusha* in Gc un Mb) bekommen hat. Dies bedeutet eine große Ehre und Freude und gibt die Gewißheit, daß der Name des Paten (und die Person selbst) nach dem Tode nicht schnell vergessen wird." Fisch (1979, p. 30) also reports that the namesakes give each other presents, the main present being an ox which the older namesake has to give to his or her young namesake. The giving of this ox

was called *kugusa edina* 'giving of the name'. The namesakes also helped each other in a number of ways during their lives.

228 In any case, it is justified to say, as Väänänen (Hän tarvitsee parhaimman uskonnon: Esitys Amboneekerien uskonnosta, undated manuscript from the 1920s/1930s, p. 16, Hp:XXXIX, FMSA) does, that Ambo children were given names that referred to circumstances, events and people.

229 Even today, the idea of changing one's name seems to be strange to the Ambos. Malua (19.9. 2000) put this clearly: "No, that is not happening in the names the fathers have given. That name remains forever."

230 Tirronen (1986, p. 22) translates *edhina lyoponto* as 'nickname, by-name'. The word *ponto* means 'on the side' (Tirronen 1986, p. 350). Hence *edhina lyoponto* could be translated literally as 'byname' or 'additional name'. The term *oshilukadhina* is translated as 'pet name; nickname'; the verb *luka* means 'name, give a name, call', and *edhina* is 'name' (Tirronen 1986, p. 22, 194).

231 In Ndonga, *iifudho* means 'breaths' (English–Ndonga Dictionary 1996, p. 31–32).

232 The Finnish missionary Birger Eriksson was the first moderator of the Evangelical Lutheran Ovambo-Kavango Church, which was registered in 1957. He arrived in the Ambo area in 1937. (Peltola 1958, p. 242–243, 269.) August Wulfhorst (Haschipala. Bilder aus dem Leben der Heiden in Ovamboland, p. 141, Vorträge und Aufsätze zur Ovambo-Mission 1910–1933. C/k:22, UEMA) also says that he was called *Aschipalla* (*Ashipala*) by the Ambo people, and Jooseppi Mustakallio (1903, p. 26) was given the name *Oshipala*.

233 Williams (1994, p. 22) claims that *Nakambale* means literally 'the person with the hat', and that when Rautanen became old the name was changed into *Nakambalekanene*, meaning 'the person with a big hat'. Aini Aarni (Muistikuva Martti Rautasesta, Martti Rautasta koskevat muistelmat kerätty 1958, Hp:110, FMSA) tells that Rautanen was also called *Egonga lja tsa muule*, 'an assegai which has sunk deep', by the Ambo people, because he knew the names of the trees and birds and many other things in the Ambo area.

234 Tirronen gives a number of typical names for oxen in his Ndonga–English Dictionary (1986), but he mentions neither *Sindongo* nor *Kasese*. It seems reasonable to assume that *Sindongo* was a name for a dark ox and Kasese for a light one.

235 Obadja Iihuhua (ELC, p. 1574) explains these names by saying that *Alukonga* is quick and *Šilandula* is happy. The verb *konga* means 'seek, search for', and *shilandula* means 'follow it' (Tirronen 1986, p. 145, 177).

236 According to Gunner and Gwala (1994, p. 1), *izibongo,* which is a plural noun, can be translated as 'praises', 'praise names' or 'praise poems'.

237 Rautanen must refer to King Kambonde kaNankwaya here, the ruler of Ondonga in 1874–1883 (Nambala 1994, p. 36). Rautanen (to the mission director 23.4.1881, Eac:5, FMSA) says that King Kambonde was not very popular among his subjects, and presumes that had the people dared, they would rather have composed libellous poems about him.

238 On the other hand, Estermann (1976, p. 172–174) cites a praise poem exalting the glorious deeds of King Mandume of Oukwanyama, which indeed mentions the name *Mandume*.

239 The years of reign are taken here from Nambala 1994, p. 36–38. The name forms that Nambala uses are slightly different: *Iipumbu yaTshilongo, Nehale lyaMpinga, Shaanika shaNashilongo.*

240 Nambala (1994, p. 38) states that Shaanika shaNashilongo reigned in Ongandjera, not Uukwaluudhi, during these years.

241 Dammann and Tirronen (1975, p. 206) call these poems *Selbstpreise* in German. Their examples were all recorded in the 1950s.

242 Dammann and Tirronen (1975, p. 207, 212) translate these names into German as 'ich des Klatchens' (*Ndiwangu*), 'kann nicht laufen' (*Kaatondoka*) and 'Schütze' (*Shuumbwa*).

243 Many Finnish sources (e.g. Savola 1924, p. 80) use the word *sukunimi* 'surname, family name' when talking about Ambo patronyms. Savola (1924, p. 76) points out that even if Ambo children got their "family name" from the father's side, the father – unlike the mother – was not regarded as a relative.

244 See Tirronen (1977, p. 43–46) for the use of the possessive concord in Ndonga.

245 The Kavangos, who are closely related to the Ambo groups, have this tradition. Both men and women are called after their first-born child, e.g. *Shapirama* 'father of *Pirama*' or *Nanankali* 'mother of *Nankali*'. Many Kavangos are also generally known by this name. (Fisch 1979, p. 37.) Teknonyms are also used among the Hereros in Namibia (Otto 1985, p. 130). They are also common in other southern African societies. Among the Zulus, for example, this practice is more common than patronymy (Koopman 1987b, p. 146).

246 When Petrus Amakali (10.10.2000) was asked why the fathers traditionally name the children in the Ambo area, he said simply: "It is the tradition. The father is the boss of the family." Indeed, the father was the head of the homestead, and thus he had a certain authority over his wives and children (Eirola 1992, p. 41). Hjort af Ornäs (1987, p. 29–30) also points out that in Oukwanyama, the role of the father was by no means marginal in his child's life. For example, the father had an important role in his daughter's initiation ceremony, and the wedding ox was brought to the father, not to the maternal uncle of the bride.

247 Kalle Koivu (Ambomaalla: Uukuambissa, Koko heimoa koskevia taikurien johtamia juhlamenoja pakanuuden aikana, information collected over the years 1909–1917, p. 61, Hp:34, FMSA) says that even if the people in Uukwambi inherited clan names from the maternal side, only the name given by the father and the father's name, which was used as a surname, were in everyday usage.

248 According to Tirronen (1986, p. 240), *mwene gwiita* means 'king'. An exact translation could be 'leader of the military forces', as *mwene* means 'possessor, owner, master, boss, leader', and *iita* is 'war, warfare; military forces' (Tirronen 1986, p. 240, 391).

249 Some sources (e.g. Haahti 1913, p. 158) also write this name as *Eeva Maria*, and some others as *Eeva-Maria* (e.g. Suomalaista raivaustyötä Afrikan erämaassa 1945, p. 18).

250 The Ambo names mentioned here (*Iipinge, Iithoko, Amutenya* and *Nangolo*) are patronyms, not names given at baptism.

251 Piirainen (to the mission director 15.6.1869, Eac:3, FMSA) tells of a baptism ceremony in the Herero area in which the baptised received names such as *Edvard, Anders, Rosalia, Cornelius, Gerta, Johannes, Asser, Minette, Efraim, Isak, Simeon, Samuel, Meta, Hulda, Ruben, Zépora, Mathilda Sofia, Lena, Sofia Johanna, Ragel* and *Elisabet*. The Finnish mission magazine Suomen Lähetyssanomia (Pakanalasten kaste Valaskalalahdella 1891, Lisälehti, p. 62) also tells of German missionaries in South West Africa who in the late 19th century baptised converts with names such as *Nikoline, Sarah Mathilda, Frits* and *Traugott*.

252 In this study, we use the term *baptismal name*, not *Christian name*, for names given at the ceremony of baptism in the Ambo area. The reason for this is that in Africa, *Christian name* is often understood to refer to non-African names only – to biblical and European names – whereas in the Ambo area, many of the names given at baptisms are Ambo names which often have Christian meanings too. A good example of the use of *Christian name* in Africa can be found in Moyo's (1996, p. 13) statement on personal names in Malawi: "Schoolgoers would have two names: an African name for the home and an English or Christian name for use at school." Moyo (1996, p. 13) even sees *English name* and *Christian name* as synonymous: "converts to the new faith ... felt strongly attracted to the acquisition of English or Christian names as they commonly came to be known". Koopman (1986, p. 22–23) has also analysed the difficulties regarding the use of the term *Christian name* in Africa.

253 Some foster children of Finnish missionaries were baptised already before these first public baptisms in the Ambo area. Weikkolin's foster daughter was baptised in 1881

and received the name *Anna Maria* (K.A. Weikkolin to the mission director 27.10.1881, Eac:5, FMSA), and Piirainen's foster daughter was given the name *Emma Mathilda* in 1882 (A. Piirainen to the mission director 23.1.1882, Eac:5, FMSA).

254   One gets the impression from Peltola (1958, p. 83–84) and Nambala (1994, p. 82) that the African names here – *Iimene, Nangolo, Shikongo, Angula, Negonya* and *Nangombe* – are all patronyms. However, Reijonen (1883, p. 71) claims that they were the former names of these baptised men.

255   One of the first Ambo Christians, Gustaw (or *Gustav*), who was baptised in the Herero area, visited king Kambonde in 1882 in order to find out what he thought about Ambo Christians. When the king heard the new name of this convert, he said: "Do not talk about new names to me, do not talk about the Word to me. We are Ndongas, we have old customs, we have our parents' customs. Are you mad?". (K.A. Weikkolin, Report for January–June 1882, Eac:5, FMSA.)

256   In the case of children, the father chose the name, which was in accordance with the Ambo tradition (Pentti 1959, p. 35–36).

257   The name *Hellevi* is based on the Finnish woman's name *Hellä* 'tender, loving', which can also be seen as a hypocoristic form of *Helena* (Vilkuna 1993, p. 75).

258   Hukka (2.3.2000), who worked as a pastor in the Elim congregation in Uukwambi in the late 1940s, said that the converts normally had names with them when they came to be baptised, and as they were mainly biblical ones, they very seldom caused any problems.

259   Namuhuja (14.4.1997) said that often when a father came to baptise his child, the pastor simply gave him a list of European and biblical names from which he could choose a suitable name.

260   *Petäjä* and *Pennanen* are both surnames of Finnish missionaries (Peltola 1958, p. 263, 268).

261   The German missionaries in the Herero area also baptised people with more than one name at the end of the 19th century. Names such as *Josefiina Nathalia* (Yrjö Roiha to the mission director 28.2.1883, Eac:6, FMSA) or *Amalia Maria* (Tärkeä kaste Hereromaalla 1891, p. 182) were fairly common.

262   *Wilhelm* is an old Germanic name which includes the semantic elements 'will' and 'helmet', and the Finnish man's name *Väinö* is derived from the name of the main character in the Finnish national epic Kalevala, *Väinämöinen* (Vilkuna 1993, p. 186, 189).

263   The German missionaries in South West Africa also pointed out that not all Hereros who had a biblical name were Christians: "Das sollte doch jeder Ansiedler wissen, daß die Mission es nicht verhindern kann, daß auch heidnische Eingeborene sich alle möglichen biblischen Namen von Patriarchen und Propheten beilegen, und daß die Weisen selbst das oftmals unterstützen, weil sie nicht imstande sind, den ursprünglichen Herero- oder Nama-Namen auszusprechen. Deshalb ist es verkehrt, jeden, der z. B. den Namen Paulus trägt, für einen Christen zu halten und daran abfällige Bemerkungen zu knüpfen." (Haussleiter 1906, p. 18.) Perheentupa (1923, p. 13) also says that the Ambos were often ashamed of their traditional names. However, it is also possible that in some cases, the missionaries misinterpreted the traditional name avoidance custom as shame.

264   German names were mainly adopted from the German missionaries in Oukwanyama. However, they were also imported into the Ambo area from the Herero area, where many Ambos were baptised by Rhenish missionaries. For example, Weikkolin (Report for April, May and June 1884, Eac:6, FMSA) tells of three Ambo men who were baptised in Omaruru with the names *Albert*, *Fritz* and *Herman*.

265   The Catholic priests who worked in the Ambo area were mainly from Germany, but also from the Netherlands (Amushila 11.10.2000).

266   Amaambo (3.4.1997) himself named his daughter *Lahja* after his English teacher Lahja Lehtonen, because she was a very good teacher. It was also important to Amaambo that the Finnish name *Lahja* means 'gift'.

267 Weikkolin (to the mission director 15.2.1883, Eac:6, FMSA) assumes that self-ishness may play a role in such namesake relationships, but that they were also based on love.

268 Oskari Tylväs was a Finnish missionary who worked in the Ambo area during the years 1902–1929 (Peltola 1958, p. 262).

269 Surnames may be given as first names in the Afrikaans naming system as well (De Stadler 1990, p. 378). However, it would be mere speculation to see the use of European surnames as baptismal names in the Ambo area as the result of this influence.

270 Lehtonen (7.11.1994) told of an Ambo woman who wanted to become a name-sake of two Finnish missionaries, Anna-Liisa Sorsa and Ulla Nenonen. She adopted the name *Ulla Sorsa* at baptism.

271 Lehtonen (2.4.1997) told of an Ambo boy who was named *Esa* after the mission-ary Hanna Porola's brother. However, it was Hanna Porola who was regarded as the namesake of the child.

272 Pentti (1959, p. 36) gives a good example of this. If a woman named *Anna* has a daughter whose name is *Maria*, and a woman named *Maria* has a daughter named *Anna*, these two women can laugh and say that they have given birth to each other. Lehtonen's (2.4.1997) story of her namesake's wedding is also illustrative. When Lehtonen went to the wedding place, the other guests were delighted and said: "The bride has arrived!"

273 Hukka (1954, p. 83) also tells of an Ambo girl who was regularly called *felani* (< *Fräulein*) in her family, because she was the namesake of a missionary.

274 Holopainen (1993, p. 136) explains how he became a "son-in-law" in Bishop Leonard Auala's family: the eldest daughter of Bishop Aula named her child after Holopainen's wife Eevaliisa, and thus Holopainen was regarded as the husband of his wife's young namesake. Kivelä (1991, p. 28), on her part, tells how she was called *omutekulu* 'grandchild' by a woman whose daughter's daughter was named after her.

275 Aarni's parents worked in the Ambo area between the years 1909 and 1946 (Peltola 1958, p. 264).

276 According to Mbenzi (24.3.1997), some Ambos also assumed Afrikaans names in order to get permission to move to Windhoek. With Afrikaans names they could be taken as Damaras, for whom moving to the capital was much easier than for the Ambo people. Mbenzi also stated that the reasons for giving Afrikaans and Finnish names in the Ambo area are clearly different, as the latter are based on friendship and real namesake relationships.

277 Levänen (1963, p. 139) tells the story of an unbaptised Ambo woman who had hoped to have a child with her Christian husband Abraham. When the woman finally got pregnant, she decided to get baptised and chose the name *Saara*; the baby boy was named *Isak*. The biblical model for this name choice is obvious.

278 This name could also be understood as a name referring to the time of the birth of the child, and not primarily as a "namesake name".

279 As the UN Commissioner for Namibia and later Special Representative of the Secretary General during the Namibian independence process, this Finn has ac-quired many namesakes in Namibia. His first name *Martti* also connects him with the Finnish pioneer missionary Martti Rautanen in the Ambo view.

280 Veikko Munyika (16.10.2000) said that his first name *Veikko* comes from the Finn-ish missionary Karl August Weikkolin. Munyika was named after a pastor's son who was originally named after Weikkolin.

281 Selma Gwamtana, who was interviewed by Nampala (2000, p. 15), claimed that in the early years of Christianity the Finnish missionaries in Ondonga had no problems with traditional names such as *Uusiku* and *Amutenya*, but as things be-gan to change, they started to refuse to baptise children with traditional names.

282 *Aune* is a Finnish form of the Greek woman's name *Agnes* (Vilkuna 1993, p. 43).

283 *Kerttu* is a Finnish form of the German woman's name *Gertrud* (Vilkuna 1993, p. 102).

284 This opinion was argued theologically: only Jesus could provide redemption, not a human being (Heikki Saari to the mission director 30.9.1905, Eac:11, FMSA).

285 Hochstrate (Bericht der Station Namakunde vom Konferenzjahr 1912–13, p. 6, C/h:52, UEMA) also claims that it was difficult to form Ambo names which could serve as a confession of faith, as the language was lacking in expressions which show something good or noble. Therefore, he concluded that it was best to let the Ambos choose their names freely.

286 Since the late 19th century, Christianity was also reflected in the names of unbaptised Ambo people. For example, a Kwanyama father who was not yet baptised but was interested in Christianity, gave his children the names *Schimue oshili* 'one thing is true', *Dimbulukeni* 'think about that', and *Hambeleni* 'praise' (Aus den Anfangstagen der Ovambomission 1904, p. 32). These name forms are typical of ones used in old German missionary literature. For example, *Schimue oshili* would be written as *Shimwe oshili* today.

287 Some missionaries also pointed out that at the beginning of the missionary work in the Ambo area, biblical and European names may have been good – perhaps even necessary – for a number of reasons, but that later the situation had changed (Walde Kivinen to the mission director 30.1.1937, Eac:38, FMSA).

288 A little later Alho wrote a letter to the mission director (11.10.1937, Eac:38, FMSA), in which he stressed that foreign names had been helpful for many Ambo converts when they had started their new lives as Christians. He also worried that indigenous names might be confusing to the Ambo people. Nevertheless, Alho supported the idea that the converts should assume both a "Christian name" and an indigenous one. This also became the prevalent custom later.

289 It seems that some missionaries also referred to the fact that in Finland, names of Finnish origin had also become popular at that time, as opposed to biblical and other foreign names (Viktor Alho to the mission director 11.10.1937, Eac:38, FMSA). Certainly, the developments in Finnish personal naming had some effect on the ideas of the Finnish missionaries in the Ambo area.

290 This may, of course, be due to the fact that the Ambo priests were for a long time under the influence of Finnish missionaries (Ihambo 7.10.2000).

291 When a number of converts at Olukonda took Ambo names at baptism, some unbaptised Ambos in the neighbourhood concluded that if the converts' names were accepted, then they would not need to be baptised (Walde Kivinen to the mission director 30.1.1937, Eac:38, FMSA).

292 *Matti* is a Finnish man's name derived from the biblical name *Mattias* or *Matteus*, and *Taavi* is the Finnish form of the biblical man's name *David*. *Sesilia* (*Cecilia*) is originally a saint's name, which was popular among women all over Europe. *Saku* is a Finnish pet form of the man's name *Sakari*, which is derived from the biblical *Sakarias*. (Vilkuna 1993, p. 48, 121–122, 152, 166.)

293 In the archives of the Finnish Evangelical Lutheran Mission in Helsinki, one can find no calendars published for the Ambo congregations between the years 1938 and 1950. One reason for this may be the Second World War. During the war (1939–1945), there were almost no connections between Finland and the Ambo area (Peltola 1958, p. 235–236), and most probably no calendars were published at that time, either.

294 The Hereros in Namibia call surnames *ozofana* (Otto 1985, p. 131), and the Xhosa word for surname is *ifani* (Neethling 1996, p. 34). Obviously, these terms are based on the Afrikaans word *van* as well. In Afrikaans, the preposition *van* 'from', which appears in many Afrikaans surnames, has developed into a noun meaning 'surname' (Neethling 1996, p. 34).

295 The Ambo Christians have generally used their fathers' baptismal names as patronyms, contrary to the Zulus, for example, who use their fathers' Zulu names for this purpose (Koopman 1986, p. 46).

296 Helenius (1930, p. 89) talks about surnames here (in Finnish: *sukunimi*), but she is obviously referring to patronyms.

297 In an earlier regulation concerning passports, which were compulsory for all indigenous people in the colony, it was ordered that such a passport should include
the name and the "byname" of the person: "Name des Inhabers (einschließlich
Beiname)" (Verordnung betreffend die Paßpflicht der Eingeborenen 1907/08 p.
20, 10.01: 2235, RKA).

298 The Hereros used patronyms for identification (Otto 1985, p. 131). The Kavangos
also used fathers' names for this purpose, and sometimes the mother's name was
added to it, e.g. *Mate zaMukuve naNasira* means 'Mate, daughter of Mukuve
(father) and Nasira (mother)' (Fisch 1979, p. 38).

299 The later form for contract workers only asked for the name of the employee
(*Name of Employee / Naam van Werknemer / Edina lomulongi*) (Kane-Berman
1972, Appendix II).

300 In a later letter, Tarkkanen also referred to the fact that there were hundreds of
people carrying the same names in the Ambo area. For this reason, he stated, a
surname would be most suitable as a register name. (Matti Tarkkanen to August
Hänninen 12.6.1931, Daa:30, FMSA.)

301 In the Ambo language, the use of the possessive concord had to be applied to
foreign names as well. Thus, names beginning with *K* typically got the possessive
concord *ka* (*Kaarina kaAndreas, Kristofina kaMateus, Kauko kaNangombe*) and
names beginning with *M* got *ga* (*Maria gaAmakali, Martha gaGideon, Mateus
gaPetrus*), whereas *ya* was used for various other kinds of names (*Anna yaShikongo,
Ester yaKleopas, Hileni yaPetrus, Johannes yaNamene, Lahja yaEdward, Selma
yaMartin*). (Namuhuja 1996, p. 88–93.)

302 The same development took place in Medieval Europe. Elements such as *filius*
and *alias*, as well as certain prepositions and relative clause elements, were mostly
deleted from the appositions which were used together with the baptismal names
of people, e.g. *Arnulfus filius Theoderici*. Gradually these appositions also developed into surnames. (Van Langendonck 1990, p. 436.)

303 This name is derived from the word *omuhuya*, meaning 'strip of (tree) bark (used
as binding material)' (Tirronen 1986, p. 87).

304 Because of the patrilineality of many southern African cultures, the adoption of
European-type surnames has been a relatively easy process for these groups, as
the inheritance of surnames follows the patrilineal line as well.

305 This is what happened among the Hereros as well, where the wife and the children also adopted the father's surname (Otto 1985, p. 131).

306 Mbenzi (24.3.1997), for example, said that his mother, together with many others, adopted her husband's surname in the mid-1980s.

307 A similar development took place among other ethnic groups in Namibia as well.
The hereditary surnames of the Kavangos were often based on the traditional or
"Christian" names of the fathers, but some Kavangos also started to use their own
bynames as surnames (Fisch 1979, p. 38). Among the Hereros, names of prominent ancestors were adopted for this purpose as well (Otto 1985, p. 131).

308 The register of the theologians of the Evangelical Lutheran Church in Namibia
(ELCIN) gives Auala's grandfather's name in the form *Awala* (Nambala 1995, p.
58).

309 According to the English–Ndonga Dictionary (1996, p. 189), "nothingness" is
okwaanasha, okwaana or *owala* in Ndonga.

310 The Kavango theologians and other non-Ambos were naturally left out of this
examination, as well as married women, who usually carry their husbands' surnames. All the other theologians of the ELCIN are included in the data, from the
first ordination in 1925 up to the year 1995.

311 Of these names, *Abraham* is not a patronym but the grandfather's name. *Andreas*
is clearly a patronym, whereas *Leonard* may be: the father's name was marked as
Leo. (Nambala 1995, p. 36, 53, 117.)

312 Munyika (16.10.2000) feels that the most important thing for the Ambo people is
that their names show that they are African and Namibian; the Ambo identity is
not very important. Mwaetako (14.10.2000), in turn, pointed out that surnames

must be African, because African names are easier for the Ambo people to remember than foreign ones.

313 Also among the Nguni peoples in South Africa, women started to use their husbands' clan names under pressure from churches and colonial bureaucrats. Nowadays women tend to return to the traditional custom of retaining their own clan name throughout life. (Herbert 1996, p. 1223.)

314 In such systems, the clan names should really be regarded as personal names too, contrary to the Ambo naming system, in which they are mere forms of address.

315 Herbert (1996, p. 1223) claims that among the Nguni peoples, "an indigenous system of patrilineal 'clan names' (Zulu *izibongo*; Xhosa *iziduko*) was converted into a system of surnames". Koopman (1986, p. 54), for his part, is of the opinion that even if the clan names are used as surnames within the "Western context", i.e. in the context of the modern society, they should still be regarded as clan names.

316 Herbert (1995, p. 2) also uses the term *birth name* to refer to "the African language name(s) bestowed sometime shortly after birth". The Ambo informants in this study usually referred to this name in English as *African name* or *Oshiwambo name*. However, as many of the baptismal names of the Ambo people are also African and Ambo names, neither of these terms is accurate enough for this purpose. The term *first name* – or *very first name* – was also used but, as it is generally used to refer to a forename, it was not suitable either. On the other hand, Pentti (1959, p. 35–36) refers to the African name given to an Ambo child before baptism as a temporary name. In many cases, the birth name is temporary by nature.

317 In other African countries, hospital births have also caused confusion in the naming systems of different ethnic groups. Herbert (1996, p. 1226) says that, as many hospitals require that names of children be submitted when the mother is admitted to the maternity ward – which is often contrary to traditional practice – children have been given names in advance by nurses or hospital administrators. These names are sometimes taken from other languages than that of the child. In the Ambo area, however, names of babies are not required in advance by hospitals (Säynevirta 12.4.1997).

318 Munyika (16.10.2000) said that his father accepted the names that the nurses had given to his brothers in hospital and never gave them other names. Since then, they have been called by those names.

319 Säynevirta (12.4.1997) stressed that the mother should also approve the name the midwives have given, because if she did not like it, the name would probably not be used at home.

320 Amushila (11.10.2000) said that if the father is absent, somebody else can choose the name, and Mwaetako (14.10.2000) stated that if the father is very young, his father is supposed to give this name.

321 Säynevirta (12.4.1997) told of a new-born baby in the Onandjokwe Lutheran Hospital who looked like an Indian and was named *Omuindia*. Tirronen (1986, p. 105) translates *Omuindia* as 'Hindu'.

322 The Kwanyama name *Hatuiikulipi* means 'where are we going?'. Abraham Malua told that he never asked his father to tell him his motive for giving this name. (Malua 19.9.2000.)

323 This is also the case among the Hereros in Namibia. Otto (1985, p. 126, 131) states that the Western name, which is received at baptism and is usually inherited from a grandparent, is a Herero's most important name in terms of frequency of usage, and it is also the one used in official documents.

324 The verb *shasha* means 'baptise' and the noun *edhina* 'name' (Tirronen 1986, p. 22, 370). This name is also referred to as *edhina lyomuntu mwene,* which is the translation for 'forename' in the English–Ndonga Dictionary (1996, p. 110); the literal translation would be 'person's own name'.

325 For example, what Koopman (1986, p. 47) says about the "European name" of the Zulus, which is often given at baptism, could not be said about baptismal names in Ambo society. Koopman says that no significance is attached to this name, and

it is therefore not subject to respectful avoidance or possible misuse for witch-craft. According to Koopman, it is also not important who gives this name, and it may be given by preachers, teachers, nurses or European employers, as well as by the parents.

326 Among the Hereros in Namibia, the father or the paternal grandfather usually gives the African "house-name" to the child, whereas the baptismal name may be given by other relatives or godparents as well. The baptismal name is often inherited from a grandparent or a godparent, but it may also be a new name. (Otto 1985, p. 128, 131.) Among the Kavangos, the father gives the African name to the child, but Fisch (1979, p. 28, 37–38) does not mention who gives the baptismal name.

327 Before independence, the contract labour system also caused delays in the giving of the name. As Hishongwa (1992, p. 104) observed: "In Owambo the naming of children was a man's prerogative. Under the contract labour system it often took several weeks, even months, for a letter to reach the father, informing him that a baby boy or girl had been born into the family. It took a long time again for the letter from the husband to reach the wife, informing her of his choice of name. Men who knew about the problems of communicating left a name for either sex before leaving for the south. Otherwise, baby boys were sometimes given their father's name, or an elder relative would take over the absent father's role of naming the infant."

328 In South Africa, De Klerk and Bosch (1996, p. 180–181) have also found that giving an additional English name for the child is nowadays more common among the Xhosa families who live in rural areas than among those living in urban areas.

329 Ihambo (7.10.2000) and Kanana (19.9.2000) also pointed out that today the Ambo people are free to give African names at baptism, on the condition that they are not insulting or express bad feelings.

330 Ihambo (7.10.2000) gave *Mwapota* 'you are naughty/rude' as an example of a "bad" name which refers to the situation in the family. Mbenzi (24.3.1997) told of a man who was angry with his wife and gave his child the name *Ndemuloloka* 'I am tired of you (or him/her)'. Another father named his child *Tyenitangi* 'say thank you', as a message to his wife whom he had to marry because she was pregnant. Kanana (19.9.2000) mentioned names with meanings such as 'leave me alone' or 'you are stupid', and Malua (19.9.2000) said that a man who is not sure if the child is his may give it a name meaning 'I doubt it'. Amaambo (3.4.1997) mentioned the name *Shimaningi* 'what have you done?' as a name containing a message from the husband to the wife who, as he sees it, has done something wrong.

331 Suzman (1994, p. 255) explains this kind of name-giving in South Africa by saying that it "provided an outlet for the regulation of social relations in the intense social interaction of small communities; it allowed people to communicate their feelings indirectly, without overt confrontation and possible conflict". According to Herbert (1999b, p. 116–117), these "friction names" are almost exclusively given by women in South Africa, whose public voices are muted in traditional communities.

332 The Ambo people also express their feelings with the naming of dogs. This is reflected in the Ambo saying: "Edhina lyombwa okumukweni ho li uvu", 'you will hear the dog's name from your neighbour' (Tirronen 1986, p. 223). In many other African communities, dog names are also used as a channel for expressing social tension (Herbert 1999b, p. 117; Koopman 1986, p. 75).

333 Mwaetako (14.10.2000) said that these names are often modified by the white employers: a man who has been baptised as *James* by the Anglicans may become *Jakob* and *Peter Pieter* when working for Afrikaans-speaking people in the south. If the workers have "difficult" Ambo names, they may also be given totally new Afrikaans names.

334 These names, given by Father Stefanus Amushila (11.10.2000), were all taken from the parish register of the Roman Catholic Mission in Oshikuku for the year 2000.

335 It seems that the Catholic Ambos have adopted Finnish names from the Lutherans. The woman's name *Rauha* means 'peace', the woman's name *Saima* is derived from the Finnish lake name *Saimaa*, and *Väinö* was explained earlier in this thesis (Vilkuna 1993, p. 145, 151).

336 This has also been a common custom among the Kavangos, who are mainly Catholics: "Bei der christlichen Taufe wird ein Name aus dem Neuen oder Alten Testament oder von einem christlichen Heiligen gewählt. Dieser Christenname steht in Dokumenten gewöhnlich vor dem traditionellen Namen. In der Praxis gebraucht man meistens aber nur einen der beiden Namen." (Fisch 1979, p. 37.)

337 According to Hiltunen (1986, p. 103), the percentage of non-Christians for the whole population in the Ambo area was 5 per cent in the 1980s.

338 As Amaambo (3.4.1997) put it, the one name is a namesake name and the other one a meaningful name.

339 At times children are named after the mother as well, but this kind of naming only expresses the father's feelings toward his wife and has nothing to do with a "real" namesake relationship (Amkongo 14.4.1997).

340 The Ambo saying "Edhina ekogidho", which means that the child will resemble his or her namesake, was cited by almost all informants (e.g. Amaambo 3.4.1997; Namuhuja 14.4.1997). The word *ekogidho* means 'joining, connecting permanently together' (Tirronen 1986, p. 137). Hence, this expression means that the name joins the namesakes permanently. A. Enkono (18.10.2000) explained this idea: "If someone names his child after somebody, one really admires that person and wants the child to become like him. The namesake is a role-model for the child. One doesn't name the child after just anybody."

341 The namesake relationship resembles the Christian godparent relationship in many respects. A godparent is also expected to take care of the child, both socially and spiritually. (Nashihanga 18.4.1997.)

342 There are different customs in different Ambo groups with regard to the namesake's obligations at the child's wedding. Typically, the namesake slaughters an ox at the wedding if he belongs to the father's family. (Amaambo 3.4.1997.)

343 Munyika (16.10.2000) reported that the Lutheran church newspaper Omukwetu had a column in the 1970s, in which meanings of many Finnish and other foreign names were given. This led to a general interest in names, and people wrote letters to the editor asking for the origin of their names. According to Munyika, this is how many Ambo people came to know the meanings of their names.

344 In many other African societies, European names have also been criticised because people do not know their meanings. In some societies, this has led to the custom of giving children names which are not European personal names but common nouns in European languages. For example, the Bapende people in Zaïre, who give names according to events taking place around the time of birth, do not borrow French names but only common nouns from the French language (Ndoma 1977, p. 92).

345 Säynevirta (12.4.1997) told of an Ambo man who named his first-born son *Kapenambudhi* 'it does not matter'. He had talked about names of children with his friends at school, and had said that when he one day has a child, he will simply name it *Kapenambudhi* – which he did.

346 *Kashimbandjola* means 'it does not stop me from being happy', and shows that someone had done something bad to the father of Enkono's mother (A. Enkono 18.10.2000).

347 Miraculously all Munyika's family members except one, who died in exile, came back to Namibia (Munyika 16.10.2000).

348 According to Tirronen (1986, p. 147, 292), *onkoshi* is 'lion' and *ekoshi* 'big lion, big boy'.

349 Only Malua (19.9.2000) remarked that a name may also be chosen only because the father likes it.

350 Mbenzi (24.3.1997) gave a good example of playing with names. He told of three Ambo men who went to work in the south with the intention of stealing some-

thing from the white farm owner. When these men came to the farm, they gave as their names *Ndapandula Wapangoshali* 'I thank, you have given me something free of charge', *Layoove Kushiinge* 'you fool, you do not know me' and *Nandekonga Kumononge* 'even if you search, you will not find me'. The farm owner obviously did not understand their language.

351 Nicknames are often used in death notices, for example, beside the official name of the person (Lehtonen 2.4.1997).

352 The missionaries working among the Ambo people were all given nicknames as well. However, they did not always know these names themselves, as they were kept secret. (Amkongo 14.4.1997.)

353 Auala tells that he started to call his wife *Aluhe* before they got married, as he was fascinated by the idea that she would always be his. He also used this name systematically for her. Only when Auala became angry at his wife, might he use her Finnish name *Aina*. (Auala 1975, p. 132–133.)

354 Budack (1979, p. 8–18) classifies the nicknames – in Afrikaans: *byname* – of the so-called Rehoboth Basters in Namibia. These nicknames refer to 1. Physical appearance, 2. Personal characteristics, 3. Events and circumstances in the person's life, 4. Other people, 5. Occupations, 6. Names of places, 7. Person's own forename or surname. Budack also regards names given to children soon after birth as nicknames. For the nicknames of the Hereros see Otto (1985, p. 130–131), and for those of the Kavangos, Fisch (1979, p. 32–37). Altogether, not much research has been done on nicknames in southern Africa (Neethling 1994, p. 89).

355 Amakali (10.10.2000) also pointed out that if the person gets angry because of his or her nickname, then it would really stick.

356 The person in question is Elieser Tuhadeleni, one of the first SWAPO activists, who was generally known by this nickname *Kahumba Kandola* (Lehtonen 7.11.1994; Holopainen 1993, p. 57).

357 According to Mbenzi (24.3.1997), the origin of this name is not known to the Ambo people today. However, one might think that it refers to Johanna Rautanen's father Martti Rautanen, whose Ambo name was *Nakambale*. Thus Johanna Rautanen would be *gwaNakambale*, daughter of Nakambale, of which *Gwanaka* could be a shortened form.

358 Lahja Lehtonen (2.4.1997) said that one of her Ambo namesakes used her nickname *Kanyeku* in her wedding invitation. The word *nyeku* denotes flinging of one's head or arm (Tirronen 1986, p. 312).

359 Munyika (16.10.2000) also remarked that Catholic names are generally regarded as difficult and Lutheran names as long, whereas Anglican names, i.e. English names, are short and therefore preferred.

360 The model for this final *h* can be found in the English Bible, which includes personal names such as *Deborah, Jonah, Noah, Obadiah* and *Sarah*.

361 The verb *mona* means 'find, obtain; experience, observe, see'. It is also used for giving birth: *Omukulukadhi okwa mono okanona* 'The wife gave birth to a child'. (Tirronen 1986, p. 229.)

362 Neethling (1994, p. 90–92) has analysed the ways in which nicknames are derived from Xhosa personal names. He presents five categories for this process: 1. Abbreviation by syllable deletion: *Mbulelo > Mbu, Nomawethu > Wethu*, 2. (Affective) Diminuation through abbreviation: *Nandipha > Nandy, Thobeka > Tobsie*, 3. Derived (shortened) with final *s/sh*: *Noluthando > Thandos, Nosipho > Sposh*, 4. Reduplication of base name syllable: *Nomvuzo > Vuvu, Zanele > Zaza*, and 5. Miscellaneous: *Bukelwa > Kenna, Zolani > Z*. Neethling (1994, p. 90) also points out that the lexical meaning of the name is largely lost in this process.

363 Beside being given to people, animals, etc., praise names are today given to many modern phenomena, such as computers and cars (Mbenzi 24.3.1997).

364 Praises of women seem to be uncommon in other African societies too, e.g. among the Zulus (Koopman 1987b, p. 160).

365 Nambala (14.4.1997) stated that if a person could not present his name properly, it could not be called a praise name.

366 According to Namuhuja (14.4.1997) *Eshilikiti* is a name for a person who can go anywhere, as he is not afraid of anything. Tirronen (1986, p. 375) translates *eshilikiti* as 'one in full attire, in full equipment, one in full armament, soldier; unknown cattle killer (wild animal)'.

367 The word *uupenda* means 'enterprising spirit or disposition ; enthusiasm; bravery; heroism'. The verb *pendapala* means 'become enterprising, enthusiastic or brave'. (Tirronen 1986, p. 339.)

368 Munyika (16.10.2000) stated that Ambo women often used manipulative power effectively and that some Ambo kings were practically ruled by women who stayed in the background.

369 The so-called "clan names" are not discussed in this subsection but in the next one, as they are generally regarded as a form of address by the Ambo people, not as names.

370 Amakali (10.10.2000) also stressed that this custom is "very powerful" in Ambo society today.

371 In general, Ambo men seem to have certain reservations about hyphenated surnames (Ihambo 7.10.2000; Munyika 16.10.2000; Nambala 14.4.1997). Munyika (16.10.2000) said that because the husband's name is put at the end of the wife's name in these, some men "feel lonely there and sometimes detached from the wife". He also pointed out that the change from the husband's name to the father's name is only a change from one male to another, and thus not in line with the spirit of women's liberation.

372 During the war of independence, however, many Ambo mothers gave their children their own surnames in order to protect them from the South African soldiers who frequently came to people's homes to search for SWAPO fighters (Amaambo 3.4.1997).

373 This is the case among the Zulus too, even if patronyms are more commonly used among the Zulus living in rural districts (Koopman 1987b, p. 145).

374 According to Braun (1988, p. 7), the term *address* "denotes a speaker's linguistic reference to his/her collocutor(s)", and *forms of address* are words and phrases used for addressing.

375 Koopman (1987b, p. 140) remarks that it is quite normal for a Zulu to go through a week or even a month being addressed by a number of different ways by other people, but not by his or her personal name.

376 Nambala (14.4.1997) said that many people in the Ambo communities have grown up without ever hearing their mother's name, as the mother is always called *meme* only.

377 Tirronen (1986, p. 271) translates *-nene* as 'big, tall, large, great; grave, serious; older', and gives *Fridanene* 'the aged Frieda' and *Nakambalekanene* 'the elder Rautanen' as examples of the use of *-nene* with personal names.

378 The use of the word *tatekulu* is a result of Kwanyama influence on Ndonga. Previously, grandfathers in Ondonga were also addressed as *kuku*. (Amaambo 3.4.1997.)

379 It is also common among other ethnic groups in southern Africa to use kinship terms as a way of respect in cases where no kinship exists. Thus, a Zulu may say politely "Sawubona baba" 'greetings, father' to an older man or "Sawubona gogo" 'greetings, granny' to an elderly woman. The term *mama* 'mother' is also used for any woman who is old enough to be a mother. (Koopman 1986, p. 39.)

380 In Ndonga, 'my/our mother' is *meme*, 'your mother' is *nyoko*, and 'his/her or their mother' *yina*, whereas 'my/our father' is *tate*, your father is *ho*, and 'his/her or their father' is *he* (Tirronen 1977, p. 19–20).

381 Säynevirta (12.4.1997) said that these terms can also be used as a way of expressing respect (*sheeli*) or disparagement (*nkelo*) for people who are not necessarily first-born or last-born.

382 Tirronen (1986, p. 368, 304) translates *omushakati* as 'third and any further child between the second and the second last child', and *ontowele* or *ontoyele* as 'second or next to the youngest child'.

383 The term *omutekulu* is also used for a man's sister's child; a great-grandchild is *omutekulululwa*. The verb *tekula* means 'foster, care for', and it also appears in the Ndonga terms for foster-parents and foster-children: *omutekulitate* 'my foster-father', *omutekuliho* 'your foster-father', *omutekulihe* ' his/her foster-father'; *omutekulimeme* 'my foster-mother', *omutekulinyoko* 'your foster-mother', *omutekuliyina* 'his/her foster-mother; *omutekulwa* 'foster-child'. (Tirronen 1986, p. 401.)

384 For example, Munyika (16.10.2000) said that his three sons, who all have both a European (or biblical) and an Ambo baptismal name, have always been known by their Ambo names only.

385 Lehtonen (2.4.1997) told of an Ambo woman who addressed her daughter, who was a Sunday school teacher, as *juffrou*. This Afrikaans term means 'lady, teacher, Miss, Madam' (Bosman *et al.* 1997, p. 47).

386 This is a general trend in South Africa as well. For example, many young Zulus use their Zulu names in all situations (Suzman 1994, p. 255).

387 Säynevirta (12.4.1997) said that the longer she has worked in the Ambo area, the less she has heard European names used in everyday life, as the Ambo people mainly use African names with each other. Säynevirta's Ambo name *Namutenya* 'midday' is also the one generally used for her by the Ambo people.

388 Kanana (19.9.2000) pointed out that the Kwanyama custom of calling women and girls by their father's clan name served to show other people which clan the father belonged to. However, if a man had no daughters but only sons, other people would not be able to identify his clan, as it would not be mentioned openly.

389 It is a general phenomenon that naming innovations arrive in the cities first, from where they spread elsewhere. As was noted earlier, the surname innovation in Europe spread from big cities to smaller towns, and finally to the countryside (Fleischer 1968, p. 85; R. Kohlheim 1996a, p. 1280).

390 Amakali (10.10.2000) felt that many biblical names, e.g. *Paul, John* and *Maria*, will remain popular also because being named after biblical characters is important to many Ambos.

391 Munyika (16.10.2000) pointed out that one reason for the decline of European names is that the influence of missionaries on Ambo culture is minimal today. European names are thus based on friendships between the Ambos only.

392 Lehtonen (2.4.1997), for example, told of an Ambo pastor who refused to baptise a child with the name *Faith* in the Ambo area.

393 Amakali (10.10.2000) did not believe that this would be a lasting trend in Ambo society, as people would eventually feel that the meaning of the name is also important. According to him, it is very important to an Ambo to be able to explain the meaning of his or her name when asked.

394 Ihambo (7.10.2000) said that many children who were born on the national Heroes' Day, are named *Hero*. His own son was baptised in 2000 as *Josef Paulus Salom Grace*. Ihambo used the name *Grace* because he felt that it was by the grace of God that the baby was a boy, as there were only daughters in the family before him. Clearly, the motive for this name is typically African – the name expresses the father's feelings – even if the name itself is English. Ihambo's (7.10.2000) daughter was also given an English name: *Rejoice*.

395 Amaambo (3.4.1997) felt that it was not possible for the Ambo people to throw away their European and biblical names, because these had been introduced in earlier times and it would now be too late to turn back. He also pointed out that the Ambos do not live in isolation today, but in a multicultural society.

Analysis of the Name Data

The Baptismal Names of the Elim, Okahao and Oshigambo Congregations, 1913–1993

Reasons for Choosing the Congregations

In the new "African-European" naming system of the Ambo people, the baptismal name is the name in which the influence of European naming practices and that of Christianity are most clearly visible. Within these names, one can also see the most significant trends in the Ambo personal naming in the 20th century: first, the adoption of European and biblical names, and later, the re-Africanisation of personal names. In order to analyse this process more carefully, we shall have a look at the baptismal names of three congregations of the Evangelical Lutheran Church in Namibia (ELCIN). Among other things, we shall examine what kind of European and biblical names have been adopted in the Ambo area, how popular these names have been at different times, and what kind of Ambo baptismal names the Ambo people have given to their children.

This analysis will be both linguistic and statistical, and it is based on a corpus containing the baptismal names of a total of 10,920 members of the Elim, Okahao and Oshigambo congregations from the period 1913–1993. These congregations are among the seven oldest congregations in the Ambo area, whose parish records were microfilmed in Namibia in 1993–94, as part of a Finnish research project on the population development in northern Namibia (Siiskonen 1994, p. 25–26). Of these congregations, Okahao was founded in 1903, and Elim and Oshigambo both in 1912 (Nambala 1995, p. 13). These congregations were chosen for this study primarily because their baptismal registers were described as reliable by the historians working with these parish records in the University of Joensuu. All these congregations also have registers of baptism since the 1910s, and there are no gaps in them.[396] It was also important that these congregations represent three different Ambo subgroups: Elim[397] is situated in Uukwambi, Okahao[398] in Ongandjera and Oshigambo in Ondonga.[399] People in these areas speak different Ambo varieties:

Map 2.

The location of the Elim, Okahao and Oshigambo congregations in the Ambo area. Timo Jokivartio 2003.

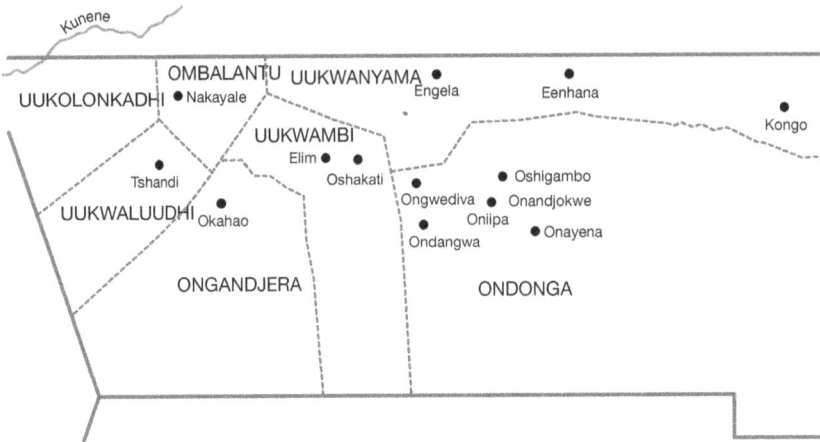

Kwambi, Ngandjera and Ndonga. Since the Finnish missionary influence, however, they have had a common written language, Ndonga, which is based on the linguistic variety of the Ndonga subgroup.

It is important to note that there have also been people in these congregations who originally belonged to other Ambo subgroups. For example, many Kwanyamas moved to Oshigambo, and to some other congregations, after the Rhenish missionaries had left Oukwanyama in 1916 (Martti Rautanen to the mission director 24.1.1917, Hp:110, FMSA). In the early 20th century, when new congregations were founded all over the Ambo area, it was also typical that the nucleus of a new congregation was composed of Christians who arrived from other communities (Notkola & Siiskonen 2000, p. 34). There are also many other reasons for migration within the Ambo area. One should note that not all members of these congregations were Ambos, even if the clear majority were. Since the early days of the Finnish missionary work, members of other ethnic groups, e.g. Damaras, have been under the influence of the Lutheran mission as well.[400] The San (Bushmen) have traditionally been close to the Ambo communities too, and intermarriage between these groups has been common (Gordon 1992, p. 27–28). Thus, it is clear that the baptismal registers of these congregations also include names of people who are not Ambos. As the San groups who live in close contact with the Bantu have had the custom of using Bantu names beside their indigenous ones (Hynönen 1981, p. 99), these people cannot always be recognised by their names either. It also seems that they have adopted the same kind of European and biblical names at baptism as the Ambo Christians have.[401] However, as these minorities are very small in the Ambo area,[402] there would be no point in making a distinction between them and the Ambos when analysing the baptismal name-giving in this area.

The names for this study were collected from the baptismal registers of the Elim, Okahao and Oshigambo congregations in such a way that the baptisms of every fifth year were included in the data, starting from the year 1913 up to the year 1993. As the microfilmed parish registers of Elim and Okahao for the year 1993 included baptisms until March only, the baptisms of the previous year 1992 were added to the 1993 data.

Until 1925, the majority of baptisms in the Ambo congregations were performed on adults (Varis 1988, p. 94), and during the following decades, the number of adult baptisms remained significant as well. In this study, adult baptisms and infant baptisms are analysed together, i.e. without distinction. This analysis will thus reveal what kind of baptismal names the Ambo people were given in different years, but it does not aim to make comparisons between the names of different age-groups. Nevertheless, one may claim that these name data represent the contemporary Lutheran Ambo population relatively well, even if the emphasis in this material is on names given between the 1950s and 1970s. In Namibia, the average life expectancy at birth is 54 years today (World Bank Atlas 2000, p. 24). Thus, the majority of people who were baptised at the beginning of the century have already died, and their share of the data may well correspond to their share of the present Ambo population. On the other hand, the names of people born in the 1980s and 1990s are slightly underrepresented in the data. In recent years, thousands of young adults have also died of AIDS, which has brought about significant changes in the demography.

Of the 10,920 baptised Ambos whose names are represented in the data, 6,028 (55.2 per cent) were women and 4,892 (44.8 per cent) men. The bigger share of women can be explained at least partly by referring to the fact that many Ambo men who worked in the south were also baptised outside the Ambo area. This material also clearly represents a rural population. In fact, there are no real cities in the Ambo area.

The baptisms were distributed fairly evenly among the three sample congregations (see figure 1).

Figure 1.

The distribution of baptisms among the three congregations of the name data: Elim, Okahao and Oshigambo (%)

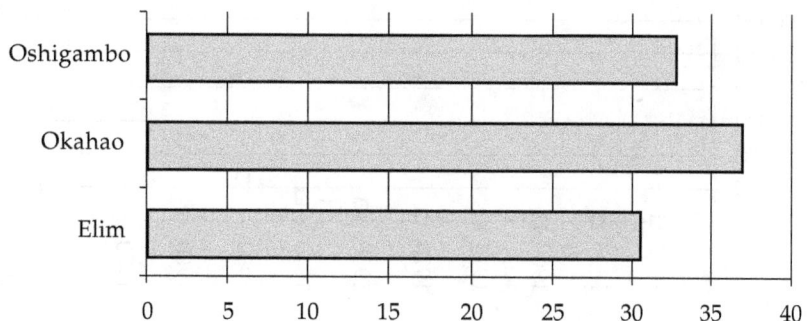

The average annual number of baptisms in one congregation is 214. As figure 2 shows, the number of baptisms in the congregations was fairly small at the beginning of the century, but grew steadily until the 1950s and 1960s. After this, the number of baptisms decreased again.

Figure 2.

The number of baptisms in the three congregations (Elim, Okahao, Oshigambo) in different years (1913–1993)

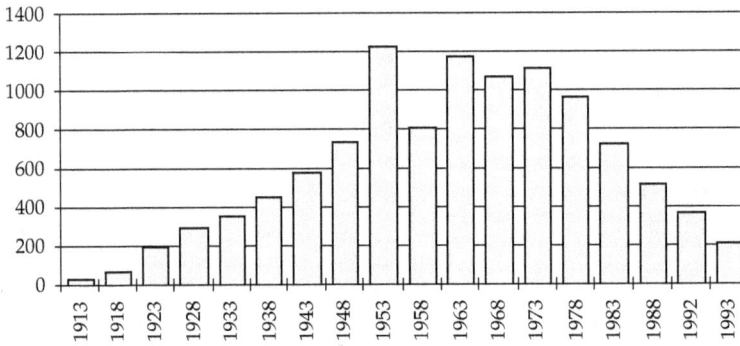

The decrease of baptisms in these congregations after the 1960s can be explained by the fact that at that time, a number of new congregations were founded in the Ambo area, and some of them were separated from these old congregations.[403] On the whole, the number of Christians in the Evangelical Lutheran Church in Namibia (ELCIN) grew steadily during the course of the 20th century (see figure 3).

Figure 3.

The number of members in the congregations of the Evangelical Lutheran Church in Namibia (ELCIN) 1883–1990. Source: Nambala 1995, p. 12.

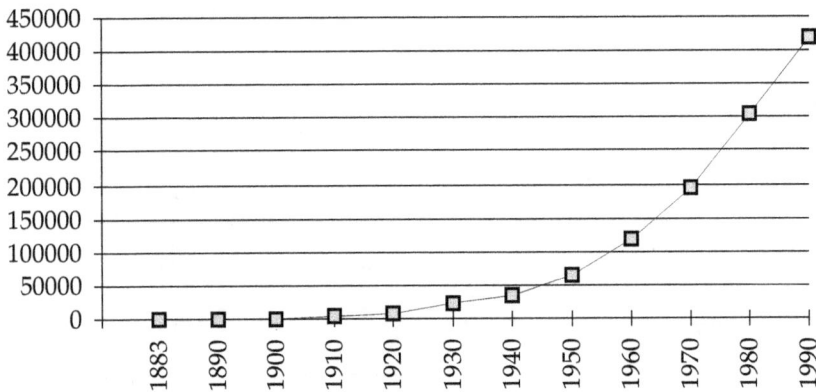

Even if the names in the baptismal registers were for the most part written clearly, collecting names was not unproblematic. At times, it was difficult to decipher names because they had been written illegibly. Some microfilmed pages were not perfectly sharp either. In some cases, the sex of the baptised person was not marked in the register, and it was impossible to judge it from the name. Because of these reasons, the baptismal names of more than 200 people had to be left out of the data. Most of the baptismal names that were left out contained unclear Ambo names, which may have been possible for an Ambo-speaking person to decipher, but not for the writer of this thesis.

At times, the entries in the baptismal registers were clearly incorrect. For example, a child could be registered to have been baptised before he or she was even born. There were also many name forms which obviously contained unintentional spelling errors, e.g. *Alberlina* instead of *Albertina* or *Gerlrud* instead of *Gertrud*. When collecting names, such forms were not corrected, as this would have made the material lose its authentic nature. The few names which were originally written with an initial small letter, however, were changed to begin with a capital letter, as they are names. Some problems were also caused by baptisms which had taken place in a certain year, and were only marked in the following years' lists. Such baptisms were not researched systematically, but the ones that were found were included in the data.

In the case of adult baptisms, the original Ambo name of the person was often given in brackets after the baptismal name, and the patronym was frequently, but not always, added as well, e.g. *Aune Ndasiluohenda* (*Kaunapaua*) *ja Kashuku* (Elim 1953), *Tobias* (*Nangolo*) *ja Nuuta* (Oshigambo 1933) or *Elisabet* (*Nuusiku*) (Elim 1973). These original Ambo names were not included in the data. Often baptismal names were also underlined, which made it easier to separate them from the other names of the converts. Sometimes the baptismal name of the person was separated from his or her other name(s) by a space.

At the beginning of the Finnish missionary work in the Ambo area, the missionaries were responsible for the parish records. After the first ordination of local pastors in 1925 (Nambala 1994, p. 86), the responsibility gradually fell upon the Ambo Christians. However, the Finns were not always satisfied with the way the Ambo pastors kept maintained the parish records. In the 1930s, the director of the Finnish Mission, Matti Tarkkanen, encouraged the missionaries to make inspections of church records in the congregations a few times a year (Matti Tarkkanen to August Hänninen 12.6.1931, Daa:30, FMSA). Some Finns also took a lot of trouble to put these records in proper order (Helenius 1930, p. 88–89).[404] One of the main reasons for the numerous errors in them was that baptisms were usually not recorded immediately after the baptism but much later (Matti Tarkkanen to August Hänninen 22.1.1931, Daa:30, FMSA). This problem was frequently taken up at the missionary conferences, e.g. at a meeting in 1937 in which it was stressed that names and numbers should be written in a clear handwriting in church records (Missionary conference in Engela and Onandjokwe 26.8.–3.9.1937, appendix 22, Dea:4, FMSA). Based on all this, it is obvious that the church records of Elim, Okahao and Oshigambo cannot be faultless either.

Variation in Name Forms

It is characteristic of the name data in this study that there is a lot of variation in the name forms, both in the European and biblical names and in the Ambo ones. There are also many reasons for these variations, both extralinguistic and linguistic ones.

Extralinguistic Reasons. The most typical extralinguistic reason for the variation in the name forms is the negligence and ignorance of the people who recorded names in the baptismal registers, i.e. missionaries, Ambo pastors and secretaries of the congregations. Many names have obviously been written in a hurry, or carelessly, as the above-mentioned forms *Alberlina* and *Gerlrud* indicate.[405] Other examples of this phenomenon are *Berla* (*Berta*), *Emmalmmanuel* (*Emmanuel*) and *Mrkus* (*Markus*). Of course, one might also suspect that *Alberlina*, for example, could be correct. However, as there are 51 cases of *Albertina* and only one *Alberlina* in the data, it is logical to assume that *Alberlina* is a spelling error. In the same way, as *Berta* appears in the data 8 times, *Bertta* (the Finnish form of the name) 22 times and *Berla* only once, *Berla* was also regarded as a misspelling. There are also some Ambo names in the data which were written incorrectly probably for the same reason, e.g. *Eluhole* (*Etuhole*), *Homaten* (*Homateni*), *Nalangwe* (*Natangwe*) and *Ndeshipand* (*Ndeshipanda*).

The ignorance of the recorder is obvious in many cases in which European and biblical names are written incorrectly. This is not surprising, as many of these names were unfamiliar to the Ambo people. German names especially seem to have been difficult for the recorders. Here are some examples:

Charlotte	*Chalotte: Charllotte: Charltotte: Salot: Salote: Sarlote*
Gertrud	*Gerdrut: Gerturd: Gerdruta: Gerdrula: Gerlrud*
Fredrik/Friedrich	*Firdrik: Fredrek: Friadrek: Fridirh: Fridrich: Fridriech*
Gottfried	*Cotfried: Gotfrid: Gotfried*
Gottlieb	*Cottlieb: Cotlieb: Gottlib*

Some Ambo names may also have been written incorrectly by Finnish missionaries who were not as familiar with Ambo names as the Ambo pastors were, even if the Finns in the Ambo area all spoke the local language. Some names in the data, especially Ambo names, may also have been misinterpreted by the writer of this thesis, due to both unclear handwriting in the baptismal registers and her limited knowledge of the Ambo languages.

The Influence of the Ambo Languages on European and Biblical Names. The other main reason for the variations in the name data is that in Ambo society, European and biblical names have often received domesticated name forms, as they have been adapted to the phonology of the Ambo languages. Such name forms, e.g. *Esitela* instead of *Ester* or

Johannesa instead of *Johannes*, are used in everyday speech, and this phenomenon is reflected in the baptismal registers as well. It seems that some pastors used Africanised name forms in the church records more frequently than others. It is impossible to judge on the basis of these records only whether these names were written in this way deliberately or not. One might suspect that by using domesticated name forms the Ambos wanted to make their baptismal names look more African, in the same way as the Finns, for example, started to use domesticated name forms of foreign names in official contexts too: *Andreas* became *Antti*, *Laurentius Lauri, Birgitta Pirkko,* etc. (Maliniemi 1947, p. 48, 50, 56).

However, this does not seem to be the case in Ambo society. According to Halolye Nashihanga (18.4.1997), domesticated name forms appear in the parish records only because the recorders did not know the correct forms of these names: "If they have written Johannesa, it is wrong." Nowadays the secretaries of the congregations also have name lists in which they can check the correct forms of the most popular foreign names (Nashihanga 18.4.1997). Amaambo (3.4.1997) and Namuhuja (14.4.1997) also stated that the pastors and the secretaries usually wrote names down in the parish records in the way they preferred, without consulting the name-givers. Hence, if the father had written the name *Estela* down on a piece of paper, the name could appear as *Ester* in the parish registers.[406]

As the recorders generally aimed to write foreign names down in their original forms, it is not surprising that Africanised name forms are a clear minority in the data. Nevertheless, as these forms are the ones most frequently used in everyday speech, it is useful to have a closer look at them. The phonotactics of Ambo has affected biblical and European names in many ways. Firstly, the fact that all syllables are open in the Ambo languages (Tirronen 1977, p. 5) has led to the addition of an extra vowel at the end of many closed syllables of foreign names.[407] Secondly, there are frequent variations between *l* and *r* in the names. This is due to the fact that the sounds which in Finnish (and many other European languages) are written with the letters *r* and *l,* are representations of the same phoneme in the Ambo languages. In the written language of Ndonga, the letter *l* has been chosen to represent this phoneme, whereas *r* appears in foreign loan words only, e.g. *oradio* 'radio', *oranda* 'rand' or *orehisteli* 'register' (Tirronen 1977, p. 5; 1986, p. 364). The fact that the Ambo languages make no significant difference between these sounds in speech is reflected in many name forms in the data, in which the original *r* of a foreign name has become *l,* or vice versa.

In the following list, there are examples of domesticated forms of women's and men's European and biblical names. In many names, one can see more than one of the above mentioned factors functioning together. For example, in the name form *Esitela*, which is based on the biblical woman's name *Ester*, there are two extra vowels which have come to form open syllables, and the letter *r* has been replaced with *l.* One can also notice that many name forms are not completely Africanised, e.g. *Estela*, in which the first syllable has remained closed. The original name form is given first, and the Africanised form(s) after it. The number of occurrences of each name form in the data is given in brackets.

Albertina: Albelitina (52: 1)
Elisabet: Elisabeta (60: 3)
Ester: Estela: Esitela (173: 3: 2)
Gloria: Grolia (0:1)
Helvi: Helivi (37: 1)
Hilaria: Hiralia (11: 1)
Hilma: Hilima (185: 10)
Hulda: Huluda (3: 1)
Katrina: Katilina (25: 1)
Klaudia: Kelaudia (37: 3)
Lahja: Lahija: Lahya (54: 2: 2)
Laura: Laula (3: 2)
Margareta: Marigaleeta (1: 1)
Mirjam: Mirjama (34: 1)
Natalia: Nataria (30: 1)
Orvokki: Orovokki (1: 1)
Petriina: Peteliina (16: 1)
Priskilla: Prisikilla (9: 1)
Rakel: Rakela (36: 1)
Saara: Saala (48: 2)
Selma: Selima (276: 4)
Serafina: Selafina (2: 1)
Sigrid: Sigirid (7: 1)
Tuulikki: Tuurikki (12: 1)
Ursula: Ulsula (0: 1)
Viktoria: Vikotoria (36: 1)

Absalom: Abisalom: Absalomo (10: 9: 3)
Armas: Arumas (25: 1)
Axel: Akisel: Akser (3: 1: 1)
Eliakim: Eliakima (6: 2)
Elkana: Elikana (3: 2)
Erkki: Erikki (12: 1)
Gabriel: Gabrieri (48: 1)
Gebhard: Gebihard (9: 1)
Gideon: Gideona (42: 1)
Gottlieb: Gottrieb (8: 1)
Hilarius: Hiralius (1: 1)
Hiskia: Hisikia (3: 1)
Jafet: Jafeta (29: 2)
Jefta: Jefuta (1: 1)
Johannes: Johannesa (215: 2)
Josef: Josefa (77: 2)
Kaleb: Kaareb: Kaareba (1: 1: 1)
Kefas: Kefasa (9: 1)
Leopold: Leopord (3: 1)
Martin: Martina: Maritin (61: 4: 1)
Nahum: Nahuma (7: 2)
Oskar: Oskal (26: 1)
Petrus: Petrusa (206: 1)
Severinus: Sevelinus (2: 3)
Simon: Simoni (88: 1)
Simson: Simsoni (8: 1)
Timoteus: Timoteusa (50: 1)
Tobias: Topiasa (47: 1)
Vilbard: Vilbald: Vilibard (17: 3: 3)
Vilhelm: Vilihema (18: 3)

Furthermore, in Ndonga, the symbol *d*, pronounced as the letter *d* in English, appears only in the combination *nd* (e.g. *pa-ndu-la* 'thank'), which is pronounced as *nd* in the English word *and*. The combination *dh* (*e-dhi-na* 'name'), on the other hand, is pronounced as *th* in the English word *this*. (Tirronen 1977, p. 12.) Thus, adding an extra *n* to some foreign names containing the letter *d* guarantees that the *d* in them will be pronounced properly:[408]

Adele: Andele (1: 1)
Adelheid: Andelheid (1: 1)
Fredrika: Fenderika: Frendrika (7: 1: 2)
Lidwina: Lindivina (0:1)
Loide: Loinde (157: 1)

Fridrich: Frindrich (4: 1)
Kennedy: Kenedy: Kenendi (1: 2: 1)
Sadok: Sandok (5: 1)

Similarly, *b*, a letter which occurs only in the combination *mb* in Ndonga (Tirronen 1977, p. 12), is sometimes replaced with *p*, e.g. *Rebekka > Repekka* and *Tobias > Topiasa*.[409] Some Finnish names which contain the letters *ä* and *ö*, unfamiliar to the Ambo people, are written with *a* and *o* in the baptismal records, e.g. *Hynönen > Hynonen, Petäjä > Petaja, Väinö > Vaino*. They are also pronounced accordingly in everyday speech. When pronouncing foreign names, the stress and the tone also follow the rules of the Ambo languages.

There also appears to be an interesting variation between *i* and *e* in many names. For this phenomenon, no obvious reason could be found:

Hilaria: Hiralia: Helalia (11: 1: 3)   *Hesekiel: Hiskiel* (6: 1)
Sesilia: Sisilia (42: 2)   *Hiskia: Heskia* (3: 2)
Vilhelmina: Velhelmina (8: 6)   *Onesimus: Onesemus* (5: 1)
Pinehas: Penehas (14: 1)
Teofilus: Teofelus: Teoferus (38: 1: 2)

Hypercorrect Name Forms. The Africanisation of names has also led to a linguistic counterreaction in the church records: the creation of hypercorrect name forms. The Ambo people know that Africanised name forms such as *Esitela < Ester* or *Johannesa < Johannes*, which include extra open syllables, are incorrect in the language of origin, and this has led to the false analogy that many open syllables which originally belonged to foreign names are also incorrect. Thus, such syllables have often been closed by apocopation of the final vowel. Examples of these are numerous in the data:

Albertina: Albertin (52: 10)   *Naftali: Naftal: Nafital* (37: 6: 2)
Debora: Debor (3: 1)   *Salomo: Salom* (25: 3)
Hilma: Hilm (185: 1)
Justiina: Justiin (9: 1)
Magdaleena: Magdaleen (22: 1)
Lovisa: Lovis (56: 5)
Rebekka: Rebek (16: 6)
Ruusa: Ruus (49: 1)
Suoma: Suom (29: 1)
Taimi: Taim (77: 4)

In other cases, vowels have been deleted from open syllables in the middle of the name, even if they are perfectly correct in the original name:

Dorotea: Dortea (10: 2)   *Augustinus: Augstinus* (4: 1)
Elisabet: Elisbet (60: 2)   *Bartolomeus: Bartlomeus* (3: 1)
Helena: Helna (151: 2)   *Benediktus: Bendiktus* (1: 1)
Kaarina: Kaarna (44: 2)   *Bonifatius: Bonfatius* (2: 1)
Hesekiel: Heskiel (6: 3)
Melkisedek: Melksedek (3: 2)
Onesimus: Onesmus (5: 7)
Potifar: Potfar (0: 1)
Sebulon: Seblon (18: 5)

Other Reasons for Variations in European and Biblical Names. There also appears to be a variation in the doubling of vowels and consonants in the European and biblical names of the data. Some of this can be explained by the fact that there is similar variation in the corresponding names in Europe as well. Hence, it is understandable that one can find name forms such as *Albertiina* and *Albertina, Berta* and *Bertta, Josefiina* and *Josefina, Justiina* and *Justina, Leena* and *Lena, Marta* and *Martta, Saara* and *Sara,* or *Aaron* and *Aron, Leevi* and *Levi, Siimon* and *Simon, Teofiilus* and *Teofilus,* and *Tiitus* and *Titus* in the Ambo material as well.[410] The majority of cases, however, seem to be due to the fact that the length of vowels and consonants does not have a similar function in the Ambo languages as it has in many European languages. Therefore, it is often difficult for the Ambo people to write down European names, which they may have heard but not seen, in the way in which they would be written in the European language.

Aina: Ainna (152: 2)	*Eero: Ero* (2: 1)
Aleta: Alleta (2: 1)	*Eino: Eeino* (17: 1)
Aune: Aunne (55: 2)	*Filemon: Filemoon* (82: 1)
Beata: Beatta (42: 6)	*Filippus: Filipus: Fiilippus* (70: 10: 1)
Elina: Elinna (30: 1)	*Iivari: Ivari* (3: 2)
Fiina: Fiinna (33: 1)	*Martti: Marti* (1: 1)
Hilkka: Hilka (10: 3)	*Matti: Mati* (7: 1)
Irja: Iirja (49: 1)	*Suikkanen: Suikanen* (0: 1)
Johanna: Johana (150: 1)	
Kaarina: Kaariina (44: 1)	
Kerttu: Kertu (7: 1)	
Koskimaa: Koskima (1: 0)	
Laina: Lainna (71: 2)	
Linda: Liinda (11: 2)	
Linnea: Linea: Liinea: Lineea: Liineea (4: 18: 2: 1: 2)	
Luise: Luisse (5: 4)	
Martta: Maartta (145: 1)	
Rauha: Rauuha (47: 1)	
Rakel: Rakkel (36: 8)	
Rebekka: Rebbeka: Rebbekka: Rebeka (16: 2: 1: 5)	
Susanna: Sussana: Susana: Suusanna (10: 2: 1: 1)	
Terttu: Tertu (18: 2)	
Tuulikki: Tuuliki: Tulikki: Tuliki (12: 6: 1: 1)	
Veronika: Veronikka (5: 1)	

The variation in name forms such as *Elisabet* and *Elizabeth, Frida* and *Frieda, Martha* and *Martta, Rut* and *Ruth, Victoria* and *Viktoria,* or *Akseli* and *Axel, Carl* and *Karl, Edvard* and *Edward, Gustaf* and *Kustaa, Michael* and *Mikael, Victor* and *Vihtori, Vilhelm* and *Wilhelm* can also be explained by similar variation in European naming systems.

Some variations in the biblical names of the data are due to the influence of different European and Ambo Bible translations. Sometimes it is a European form of the name that is used, e.g. *Eeva, Elizabeth, Martta, Ruth,*[411] but most commonly a form that can be found in the Ndonga

Bible translations. The New Testament was published in Ndonga as early as 1903, and the whole Bible in 1954 (Tirronen 1977, p. 11). In 1977, a new edition of the 1954 translation was published, which followed the new standard orthography of Ndonga, and a new translation came out in print in 1986. There are differences in personal names in all these translations.[412] Here are examples of variations in the data which can be seen to originate from the differences between the Ndonga Bible translations (Ombibeli Ondjapuki moshindonga 1954; Ombimbeli Ondjapuki 1977; Ombimbeli Ondjapuki 1986):

Magdaleena: Magdalena
Rebeka: Rebekka

Abiatar: Abjatar
Abisai: Abisaji
Aser: Asser
Beñamin: Benjamin
Elia: Elija: Elias
Eliakim: Eljakim
Enok: Henok
Hiskia: Hiskija
Jeremia: Jeremija
Linius: Linus

Orthographies and Varieties of the Ambo Languages. There appears to be a lot of variation in the Ambo names of the data as well. This is mainly due to the various changes that have taken place in the orthography of Ndonga during the 20th century. These changes have for example led, in certain contexts, to the following replacements of letters: $u > w$, $j > y$, $š > sh$ and $z > d > dh$ (Fourie 1992, p. 17). Here are some examples in the data of this kind of variation:[413]

Aluẓilu: Aludilu: Aludhilu
Cikameni: Thikameni
Gandjomuenjo: Gandjomuenyo: Gandjomwenjo
Iijaloo: Iyaloo: Jaloo
Kaunapaua: Kaunapawa
Kaushiuetu: Kaushiwetu
Muaẓina: Muadina: Mwadhina
Mueneni: Mweneni
Naluendo: Nalwendo
Namŭteña: Namŭteñja: Namutenya
Napopje: Napopye
Natangue: Natangwe
Ndaguedha: Ndagwedha
Ndakulilua: Ndakulilwa
Ndapeua: Ndapewa
Ndasiluohenda: Ndasilwohenda
Njanjukueni: Njanjukweni: Njanyukweni: Nyanjukweni: Nyanyukueni: Nyanyukweni
Šigueẓa: Shigueda: Shiguedha: Shigwedha
Šikongo: Shikongo
Šoopala: Shoopala
Uujuni: Uuyuni

Uilika: Wilika
Ẓiginina : Diginina: Dhiginina
Ẓimbulukueni: Dhimbulukueni: Dhimbulukweni

In those Lutheran congregations in which Ndonga was used as a written language, as is the case in Elim, Okahao and Oshigambo, names have generally been recorded in the baptismal lists according to the Ndonga orthography. However, one can find dialectal name forms in these parish records too. In Elim, for example, Kwambi names were usually written down in the Ndonga form in the late 1940s, but the local pastors sometimes wrote them in their Kwambi forms as well (Hukka 2.3.2000). There are also quite a number of Kwanyama names in the data. The following variation of name forms originates in the differences between Ndonga (left) and Kwanyama (right):[414]

Elago: *Helao* 'luck, happiness'
Hilifa: *Nghilifa* 'I do not tend cattle'
Hilifavali: *Nghilifavali* 'I do not tend cattle anymore'
Iita: *Heita* 'war'
Shandje: *Shange* 'my'
Uugwanga: *Hauwanga* (< *oshigwanga* 'herb')
Uusiku: *Haufiku* 'night'

General Remarks on the Name Data

The Number of Names. One of the major changes in the Ambo naming system has been the adoption of multiple personal names, which was not characteristic of the traditional Ambo system. Many Ambos have received more than one name at baptism. The name data for this study include the baptismal names of 10,920 people, but altogether, the number of different names is 16,643.[415] Hence, the average number of names per individual is 1.5. Almost half (44.5 per cent) of the people whose names were included in the corpus have two or more baptismal names. It is obvious that this custom is due to European influence on the Ambo naming system. As we have seen, there were examples of this phenomenon already among the first baptisms. The first Ambo kings were baptised as *Eino Johannes* and *Martin Elifas*, for instance (Peltola 1958, p. 143). However, having more than one name was not the only European model for the Ambo people. Of all the Finnish missionaries who worked in the Ambo area between the years 1870 and 1959, 27 per cent had one name only (Peltola 1958, p. 259–277).[416]

The popularity of multiple baptismal names can primarily be explained by the advent of Ambo baptismal names. People who chose to bestow African baptismal names on their children generally gave these names beside a European or biblical name. Those who were content with using Ambo names as unofficial "home-names" only typically gave only one European or biblical baptismal name to their children. Examples of single Ambo names are extremely rare in the data. The adoption of Ambo baptismal names has thus led to the increase of multiple baptismal names, which is a typical phenomenon in European naming systems. Once again, the desire to Africanise personal names has led to the Europeanisation of the naming system in some other respects. One reason for the adoption of multiple baptismal names in the Ambo congregations may also be that this practice made it possible to combine several motives in name-giving. One of the names may be given as a namesake name, another one as a name referring to the circumstances around the birth, and so on (Amaambo 3.4.1997).

Figure 4.

Percentages of men and women in the data who have one, two, three or four baptismal names

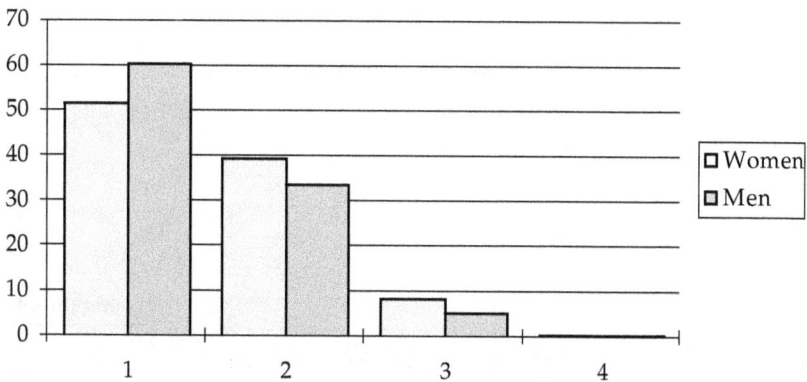

As figure 4 shows, multiple baptismal names are more common among the women than among the men in the data. It is difficult to find any single reason for this. It may partly be explained by a European model: of all the Finnish female missionaries who worked in the Ambo area between the years 1870 and 1959, 81.1 per cent had more than one fore-name, whereas among the male missionaries, the corresponding percentage is 55.6 (Peltola 1958, p. 259–277).[417] Figure 4 also reveals that the number of Ambos carrying four names is minimal. In the Lutheran Ambo congregations, three names has been the general maximum for names given at baptism (Amkongo 14.4.1997; Nashihanga 18.4.1997). This rule was introduced because of the limited space for names in the baptismal registers (Lehtonen 17.11.1994).

There is also a geographical variation in the number of baptismal names given to an individual (see figures 5 and 6). Multiple names are most common in Okahao, where 73.6 per cent of women and 57.3 per cent of men have more than one name. Single names, in turn, are most common in Elim, where 73.6 per cent of women and 79.9 per cent of men have received one baptismal name only. These differences can be explained at least partly by the varying attitudes of missionaries and Ambo pastors towards African baptismal names. As we have seen, some of them were willing to accept Ambo baptismal names much earlier than others.

Figure 5.

Percentages of women in different congregations who have one, two, three or four baptismal names

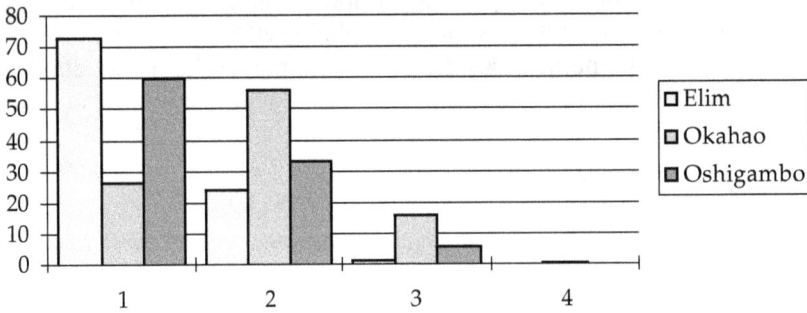

Figure 6.

Percentages of men in different congregations who have one, two, three or four baptismal names

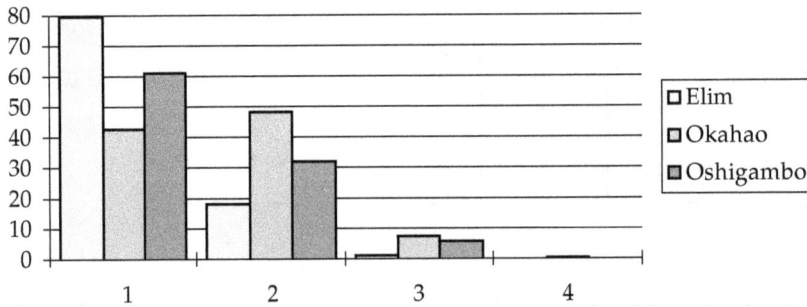

The giving of multiple baptismal names increased clearly in the church in the course of the 20th century. In the 1920s, the proportion of baptisms with more than one name was 4.5 per cent, whereas in the 1990s their proportion had grown up to 78.8 per cent of all baptisms. The giving of multiple baptismal names has increased at the same pace among the women and the men (see figure 7).[418]

Figure 7.

Percentages of women and men who have received more than one name at baptism (1910s–1990s)

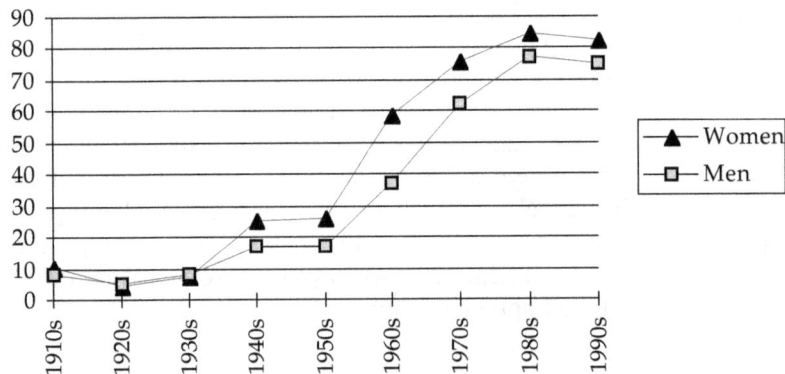

Hyphenated Names. There are also many hyphenated names in the data. Even if such a name type is of European origin in the Ambo naming system, its usage differs considerably from that in European countries. In Europe, hyphenated names have generally developed from specific popular combinations of names. In Finland, for example, *Maria Elisabet* became *Maija-Liisa* and *Anna Kristiina Anna-Stiina*, and later new hyphenated names were formed using the same model: *Sanna-Mari, Suvi-Tuuli* 'summer wind', etc.[419] It is a fact that some of these names have become very popular, e.g. *Anna-Kaisa, Anne-Mari, Juha-Matti* and *Jukka-Pekka*, and many of them also have compound name forms, e.g. *Annakaisa, Annemari, Juhamatti* and *Jukkapekka*. (Kiviniemi 1982a, p. 185–187; 1993, p. 22–29.)

In the name data for this study, hyphenated names which are common – or at least probable as hyphenated names – in Europe, are extremely rare. Examples of these are *Aina-Lovisa, Anna-Maria, Eevi-Lydia, Eva-Berta, Ida-Maria, Kaino-Lovisa, Kerttu-Maria, Maria-Magdalena, Sirkka-Lisa* and *Eino-Johannes*[420.] Many European hyphenated names also appear as two single names in the corpus. For example, in Okahao the Finnish name *Anna-Liisa*, which most probably refers to the missionary Anna-Liisa Sorsa (Peltola 1958, p. 272), appears regularly as *Anna Liisa* or *Anna Lissa* (7 occurrences). The other hyphenated names in the data which consist of European and/or biblical names, are not common in Europe, even if they are not totally impossible in European naming systems either, e.g. *Elizabet-Bergita, Elizabeth-Laina, Foibe-Saara, Helena-Eine, Katrina-Marta, Lahja-Evangeline, Margaleeta-Angela, Paulina-Katriina, Saara-Saima; Andreas-Petrus, David-George, Filippus-Jason, Gabriel-Hosea, Henok-Viktor, Natanael-Gotfrid, Petrus-Johannes, Teodor-Robert.*

The most common hyphenated names in the data are names which consist of both European or biblical and Ambo names. Examples of these are: *Aino-Nangula, Etuhole-Agnes, Justina-Iyaloo, Kondjashili-Hilda, Ndilimeke-Saima, Nuugwanga-Rut; Aaron-Pendapala, Armas-Tonata, Daniel-Tuhafeni, Erastus-Natangwe, Heikki-Tangeni, Juuso-Uusiku, Natangwe-Hendrik, Nuuyoma-Wilbard, Risto-Shivute, Sakaria-Megameno.*[421] Hyphenated names consisting of Ambo names only are rare, but examples of them can be found as well, e.g. *Ndapewa-Hanganeni* for a woman and *Tuhafeni-Mekondjo* for a man.

An interesting phenomenon in the data is hyphenated names that consist of three or more components. A good example of these is *Leopold-Meke-Ndati-Tangi* 'Leopold-in the hand-I said-thank you' (e+a+a+a), in which the first name is European and the other three Ambo names. Other examples are *Aili-Loide-Ndeshimona* (e+b+a), *Elina-Mariyatta-Ndapewoshali* (e+e+a), *Elise-Laina-Naambo* (e+e+a), *Emma-Tangi-Kornelia* (e+a+e), *Helvi-Hilma-Ndinelago* (e+e+a), *Saara-Toini-Nyanyukweni* (b+e+a); *David-Nambili-Tangeni* (b+a+a), *Elago-Sondaha-Nabot* (a+a+b), *Elifas-Tangeni-Nayiloke* (b+a+a), *Immanuel-Martin-Inekela* (b+ e+a), *Ismael-Elago-Jimmy* (b+a+e), *Lot-Spener-Nangolo* (b+e+a), *MwadhinaDhiginina-Otulina* (a+a+a), *Toivo-Emil-Natangue* (e+e+a).[422]

It seems that hyphenated names can be formed from almost any names, and they resemble greatly the other name combinations in the data. It is clear that these formations are not hyphenated names in the European sense. Rather, they look like ordinary combinations of baptismal names which only happen to be attached to each other with a hyphen. This observation is supported by the Ambo informants used for this study. According to Hans Namuhuja (14.4.1997), some Ambo pastors have simply had the habit of writing names down in this way in church records, in order to show that the names belong together. In everyday life, these names are often written without a hyphen, and people are usually addressed by one name only.[423] In general, it seems that the hyphens which appear in these official documents are not important to the name-bearers.[424] Thus, one may claim that the difference between hyphenated names and name combinations is not significant to the Ambo people. Because of this, the names which appear in these hyphenated forms are also analysed as separate names in this study.

Figure 8.

The proportion of women in different congregations who carry hyphenated names consisting of two, three or four names (%)

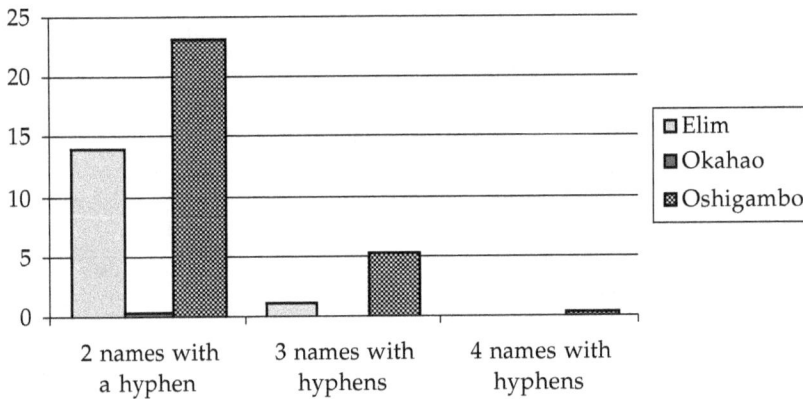

Figure 9.

The proportion of men in different congregations who carry hyphenated names consisting of two, three or four names (%)

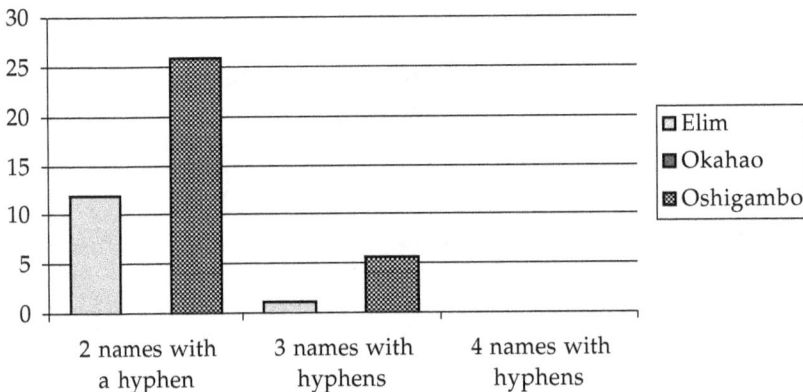

Figures 8 and 9 show how hyphenated names are distributed unevenly among the three congregations of the data. In the baptismal registers of the Okahao congregation, there are almost no hyphenated names, whereas in Elim and Oshigambo hyphenated names consisting of two names are very common, and those consisting of three names are also relatively common in Oshigambo. This variation shows that there is no uniform practice in regard to hyphenated names in the Ambo congregations. The pastors and secretaries of the congregations have simply recorded name combinations in two different ways: either with or without hyphens.

Figure 10.

The proportion of men and women in the data who carry hyphenated names (1910s–1990s) (%)

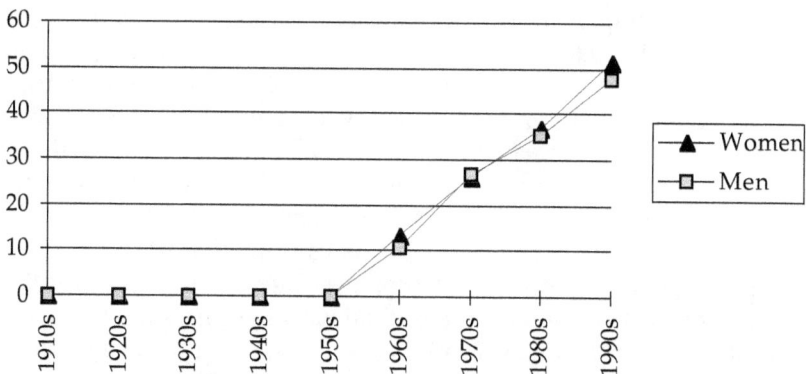

Hyphenated names started to become common in both women's and men's names in the 1960s. Figure 10 shows how this new name type – or rather: a new way of recording names – became popular within a few decades only. In the 1990s, roughly half of the baptised children in the data (49.7 per cent) were given a name which contained a hyphen.[425] This shows that using hyphens for names had really become a fashion in Ambo society, or at least in the parish records.

Women's Names and Men's Names. In the traditional Ambo naming system, women and men often carried the same names, even if there were also names which had both feminine and masculine forms, e.g. *Angula* 'morning' for a boy and *Nangula* for a girl, and *Uukongo* 'hunting' for a boy and *Nuukongo* for a girl. In European systems, names are much more clearly divided into genders, and the percentage of names which may be used for either sex is typically very small. In Finland, the law on first names, which was enacted in 1945 and amended in 1993, even prescribes that a boy should not be given a woman's name and a girl a man's name (Kiviniemi 1993, p. 31, 165–166).[426] Making such a clear distinction between men's and women's names obviously was a new practice for the Ambo people. Nevertheless, they adopted it together with European and biblical names.

As far as European and biblical names are concerned, the distinction between male and female names has not been complete in the Ambo naming system. At times, women were given men's names, and vice versa. This phenomenon can also be seen in the name data: some Ambo women were given names such as *Abia, Augustinus, Erkki, Felix, Filemon, Jekonia, Kornelius, Steven* and *Wilbard*, and some men have the names *Alli, Ida, Riika* and *Sofia,* which look more like women's names. How can this be explained? Is it possible that the sex of these people is marked incorrectly in the baptismal list? In many cases, this does not seem to be the explanation, as these people often have additional names which are typical of their sex, e.g. *Aune Felix, Ester-Wilbard, Frieda-Steven, Ruusa-Erkki-Ndaetelwa* and *Teobolina Augustinus* for women, and *Isak-Ida* or *Alli Olli Kamati* 'little boy' for men. In some cases, it also seems as if the names of the opposite sex do not refer to the child, but to some other person. For example, the girl's name *Fenni-Filemon-Ligola* 'cheer, jubilate' might include a message for a person named Filemon: that he should be cheerful because of the child, for example. Similarly, with the boy's name *Sakaria-Sofia-Tangi* 'thank you', the father might express his gratitude to a woman named Sofia; maybe he is thanking his wife for the child. Some of these name forms may originally be names of the opposite sex too. For example, the name which was written as *Ida* in the baptismal list, might refer to the Ambo man's name *Iita* 'war'. However, it is impossible to prove such assumptions. Surely, one reason for this phenomenon is also that the Ambos did not always know if a particular European or biblical name was originally a man's or a woman's name.

On the other hand, it is generally known that in Ambo society, names of the opposite sex have sometimes deliberately been given as baptismal names because of the namesake custom, even if this is not common. Lehtonen (2.4.1997) for example tells of a girl who was born in an Ambo house and was named *Elifas* after the master of the house. Later this woman got married to her namesake and started to use the name *Elifasina*.

Beside typical men's and women's names, there are also many European and biblical names in the data which are gender-neutral. European surnames are good examples of this, even if Ambo boys are normally named after males and girls after females. Hence the gender element, absent in the surname, is, in a sense, added to it. Here are some examples of Finnish surnames given as baptismal names in the Ambo area; the names of the original bearers of these names, who are all Finnish missionaries, are also given here (f and m in the brackets refer to the sex of the name-bearer):

Antila (f)[427]	< Miina (Vilhelmiina) Anttila (Peltola 1958, p. 266)
Koskima (f)	< Laimi Koskimaa (Peltola 1958, p. 268)
Salmi (f)	< Raija Salmi (Personnel archives of the Finnish Evangelical Lutheran Mission)
Soini (f, m)	< Aino Soini (Peltola 1958, p. 269)
Hynonen (m)	< Erkki Hynönen (Peltola 1958, p. 268)
Lehto (m)	< Erkki Lehto (Peltola 1958, p. 264)
Pentti (m)	< Elias Pentti (Peltola 1958, p. 271)

Petaja (m)	< Kalle (Kaarlo) Petäjä (Peltola 1958, p. 263)
Petenen (m), *Pettenen* (m)	< August Pettinen (Peltola 1958, p. 261)
Rautanen (m)	< Martti Rautanen (Peltola 1958, p. 259)
Suikanen (m)	< Olli Suikkanen (Peltola 1958, p. 266)
Tylves (m)	< Oskari Tylväs (Peltola 1958, p. 262)

Other European surnames in the data are either names of well-known people, typically of politicians and historical characters, or surnames of Namibians of European origin: *Achrenius* (m), *Bekker* (m), *Dias* (m), *Edison* (m), *Kennedy* (m), *Nixon* (m), *Pretorius* (m), *Spener* (m), *Waldheim* (m), *Wilson* (m). Of these, the surnames *Bekker, Pretorius* and *Wilson* appear in the Namibian telephone directory (Telecom Namibia 92/93), and they may well be adopted from Namibians of European origin. The other names could refer to the following well-known characters, even if other explanations are possible too: Abraham or Antti Achrenius (Finnish hymn writers)[428], Bartholomew Diaz, Thomas Alva Edison, John F. Kennedy, Richard Nixon, Philipp Jakob Spener[429] and Kurt Waldheim.

Biblical place-names are also basically gender-neutral. Here are examples of them in the data: *Eben-Eser* (f)/ *Ebenhaezer* (f)/ *Ebben-Eser* (m), *Mahanaem* (f, m)/ *Mahanaema* (f)/ *Mahnaem* (f)/ *Mahanaim* (f), *Jordan* (m), *Sioni* (m). There are also a number of gender-neutral names in the data which are common words in European languages or words referring to the Christian culture:

Agnus (m)	< Latin *agnus* 'lamb'
Dezember (f)	< German *Dezember* 'December'
Epefinia (f)	< Greek *epifaneia* 'Epiphany'
Frendj (m)	'friend'
Happy (f)	'happy'
Hosiana	< Hebrew *hoshi'ana* 'hosanna'
Januarie (m)	< Afrikaans *Januarie* 'January'
Jehova (f)	< Hebrew *JHWH* 'God'
Junior (m)	'junior'
Krismes (f)	'Christmas'
Lucky (f)	'lucky'
Niewejaar (f)	< Afrikaans *Nuwejaar* 'New Year'
Remember (f)	'remember'
Sondag (f, m)	< Afrikaans *Sondag* 'Sunday'
Thankyou (m)	'thank you'

Many of these names are in English or Afrikaans, and some of them actually look like translations of common Ambo names which also appear in the data, e.g. *Happy, Lucky* < *Elago* or *Nelago, Thankyou* < *Ndapandula* or *Tangi, Remember* < *Dhimbulukweni*. Many of these names also seem to refer to the time of the birth, just as many Ambo names typically do: *Dezember, Epefinia, Januarie, Krismes, Niewejaar* and *Sondag*. Obviously, these names are given according to the same principles as many Ambo names. On the whole, names of this kind are very rare in the data.

However, one might expect that especially names which are common words in the English language might become more popular in the Ambo area, as a consequence of the popularity of the English language.

There are 1,715 different forms of Ambo names in the data. Of these, 208 (12.1 per cent) occur both as women's and men's names. It should be noted, however, that some names which occur with only men or women in the data may well be used by the opposite sex too, even if there are no examples of this in the data. On the other hand, there are specific Ambo names which seem to be typical of either sex. The Ambo names which have male and female forms, the latter being formed with the name-deriving formative *na-/n-*, are clear examples of these: *Amutenya* and *Namutenya* (< *omutenya* 'midday'), *Elago* and *Nelago* (< *elago* 'luck, happiness'), *Iita* and *Niita* (< *iita* 'war').[430] Names which are semantically marked as either for men or for women also belong to this group, e.g. *Nekulu* 'mother of the family' and *Takatsu* 'she shall grind' for girls, and *Kamati* 'little boy' and *Omusamane* 'married man, head of the house' for boys. Many traditional Ambo names which appear in the data are also generally understood to be either women's or men's names. According to Tirronen (1986, p. 6, 98, 237, 249, 250, 270), *Mutaleni*, *Nandjelo* and *Nankali* are women's names, for example, whereas *Amakali*, *Iimene* and *Nehale* are traditionally men's names.

There are also newer Ambo names which have become very popular among the Ambo people and are much more common among either sex, even if they are not linguistically marked as female or male names. Names such as *Magano* 'gift', *Ndinelago* 'I have luck/happiness' and *Ndakulilwa* 'I am redeemed' have developed into typical women's names, whereas *Natangwe* 'may He be praised' and *Pendapala* 'be brave/energetic', for example, are more common among the men.

The Most Popular Names

The Most Popular Names for Women and Men. Not surprisingly, some names are much more common than others in the name data for this study. The most popular of these are carried by 4 to 6 per cent of all Ambo men or women in the data. In this subsection, we shall look at the popular first given names and the subsequent given names separately. Of these, the first mentioned ones are typically European and biblical names, whereas the latter ones are mainly Ambo names.

Among the women's first given names, one can find 633 different name forms. As there are 6,028 baptised women in the data, the average number of bearers for each name form is 9.5. The following list shows the "top twenty" first given names of women in the data, both in absolute numbers and as a percentage. Name forms that are obviously variants of the same name, e.g. *Hilma, Hilm* and *Hilima*, are counted together here.

1.	*Selma* 266 + *Selima* 4	270	4.5
2.	*Maria*	236	3.9
3.	*Martta* 140 + *Marta* 61 + *Martha* 1 + *Maartta* 1	203	3.4
4.	*Hilma* 175 + *Hilm* 1 + *Hilima* 10	186	3.1
5.	*Ester* 169 + *Estela* 3 + *Esitela* 2	174	2.9
6.	*Aina* 150 + *Ainna* 2	152	2.5
7.	*Johanna* 145 + *Johana* 1	146	2.4
8.	*Loide* 141 + *Loinde* 1	142	2.4
9.	*Helena*	141	2.3
10.	*Anna*	114	1.9
11.	*Josefina* 90 + *Josefiina* 11 + *Josofina* 1 + *Jasofina* 1	103	1.7
12.	*Emilia* 93 + *Emiilia* 1 + *Emilja* 1 + *Emielia* 1 + *Emiliha* 1 + *Emmilia* 1	98	1.6
13.	*Hilja* 90 + *Hilya* 3 + *Hilija* 1 + *Hilia* 1	95	1.6
14.	*Hileni* 85 + *Hilen* 1	86	1.4
15.	*Hertta*	84	1.4
16.	*Paulina* 61 + *Pauliina* 22	83	1.4
17.	*Elisabet* 60 + *Elisabeta* 3 + *Elisabeth* 3 + *Elisbet* 2 + *Elizabeth* 13 + *Elizabet* 1	82	1.4
18.	*Albertina* 51 + *Albertin* 10 + *Albertiina* 13 + *Albertiin* 3 + *Alberlina* 1 + *Alberiitina* 2 + *Albelitina* 1	81	1.3
19.–20.	*Frida* 42 + *Frieda* 33	75	1.2
	Taimi 71 + *Taim* 4	75	1.2

On average, these twenty names have 131 name-bearers each, and their bearers account for almost half (43.6 per cent) of the women in the data. The bearers of the most popular ten names represent a little less than one third (29.3 per cent) of all women.[431] These names have thus been very popular among the Ambo people. All these names are of European or biblical origin. The most popular of them, *Selma*, seems to refer to Selma Rainio, the first European medical doctor in the Ambo area, who worked there between the years 1908 and 1939. This name was also carried by the missionaries Selma Santalahti and Selma Markkanen. (Peltola 1958, p. 263, 264, 266.) Many other of these names are also of Finnish origin, e.g. *Aina, Hertta, Hilja, Hilma* and *Taimi*. Some of these names have been common in many European countries, e.g. *Albertina, Emilia* and *Frida/Frieda*. Of these, *Frida/Frieda* obviously refers to Frieda Rautanen, wife of the missionary Martti Rautanen. The biblical names in this list are, for the most part, names that are popular among Christian women all over the world, e.g. *Elisabet, Ester, Johanna* and *Maria*. On the other hand, the biblical name *Loide*, which is quite uncommon elsewhere, has become surprisingly popular among the Ambos.

Among the men's first given names, one can find 708 different name forms. As there are 4,892 baptised men in the data, the average number of bearers for each name form is 6.9, i.e. a little less than the corresponding number for women. The "top twenty" list of men's first given names is as follows (both in terms of absolute numbers and percentage):

1.	*Johannes* 206 + *Johannesa* 2 + *Johanns* 1	209	4.3
2.	*Petrus* 192 + *Petrusa* 1	193	3.9
3.	*Andreas* 154 + *Andrias* 4 + *Andreds* 1	159	3.3
4.	*Paulus* 136 + *Paulusa* 3 + *Paulu* 1 + *Palus* 1	141	2.9
5.	*David*	126	2.6
6.	*Tomas* 112 + *Tomasa* 2 + *Thomas* 1	115	2.4
7.	*Mateus* 79 + *Matteus* 22 + *Matheus* 1 + *Maateus* 1 + *Mateu* 1	104	2.1
8.	*Erastus*	89	1.8
9.	*Simon* 84 + *Simoni* 1 + *Siimon* 2 + *Siimoni* 1	88	1.8
10.	*Filemon* 80 + *Filemoni* 1 + *Filemoon* 1 + *Filimoni* 1	83	1.7
11.	*Filippus* 70 + *Filipus* 10 + *Filippu* 1	81	1.7
12.	*Josef* 74 + *Josefa* 2	76	1.6
13.	*Sakaria* 74 + *Sakarias* 1	75	1.5
14.	*Martin* 60 + *Martina* 4 + *Marttina* 1 + *Martti* 1 + *Marti* 1 + *Maritin* 1	68	1.4
15.	*Samuel* 58 + *Samue* 1	59	1.2
16.	*Immanuel* 49 + *Immanuela* 1 + *Immanue* 1 + *Immanel* 1 + *Imanuel* 1	53	1.1
17.	*Sakeus*	52	1.1
18.–19.	*Timoteus* 48 + *Timoteusa* 1	49	1.0
	Titus 44 + *Tiitus* 5	49	1.0
20.–21.	*Gabriel* 47 + *Gabrieri* 1	48	1.0
	Tobias 47 + *Topiasa* 1	48	1.0

These twenty names have 96 name-bearers on average, and their bearers form a good third (39.2 per cent) of the men in the data.[432] The bearers of the most popular ten names represent a good fourth (26.8 per cent) of these men. Hence, the most popular men's names are slightly less popular than the most popular women's names.

As far as the origin of names is concerned, this list differs considerably from that of women: almost all names in the men's list are of biblical origin. Many of these names and their hypocoristic forms are very popular all over the Christian world, as they are names of the disciples of Jesus and the apostles, e.g. *Andreas, Johannes, Petrus, Paulus* and *Tomas*. On the other hand, some biblical names that are not very common elsewhere have become surprisingly common among the Ambo people, e.g. *Erastus, Immanuel* and *Sakeus*. The only European name in the list is *Martin*, a name obviously referring to the Finnish missionary Martti (Martin) Rautanen (Peltola 1958, p. 259).

The lists of the most popular subsequent given names look fundamentally different, as there are mainly Ambo names on them. The data contain 3,486 names that are given for women as second, third or fourth baptismal names, and there are 2,918 women bearing these names. Among these names, one can find 1,129 different name forms. Each name form thus has 3 occurrences on average – and also 3 name-bearers, as the same name never occurs twice in the combination of baptismal names of a single woman. The "top twenty" list of these names looks like this (the percentage figures show the number of these name forms of all the occurrences of subsequent women's names in the data):

1.	*Magano* 187 + *Omagano* 12 'gift'	199	5.7
2.	*Ndinelago* 157 + *Ndinelaago* 1 + *Dinelago* 1 'I am happy/lucky'	159	4.6
3.	*Ndapewa* 82 + *Ndapeua* 56 + *Nndapeua* 1 'I was given'	139	4.0
4.	*Nelago* 110 + *Nelaago* 3 'luck/happiness'	113	3.2
5.	*Ndakulilua* 40 + *Ndakulilwa* 26 'I am released, redeemed'	66	1.9
6.	*Ndapanda* 'I took a liking (to it), I approved (of it)'	59	1.7
7.	*Njanjukueni* 17 + *Njanjukweni* 10 + *Njanyukweni* 2 + *Nyanyukweni* 17 + *Nyanyukueni* 4 + *Nyanjukweni* 6 'rejoice'	56	1.6
8.	*Nangula* 'morning'	54	1.5
9.	*Ndahambelela* 'I praise'	53	1.5
10.	*Namutenja* 33 + *Namutenya* 10 + *Namuteña* 4 'midday'	47	1.3
11.	*Ndilimeke* 'I am in the hand'	44	1.3
12.–13.	*Ndapandula* 'I thank'	41	1.2
	Ndeyapo 28 + *Ndejapo* 13 'I came/arrived'	41	1.2
14.–16.	*Niita* 'war'	38	1.1
	Panduleni 'thank'	38	1.1
	Ndasiluohenda 21 + *Ndasilwohenda* 16 + *Ndasilohenda* 1 'I have received mercy'	38	1.1
17.	*Natangwe* 21 + *Natangue* 16 'may He be praised'	37	1.1
18.	*Nangombe* 'ox'	34	1.0
19.	*Maria*	28	0.8
20.	*Mpingana* old personal name[433]	27	0.8

All names in this list are Ambo names, except for the biblical *Maria*, which ranks 19th in the list. On average, these names have 66 occurrences as subsequent baptismal names, and their share of all the second, third or fourth baptismal names of women is a good third (37.6 per cent). Thus, the most popular subsequent given names are not as popular as the most popular first given names. Four of these names, however, cover more than 3 per cent of all the subsequent women's names.

The name data for this study contain 2,237 names which are given for men as second, third or fourth baptismal names, and there are 1,938 men bearing these names. Among these names, one can find 1,076 different name forms. Each name form has thus 2 occurrences on average – and also 2 name-bearers. The "top twenty" list of these names is as follows (both in terms of absolute numbers and percentage):

1.	*Natangwe* 99 + *Natangue* 34 'may He be praised'	133	5.9
2.	*Panduleni* 51 + *Pandulen* 3 'thank'	54	2.4
3.	*Tangeni* 'thank, praise'	47	2.1
4.–5.	*Elago* 'luck/happiness'	44	2.0
	Ndeshipanda 43 + *Ndeshipand* 1 'I took a liking to it, I approved of it'	44	2.0
6.–7.	*Shaanika* old personal name	25	1.1
	Mekondjo 'in a battle'	25	1.1
8.	*Iiyambo* 10 + *Iyambo* 2 + *Iijambo* 8 + *Ijambo* 1 old personal name[434]	21	0.9
9.	*Iita* 'war'	20	0.9
10.	*Hafeni* 'be happy'	19	0.9
11.	*Shikongo* 16 + *Sikongo* 2 old personal name[435]	18	0.8

12.–15.	*Amutenja* 11 + *Amutenya* 6 'midday'	17	0.8
	Angula 'morning'	17	0.8
	Kondjeni 16 + *Kondyeni* 1 'fight'	17	0.8
	Pendapala 'be brave/energetic'	17	0.8
16.	*Iipinge* old personal name[436]	16	0.7
17.–19.	*Megameno* 'under protection/patronage'	15	0.7
	Tuutaleni 9 + *Tutaleni* 6 'let us look'	15	0.7
	Uushona 'smallness, littleness'	15	0.7
20.	*Petrus*	14	0.6

As was the case with the corresponding list of women's subsequent names, almost all names in this list are Ambo names. The only exception is the biblical *Petrus*, which ranks 20th in the list. On average, these names have 30 occurrences as subsequent given names, and their share of all the second, third or fourth baptismal names for men is a good fourth (26.6 per cent). Only one of these names is so popular that its share is more than 3 per cent, whereas women have four such names. On the other hand, the name *Natangwe* 'may He be praised', with its share of 5.9 per cent, is more popular than any of the women's subsequent names.

Temporal Variation in Popular Names. In this subsection, we shall look at developments in the popularity of the most common names in the Ambo area in the course of the 20th century. Let us start by comparing the lists of the most popular first given names of women in the 1920s and in the 1990s (given in absolute terms and as a percentage):

1920s

1.	*Selma*	15	5.2
2.–3.	*Frida* 6 + *Frieda* 3	9	3.1
	Maria	9	3.1
4.–8.	*Albertina* 7 + *Albertiina* 1	8	2.8
	Helena	8	2.8
	Hilma	8	2.8
	Marta 4 + *Martta* 4	8	2.8
	Suoma	8	2.8
9.–11.	*Anna*	7	2.4
	Jakobina 5 + *Jakobiina* 1 + *Jakopiina* 1	7	2.4
	Johanna	7	2.4

1990s

1.	*Selma*	14	4.6
2.–5.	*Hilma*	10	3.3
	Johanna	10	3.3
	Maria	10	3.3
	Marta 8 + *Martta* 2	10	3.3
6.	*Helena*	8	2.6
7.–8.	*Elisabet* 5 + *Elizabeth* 2	7	2.3
	Ester	7	2.3
9.–12.	*Emilia*	6	2.0
	Monika	6	2.0
	Paulina	6	2.0
	Taimi 5 + *Taim* 1	6	2.0

Even if the number of baptised women in the 1920s (289) and 1990s (303) is not large, these lists are most illuminating. The most popular name in both of these lists is the European *Selma*, and many other names appear in both lists too: the biblical names *Johanna, Maria* and *Marta*, and the European (Finnish) names *Helena* and *Hilma*.[437] From the Finnish point of view, it is interesting to note that many names which were popular in Finland at the beginning of the 20th century but went out of fashion later, e.g. *Hilma, Selma* and *Taimi*, were still popular in the Ambo area in the 1990s.[438]

In the data, there are 203 men baptised in the 1920s and 276 in the 1990s. The lists of the most popular first given names of men over these decades also resemble each other:

1920s

1.	*Simon* 8 + *Siimon* 2	10	4.9
2.	*Teofilus* 5 + *Teoferus* 2	7	3.4
3.–5.	*Andreas*	5	2.5
	Johannes	5	2.5
	Petrus	5	2.5
6.–18.	*David*	4	2.0
	Gabriel	4	2.0
	Jeremia	4	2.0
	Joel 3 + *Jooel* 1	4	2.0
	Jona 3 + *Joona* 1	4	2.0
	Josef	4	2.0
	Sakaria	4	2.0
	Sakeus	4	2.0
	Samuel	4	2.0
	Silvanus	4	2.0
	Tobias	4	2.0
	Tomas	4	2.0
	Vilhelm 3 + *Wilhelm* 1	4	2.0

1990s

1.	*Johannes*	16	5.8
2.–3.	*Andreas*	11	4.0
	Filemon	11	4.0
4.–5.	*Sakeus*	9	3.3
	Tomas	9	3.3
6.–7.	*Paulus*	8	2.9
	Petrus	8	2.9
8.	*Mateus*	7	2.5
9.–11.	*David*	6	2.2
	Martin 5 + *Martina* 1	6	2.2
	Sakaria	6	2.2

There are altogether seven names which appear in both lists, and all of them are biblical: *Andreas, David, Johannes, Petrus, Sakaria, Sakeus* and *Tomas*.[439] Most of the other names in these lists are biblical as well, and only two are European: *Vilhelm* in the 1920s and *Martin* in the 1990s. Biblical names have thus retained their popularity among the Ambo men in the course of the 20th century.

This temporal analysis of the most popular first given names of women and men reveals that the changes in baptismal names have not been significant: the same names have largely retained their popularity during the course of the 20th century. In this respect, the personal nomenclature of the Ambo people differs greatly from that of the Finns and other Europeans. The contemporary European naming systems are characterised by naming fashions which change with every generation, and even more rapidly. These changes are explained by the fact that people do not usually want to give their children names of the preceding generation because of the various personal connotations that are attached to these names (Kiviniemi 1993, p. 45). In the Ambo culture, the thinking is totally different: names of the preceding generation are given to babies particularly because of the links between these names and the people who bear them. The traditional namesake custom has thus led to a situation in which the same names are transferred from one generation to another, and in which there is not much space for new names in the naming system. On the other hand, the practice of giving children Ambo names as subsequent baptismal names has brought the name-givers the freedom to choose other kinds of names as well, and also to create new names.

Let us now look more closely, from a temporal point of view, at the "top names" of Ambo women and men, which were given in the previous subsection. The most popular name for the Lutheran Ambo women in the 20th century, as a first given name, seems to be the European *Selma*, which was adopted from Finnish missionaries, especially from Selma Rainio, the founder of the Onandjokwe hospital. Since the 1920s, the occurrence of this name amongst the first given names of women in the data has been more than 3 per cent, and in the 1950s, it was even more than 6 per cent (see figure 11). The name *Selma* is not common as a second, third or fourth given name: it occurs 10 times only as a subsequent baptismal name in the data.

Figure 11.

The proportion of women in the data who have the name Selma/Selima as their first baptismal name (1913–1993) (%)

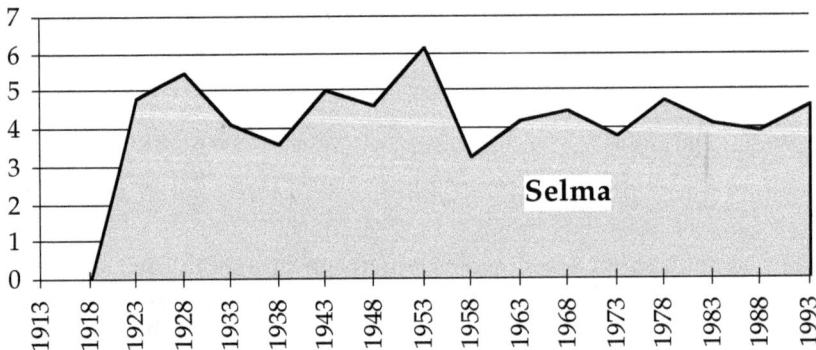

The second most common name in the list of women's first given names is the biblical *Maria*, which has also been popular throughout the 20th century (see figure 12). This name also appears 28 times as a subsequent baptismal name. *Maria* was a common name among the Finnish missionaries in the Ambo area too. Beside Maria Ala-Nikula, Maria Alen, Maria Hottinen, Maria Roiha, Maria (Maikki) Savola and Maria Wehanen, many Finnish women in the Ambo area had this name as a subsequent baptismal name (Peltola 1958, p. 259–277).

Figure 12.

The proportion of women in the data who have the name Maria as their first baptismal name (1913–1993) (%)

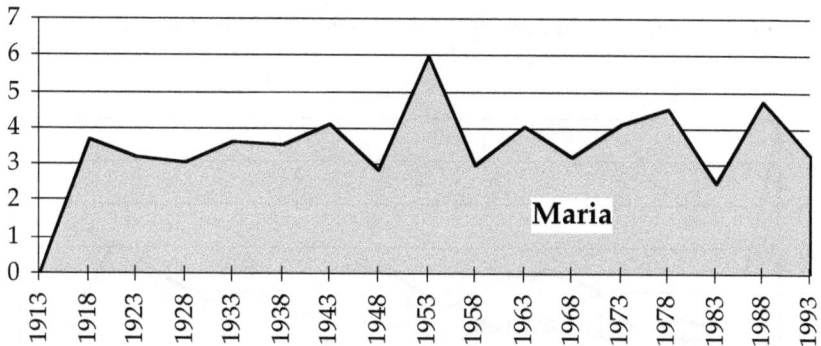

The same phenomenon can be seen with the third most common name in the list of women's first given names, *Martta*: its popularity has remained stable throughout the century (see figure 13).[440] This name is originally biblical, but it has also had Finnish name-bearers in the Ambo area, e.g. Martta Paavola and Martta Wäänänen (Peltola 1958, p. 272, 263).

Figure 13.

The proportion of women in the data who have the name Martta/Marta/Martha/Maartta as their first baptismal name (1913–1993) (%)

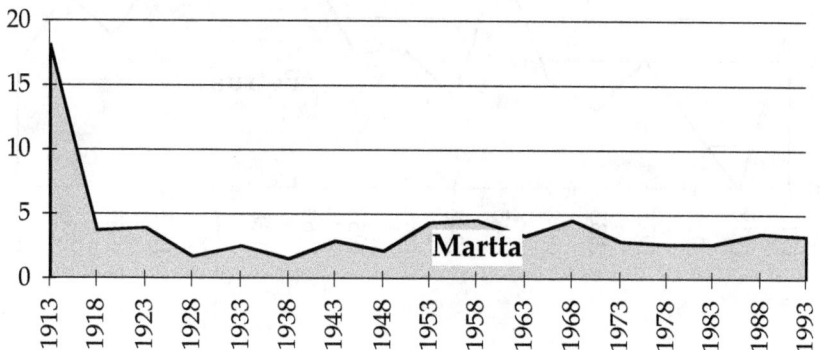

The most popular names in the list of first given names of men are the biblical *Johannes*, *Petrus* and *Andreas*, which have been relatively common among the Ambo Christians throughout the 20th century. The share of these names amongst the first given names of men is more than 2 per cent for most of the period 1913–1993 (see figures 14, 15 and 16).[441] Beside Johannes Syrjä, whose first baptismal name was *Johannes*, some Finnish missionaries have had *Johannes* as a subsequent baptismal name (Peltola 1958, p. 267, 259–277). The names *Petrus* and *Andreas*, however, do no occur as such among the names of Finnish missionaries. Of these names, *Johannes* appears 9 times, *Petrus* 14 times,[442] and *Andreas* only once as a subsequent baptismal name in the data.

Figure 14.

The proportion of men in the data who have the name Johannes/Johannesa/ Johanns as their first baptismal name (1913–1993) (%)

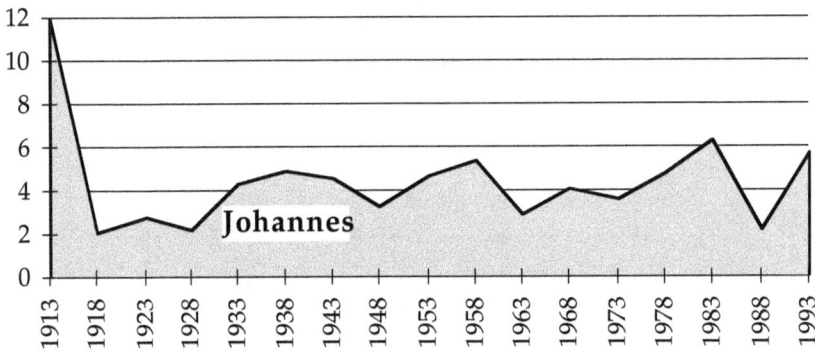

Figure 15.

The proportion of men in the data who have the name Petrus/Petrusa as their first baptismal name (1913–1993) (%)

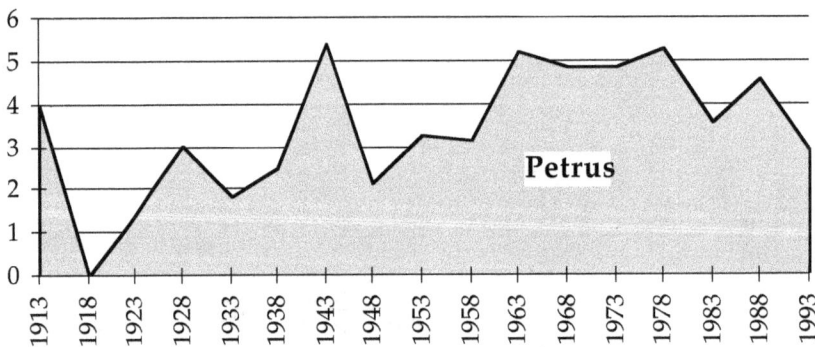

Figure 16.

The proportion of men in the data who have the name Andreas/Andrias/ Andreds as their first baptismal name (1913–1993) (%)

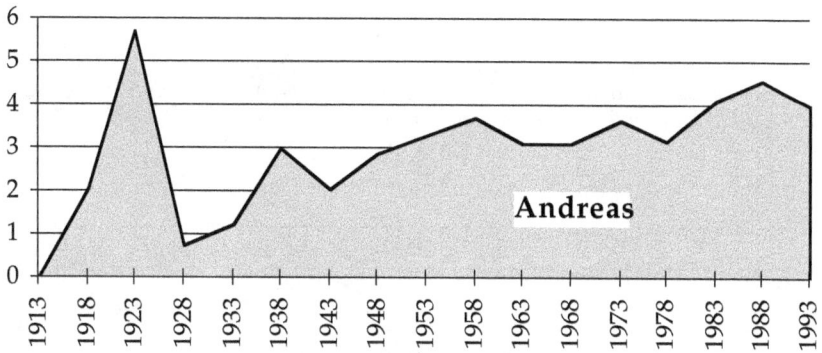

The changes in the popularity of the most common subsequent baptismal names look fundamentally different. As these names, which are almost exclusively Ambo, started to become common especially in the 1950s and 1960s, there would be no sense in making comparisons between the most popular subsequent baptismal names in the 1920s and 1990s, as was done with the first baptismal names. However, let us look at the developments in the popularity of the most common subsequent names. The most popular women's subsequent name, *Magano/Omagano* 'gift' has been common since the 1960s (see figure 17).[443] At times, it has been given to more than 5 or 6 per cent of the baptised girls. This name also appears 11 times (*Magano* 10 times, *Omagano* once) as a first given name in the data.

Figure 17.

The proportion of women in the data who have the name Magano/Omagano as a second, third or fourth baptismal name (1913–1993) (%)

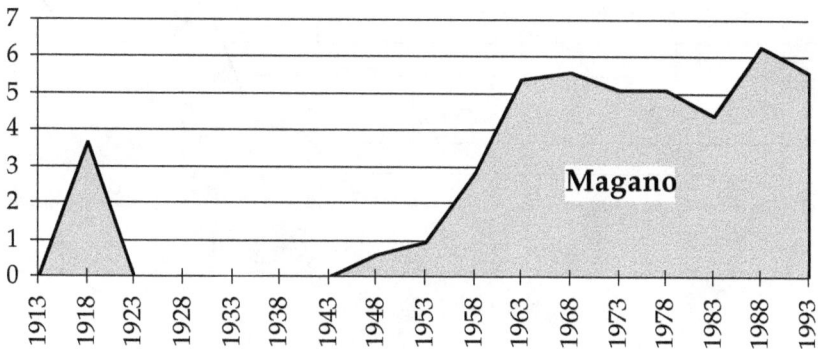

The second most common subsequent name of women is *Ndinelago* 'I have luck/ happiness', which has also become popular especially since the 1950s and 1960s (see figure 18). This name also appears 5 times as a first given name in the women's name data.

Figure 18.

The proportion of women in the data who have the name Ndinelago/Ndinelaago/ Dinelago as a second, third or fourth baptismal name (1913–1993) (%)

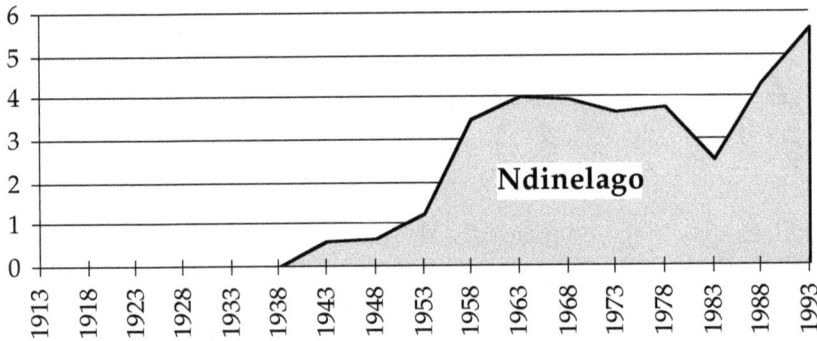

The most popular men's subsequent name, *Natangwe* 'may He be praised', as well as the second most common one, *Panduleni* 'thank', have also been very common since the 1960s (see figures 19 and 20). The name *Natangwe* also appears 5 times and the name *Panduleni* 3 times as a first given name in the data.

Figure 19.

The proportion of men in the data who have the name Natangwe/Natangue as a second, third or fourth baptismal name (1913–1993) (%)

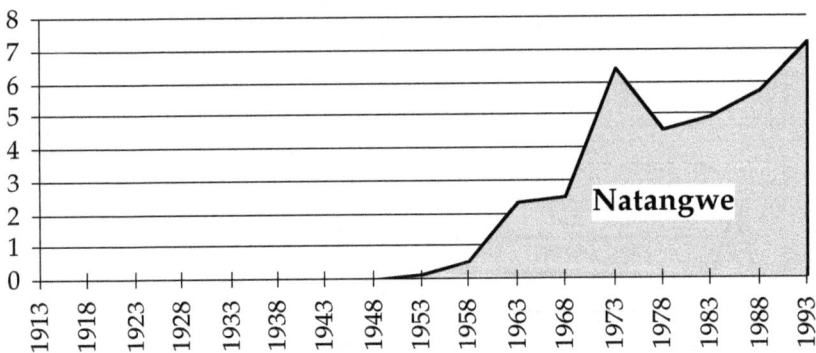

Figure 20.

The proportion of men in the data who have the name Panduleni/Pandulen as a second, third or fourth baptismal name (1913–1993) (%)

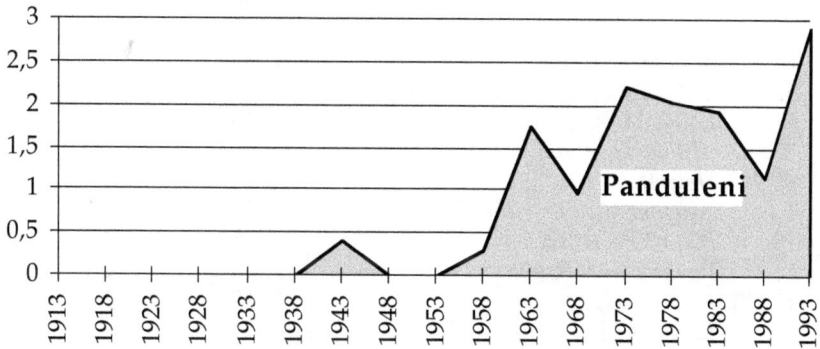

Regional Variation in Popular Names. Beside temporal variation, there also appears to be a regional variation in the popularity of baptismal names in the Ambo area. In this subsection, the focus will be on the first given names, which are often bestowed as namesake names. As the Ambo people have usually named their children after people who live near them and with whom they are in frequent contact, i.e. friends, family members, teachers, local missionaries, etc., it is understandable that many names are more common in some places than in others.

Judging from the baptismal registers only, it is impossible to say if a particular name has been given as a namesake name or not. However, in the name data for this study, one can find a few examples of name pairs which could be explained by a namesake relationship. Especially in cases in which the namesakes share more than two names or carry a combination of two names which is not common elsewhere, this looks quite obvious. For example, in the Okahao data there is a woman baptised as *Margaret Rose Ndinelago* in 1968 and another one as *Margalleta Rose Ndinelago* in 1993. In the Elim data one can find one *Rauha Fiina* baptised in 1948, one *Rauha-Fiina* in 1963, and yet another *Rauha-Fiina* in 1988. As these three women also represent different generations, it is possible that this is a real "namesake chain". On the other hand, the repetition of combinations of certain popular names, e.g. *Aina Magano* or *Selma Ndinelago*, should primarily be explained by the general popularity of these names, even if there most probably are namesake relationships behind these name combinations too. In some cases, the regional popularity of a particular name may also be due to a local naming fashion: a name which has been chosen by one name-giver, may also be given by many others who find it suitable as a baptismal name.

The lists of the most popular first given names of women in the Elim, Okahao and Oshigambo congregations show that many popular names are common in all three congregations. In all these "top twenty" lists (1913–1993), one can find the names *Aina, Helena, Hilma, Johanna, Maria, Martta* and *Selma*. These seven names are all European (Finnish) or biblical of origin, and so are most of the other names in these lists too.

Name		Number	Percentage
Elim			
1.	*Maria*	66	3.6
2.	*Selma*	54	3.0
3.	*Martta* 34 + *Marta* 19	53	2.9
4.	*Aina* 49 + *Ainna* 1	50	2.7
5.	*Johanna* 47 + *Johana* 1	48	2.6
6.	*Laina* 44 + *Lainna* 2	46	2.5
7.	*Hilma* 42 + *Hilm* 1	43	2.4
8.–9.	*Helena*	39	2.1
	Josefina 36 + *Josefiina* 3	39	2.1
10.	*Hilja* 33 + *Hilya* 3	36	2.0
11.	*Paulina* 27 + *Pauliina* 7	34	1.9
12.–13.	*Laimi*	32	1.8
	Elisabet 21 + *Elisabeta* 2 + *Elisbet* 2 +		
	Elizabet 1 + *Elizabeth* 6	32	1.8
14.	*Loide* 27 + *Loinde* 1	28	1.5
15.	*Saima*	27	1.5
16.–17.	*Aili*	25	1.4
	Rauna	25	1.4
18.–19.	*Emilia*	24	1.3
	Toini	24	1.3
20.	*Alina*	23	1.3
Okahao			
1.	*Loide*	98	4.3
2.	*Selma* 88 + *Selima* 1	89	3.9
3.	*Hertta*	84	3.7
4.	*Ester*	80	3.5
5.	*Aina*	74	3.3
6.	*Hilma*	70	3.1
7.	*Josefina* 51 + *Josefiina* 6 + *Josofina* 1	58	2.6
8.	*Maria*	57	2.5
9.	*Martta* 48 + *Marta* 1 + *Maartta* 1	50	2.2
10.	*Irja* 46 + *Iirja* 1	47	2.1
11.	*Johanna*	46	2.0
12.–13.	*Anna*	40	1.8
	Taimi	40	1.8
14.–16.	*Helena*	39	1.7
	Hilja	39	1.7
	Lahja 36 + *Lahija* 2 + *Lahya* 1	39	1.7
17.	*Julia*	37	1.6
18.	*Aune*	30	1.3
19.	*Kristofina* 27 + *Kristofiina*	29	1.3
20.	*Laimi*	28	1.2
Oshigambo			
1.	*Selma* 124 + *Selima* 3	127	6.5
2.	*Maria*	113	5.8
3.	*Martta* 58 + *Marta* 41 + *Martha* 1	100	5.1
4.	*Hilma* 63 + *Hilima* 10	73	3.7
5.	*Ester* 67 + *Estela* 3 + *Esitela* 2	72	3.7

6.–7.	*Frieda* 32 + *Frida* 27 + *Filita* 4	63	3.2
	Helena	63	3.2
8.	*Anna*	57	2.9
9.	*Hileni*	53	2.7
10.	*Johanna*	52	2.7
11.	*Emilia* 46 + *Emiilia* 1	47	2.4
12.	*Albertina* 22 + *Albertiina* 11 +		
	Albertin 10 + *Albertiin* 3	46	2.4
13.	*Saara* 36 + *Saala* 2	38	1.9
14.	*Elisabet*	35	1.8
15.	*Paulina* 16 + *Pauliina* 13	29	1.5
16.	*Aina* 27 + *Ainna* 1	28	1.4
17.	*Sofia*	27	1.4
18.	*Ruusa* 25 + *Ruus* 1	26	1.3
19.	*Monika*	24	1.2
20.	*Lovisa* 19 + *Lovis* 4	23	1.2

There are also clear differences between the popularities of these names in the three congregations. For example, *Loide* is much more common in Okahao than elsewhere, and *Ester* is very popular in Okahao and Oshigambo but not in Elim. The name *Hertta* also appears in the Okahao "top twenty" list only, and *Frieda* in the Oshigambo list only. Of these "top twenty" names, *Hertta* (84 occurrences) and *Irja/Iirja* (47 occurrences) are "unique" in the sense that they have a good number of occurrences in one congregation only, which is Okahao. Interestingly, one can find unique names in Okahao among the less popular names as well: *Ebba* (16 occurrences in Okahao: 0 elsewhere), *Gertrud* (22: 0) and *Sylvi/Syilvi* (16: 0). The women's names in Elim and Oshigambo are much more mixed. However, there are some names which are common in either of these congregations but rather rare elsewhere. Typical names for Elim are *Loise* (14: 2), *Saima* (27: 8) and *Susanna/Susana/Suusanna* (11: 1), for example, and typical for Oshigambo are *Frieda/Frida* (63: 16), *Ida/Iida* (9: 2), and *Sofia* (27: 9). The names *Ilona* (14: 0) and *Reeta/Reta/Retta* (9: 0) also occur in Elim only.

The lists of the most popular first given names of men in Elim, Okahao and Oshigambo (1913–1993) also show that many names are common in all these congregations: the biblical names *Andreas, David, Erastus, Filippus, Johannes, Paulus, Petrus* and *Tomas* appear among the "top twenty" names of every congregation.

Name		**Number**	**Percentage**
Elim			
1.	*Petrus*	46	3.1
2.	*Johannes* 43 + *Johanns* 1	44	2.9
3.	*Erastus*	39	2.6
4.	*Andreas* 32 + *Andrias* 3	35	2.3
5.	*Paulus*	32	2.1
6.	*Simon* 30 + *Simoni* 1	31	2.1
7.–8.	*Festus*	28	1.9
	Tomas	28	1.9

9.–10.	*Immanuel* 24+ *Imanuel* 1 + *Immanel* 1 +		
	Immanue 1	27	1.8
	Lukas 22 + *Luukas* 5	27	1.8
11.–12.	*Efraim* 22 + *Efraima* 2	24	1.6
	Junias	24	1.6
13.	*Martin* 18 + *Martina* 2 + *Marti* 1 + *Martti* 1 +		
	Marttina 1 + *Maritin* 1	24	1.6
14.	*Gabriel*	22	1.5
15.–16.	*Naftali* 17 + *Nafital* 2 + *Nafitali* 1 + *Naftal* 1	21	1.4
	Silas	21	1.4
17.	*Filippus* 14 + *Filipus* 4 + *Fiilippus* 1	19	1.3
18.–20.	*David*	18	1.2
	Epafras	18	1.2
	Lasarus 17 + *Lazarus* 1	18	1.2

Okahao

1.	*Andreas* 75 + *Andreds* 1	76	4.3
2.	*Petrus*	71	4.0
3.	*David*	69	3.9
4.	*Johannes*	68	3.9
5.	*Paulus*	60	3.4
6.	*Tomas*	42	2.4
7.	*Simon* 38 + *Siimon* 2	40	2.3
8.	*Timoteus*	34	1.9
9.	*Matteus* 21 + *Mateus* 12	33	1.9
10.	*Vaino* 30 + *Waino* 2	32	1.8
11.	*Benjamin* 22 + *Benjamen* 3 + *Beñamen* 2 +		
	Beñamin 1 + *Benyamen* 1 + *Benyamin* 1	30	1.7
12.–13.	*Erastus*	29	1.6
	Filippus 26 + *Filipus* 3	29	1.6
14.	*Josef*	27	1.5
15.	*Samuel* 24 + *Samue* 1	25	1.4
16.–17.	*Ananias*	24	1.4
	Sakeus	24	1.4
18.	*Titus*	22	1.2
19.–20.	*Eliaser*	19	1.1
	Filemon	19	1.1

Oshigambo

1.	*Johannes* 95 + *Johannesa* 2	97	6.0
2.	*Petrus* 75 + *Petrusa* 1	76	4.7
3.	*Mateus* 53 + *Matheus* 1 + *Maateus* 1	55	3.4
4.	*Sakaria* 51 + *Sakarias* 1	52	3.2
5.–6.	*Andreas* 47 + *Andrias* 1	48	3.0
	Paulus 44 + *Paulusa* 3 + *Paulu* 1	48	3.0
7.	*Filemon* 44 + *Filemoni* 1 + *Filemoon* 1 +		
	Filimoni 1	47	2.9
8.	*Tomas* 42 + *Tomasa* 2 + *Thomas* 1	45	2.8
9.	*David*	39	2.4
10.	*Filippus* 30 + *Filipus* 3 + *Filippu* 1	34	2.1
11.–12.	*Josef* 31 + *Josefa* 1	32	2.0
	Martin 31 + *Martina* 1	32	2.0
13.	*Gideon* 25 + *Gideona* 1	26	1.6

14.	*Jeremia* 24 + *Jeremija* 1	25	1.5
15.	*Samuel*	24	1.5
16.–17.	*Sakeus*	22	1.4
	Teofilus 16 + *Teofiilus* 4 + *Teoferus* 2	22	1.4
18.–19.	*Erastus*	21	1.3
	Vilhelm 14 + *Vilihema* 3 + *Wihema* 1 +		
	Wilhelm 2 +*Wilhem* 1	21	1.3
20.	*Tobias* 17+ *Topiasa* 1	18	1.1
21.–23.	*Jason*	17	1.0
	Lasarus	17	1.0
	Leonard	17	1.0

These lists show that there is a regional variation among the men's names too. For example, the names *Efraim*, *Festus* and *Immanuel* only appear in the "top twenty" list of Elim, *Benjamin*, *Timoteus* and *Vaino* on that of Okahao, and *Gideon*, *Jeremia* and *Sakaria* on that of Oshigambo. Among the men's "top twenty" names there are no names appearing in one congregation only. This may be explained by the fact that most of the men's popular first given names are biblical, and the models for these names, biblical characters, were similarly "present" in all congregations, contrary to the European missionaries whose names are most common in those areas where they have worked. However, there is one example of a European name which appears in one of these lists only, the Finnish *Vaino/Waino* (< *Väinö*). This name has 32 occurrences in the Okahao data, and 7 occurrences in other congregations. Among the less popular men's names, there are a few examples of unique names as well: the Finnish name *Juuso* in Oshigambo (10: 0) and the European *Maks* (< *Max*) in Okahao (11: 0). The other European names in the "top twenty" lists, *Leonard*, *Martin* and *Vilhelm*, were distributed fairly evenly among the three congregations, and the same could be said about many of the less popular European names in the data, e.g. *Armas*, *Eino*, *Frans*, *Oskar*, *Reinhold* and *Toivo*.

It is clear that the regional variation of names is an existing phenomenon in the Ambo area. In the case of European names, this was originally due to the fact that there were different missionaries working in different congregations, and hence the names that were adopted from the Europeans were different as well. Part of this variation may also be explained by the fact that some Ambo people were more popular as namesakes than others. Local naming fashions could also play a role in this phenomenon. Based on all this, one may assume that had there been more congregations chosen for this study, the variety of names in the data would have been wider as well.

The Classification and Analysis of the Name Data

Classification Principles

In order to analyse the baptismal names in the data with regard to their origins, the names were divided into four classes: 1. Biblical names, 2. European names, 3. Ambo names, and 4. Other names. At first, it seemed obvious that there were mainly biblical, European and Ambo names in the data, and separating the Ambo names from the biblical and European ones was quite simple. The distinction between the biblical and European names was a more difficult issue, however.

The main reason for this difficulty was that many names that are in general use in Europe are also biblical in origin, and they often have domesticated name forms which do not much resemble the original names in the Bible. Because of this, these name forms are not primarily regarded as biblical names in Europe, but as names belonging to the "national" nomenclatures of the countries in question. For example, the names *Liisa, Maija, Juho* and *Matti* are generally regarded as typical Finnish forenames, even if they are derived from the biblical names *Elisabet, Maria, Johannes* and *Mattias/Matteus* (Vilkuna 1993, p. 96, 112, 116, 121). Thus, the problem was whether such name forms be classified as biblical names or European names in this study. Classifying them as biblical names would undoubtedly be historically correct, but the name lists that one would get this way would not look very biblical. In many cases, it would also be impossible to judge if a particular name really is derived from a biblical name or from some other source, as many European name forms have various origins.

One could also suggest that the class of European names should be limited to names which have their roots in European languages. However, this would be very problematic, as it is often impossible to say if the origins of a particular name really are European or not. This kind of solution would also make the class of European names very small, as many names commonly used in Europe have their origins in the Bible or are borrowed from various non-European cultures. Moreover, to make this even more complicated, many biblical names are also European in origin, as they are Greek and Latin names, and separating them from the other biblical names would be a hopeless task. Hence, it is obvious that this kind of classification would not serve the purposes of this study either.

Should all names which are commonly used in Europe be classified as European names then, regardless of their origins? If so, many but not all biblical names that are used by the Ambo people would end up in this group as well. Or could the solution be that some names in the data should be classified as both biblical and European? This solution would perhaps correspond best to the actual situation in Ambo society, but such a double classification would make the analysis of the data very complicated. To avoid these problems, one might also feel tempted to classify all biblical and European names in the data into one single class. However, with such a solution a lot of information would be lost and hence no comparisons could be made between the popularity of biblical and European names in Ambo society.

The name data in this study also leads one to wonder if there would be any sense in classifying European names into further subgroups: Finnish names, German names, Afrikaans names and English names. It is clear that names such as *Armas* 'beloved' and *Orvokki* 'violet' are Finnish names, whereas *Friedrich* and *Gottfried* are German, for example.

230

However, this would also be very complicated, as many European names, e.g. *Emilia, Selma, Frans* and *Otto*, are in general use in several European countries and are not typical to one naming system only. Altogether, the personal nomenclatures in different European countries contain a large number of borrowed names from other European naming systems, as well as from various non-European naming systems.

After all these considerations, the name data were classified into four groups in such a way that one name could belong to one class only. No subclasses were formed either. Let us look at these classes and the criteria for the classification of names more closely here.

Biblical Names. In this study, the term *biblical name* is reserved for names which can be found in the Bible and which appear in the data either exactly as they are in the Old or the New Testament, or in a slightly modified form. These names are usually personal names of biblical characters, but biblical place names (e.g. *Jordan*) and expressions (e.g. *Hosiana*) appear as well. Domesticated Ambo forms of biblical names are also included in this class. Hence, the name forms *Estela* and *Esitela* were put into this class together with *Ester*, and *Johannesa* with *Johannes*. Names which could not be interpreted as Ambo forms of biblical names but resembled them to a great extent, were also included, e.g. *Maateus* and *Mateu* beside *Mateus*. The biblical origin of these names was checked both in the Finnish reference books of the Bible (Vuorela 1951, 1954) and the Ndonga Bible translations (Ombibeli Ondjapuki moshindonga 1954; Ombimbeli Ondjapuki 1977; Ombimbeli Ondjapuki 1986). European hypocoristic forms of biblical names, e.g. *Maija* and *Matti*, were left out of this class and regarded as European names. Some abbreviated forms of biblical names were classified into this class, however, as it seemed that they had been developed in the Ambo area and were thus not borrowed from the Europeans, e.g. *Stefa < Stefanus* and *Teemus, Temus < Nikodemus*.

Hence, names which appear in the Bible were classified into this group, irrespective of whether they are commonly used in Europe or not. The name *Maria*, for example, was classified as a biblical name in this study, even if it may often have been given in the Ambo area after some European woman carrying the name, rather than from its biblical reference. This was a practical solution too: with the assistance of the reference books of the Bible and the different Bible translations, it was easy to separate these names from the other names in the data. The Bible has also had a very important role in the life of the Ambo people, and thus one may assume that the biblical character of the name has been of importance also in cases in which these names have been given after Europeans. In the Ambo context, emphasising the biblical nature of names at the expense of the European aspect may thus be seen as justified. It is also a fact that in any onomastic classification in which a name belongs to one class only, one classification motive must be given a preference over the others.

European Names. This class contains names that the Ambo people have adopted from the Europeans, as well as from the Namibians of European origin, with whom they have been in close contact – except for the biblical names carried by these people. Some European names in the data can also be explained as coming from the influence of education and media, which have brought people and events outside the Ambo area closer to the Ambo people.

There are many Finnish names in this class. Some of them originate in the Finnish language, e.g. *Kaino* 'shy' and *Lahja* 'gift' for women, and *Armas* 'beloved' and *Oiva* 'very good' for men. Some of them are originally biblical or adopted from other European naming systems, but are generally regarded as Finnish names because of their Finnish form, e.g. *Kerttu < Gertrud, Maija < Maria, Heikki < Henrik, Vihtori < Victor* (Vilkuna 1993, p. 73, 102, 116, 185). There are also many German, English and Afrikaans names in this class, including common hypocoristic forms of biblical names in these naming systems, e.g. *Jack < John* (*Johannes*) in the English one. Many names in this class are also common in several European naming systems, e.g. *Emilia, Viktoria, Axel* and *Leonard*. Domesticated Ambo forms of European names are also included in this class, e.g. *Hilima* together with *Hilma* and *Vilihema* with *Wilhelm*. European surnames and their Ambo forms are found in this class as well. Names that are not typically used as personal names in European naming systems but refer to various aspects of European culture, e.g. *Junior* and *Origenes*, were also classified as European names in this study.

The origins of these names were checked in various European name books – German, English, Afrikaans, Dutch – which are listed in the bibliography of this study under the title Books of Reference. The main source for Finnish names was the list of the most common 5,000 names of the Finns since the late 19th century, presented by Kiviniemi (1982a, p. 249–348). The main source for the surnames used in Namibia was the Namibian telephone directory (Telecom Namibia 92/93), and the ones for the names of Finnish missionaries were Peltola 1958 (p. 259–277) and the personnel archives of the Finnish Evangelical Lutheran Mission in Helsinki.

Ambo Names. The third class contains Ambo names, which were for the most part easy to differentiate from the biblical and European names. Most of these names also turned out to be semantically transparent. The Ndonga–English Dictionary (Tirronen 1986) was most useful for the identification and translation of these names, together with the expertise of Ms. Lahja Lehtonen and Ms. Riikka Halme, who assisted with the translation of the Ndonga and Kwanyama names respectively.

There were some names in the data which could be interpreted as both Ambo and biblical or European names, e.g. *Hileni* and *Niilo*. In such cases, the name was classified according to the most probable interpretation. For example, names which occurred more commonly as a first given name or as the only baptismal name of the person, especially in the early 20th century, were more likely to be European or biblical than Ambo.

It is also possible that some of the names which were classified as Ambo in this study are in fact Ambo forms of biblical or European names, even if the origins of these names were impossible to trace. A profound analysis of all these names would have been too laborious a task, considering the general aims of this study. Hence, names which looked phonotactically like Ambo ones and could not be interpreted as Ambo forms of certain biblical or European names were classified as Ambo. It should be noted that all Ambo names in the data are not Ndonga or Kwanyama but represent other Ambo varieties as well, and tracing their meanings should be left to the specialists in Ambo linguistics. Nevertheless, hundreds of the Ambo names in the data could be translated, which was sufficient for an analysis of the morphology and semantics of these names.

Other Names. This class contains names which could not be classified otherwise, as their origins remained unclear. Many of these name forms look as if they were biblical or European in origin, but it was impossible to find out what the original name was. This group also includes abbreviated names which most likely refer to particular existing names, e.g. *K.* and *Nd.*, even if it is difficult to say what these names might be.

Biblical Names

Remarks on the Biblical Names in the Data. Earlier, we saw that biblical names were found among the most popular names in Ambo society. In the list of the twenty most popular first given names of women in the data, there are 6 biblical names: *Maria, Martta, Ester, Johanna, Loide* and *Elisabet.* In the corresponding list of men's names, all but one is biblical: *Johannes, Petrus, Andreas, Paulus, David, Tomas, Mateus, Erastus, Simon, Filemon, Filippus, Josef, Sakaria, Samuel, Immanuel, Sakeus, Timoteus, Titus* and *Gabriel.* Thus, one may say that biblical names have become an important part of Ambo personal nomenclature. Of the 16,643 name occurrences in the data, 5,671, i.e. one third (34.1 per cent), turned out to be biblical.

Biblical names are much more common as first given names than as subsequent given names. Of the 10,920 first given names in the data 5,419, i.e. roughly half (49.6 per cent) are biblical. Of the 5,723 subsequent given names, only 252 (4.4 per cent) belong to this class.

Adopting biblical names at baptism has been common everywhere in the world where people have embraced Christianity. Names of the central characters in the New Testament, e.g. the apostles and the disciples of Jesus, have become common. Hence, it is not surprising that the top names in the Christian world, such as *Elisabet, Maria, Andreas* and *Johannes,* appear among the most popular names in Ambo society too. This may partly be explained by a European model: these names have also been commonly used by the Europeans living in Namibia. However, it is impossible to judge on the basis of the name data only if a particular name was originally given after some European carrying this name, or because of its connection with a biblical character, or both. Here are some examples of biblical names in the data which might have been given after Finnish missionaries as well: *Eeva, Elisabet, Ester, Johanna, Lea, Lydia (Lyydia), Maria, Martta, Mirjam, Rakel; Elias, Gabriel, Isak, Johannes, Samuel, Tobias* (Peltola 1958, p. 259–277).

Some biblical names, e.g. *Eeva* and *Martta*, may also appear in a Finnish form because they were recorded in the church registers by Finnish missionaries or Ambo pastors to whom Finnish name forms were familiar, not necessarily because other Finns had had these names. Many biblical names may also be adopted from other Europeans in Namibia, e.g. *Dina, Hanna, Julia, Klaudia, Sara* and *Susanna* for women, and *Adam, Andreas, Daniel, David, Michael* and *Thomas* for men. On the other hand, there are many biblical names in the data which hardly have European models in Namibia, as these names are not popular names in European naming systems, e.g. *Bilha, Loide, Mahanaem, Peninna* and *Sipora* for women, and *Abisai, Epafroditus, Jerobeam, Onesimus* and *Sosipater* for men. Some of these names have also become surprisingly popular in the congregations studied for this thesis, especially the women's name *Loide* (157 occurrences in the data) and the men's names *Erastus* (89), *Festus* (49), *Junias* (40) and *Naftali* (46).[444] This phenomenon shows that the Ambo people have not simply followed the European model when adopting biblical names in their personal nomenclature.

The difference between the women's and men's names in this class is striking. Of the men's first given names 79.5 per cent (3,887) belong to this class, whereas the share of biblical names of the women's first given names is only 25.4 per cent (1,532), the majority of them being European names. The corresponding numbers for subsequent given names are 6.7 per cent (149) for men and 3.0 per cent (103) for women. There are many reasons for this difference. It is generally known that there are more male than female characters in the Bible, e.g. all the apostles and the twelve disciples of Jesus were men. Hence, there have been more biblical names for men to choose from, and this seems to be reflected in the names of the Ambo Christians as well.

Another explanation for this difference between men and women seems to be that Finnish female missionaries have had a very significant role in the missionary work carried out in the Ambo area. Since 1910, the number of Finnish female missionaries in South West Africa, i.e. in the Ambo area and in Okavango, was higher than that of male missionaries, and since the end of the 1920s, even the number of unmarried female missionaries was clearly higher than that of male missionaries (Kena 2000, p. 13–14).[445] In 1971, for example, out of a total of 102 Finnish missionaries 79 were women (Tötemeyer 1977, p. 21). Many Finnish women also worked as teachers, nurses and midwives, which led to the development of close relationships between them and the local people (Kena 2000, p. 194). Hence, it is not surprising that Finnish women were often chosen as namesakes for Ambo children. The Ambo informants of this study also emphasise that Ambo children have often been named after teachers and nurses (Amaambo 3.4.1997). Altogether, it seems to be both the number of Finnish female missionaries and the roles that they had in missionary work that explain this difference.

The Biblical Names of Women. The following list contains all the women's names in the data which were classified as biblical names. The numbers after the names show the number of occurrences of these names as first given names and as subsequent given names; the latter ones are given after a plus sign (+). Names which are to be found in the Old Testament are marked with OT, and the New Testament names with NT; many names also appear in both of them. The name forms in the Ndonga Bible translations (1954, 1977 and 1986) are set in boldface, and when a difference needs to be made between them, also with NB 1954, NB 1977 and NB 1986. In some cases, name forms in the Finnish Bible translations (Pyhä Raamattu 1938, Raamattu 1992) are given as well, and they are marked with FB. The sign (mn) indicates that the name is originally a man's name, not a woman's name.

The list also includes references to the use of these biblical names in European naming systems. The name forms listed after F are names that have been in common use in Finland. Names that have been carried by Finnish missionaries in the Ambo area are listed after FM. The letters G, A and E refer to name forms used in the German, Afrikaans and English naming systems respectively. Many of these name forms are similar to the ones in the Bible translations of these languages, but European hypocoristic forms of biblical names are given as well. Additional explanations for some name forms are given too. If the name is used for the same sex as in the Bible and in the same form, there is no need for further explanations.

Abia 1, *Abias* + 1. OT, NT (mn) (see the list of biblical men's names). The final *s* in the form *Abias* may be explained by the influence of the final *s* in many other biblical men's names, e.g. **Barnabas** or **Elifas**. The full names of these two women are **Abia** *Namupa* and *Loise Abias*.

Ada 1. OT. In the Ambo area, this name may also be of European origin, in which case it could be an abbreviated form of German women's names beginning with *Adel-*, e.g. *Adelheid*. F: *Aada*, **Ada**, G: **Ada**, *Adda*, A: **Ada**, E: **Ada**, *Adah*.

Apolonia 1. NT place name. NB: **Apollonia**. In Europe, this name can also be traced back to a 3rd-century Alexandrian martyr, a female saint named **Apollonia**. G: **Apollonia**, E: *Appoline*.

Bilha 9. OT.

Debor 1, **Debora** 3. OT. F: **Debora**, G, A: **Debora**, *Deborah*, E: *Deborah*.

Delila 4. OT. F: **Delila**, G, A: **Delila**, *Delilah*.

Diina 16, **Dina** 6. OT. In Europe, **Dina** can also be seen as an abbreviated form of women's names such as *Bernhardina* and *Gerhardina*. FB: *Diina, Dina*. F: *Dina*, G: **Dina**, *Dinah*, A: **Dina**, *Dinah, Diena*, E: *Dinah*.

Eben-Eser + 1, *Ebenhaezer* + 1. OT place name. This name also occurs as a man's name in the data (see the list of biblical men's names).

Eeva 3, **Eva** 8. OT, NT. F, FM: *Eeva, **Eva***, G: **Eva**, A, E: **Eva**, *Eve*.

Elisabet 60, *Elisabeta* 3, *Elisabeth* 3, *Elisbet* 2, *Elizabet* 1, *Elizabeth* 13. NT. F: **Elisabet**, *Elisabeth*, FM, G: *Elisabeth*, A: **Elisabet**, *Elisabeta, Elisabetta, Elizabet, Elizabeta, Elizabetta, Elizabeth*, E: *Elisabeth, Elizabeth*.

Esitela 2, *Estela* 3, **Ester** 169 + 4. OT. F: **Ester**, *Esteri, Esther*, FM: **Ester**, *Esteri*, G, E: *Esther, Hester*, A: **Ester**, *Esther, Hester*.

Eunike 17 + 2, *Heunike* + 1. NT. FB: *Eunika,* **Eunike**. F: *Euniika, Eunika*, A, E: *Eunice*.

Felix + 1. NT (mn). NB: **Feliks**, FB: *Feeliks, Felix*. The full name of this woman is *Aune Felix*. F (mn): *Feeliks,* **Feliks**, *Felix*, A (mn): **Feliks**, *Felix*, G (mn), E (mn): *Felix*.

Filemon + 1. NT (mn) (see the list of biblical men's names). The full name of this Ambo woman is *Fenni* **Filemon** *Ligola*.

Foibe 25 + 3. NT. A: *Febe, Phebe, Phoebe*, E: *Phoebe*.

Hanna 20 + 1. OT, NT. F: **Hanna**, G, A: **Hanna**, *Hannah*, E: *Hannah*.

Hofen + 1. OT (mn). NB: **Hofni**. This name form may be based on the biblical man's name **Hofni**, which appears among the men's names also as *Hofeni* and *Hofen* (see the list of biblical men's names). The full name of this Ambo woman is *Kristofina Nelago Timomukuathi Hofen*.

Jekonia 1. OT, NT (mn) (see the list of biblical men's names). The full name of this Ambo woman is **Jekonia** *Ndeshihala*.

Johana 1, **Johanna** 145 + 5. NT. F, FM, G: **Johanna**, A, E: *Joanna,* **Johanna**.

Julia 54 + 4, *Julila* 1. NT. F: **Julia**, *Juulia*, G: **Julia**, *Julie*, A, E: **Julia**.

Kelau 1, *Kelaudia* 3, *Klalaudia* 1, **Klaudia** 36 + 1. NT. In the name forms *Kelau* and *Kelaudia* the vowel *e* serves to make the consonant combination *kl* easier for the Ambo people to pronounce. F, G: *Claudia,* **Klaudia**, A, E: *Claudia*.

Kornelius 1. NT (mn) (see the list of biblical men's names). The full name of this woman is **Kornelius** *Ndapeua*.

Lea 17. OT. 1954 NB: **Leja**. F: **Lea**, *Leea*, FM, G: **Lea**, A: **Lea**, *Leah*, E: *Leah*.

Lidia 18 + 1, *Liidia* 1, *Lydia* 21 + 6, *Lyidia* 1. NT. FB: *Lyydia*. F: **Lidia**, *Liidia*, *Lydia*, *Lyydia*, FM: *Lyydia*, G, E: *Lydia*, A: **Lidia**, *Lydia*.

Loide 141 + 16, *Loinde* 1. NT. FB: *Loois*, A: *Lois*, *Loïs*, *Loïsa*, E: *Lois*. In the Afrikaans naming system, the name *Loïs* can also be seen as an abbreviated form of *Heloïse* or as a variant of *Louise*.

Maartta 1, **Marta** 61 + 1, *Martha* 1, *Martta* 140 + 5. NT. FB: *Martta*. F: **Marta**, *Martha*, *Martta*, FM: *Martta*, A, G: **Marta**, *Martha*, *Marthe*, E: *Martha*.

Magdaleen 1, **Magdaleena** 20 + 2, *Magdalen* 2, **Magdalena** 17 + 1. NT. 1954 NB: **Magdaleena**, 1977 NB, 1986 NB: **Magdalena**. F, FM: **Magdaleena**, **Magdalena**, G: **Magdalena**, *Magdalene*, A: **Magdalena**, *Magdalene*, *Magdaline*, E: *Madeline*, *Magdalen*.

Maha 1, *Mahanaem* 4, *Mahanaema* 1, *Mahnaem* 1, **Mahanaim** +1. OT place name. 1954 NB, 1986 NB: **Mahanajim**, 1977 NB: **Mahanaim**. *Maha* might be an abbreviated form of this name.

Maria 236 + 28. NT. F: *Mariia*, **Maria**, FM, G, A, E: **Maria**.

Miriama 1, **Mirjam** 34, *Mirjama* 1, *Mirjami* 1 + 2. OT. 1954 NB: **Mirijam**, 1977 NB: **Miriam**, 1986 NB: **Mirjam**. F: **Miriam**, **Mirjam**, *Mirjami*, FM: **Mirjam**, G, A: **Miriam**, **Mirjam**, E: **Miriam**.

Naema 1 + 1, **Naemi** 11 + 1, *Naomi* 1 + 1. OT. FB: *Noomi*. F: *Naema*, **Naemi**, *Naima*, *Naimi*, *Noomi*, G: **Naemi**, *Noemi*, A: *Naome*, *Naomi*.

Peninna 4. OT. F: **Peninna**.

Prisikila 1, *Prisikilla* 1, **Priskila** 5, *Priskilla* 9. NT. G, A, E: *Priscilla*.

Rakel 36, *Rakela* 1, *Rakkel* 7 + 1. OT, NT. F: *Raakel*, *Raakeli*, *Raakkel*, *Raakkeli*, *Rachel*, **Rakel**, FM: **Rakel**, G: *Rachel*, *Rahel*, A: *Rachel*, *Rachele*, *Rachell*, *Ragel*, E: *Rachel*.

Rebbek 2, *Rebbeka* 2, *Rebbekka* 1, *Rebek* 6, **Rebeka** 5, **Rebekka** 16, *Repekka* 1. OT, NT. 1954 NB (OT), 1977 NB (OT, NT), 1986 NB (NT): **Rebeka**, 1954 NB (NT), 1986 NB (OT): **Rebekka**. F: *Rebecca*, *Rebecka*, **Rebekka**, *Repekka*, G: **Rebekka**, A: *Rebecca*, **Rebekka**, *Rebeka*, E: *Rebecca*, *Rebekah*.

Rut 2 + 1, *Ruth* 2, *Ruthu* 1, *Rutt* 1, *Ruut* 2. OT, NT. F: **Rut**, *Ruth*, *Ruut*, *Ruuth*, G, E: *Ruth*, A: **Rut**, *Ruth*.

Saala 2, *Saara* 47 + 1, **Sara** 9. OT, NT. 1954 NB (OT): **Saraji**, 1977 NB (OT), 1986 NB (OT): **Sarai**. FB: *Saara*. F: *Saara*, **Sara**, *Sarah*, G: **Sara**, *Sarah*, *Zara*, *Zarah*, A, E: **Sara**, *Sarah*.

Salome 2 + 2. NT. F, FM, G, A, E: **Salome**.

Sipora 1. OT. 1986 NB: **Sippora**. G: *Zippora*.

Sosanna 1, *Sosana* + 1, *Sossanna* 1, *Sossana* + 2, *Susana* 1, **Susanna** 8 + 2, *Sussana* 2, *Suusanna* 1. NT. F: *Susan, Susann,* **Susanna**, *Susanne,* G: **Susanna***, Susanne, Suzanne,* A: **Susanna***, Susannah, Susanne, Suzanna, Suzanne,* E: *Susan, Susannah.*

Tabita 1. NT. A: **Tabita***, Tabitha,* E: *Tabitha.*

The Biblical Names of Men
The following list presents all the men's names in the data which were classified as biblical names, in the same way as biblical women's names were presented above. The sign (wn) indicates that the name is originally a woman's name, not a man's name. Names that are common to both sexes are marked with (wn, mn).

Aaron 10, *Aron* 15 + 1, *Arona* 2. OT. F: **Aaron***, Aaroni, Aron,* G: **Aaron***, Aron,* E: **Aaron***.*

Abed 29, *Abed-Nego* 1, **Abednego** 1. OT. *Abed* may be an abbreviated form of **Abednego***.*

Abel 9. OT. FB: *Aabel,* **Abel***.* F: *Aabel, Aapel, Aapeli,* **Abel***,* A: **Abel***, Abell,* G, E: **Abel***.*

Abia +1. OT, NT. 1954 NB (OT), 1986 NB (OT): **Abija***.* FB: **Abia***.* This name also occurs as a woman's name in the data (see the list of biblical women's names).

Abiafal 1, **Abiatar** 4, *Abiatra* 1, *Abijatar* 2, **Abjatar** 4. NT. 1954 NB, 1977 NB: **Abjatar***,* 1986 NB: **Abiatar***.* FB: **Abjatar***.* The letter *f* in the first name form may be due to misreading or misspelling.

Abineel 4, *Abinel* 2, *Abiniel* 1, **Abner** 15, *Abniel* 2. OT. F, E: **Abner***.*

Abisai 12, **Abisaji** 1. OT. 1954 NB: **Abisaji***,* 1977 NB, 1986 NB: **Abisai***.*

Abisalom 9, *Abisalomo* 2, **Absalom** 10, *Absalomo* 3. OT. F, G, E: **Absalom***.*

Abraham 39. OT. FB: *Aabraham,* **Abraham***.* F: *Aabraham, Aapraham, Aaprahami,* **Abraham***,* G, A, E: **Abraham***.*

Adam 1. OT. F: *Aadam, Aatam, Aatami,* A: **Adam***, Adahm,* G, E: **Adam***.*

Agrippa 1. NT.

Ahas 3. OT.

Akitofel 6, *Aktofel* 6 + 1, *Aktofer* 1. OT. 1954 NB, 1986 NB: **Ahitofel***,* 1977 NB: **Akitofel***.*

Alfeus 21. NT. A: **Alfeus***, Alpheus.*

Ammon 3, **Amon** 2. OT, NT. G: **Amon***.*

238

Amos 2. OT. 1986 NB: *Amoz*. F: *Aamos*, *Amos*, G, A, E: *Amos*.

Anania 1, *Ananias* 32 + 2. NT. FB, F: *Ananias*.

Andreas 154 + 1, *Andreds* 1, *Andrias* 4. NT. The second *d* in *Andreds* is most probably due to misreading or misspelling. F: *Andreas*, *Andres*, *Antreas*, G: *Andreas*, *Andres*, A: *Andreas*, *André*, *Andries*, *Andrew*, E: *Andrew*.

Andronikus 1. NT.

Aser 1, *Asser* 14, *Asseri* 1. OT. 1954 NB, 1977 NB: *Asser*, 1986 NB: *Aser*. F: *Asser*, *Asseri*.

Augustu 1, *Augustus* 4. NT. A: *Augustus*, E: *Augustus*. The name form *Augustu* may also refer to *August*, which is a European abbreviated form of *Augustus* (see the list of European men's names).

Barakia 1, *Barakias* 3, *Barasias* 1. NT.

Barnabas 2. G, A: *Barnabas*. NT.

Bartlomeus 1, *Bartolomeus* 3. NT. F: *Bartolomeus*, G: *Bartholomäus*, A: *Bartholomeus*, *Bartolomeus*, *Bartholomew*, *Bartolomeüs*, E: *Bartholomew*.

Beñamen 2 + 1, 5, *Beñamin*, *Benjamen* 7 + 1, *Benjamin* 25, *Benyamen* 1, *Benyamin* 1. OT. 1954 NB: *Beñamin*, 1977 NB, 1986 NB *Benjamin*. F, G, A: *Benjamin*.

Betuel 4. OT. 1954 NB: *Betujel*.

Biliam 1. OT. 1954 NB: *Bilejam*, 1977 NB, 1986 NB: *Bileam*.

Boas 1. OT.

Dan 1. OT. FB: *Daan*, *Dan*, F: *Dan*, *Dani*, G: *Dan*, A: *Daan*, *Dan*, E: *Dan*, *Danny*. In the Ambo context, as well as in Europe, this name can also be seen as an abbreviated form of the biblical *Daniel*.

Daniel 34 + 6. OT. 1954 NB: *Danijel*. F, G, E: *Daniel*, A: *Daniël*.

David 126 + 5. OT, NT. F: *Daavid*, *David*, G, E: *David*, A: *David*, *Dawid*.

Ebben-Eser + 1. OT place name. NB: *Eben-Eser*. This name also occurs as a woman's name in the data (see the list of biblical women's names). A (mn): *Ebenaeser*, *Ebeneser*, *Ebenezer*, *Ebenhaeser*, *Ebenhaezer*, E (mn): *Ebenezer*.

Efraim 36 + 1, *Efraima* 2. OT, NT. 1954 NB (OT): *Efrajim*. F: *Efraim*, G, E: *Ephraim*.

Elaser 1, *Eliaser* 23 + 2, *Elieser* 16, *Eliser* 1. 1954 NB (NT), 1977 NB (OT, NT), 1986 NB (OT, NT): *Elieser*, 1954 NB (OT): *Elijeser*, 1954 NB (NT), 1977 NB (NT), 1986 (OT, NT): *Eleasar*. F: *Eleasar*, E: *Eleazar*.

Eli 1. OT, NT. 1954 NB (NT), 1977 NB (NT): *Eeli*. F: *Eeli*, *Eli*, A: *El*, *Eli*, *Elie*, E: *Eli*.

Elia 21 + 1, *Elija* 1, *Elias* 11. 1954 NB (OT): *Elija*, 1954 NB (NT), 1977 NB (NT): *Elias*, 1977 NB (OT), 1986 NB (OT, NT): *Elia*. F: *Elia*, *Elias*, *Elijas*, FM, G: *Elias*, A: *Elia*, *Elias*, *Elija*, E: *Elias*, *Elijah*.

Eliab 1. OT. 1954 NB: *Elijab*.

Eliakim 5 + 1, *Eliakima* 2, *Eliakimi* 1, *Eliekima* 1, *Elijakim* 1, *Eljakim* 7. 1954 NB (OT), 1986 NB (OT): *Eljakim*, 1954 NB (NT), 1977 NB (OT, NT), 1986 NB (NT): *Eliakim*. FB: *Eljakim*.

Elifas 22 + 1, *Elipas* 1. OT.

Elikana 2, *Elkana* 3, *Elkanus* 1. OT. *Elkanus* may be formed from *Elkana* after the model of other biblical men's names ending with *-us*, e.g. *Erastus*, *Festus* and *Lasarus*. E: *Elkanah*.

Eneas 1. NT. E: *Aeneas*.

Enok 2, *Henok* 13. NT. 1954 NB, 1977 NB: *Enok*, 1986 NB: *Henok*. F: *Eenok*, *Eenokki*, *Enok*, G: *Enoch*, *Henoch*, A: *Enoch*, *Henoch*, *Henog*, E: *Enoch*.

Enos 5 + 3. OT, NT. A: *Enos*.

Epafras 25 + 1. NT.

Epafrasditus 1. A contamination of the biblical men's names *Epafras* and *Epafroditus*?

Epafroditus 2. NT.

Erastus 89. NT. A: *Erastus*.

Esra 2. F: *Esra*, G: *Esra*, *Ezra*, E: *Ezra*. OT.

Fanuel 18. NT.

Fares 1. NT.

Festus 46 + 2, *Fesitus* +1. A: *Festus*. NT.

Fiilippus 1, *Filippu* 1, *Filippus* 70, *Filipus* 10. NT. F: *Filippus*, G: *Philipp*, A: *Filippus*, *Philippus*, E: *Philip*.

Filemon 80 + 2, *Filemoni* 1, *Filemoon* 1, *Filimoni* 1 + 1. NT. F: *Filemon*, A: *Filemon*, *Philemon*, E: *Philemon*.

Fortunatus 1. NT. G: *Fortunat*, *Fortunatus*, E: *Fortunatus*.

Gabriel 47 + 1, *Gabrieri* 1. OT, NT. F: *Gaabriel*, *Gabriel*, FM, G, E: *Gabriel*, A: *Gabriel*, *Gabriël*.

Gaijus 1. NT. NB: **Gaius**, FB: *Gajus,* **Gaius**. F: *Caius, Kaijus, Kaius,* G: *Cajus, Kajus,* E: *Caius,* **Gaius**.

Gerson 1 + 1. OT. G: **Gerson**, E: *Gershom.*

Gideon 42, *Gideona* 1. OT, NT. 1954 NB (OT): **Gidejon**. F, G, E: **Gideon**, A: **Gideon**, *Gidion.*

Hagaia 1, **Haggai** 1. OT. 1954 NB: **Haggaji**.

Hanas 1. NT. NB: **Hannas**. *Hanas* may also refer to the European *Hans* (see the list of European men's names).

Hebron 1. OT place name.

Hesekiel 6, *Heskiel* 3, *Hiskiel* 1. OT. 1954 NB: **Hesekijel**. F: **Hesekiel**, G: *Ezechiel*, E: *Ezekiel.*

Heskia 2, *Hisikia* 1, **Hiskia** 3, **Hiskija** 1. OT, NT. 1954 NB (OT), 1986 NB (OT): **Hiskija**, 1954 NB (NT), 1977 NB (OT, NT), 1986 NB (NT): **Hiskia**. F: **Hiskia**, *Hiskias*, E: *Hezekiah.*

Hofen 2 + 2, *Hofeni* 2 + 2, *Hofin* 4, *Hofini* 1, **Hofni** 4 + 2. OT.

Hosea 21 + 1. OT, NT. 1954 NB (OT): **Hoseja**. G: **Hosea**.

Hosiana + 1. NT. An exclamation in Hebrew: *hoshi'ana* 'hosanna, help'. NB: **Hosianna**. E: *Hosanna* (w, m).

Imanuel 1, *Immanel* 1, *Immanue* 1, **Immanuel** 49 + 2, *Immanuela* 1. OT, NT. F: *Imanuel*, **Immanuel**, G, A, E: **Immanuel**.

Isai 8. OT, NT. 1954 NB (OT): **Isaji**.

Isak 27. OT, NT. 1954 NB (OT), 1977 NB (OT): **Isaak**, 1954 NB (NT), 1977 NB (NT), 1986 NB (OT, NT): **Isak**. F: *Iisak, Iisakki*, **Isak**, FM: **Isak**, G: *Isaak*, A: *Isaac, Isaak, Isac,* **Isak**, *Izaak, Izak*, E: *Isaac, Izaak.*

Isaskar 2, *Isaskari* 1. OT, NT.

Ismael 13. OT. 1954 NB: **Ismajel**. F: **Ismael**.

Israel 15. OT, NT. 1954 NB (OT): **Israjel**, 1954 NB (NT), 1977 NB (OT, NT), 1986 NB (OT): **Israel**, 1986 NB (OT, NT): **Israeli**, F, G, E: **Israel**. This name appears in the Bible both as a personal name and as the name of a nation.

Jaason 1, **Jason** 40 + 4. NT. A: **Jason**, *Jasson*, E: **Jason**.

Jafet 27 + 2, *Jafeta* 2. OT. F: *Jaafet*, **Jafet**, *Jahvet, Jahvetti*, E: *Japhet, Japheth.*

Jairus 7. NT.

Jakob 17, *Jakobo* 2. OT, NT. F: *Jaakob, Jaakop, Jaakoppi, Jacob,* **Jakob**, G, A: *Jacob,* **Jakob**, E: *Jacob*.

Jefta 1, *Jefuta* 1. OT, NT. E: *Jephtah*.

Jekonia 3. OT, NT. 1954 (OT): **Jekońa, Jekonija**, 1977 (OT): **Jekonia**, 1986 (OT): **Jojakin**. This name also occurs as a woman's name in the data (see the list of biblical women's names).

Jeremia 36, *Jeremija* 1. OT, NT. 1954 NB (OT): **Jeremija**. F: **Jeremia**, *Jeremias*, G: *Jeremias*, A: **Jeremia**, *Jeremiah, Jeremias*, E: *Jeremiah, Jeremy*.

Jerobeam 9 + 1, *Jerobeas* 1. OT. 1954 NB: **Jerobejam**.

Jesaja 17 + 2, *Jesaya* 6. OT. F: *Esaias, Esaijas, Esajas*, A: *Esaias, Jesaias,* **Jesaja**, *Jesajas*, E: *Isaiah*.

Joas 1. OT.

Job 8. OT, NT. F, G, A, E: **Job**.

Joel 30 + 1, *Jooel* 1. OT, NT. F: **Joel**, *Joeli, Jooel*, A: *Joël*, E: **Joel**.

Johannes 206 + 9, *Johannesa* 2, *Johanns* 1. NT. F, FM, G, A: **Johannes**, E: *John*.

Jolam + 1, **Joram** 1, *Jorama* 3. OT, NT. 1954 NB (OT), 1977 NB (OT): **Hadoram**. These name forms may also be based on the Finnish man's name *Jorma*, which is derived from the biblical **Jeremia**. F: *Jorma*.

Jona 14 + 3, **Jonas** 32, *Joona* 2. OT, NT. 1954 NB (NT): **Jonas**. FB: *Joona*. F: **Jonas**, *Joona, Joonas*, G: **Jonas**, A: *Jon,* **Jona**, *Jonah,* **Jonas**, E: *Jonah,* **Jonas**.

Jonatan 3, *Jonatana* 1. OT. F: **Jonatan**, *Jonathan, Joonatan*, G, E: *Jonathan*, A: **Jonatan**, *Jonathan*.

Jordan 1. OT and NT place name (river). G, E: **Jordan**.

Josafat 5. OT, NT.

Josef 74 + 3, *Josefa* 2. OT, NT. F: *Joosef, Joosep, Jooseppi,* **Josef**, *Josep, Joseph*, G: **Josef**, *Joseph*, A: **Josef**, *Joseph, Jozef*, E: *Joseph*.

Josia 3. OT, NT. 1954 NB (OT): **Josija**. G: **Josia**, *Josias*, A: **Josia**, *Josiah, Josias*, E: *Josiah*.

Josua 8. OT, NT. F: *Joosua,* **Josua**, G: **Josua**, A: *Joshua,* **Josua**, *Jozua*, E: *Joshua*.

Judas 1. NT. In the New Testament, there are many male characters with this name. As it also belonged to Judas Iscariot, the disciple who betrayed Jesus, it has not been popular in Europe either. E: *Jude*.

Julius 16. NT. F, G, A, E: **Julius**.

Junia 1, **Junias** 38 + 1. NT. A: *Junia, Junius*.

Justus 4. NT. F, G, A: **Justus**.

Kaanana 1. OT. 1954 NB, 1977 NB: **Kanaan**, 1986 NB: **Kaanan**.

Kaareb 1, *Kaareba* 1, **Kaleb** 1. OT. F: *Kaaleb, Kaaleppi*, **Kaleb**, E: *Caleb*.

Karpus + 1. NT.

Kefas 8 + 1, *Kefasa* 1. NT. A: *Cefas, Cephas, Sefas*.

Keleopas 1, **Kleopas** 17, *Kleupos* 1. NT. F: *Kleofas*.

Klemens 2. NT. F: **Klemens**, G: *Clemens*, **Klemens**, A: *Clemence, Clemens*, **Klemens**, E: *Clement*.

Kornelius 9, *Kronelius* 1. NT. G: *Cornelius, Kornel*, **Kornelius**, A: *Cornelis, Cornelius, Korneels, Kornelis*, **Kornelius**, E: *Cornelius*.

Laban 1. OT.

Lamek 13. OT, NT.

Lasarus 37 + 3, *Lazarus* 1. NT. G: *Lazar*, A: **Lasarus**, *Lazarus*, E: *Lazarus*.

Lebbeus + 1, *Lebeus* 1 + 1, *Rebeus* 2. NT. **Lebbeus** appears in the 1954 and 1977 Ndonga Bible translations only, not in the 1986 translation. First, this disciple of Jesus was referred to as 'Lebbeus, whose byname is Taddeus' ("naLebbeus, edhina lye lyoponto Taddeus"), and later as "Taddeus" only (Mateus 10: 3). The same has happened in the Finnish Bible translations (1938 and 1992).

Leevi 11 + 1, **Levi** 3 + 2. OT, NT. FB: *Leevi*. F: *Leevi*, **Levi**, E: **Levi**.

Liinus 2, **Linius** 1, **Linus** 7. NT. 1954 NB, 1977 NB: **Linius**, 1986 NB: **Linus**. FB: *Liinus, Linos*. F: *Liinus*, G, A: **Linus**.

Liisias 1, **Lisias** 20, *Lisiasa* 2, *Lisijas* 1. NT.

Lot 9 + 1. OT, NT. A: **Lot**, *Lothar*.

Lukas 41, *Luukas* 6. NT. FB: *Luukas*. F: **Lukas**, *Luukas*, G, A: *Lucas*, **Lukas**, *Luke*, E: *Lucas, Luke*.

Lukius 4 + 1. NT. G: *Lucius, Luzius*, A, E: *Lucius*.

Maateus 1, *Mateu* 1, **Mateus** 79 + 1, *Matheus* 1, *Matteus* 22 + 2. NT. F: **Mateus**, *Matheus, Matteus*, G: *Matthäus*, A: *Matteus, Mattheus, Matthew*, E. *Matthew*.

Mahanaem 1. OT place name. 1954 NB, 1986 NB: *Mahanajim*, 1977 NB: **Mahanaim**. This name also appears as a woman's name in the data (see the list of biblical women's names).

Malakia 16 + 1, *Malakias* 2. OT. 1954 NB: **Malejaki**, 1977 NB: **Malakia**, 1986 NB: **Maleaki**. FB: *Malakia*. F: *Malakias*, E: *Malachi*.

Markus 12 + 1, *Mrkus* 1. NT. F, G: **Markus**, A: *Marcus*, **Markus**, E: *Marcus, Mark*.

Matatias 2. NT. 1954 NB, 1977 NB: **Matatia**.

Matias 17. NT. F: *Mathias*, **Matias**, *Matiias, Matthias, Mattias*, G, E: *Matthias*, A: *Mathias*, **Matias**, *Matthias*.

Melkisedek 3, *Melkisedeki* 1, *Melksedek* 1 + 1. OT, NT. E: *Melchisadek*.

Metusala 3, *Metusalem* 4. OT. E: *Methuselah*.

Michael 1, **Mikael** 16 + 1. OT, NT. F: *Micael, Michael, Mickael, Miikael, Miikkael*, **Mikael**, *Mikaeli*, G, E: *Michael*, A: *Michael, Michail, Michiel, Migael*.

Miika 1, **Mika** 12 + 1. OT. FB: *Miika*. F: *Miika*, **Mika**, E: *Micah*. In Finland, **Mika** is an abbreviated form of the biblical **Mikael**.

Misael 1. OT. 1954 NB: **Mišael**, 1977 NB, 1986 NB: **Mishael**.

Moses 26 + 1. OT, NT. F: *Mooses*, **Moses**, G, E: **Moses**.

Nabot 1 + 1. OT.

Nafital 2, *Nafitali* 1, *Naftal* 6, **Naftali** 36 + 1. OT.

Nahas 1. OT. 1986 NB: **Nahash**.

Nahum 7, *Nahuma* 2. OT, NT. E: **Nahum**.

Nason 1. OT, NT. 1954 NB (OT), 1977 NB (OT): **Nahason**, 1954 NB (NT), 1977 NB (NT), 1986 NB (NT):**Nahasson**, 1986 NB (OT): **Nakshon**, 1954 NB (NT), 1977 NB (NT): **Naasson.** FB: **Nahasson**, *Nahson*.

Natan 4. OT, NT. G, E: *Nathan*, A: **Natan**, *Nathan*.

Natanael 13 + 3. NT. F: **Natanael**, G: *Nathanael*, A: **Natanael**, *Nataniel, Nathanael*, E: *Nathanael, Nathaniel*.

Nehemia 5 + 1. OT. 1954 NB: **Nehemija**. F: *Nehemias*, E: *Nehemiah*.

Neri 1. OT, NT. NB (OT): **Ner**.

Nikanor 16. NT. F: **Nikanor**.

Nikodemus 27 + 1, *Nikodemusa* 1, *Teemus* 5, *Temus* 2. NT. The name forms *Teemus* and *Temus* seem to be abbreviated forms of *Nikodemus*. FB: Nikodeemus, *Nikodemos*. F: *Nikodeemus*, *Nikodemus*, *Teemu*, G: *Nikodemus*, E: *Nicodemus*.

Noa 6, *Noua* 1. OT, NT. 1954 NB, 1977 NB: *Noa*, 1986 NB: *Noowa*. F: *Noa*, *Noak*, G, E: *Noah*.

Obadja 3. OT. G: *Obadja*, E: *Obadiah*.

Obed 2. OT, NT.

Olimpas (Orpas) 1. NT. FB: *Olympas*. The name *Orpas*, which is put in brackets after the name *Olimpas* in the baptismal register, does not occur in the Bible. NB (OT, wn): *Orpa*. E: *Olympias*.

Onesemus 1, *Onesimus* 5, *Onesmus* 7. NT.

Onesiforus + 1. NT.

Palus 1, *Paulu* 1, *Paulus* 136 + 5, *Paulusa* 3. NT. F: *Paul, Pauli, Paulus*, G, E: *Paul*, A: *Paulus*.

Penehas 1, *Pinehas* 14. OT. E: *Phineas, Phinehas*.

Petrus 192 + 14, *Petrusa* 1. NT. F: *Petrus*, FM: *Pietari*, A: *Petros, Petrus, Pieter,* G, E: *Peter*.

Pilatus 2. NT.

Potfar 1. OT. NB: *Potifar*.

Rehabeam 13, *Rehabiam* 1. OT, NT. 1954 NB (OT): *Rehabejam*.

Ruben 13 + 1, *Ruuben* 1. OT, NT. F: *Ruben*, *Ruuben*, G: *Ruben*, A: *Reuben, Ruben*, E: *Reuben*.

Rufus 1, *Ruufus* 1. NT. F, G, A, E: *Rufus*.

Sadok 5, *Sandok* 1. OT, NT. 1986 NB (OT): *Zadok*.

Sadrak 3. OT. 1986 NB: *Shadrak*.

Sakaria 74 + 2, *Sakarias* 1. NT. F: *Sakari*, *Sakaria*, *Sakarias*, *Zacharias*, FM: *Sakari*, G: *Zacharias*, A: *Sagaria, Sagarias, Zacharia, Zacharias, Zacharya*, E: *Zacharias, Zachary*.

Sakeus 52 + 1. NT. F: *Sakeus*, A: *Saggeus, Zacheus*.

Salatiel 5 + 1. OT, NT. 1954 NB (OT): *Sealtijel*, 1977 NB (OT): *Sealtiel*, 1986 NB (OT): *Shealtiel*. FB: *Sealtiel*. E: *Salathiel*.

Salmo + 1, *Salom* 3, **Salomo** 25. OT, NT. F: **Salomo**, *Salomon, Salomoni*, G: *Salomon*, A: *Salamon*, **Salomo**, *Salomon, Solomon*, E: *Solomon*.

Salmon 1. OT, NT. 1954 NB (OT), 1977 NB (OT): **Salmona**, 1986 NB (OT): **Zalmona**. This name form in the data may also be based on the biblical **Salomo**. A: **Salmon**.

Samue 1, **Samuel** 58. OT, NT. 1954 NB (OT): **Samujel**. F: *Saamuel*, **Samuel**, *Samueli*, FM: **Samuel**, G, A, E: **Samuel**.

Saul 1. OT, NT. 1986 NB (OT): **Shaul**, 1986 NB (NT): **Saulus**. F: **Saul**, *Sauli*, A: **Saul**, **Saulus**, E: **Saul**.

Sdefanus 1, *Stefa* 1, **Stefanus** 27 + 1, *Sttefanus* 1. NT. *Stefa* may be an abbreviated form of **Stefanus**. In the New Testament, there is also a man's name **Stefanas**. F: **Stefanus**, G: *Stefan, Stephan*, A: **Stefanus**, *Stephanus, Stefan, Stephan*, E: *Stephen*.

Sebedeus 1. NT.

Seblon 4 + 1, **Sebulon** 17 + 1. OT, NT.

Sefania 1. OT. 1954 NB: **Sefańa**, 1977 NB, 1986 NB: **Sefanja**. F: *Sefania, Sefanias*, A: **Sefanja**, *Zefanja*, E: *Zephaniah*.

Sem 39. OT, NT. F: **Sem**, *Semi, Semmi*.

Sema 2, *Semae* 1. OT. 1986 NB: **Shema**. In the New Testament (NB 1954; NB 1977; NB 1986), there is also a man's name **Semei**, on which the form *Semae* may be based. **Sema** could also be interpreted as an Ambo form of the biblical man's name **Sem**.

Setta 1. OT, NT. NB: **Set**. F: *Seet, Seeti*, **Set**, *Seth, Setti*, E: *Seth*.

Siimon 2, *Siimoni* 1, **Simon** 84 + 4, *Simoni* 1. NT. F: *Siimon, Siimoni*, **Simon**, G, A, E: **Simon**.

Sila 1, **Silas** 39 + 2. NT. F: *Siilas*, E: **Silas**.

Silvanus 16 + 3. NT. G: *Silvan*, **Silvanus**, A, E: **Silvanus**.

Simeon 40, *Simion* 4. OT, NT. F: *Siimeon*, **Simeon**, *Simeoni*, G, A, E: **Simeon**.

Simson 8, *Simsoni* 1. OT, NT. F: **Simson**, G: *Samson*, **Simson**, E: *Samson, Sampson*.

Sioni + 1. OT, NT place name (mountain). 1954 NB (OT): **Sijon**, 1977 NB (OT): **Sion**.

Sosipater 1. NT.

Teofelius 1, *Teofelus* 1, *Teoferus* 2, *Teofiilus* 4, **Teofilus** 36 + 2. NT. F: *Teofiilus*, **Teofilus**, G: *Theophil, Theophilus*, A: *Theofilus, Theophilus*, E: *Theophilus*.

Thomas 1, **Tomas** 112 + 3, *Tomasa* 2. NT. F: *Thomas*, **Tomas**, *Tuomas*, A: *Thomas*, **Tomas**, G, E: *Thomas*.

Tiitus 5, **Titus** 44. NT. F: *Tiitus*, **Titus**, G, E: **Titus**.

Timoteus 48 + 2, *Timoteusa* 1. NT. F: **Timoteus**, G: *Timotheus*, A: **Timoteus**, *Timotheus*, E: *Timothy*.

Tobias 47, *Topiasa* 1. OT NB 1954, NB 1986: **Tobija**, NB 1977: **Tobia**. FB: **Tobia**. F: *Tobias*, *Topia*, *Topias*, FM: *Tobias*, G, A: *Tobias*, E: *Tobias*, *Toby*.

European Names

Remarks on the European Names in the Data. Beside biblical names, names of European origin have become very common in the Ambo area as a result of European cultural influence. Among the twenty most popular women's first given names in the data, 14 names were classified as European names: *Selma, Hilma, Aina, Helena, Anna, Josefina, Emilia, Hilja, Hileni, Hertta, Paulina, Albertina, Frida* and *Taimi*. In the corresponding list of men's names, there is only one European name: *Martin*. Other popular European men's names in the data are *Vaino* (45 occurrences), *Wilbard* (42), *Leonard* (40), *Frans* (37), *Vilhelm* (37), *Oskar* (29), *Armas* (26), *Toivo* (23), *Vilho* (22), *Reinhold* (21) and *Eino* (18).

Of the 16,643 name occurrences in the data, 5,453, i.e. almost one third (32.8 per cent), are of European origin. Just as was the case with biblical names, European names are much more common as first given names than as subsequent given names. Of the 10,920 first given names in the data, 5,090, i.e. roughly half (46.6 per cent), are European. Of the 5,723 subsequent given names, only 363 (6.3 per cent) belong to this class. This is because the majority of subsequent given names in the data are Ambo.

There is also a clear difference between the names of women and men in this class. Of the women's first given names 70.7 per cent (4,264) belong to this class, whereas the share of European names of the men's first given names is only 16.9 per cent (826). The first given names of women are thus predominantly European, while the men's first given names are predominantly biblical. The corresponding numbers in subsequent given names are 8.0 per cent for women (278) and 3.8 per cent (85) for men.

Many, if not most, European names in the data are of Finnish origin, but there are also names which are common among the Namibians who have their roots in Europe. Hence, beside names adopted from Finnish missionaries, there are also German, Afrikaans and English names in the data. Let us look at examples of names typical of these groups:

Finnish women's names: *Aila, Aili, Aina, Aini, Aino, Aune, Helmi, Helvi, Hilja, Hilkka, Impi, Inkeri, Irja, Kaino, Kaisa, Kerttu, Lahja, Laimi, Laina, Lempi, Lilja, Lyyli, Maija, Maila, Orvokki, Raili, Rauha, Rauna, Ruusa, Saija, Saima, Saimi, Siiri, Sirkka, Sirpa, Siviä, Suoma, Sylvi, Taimi, Terttu, Toini, Tuulikki.*

Finnish men's names: *Armas, Arvo, Eero, Eino, Erkki, Esko, Heikki, Juho, Juuso, Lauri, Matti, Mauno, Mikko, Oiva, Paavo, Pentti, Risto, Simo, Tauno, Toivo, Urho, Vaino (< Väinö), Veijo, Veikko, Vilho, Viljo.*

German women's names: *Adelheid, Auguste, Elise, Frieda, Hilde, Menette (< Minette), Mestilde (< Mechthilde), Ottilie, Renatte (< Renate).*

German men's names: *Bernhard, Friedrich, Gebhard, Gerhard, Gottfried, Gottlieb, Helmut, Reinhold, Willebrand, Willehard.*

Afrikaans women's names: *Aleta, Bernardina, Evalina, Hariana (< Ariana), Hendrika, Hendrina, Letta, Saarti (< Saartjie).*

Afrikaans men's names: *Arbertus (< Albertus), Antonius, Ati (< At, Attie), Darius, Hendrik, Jakobus, Reinert, Sebastianus.*

English women's names: *Jennifer, Jenny, Nancy, Rose.*

English men's names: *Barry, Cenneth (< Kenneth), Charles, Elvis, George, Henry, Jack, Jimmy, Marvin.*

Beside these names, there are also many names in the data which are common to most of these naming systems. The reason for this is that many personal names have been adopted from one naming system to another in Europe. Hence, there are names of German origin in the Finnish system, names of English origin in the German system, etc. The German and Afrikaans naming systems especially have common names, because of common linguistic roots. The Finnish naming system is more different, mainly due to the large number of names originating in the Finnish language. These became popular in Finland after the national awakening in the 19th century, e.g. *Impi* 'maiden', *Kaino* 'shy', *Lahja* 'gift', *Lempi* 'love', *Orvokki* 'violet'; *Armas* 'beloved', *Oiva* 'very good', *Toivo* 'hope', *Veikko* 'brother'. Here are some examples of the "Pan-European" names in the data:

Pan-European women's names: *Albertina/Albertiina, Alma, Amalia, Beata, Berta/Bertta, Charlotte, Ella, Elma, Emilia, Emma, Evelina/Eveliina, Hilaria, Hilda, Hilma, Hulda, Ida, Josefina/Josefiina, Juliana, Laura, Leena/Lena, Liina/Lina, Linda, Liisa/Lisa, Monica/Monika, Natalia, Nina, Olivia, Paula, Rosa, Selma, Sofia, Victoria/Viktoria.*

Pan-European men's names: *Adolf, Albin, Alfred, Aksel/Axel, Alfons, Arnold, Edvard/Edward, Frans, Hans, Herman, Jan, Leonard, Leopold, Martin, Nestor, Oskar/Oskari, Otto, Robert, Rudolf, Victor/Viktor, Vilhelm/ Wilhelm.*

Many names in the data are also originally names of non-biblical saints, or names which refer to the Christian culture without being biblical names. Examples of such names are:[446]

Women's non-biblical Christian names: *Agnes, Anastasia, Angela, Anna/ Anne, Birgitta, Dorotea, Ebba, Epefinia (< epifaneia), Gertrud, Hedvig, Helena, Hilda, Jehova, Juliana, Justina, Katrina, Krismes, Kristina, Lusia, Margaret, Marian, Monica/Monika, Paula, Sesilia, Ursula, Valeria, Veronika, Victoria/Viktoria.*

Men's non-biblical Christian names: *Augustinus, Achrenius, Agnus, Albert, Aleksander, Ambrosius, Barry, Benediktus, Bonifatius, Charles, Dennis, Edward, Erasmus, Fredinad (< Ferdinand), George, Germanius (< Germanus), Geron, Henry, Hilarius, Ignatius, Ireneus, Josse, Kansius (< Canisius), Keneth, Kosmas (< Cosmas), Kristian, Leonard, Martin, Modestus, Niklas (< Nicholas), Olavi (< Olaf), Oligenes (< Origenes), Patrik (< Patrick), Pius, Robert, Sebastianus, Severinus, Teodor, Viktor.*

It is important to note that many of these names are ordinary first names in many European naming systems and thus not primarily regarded as saints' names today. As the saints do not have any special religious significance for the Lutheran Ambos, it is reasonable to assume that they have adopted these names mainly because they are names carried by Europeans, not because they refer to specific saints. Some of these saints' names, e.g. *Bonifatius, Ireneus* and *Pius*, may also be adopted from Anglican and Catholic Ambos after whom the Lutheran Ambos have named their children.

Beside names that are common forenames in European naming systems, many names in the data are originally European surnames (*Hynonen, Nixon*) or have their origins in European languages (*Happy, Dezember*).

The European Names of Women. The following list contains all the women's names in the data which were classified as European names. The numbers after the names show the number of occurrences of these names as first given names and as subsequent given names; the latter ones are given after a plus sign (+). The list also includes references to the use of these names in different European naming systems. The name forms listed after the letter F are names that have been in common use in Finland. Names that have been carried by Finnish missionaries in the Ambo area are marked with FM. The letters G, A and E refer to name forms used in the German, Afrikaans and English naming systems. In some cases, names from the Dutch naming system, which is historically close to the Afrikaans one, are given as well, and they are marked with H. Names that also appear as surnames in Namibia are marked with N (sn), and the surnames of Finnish missionaries with FM (sn).

The sign (mn) indicates that the name is originally a man's name, not a woman's name. Names that are common to both sexes are marked with (wn, mn). Additional explanations for names and name forms are given as well.[447] Finnish names which are semantically transparent are translated.

Adele 1, *Andele* 1. F: *Adeele, Adela, Adele, Adèle,* FM: *Adèle,* G: *Adela, Adele, Adely,* A: *Adela, Adele, Adèle, Adella, Adelle,* E: *Adela.* These name forms are based on *Adelheid.*

Adelheid 1, *Adleheid* 1, *Andelheid* 1. F, E: *Adelaide*, G: *Adelaide, Adelheid,* A: *Adelaide, Adalheid, Adelheid.* An old German name consisting of two parts meaning 'noble' and 'kind, sort'.

Agenus 4 + 1, *Agnes* 1 + 1. F, FM, G, A, E: *Agnes.* The name form *Agenus* may also be based on the Latin word *agnus* 'lamb'(see the list of European men's names). Agnes (d. c. 305) was a virgin martyr of Rome; her name means 'chaste, pure'.

Aila 1. F, FM: *Aila. Aila* and the following *Aili* are Finnish names originating in Lapland.

Aili 57 + 3. F, FM: *Aili,* E: *Ailie.* See *Aila.*

Aina 150 + 2, *Ainna* 2. F: *Aina,* G: *Eina.* The Finnish word *aina* means 'always', but the personal name *Aina* is not generally connected with this word. The name first became common among the Swedish-speaking Finns. In Estonia, *Aina* is seen as a variant of *Anna.*

Aini 4. F, FM: *Aini.* A name based on the Finnish names *Aina* and *Aino.*

Aino 12. F, FM: *Aino.* A name originating in the Finnish national epic Kalevala. The name is derived from the Finnish word *ainoa* 'the only one'.

Albelitina 1, *Alberiitina* 2, *Alberlina* 1, *Albertiin* 3, *Albertiina* 13, *Albertin* 10, *Albertina* 51 + 1. F: *Albertiina, Albertina, Alpertiina,* FM, A: *Albertina, Albertine,* G: *Albertina, Albertine,* E: *Albertine.* A female form of *Albert* (see *Arbertus* in the list of European men's names).

Aleta 2, *Alleta* 1. G: *Aletta, Alette,* A: *Alet, Aleta, Aletta,* E: *Alethea. Aletta* is a variant of *Adelheid.*

Ali 1, *Alli* 3. F: *Alli,* G: *Alli, Ally,* A: *Alli, Allie.* As a Finnish name, *Alli* means 'old squaw, long-tailed duck'. In Europe, it is generally interpreted as an abbreviated form of various women's names beginning with *Al-,* e.g. *Alfhild, Alida, Alina* and *Alisa.*

Aliina 8, *Alina* 45 + 1. F: *Aliina, Alina,* FM: *Alina,* G: *Alina, Aline,* A: *Alien, Alina, Aline,* E: *Aline.* Possible origin: *Adelinde/Adeline.*

Alisa 5. F: *Alice, Aliisa, Aliise, Aliisi, Alisa, Alise, Alisi,* FM: *Aliisa, Aliisi, Alice,* G, E: *Alice,* A: *Alice, Alisa, Aliza, Alyssa.* Possible origins: *Adelheid,* **Elisabet** (see the list of biblical women's names).

Alma 13. F, FM, G, A, E: *Alma.* A name based on the Latin word *alma* 'loving, kind' or the river Alma in the Crimea.

Aloisia 1. G: *Aloisia, Aloysia,* A: *Aloïse,* E: *Aloisia.* A female form of *Aloysius,* the name of a 16th century Spanish saint Aloysius Gonzaga.

Alvina 1. F: *Alviina, Alvina,* G: *Alwine,* A: *Alewina, Alwina.* Possible origins: *Adolfina, Alf.*

Amalia 16 + 1. F: *Amaalia, Amalia,* FM: *Amalia,* G: *Amalia, Amalie,* A: *Amalea, Amalia, Amalie, Amelia,* E: *Amelia.* This name may have German, Greek, Latin or Hebrew origins. The element *amal-* in many old German names may mean 'labour'.

Anastasia 1. F, G, E: *Anastasia,* A: *Anastasia, Anastassia, Anastassja.* Anastasia was a Roman martyr (d. c. 304), whose name is based on the Greek word *anastasis* 'resurrection'.

Angela + 1. F, G, E: *Angela,* A: *Angela, Angèle.* A woman's name derived from the Greek man's name *Angelos* 'messanger, angel'. *Angela* is also a saint's name: the foundress of the Ursuline nuns was Angela Merici (1474–1540).

Angelina 1. F: *Angeliina, Angelina,* G: *Angelina, Angeline,* A, E: *Angelina.* A variant of *Angela.* Also a saint's name.

Anna 114 + 1. F, FM, G, A, E: *Anna.* According to the Christian tradition, the mother of the Virgin Mary was Anna. This name, which is related to the Hebrew name *Hannah* 'grace', does not appear in the Bible as such.

Anne 1. F, G, A, E: *Anne.* A variant of *Anna.*

Anneli 1, *Annelie* 1. F, G, A: *Anneli, Annelie,* FM: *Anneli.* A variant of *Anna.*

Anni 1. F: *Anni, Annie,* FM, G: *Anni,* A, E: *Annie.* A variant of *Anna.*

Annikki + 2. F, FM: *Annikki,* A: *Anneke, Annekie.* A variant of *Anna.*

Antila + 1. FM (sn): *Anttila.* One of the Finnish female missionaries in the Ambo area was Vilhelmiina (Miina) Anttila (Peltola 1958, p. 266). The full baptismal name of this Ambo woman is *Miina Antila.*

Auguste 24. F: *Augusta, Aukusta,* FM, E: *Augusta,* G, A: *Augusta, Auguste.* A female form of *August* (see the list of European men's names).

Augustina 1. F: *Augustina,* G, A: *Augustina, Augustine.* A female form of *Augustinus* (see the list of European men' names).

Augustinus + 1. This Ambo woman has a man's name (see *Augustinus* in the list of European men's names). Her full baptismal name is *Teobolina Augustinus.*

Aune 53 + 2, *Aunne* 2. F, FM: *Aune.* A Finnish form of *Agnes.*

Aurelia 1. F, E: *Aurelia,* G: *Aurelia, Aurelie,* A: *Auralea, Auralia, Aurelia, Aurelie.* A female form of *Aurelius,* which is based on the Latin word *aurum* 'gold'.

Barbro + 1. F, G, A: *Barbro.* A Swedish form of *Barbara*; a saint's name based on the Greek word *barbaros* 'alien, foreigner'.

Beada 1, *Beata* 38 + 4, *Beatt* 1, *Beatta* 6. F: *Beada, Beata,* G: *Beata, Beate,* A, E: *Beata.* A name derived from the Latin *beatus* 'happy, beatified'.

251

Benita 1. F, G, E: *Benita*. A Spanish abbreviated form of *Benedicta* < *Benedictus* (see the list of European men's names). In the Ambo area, this name probably came into the naming system as an adoption from the Portuguese of Angola.

Bergita + 1, *Bergite* 1. F: *Birgetta, Birgitta, Birgitte, Birkitta, Brigitta, Brigitte, Pirketta, Pirkitta,* G: *Birgit, Birgitta, Brigitta, Brigitte,* A: *Brigid, Brigit, Brigitta, Brigitte,* E: *Bridget*. St. Bridget (Birgitta) (1303–73) is the patron saint of Sweden. Her name refers to the Celtic fire goddess *Brighid*.

Berla 1, *Berta* 7 + 1, *Bertta* 21 + 1. F: *Berta, Bertha, Bertta,* FM: *Bertta,* G, A: *Berta, Bertha,* E: *Bertha*. The name form *Berla* may be explained by the carelessness of the recorder: the *l* in it should be *t*. Possible origins: *Alberta, Gundeberta, Herberta, Huberta, Berthilde*. The original element *bertha* in these names means 'bright'.

Bernardina 1. G: *Bernhardine,* A: *Bernadina, Bernadine, Bernardina, Bernhardina*. A female form of *Bernard/Bernhard* (see the list of European men's names).

Chalotte 3, *Charllotte* 1, *Charlotte* 2, *Charltotte* 1, *Salot* 2, *Salote* 1, *Sarlote* 6, *Sarlotte* 1 + 1, *Šarlotta* 1. F: *Charlotta, Charlotte, Saarlotta, Sarlotta,* FM: *Charlotta,* G: *Carlota, Carlotta, Charlotte,* A: *Carlotta, Charlot, Charlotta, Charlotte, Karlotta,* E: *Charlotte*. A female form of *Carlo* and *Charles* (see *Carl/Karl* in the list of European men's names).

Dezember + 1. A German word meaning 'December'.

Ditrid + 1. G: *Diethild, Diethilde, Dietlind, Dietlinde,* G (mn): *Dietfried. Dietfried* is an old German name with elements meaning 'people' and 'peace'.

Dorodea 2, *Dorotea* 10, *Dortea* 2. F: *Dorotea, Dorothea,* G, E: *Dorothea,* A: *Dorathea, Dorethea, Dorotea, Dorothea*. The Greek name of the virgin martyr Dorothea (d. c. 313) means 'gift of God' (see also *Teodor* in the list of European men's names).

Ebba 16. F, FM, A: *Ebba,* G: *Eba, Ebba*. A Nordic name related to *Ebbe. Ebba/Ebbe* is also a saint's name.

Eevi 1, *Evi* 8. F: *Eevi, Evi,* FM: *Eevi,* G: *Evi,* A: *Evi, Evie, Ewie*. In Ndonga, *Evi* means 'ground, soil, earth, sand; globe, earth (our planet); country, land; corn' (Tirronen 1986, p. 463). However, as many of these names appear as first given names in the 1940s and sometimes as the only baptismal name of the person, they were assumed to be of European origin. A variant of **Eeva/ Eva** (see the list of biblical women's names).

Eine + 1. F, FM: *Eine*. A Finnish name probably connected with the man's name *Eino* (see the list of European men's names).

Eliina 3, *Elina* 29 + 1, *Eline* 1, *Elinna* 1. F: *Eliina, Elin, Elina, Elna,* FM: *Elina,* G: *Elin, Elina,* A: *Elina, Elna, Elne*. Variants of *Helena*.

Elika 1, *Erikka* 2. F: *Eerika, Erica, Eriika, Eriikka, Erika, Erikka,* G: *Erika,* A: *Erica, Ericha, Erika,* E: *Erica.* A female form of *Eric/Erik* (see *Erikki/ Erkki* in the list of European men's names).

Elisa 1. F: *Eliisa, Elisa, Elissa, Elsa,* FM: *Eliisa,* G: *Elisa, Elsa,* A: *Elisa, Eliza, Elsa, Elza,* E: *Elsa,* E (mn): *Elisha.* As a woman's name, *Elisa* is an abbreviated form of **Elisabet** (see the list of biblical women's names). The biblical name **Elisa** is a man's name.

Elise 12 + 2, *Elisse* 1. F: *Eliise, Elise, Else,* G: *Elise, Else,* A: *Elise, Elize, Else.* A variant of **Elisabet** (see the list of biblical women's names).

Ella 1. F, G, A, E: *Ella.* A variant of *Elina < Helena* or an independent name.

Elli 13. F, G: *Elli, Elly,* FM: *Elli,* A: *Elli, Ellie.* Possible origins: *Helena, Elina, Ellen, Eleonora.*

Elma + 1. F, FM, G, A, E: *Elma.* A common abbreviated form in many European naming systems, which may have various origins, e.g. *Else-Marie, Guglielma, Ihanelma.*

Emielia 1, *Emiilia* 1, *Emilia* 93 + 2, *Emiliha* 1, *Emilja* 1, *Emmilia* 1. F: *Emiilia, Emilia, Emilie,* FM: *Emilia,* G: *Emilia, Emilie, Ämilia,* A: *Emelia, Emilia, Emilie,* E: *Emilia, Emily.* A female form of *Emil* (see the list of European men's names).

Emma 30. F, FM, G, A, E: *Emma.* Possible origins: *Emelia, Emilia, Emerentia.*

Emmi 1. F, G: *Emmi, Emmy,* A: *Emmi, Emmie.* Possible origins: *Emelia, Emilia, Emerentia.*

Enderina 1, *Endrina* 1, *Hedriina* 1, *Hedrina* 1, *Hendelina* 4 + 1, *Henderiina* 2, *Henderina* 3, *Hendriina* 9, *Hendrina* 19 + 2. G: *Hendrina,* A: *Hendrien, Hendrina.* A female form of *Hendrik* (see the list of European men's names). See also *Hendrika.*

Epefinia 1. H: *Epifania, Epiphania.* The Greek word *epifaneia* means 'Epiphany'. In Ndonga, Epiphany is *Esiku lyaapagani.*

Erkki + 1. F (mn), FM (mn): *Erkki,* H: *Ereke, Erke, Erkie.* (See *Erikki/Erkki* in the list of European men's names.)

Eufemia 2. F: *Eufeemia, Eufemia,* G: *Eufemia, Eufemie, Euphemia, Euphemie,* E: *Euphemia.* This saint's name is based on a Greek word meaning 'auspicious speech, honour, good repute'.

Evalina 1, *Eveliina* 3, *Evelina* 20 + 2. F: *Eveliina, Evelina, Evelyn,* G: *Eveline, Evelyn,* A: *Evalina, Evaline, Evelina, Eveline, Evelyn,* E: *Eveleen, Evelina, Evelyn.* These name forms are based on the old German name *Avelina < Avi*; the Latin form is *Evelina.*

Evangelina + 1, *Evangeline* 1 + 1. G, E: *Evangeline*. This name is based on the Greek word *euangelion* meaning 'Gospel'. The name seems to have been invented by Longfellow for his narrative poem *Evangeline*.

Faustina 2. G: *Faustina, Faustine. Faustinus* is the name of a male saint.

Feinni 1, *Fenni* 25, *Fennie* 1, *Feni* + 1. G: *Fine, Fini, Finne, Finni*, H: *Fen, Fenna, Fenne, Fennie, Fenny*, A: *Fenna, Fini, Finie*. These name forms are based on women's names ending with *-fine*, e.g. *Josefine*, as well as on the man's name *Fennechienus*.

Fenderika 1, *Frederik* 1, *Frednika* 1, *Fredriika* 1, *Fredrika* 6 + 1, *Frendrika* 2, *Prendrika* 1. F: *Fredriika, Fredriikka, Fredrika, Reetriika, Reetriikka*, FM, G: *Friederike*, A: *Frederica, Frederika, Friederike*, E: *Frederica*. A female form of *Fredrik* (see the list of European men's names).

Fiina 29 + 4, *Fiinna* 1. F: *Fiina*, G: *Fiene, Fina*, A: *Fien, Fina*. These name forms are based on women's names ending with *-fina/-fiina*, e.g. *Adolfina* and *Josefiina*.

Filipa + 1. G, E: *Philippa*, A: *Felippa, Filippa, Philippa*. A female form of *Philip* (see **Filippus** in the list of biblical men's names).

Filita 4, *Frida* 42 + 3, *Frieda* 33. F: *Frida, Friida*, FM: *Frieda*, G: *Frida, Frieda, Friede*, A: *Freda, Frida, Frieda*. The original bearer of this name in the Ambo area was Frieda (Anna Friederike) Rautanen, wife of the Finnish missionary Martti Rautanen (Peltola 1958, p. 259). *Filita* is interpreted as an Ambo form of this name; it was given as the only baptismal name for four women in the 1930s and 1940s. *Frieda* is an abbreviated form of German names such as *Elfriede* and *Friederike*.

Fransiina 5, *Fransin* 1, *Fransina* 12. F: *Fransiina, Fransina*, G: *Francine, Franzine*, A: *Francina, Francine, Fransina*. A female form of *Frans* (see the list of European men's names).

Gerdrula 1, *Gerdrut* 1, *Gerdruta* 3, *Gerlrud* 1, *Gertrud* 14 + 3, *Gerturd* 2 + 1. F: *Gertrud*, G: *Gertraud, Gertraude, Gertraut, Gertrud, Gertrude*, A: *Geertruida, Gertrud, Gertrude, Gertruida*, E: *Gertrude*. An old German name including elements which mean 'spear' and 'strength'. Also a saint's name. The name form *Gerlrud* may be due to the carelessness of the recorder of this name: the *l* in it should be *t*.

Gertta 1. F: *Gerda, Greeta, Greetta, Greta*, G: *Geerd, Geerta, Geerte, Geertje, Gerda, Gerta, Greta, Grete, Grethe*, A, E: *Gerda*. This name form may also refer to the name *Hertta* (see *Hertta*). Possible origins: *Gertrud, Gerhard* (mn), *Gert* (mn). *Greta* < *Margareta*.

Grolia + 1. G, A, E: *Gloria*. A Latin word meaning 'glory'.

Halian 1, *Haliana* 1, *Hariana* 1. F, E: *Adriana*, G: *Adriane, Ariane*, A: *Adriana, Ariana, Arianna*. *Adriana* is a female form of *Adriaan*.

Happy + 1. E (wn, mn): *Happy*. This name may also be a translation of some Ambo name with the same meaning, e.g. *Nelago* 'luck, happiness' or *Ndinelago* 'I have luck, happiness'.

Hedvig 2. F, FM: *Hedvig*, G, A: *Hedwig*. St. Hedwig, duchess of Silesia, was a medieval saint. Her name has been interpreted as containing two words meaning 'battle'.

Helalia 3, *Helaria* 2, *Heralia* 1, *Hilalia* 1, *Hilaria* 11, *Hileria* 1, *Hiralia* 1. F, G, A: *Hilaria*, E (wn, mn): *Hilary*. A female form of *Hilarius* (see the list of European men's names).

Helemi 1, *Helmi* 8. F, FM: *Helmi*, A: *Helmi, Helmie*. The Finnish name *Helmi* means 'pearl'. In Finland, as elsewhere in Europe, this name may have originated in *Vilhelmiina/Wilhemina*.

Helena 141 + 10, *Hellen* + 1, *Helna* 2. F: *Heleena, Helen, Helena, Helene, Hellen, Helleni, Hellin,* FM: *Helena, Hellin, Hélène,* G: *Helen, Helena, Helene,* A: *Heleen, Helen, Hélène, Helena, Helene,* E: *Helen.* A Greek name meaning 'the bright one'. Also a saint's name.

Helivi 1, *Helvi* 33 + 4. F, FM: *Helvi*, G: *Helvi, Helwi*. A Finnish variant of *Hedvig*. In Germany, this name can be explained as coming from Finnish.

Hella 2. F: *Hella*, G: *Hela, Hella*. Possible origins: *Eleonoora*, **Elisabet**, *Helena*. In the Ambo context, this name form may also be a variant of *Ella*.

Helly + 1. F: *Heli, Helli, Helly*, G: *Heli, Hely*, A: *Helie*. Possible origin: *Helena*. In the Ambo context, this name form may also be a variant of *Elli*.

Helma 1. F: *Helma*, A, G: *Helma, Herma*. *Helma* is a variant of *Wilhelmina*, *Herma* of *Hermana* < *Herman*. In the Ambo context, this name form may also be a variant of *Elma*.

Hendrika 1. F: *Henriika, Henriikka, Henrika, Henrikka*, G: *Hendrika, Hendrike, Hendrikje, Henrika, Henrike*, A: *Hendrieka, Hendrika, Henrika*. A female form of *Hendrik* (see the list of European men's names).

Henneriette 1. F: *Henrietta, Henriette*, G: *Henriette, Heinriette*, A: *Henrietta, Henriëtta, Henriette, Henriëtte*, E: *Henrietta*. A female diminutive form of *Henri* (see *Henry* in the list of European men's names).

Heni + 1, *Henni* 2. F, G: *Henni, Henny*, A: *Henni, Hennie*. Possible origins: *Hendrika, Henriëtta, Henriikka*.

Hermea 1. G, A: *Herma, Hermia*, E: *Hermia*. Possible origins: *Herman* (mn), *Hermes* (mn), *Hermingard*.

Hertta 84 + 3. F: *Hertha, Hertta*, G: *Herta, Hertha*. Originally an old German name based on the god named Nerthus.

Hilda 41 + 1. F, FM, G, E: *Hilda*, A: *Hilda, Hylda*. St. Hilda was a 7th century saint. This name may be based on the old Scandinavian name *Hildr*, or it may be an abbreviated form of names such as *Hildegard* or *Mathilda*.

Hilde 1. F, G, A: *Hilde*. See *Hilda*.

Hilen 1, *Hileni* 85 + 1. F: *Ireene, Irene,* G: *Ireen, Irene,* H: *Hillena, Hillina, Hylena, Irena, Irene, Irenea,* A: *Ileana, Ilene, Irena, Irene,* E: *Irene.* According to one explanation, the common name *Hileni* is an Ambo form of *Irene* (Lehtonen 17.11.1994), a name based on a Greek word meaning 'peace', or a female form of *Ireneus* (see the list of European men's names). The Afrikaans form *Ilene* is a variant of *Aileen, Eileen* or *Helena.* The Ambo verb *hila* means 'pull' (Tirronen 1986, p. 72), and *hileni* is the plural imperative form of it. However, as *Hileni* appears as the only baptismal name for a number of Ambo women baptised since the 1920s, a European derivation seems more probable here.

Hilia 1, *Hilija* 1, *Hilja* 90 + 1, *Hilya* 3. F, FM: *Hilja.* This name originates in the Finnish word *hiljainen* 'silent'. In the Ambo context, these name forms may also be based on the name *Irja.*

Hilima 10, *Hilm* 1, *Hilma* 175 + 10. F, FM, G: *Hilma.* An abbreviated form of German names including the element *helm* 'helmet', e.g. *Helmgund* and *Wilhelmine.*

Hilka 2 + 1, *Hilkka* 9 + 1. F, FM: *Hilkka,* G: *Hilka, Hilke.* In Finland, this name is based on the Finnish word *hilkka* 'bonnet, hood'.

Hulda 2 + 1, *Huluda* 1. F, G: *Hulda,* A, E: *Hulda, Huldah.* An old Scandinavian name meaning 'muffled, covered'.

Ida 10, *Iida* 1. F: *Ida, Iida, Iita,* FM: *Ida, Iida,* G, E: *Ida,* A: *Ida, Ita, Yda.* There are a number of explanations for this name, most of which claim that it originates in the Germanic languages.

Iirja 1, *Irja* 46 + 3. F, FM: *Irja.* A female form of the Low German man's name *Irg* = *Georg,* which was adopted by Finland from Estonia.

Ilona 14 + 1. F, FM, G: *Ilona,* A: *Ilona, Illona.* A Hungarian form of *Helena.*

Imbi 1, *Impi* 1. F, FM: *Impi.* A Finnish name meaning 'maiden'.

Ina 9, *Inna* 4 + 1. F: *Ina, Iina, Inna,* G: *Ina,* A: *Ina, Inna.* An abbreviated form of women's names ending with *-ina,* e.g. *Carolina, Katharina* and *Wilhelmina.*

Inkeri 3 + 1. F: *Inger, Inker, Inkeri,* FM: *Inkeri.* A Finnish form of the Scandinavian *Ingrid.*

Jakobiina 13, *Jakobina* 22 + 3, *Jakopiina* 2. F: *Jakobina,* G: *Jakobine,* A: *Jacobina, Jakobina,* E: *Jacobina.* A female form of **Jakob** (see the list of biblical men's names).

Jasofina 1. This name form may be a contamination of *Jakobina* and *Josefina.*

Jehova + 1. This name refers to the God of the Old Testament. However, it does not appear in the Bible as such. The full name of this woman is *Fenni Jehova Tuyenikelao* ('let us go to happiness').

Jennifer + 1. F, G, E: *Jennifer*, A: *Jenefer, Jenifer, Jennifer.* A variant of *Guinevere*, which was the name of the wife of King Arthur.

Jenny 1. F, G: *Jenni, Jenny*, A: *Jen, Jenni, Jennie*, E: *Jenny.* Possible origins: *Geneviève, Jane, Janet, Jennifer, Joanna.*

Jollin + 1. G: *Jorina, Jorine, Jorinna*, A: *Jolina, Joline, Jolinde.* The Afrikaans forms are based on *Jolanda.*

Josefiina 11 + 1, *Josefina* 90 + 3, *Josofina* 1. F: *Joosefiina, Joosefina, Josefiina, Josefina*, FM: *Josefina*, G: *Josefine, Josephine*, A: *Josefina, Josefine, Josephina, Josephine*, E: *Josephine.* A female form of ***Josef*** (see the list of biblical men's names).

Juliana 1. F: *Juliaana, Juliana, Juljaana, Juljana*, G, E: *Juliana*, A: *Julian, Juliana.* St. Juliana was a 4th century virgin martyr. Her name is based on the man's name *Julianus* < ***Julius*** (see the list of biblical men's names).

Jusitina 1, *Justiin* 1, *Justiina* 9, *Justina* 36 + 1, *Justine* 1. F: *Justiina, Justina*, G, A: *Justina, Justine*, E: *Justina.* A female form of the man's name *Justinus* < ***Justus*** (see the list of biblical men's names). Also a saint's name: Justina was a martyr of Antioch, c. 300.

Kaariina 1, *Kaarina* 39 + 5, *Kaarna* 2. F: *Carin, Carina, Kaarin, Kaarina, Kariina, Karin, Karina*, FM: *Kaarina, Karin*, G: *Carina, Karen, Karin, Karina*, A: *Carin, Carina, Karen, Karena, Karien, Karin, Karina*, E: *Karen.* *Kaarina* is a Finnish form of *Katariina/Katharina.*

Kaija 1 + 1. F, FM: *Kaija*, G: *Kaja*, H: *Caia, Caja, Kaja.* *Kaija* is a Finnish abbreviated form of *Katariina.*

Kaino 14 + 1. F (wn, mn), FM (wn): *Kaino.* A Finnish name meaning 'shy'.

Kaisa 3. F, FM: *Kaisa, Kaisu.* A Finnish abbreviated form of *Katariina/ Katharina.*

Karlolina 1, *Karoliina* 5 + 1, *Karolina* 17 + 1. F: *Caroliina, Carolin, Carolina, Caroline, Karoliina, Karolina, Karoline*, FM: *Karolina*, G: *Carolin, Carolina, Caroline, Karolina, Karoline*, A: *Carolina, Carolyn, Karolina*, E: *Caroline.* A female form of *Carolus* (see *Carl/Karl* in the list of European men's names).

Katilina 1, *Katriina* 14 + 1, *Katrina* 25. F: *Catarina, Catharina, Katariina, Katarina, Katharina, Katriina, Katrin, Katrina*, FM: *Katharina*, G: *Catharina, Katarina, Katharina, Katharine*, A: *Catalina, Catarina, Catharina, Katarina, Katharina, Katharine, Katrien, Katrina*, E: *Catharine, Catherine, Katharine, Katherine.* There are many female saints carrying the name *Catherine/Katharine.* The Greek word *katharos* means 'pure'.

Kelmedina 1, *Klementina* 1. G: *Clementine, Klementine*, E: *Clementina, Clementine.* A female form of the name *Clement* (see ***Klemens*** in the list of biblical men's names).

Kerttu 6 + 1, *Kertu* 1. F, FM: *Kerttu*. A Finnish form of *Gertrud*.

Kiristi 1. F, FM: *Kirsti*, G: *Kirsten, Kirstin*, A: *Kristin*, E: *Kirsten, Kirsty*. These name forms are variants of *Christina/Kristina*.

Korneelia 1, *Kornelia* 10 + 2, *Kronelia* 2. G, A: *Cornelia, Kornelia*, E: *Cornelia*. A female form of the Latin name *Cornelius* (see **Kornelius** in the list of biblical man's names).

Koskima + 1. FM (sn): *Koskimaa*. One of the Finnish female missionaries in the Ambo area was Laimi Koskimaa (Peltola 1958, p. 265). The full baptismal name of this Ambo woman is *Hilma Koskima*.

Krismes + 2. This name refers to the word meaning 'Christmas' (English: *Christmas*, Afrikaans: *Kersfees, Krismis*. Finnish: *joulu*, German: *Weihnachten*, Ndonga: *okrismesa*).

Kristiina 1, *Kristina* 4. F: *Christiina, Christin, Christina, Christine, Cristiina, Cristina, Cristine, Kristiina, Kristiine, Kristin, Kristina, Kristine*, G: *Christin, Christina, Christine, Kristin, Kristina, Kristine*, A: *Christiana, Christiane, Christien, Christina, Christine, Kristiane, Kristien, Kristina*, E: *Christina, Christine*. St. *Christina* was a virgin martyr. Her name is a female form of *Christian* (see *Kristian* in the list of European men's names).

Kristofenia 1, *Kristofiina* 10, *Kristofina* 42 + 3. G: *Christophine*, A: *Christoffelina*, H: *Christoffelina, Christoffine, Christophina*. A female form of *Kristof* (see the list of European men's names).

Kustaava 2, *Kustava* 2. F: *Gustaava, Gustava, Kustaava, Kustava*, FM, G: *Gustava*, A: *Gusta*. *Kustaava* is a Finnish form of *Gustava*, which is a female form of *Gustav* (see *Gustaf* in the list of European men's names).

Lahija 2, *Lahja* 52 + 2, *Lahya* 2. F, FM: *Lahja*. A Finnish name meaning 'gift'.

Laima 1. This name form may be a contamination of the Finnish names *Laimi* and *Laina*, which are both popular in the Ambo area – or a misspelling. In Europe, *Laima* is a Latvian name, from which the name *Laimi* is derived.

Laimi 66 + 1. F, FM: *Laimi*. See *Laima*.

Laina 66 + 5, *Lainna* 2. F, FM: *Laina*. One of the new names which became popular in Finland in the 19th century.

Laula 2, *Laura* 3. F, G, A, E: *Laura*. A name connected with the Latin word *laurus* 'laurel, bay tree'. Also an abbreviated form of *Laurencia*, which is a female form of *Laurence* < *Laurentius* (see *Lauri* in the list of Europen men's names).

Laulinda + 1. F: *Lauriina*, G: *Laurine*, A: *Laurina, Laurinda, Laurine*, E: *Laurinda*. A variant of *Laura*.

Lavinia 2. G, A, E: *Lavinia*. Lavinia is the wife of Aeneas in the Roman mythology.

Leena 37 + 6, *Lena* 1. F: *Leena, Lena,* FM: *Leena,* G, A, E: *Lena.* Possible origins: *Helena,* **Magdalena** (see the list of biblical women's names).

Leila 1. F, FM, E: *Leila,* G: *Leila, Leilah, Lejla, Leyla,* A: *Leila, Leilah, Lelah.* An Arab and Persian name meaning 'night'.

Lembi 2, *Lempi* 9. F, FM: *Lempi.* A Finnish name meaning 'love'.

Leokaldia 1, *Leokalidea* 1. G: *Leocadia, Leokadia, Leokadie.*

Letesia 1, *Letisia* 2. G: *Laetitia, Letitia, Letizia, Lätitia, Lätizia,* A: *Laeticia, Laetitia, Leticia, Letitia,* E: *Laetitia, Lettice.* The Latin word *laetitia* means 'gladness'.

Letha 1, *Letta* 2. G, A: *Letta.* The Afrikaans name *Letta* is an abbreviated form of *Aletta.* In the Ambo context, these name forms may also be based on the names *Greta, Reeta, Reta,* etc. (see *Gertta* and *Reeta/Reta*).

Lida 1. F: *Lida, Liida,* G: *Lida, Lidda, Lyda,* A: *Lida.* Possible origins: *Alida, Ludmilla.*

Liina 25 + 3, *Lina* 3. F: *Liina, Lina,* FM: *Liina,* G: *Lina,* E: *Lina, Lyn, Lynn, Lynne,* A: *Lin, Lina, Lynn.* An abbreviated form of names ending with *-lina* or *-liina,* e.g. *Aliina/Alina, Elina, Eveliina/Evelina, Karoliina/Karolina* and *Melina.*

Liinda 2, *Linda* 11. F, FM, G, E: *Linda,* A: *Linda, Lynda.* Possible origins: *Alinda, Belinda, Melinda, Rosalinda, Theolinda.* The old German *Linda* means 'serpent'. The name forms in the data could also be Ambo forms of *Lida.*

Liinea 2, *Liineea* 1 + 1, *Linea* 18, *Lineea* 1, *Linnea* 4. F: *Linea, Linnea, Linnéa,* FM: *Linnéa,* A: *Linne, Linné, Lynne.* In Finland, the name *Linnea* refers to the famous Swedish botanist Karl von Linné.

Liisa 3 + 9, *Lisa* + 1, *Lissa* + 4. F: *Liisa, Lisa,* FM: *Liisa,* G: *Lies, Liesa, Lisa, Lissa,* A: *Lisa, Lissa, Liza.* A variant of **Elisabet** (see the list of biblical women's names).

Liise + 1. F: *Liise, Lise,* G: *Lies, Liese, Lise, Lisse,* A: *Lise, Lize.* A variant of **Elisabet** (see the list of biblical women's names).

Lilja 10 + 1. F: *Lilja, Lilia,* FM: *Lilja.* A Finnish name meaning 'lily'; also a hypocoristic form of **Elisabet** (see the list of biblical women's names).

Lilli 1, *Lylly* 1. F, G: *Lili, Lilli, Lilly, Lily,* A: *Lili, Lilie, Lilli, Lillie,* E: *Lily.* Possible origins: **Elisabet**, *Karoliina, Liliana, Lilja.*

Lindivina 1. G: *Ledwina, Lidwina, Lidwine.*

Loise 16 + 1, *Luise* 4 + 1, *Luisse* 3 + 1. F: *Louise, Luise,* FM: *Luise,* G: *Loisa, Louisa, Louise, Luisa, Luise,* A: *Loisa, Louisa, Luisa, Luise, Luiza, Luize,* E: *Louisa, Louise.* One of the female missionaries of the Finnish Mission in the Ambo area was the Estonian-born Luise Lehto (Peltola 1958, p. 264). The French woman's name *Louise* is a female form of *Louis* (< *Ludwig*).

Lotta 3 + 1, *Lotte* 1. F: *Lotta, Lotte,* G: *Lotte, Lotti, Lotty,* A: *Lotta, Lotti, Lottie,* E: *Lottie.* Abbreviated forms of *Charlotta* and *Charlotte.*

Lovis 5, *Lovisa* 50 + 6. F, FM: *Loviisa, Lovisa,* H: *Lowiese. Loviisa* and *Lovisa* are Finnish-Swedish forms of *Louise.* (See also *Loise/Luise/Luisse.*)

Lucky + 1. An English word. In the same way as *Happy,* this name could be a translation of some Ambo name with the same meaning, e.g. *Nelago* 'luck, happiness' or *Ndinelago* 'I have luck, happiness'.

Lusaria 1, *Rosalia* 28, *Rosared* 1, *Rosaria* 1 + 1. F: *Rosalia, Rosalie,* G: *Rosalia, Rosalie, Rosaria,* A: *Rosalia, Rosalie, Rozalia, Rozalie,* E: *Rosalie.* The *d* at the end of *Rosared* may be due to misspelling or misreading, the intended letter may be *a.* The Latin word *rosalia* refers to an annual ceremony in which garlands of roses were hung on tombs. *Rosalia* is also a name of a 12th century Sicilian saint.

Lusia 28 + 1, *Luusia* 5, *Rusia* 1. F: *Lucia, Lusia,* G: *Lucia, Lucie, Lusia, Luzia, Luzie,* A: *Lucia, Lucie, Lusia,* E: *Lucia, Lucy.* St. Lucia was a virgin martyr (d. 304); her name is derived from the Latin word *lux* 'light'.

Lusiina + 1. F: *Lucina, Lusiina, Lusina,* G: *Luciane,* A: *Luciana, Lucina, Lucinda,* E: *Lucinda.* A variant of *Lucia.*

Lyyli 2. F, FM: *Lyyli.* A Finnish form of *Lydia* (see **Lidia** in the list of biblical women's names and *Lilli/Lylly* in this list).

Maadi 1. G: *Madi, Mady, Maidi, Maud,* A: *Maddi, Maddie,* E: *Maud, Maude.* Possible sources: **Magdalena** (see the list of biblical women's names), *Matilda.*

Maija 2 + 2. F: *Maija, Maja,* FM: *Maija,* G, A: *Maja.* The Finnish name *Maija* is a variant of **Maria** (see the list of biblical women's names). For *Maja,* there are many possible origins, for example in the Greek, Roman and Indian mythologies.

Maila 3. F, FM: *Maila.* A Finnish variant of **Maria** (see the list of biblical women's names).

Maire 1. F, FM: *Maire,* E: *Máire.* In Finland, this name is based on the Finnish word *maire* or *mairea* 'lovely, sweet'.

Maliana 1, *Marian* 1, *Mariana* 14, *Marianna* 8, *Marianne* 1, *Marjana* 1, *Marjanna* 3. F: *Mariaana, Marian, Mariana, Mariann, Marianna, Marianne, Marjaana, Marjana, Marjanna, Marjanne,* FM: *Marjaana,* G: *Mariana, Mariane, Marianne, Marijana,* A: *Marian, Mariana, Marianna, Marianne,*

Marina, Maryn, Maryna, E: *Marianne*. The French name *Marianne* is based on the names *Marie* and *Anne*, which refer to the mother and grandmother of Jesus. *Marian* is also a saint's name.

Malita 2. F: *Maarit, Maarita, Marit, Marita, Maritta*, FM, A: *Marita*, G: *Marit, Marita, Maritta*. *Marita* is a Spanish variant of **Maria**. The name form *Malita* could also be an Ambo form of **Marta**. (See **Maria** and **Marta** in the list of biblical women's names.)

Margaleeta 1, *Margaleta* 2, *Margalleta* 1, *Margaret* 1, *Margareta* 1, *Marigaleeta* 1. F: *Margareeta, Margareetta, Margaret, Margareta, Margarete, Margareth, Margaretha, Margarethe, Margaretta, Margarita*, FM: *Margareta*, G: *Margareta, Margarete, Margaretha, Margarethe, Margarita, Margarte, Margherita, Marghitta*, A: *Margaret, Margareta, Margarete, Margaretha, Margarethe, Margaretta, Margarita, Margrita*, E: *Margaret*. There are many female saints named *Margaret;* the name is based on a Greek word meaning 'pearl'.

Mariyatta + 1. F: *Mariatta, Marietta, Marjatta*, FM: *Marjatta*, G: *Marietta*, A: *Marieta, Mariëtta*. In Finland, *Marjatta* is based on the names **Maria** and *Marketta* < *Margareta*.

Marja 1. F, FM, A, G: *Marja*. This name form could also refer to the biblical name **Maria**, but as *Marja* is the name of a Finnish missionary, it is classified as a European name here. In Finnish, the word *marja* means 'berry', but the name *Marja* is also understood to refer to **Maria** (see the list of biblical women's names).

Matilda 1, *Matilde* 1. F: *Mathilda, Matilda, Matilta*, FM, A: *Mathilda, Mathilde, Matilda*, G: *Mathilde*, E: *Matilda*. An old German name consisting of elements meaning 'might, strength' and 'battle, strife'.

Maura 1. F, G, A: *Maura*. This name may have Celtic or Russian (*Mavra*) origins, or be a variant of the biblical **Maria** (see the list of biblical women's names).

Menet 1, *Menete* 16, *Menette* 2. G: *Minette*, H: *Mennette, Minetta, Minette*. The wife of the Rhenish missionary Gottlieb Viehe, who worked in South West Africa, was Minette (K.L. Tolonen to the mission director 12.6.1869, Eac:3, FMSA; B/cII:32, UEMA). *Minette* is a derivative of *Mina* (see *Miina/ Mina*).

Mestilde 1. G: *Mechthild, Mechthilde*, A: *Metilda, Metilde*.

Miina 15 + 1, *Mina* 1. F: *Miina, Mina, Minna*, FM: *Miina*, G, E: *Mina, Minna*, A: *Mien, Miena, Mina*. Abbreviated forms of names ending with - *miina* or -*mina*, e.g. *Abrahamina, Hermina, Jacomina, Vilhelmiina/ Wilhelmina*.

Monica + 1, *Monika* 64 + 5. F: *Monica, Monika, Moonika*, G, A: *Monica, Monika*, E: *Monica*. A saint's name: St. Monica (332–87) was the mother of St. Augustine (Augustinus). This name could also be seen as an Ambo name: the verb *monika* means 'be visible, be seen, be found, appear' (Tirronen 1986, p. 229).

Nancy + 1. F, G, A, E: *Nancy*. An English variant of *Anna*.

Natalia 29 + 1, *Nataria* 1. F: *Natalia, Natalie, Nathalia, Nathalie,* FM: *Natalia,* G: *Natalia, Natalie, Nathalie,* A: *Natalia, Natalie, Natalya,* E: *Natalia, Natalie*. This name originally refers to Christmas: in the Middle Ages, the Latin term *natale Domini* 'birth of the Lord' was used for Christmas Day. St. Natalia is a saint of the Orthodox Church, and the name is especially common in Russia.

Niilo + 1. F (mn): *Niilo*. See *Niilo* in the list of European men's names.

Nina + 1. F: *Nina, Niina,* G, A, E: *Nina*. A Russian hypocoristic form of *Anna*.

Niewejaar + 1. This name refers to the Afrikaans word *Nuwejaar* 'New Year'.

Noise + 1. An English word.

Olivia 26 + 5. F: *Oliivia, Olivia,* G, E: *Olivia,* A: *Oliva, Olivia*. The Latin word *oliva* means 'olive'. *Oliva* is also a saint's name. *Olivia* has also been connected with the man's name *Oliver*.

Orovokki + 1, *Orvokki* + 1. F, FM: *Orvokki*. A Finnish name meaning 'violet'.

Otilie 1, *Ottilia* 17, *Ottilie* 7. F: *Ottiilia, Ottilia,* G: *Ottilie,* A: *Ottilia, Ottilie,* E: *Ottilia*. A female form of *Otto* (see the list of European men's names) or an independent German name based on the word *othal* 'fatherland'. St. Ottilia was a 7th century virgin who became the patron saint of Alsace.

Paula 1. F, FM, G, A, E: *Paula*. A female form of **Paulus** (see the list of biblical men's names). Also a saint's name. In Finland, this name is also connected with the Finnish word *paula* 'string, cord, snare, springe, net, trap, toils'.

Pauliina 22, *Paulina* 61 + 2. F: *Pauliina, Paulina, Pauline,* G: *Pauline,* A, E: *Paulina, Pauline*. A variant of *Paula*, or a female form of *Paulinus* (< **Paulus**).

Peteliina 1, *Petelina* 1, *Petriina* 16, *Petrina* 18 + 1. F: *Petriina,* A: *Petrina*. A female form of **Petrus** (see the list of biblical men's names).

Raila 1 + 2. F: *Raila*. A Finnish name belonging to a group of names such as *Aila, Aili, Maila, Maili, Raila* and *Raili*. This name may be linked to **Rakel** (see the list of biblical women's names).

Raili 3. F, FM: *Raili*. See *Raila*.

Rauha 44 + 3, *Rauuha* 1. F, FM: *Rauha*. A Finnish name meaning 'peace'.

Rauna 36 + 1. F, FM: *Rauna*. This Finnish name may be derived from the Scandinavian name *Ragnhild*.

Rautia 1. F (mn, sn): *Rautia,* FM (sn): *Rautanen, Rautaheimo*. This name is a rarely occurring man's name and surname in Finland. The old Finnish word *rautia* means 'smith' (Mikkonen & Paikkala 1992, p. 493).

Reeta 7, *Reta* 1, *Retta* 1. F: *Greeta, Greetta, Greta, Reeta, Reetta,* FM, E: *Greta,* G: *Greet, Greda, Gret, Greta, Grete, Reta,* A: *Greta, Grete, Gretha, Grethe, Reta, Retha.* These name forms are based on *Margareta.*

Regiina 1, *Regina* 2. F: *Regiina, Regina,* FM, E: *Regina,* G: *Regina, Regine,* A: *Regina, Regine, Régine.* The Latin word *regina* means 'queen'; this name has been interpreted as referring to the Virgin Mary as the Queen of Heaven.

Reginalda 1. G (mn), E (mn): *Reginald,* A (mn): *Reginald, Reinald, Reinaldus.* This man's name is based on the old German name *Reginold,* from which the name *Reinhold* is also derived (see the list of European men's names).

Remember + 1. An English word. This name could also be a translation of the Ambo name *Dhimbulukweni* 'remember'.

Renatte 1. F, G: *Renata, Renate,* A: *Renata, Renate, Renetta, Renette.* A German woman's name based on the Latin word *renatus* 'born again'.

Riikka 2. F: *Riika, Riikka,* G, A: *Rika.* These name forms are based on women's names ending with *-rika* or *-riikka,* e.g. *Diederika, Fredrika, Hendrika, Henriikka, Ulrika.*

Ritta 1. F: *Briita, Briitta, Brita, Britta, Priita, Priitta, Riita, Riitta, Rita,* FM: *Brita, Riitta,* G: *Brita, Britt, Britta, Rita,* A: *Britt, Britta, Rieta, Rita,* E: *Rita.* These name forms are based on *Rita < Margareta* or *Brita < Brigitta* (see *Bergita/Bergite*).

Ronde 1. G: *Rhonda, Roda, Rodegard, Rodehild, Rodehilde, Ronda,* A: *Rhoda, Rhode, Roda,* E: *Rhoda, Rhode, Rhodie, Rhonda.* The name *Rhoda > Rhode* is probably a Greek name based on a word meaning 'rose'.

Rosa 3. F: *Roosa, Rosa,* FM, G, A, E: *Rosa.* A latinisation of the name *Rose.* *Rose* + 2. F, G, A, E: *Rose.* Although this name has been identified with the rose flower, it may originally refer to an old German word *(h)ros* meaning 'horse'.

Roti 1. G: *Lotte, Lotti, Lotty,* A: *Lotti, Lottie,* E: *Lottie, Lotty.* Variants of *Charlotte.*

Rusa 1, *Ruus* 1, *Ruusa* 47 + 2. F: *Ruusa.* A Finnish form of *Rosa.*

Saarti 2, *Sarti* 1, *Sartti* 2. A: *Saartji, Saartjie.* Variants of **Sara** (see the list of biblical women's names).

Sabiina 1 + 1. F: *Sabiina, Sabina, Sabine,* G: *Sabina, Sabine,* A: *Sabien, Sabina, Sabine,* E: *Sabin, Sabina.* The Latin *Sabina/Sabinus* 'Sabine man/ woman' was a common Roman cognomen. *Sabinus* is also a male saint's name.

Saija 1. F, FM: *Saija.* A Finnish hypocoristic form of *Saara* (see **Sara** in the list of biblical women's names). *Saija* is also the nickname of the Finnish missionary Sävy Vilkuna (Lehtonen 17.11.1994).

Saima 35 + 5. F, FM: *Saima*. A Finnish name derived from the lake name *Saimaa*..

Saimi 6. F, FM: *Saimi*. A Finnish name based on the name *Saima* (see *Saima*).

Salmi 1. F, FM (sn): *Salmi*. One of the Finnish female missionaries in the Ambo area was Raija Salmi (Personnel archives of the Finnish Evangelical Lutheran Mission, Helsinki). *Salmi* is not a common woman's name in Finland.

Sarafina 1, *Selafina* 1, *Serafina* 2. F: *Serafia, Serafiia, Serafiina, Serafina*, FM: *Serafia, Serafina*, G: *Seraphine*, E: *Seraphina*. A Latin female derivative of the Hebrew word *seraph* 'noble, burning one'. Also a saint's name.

Savelia 1. G: *Xaveria*, A: *Xaviera*, H: *Saveria, Xaveria*. *Xaviera* is an Arabic name meaning 'bright, shining'.

Secilia 1, *Sesilia* 41 + 1, *Sisilia* 1 + 1. F: *Cecilia, Cesilia, Secilia, Sesiilia, Sesilia, Sisilia*, FM: *Cecilia*, G: *Cecilie, Cäcilia, Cäcilie, Zäcilie, Zäzilia, Zäzilie*, A: *Cecelia, Cecilia, Cecily, Cécile*, E: *Cecilia, Cecily, Cicely*. A name of a female Roman saint which is based on the Roman family name *Caecilius*.

Selima 4, *Selma* 266 + 10. F, FM, G: *Selma*, A: *Selama, Selma. Zelma*. This name may have Celtic origins or be based on *Anselma* or **Salome** (see the list of biblical women's names).

Senia 2, *Senja* 10 + 2. F: *Senia, Senja, Xenia*, G: *Xenia*, A: *Xenia, Zenia*. *Senja* is an Eastern Finnish form of the Greek name *Xenia*. This name also occurs as a saint's name in the Orthodox Church and is especially common in Russia.

Sieli 1, *Siili* 1, *Siiri* 4. F, FM: *Siiri*, G: *Siri*. *Siiri* is a Finnish variant of the Scandinavian name *Sigrid* which includes elements meaning 'to win' and 'to ride'. The *ie* in the name form *Sieli* may be explained as coming from German or Afrikaans influence.

Sigirid 1, *Sigrid* 7, *Sigried* 1. F, E: *Sigrid*, G: *Siegrid, Sigrid*. See *Siiri*.

Silvia 9, *Sulvia* + 1, *Sylivia* + 1, *Sylvia* 14 + 1. F, G, E: *Silvia, Sylvia*, FM: *Sylvia*, A: *Silvia, Sylvia, Zilvia, Zylvia*. The name *Silvia* is based on the Latin word *silva* 'forest'.

Sirkka 2. F, FM, G: *Sirkka*. The Finnish name *Sirkka* refers to several words meaning 'seed leaf' (*sirkkalehti*), 'cricket' (*heinäsirkka*) and 'yellowhammer' (*keltasirkku*). In Germany, this name can be attributed to Finnish influence.

Sirpa 1. F: *Sirpa*. A new Finnish formation which can be understood to refer to the word *sirpale* 'broken piece, fragment, chip'.

Siviä + 1. F: *Siveä, Siviä*, FM: *Siviä*. A Finnish name meaning 'chaste'.

Sofia 36 + 4. F: *Sofi, Sofia, Sofie, Sofiia, Sohfia, Sohvi, Sohvia*, FM: *Sofia*, G: *Sofia, Sofie, Sophia, Sophie*, A: *Sofia, Sofie, Sophia, Sophie, Zofia, Zofie, Zophia*, E: *Sophia, Sophie*. A Greek name meaning 'wisdom'.

Soini 2. F (wn, mn), FM (sn): *Soini*. One of the Finnish female missionaries in the Ambo area was Aino Soini (Peltola 1958, p. 269). *Soini* is not a common first name in Finland and appears both among women and men. The full baptismal names of these Ambo women are *Soini* (1953) and *Soini Niita* (1992).

Sondag + 1. An Afrikaans word meaning 'Sunday'.

Steven + 1. A (wn): *Stevani, Stevanie, Stevie,* G (mn), A (mn), E (mn): *Steven,* N (sn): *Stevens*. This name may be based on a European man's name or a surname. The full baptismal name of this Ambo woman is *Frieda Steven*. See also *Sdefanus/**Stefanus*** on the list of biblical men's names.

Suama 6 + 1, *Suom* 1, *Suoma* 28 + 1. F, FM: *Suoma*. This Finnish name, which means 'given', has been explained as referring to the idea of God's gift: *Jumalan suoma* 'given by God'.

Syilvi 1, *Sylvi* 15 + 3. F, FM: *Sylvi,* G: *Silvie, Sylvie,* A: *Silvi, Silvie, Sylvi, Sylvie*. See *Silvia/Sylvia*.

Tabea 2, *Tabeija* 1. G: *Tabea,* H: *Tabeia*. This name is based on **Tabita** (see the list of biblical women's names).

Taim 4, *Taimi* 71 + 6. F, FM: *Taimi*. A Finnish name meaning 'plant'.

Taina 4. F, FM, G: *Taina*. A Finnish form of the Russian name *Tatjana*.

Teoboliina 2, *Teobolina* 3, *Teopoliina* 4, *Teopolina* 17 + 1, *Teopopina* 1. G: *Teudelinde, Theodelinda, Theodelinde, Theodolinde, Theudelinde,* H: *Teubelina, Theodorina*. The Dutch name *Teubelina* is based on the man's name *Theobald*, which is an old German name consisting of elements meaning 'folk, people' and 'bold'.

Teresia 6 + 1, *Tresia* 2. F: *Teresa, Terese, Teresia, Teressa, Theresa, Therese, Theresia,* FM: *Thérèse,* G: *Teresa, Terese, Theresa, Therese, Theresia,* A: *Tercia, Teresa, Terese, Teresia, Tersia, Theresa, Therese, Theresia, Thereza, Thérèse,* E: *Theresa*. These name forms are based on the saint's name *Theresa/Theresia*. The etymology of this name is not clear.

Teresina + 1, *Tersina* 1. G: *Theresina*. A derivative of *Theresia*.

Terttu 15 + 3, *Tertu* 2, *Terutu* 1. F, FM: *Terttu*. A Finnish name meaning 'cluster (of berries), raceme'.

Toini 42 + 3. F, FM: *Toini,* A: *Toinette, Toni, Tonie*. Possible origins: *Antonia, Antoinette*.

Tuliki 1, *Tulikki* 1, *Tuuliki* 5 + 1, *Tuulikki* 10 + 2, *Tuurikki* 1. F, FM: *Tuulikki*. A Finnish name originating in the Finnish national epic Kalevala. The Finnish word *tuuli* means 'wind', and *-kki* is a typical ending of Finnish women's names.

Tusnelde 5 + 1. G: *Thusnelda*, H: *Thusnelda, Tusnelda*. The etymology of this name is unclear.

Ulla + 1. F, FM, G: *Ulla*, A: *Ula, Ulla*. Possible origins: *Ulrika, Ursula*.

Ulsula 1. F, G, A, E: *Ursula*. A saint's name derived from the Latin word *ursa* 'bear'.

Valeria 1. F, A: *Valeria*, G, E: *Valeria, Valerie*, A: *Valaree, Valarie, Valary, Valeria, Valerie, Valérie*. A saint's name based on the Roman family name *Valerius*.

Velemiina 1, *Velemina* 2, *Velhelemina* 1, *Velhelmina* 6, *Vilhelemiina* 1, *Vilhelmiina* 2, *Vilhelmina* 8, *Wilhelmina* 10. F: *Vilhelmiina, Vilhelmina, Wilhelmiina, Wilhelmina*, FM: *Vilhelmiina, Wilhelmiina, Wilhelmina*, G: *Wilhelmina, Wilhelmine*, A: *Vilhelmina, Wilhelmena, Wilhelmina, Wilhelmine, Wilhelminia, Wilamina, Willemien, Willemina, Wilmena, Wilmina*, E: *Wilhelmina*. Female forms of *Vilhelm/Wilhelm* (see the list of European men's names).

Veronika 4 + 1, *Veronikka* 1, *Voronika* 1. F, A: *Veronica, Veronika*, G: *Veronika*, E: *Veronica*. A saint's name which has been explained to refer to both the Latin word *veritas* 'truth' and the Greek word *eikon* 'picture, icon'.

Victoria 1, *Vihtoria* 8, *Vikotoria* 1, *Viktooria* 2, *Viktoria* 34 + 2, *Viktoriia* 2, *Vistoria* 10. F, G, A: *Victoria, Viktoria*, E: *Victoria*. A name of a Roman virgin martyr; the Latin word *victoria* means 'victory'.

Viktoriina 2, *Viktorina* 16 + 1, *Vistolina* 1, *Vistoriina* 5, *Vistorina* 17. F: *Vihtoriina, Vihtorina, Viktoriina, Viktorina*, G: *Victorine, Viktorina, Viktorine*, A: *Victorina, Victorine, Viktorina, Viktorine*. A derivative of *Viktoria*.

Wantful 1. An invention based on the English language.

Wappu 1. F, FM: *Vappu*. A Finnish form of the German name *Walburg*, which is also a saint's name.

Wilbard + 1. This Ambo woman has been given a European man's name (see *Wilbard* in the list of European men's names). Her full baptismal name is *Ester Wilbard*.

The European Names of Men. The following list presents all the men's names in the data which were classified as European names, in the same way as European women's names were presented above. The sign (wn) indicates that the name is originally a woman's name, not a man's name. Names that are common to both sexes are marked with (wn, mn).

Aagustinus 1, *Augstinus* 1, *Augustinus* 4. F: *Augustinus*, G, A: *Augustin*, H: *Augustijn, Augustinus*, E: *Augustine*. This name refers to St. Augustine (Augustinus), one of the Fathers of the Church. *Augustinus* is a Latin diminutive of *augustus* 'venerable, consecrated'.

Achrenius 1. F (sn): *Achrenius*, H: *Acronius*. This name may refer to the Finnish hymn writers Abraham and/or Antti Achrenius. There are several hymns, e.g. 145, 193, 225 and 409, written by these men in the hymn book of the Evangelical Lutheran Church in Namibia (Omaimbilo gOngerki Onkwaevangeli pa Luther yOwambokavango I. 1967). The full baptismal name of this Ambo man is *Achrenius Edison Elago*.

Adlof 1, *Adolf* 3. F: *Aadolf, Aadolffi, Adolf,* G: *Adolf, Adolph,* A: *Adolf, Adolph, Adolphus,* E: *Adolphus. Adolf* is an old German name consisting of two elements meaning 'noble' and 'wolf'.

Agnus 1. A, E: *Angus.* This name seems to be based on the Latin word *agnus* 'lamb': *Agnus Dei* 'Lamb of God'.

Akisel 1, *Aksel* 2, *Akseli* 1, *Akser* 1, *Axel* 3. F: *Aksel, Akseli, Axel,* FM: *Aksel,* G: *Axel.* A Danish form of the Hebrew **Absalom** (see the list of biblical men's names). These name forms could also be based on the name *Alex* (see *Aleks*).

Alarikki + 1. F, FM: *Alarik,* G: *Alarich, Alrich, Alrik,* E: *Alaric.* An old German name consisting of two elements meaning 'all' and 'ruler'.

Albin 5, *Albina* 2. F: *Albiin, Albiinus, Albin, Albinus, Alpiin, Alpiini, Alpiinus, Alpin, Alpinus,* FM: *Albin, Albinus,* G: *Albin, Albinus, Albwin, Albuin,* A: *Albinus,* E: *Albin, Albion. Albinus* is a saint's name based on the Latin word *alba* 'white'.

Aleks 1. F: *Aleksi, Aleksis, Alex,* G: *Alex,* A: *Alex, Alexis, Alexius,* E: *Alexis.* An abbreviated form of *Alexander.*

Aleksander 1. F: *Aleksander, Aleksanter, Aleksanteri, Alexander,* FM: *Alexander,* G, E: *Alexander,* A: *Aleksander, Alexander, Alexandre.* The Greek name *Alexandros* means 'defender, protector'. Also a saint's name.

Alferd 1, *Alfird* 1, *Alfred* 1, *Alfrid* 5, *Alfrieda* 1, *Alfrird* 1. F: *Alfred, Alfrid,* G: *Alfred, Alfried,* A: *Alfred, Alfredus,* E: *Alfred.* An old English name consisting of two elements meaning 'elf' and 'counsel'; the name of Alfred the Great (849–901).

Alfons 1. F: *Alfons, Alfonso,* G: *Alfons,* A: *Alfons, Alfonse, Alfonso, Alfonsus, Alphonse,* E: *Alphonso.* An old German name consisting of two elements meaning 'noble' and 'ready, apt'.

Alli 1. F, G: *Ali,* A (wn, mn): *Ali, Alie, Alli, Allie,* A (mn): *Al,* F (wn): *Alli.* These male forms are based on names beginning with *Al-,* e.g. *Alan, Albert, Alexander, Alfons* and *Alfred.* (See also *Ali/Alli* in the list of European women's names.)

Ambrosius 4. F: *Ambrosius,* G: *Ambros, Ambrosius,* E: *Ambrose.* St. Ambrose (Ambrosius) was a 4th century bishop of Milan; the Greek word *ambrosios* means 'pertaining to the immortals'.

Annesa 1. F, G, A: *Hannes.* A German abbreviated form of **Johannes** (see the list of biblical men's names).

Andolofa 1. H: *Andolph*. This name could also be an Ambo form of *Adolf*.

Antonius 1. F: *Anton, Antoni, Antton, Anttoni,* G: *Anton, Antonius,* A: *Anthonie, Anton, Antonie, Antonius, Antoon,* E: *Anthony, Antony*. St. Antony (Antonius) was a famous Egyptian ascetic; *Antonius* is a Roman family name.

Arbertus 1. F: *Albert, Albertti, Alpert, Alpertti,* G: *Albert, Aribert,* A: *Albert, Albertus,* E: *Albert*. The old German name *Adalbertus* includes two elements meaning 'noble' and 'bright'.

Armas 25, *Arumas* 1. F, FM, G: *Armas*. A Finnish name meaning 'beloved'. In Germany, this name can be explained as being derived from the Finnish.

Arnold + 1. F, E: *Arnold,* G: *Arnold, Arnolt,* A: *Arnold, Arnoldt, Arnoldus, Arnolt*. The old German name *Arenvald* consists of two elements meaning 'eagle' and 'power'.

Aro 1. F: *Aaro, Aro, Arvo,* F (sn): *Aro,* FM (sn): *Alho,* G: *Alo, Allo*. This name could also refer to the biblical **Aaron**/*Aron* (see the list of biblical men's names).

Arvo 2. F, FM: *Arvo*. A Finnish name meaning 'value, worth, dignity'.

Ati + 1. A: *Ad, At, Atti, Attie*. An Afrikaans form of *Adriaan*, which is based on the Latin name *Hadrianus* 'of the Adriatic'.

Auguste 2. F: *August, Augusti, Aukust, Aukusti,* FM, G, A: *August*. The Latin word *augustus* means 'venerable, consecrated' (see **Augustus** in the list of biblical men's names).

Barry 1. E, N (sn): *Barry*. An Irish name based on a word meaning 'spear'. Also a saint's name.

Bekker 1. N (sn): *Becker, Bekker*. *Bekker* is an Afrikaans surname in Namibia. This baptismal name could also be based on the German surname *Becker,* which occurs in Namibia as well. A possible source for this name form is also the biblical man's name **Beker**, which appears in the Old Testament.

Bendiktus 1, *Benediktus* 1. G: *Benedikt, Benediktus,* A: *Benedict, Benedictus, Benedikt, Benediktus,* E: *Benedict*. St. Benedict (c.480–c.550) was the founder of the Benedictine Order; the Latin word *benedictus* means 'blessed'.

Benhard 3, *Bernaldu* 1, *Bernhard* 3. F, FM: *Bernhard,* G: *Bernald, Bernard, Bernhard,* A: *Bernard, Bernardt, Bernardus, Bernhard, Bernhardt, Bernhardus,* E: *Bernard*. The old German name *Berinhard* is a compound of elements meaning 'bear' and 'stern'.

Bokkie + 1. G: *Boke,* H: *Boke, Bokke, Bocke, Boek,* N (sn): *Bock, Bok*. The Afrikaans word *bokkie* 'little goat' is also used as a nickname in Namibia (Voipio-Vaalas 15.8.1995). *Bock* and *Bok* are also common surnames among the German and Afrikaans-speaking people in Namibia.

Bonfatius 1, *Bonifasius* 1, *Bonifatius* 2. G: *Bonifacius, Bonifatius, Bonifaz, Bonifazius,* A: *Bonifacius,* E: *Boniface.* The name of a 3rd century martyr saint, which was later adopted by many popes. The Latin word *bonifacius* means 'well-doer'.

Carl + 1, *Karl* 1. F: *Carl, Carlo, Kaarl, Kaarle, Kaarlo, Karl, Karlo,* FM: *Carl, Kaarle, Kaarlo, Karl,* G: *Carel, Carl, Carlo, Carolus, Karel, Karl,* A: *Carel, Carl, Charl, Karel, Karl, Sarel,* E: *Carl, Charles.* An old German name meaning 'man'. Also a saint's name.

Cenneth 1, *Keneth* 1. F: *Kennet, Kenneth,* A, E: *Kenneth.* A Gaelic name which was common especially in Scotland. Also a saint's name.

Charles + 1. F, G, A, E: *Charles.* See *Carl/Karl.*

Cotfried 1, *Gotfried* 1, *Gotfrid* + 1, *Gottfried* + 1. F: *Gottfrid, Gottfried,* G: *Gottfried,* A: *Godfrey, Godfried, Gotfried, Gottfried,* E: *Geoffrey, Godfrey, Jeffrey.* An old German name including two elements meaning 'god' and 'peace'.

Cottlieb 2, *Gotlieb* 1, *Gotriba* 1, *Gottlib* 2, *Gottlieb* 7 + 1, *Gottrieb* 1. F, G: *Gottlieb,* A: *Gotlieb, Gottlieb.* An old German name consisting of two elements meaning 'god' and 'love'.

Dalius 1, *Darius* 2. A, N (sn): *Darius,* G: *Dario.* The name of various Persian kings, with many possible derivations.

Denis 3, *Dennis* 1. F, G, E: *Denis, Dennis,* A: *Denis, Dennis, Dennys, Denys,* N (sn): *Dennis.* This name is based on the Greek name *Dionusios* 'of Dionysos', which appears in the New Testament (NB: **Dionisius**); the Latin form is *Dionysius.* Also a saint's name.

Dias + 2. G, H: *Diaz.* The full baptismal names of these Ambo men are *Bartolomeus Dias* and *Armas Iita Dias.* These names seem to refer to the Portuguese explorer Bartholomew Diaz.

Diogenes 3, *Diyongenus* 1. G: *Diogenes.* This name seems to refer to the famous Greek philosopher Diogenes.

Dion 1. G: *Dion, Dionys,* A: *Deon, Dion,* E: *Dion.* Possible origins: **Gideon**, *Dionysius.*

Edison + 1. This name may refer to Thomas Alva Edison (1847–1931), the inventor of the electronic lamp and other technical instruments. The full name of this man is *Achrenius Edison Elago.*

Edvard 2, *Edward* 4. F: *Edvard, Edvart, Edvartti, Edward, Eedvard, Eetvartti,* G: *Eduard, Edward,* A: *Edouard, Eduard, Edward, Edwardus,* E: *Edward.* An old English name containing two elements meaning 'rich, happy' and 'ward, guardian'. Also a saint's name.

Eeino 1, *Eino* 17. F, FM: *Eino.* A Finnish form of the German man's name *Enewald.*

Eero 2, *Ero* 1. F, FM: *Eero*. A Finnish form of *Eerik* (see *Erikki/Erkki*).

Elis 1. F: *Eelis, Elis*, G: *Elis*. This name is based on the Hebrew name **Elisa**, which appears in the Old Testament, or on its Latin form *Elisaeus/Eliseus*.

Ello 1. F, FM: *Eero*, G: *Elo, Hello*. See *Eero*.

Elvis 1. G, A: *Elvis*. This name could refer to the American singer Elvis Presley. The full baptismal name of this man is *Elvis-Nixon Tangeni* (1978).

Emil + 1. F: *Eemeli, Eemil, Eemili, Emil*, FM, G: *Emil*, A: *Aemil, Aemilius, Emiel, Emil, Emile, Emilius*. This name is based on the Roman family name *Aemilius*.

Emirich 1. F: *Emerik*, G: *Emerich, Emmerich*, E: *Emery*. An old German name, which is a compound formed from the stem *Im-* or *Em-* and *ric* 'ruler'; the latinised form is *Emericus*.

Emmalmmanuel 1, *Emmanuel* 1. F, G: *Emanuel, Emmanuel*, FM, E: *Emanuel*, A: *Emmanuel*. *Emanuel* is a Latin-Greek form of the Hebrew name **Immanuel** (see the list of biblical men's names).

Erasmus 10. F, G, A, E, N (sn): *Erasmus*. This name is based on a Greek word meaning 'beloved, desired'. Also a saint's name and the name of the Dutch scholar and reformer Desiderius Erasmus (1465–1536).

Erikki 1, *Erkki* 11 + 1. F: *Eerik, Eerikki, Eric, Erich, Erik, Erikki, Erkki*, FM: *Erik, Erkki*, G: *Erich, Erik, Erk*, A: *Eric, Erich, Erik, Eryk*, E: *Eric*. *Erik* < *Eirik* is an old Scandinavian name consisting of two elements meaning 'alone' or 'always' and 'kingdom, ruler'. *Erkki* is a Finnish form of this name.

Esko 1. F: *Esko*, H: *Esgo, Eske*. *Esko* is a Finnish form of the old Scandinavian name *Eskil*.

Evald 2. F: *Evald*, G: *Ewald*, A: *Ewald, Ewaldus*. An old German name consisting of two elements meaning 'law' and 'power, ruler'.

Evalistus 2. G: *Evarist, Evaristus*, H: *Evarest, Evariest, Evarist, Evaristus*. A saint's name.

Felitiman 1. N (sn): *Feldmann*. This name seems to be based on the German surname *Feldmann*, which is used in Namibia.

Firdrik 1, *Fredrek* 1, *Fredrik* 1 + 1, *Friadrek* 1, *Fridirh* 1, *Fridrich* 4, *Fridriech* 1, *Fridrik* 2, *Friedrich* 1, *Frindrich* 1. F: *Frederik, Fredrik, Fredrikki, Freedrik, Friedrich, Reetrik, Reetrikki, Rietrikki*, FM: *Fredrik*, G: *Frederic, Frederich, Frederick, Frederik, Fredrich, Fredrik, Friedrich*, A: *Frederic, Frederich, Frederick, Frederik, Frederikus, Friedrich*, E: *Frederic, Frederick*. An old German name consisting of elements meaning 'peace' and 'ruler'.

Frans 34 + 2, *Fraz* 1. F, G: *Frans, Franz*, FM, A: *Frans, Frantz, Franz*. An abbreviated form of the saint's name *Franciscus*, which means 'Frenchman'.

Fredinad 1. F: *Ferdinand, Ferdinant,* G, E: *Ferdinand,* A: *Ferdinand, Ferdinandus, Fernand, Fernandus.* An old German name consisting of elements meaning 'peace' and 'brave', or 'journey' and 'risk, venture'. Also a saint's name.

Frendj 1. F, G, A: *Fred,* E: *Fred, Friend.* This name seems to be based on the English word *friend.* In England, *Friend* also occurs as a man's name. This name form could also be an Ambo form of *Fred.*

Fried 1. G, A: *Fried.* An abbreviated form of *Frederik/Friedrich* or *Gottfried.*

Gebhard 9, *Gebihard* 1. G: *Gebhard,* N (sn): *Gebhardt.*

Gehad 1, *Gehard* 1. These name forms may be based on either *Gebhard* or *Gerhard.*

George 2 + 1. F, G: *Georg, George,* A: *Georg, George, Georgie, Georgius,* E: *George.* This name is based on the Greek word *georgos* 'farmer'. St. George (d. c. 303) is the patron saint of England.

Gerhard 2. F, G: *Gerhard,* A: *Geerhard, Gerard, Gerhard, Gerhardt, Gerhardus.* An old German name with elements meaning 'spear' and 'hard'.

Germanius + 1. G: *German, Germanus,* E: *German.* The Latin name *Germanus* 'German' is also a saint's name.

Geron 1. G: *Gereon, Gerion,* H: *Gero, Geron. Geron/Gereon* is a saint's name.

Gustaf 4, *Kustaa* 1, *Kustaf* 1. F: *Gustaf, Gustav, Kustaa, Kustavi,* FM: *Gustaf, Kustaa,* G: *Gustaf, Gustav,* A: *Gustaaf, Gustaf, Gustav, Gustave, Gustavus,* E: *Gustavus.* This name, which has become common especially in Sweden, may have German or Slavic origins.

Halloway 1. E (sn): *Halloway.*

Hans 2 + 1. F, A: *Hans,* G: *Hanns, Hans.* An abbreviated form of **Johannes** (see the list of biblical men's names).

Heikki 4 + 4. F, FM: *Heikki,* A: *Hekkie.* A Finnish form of *Henrik/Heinrich.*

Heiko 1. G: *Heiko.*

Helmut 1. F: *Helmut, Helmuth,* G: *Hellmut, Hellmuth, Helmut, Helmuth,* A: *Hellmut, Helmut, Helmoed, Helmoet, Helmuth.* An old German name which has been explained to mean 'brave protector'.

Hendrik 1 + 3. F: *Hendrik, Henrik, Henrikki, Hentrikki,* FM: *Hendrik, Henrik,* G: *Endric, Endrich, Endrik, Heinrich, Hendrich, Hendrik, Hendryk, Henrich, Henrick, Henrik,* A: *Hendrik, Hendrikus, Henricus, Henrikus.* An old German name consisting of elements meaning 'home, house' and 'ruler'. Also a saint's name: St. Henry (Henrik) is the patron saint of Finland. One of the missionaries of the Finnish Mission in the Ambo area was the Estonian Hendrik Tuttar (Peltola 1958, p. 262).

Henry 1. F, G: *Henri, Henry,* A: *Hendrie, Henri, Henry,* E: *Henry.* A variant of *Hendrik/Heinrich.* See *Hendrik.*

Herman 7 + 4. F: *Herman, Hermann, Hermanni,* G: *Herman, Hermann, Herrmann,* A: *Herman, Hermann, Hermanus,* E: *Herman.* An old German name consisting of elements meaning 'host, army' and 'man'.

Herneus 1, *Ireneus* 1. F: *Ireneus,* G: *Herenäus, Irenaeus, Ireneus, Irenäus,* A: *Hernus. Irenaeus* is a saint's name based on a Greek word meaning 'peace'.

Hilarius 1, *Hiralius* 1. F: *Hilari, Hilarius, Hillari,* G, A: *Hilarius,* E: *Hilary. Hilarius* is a name of a 4th century saint, bishop of Poitiers; the Latin word *hilarus* means 'cheerful'.

Hynonen 1. FM (sn): *Hynönen.* One of the Finnish male missionaries in the Ambo area was Erkki Hynönen (Peltola 1958, p. 268). *Hynonen* is the only baptismal name of this Ambo man.

Ida + 1. This Ambo man seems to have been given a European woman's name (see the list of European women's names). His full baptismal name is *Isak Ida.* The name *Ida* could also refer to the Ambo name *Iita* 'war'.

Ignatius 7. F, E: *Ignatius,* G: *Ignatius, Ignaz,* A: *Ignaas, Ignatius.* A saint's name with an unknown etymology.

Iivari 3, *Ivari* 2. F: *Iivar, Iivari, Ivar, Ivari,* G: *Ivar, Iwar,* A: *Ivar.* An old Scandinavian name meaning 'fighter with a bow'.

Jaakon 1, *Jakko* 1. F, FM: *Jaakko,* G: *Jago, Yago,* A: *Jac, Jaco, Jako.* These name forms seem to be based on **Jakob** (see the list of biblical men's names).

Jack 1. F, G, A, E: *Jack.* An English pet form for *John* < **Johannes** (see the list of biblical men's names).

Jakobus 1. A: *Jacobus, Jakobus.* This Afrikaans name is based on **Jakob** (see the list of biblical men's names).

Jan 1 + 1, *Janna* 1. *Janna* could be an Ambo form of *Jan.* F: *Jan, Jani,* G: *Jan, Jahn,* A, E: *Jan. Jan* is a variant of **Johannes** (see the list of biblical men's names).

Januarie 1. An Afrikaans word meaning 'January'. N (sn): *Januarie.*

Jimmy + 2. F: *Jim, Jimi, Jimmy,* G, A, E: *Jim, Jimmy.* An English pet form for *James* < **Jakob** (see the list of biblical men's names).

Joakim 1. F: *Joachim, Joakim,* G, E: *Joachim,* A: *Joachem, Joachim, Joagim.* According to Christian tradition, the father of the Virgin Mary was *Joakim,* which explains the popularity of this name in Europe. In the Old Testament, there is also a man's name **Jojakim**. The Hebrew name *Jehoiachim* has been explained to mean 'May Jehovah raise up, exalt'.

Jokkie + 1. G: *Jock, Jocki, Jocky, Joggi, Joki, Joky,* A: *Jock, Joggie,* E: *Jock.* This name may also be based on the Afrikaans word *jokkie* 'jockey'.

Josse + 1. G: *Joos, Jos, Joss, Josse,* A: *Joos, Jos, Jose, José,* E: *Jos, Josh, Josse.* These European name forms are based on various names starting with *Jos-,* e.g. *Josef, Joshua, Josiah* and *Josias. Josse (Judoc)* is also a saint's name.

Juho 1. F, FM: *Juho.* A Finnish form of *Juhani* < **Johannes** (see the list of biblical men's names).

Junior + 1. An English word. The full name of this boy is *Thankyou Naftali Junior.*

Juuso 10. F: *Juuso.* A Finnish form of **Josef** (see the list of biblical men's names).

Kansius 1. H: *Canisius.* A saint's name: Peter Canisius (1521–97) was a Jesuit priest, writer and educator.

Kenedy + 2, *Kenendi* + 1, *Kennedy* 1, *Kennedi* + 1. These names seem to refer to president John F. Kennedy or the other famous Kennedies in the United States. The full names of these men are *Kennedy Kaunda* (1973), **Sakeus** *Kenedy Tetekela* (1988), *Rebeus Kenendi Ndayaamena* (1988), **Johannes** *Kennedi Ndemufayo* (1988) and **Andreas** *Tuyeni Kenedy Natangwe* (1993).

Kiljana 1. FM, G: *Kilian.* One of the Finnish missionaries in the Ambo area was Kilian Sulo Alarik Aarni (Peltola 1958, p. 264).

Kosmas 2. G: *Cosmas, Kosmas.* A saint's name based on a Greek word meaning 'order'.

Krisian 1, *Kristian* 10, *Kristiana* 2. F: *Christian, Cristian, Kristiaani, Kristian, Ristian,* FM, E: *Christian,* G: *Christian, Kristian,* A: *Christiaan, Christian, Kristiaan, Kristian, Krystiaan.* A name based on the Latin word *christianus* 'a Christian'.

Kristi + 1. G: *Chris, Christ, Christe,* A: *Christie, Kristie.* An abbreviated form of *Christian/Kristian.*

Kristof 16 + 1. F: *Christoffer, Christopher, Kristofer, Kristoffer,* G: *Christof, Christoffer, Christoph, Christopher, Kristof,* A: *Christof, Christoff, Christoffel, Christoph, Christopher, Kristof, Kristoff, Kristoffel, Kristoph, Kristophe,* E: *Christopher.* A name based on the Greek *Kristoforos* 'bearing Christ'. Also a saint's name.

Lauri 1. F: *Lauri,* G: *Lauritz,* A: *Laurie, Lauritz. Lauri* is a Finnish form of the Latin saint's name *Laurentius* 'of Laurentium'; this place name refers to the bay tree.

Lehto 5. FM (sn): *Lehto.* One of the Finnish missionaries in the Ambo area was Erkki Lehto (Peltola 1958, p. 264).

Leonard 39 + 1. F: *Leonaarti, Leonard, Leonart, Leonarti, Leonartti, Leonhard,* FM: *Leonhard,* G: *Leonard, Leonhard, Lienhard,* A: *Leendert,*

Leonard, Leonardus, Leonhard, Lionard, E: *Leonard.* An old German name consisting of two elements meaning 'lion' and 'hardy, bold'. Also a saint's name.

Leopold 3, *Leopord* 1. F, G, E: *Leopold,* A: *Leopold, Leopoldus.* An old German name consisting of two elements meaning 'people' and 'bold'.

Levena + 1. G: *Leven, Levin, Lewin,* H: *Levien, Lieven.* The Dutch forms refer to St. Lebuinus.

Maks 11. F: *Maks, Max,* G: *Max,* A: *Max, Maximiliaan, Maximillian,* E: *Maximilian.* Possible origins: *Maximus, Maximinus* and *Maximilian* which are all based on the Latin word *maximus* 'the greatest'. *Maximilian* is a contamination of two Roman names: *Maximus* and *Aemilianus.*

Maritin 1, *Marti* 1, *Martin* 60 + 1, *Martina* 4, *Martti* 1, *Marttina* 1. F, FM: *Martin, Martti,* G, E: *Martin,* A: *Maarten, Maartin, Marten, Marthinus, Martin, Martinus, Martyn. Martin* is based on the Latin name *Martinus,* which is the diminutive form of *Martius* 'of Mars'. Also a saint's name. *Martti* is the Finnish form of this name. The original model for this name in the Ambo area was the Finnish missionary Martti (Martin) Rautanen (Peltola 1958, p. 259). Martin Luther and Martti Ahtisaari may also have served as models for some of these names.

Marvin + 1. G, E: *Marvin.*

Mati 1, *Matti* 7. F, FM: *Matti,* G: *Mat, Matti,* A: *Matt, Mattie.* Variants of *Mattias* and *Matteus* (see **Mateus** and **Matias** in the list of biblical men's names). The name form *Mati* could also refer to the Ambo word *omumati* 'boy, youngster' (Tirronen 1986, p. 206).

Mauno 2. F, FM, G: *Mauno.* A Finnish form of *Magnus,* a Latin name meaning 'great'. In Germany, *Mauno* can be explained as Finnish influence.

Mikko + 1. F, FM: *Mikko.* A Finnish form of **Mikael** (see the list of biblical men's names).

Modestus 1. G: *Modest, Modesto, Modestus,* H: *Modest, Modestus.* A saint's name based on the Latin word *modestus* 'modest'.

Nestor 4. F: *Nestor, Nestori,* FM, G: *Nestor.* A Greek name referring to the military commandor Nestor in the Trojan war.

Niilo 5. F: *Niilo,* A: *Niel,* E: *Neil.* A Finnish form of *Nikolaus* (see *Niklas*). The Afrikaans form *Niel* may originate from *Nicholas* or *Nataniel* and the English form *Neil/Niall/Nigel* seems to be an independent name. *Niilo* could also be interpreted as an Ambo name (< *na + iilo*), in which case it could be derived from *okalo* 'ripening period of corn and fruit, brewing period of marula beer' (Tirronen 1986, p. 187). However, as this name appears among the men's names as the first baptismal name only and once as the only name of the person, it was classified as a European name. It also occurs once as a subsequent name among the women in the data; the full baptismal name of this woman is *Martta Niilo* (see *Niilo* in the list of women's European names).

Niklas 1. F: *Nicholas, Nicklas, Niclas, Nicolas, Niklas, Nikolas, Nikolaus,* G: *Niklas, Niklaus,* A: *Nicholaas, Nicholas, Nicolaas, Nicolas, Nieklaas, Niklaas, Niklas, Nikolaas, Nikolas,* E: *Nicholas. Nikolaos* is a Greek name consisting of elements meaning 'victory' and 'folk, people'; the Latin form of this name is *Nicolaus.* Also a saint's name (St. Nicholas, Santa Claus).

Nikolae 1, *Nikolai* 1. F: *Nikolai, Nikolaj,* G: *Nicolai, Nikolai.* A Russian form of *Nicolaus.*

Nixon + 1. This name may refer to Richard Nixon, the former president of the United States (see the name *Elvis* above).

Oiva 10, *Oiwa* 1. F: *Oiva.* A Finnish name meaning 'excellent, very good'.

Olavi 4, *Olvi* + 1. F: *Olav, Olavi,* FM: *Olavi,* G, E: *Olaf,* A: *Olaf, Olav.* An old Scandinavian name. St. Olaf is the patron saint of Norway. *Olavi* is the Finnish form of this name.

Oligenes 1. This name refers to Origenes, one of the Fathers of the Church.

Olli + 1. F, FM: *Olle, Olli,* A: *Ollie.* A variant of *Olavi/Olaf.*

Oskal 1, *Oskar* 24 + 2, *Oskari* 2. F: *Oscar, Oskar, Oskari,* FM: *Oskari,* G, A: *Oscar, Oskar,* E: *Oscar.* An old English name consisting of elements meaning 'god' and 'spear'. The son of Ossian in Ossianic poems.

Otto 1. F, FM, G, E, N (sn): *Otto,* A: *Otho, Otto.* An old German name meaning 'rich'.

Paavo 5. F, FM, G: *Paavo.* A Finnish form of *Paavali* < **Paulus** (see the list of biblical men's names). In Germany, this name can be ascribed to Finnish influence.

Patrik + 1. F: *Patric, Patrick, Patrik,* G: *Patric, Patrick, Pattrick, Pattrik,* E: *Patrick.* St. Patrick is the patron saint of Ireland. The name is based on the Latin word *patricius* 'nobleman'.

Pentinen 1. FM (sn): *Pentikäinen, Pentti, Pettinen.*

Pentti 1. F, FM (sn): *Pentti.* One of the Finnish missionaries in the Ambo area was Elias Pentti (Peltola 1958, p. 271). However, as Pentti arrived in the Ambo area in 1948 and the Ambo man carrying this name was baptised in 1918, this name must refer to the Finnish forename *Pentti,* which is derived from *Benediktus.*

Petaja 2. FM (sn): *Petäjä.* One of the Finnish missionaries was Kalle Petäjä who worked among the Ambo people between the years 1907 and 1953 (Peltola 1958, p. 263). The full baptismal names of these two men are *Petaja* (1953) and *Petaja Angala* (1953).

Petela 3. G, F, A, E: *Peter.* A variant of **Petrus** (see the list of biblical men's names).

Petenen 1, *Pettenen* + 1. FM (sn): *Pettinen*. One of the Finnish missionaries in the Ambo area was August Pettinen (Peltola 1958, p. 261).

Pius 2 + 1. G: *Pius*. A saint's name which has been common among the popes. The Latin word *pius* means 'pious'.

Pretorius 1. N (sn): *Pretorius*. A common Afrikaans surname.

Rafael 2. F: *Raafael, Rafael*, G: *Rafael, Raffael, Raphael*, E: *Raphael*. A Hebrew name meaning 'God has healed'; the name of one of the three archangels in the apocryphal Book of Tobit.

Rautanen 1. This name may refer to the Finnish missionary Martti Rautanen, or to someone else in his family (Peltola 1958, p. 259, 262). FM (sn): *Rautanen*.

Reinert 1. G: *Reiner, Reinhard*, A: *Rainard, Raynard, Reinart, Reinert, Reinhard, Renard*, N (sn): *Reinert*. *Reinhard* is an old German name consisting of elements meaning 'counsel, wisdom' and 'hardy, bold'.

Reinhold 20 + 1. F, FM, G: *Reinhold*, A: *Reinhold, Reinhoud, Reinold, Reinoud, Reynold*. An old German name consisting of two elements which mean 'counsel, wisdom' and 'power'.

Riika + 1. G: *Rick, Riek, Rik*, A: *Ric, Rick, Riek, Ryk*. *Riika* is also a European woman's name (see *Riikka* in the list of European women's names). The full baptismal name of this person is *Angula Riika*. The male forms *Rick, Riek*, etc. are derived from names such as *Eric, Frederik, Diederik, Richard* and *Ulrich*.

Risto 7. F, FM, G: *Risto*, H: *Rist*. A Finnish name based on *Kristoffer* and *Kristian*. In Germany, this name can be attributed to Finnish influence.

Robert + 1. F: *Robert, Roobert, Roopert, Roopertti*, G, E: *Robert*, A: *Robert, Robertus*. An old German name consisting of two elements meaning 'fame' and 'bright'. Also a saint's name.

Rudolf 1. F: *Rudolf, Ruudolf*. FM, G, E: *Rudolf*, A: *Roedolf, Rudolf, Rudolph*. An old German name consisting of two elements meaning 'fame' and 'wolf'.

Sebastianus 1. F, G, E: *Sebastian*, A: *Sebastiaan, Sebastian*, H: *Sebastiaan, Sebastianus*. St. Sebastian (Sebastianus) was a Roman martyr; the name *Sebastianus* means 'of Sebastia'.

Sevelinus 3, *Severinus* 2. F: *Severi, Severin*, G: *Severin, Severinus*. A saint's name: *Severinus* is the other name for St. Boethius, the Roman philosopher and martyr. The name is based on the Latin word *severus* 'severe'.

Severus 5 + 1. F, H: *Severus*. A Roman family name. See *Severinus*.

Sofia + 1. The woman's name *Sofia* (see the list of European women's names) has been given to a male child here. The full name of this man is *Sakaria Sofia Tangi*.

Simo 1. F: *Simo*, A: *Sim*. A Finnish abbreviated form of **Simon** and **Simeon** (see the list of biblical men's names).

Soini 1. F (wn, mn), FM (sn): *Soini*. One of the female Finnish missionaries in the Ambo area was Aino Soini (Peltola 1958, p. 269). *Soini* is also not a common first name in Finland, but it has been used by both women and men. This name also appears as a woman's name in the data (see the list of European women's names). As Aino Soini arrived in the Ambo area in 1948 and the man in question was baptised in 1918, this name cannot be based on Aino Soini's surname.

Sondag + 2. An Afrikaans word meaning 'Sunday'.

Spener + 1. G (sn): *Spener*. This name may refer to Philipp Jakob Spener who was the other leader – beside Francke – of the pietist movement in the 17th century Germany (Christensen & Göransson 1974, p. 380).

Suikanen 1. FM (sn): *Suikkanen*. One of the Finnish missionaries in the Ambo area was Olli Suikkanen (Peltola 1958, p. 266). *Suikanen* is the only baptismal name of this man, who was baptised in 1963.

Tauno 5 + 2, *Taunoe* 1, *Taunu* + 1. F, FM: *Tauno*. A Finnish name meaning 'accommodating, compliant, docile'.

Teodor 6 + 2. F: *Teodor, Theodor*, G: *Theodor*, A: *Theodoor, Theodor, Theodore, Theodorus*, E: *Theodore*. A Greek name meaning 'gift of God'. Also a saint's name.

Thankyou 1. An English expression: *thank you*.

Timo 1. F, FM: *Timo*, G: *Thiemo, Tiemo, Timmo, Timo*, A: *Tim, Timmo, Timo*, E: *Tim, Timothy*. An abbreviated form of **Timoteus** (see the list of biblical men's names).

Toivo 21 + 2. F, FM: *Toivo*. A Finnish name meaning 'hope'.

Tylves 3. FM (sn): *Tylväs*. One of the Finnish missionaries in the Ambo area was Oskari Tylväs (Peltola 1958, p. 262). The full baptismal names of these men are *Tylves* (1943), *Tylves Shikongo Nghidingua* (1973) and *Tylves Natangwe* (1978).

Uno 1, *Uuno* 1. F: *Uno, Uuno*, G: *Unno*. A name based on the Latin word *unus* (Italian: *uno*) 'one, only'. It has become popular especially in the Nordic countries.

Urho 1. F, FM: *Urho*. A Finnish name meaning 'hero, brave fighter'.

Usiko 1. F: *Usko*. *Usko* is a Finnish name meaning 'faith'.

Vaino 35 + 6, *Väinä* 2, *Waino* 2. F, FM: *Väinö, Wäinö*. A Finnish name originating in the Finnish national epic Kalevala; *Väinämöinen* is the main character of this epic.

Veijo 3. F: *Veijo*. A Finnish name based on the name *Veikko*.

Veikko 4 + 1, *Veiko* + 1. F, FM: *Veikko*. A Finnish name meaning 'brother'.

Veni 2, *Venni* 2. F: *Venni*. A Finnish name derived from the name *Verneri* < *Werner*.

Verner 8. F: *Verner, Verneri, Werner*, FM: *Verner*, G: *Werner, Wernher*, A: *Werner*. An old German name, a compound of elements meaning 'folk' and the folkname *Varin*.

Victor 1, *Vihito* 1, *Vihtor* 1, *Vihtori* 3, *Viktor* 6 + 1, *Viktori* 4. F: *Vihtor, Vihtori, Viktor, Viktori*, FM: *Viktor*, G, A: *Victor, Viktor*, E: *Victor*. The Latin name *Victor* means 'conquerer'; it is the name of many saints.

Vilbald 3, *Vilbard* 17, *Vilbardt* 1, *Vilibard* 3, *Vilpard* + 1, *Wibard* 1, *Wilbard* 14 + 1, *Wilpad* 1, *Willebrand* 1. G: *Wibald, Wigbald, Wilbelt, Wilbert, Wilbrand, Willebald, Willebrand, Willibald, Willibert, Willibrand. Willebald/ Willibald* was an Anglo-Saxon saint who lived in the 8th century.

Vilhelm 18, *Vilihema* 3, *Wihema* 1, *Wilhelm* 12, *Wilhelma* 1, *Wilhem* 1, *Wilhema* 1. F: *Vilhelm, Vilhelmi, Wilhelm, Wilhelmi*, FM: *Vilhelm*, G: *Wilhelm*, A: *Wilhelm, Willem, William*, E: *William*. An old German name consisting of two elements meaning 'will' and 'helmet'. Also a saint's name.

Vilho 19 + 1, *Viliho* 1, *Wilho* 1. F: *Vilho, Wilho*. A Finnish variant of *Vilhelm/ Wilhelm*.

Vili 1, *Viliheiki* 1. F: *Heikki, Vili*, FM: *Vili-Heikki*, G: *Willi, Willy*, A: *Willie, Willy*. The name *Viliheiki* also appears as *Vili-Heikki* in the church registers. This name may be given after the son of the Finnish missionary Heikki Saari, Vili-Heikki Saari (Personnel archives of the Finnish Evangelical Lutheran Mission, Helsinki). *Vili* is a Finnish variant of *Vilhelm/Wilhelm*. See also *Heikki* in this list.

Viljo 1. F: *Viljo*, H: *Wiljo*. A Finnish name meaning 'the best, very good'; also a variant of *Vilhelm* < *Wilhelm* and *Viljami* < *William*.

Waldheim + 1. This name may refer to the former general secretary of the United Nations, Kurt Waldheim.

Willehard 1. F: *Vilhard, Villehad, Villehard, Villhard, Willehard*, FM: *Willehad*, G: *Willehad, Willehard*. St. Willehad (d. 789) was bishop of Bremen. The name has been explained to mean 'eager fighter' or 'quarreller'.

Wilson 1. G: *Wilson*, N (sn): *Wilson*. An English surname, originally a diminutive form of *William*.

Zee 1. A Dutch word meaning 'sea'; the corresponding Afrikaans word is *see*. N (sn): *Zeelie, Zeeman*.

Ambo Names

Remarks on the Ambo Names in the Data. Ambo names, i.e. names that are derived from nouns, verbs and other elements in the Ambo languages, form the third main group in Ambo baptismal nomenclature. Of the 16,643 name occurrences in the data, 5,367, i.e. almost one third (32.3 per cent), are Ambo names. These names are extremely rare as first given names, but very common as subsequent baptismal names. Of the first given names in the data, 309 names (2.8 per cent) are Ambo names, whereas 5,058 (88.4 per cent) of the subsequent given names belong to this class. With regard to the popularity of Ambo names, the names of women and men have a similar profile. Of the first given names of women 184 (3.1 per cent) are Ambo names, while of those of men 125 (2.6 per cent). The corresponding numbers in subsequent given names are 3,075 (88.2 per cent) for women and 1,983 (88.6 per cent) for men.

A characteristic of this class is the wide variety of name forms: there are altogether 1,715 different name forms among the Ambo names in the data. This can be explained partly by the various orthographic changes and linguistic differences between the Ambo varieties. Hence, there are such name pairs in the data as *Uusiku* and *Haufiku*, which are Ndonga and Kwanyama forms for 'night', or *Njanjukueni* and *Nyanyukweni* 're-joice', which in turn represent different orthographies in these languages. A more important reason for this variation, however, is that Ambo names are typically not selected from a repertoire of names that occur with high frequency, but are very often created by the name-giver using the linguistic resources of the Ambo languages. Because of this, it may not be surprising that the majority of Ambo names in the data occur once only. It is also characteristic of Ambo names that many of them may be conferred on both sexes. As many as 12.1 per cent of the different Ambo name forms in the data appear both as men's and women's names. It is also interesting to note that a little less than one third of the names in the 1938 Ambo name-day calendar (Ondjalulamasiku Jomumvo 1938), 115 names altogether, can be found in the data, even if not always in an exactly similar form.

Even if many Ambo names are new creations, there are some of them which have become very popular as baptismal names. The lists of the twenty most popular subsequent given names of women and men, which were presented earlier in this study, show what kind of names these are. Of the twenty names in the women's list, 19 were Ambo names: *Magano, Ndinelago, Ndapewa, Nelago, Ndakulilwa, Ndapanda, Nyanyukweni, Nangula, Ndahambelela, Namutenya, Ndilimeke, Ndapandula, Ndeyapo, Niita, Panduleni, Ndasilwohenda, Natangwe, Nangombe* and *Mpingana*. Similarly, 19 names in the men's list are Ambo names: *Natangwe, Panduleni, Tangeni, Elago, Ndeshipanda, Shaanika, Mekondjo, Iiyambo, Iita, Hafeni, Shikongo, Amutenya, Angula, Kondjeni, Pendapala, Iipinge, Megameno, Tutaleni* and *Uushona*.[448] As can be seen, the names *Natangwe* and *Panduleni* appear in both lists. The difference between male and female Ambo names was also discussed earlier.

There is one name in this class which was classified as an Ambo name, even if it could also be understood as a Finnish name: *Kauko*. As a Finnish man's name, *Kauko* is a derivative of *Kaukomieli*, a name used for *Lemminkäinen*, one of the main characters in the Finnish national epic Kalevala (Vilkuna 1993, p. 101). As an Ambo name, *Kauko* could contain the idea 'the world is no better elsewhere'. This name occurs both among the men's and women's names in the data. Four women have it as a subsequent baptismal name (e.g. *Elina Kauko* and *Eva Kauko Ndapanda*), six men as a subsequent baptismal name (e.g. *Erastus Kauko* and *Martin Kondjashili Kauko*), and one man as his only baptismal name. All the other names in the data which could have been interpreted either as Ambo or as European, *Evi, Hileni, Monika, Mati* and *Niilo*, were classified as European names.

Morphology of Ambo Names. In African languages, the name-forming process is typically a derivational one: names are derived from some primary source in the language, such as nouns, verbs, adjectives, noun phrases and clauses (Koopman 1979b, p. 153). In this subsection, we shall look at the most common methods used for constructing personal names in the Ambo languages: 1. Deriving names from nouns, 2. Deriving names from verbs, 3. Deriving names from clauses, and 4. Deriving names from other linguistic sources. The examples of names that are given here are almost exclusively Ndonga names.

Deriving Names from Nouns. There are many ways to derive personal names from nouns in the Ambo languages. The original stem of the noun may occur in the name with or without a prefix, or with part of the prefix only. Female names are often derived from nouns with the name-deriving formative *na-/n-*, whereas in male names the *o* of the prefix is often replaced by *a*. There are also names which consist of nouns and locative prefixes, for example.

Names without a Prefix (Class 1a). Names that are derived from singular nouns belonging to class 1a in the Ambo languages do not contain a prefix, as there is no prefix for the nouns of this class in the singular form. For example, the singular form of the word meaning 'friend' is *kuume* and the plural form is *oo/kuume*.[449] This noun class consists mainly of kinship terms (e.g. *tate* 'my father', *oo/tate* 'our fathers') and loan words referring to people (e.g. *ndohotola* 'doctor', *oo/ndohotola* 'doctors'). (Tirronen 1977, p. 19–20; 1986, p. c.) Here are examples of such names in the data:

Kuku < *kuku* 'my grandmother'
Kuume < *kuume* 'friend'
Mbushandje < *mbushandje* 'my namesake'
Namupa < *namupa* 'the only daughter among more brothers'
Nekulu < *nekulu* 'mother of the family, madam'
Tate < *tate* 'my father, mister'

Names with the Whole Prefix. Many names in the data contain the whole prefix of the noun, beside the noun stem itself. Here are examples of such names, both in the singular and plural form:

Aantu < pl. *aa/ntu; omu/ntu* 'man, human being'
Egameno < *e/gameno* 'protection, patronage'
Egumbo < *e/gumbo* 'homestead, house, home'
Ekelyombili < *e/ke lyombili* 'hand of peace'
Einekelo < *e/inekelo* 'confidence, faith, trust'
Ekondo < *e/kondo* 'hoof'
Elago < *e/lago* 'happiness, luck'
Eloolo < *e/loolo* 'abundance, profusion, plenty, good harvest'
Iigonda < *ii/gonda* 'engagement gifts'
Iilende < pl. *ii/lende; oshi/lende* 'leader, hero'
Iilonga < pl. *ii/longa; oshi/longa* 'work, task, occupation'
Iimbondi < pl. *ii/mbondi; oshi/mbondi* 'any herbaceous plant, herb, weed'
Iimongwa < pl. *ii/mongwa; oshi/mongwa* 'brackish nature, salinity'
Iipumbu < pl. *ii/pumbu; oshi/pumbu* 'group of tall trees in a desert wasteland'
Iita < *ii/ta* 'war, warfare'
Omagano < *oma/gano* 'gift, present'
Omalovu < *oma/lovu* 'beer'
Omuna < *omu/na* 'someone's child'
Omusamane < *omu/samane* 'married man, head of the house'
Omuwa < *omu/wa* 'royal person, prince, princess, lord'
Uulumbu < *uu/lumbu* 'famine, drought, depression'
Uuyuni < *uu/yuni* 'world, era'

Names without the Initial Vowel of the Prefix. In many names, the prefix of the noun appears in an abbreviated form: the first vowel, i.e. the pre-prefix, is missing. Thus, *oshi-* has become *shi-, oma- ma-, omu- mu-*, etc. Here are examples of this phenomenon in the data:

Katili < *oka/tili* 'envy, jealousy, long thin stem (of calabash)'
Lugodhi < *olu/godhi* 'hostility, fight, battle, contest'
Lukongo < *olu/kongo* 'disadvantage, inconvenience, drawback, seeking'
Magano < *oma/gano* 'gift, present'
Malenga < pl. *oma/lenga; e/lenga* 'adviser, counsellor, officer'
Mayenge < pl. *oma/yenge; e/yenge* 'a small piece of ostrich eggshell to be made into a pearl by drilling a hole and rounding it (also a ready-made pearl)'
Mukuilongo < *omu/kwiilongo* 'stranger, foreigner'
Mumbala < *omu/mbala* 'courtier, chamberlain'
Munondjene < *omu/nondjene* 'one with bad luck';
o/ndjene 'bad luck, misfortune'
Mupaja < *omu/paya* 'big belt, girdle'
Mupolo < *omu/polo* 'bridge of the nose, forehead'
Muyenda < *omu/yenda* 'visitor, guest'
Shikwambi < *oshi/kwambi* 'Kwambi dialect or habit'
Shilongo < *oshi/longo* 'country, state, kingdom'
Shilumbu < *oshi/lumbu* 'white man'
Shimanya < *oshi/manya* 'iron ore'
Shimbili < *oshi/mbili* 'bad peace' < *o/mbili* 'peace, harmony, reconciliation, apology'

In some cases, in which the prefix consists of one vowel only, this has led to the deletion of the whole prefix:

Hango < *o/hango* 'wedding'
Hupitho < *e/hupitho* 'saving, rescue, salvation'
Lago < *e/lago* 'happiness, luck'
Mvula < *o/mvula* 'rain'
Ndjalo < *o/ndjalo* 'area, surface'
Ndjodhi < *o/ndjodhi* 'dream'
Ngula < *o/ngula* 'morning, before noon'
Ngunga < *o/ngunga* 'debt, rain'
Pongo < *e/pongo* 'homeless person, wanderer, tramp, poor person'

Names Formed with <u>A-</u>. In many names which are derived from nouns with a prefix beginning with the letter *o*, the *o* has been changed into an *a*. This phenomenon is typical of male names, but such names can be found among the women as well. In Ndonga, *a-* can be used to denote a person who has a particular characteristic. For example, *amutse* (< *omu/tse* 'head') means 'big-headed', *amagulu* (< pl. *oma/gulu; oku/gulu* 'leg') 'long-legged' and *amupunda* (< *omu/punda* 'potbelly') 'big-bellied'. (Tirronen 1986, p. 1, 52, 356, 433.) In addition, *a-* is commonly used as a name-deriving formative:

Aludhilu < *olu/dhilu* 'transfer of homestead'
Alugodhi < *olu/godhi* 'hostility, fight, battle, contest'
Amadhila < pl. *oma/dhila; e/dhila* 'big bird, aeroplane, kudu horn as a wind-instrument in an initiation ceremony'
Amalovu < *oma/lovu* 'beer'
Ambambi < *o/mbambi* 'duiker buck, frost'
Ambata < *o/mbata* 'reluctance to work, unwillingness to work'; *ambata* 'gainsayer'
Ambili < *o/mbili* 'peace, harmony, reconciliation, apology'
Ambuga < *o/mbuga* 'desert wasteland, wilderness, uninhabited area'
Ambunda < *o/mbunda* 'back, loins, hips'; *ambunda* 'one with an exceptional back'
Amupaja < *omu/paya* 'big belt, girdle'
Amupala < *omu/pala* 'big bad face' < *oshi/pala* 'face'
Amupolo < *omu/polo* 'bridge of the nose, forehead'
Amupembe < *omu/pembe* 'white tail-hairs among black ones'
Amupunda < *omu/punda* 'potbelly'
Amushe < *omu/she* 'raisin-bush'
Amushila < *omu/shila* 'tail, whisk (broom), lash, thong'
Amvula < *o/mvula* 'rain'
Angombe < *o/ngombe* 'beast, head of cattle, dullard, ignorant person, tick, mark of checking'
Anguwo < *o/nguwo* 'blanket made of a skin, used also as an umbrella, dress, garment'
Ankama < *o/nkama* 'strength, firmness'
Ankonga < *o/nkonga* 'wedding'
Ashikongo < *oshi/kongo* 'search for girls to the chief's court'
Ashikoto < *oshi/koto* 'passenger-coach, cabin'
Ashilungu < *oshi/lungu* 'small lip (with negative meaning)'
Asino < *o/sino* 'gemsbok, oryx'

Names Formed with *Na-/N-*. Many names in the data are also formed by prefixing *na-/n-* to the noun. In Ndonga, the morpheme *na-/n-* means 'with, and, along, according to, all over, also, too, as well'. Personal nouns can also be formed with *na-/n-* being prefixed to the noun. For example, *omu/nandunge* 'clever/intelligent person' is derived from *oo/ndunge* 'intelligence, thoughtfulness' and *omu/nedhina* 'well-known/famous person' from *e/dhina* 'name/title'. (Tirronen 1986, p. 22, 242, 249, 269, 270.) *Na-/N-* is commonly used as a name-deriving formative, especially for female names. In many names, the first vowel of the original prefix is replaced by the *a* in *na-* (e.g. *na + o/hango > Nahango*), but in certain contexts it remains unchanged (e.g. *na + e/gumbo > Negumbo*). Here are more examples:

Nahambo < *o/hambo* 'cattle-post (remote pasture), pen for oxen'
Nahango < *o/hango* 'wedding'
Nahenda, Nohenda < *o/henda* 'mercy, pity'
Namalunga < pl. *oma/lunga*; *e/lunga* 'big thief'
Namatanga < pl. *oma/tanga*; *e/tanga* 'pumpkin, ball, group, team, armed force'
Namatsi < pl. *oma/tsi*; *oku/tsi* 'ear'
Nambili, Nombili < *o/mbili* 'peace, harmony, reconciliation, apology'
Nambahu < *o/mbahu* 'locust'
Nambala < *o/mbala* 'hastiness, quickness; chief's dwelling, court, palace; bald-headedness'
Nambalu < *o/mbalu* 'disaster, evil, mischief, fatty spot on the surface of sauce, soup, etc.'
Nambudhi < *o/mbudhi* 'matter of dispute, discord, strife, quarrel'
Namene < *o/mene* 'early in the morning'
Nameya < *ome/ya* 'water, liquid, juice, liquor, alcohol'
Nampweya < *o/mpweya* 'smoothness and roundness'
Namuenjo, Namwenjo < *omw/enyo* 'soul, spirit, mid, life'
Namupunda < *omu/punda* 'potbelly'
Nandigolo < *o/ndigolo* 'shout of joy'
Nandjambi < *o/ndjambi* 'boys' group to help somebody, bee, reward, salary'
Nandjungu < *o/ndjungu* 'diligence, energy, activity'
Nankalu < *o/nkalu* 'battle-cry, rallying cry'
Nashilongo < *oshi/longo* 'country, state, kingdom'
Negoli < *e/goli* 'bend, curve'
Nekandjo < *e/kandjo* '(single) time, occasion, stride, bound, leap, charge of shot'
Nendongo < *e/ndongo* 'syphilis, pitch-black colour'
Negumbo < *e/gumbo* 'homestead, house, home'
Nehale < *e/hale* 'passage-yard, court'
Niimpungu < pl. *iimpungu*; *oshi/mpungu* 'mound on which corn is grown, flower bed, table, list'
Niipindi < *ii/pindi* 'merchandise'
Niitula < pl. *ii/tula*; *oshi/tula* 'settler's temporary dwelling'
Nuuta < *uu/ta* 'bow, arch, weapons, game being hunted'
Nuuyoma < *uu/yoma* 'cowardice'

Names Formed with *Ka-*. Many names in the data are also formed by prefixing *ka-* to the noun concerned. In Ndonga, *ka-* can be translated as 'of the type of'. For example, the name *Kashilumbu* is derived from *oshi/lumbu* 'white man'. (Tirronen 1986, p. 118, 195.) There are examples of such names both among the women's and the men's names in the data. It should be noted, however, that many of these names may also be interpreted as being based on the diminutive form of the noun. These are formed by replacing the normal prefix of the noun by the prefix *oka-*, e.g. *oka/nime* 'small lion' < *o/nime* 'lion', *oka/menye* 'small springbok' < *o/menye* 'springbok', or *oka/pongo* 'small homeless person' < *e/pongo* 'homeless person'.

Kakololo < *e/kololo* 'coughing, removing of fruit pulp and seeds from a pumpkin, cave'
Kakunde < *e/kunde* 'bean, kind of intoxicating drink'
Kalenga < *e/lenga* 'adviser, counsellor, officer'
Kambala < *o/mbala* 'hastiness, quickness; chief's dwelling, court, palace; bald-headedness'
Kambonde < *o/mbonde* 'area growing low Kalahari Christmas-trees' or *e/mbonde* 'chamber pot' or *oka/mbonde* 'kind of string of pearls'
Kamene < *o/mene* 'early in the morning'
Kamenye < *o/menye* 'springbok'
Kampelo < *o/mpelo* 'allegation that one alone is obliged to work while his/her companions have got it easy' (or < *oka/mpelo* 'little allegation that ...')
Kamulilo < *omu/lilo* 'fire'
Kamwene < *mwene* 'owner, master, boss, leader'
Kanjama < *o/nyama* 'meat, flesh'
Kanime < *o/nime* 'lion'
Kapongo < *e/pongo* 'homeless person, wanderer, tramp, poor person'
Kayamba < *-yamba* 'well-to-do, rich, wealthy'

Names Formed with a Locative Prefix. Many names in the data appear with a locative prefix: *ku-*, *mu-* or *pu-*. The prefix *ku-* denotes a distant place and often also direction, *mu-* denotes being in something ('in, inside'), and *pu-* indicates immediate proximity. (Tirronen 1977, p. 89, 91, 97, 101.) Examples of such names are:

Kelago < *ku* + *e/lago* 'luck, happiness'
Kombala < *ku* + *o/mbala* 'hastiness, quickness; chief's dwelling, court, palace; bald-headedness'
Kombanda < *ku* + *o/mbanda* 'surface, top'; *kombanda* 'on the top, on the other side, beyond, after (a time)'
Megameno < *mu* + *e/gameno* 'protection, patronage'
Meitaalo < *mu* + *e/itaalo* 'belief, faith, creed'
Meke < *mu* + *e/ke* 'palm of the hand'
Mekololo < *mu* + *e/kololo* 'coughing, removing of fruit pulp and seeds from a pumpkin; cave, cavern, hollow'
Mekondjo < *mu* + *e/kondjo* 'fighting, struggling'
Melago < *mu* + *e/lago* 'luck, happiness'
Menongelo < *mu* + *e/nongelo* 'school'
Metine < *mu* + *E/tine* 'Thursday'
Metumo < *mu* + *e/tumo* 'sending, mission'
Mohole < *mu* + *o/hole* 'love'
Mondjila < *mu* + *o/ndjila* 'line, path, road, course, way, journey, method, way of behaving'
POmbili < *pu* + *o/mbili* 'peace, harmony, reconciliation, apology'

Deriving Names from Verbs. Personal names which are derived from verbs are very common in the data. Many of them appear in the imperative mood, but other verb forms occur with high frequency as well.

Imperative singular
Dhiginina 'persevere in, persist in, keep on, be steadfast'
Hambelela 'praise, glorify'
Hekeleka 'comfort, console'
Homata 'arm yourself, equip yourself with arms'
Ilonga 'learn, study'
Inekela 'hope, wish, trust in/to, confide in, rely on'
Kaminina 'hide in your fist, hide your things for the needy'
Kondja 'fight, struggle, wrestle, strive'
Konga 'look for, seek, search for, hunt'
Kwatha 'help'
Ligola 'cheer, jubilate'
Londoloka 'climb down, descend, get down'
Minikila 'shine on, lighten, enlighten, illuminate, shade your eyes with your hand to see better'
Nyanyukwa 'be glad, become delighted, rejoice'
Shambekela 'receive with cupped hands'
Sheya 'deliberate or consider especially, intend'
Simaneka 'honour, pay honour to a person, have respect for, esteem (highly)'
Tanga 'praise, extol, glorify'
Tegamena 'wait for, expect, hope, look forward to, anticipate'
Tegelela 'wait for, expect'
Thikamena 'oppose, stand godparent to a child'
Tonata 'come open (eyes), awake out of sleep, become visible, become spiritually awakened'
Vulika 'obey, be obedient, submit yourself, be possible'
Vululukwa 'rest, be at rest, take some repose'
Wilika 'lead, conduct, direct, derive'

Imperative plural
Angaleni < angala 'beware of, look out (for)'
Dhiladhileni < dhiladhila 'think, meditate, imagine, consider'
Dhimbulukweni < dhimbulukwa 'remember, recall'
Endeleleni < endelela 'move rapidly, hurry, hasten'
Fileni < fila 'fill up (a pit, a hole), earth up (plants)'
Fudheni < fudha 'breathe'
Galukeni < galuka 'come back, return'
Gongaleni < gongala 'come together, gather'
Gundjileni < gundjila 'calm oneself, become quiet, compose oneself'
Hanganeni < hangana 'unite, join together, form an alliance'
Igandjeleni < igandjela 'expose/devote oneself to something or someone'
Ileni < ila 'come for'
Indileni < indila 'ask, request, demand, beg, apply for'
Ipuleni < ipula 'ask oneself, ask in one's mind, ponder, deliberate, become disturbed'
Kotokeni < kotoka 'be on one's guard, be careful, look out, notice'
Landuleni < landula 'follow'
Longeni < longa 'work, labour, function, act, teach'
Loteni < lota 'abate (wind, rain, hate, etc.), cease to flow, become quiet/calm'

285

Matukeni < matuka 'run, flow, come or get open (the lid of a granary)'
Nangeni < nanga 'lose flesh, lose weight, get thinner'
Ningeni < ninga 'do, make, treat, handle, get, grow, turn, become'
Panduleni < pandula 'thank, praise, acclaim, resign, give up a post'
Pashukeni < pashuka 'come open, open'
Pendukeni < penduka 'wake, become enlivened'
Popjeni < popya 'talk, speak, slander, vilify, calumniate'
Taleni < tala 'look at, view, regard, consider, observe, behold'
Tileni < tila 'fear, be afraid'

Other verb forms

Inamuvulwa < inamu vulwa 'you (pl.) are not tired (have not tired), do not get tired'; *vulwa* 'get tired, become weary, become fatigued'
Inamuuluma < inamu uluma 'you (pl.) did not hurry (have not hurried), do not hurry'; *uluma* 'hurry, hasten'
Inotila < ino tila 'you (sing.) are not afraid (have not been afraid), be not afraid'; *tila* 'fear, be afraid'
Kandali < kanda li 'I was not'
Mualele < omwa lele 'you (pl.) ruled/looked after'; *lela* 'reign, rule, take care of, look after, tend, nurse (child)'
Muatantandje < omwa tanta ndje 'you (pl.) have threatened me'; *tanta* 'be determined, act resolutely against somebody, threaten, dance, jump, hop for joy'
Mwaalele < omwa alele 'you (pl.) stretched wide open, you crucified'; *alela* 'stretch wide open, crucify, burn on the bottom'
Mwadhina < omwa dhina 'you (pl.) have despised'; *dhina* 'despise, scorn, disregard'
Naapopye < naa popye 'let them speak'; *popya* 'talk, speak, slander, vilify, calumniate'
Ndafudha < onda fudha 'I breathe'; *fudha* 'breathe'
Ndaithanua < onda ithanwa 'I am called'; *ithana* 'call, summon, name'
Ndakoko < onda koko 'I grew old'; *koka* 'grow, develop, grow old, pull, tug'
Ndakoneka < onda koneka 'I have noticed / found out'; *koneka* 'notice, find out, discover, investigate'
Ndakundana < onda kundana 'I came (have come) to know'; *kundana* 'hear of something, come to know, learn'
Ndatelela < onda telela 'I wander about, I am always on the move'; *telela = telagana* 'wander about, roam, move restlessly, be always on the move'
Ndatinda < onda tinda 'I refuse'; *tinda* 'refuse'
Ndina < ondi na 'I have'; *na* 'have, possess, own'
Ondahala < onda hala 'I want'; *hala* ' be willing, want, court a girl'
Taakondjo < otaa kondjo 'they fight'; *kondja* 'fight, struggle, wrestle, strive'
Taanjanda < otaa nyanda 'they play/dance'; *nyanda* 'gallop, play, act, dance'
Taati < otaa ti 'they say'; *tya* 'say, tell, remark, mean'
Takatsu < ota ka tsu 'he/she shall pound'; *tsa* 'pound, stick, stab'
Tamukondjo < otamu kondjo 'you (pl.) fight'; *kondja* 'fight, struggle, wrestle, strive'
Tapopi < ota popi 'he speaks'; *popya* 'talk, speak, slander, vilify'
Toti < oto ti 'you (sing.) say; *tya* 'say, tell, remark, mean'
Tuna < otu na 'we have'
Twapewa < otwa pewa 'we have been given'; *pa* 'give somebody something, offer, admit'

Deriving Names from Clauses. Ambo personal names may also be derived from whole clauses or sentences:

Hinasha < hi na sha 'I have nothing'
Inamushidhimbwa < inamu shi dhimbwa 'you (pl.) have not forgotten it, do not forget it'
Kalaputse < kala putse 'stay with us / at our house'
Kandalipo < kanda li po 'I was not here'
Katulimondjila < katu li mondjila 'we are not right / on the way'
Katunashili < katu na shili 'we do not have the truth'
Mutaleninohenda < mu taleni nohenda 'look at him/her with mercy'
Mwetulamba < omwe tu lamba 'you (pl.) (have) followed us'
Ndalikokule < onda li kokule 'I was far away'
Ndamonekuatho < onda mona ekwatho 'I have found/received help'
Ndapeuoshilonga < onda pewa oshilonga 'I was given a task/duty'
NDathigwapo < onda thigwa po 'I was left/deserted here'
Ndatindangi < onda ti ndangi 'I said thank you'
Ndejapo, Ndeyapo < onde ya po 'I came here'
Ndeshipewa < onde shi pewa 'it was given to me'
Ndilimeke < ondi li meke 'I am in the hand'
Ndilimekondjo < ondi li mekondjo 'I am in a battle'
Ndilipo < ondi li po 'I am here'
Ndinaetegameno < ondi na etegameno 'I have hope'
Ndinelago < ondi na elago 'I have luck/happiness (I am lucky/happy)'
Ndinomukwathi < ondi na omukwathi 'I have a helper/assistant'
Ondemutega < onde mu tega 'I have been waiting for him/her'
Otulimegameno < otu li megameno 'we are under protection, patronage'
Talohole < tala ohole 'look (sing.) at love'
Tilomalenga < tila omalenga 'be (sing.) afraid of the advisors/councellors/officers'
Tulipohamba < otu li pohamba 'we are near the king/chief'
Tunekwatho < otu na ekwatho 'we have help/assistance'
Tunuuyelele < otu na uuyelele 'we have clearness/clarity/brightness'

Deriving Names from Other Linguistic Sources. There are also Ambo names which are derived from other linguistic sources than the above mentioned: pronouns, adverbs, numerals, etc. However, they are very rare in the data:

Andija < andiya 'please, wait for a while that I....'
Ayihe < ayihe 'whole, all'
Eeno < eeno 'yes'
Gaali < gaali 'two'
Iyaloo < iyaloo 'good, excellent'
Jandje < yandje 'my'
Kamana < kamana 'first-class, first-rate'
Komesho < komesho 'ahead, further, in future' (Kwanyama form)
Kumwe < kumwe 'one, total'
Nande < nande 'at all, in the least, even'
Nena < nena 'in that case, then, today' (or 'disappear, vanish, get lost')
Natango < natango 'still, yet, until now' (or *< na + o/tango* 'sun, day')
Ndangi, Tangi < ndangi, tangi 'thank you, thanks'
Ngeno < ngeno 'if only'
Popepi < popepi 'near, nearby, close by, in the vicinity, in the neighbourhood'
Shandje < shandje 'my' or 'at the very moment, immediately'
Tango < tango 'firstly' (or *< o/tango* 'sun, day')

Semantics of Ambo Names. In this subsection, we aim to present a semantic analysis of the Ambo names in the name data. This will be done purely on the basis of the lexical meanings of these names, as there is no additional information available about the motives for the giving of these names. Herbert (1999a, p. 216; 1999b, p. 122) has pointed out that a distinction between meaning and significance is crucial when analysing African personal names. For example, all Zulu speakers would recognise that the name *Zwelibanzi* means 'the country is wide', but they could not guess that this name was chosen by the father because the family had just moved from their rural home to a big city (Herbert 1999a, p. 216). Similarly, the Ambo people have given names such as *Omalovu* 'beer' or *Tileni* 'be afraid' to their children, but the significance of these names is not apparent without further knowledge of the name-giving motives. As was noted earlier in this thesis, it is also typical of Ambo baptismal names that the name itself is only the beginning of a longer sentence which may refer to various ideas and events in the name-giver's life (Mbenzi 24.3.1997). For example, the name *Katwali* 'we did not', which Shekutaamba Nambala (14.4.1997) gave to his son, refers to many things that Nambala's family did not do at the time the child was born: they did not attend the funeral of Nambala's mother, they did not have money, and they did not have their child born in the United States. Therefore, it would be useless to try to trace the "real" meanings of these names by looking at the names only. Of course, one may guess that *Namvula* 'rain', for example, is a name given to a child who was born on a rainy day, but such assumptions can never be anything more than guesses.

One should also remember that many Ambo baptismal names are given as namesake names, and in such cases the primary significance of the name is not in the lexical meaning of the name but in its connection with a particular person. Many names in the data, such as *Amunyela, Iipumbu, Kambonde, Mpingana* and *Nehale*, are also very old personal names in the Ambo culture, which may be given primarily because they are known to be traditional Ambo personal names, not because of their lexical meanings. The meanings of some of these names, e.g. *Amunyela*, have also become obscure to Ambo people today.

In this analysis, the Ambo names in the corpus were assigned to ten classes according to their lexical meanings: 1. Names reflecting joy, happiness and gratefulness, 2. Names reflecting religious ideas and feelings, 3. Names reflecting other feelings, 4. Names as maxims, 5. Names referring to time and events, 6. Names referring to family and community, 7. Names describing physical appearance, 8. Names referring to agricultural work, 9. Names referring to wild animals and plants, and 10. Other names. It should be noted that this classification is not the only possible one. Nevertheless, by introducing these classes it is possible to focus on a number of important semantic aspects of Ambo names.[450]

Names Reflecting Joy, Happiness and Gratitude. Names which reflect joy, happiness and gratitude are very popular in the Ambo culture, as well as in many other African societies (Herbert 1996, p. 1226). There are plenty of examples of such names in the data. With these names, the name-giver undoubtedly wanted to express his positive feelings after the birth of the child. Many of these names also express the idea that the child is a gift.

> *Elago, Helao, Lago, Nelago* ('happiness, luck'), *Hafeleinge* ('be glad of me'), *Hafeni, Nyanyukwa, Nyanyukweni* ('be glad'), *Hambelela, Hambeleleni* ('praise'), *Iijaloo, Iyaloo, Jaloo* ('good, excellent'), *Ilenikelago* ('come to luck/happiness'), *Joleni* ('laugh'), *Ligola, Ligoleni* ('cheer, jubilate'), *Magano, Omagano* ('gift, present'), *Melago* ('in luck/happiness'), *Mwahafa* ('you are glad'), *Nambili* ('peace'), *Natumutange* ('let us thank/praise him/ her'), *Nandigolo* ('shout of joy'), *Ndaetelwa* ('something was brought to me'), *Ndahafa, Ndanyanyukwa, Ndinehafo* ('I am glad'), *Ndahambelela* ('I praise'), *Ndangi, Tangi* ('thank you'), *Ndapandula* ('I praise/thank'), *Ndapeua, Ndapewa* ('I was given'), *Ndapeuapeke* ('I was given in the hand'), *Ndapewomagano, Ndapewoshali* ('I received a present'), *Ndatindangi, Ndatitangi* ('I said thank you'), *Ndeshimona* ('I found/got it'), *Ndeshipewa* ('I received it'), *Ndinelago* ('I am happy/lucky'), *Nenyanyu* ('joy'), *Panduleni, Tanga, Tangeni* ('praise, thank'), *Pandulo* ('thanking, thanks'), *Penehafo* ('there is a joy'), *Penelao* ('there is luck/happiness'), *Shali* ('free of charge, gift'), *Shambekela, Shambekeleni* ('receive with cupped hands'), *Taamba, Taambeni* ('receive'), *Tanganatango* ('praise still') *Tuhafeni, Tunyanyukweni* ('let us be glad'), *Tunelago* ('we have luck/happiness'), *Tunenyanyu* ('we have a joy'), *Tujenikelago, Tuyenikelago* ('let us go to luck/happiness'), *Tujoleni, Tuyoleni* ('let us laugh'), *Twapewa* ('we have been given').

Names Reflecting Religious Ideas and Feelings. This group of names is closely connected with the previous group, as names reflecting happiness and gratefulness often reflect religious feelings as well. Herbert (1996, p. 1226) has pointed out that in a survey of six cultural groups in southern Africa, the dominant name type was one in which some praise, thanks, or other message was linked to Christian beliefs. These kinds of names are very common among the Ambo people as well:

> *Etuhole* ('he loves us'), *Gamena* ('protect, shield'), *Halolye* ('his will'), *Hupitho* ('saving, salvation'), *IlakOmwene* ('come to the Lord'), *LjOmuwa* ('of the Lord'), *Megameno* ('under protection/patronage'), *Meitaalo* ('in faith'), *Metumo* ('in the mission work'), *Mulanduleni* ('follow him'), *Nahambelelwe, Napandulwe, Natangwe* ('may he be praised'), *Nahenda, Nohenda* ('mercy'), *Ndakulilwa, Ndamanguluka* ('I am redeemed/released'), *Ndamonohamba* ('I have found a king/chief'), *Ndamonohenda, Ndasilwohenda* ('I have found/received mercy'), *Ndatuminua, Ndatuminwa* ('I have been sent'), *Ndayambekwa* ('I am blessed'), *Ndilimegameno* ('I am under protection/patronage'), *NdinOmukulili* ('I have a Redeemer'),

Ndinomugameni ('I have a protector/guardian'), *Nekulilo* ('redeeming, redemption'), *Otulimegameno* ('we are under protection/patronage'), *Peneyambeko* ('there is a blessing'), *Penomukuathi, Penomukwathi* ('there is a helper'), *Penoshinge* ('there is glory'), *Taambeyambeko* ('receive a blessing'), *TangOmuwa* ('praise the Lord'), *Tuakulilua* ('we are redeemed/released'), *Tukondjenimeitaalo* ('let us fight in faith'), *Tulimegameno* ('we are under protection/patronage'), *Tulipohamba* ('we are with the king/chief), *Tulipomwene* ('we are with the Lord'), *Tunatate* ('we have a father'), *Tunejambeko* ('we have a blessing'), *Tunekwatho* ('we have help'), *Tunomukwathi* ('we have a helper'), *Tunomuwiliki* ('we have a leader'), *Tuajambekua* ('we are blessed'), *Tuwilika* ('lead us'), *Tuyakula* ('look after us, help us'), *Tuyambeka* ('bless us'), *Uilika, Wilika* ('lead, direct').

Names Reflecting Other Feelings. Some names reflect other kinds of feelings, including negative ones such as sadness or fear. In most cases, these names seem to express the state of mind of the father who gave the name. Some of these names may also be intended as messages to other people (e.g. *Nghipandulwa* 'I have not been thanked, I will not be thanked').

Hekeleka ('comfort, console'), *Hinasha* ('I have nothing'), *Kapenambili* ('there is no peace'), *Kaunahafo* ('there is no joy'), *Mutaleninohenda* ('look at him/her with mercy'), *Ndahekelekwa* ('I have been comforted'), *Ndahekumuna* ('I sob'), *Ndahepuluka* ('I am free from distress'), *Ndahepa* ('I lack something'), *Ndajuulukua* ('I long/miss'), *Ndakumwa* ('I am surprised'), *Ndalila* ('I cry'), *Ndalimbililua* ('I doubt / have doubts about'), *Ndalulilua* ('I worry, I have difficulties'), *Ndapanda* ('I am fond of, I accept'), *Ndatega, Ndategelela* ('I wait/expect'), *Ndatila* ('I am afraid'), *Ndavulwa* ('I am tired'), *Ndekutega* ('I wait(ed) for it/you'), *Ndemutega, Ondemutega* ('I wait(ed) for him/her'), *Ndemutila* ('I am afraid of him/her'), *Ndemuvula* ('I tolerate/stand him/her'), *Ndeshihala* ('I want(ed) it'), *Ndeshihaluka* ('it frightens me'), *Ndeshipanda* ('I am fond of it/you, I accept it/you'), *Ndiholetate* ('I love my father'), *Ndiinekela* ('I trust'), *Ndikuhole* ('I love you'), *Ndilinaua, Ndilinawa* ('I am well'), *Ndinaetegameno* ('I have hope'), *Ndinombili* ('I have peace'), *Nghipandulwa* ('I have not been thanked'), *Ondahala* ('I want'), *Penouike* ('there is being alone'), *Talahole, Talohole* ('look at love'), *Tongeni* ('groan, moan'), *Tujambula* ('encourage us').

Names as Maxims. Many of the Ambo names in the data seem to be intended as some kind of maxim or guiding principle for the child's life (e.g. *Kalaneinekelo* 'live in trust'), or as request or advice to other people in the community (e.g. *Mupandeni* 'take a liking to him/her, accept him/her').

Angala, Angaleni ('beware of, look out (for)'), *Dhameni* ('clutch, stick fast to'), *Dhiginina, Ƶiginina* ('persevere/persist in, be steadfast'), *Dhiladhileni* ('think, meditate, consider'), *Dhimbulukweni* ('remember'), *Efaishe* ('leave everything'), *Endelela, Endeleleni* ('hurry, hasten'), *Fiindje* ('become like me'), *Gongaleni* ('come together, gather'), *Hanganeni* ('unite, join together'), *Igandjeleni* ('expose/devote yourself to something or someone'), *Ileni* ('come for'), *Ilonga* ('learn, study'), *Inamutila, Inotila* ('be not afraid'), *Indila, Indileni* ('ask, beg'), *Inekela, Inekeleni, Linekela* ('trust in/to'), *Inodhimbwandje* ('do not forget me'), *Ipuleni* ('ponder, deliberate'), *Itula* ('devote yourself, meddle with'), *Jelukeni* ('rise, be exalted'), *Kalaneinekelo* ('live in trust'), *Kalonge* ('go to work'), *Konga, Kongeni* ('look/search for'), *Kongenielago* ('search for luck/happiness'), *Kongondunge* ('search for understanding/ intelligence'), *Kotokeni* ('be careful, look out'), *Leshanomuenjo* ('read with a spirit'), *Longeni* ('work'), *Mupandeni* ('take a liking to him/her, accept him/her'), *Mutaleni* ('look at him/her'), *Mutileni* ('be afraid of him/her'), *Pandeni* ('take a liking to, accept'), *Pendapala, Pendapaleni* ('become enterprising/enthusiastic/brave'), *Pendukapo, Pendukeni* ('wake up, become enlivened'), *Popjeni* ('talk, speak'), *Pukulukeni* ('be set right, be corrected'), *Shikongeni* ('search for it'), *Shipandeni* ('take a liking to it'), *Shitaleni* ('look at it'), *Simaneka* ('honour, have respect for'), *Simanekohamba* ('honour the chief/king'), *Talapombanda* ('look high up'), *Talamondjila* ('look on the way'), *Taleni* ('look'), *Tegamena, Tegelela, Tegeleleni* ('wait for, expect'), *Tegomukuathi* ('wait for a helper'), *Thikameni* ('stand up, depart'), *Tileni* ('be afraid'), *Tilenuuyuni* ('be afraid of the world'), *Tilomalenga* ('be afraid of the counsellors/officers'), *Tiloveta* ('be afraid of the law'), *Tonata, Tonateni* ('awake out of sleep, become spiritually awakened'), *Tutaleni* ('let us look'), *Tuyeni* ('let us go'), *Uveni* ('feel/hear/understand/obey'), *Vulika, Vulikeni* ('obey, be obedient'), *Vululukwa, Vululukweni* ('rest').

Names Referring to Time and Events. Many of the Ambo names in the data indicate the time of the day or the year the baby was born, weather conditions, or specific events occurring at the time of the birth. Some of these names are among the most popular Ambo names, e.g. *Angula, Nangula* 'morning' and *Amutenya, Namutenya* 'midday'. Many names also seem to refer to the long wartime and independence struggle in Namibia, or to discord in the family or wider community. Some of these names may also be understood as social messages which the name-giver has directed to other people in the community (e.g. *Mweneni* 'be quiet').

Names referring to time
Amutenya, Namutenya ('midday'), *Angula, Nangula, Ngula* ('morning'), *Haufiku, Nuusiku, Uusiku* ('night'), *Metine* ('on Thursday'), *Nakwenje* ('spring'), *Namene* ('early in the morning'), *Nathinge* ('summer'), *Penethimbo* ('there is time'), *Pethimbo* ('in due time'), *Sondaha* ('Sunday').

Names referring to weather conditions and other natural phenomena
Amukwaya ('fog, mist'), *Amvula, Emvula, Namvula, Mvula* ('rain'), *Endjala, Nandjala* ('hunger, famine'), *Nailoke, Nayiloke* ('may it rain'), *NdinoOmvula* ('I have rain, this is the rain/year'), *Nefundja* ('flood'), *Uulumbu* ('drought, depression').

Names referring to war or friction in the community
Alugodhi, Lugodhi ('hostility, fight'), *Gundjileni* ('calm down'), *Heita, Iita, Niita* ('war'), *Homata, Homateni* ('arm yourself, equip yourself with arms'), *Kondja, Kondjeni* ('fight'), *Kondjashili* ('fight truly/really'), *Kondjela, Kondjeleni* ('fight on behalf of'), *Kondjelomuenjo* ('fight for life/soul'), *Loteni* ('become quiet/calm'), *Mekondjo* ('in a battle'), *Muakondja, Mwakondja*

('you have fought'), *Muatantandje* ('you have threatened me'), *Mueneni, Mweneni* ('be quiet'), *Muetulundila* ('you have slandered us'), *Munageni* ('cast him/her away'), *Mwadhina* ('you (pl.) have despised'), *Mwetugwedha* ('you have harangued/preached to us'), *Namalwa* ('difficulties, troubles'), *Naapopye* ('let them speak'), *Naatye* ('let them say'), *Nambalu* ('disaster, evil, mischief'), *Nambudhi* ('discord, quarrel'), *Nandeinotya* ('do not speak at all, even if you didn't say'), *Ndakondja* ('I fight'), *Ndilimekondjo* ('I am in a battle'), *Ndumbo, Nondumbo* ('discord, conflict, revolt'), *Penekondjo* ('there is a battle'), *Shityani* ('cheekiness, impudence, stubbornness'), *Taakondjo* ('they fight'), *Taapopi* ('they speak'), *Tukondjeni* ('let us fight'), *Tulimekondjo* ('we are in a battle'), *Tulimiita* ('we are in the war'), *Tumueneni, Tumweneni* ('let us be quiet').

Names referring to other events
Aludhilu, Aluzilu ('transfer of homestead'), *Ankonga* ('wedding'), *Ashikongo, Shikongo* ('search for girls to the chief's court'), *Eloolo* ('abundance, good harvest'), *Hango, Nahango* ('wedding'), *Iigonda* ('engagement gifts'), *Nekongo* ('seeking, searching'), *Shiponga* ('danger, accident, misadventure').

Names Referring to Family and Community. This class contains names which refer to the child's position in the family, his or her sex, social environment, etc.

Amakali, Enkali, Nankali ('survivor, death lamentation'; name of a child whose father died before the name-giving), *Iipinge, Mpingana* (names given to a child after someone else in the family has died), *Kamati* ('small boy'), *Kapongo* ('small homeless one'), *Kuku* ('my grandmother'), *Mbushandje* ('my namesake'), *Namukuambi* ('member of the Kwambi tribe, kind of herb'), *Namupa, Namupasita* ('the only daughter among more brothers'), *Nankelo* ('the youngest child'), *Nehoja* (the name of a single boy among his sisters or a single girl among her brothers), *Nekulu, Nekuru* ('mother of the family, madam'), *Nuukwawo* ('his, her or their family-circle'), *Omuna* ('someone's child' or 'you have, there is'), *Omusamane* ('married man, head of the house'), *Shiinda* ('neighbour'), *Šilume* ('despised male person'), *Tate* ('my father'), *Tatekulu* ('my grandfather'), *Tunakuku* ('we have a grandmother').

Names Describing Physical Appearance. Some Ambo names in the data seem to describe the physical appearance of the child:

Ambunda ('back, loins, hips'), *Amukušu, Mukushu* ('coloured person, person with a light brown complexion), *Amupala, Namupala* ('big bad face'), *Amupolo, Mupolo, Namupolo* ('bridge of the nose, forehead, one with beautiful features'), *Amupunda, Namupunda* ('potbelly'), *Ashilungu* ('small lip'), *Ashipala* ('face'), *Namatsi* ('ears'), *Nampweja, Nampweya* ('smoothness and roundness'), *Namule* ('tall person'), *Nandjelo* ('handsome features, pleasant appearance'), *Nantongo* ('dot, spot, speckle'), *Nuugulu* ('thin legs'), *Shikesho* ('wrist'), *Shilumbu* ('white man').

Names Referring to Agricultural Work. Many names in the data refer to the sources of livelihood of the Ambo people: farming, cattle raising, hunting and various works in the homestead. The fact that Ambo girls are expected to pound corn and boys to tend cattle is reflected in these names:

> *Amalovu, Omalovu* ('beer'), *Angombe, Nangombe* ('beast, head of cattle'), *Egumbo, Negumbo* ('homestead, house'), *Haukongo, Nuukongo* ('hunting'), *Hilifa* ('I do not tend (cattle)'), *Hilifavali* ('I do not tend (cattle) anymore'), *Kakuneni* ('go to plant seeds'), *Kakandeni* ('go to milk'), *Nahambo* ('cattle-post, pen for oxen'), *Naitsuwe, Nayitsuwe* ('may there be pounding'), *Nalijele* ('may he/she winnow it (corn)', 'may it become light/clean'), *Namatanga* ('pumpkins, balls, groups, armed forces'), *Negonga* ('assegai, kind of play with marula stones'), *Nehale* ('passage-yard'), *Niimpungu* ('mounds on which corn is grown, flower beds'), *Nuuta* ('bow, arch, weapons, game being hunted'), *Nyowa* ('millet porridge')[451], *Shikokola* ('newly cleared plot of land' or 'clear it'), *Taatsu* ('they pound'), *Takatsu* ('she shall pound'), *Tudheni* ('pluck, pick, tear loose').

Names Referring to Wild Animals and Plants. This class contains names which refer to wild animals and plants. Obviously, many of these names could be construed as referring to events occurring at the time of the birth or as names describing the child. Nevertheless, as they form a clear semantic group in the data, they are presented separately here.

> *Amadhila, Namadhila* ('big birds, aeroplanes'), *Ambambi* ('duiker buck, frost'), *Amushe* ('raisin-bush'), *Angolo, Nangolo* ('zebra, knee, elbow'), *Asino* ('gemsbok, oryx'), *Elindi* ('potbelly cricket'), *Iimbondi* ('herb, weed'), *Iipumbu* ('groups of tall trees in a desert wasteland'), *Kamenye* ('small spring-bok'), *Kanime* ('small lion'), *Nambahu* ('locust'), *Namukua* ('baobab tree'), *Namulo* ('scent of game'), *Nandjamba* ('elephant, fearless person'), *Nandjele* ('squirrel, one who is good in climbing, worth, value, rate'), *Nangolo* ('zebra, knee, elbow'), *Nanguti* ('pigeon, dove'), *Nekua, Nekwa* ('fruit of baobab, buttock skin, leather trousers'), *Ngeno* ('long fresh pole of Kalahari Christmas tree'), *NKoshi* ('lion'), *Nokadhidhi* ('small ant'), *Nuušekete* ('chirping, twittering, rustling').

Other Names. Beside names which could be classified into the above presented semantic classes, there were a number of Ambo names in the data which could not be assigned to any of them. Many of these names obviously stand for longer sentences and ideas which only the name-giver knows.

> *Aantu* ('people'), *Aantuyoye* ('your people'), *Andija* ('please, wait for a while that I....'), *Ayihe* ('whole, all'), *Eeno* ('yes'), *Gaali* ('two'), *Ileni mo* ('come in'), *Jandje* ('my'), *Kandali* ('I was not'), *Kashinasha* ('never mind'), *Kauna* ('it does not have'), *Kaushiwetu* ('[the world] is not ours'), *Kombanda* ('on

the top, on the other side, beyond, after (a time)'), *Kumwe* ('one, total'), *Mejo* ('at the coming'), *Nande* ('at all, in the least, even'), *Natango* ('still, yet, until now'), *Ndatala* ('I look at, I consider'), *Ndati* ('I said'), *Ndeshitiwa* ('it was said to me'), *Ndina* ('I have'), *Negoli* ('bend, curve'), *Nena* ('in that case, then, today), *Ntsilu* ('beret, leather cap'), *Omuenjo* ('soul, spirit, life'), *Oyandje* ('(it) is mine, (they) are mine'), *Popepi* ('near, close by'), *Tango* ('firstly'), *Toti* ('you say'), *Tuna* ('we have'), *Uujuni* ('world').

These kinds of names usually cannot be explained by the other baptismal names of the person either. Hence, of name combinations such as *Paulus Natango* or *Lovisa Kandali* one cannot guess what the names *Natango* 'still, yet' or *Kandali* 'I was not' could refer to. However, in some cases the names of the person were semantically linked to each other. Examples of these are *Leopold-Meke-Ndati-Tangi* 'Leopold-in the hand-I said-thank you' and *Daniel Halolyoye Kwatha Aantuyoye* 'Daniel-his will-help-your people', *Titus Tuna Iita* 'Titus-we have-war', *Gottlieb Namupolo Ndina Omuwa* 'Gottlieb-one with beautiful features-I have-the Lord', *Filemon Josef Tangeni Omuwene* 'Filemon-Josef-thank-the Lord', *Irja Mejo ljOmuwa* 'Irja-at the coming-of the Lord'.

The Ambo Names of Women. The list of Ambo names for women in the name data, given in Appendix 2, contains all the women's names in the data which were classified as Ambo names. The numbers after the names show the number of occurrences of these names as first given names and as subsequent given names; the latter ones are given after a plus sign (+). No additional information is given about these names in the list, which is the reason why the Ambo names in the data are given in an appendix only.

The names in this list which represent old Ambo orthographies and have special orthographic symbols in them which are not used today are given in a simplified form. For example, the name forms *Namŭteńa* (Elim 1943), *Ndemŭšikula* (Oshigambo 1943), *Šišigona* (Okahao 1938) and *Ẕiginina* (Elim 1958) are given as *Namutena, Ndemušikula, Šisigona* and *Ẕiginina* here.

Other names appear in this list in the same form as they are in the baptismal registers. Some names, however, could have been interpreted in more than one way because of illegible handwriting, but only one possible interpretation is given here.

The Ambo Names of Men. The list of Ambo names for men in the data, given in Appendix 2 as well, contains all the men's names in the data which were classified as Ambo. Again, the numbers after the names show the number of occurrences of these names as first given names and as subsequent given names; the latter ones are given after a plus sign (+). The names in this list which come from old Ambo orthographies and originally had special orthographic symbols in them are also given in a simplified form.

Other Names

Remarks on the Other Names in the Data. Eventually, the number of names which could not be classified as biblical, European or Ambo names turned out to be minimal in the data. Only 152 name occurrences, or 0.9 per cent of the total of 16,643 name occurrences in the data, ended up in this class. The share of these "other names" of all women's names is 0.8 per cent (78 occurrences) and that of men's names 1.0 per cent (74 occurrences). Of all first given names in the data 0.9 per cent (102 occurrences) were classified into this class, and the share of them among all subsequent names is the same 0.9 per cent (50).

This class contains many kinds of names whose origins remained unclear. Many of them resemble European names in form, but it was impossible to judge what the original name could be. Examples of such names are *Auna, Benifalus, Deimunde, Galotte, Hernelde, Loini* and *Salma* among the women's names and *Alekraus, Broteus, Brunnar, Drauhot, Folobianus, Lobard* and *Maritselius* among the men's names. No clear origins of these names could be found in the various European name books that were used for the analysis of the data. Some of them seem to resemble particular European names, e.g. *Galotte* the common name *Charlotte*, but not to such an extent that they could have been interpreted as variants of these. Some of these names may also be based on rare saints' names, some on the various kinds of names (first names, surnames or nicknames) of the Namibians who have their origins in Europe. Some of these names may also be so rare as European first names and surnames that they do not appear in European name books. It also seems that some of these are mixtures of two or more names which the name-giver vaguely remembers.

Many names in the data looked biblical, but it was impossible to prove their biblical origin. Therefore, they ended up in this class as well. Examples of these are *Elom* and *Enas* among the women's names and *Elodan, Esar, Iammael* and *Jorlam* among the men's names. It is possible that credible explanations could be found for these names as well, even if they are not apparent.

A specific type of names in this group are abbreviated ones which most likely refer to particular existing names, e.g. *K.* and *Nd.* It is impossible to say on the basis of the baptismal registers only if this is the way the name-giver wanted the name to be written, or if the original name was shortened in the baptismal list by the recorder of the name. It seems possible that in some cases, the name-giver deliberately wanted to give the child such a name. Most of these names are given as subsequent names, e.g. *Josefiina Nd., Selma Ndinomukuathi Mag., Melkisedek A.* and *Mikael K.* For some of these names, it is quite easy to guess what names they might refer to. For example, the above mentioned *Mag.* could well refer to the common woman's Ambo name *Magano* 'gift'. Nevertheless, as one cannot be sure of such guesses, these names were classified as "other names" as well.

This class also contains names which are neither biblical, European or Ambo names nor obscure names. Examples of these are the man's name *Gaddafi*, which most likely refers to Moammar Gaddafi, the ruler of Libya, or *Setson*, which includes both a biblical (*Set*) and European (-*son*) element.

The majority of these name forms appear in the data once only. However, there were some relatively popular names in the data which ended up in this class as well, e.g. *Eviste* and *Loini* among the women's names.

The Other Names of Women. The following list contains all the women's names in the data that were classified as "other names". The numbers after the names – once again – show the number of occurrences of these names as first given names and as subsequent given names; the latter are given after a plus sign (+). The list also includes references to the use of names in European naming systems, in the same way as on the previous lists of biblical and European names. Additional explanations for some names and name forms are given as well.

Auna 1. F: *Aina, Aini, Aino, Ainu, Anja, Anna, Aula, Aune, Auni, Auno, Rauna*, G: *Anna, Eina*, A: *Agna, Ana, Anja, Anna*, E: *Anna*. This name resembles many Finnish women's names which also appear in the data, e.g. *Aina, Aini, Aino, Aune* and *Rauna* (see the list of European women's names). The name *Agna* is also quite similar in form. However, the form *Auna* does not appear as such in any of the European name books utilised for this study.

Benifalus + 1. This name resembles the male saint's name *Bonifatius*, which also occurs in the data (see the list of European men's names).

Deimunde 1. G: *Raimunde, Reimunde*, A: *Raimona, Raimonda*.

Dekora + 1. A: *Delora*. This name resembles the biblical name **Debora** (see the list of biblical women's names). The name *Delora* is a variant of *Dolores*.

Elom + 1.

Enas + 1. G, A: *Ena*, H: *Ena, Enna*. This name could also be based on the biblical man's name **Eneas** or **Enos** (see the list of biblical men's names).

Evindina 3 + 1. H: *Everdien, Everdina, Everina, Everlina*, A: *Evadne*. In the Swedish naming system, there is a man's name *Evind*, which is based on the Norwegian name *Ejvind* (Johansson 1991, p. 31, 35). In the Ambo languages, *evi ndina* means 'I have the land' or 'the land I have'. This name also appears as the only baptismal name of the person (1968).

Eviste 7. F: *Eeva-Stiina, Eevastiina, Evastiina, Evita*, A: *Evette, Evita*.

Frina 1. This name could be a shortened form of *Fransina*, or a variant of *Frieda/Frida* (see the list of European women's names).

Galotte 1. This name form could be based on *Charlotte* (see the list of European women's names).

Hernelde 1. G, H: *Herlinde*.

I. + 1.

Jo. 1. This abbreviation could refer to the biblical name **Johanna** (see the list of biblical women's names).

Lalungek + 1.

Leetis + 1. This name resembles various name forms based on the Latin word *laetitia* 'gladness', e.g. *Lettice* (see *Letesia/Letisia* in the list of European women's names).

Lelli 1. A: *Lela, Lelah,* A (sn): *Lelie, Lely,* H: *Lelia.* This name could also be based on *Lilli* (see the list of European women's names).

Loini 26 + 1, *Lonia* + 1. F: *Leonda, Leonie, Louna,* G: *Leona, Leonia, Leonie, Loana, Lona, Loni, Lonni, Lonny, Ronja,* H: *Leona, Leoni, Leonia, Leune, Lon, Loni, Lonie, Lonnie, Rona,* E: *Rhona.* The name *Loini* reminds one of the Finnish name *Toini* (see the list of European women's names), as well as of the biblical **Loide** (see the list of biblical women's names).

Mag. + 1. This abbreviation may refer to the Ambo name *Magano* (see the list of women's Ambo names in Appendix 2).

Malijao 1. This name could refer to the biblical **Maria** (see the list of biblical women's names).

Namu. + 1. This name seems to refer to some Ambo name beginning with *Namu-,* such as *Namutenya* or *Namupala* (see the list of women's Ambo names in Appendix 2).

Nd + 1, *Nd.* + 7. These names seem to refer to some Ambo name(s) beginning with *Nd-,* such as *Ndahambelela* or *Ndakulilwa* (see the list of women's Ambo names in Appendix 2).

Ndanj. + 2. These names seem to refer to some Ambo name(s) beginning with *Ndanj-,* such as *Ndanjanjukua* (see the list of women's Ambo names in Appendix 2).

Ndasilwo. + 1. This abbreviation could refer to the Ambo name *Ndasilwohenda* (see the list of women's Ambo names in Appendix 2).

Ny. + 1. This name may refer to some Ambo name beginning with *Ny-,* such as *Nyanyukweni* (see the list of women's Ambo names in Appendix 2).

Peth. + 1. The only Ambo name beginning with *Peth-* in the data is *Pethimbo* (see the list of men's Ambo names in Appendix 2).

Retticka 1. This name form could be based on *Fredrika* (see the list of European women's names).

Saio 1. This name could refer to the Finnish woman's name *Saija* (see the list of European women's names).

Salma 1. This name resembles the European names *Selma* and *Saima* (see the list of European women's names), as well as the biblical name **Salome** (see the list of biblical women's names).

Sylkia 1. This name could be based on the European name *Sylvia* (see *Silvia/ Sylvia* in the list of European women's names).

T + 2, *T.* + 1.

Tw. + 1. This abbreviation could refer to some Ambo name beginning with *Tw-*, such as *Tweuthigilwa* (see the list of women's Ambo names in Appendix 2).

Uukoo + 1. The Finnish way of reading the combination *UK*.

The Other Names of Men. The following list presents all the men's names in the data that were classified as "other names", in the same way as the "other names" of women were presented in the previous subsection.

A. + 1.

Alekraus 1. This name may have something to do with *Aleksander* (see the list of European men's names).

Apenr 1. This name could refer to the biblical **Abner** (see the list of biblical men's names).

Arinne 1. F: *Aarne, Arne,* FM: *Aarne,* G: *Arn, Arne,* H: *Arne,* A: *Arni, Arnie, Arno.*

Bauken 1. G, H: *Bauke,* H (wn): *Bauckien, Bauke, Boukien.* The Dutch name book (Van der Schaar 1992, p. 122) also gives *Bauken* as a 15th century variant of *Baldewinus.*

Bedeka + 1. G (wn): *Bodeke.* The Afrikaans word *bedek* means 'covered, concealed, disguised, veiled, covert (threat); cover up, conceal'.

Betie + 1. F: *Pertti,* G: *Bert,* F (wn), G (wn): *Betti, Betty,* E: *Bert, Bertie,* E (wn): *Betty,* H: *Bet, Bete, Bert, Bertie,* H (wn): *Bet, Betty,* A: *Bert, Berti, Bertie,* A (wn): *Betti, Bettie.* The man's name *Bert/Bertie* is an abbreviated form of many men's names including the German element *bert*, e.g. *Albert, Bertram, Herbert, Robert* (see the list of men's European names) and *Siebert.* The woman's name *Bettie/Betty* is a hypocoristic form of the biblical **Elisabet** (see the list of biblical women's names).

Broteus 1. G, A, H: *Brutus.*

Brunnar 1. F: *Bror, Bruno, Brunolf, Bruuno,* G: *Brun, Brunger, Brünje, Brunno, Bruno, Brunold,* A: *Bruno, Burnhard,* H: *Broen, Bruining, Brun, Brune, Bruno,* E: *Bruno.*

Drauhot 1. G, H: *Traugott.*

Eelu 1 + 1, *Elu* + 1. F, FM: *Eero*, A, H: *El.*

Elodan 1.

Enerek 1. This name could be based on *Hendrik* (see the list of European men's names).

Erkon 1. G: *Ercken, Erk, Erken, Erkenwald, Erko, Erkonwald, Erkonwalt,* H: *Erk, Herk, Herko.*

Esar 1. This name could be based on the biblical man's name *Eesarhaddon*, which appears in the Old Testament. In the Ndonga Bible translations, however, this name occurs in the forms **Asarhaddon** and **Assarhaddon**.

Evatta 1. This name could be based on *Evald* (see the list of European men's names).

Febron 1. G (wn): *Febronia*, H (wn): *Febronia, Febronie.* The Old Testament place name **Hebron** appears as a man's name in the data (see the list of biblical men's names).

Fiyoo. + 1.

Folobianus 1.

Gaddafi + 1. This name seems to refer to Moammar Gaddafi, the ruler of Libya. As this surname is neither a biblical, a European or an Ambo name, it was classified in this class.

Galius 1. This name could be based on the biblical **Gaius** (see the list of biblical men's names). H: *Galenus, Gallus,* H (wn): *Galia.*

Gereven + 1. G: *Gerebern*, A: *Gerben*, H: *Geerben, Gerben, Gerbern.*

Helengous 1.

Hilkanus 1. This name could be based on *Elkanus*, a variant of the biblical name **Elkana** (see the list of biblical men's names).

Horald 1. G, H, E: *Harold.*

Iammael 1. This name looks like an abbreviated form of **Immanuel** (see the list of biblical men's names).

Jakok 1. This name could refer to the biblical **Jakob** (see the list of biblical men's names).

Janas 1. G: *Janes, Jannes,* G (sn): *Jannasch,* A: *Jans,* H: *Janis, Jannes, Jannis.*

Jorlam 1. F: *Jorma.* This name could be based on the biblical man's name **Joram** or the place name **Jordan** (see the list of biblical men's names).

K. + 1.

Kones 1, *Konias* 2, *Konis* 4, *Kons* 1. F: *Konsta, Konstantin, Konstantinus,* G: *Constans, Constant, Constantin, Constantinus, Konstans, Konstantin, Konstanz, Konz,* A: *Constand, Constans, Constant, Constantin, Constantinus, Constantius, Constantyn, Konstand, Konstans, Konstant, Konstantyn, Konstanz,* H: *Constans, Constant, Constantijn, Constantinus, Konstans, Konstant,* E: *Constant, Constantin.*

Lebi 1. This name may have something to do with the biblical man's name **Levi**, or **Lebbeus** (see the list of biblical men's names). H: *Lebbe, Lebbert.*

Likius 9 + 1. This name may be based on the biblical place name **Likia/ Liikia** (New Testament). G, H: *Eligius.*

Lius 1. G: *Lois,* H: *Livius.* This name form may also be based on the biblical **Linus** (see the list of biblical men's names).

Lobard 1. F, H, E: *Leopold,* G: *Leobard, Lebold, Leopold.* (See *Leopold* in the list of European men's names.) N (sn): *Lombaard, Lombard.*

MalLinus 1. This name could be formed from two names, e.g. **Malakia** + **Linus** (see the list of biblical men's names).

Maritselius 1. G: *Maurelius, Mauritius, Maurits, Mauritz, Mauriz,* H: *Maurits, Mauritius,* N (sn): *Maritz.*

Massay + 1.

Muskin 1. H: *Muske.*

Nata. + 1. This abbreviation may refer to the biblical name **Natanael** (see the list of biblical men's names) or some Ambo name beginning with *Nata-*, e.g. *Natangwe* (see the list of men's Ambo names in Appendix 2).

Nd. + 2. This abbreviation may refer to some Ambo name beginning with *Nd-*, e.g. *Ndeshipanda* (see the list of men's Ambo names in Appendix 2).

P. + 1.

Passa + 1. G: *Pascha, Paschalis,* H: *Paschalis.* This name could also be based on the Ambo word *Opaasa* 'Easter'.

Potela 1. This name could be based on the English word *bottle.*

Risett 1. G: *Ridsert,* H: *Ridzert.*

Setson 1, *Set-Son* + 1. This name contains both a biblical and a European element. The original bearer of this name in the Ambo area seems to be Rev. Set Son Shivute (Nambala 1995, p. 194), who originally had the name **Set** (see the list of biblical men's names) without *Son.* Later he added the European element *Son* to it, which typically occurs in many European surnames, e.g. *Anderson* (Voipio-Vaalas 15.8.1995).

Sh. + 1.

Sivas 1. In the Bible (Old Testament), **Sivan** is the name of a month.

Tirives + 1. FM (sn): *Tylväs.*

Vean 1. F, FM: *Väinö, Wäinö.*

Vellinus 1, *Welrinus* 2. A: *Verenus, Verinus, Vourinus.*

Visapa + 1. F (sn): *Visapää.* Master Niilo Visapää from Finland made a journey to the Ambo area in 1937 (Lehtori Niilo Visapään matka Namibiaan 1937, Eurooppaa ja Afrikkaa, Hk:2, FMSA). The name was given in 1963.

Voni 1. FM (sn): *Von Schantz,* H (wn): *Von, Vonnie, Vonny.*

Trends in the Baptismal Name-Giving of the Ambo People, 1913–1993

Biblical, European and Ambo Baptismal Names in the Data

In this section, we shall present a statistical analysis of the names in the name data for this study with regard to their origins. All in all, the 16,643 names of the 10,920 baptised Ambos were distributed fairly evenly among biblical, European and Ambo names. Each of these classes covers more than 30 per cent of the whole name data, whereas the share of "other names" is minimal, only 0.9 per cent (see figure 21).

Figure 21.

The distribution of names in the data among biblical, European, Ambo and other names (%)

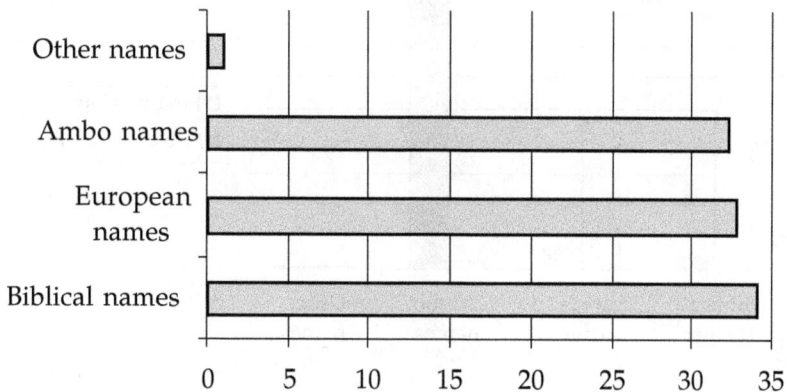

301

However, if one looks separately at the names of women and men, one can see clear differences between these four groups. The biggest group among the women's names is European, while the dominant group among the men's names is biblical (see figure 22).

Figure 22.

The distribution of names among biblical, European, Ambo and other names among the women and men in the data (%)

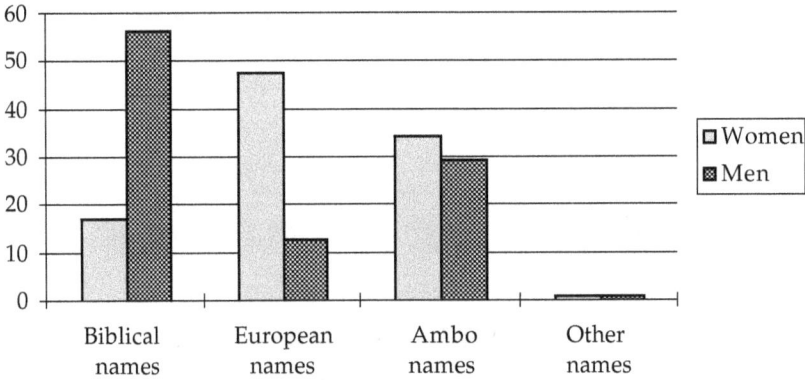

The difference between the first given names and the subsequent (second, third and fourth) given names is also significant in this respect. The first given names are predominantly biblical and European, whereas the subsequent given names are almost exclusively Ambo (see figure 23).

Figure 23.

The distribution of the first given names and the subsequent ones in the data among biblical, European, Ambo and other names (%)

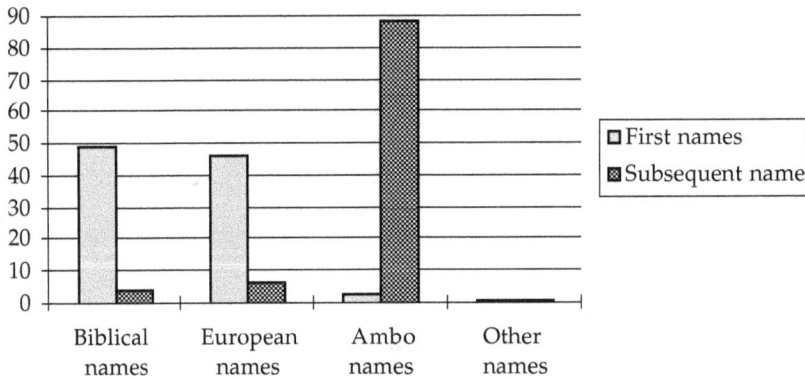

Again, there is a clear difference between the first and subsequent given names of men and women: even if the subsequent given names of both women and men are for the most part Ambo, the majority of the first given names of women are European and those of men biblical (see figures 24 and 25).

Figure 24.

The distribution of the first given names and the subsequent given names of women among biblical, European, Ambo and others (%)

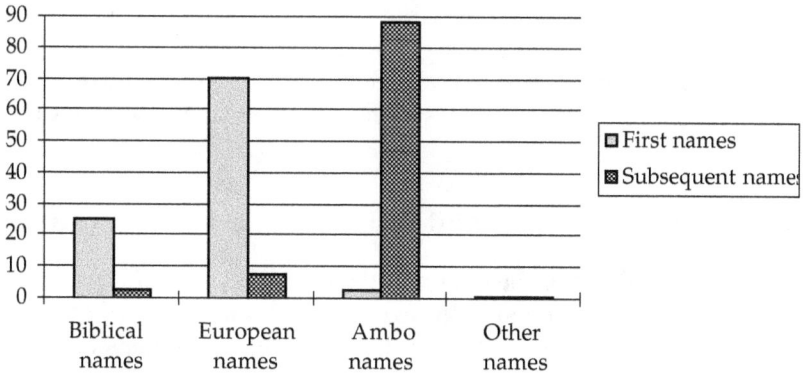

Figure 25.

The distribution of the first given names and the subsequent given names of men among biblical, European, Ambo and others (%)

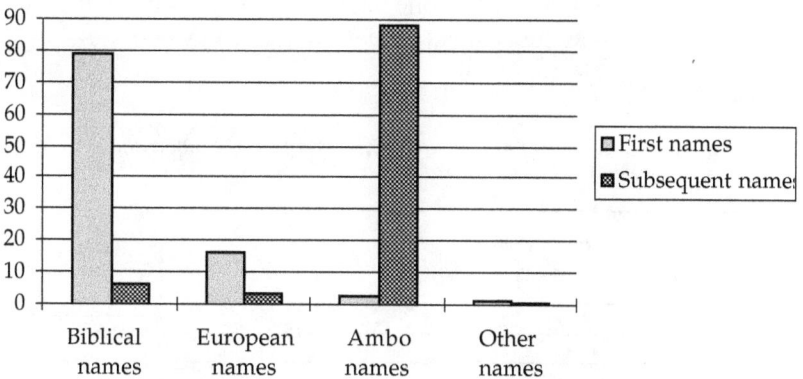

As was noted earlier, the name data for this study appear to represent the contemporary Lutheran Ambo population relatively well. Hence, one may conclude that more than 90 per cent of the Lutheran population in the Ambo area have a European or biblical name as their first baptismal name and that nearly 90 per cent of the subsequent baptismal names of these people are Ambo names. Typical name combinations for women are thus of the type "European name + Ambo name", e.g. *Aina Ndakulilwa* or *Selma Magano*, whereas the most common combinations for men are of the type "biblical name + Ambo name", e.g. *Johannes Natangwe* or *Petrus Panduleni*. Nevertheless, many other combinations appear in the data as well. Among the women one can find baptismal names such as *Bertta Suama Raila* (e+e+e), *Elisabet Penehafo* (b+a), *Inamuvulua Nambula Simanekohamba* (a+a+a) and *Shekupe Aili* (a+e). Similarly, among the men there are combinations such as *Ananias Vilho* (b+e), *David Timoteus* (b+b), *Matti Oskar* (e+e), *Ineekela Otulimegameno* (a+a), *Kleopas Uusiga Vaino* (b+a+e) and *Ndejapo Jesaja* (a+b).

As the baptismal names of the Anglican and Catholic Ambos resemble greatly those of the Lutherans – with some exceptions though, which were taken up earlier – this overall picture can be claimed to portray relatively well the baptismal names of the whole population in the Ambo area.

Changes in the Popularity of Biblical, European and Ambo Names

A diachronic analysis of the data reveals how the popularities of biblical, European and Ambo names have changed in the course of the 20th century. Altogether, radical changes in the baptismal nomenclature of the Ambo people have taken place between the years 1913 and 1993. The share of biblical and European names has decreased clearly, while Ambo names have gained popularity as baptismal names (see figures 26, 27 and 28). The share of Ambo names of all baptismal names started to grow especially in the 1950s when it became customary for the Ambo people to give children more than one baptismal name, as the names that have been bestowed as subsequent names are mainly Ambo.

Figure 26.

The share of biblical names of all the name occurrences of women and men in the data over the years 1913–1993 (%)

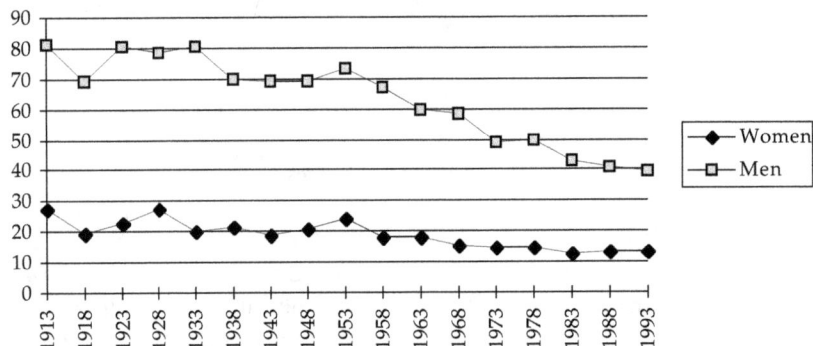

Figure 26 shows how the share of biblical names has become smaller over the years, especially among men, where their share has diminished from roughly 80 per cent to roughly 40 per cent of all men's names.

Figure 27.

The share of European names of all the name occurrences of women and men in the

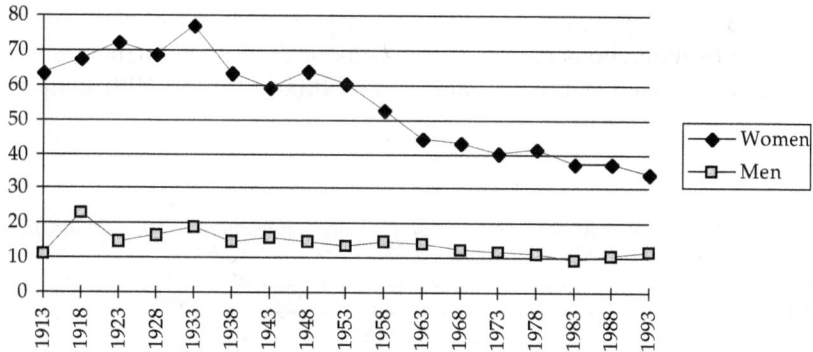

data over the years 1913–1993 (%)
The share of European names of all baptismal names has also decreased over the years, particularly among women (see figure 27). In the course of the century, the proportion of these names has diminished from almost 80 per cent to one third only.

Figure 28.

The share of Ambo names of all the name occurrences of women and men in the data over the years 1913–1993 (%)

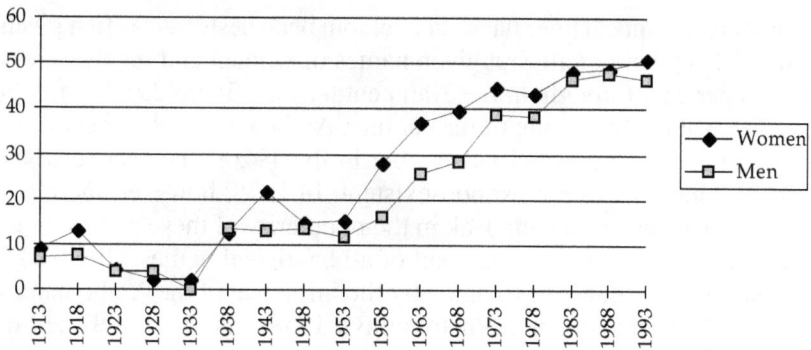

The proportion of Ambo names, however, has developed in the same way among the women and the men, from typically less than 10 per cent at the beginning of the century to roughly half of all baptismal names of both women and men in the 1990s (see figure 28). It is not surprising that the most dramatic growth took place after the 1950s, as that is when the struggle for the independence of Namibia started to inspire people all over the Ambo area and national organisations were founded to serve that purpose. Clearly, national awakening gave a strong impetus to the adoption of indigenous names in the Ambo area, a phenomenon which also characterised personal naming in Finland in the 19th century (Kiviniemi 1993, p. 97).

Figure 29.

The share of Ambo names of all the first given names of women and men in the data over the years 1913–1993 (%)

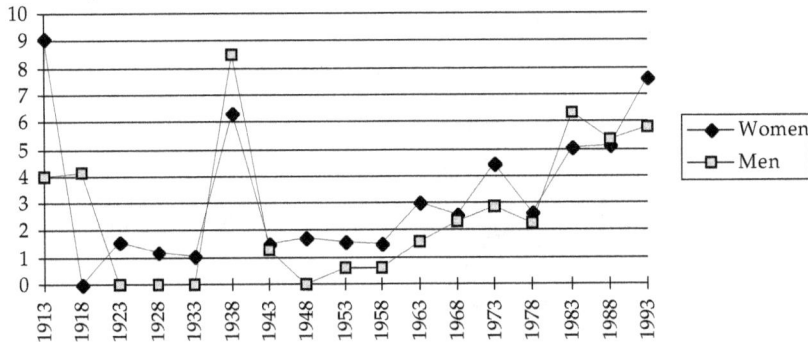

Interestingly, Ambo names have very seldom been bestowed as first given names. Their share of all first given names of women and men was less than 10 per cent throughout the 20th century (see figure 29). Figure 29 shows that at the beginning of the century, Ambo names were occasionally bestowed as baptismal names, but in the 1920s, their share of all baptismal names was almost non-existent. In 1938, however, there appears to have been a sudden peak in the popularity of these names: their share increases to a good 7 per cent of all baptismal names. Obviously, this phenomenon can be explained by the influence of the Ambo name-day calendar (Ondjalulamasiku Jomumvo 1938) that was published in that year. The effect of this calendar on the baptismal name-giving of the Ambo people was only temporary. In the 1940s, as the figure 29 shows, the Ambos returned to their previous custom of bestowing European and biblical names as first baptismal names. The share of Ambo names of all first given names started to grow again after the late 1950s, but in the early 1990s, their share was still roughly 7 per cent of all first given names.

The name data for this study end in the year 1993, but the names in the baptismal registers of the Elim, Okahao and Oshigambo congrega-

306

tions for the years 1998–2000 show no significant changes in this matter in the late 1990s. The majority of first given names in these registers are biblical and European, whereas the subsequent names are predominantly Ambo. On the other hand, it is important to note that in the Ambo naming system, the order of baptismal names is not as significant as it is in many European naming systems, where the first given name is typically the most commonly used name of the person, while the subsequent names are much less important. Often, the name that is used in everyday life in Ambo society is the Ambo baptismal name of the person, not the first biblical or European one.

Although African names have become more popular recently, the Ambo people seem to keep to the custom that the child also receives a biblical or European name. The first baptismal name is typically biblical or European whereas the subsequent ones are Ambo names.

NOTES

396 The parish registers of Olukonda (Ondonga) and Eenhana (Oukwanyama) were defective, whereas those of Tshandi (Uukwaluudhi) and Nakayale (Ombalantu) contained registers of baptisms since the 1950s only.

397 The Ambo name of this village is *Onashiku* (Nambala 1995, p. 13).

398 The Okahao congregation has also been called Rehoboth and Nakeke during its history (Notkola & Siiskonen 2000, p. 34).

399 Notkola and Siiskonen (2000, p. 34–38) give more information about these three congregations and their history.

400 See for example Yrjö Roiha's report 26.4.–26.7.1883 (Eac:6, FMSA).

401 Ida Weikkolin (1888, p. 1) says that in the year 1882, 12 of the 54 pupils in her school were San girls who had Ambo names such as *Nambahu, Nankali, Nangolo* and *Omipolo*, and Hynönen (1963, p. 107) mentions a baptism in Nkongo, in which San people whose Ambo names were *Nambahu, Haindongo, Shijoja, Muandingi* and *Nangula* were baptised as *Samuel, Eino, Sadrak, Helena* and *Tabita*. Hynönen (1981, p. 225) also states that especially in Ongandjera, the San have been assimilated into the Ambo population to such an extent that they have even forgotten their own language.

402 According to one estimate, the total number of 200,253 people in the Ambo area in 1951 included 2,449 San people (Notkola & Siiskonen 2000, p. 19).

403 The Elim congregation was first divided in 1943, Okahao in 1954, and Oshigambo in 1966 (Notkola & Siiskonen 2000, p. 35, 38).

404 Helenius (1930, p. 88–89) says that in Engela, it took several years before the church records were finally in order, and that even then, there were most probably a lot of errors and omissions.

405 Such negligence is typical of these church records in general. A person's name may be written in many different ways on different occasions, e.g. *Vili-Heikki, Viliheiki* and *Viliheik*. This shows that the correct way of spelling a person's name was not taken as seriously in the Ambo culture as it is in Finland, for example, where names such as *Elina* and *Eliina, Ester* and *Esteri, Marita* and *Maritta*, are nowadays regarded as different names, because they are spelt differently.

406 This practice was obviously common in Finland in the Middle Ages too. If the parents wanted their child to be named *Uoti*, for example, the pastor recorded the name as *Olof* – i.e. in the original Swedish form – in the parish records (Kepsu 1991, p. 33).

407   On the other hand, there is also a preference for open syllables in Finnish, even if it is not as systematic as in the Bantu languages. Therefore, Finnish names (e.g. *Aina, Taimi, Eino, Toivo*) have generally been easier for the Ambo people to adopt than German names (e.g. *Adelheid, Friedrich*), for example.

408   Savola states in his Ndonga grammar (1908, p. 1–2) that the *d* in foreign words is pronounced either as *t* or as *nd* by the Ndonga speakers.

409   In some cases, this could also be explained as Finnish influence. Originally, the sound *b* did not occur in the Finnish language, and hence the letter *b* has been replaced with *p* in many Finnish personal names, e.g. *Abel > Aapeli, Albert > Pertti, Jaakob > Jaakoppi, Tobias > Topias; Birgitta > Piritta, Valborg > Valpuri* (Vilkuna 1993, p. 25, 30, 89, 173; 46, 182). Savola (1908, p. 1) states that the *b* in foreign words is pronounced either as *p* or *mb* by the Ndonga speakers.

410   The name forms with doubled vowels or consonants are all Finnish forms.

411   Of these, *Eeva* and *Martta* are Finnish forms, whereas *Elizabeth* and *Ruth* are typically English.

412   When the Ndonga New Testament was being translated at the beginning of the 20th century, the Finnish missionaries decided to use international name forms of biblical names, not domesticated Ambo forms (Peltola 1994, p. 264). Because of this decision, the Ndonga translations are more similar –with regard to names – to European Bible translations than many other African Bible translations.

413   Some forms in this list are also mixtures of different orthographies, which shows that in practice, the orthographic systems of Ndonga have been rather unstable.

414   Fourie (1992, p. 17, 20) shows the historical developments in both Ndonga and Kwanyama orthographies.

415   Hyphenated names are not treated as single names but as separate names in this study. However, there are some exceptions to this among the biblical names: *Eben-Eser* and *Abed-Nego*.

416   In Finland, giving children more than one first name is a relatively recent phenomenon. At the end of the 19th century, roughly half of the Finns still had one name only (Kiviniemi 1993, p. 14–15).

417   Today, roughly 5 per cent of people in Finland have one forename only. The differences between men and women are not significant in this respect. (Kiviniemi 1993, p. 15.)

418   In the two earlier theses on Ambo anthroponymy of the writer (Saarelma-Maunumaa 1995, p. 53; 1997, p. 118), the curve in the corresponding diagram showing the increase of multiple baptismal names among the men is incorrect, but the mistake is corrected here.

419   In Finland, hyphenated names began to appear among the Finnish-speaking population at the end of the 19th century, at the same time as in Scandinavia and Germany. However, it was only in the 1940s that they became fashionable in Finland. (Kiviniemi 1982a, p. 186; 1993, p. 22–23.)

420   This name most probably refers to King Kambonde kaNgula, who was baptised as *Eino Johannes* (Nambala 1994, p. 36; Peltola 1958, p. 143).

421   The origins and meanings of all these names – and the others mentioned in this section – will be analysed later in this study.

422   In France, hyphenating more than two names is also possible, e.g. *Hippolyte-François-Louis-Marie-Alphonse* (Ashley 1996, p. 1218).

423   Namuhuja's (14.4.1997) baptismal name was originally written as *Hans-Daniel* in the church registers, but he stressed that it is not one name but two names. In everyday life, only *Hans* has been used.

424   On the other hand, Lehtonen (2.4.1997) reported that after hyphenated names had come into use, they became fashionable and many Ambos used hyphenated forms of their names, even if they originally did not contain a hyphen.

425   In this respect, Ambo baptismal names differ greatly from those of the Finns. In Finland, the proportion of people having a hyphenated name remained less than 9 per cent in the course of the 20th century (Kiviniemi 1993, p. 23).

426 There are also exceptions to this rule, even if they are extremely rare. For example, the names *Ensi, Kaino* and *Rauni* appear as both women's and men's names in Finland (Kiviniemi 1982a, p. 193).

427 The full baptismal name of this woman is *Miina-Antila*.

428 There are several hymns written by these men in the hymn book of the Evangelical Lutheran Church in Namibia (Omaimbilo gOngerki Onkwaevangeli pa Luther yOwambokavango I. 1967).

429 Spener was the other leader, beside Francke, of the pietist movement in 17th century Germany (Christensen & Göransson 1974, p. 380).

430 In many Bantu languages, there are rather complicated ways to derive female and male names from linguistic elements. See for example Koopman's article "Male and female names in Zulu" (1979b).

431 This is a large number, but not as much as in many naming systems in Medieval Europe, which were characterised by the decline in the name stock after the adoption of "Christian" names. In the 14th century Regensburg in Germany, for example, the most common ten names covered 78 per cent of all women and 63 per cent of all men (V. Kohlheim 1977a, p. 453, 421).

432 As the names *Gabriel* and *Tobias* (20.–21.) have the same number of occurrences in the data, they were both included in this list, even if this made the list include 21 names instead of 20. Naturally, only one of them was included in these calculations.

433 In Ndonga, the verb *pingana* means 'come into place of', and the noun *omupingeni* 'substitute, one who replaces another' (Tirronen 1986, p. 343–44). According to Mateus Angolo from Ongandjera (ELC, p. 1382–1383) and Johannes Kaukungua from Oukwanyama (ELC, p. 1473–1474), *Mpingana* is a name given to a child after someone else in the family has died. Tirronen (1986, p. 232) states that *Mpingana* is a man's name.

434 According to Mateus Angolo from Ongandjera (ELC, p. 1382–1383) and Johannes Kaukungua from Oukwanyama (ELC, p. 1473–1474), the name *Iijambo* was given to a child who was born when the father was at *ohambo* ('cattle-post').

435 In Ndonga, *oshikongo* means 'search for girls for the chief's court' (Tirronen 1986, p. 145).

436 According to Mateus Angolo from Ongandjera (ELC, p. 1382–1383) and Johannes Kaukungua from Oukwanyama (ELC, p. 1473–1474), *Iipinge* is a name given to a child after someone else in the family has died. See also the explanation for *Mpingana* in the list of women's most popular subsequent names.

437 In Finland, the lists of the most popular ten names of women in the 1920s and 1980s have no names in common, and those of the "top twenty" names have only one: *Anna* (Kiviniemi 1982a, p. 205, 207).

438 *Hilma* was among the most popular ten women's names in Finland during the years 1880–1909, after which its popularity decreased rapidly. At the same time, the popularity of *Selma* varied between the ranks 12 and 33, after which it also became unpopular. The name *Taimi* was most popular in Finland in the 1910s and 1920s, when it was the 18th most common name. (Kiviniemi 1982a, p. 204–205.)

439 If one compares the lists of the most popular ten names of men in Finland in the 1920s and 1980s, one cannot find a single common name. In the lists of the "top twenty" names, there is only one name in common: *Matti*. (Kiviniemi 1982a, p. 209, 211.)

440 The peak in the year 1913 can be explained by the fact that there happened to be 2 women with the name *Martta* among the total of 11 baptised women of that year.

441 The peak in the year 1913 in figure 14 can be explained by the fact that there happened to be 3 men with the name *Johannes* among the 25 baptised men of that year. Similarly, the peak in the year 1923 in figure 16 is due to the fact that there were 4 men with the name *Andreas* among the 70 men baptised that year.

442   Of these occurrences, 7 are attached to the name *Simon: Simon Petrus*, which is the name of one of the disciples of Jesus in the Bible.

443   The peak in the year 1918 is due to one woman who was baptised as *Magano* among the 27 baptised women of that year.

444   The names *Erastus* and *Festus* have also been used by the Afrikaans-speaking people in southern Africa (Van Rooyen 1994, p. 92, 94), but they are not typical of Finnish, German or English naming systems.

445   Kena (2000, p. 13) gives the statistics of Finnish female and male missionaries in South West Africa up to the year 1945. The first unmarried female missionaries arrived in the Ambo area in 1909, and of all the 256 Finns working in this area between the years 1870–1958, 175 (68.4 per cent) were women (Peltola 1958, p. 259–277, 154). Altogether, since the beginning of the 20th century, roughly two thirds of all the missionaries of the Finnish Evangelical Lutheran Mission in different countries have been women (Kena 2000, p. 5).

446   These saints' names were checked in the Oxford Dictionary of Saints (Farmer 1996), which includes the names of 1,250 saints from all over the Christian world.

447   The etymologies for these names were taken from the various name books listed in the bibliography under the title Books of Reference. The explanations that are given here are very brief and superficial, and sometimes one explanation is given preference over others. In general, it was easy to find information on these names in European name books. However, these books are not perfectly reliable, and many mistakes may have been copied from one book to another. Sometimes these books also give contradictory information about the origins of these names. Thus, it is possible that there are mistakes in this list too.

448   The meanings of these names were also given in these lists.

449   In this presentation, the prefix is separated from the stem with a forward slash (/) as in Tirronen's Ndonga–English Dictionary (1986).

450   African onomasticians have presented semantic typologies for the names in many African societies. For example, Ebeogu (1993, p. 133) classifies the Igbo names in Nigeria into 12 categories: 1. Gods and deities, 2. The good and the virtuous, 3. Kinship, 4. Natural phenomenon, 5. Social concepts, 6. The Calendar, 7. Titles, 8. Evil and non-virtuous, 9. Natural and physical objects, 10. Parts of the body, 11. Material assets, and 12. Occupations. Amin (1993, p. 10–13) presents eight main groups for the names of the Akan and Ewe peoples in Ghana: 1. Death-related names, 2. Birth-related names, 3. God-related names, 4. Names related to the gift of life, 5. War-related names, 6. Names related to the extended family, 7. Advisory names, and 8. Other categories: Recurrent death names, Drinking bar/fun names, Nonsense names and Role names. These categories also include nicknames.

Zulu names have for example been classified according to the social category to which they point: 1. Mother, 2. Father, 3. Community, 4. Birth circumstances, 5. Child, 6. Religion, 7. Extended family, 8. Child's sex and birth order, 9. Other (Suzman 1994, p. 262–263). See also Von Staden's (1987, p. 178–182) semantic typology for Zulu names. Herbert and Bogatsu (1990, p. 9–10) have classified Sotho and Tswana names into three broad categories: 1. Emotion-related names, 2. Religious-oriented names, and 3. Family continuity names. Elsewhere Herbert (1995, p. 3) presents 9 categories for Tsonga names: 1. Family structure, 2. Christian religion, 3. Emotional state / reaction to birth, 4. Relationships within family, 5. Criticism, complaint, friction, 6. Circumstances of family/household, 7. Circumstances having to do with pregnancy, delivery, or appearance of baby, 8. Protective, 9. Ancestor's name.

As African anthroponymic systems differ from each other in many respects, they obviously need different kinds of semantic categories as well. By presenting various categories for one anthroponymic system, onomasticians have also been able to emphasise different aspects within one system.

451   The noun *enyowa* means 'millet porridge cooked in manketti fruit pulp; species of bulbous plant used to season goat milk', and the verb *nyowa* 'take stealthily, pinch, pilfer' (Tirronen 1986, p. 316).

Analysis of the Changes is the Ambo Anthroponymic System: Conclusion

Structural Analysis of the Changes in the Ambo Naming System

The anthroponymic system of the Ambo people has undergone radical changes since the late 19th century, mainly due to European cultural influence and the adoption of Christianity. The available data show that some elements of the traditional Ambo naming system have disappeared in this process, some have survived – often in a modified form – and many new elements have been adopted. All this has led to the transformation of the Ambo naming system, even to such an extent that it is justified to refer to the new "African-European" naming system that has come to replace the traditional African one. In this section, we shall analyse this process from a structural point of view.

This analysis is based on the theoretical ideas presented at the beginning of this study. Thus, we see the anthroponymic system of the Ambo people as an organised system which consists of individual elements (different types of personal names) and of the ways in which they are structured in this system. This naming system is understood to be a subsystem of the Ambo language system. The Ambo language system, in turn, is seen as part of the Ambo culture, which thus forms the extralinguistic environment for the naming system. In this study, we have seen that the sociocultural changes that have taken place in the Ambo culture in the 20th century, have affected the naming system of the Ambo people in various ways. In this process, not only the elements of this system but also its organisation have changed, which has led to significant changes in the function of this system in society. Let us have a closer look at this process.

The traditional Ambo naming system consisted of four kinds of names given to an individual:

1. The temporary name given soon after birth
2. The real name given at the naming ceremony
3. The patronym, i.e. the father's name (a collective byname)
4. Praise names and other kinds of nicknames (individual bynames)

The new "African-European" naming system also consists of four kinds of names:

1. The name given soon after birth (birth name)
2. The baptismal name(s) given at the ceremony of baptism
3. The hereditary surname (a collective byname)
4. Praise names and other kinds of nicknames (individual bynames)

In both naming systems, the child is given an unofficial name soon after birth, and the "real" name, i.e. the "true" name of the person, which is not changed later in life, is given at a naming ceremony somewhat later. Both systems include a systematically used collective byname which connects the individual with a wider kin-group. Similarly, praise names and other kinds of nicknames belong to both systems. Because of this, one might feel tempted to state that the baptismal name has simply come to serve the function of the real name and the surname that of the patronym, and that the name types 1 and 4 have remained the same. However, if one looks at these names and their functions more closely from different viewpoints, one can see that the process has been much more complicated.

Changes in Names

In the traditional naming system of the Ambo people, personal names were exclusively Ambo names, i.e. names that were derived from the Ambo languages. Some of them were old personal names which had been in use for generations, but many of them were new names created by the name-giver. These kinds of names also belong to the new naming system. Today, the names given to babies soon after birth are mainly Ambo names, and so are roughly half of the baptismal names. The surnames of the Ambo people are also based on traditional Ambo personal names, and nicknames are typically derived from the Ambo languages as well. The morphological and semantic principles used for the formation of new Ambo names have also been largely retained. Hence, Ambo names as such have not disappeared in the process, even if some old names may not be used anymore, and there are many new Ambo names which were not used in the old times, e.g. names that reflect Christian beliefs.

In addition to retaining Ambo names, however, the new naming system contains biblical names and names that have been adopted from different European naming systems and European languages. These foreign names are mainly given as baptismal names, but one can find them among the birth names, surnames and nicknames too. Some of the foreign names have been adopted as such, but typically they appear in a modified form, especially in everyday speech. Thus, the old system, which included Ambo names only, has been replaced by a new system which includes both African and European/biblical names. It is important to note here that the adoption of foreign names has caused changes in the structure of the naming system, but not in its organisation.

Changes in Name-giving Motives and in the Functions of Names

Beside changes in individual names, there have also been changes in the name-giving motives and in the functions of different name types. The reasons for the giving of birth names in the new system are more or less similar to the ones in the old system. These names usually express the name-giver's feelings or refer to various circumstances at the time of the birth. In both systems, this name serves as a temporary name for the child at a time when it is not yet properly named, even if it may remain in use as a nickname too. In the old system, the real name of the person was typically a namesake name, and there were various social responsibilities attached to the namesake relationship. In the new system, this function has been attached to the baptismal name, which is often given as a namesake name. However, as the Ambo people typically receive more than one baptismal name, other functions are attached to these names as well. With the advent of Ambo baptismal names, many of the name-giving motives which were characteristic of temporary names were applied to these names, whereas the foreign baptismal name was often bestowed as a namesake name. The Ambo baptismal names typically reflect the father's feelings and refer to various circumstances around the time of the birth, in the same way as the birth names do. Hence, the functions of the real name in the old system and the baptismal name(s) in the new system are partly different, which has caused changes in the organisation of the Ambo naming system.

In the old system, the collective byname of the person was always his or her father's name. In the new system, the collective byname of the person is a surname, which is typically the name of a paternal forefather which has been chosen to become hereditary in the family. These names both refer to the family, but in a different way: the patronym linked the person with his or her father and with all the other children of the same father, whereas the surname typically links the members of a nuclear family, as well as of some other nuclear families from the father's side. Therefore, the function of these names in the society is different. The surname also came to serve various administrative functions in the modern society, and together with the baptismal name(s), it forms the official name of the person. Hence, the system involving the use of a single name, beside which a patronym was used, was changed into a system of multiple first names and a hereditary surname. This was a major change in the organisation of the Ambo naming system.

Changes in Naming Customs and Religious Ideas Attached to Personal Names

In the old system, an Ambo child usually received his or her temporary name at home soon after birth. This name was typically given by a woman who was present at the delivery. In the new system, the birth name is often bestowed by a midwife in hospital, or by the father. In the old system, the real name was bestowed at a special name-giving ceremony which took place at the child's home. This ceremony was followed by other ceremonies in which the namesake relationship was confirmed. In the new system, the child typically receives its "real" name at the Christian baptism, which takes place in the church. The traditional namesake ceremonies have also been reduced to a simple ceremony which takes place some time before the wedding of the child.

The religious ideas attached to personal names have changed as well. Traditionally, the name was seen as part of the soul of the person, and personal names were used for various ritual purposes. Today, the connection between the person and his or her name is also regarded as close, but this idea is often attached to Christian beliefs. Many Ambos want to name their children after other Christians, with the idea that the child will inherit the personal characteristics of his or her namesake.

African and European Elements

The change in the Ambo naming system can also be analysed from the point of view of African and European elements. Clearly, the Ambo people have chosen some European elements for their naming system and rejected others. Many elements may have been adopted because the culture they came from was considered superior. Obviously, many of them also filled a conscious need at the time when they were adopted. On the other hand, many African elements survived in the process. Hence, the result of this change is not a totally Europeanised naming system, but a new system which includes elements of both African and European origin.

Besides retaining a large number of Ambo names, the namesake custom is one of the Ambo elements that have survived in the process. The social functions attached to the namesake's role have been preserved, even if in a modified form. Today, the namesake is expected to buy school clothes for the child, for example. The old practice of giving the child an Ambo name soon after birth has also been preserved, as well as the custom of giving praise names and composing praise poetry. Ambo baptismal names are also given according to similar principles as in the old times, even if many of these names also refer to Christian beliefs.

Interestingly, many African elements, e.g. the namesake custom, have in fact Europeanised the Ambo naming system. As many Europeans were chosen as namesakes for the Ambos, this led to the adoption of new European names in the Ambo personal nomenclature. In addition, when the Ambo people name their children after other Ambos, it is often the European or biblical name of the person that is chosen as a namesake name. The old patronymic custom, in turn, has led to the Europeanisation of patronyms, as the names of the fathers gradually became European or biblical as a consequence of Christian baptisms. The advent of Ambo baptismal names also led to the use of multiple baptismal names, which is a typical feature in European naming systems. Similarly, the adoption of certain European naming customs has led to the Africanisation of personal names. For example, the adoption of the surname system made it possible for the Ambo people to start using Ambo surnames instead of European and biblical patronyms. All this shows that in the new "African-European" naming system, African and European elements are merged into each other in a dynamic way.

Sources of the Change

In the theoretical introduction for this study, we listed six possible sources for a change in an anthroponymic system:

1. The anthroponymic system itself
2. Its linguistic environment
3. Its extralinguistic environment, i.e. the social system or culture
4. Another anthroponymic system
5. Another language
6. Another social system or culture

When analysing the changes in the Ambo naming system, we have emphasised only some of these. We have shown that the onomastic changes in the Ambo area originate mainly from the changes in the Ambo culture which were caused by the adoption of Christianity and the influence of various European cultures on the life of the Ambo people (in the form of missionary work and colonialism). The influence of European naming systems and languages is also apparent in the Ambo naming system, as foreign names have been adopted both from European naming systems (e.g. *Adelheid, Charles, Lahja*) and European languages (*Remember, Sondag*).

However, there are also internal factors which explain some of the developments in the Ambo naming system. For example, the changes in the Ambo linguistic varieties – phonological, morphological, lexical, orthographic, etc. – have caused changes in Ambo names too, as these names are based on ordinary words and clauses in these linguistic varieties. Many of the changes in the Ambo culture which have been reflected in personal names may not be explained purely by European influence either (Malan 1978, p. 264–265). Some changes can also be explained by the developments in the anthroponymic system itself. For example, the adoption of surnames was largely due to the fact that after the adoption of European and biblical names, the patronymic system could not serve the function of differentiating people, as too many people in the community had similar names, e.g. *Selma Mateus*. However, it is often impossible to define the original sources for the various changes in the Ambo naming system, as onomastic change is typically caused by several internal and external factors working together.

Altogether, as the entire Ambo naming system has been reorganised and its functions in the society have changed accordingly, the naming system of the Ambo people at the end of the 20th century is not the same as it was at the beginning of the century.

Comparison between the Anthroponymic Changes in the Ambo Area and in Medieval Europe

In this section, we aim to compare the changes in the Ambo naming system with the changes that took place in European naming systems particularly in the Middle Ages. These changes, as will be seen, share many common characteristics. However, let us look at the developments in the Ambo naming system first.

From a historical point of view, the development of the Ambo personal naming system can be divided into five stages: 1. The period of traditional Ambo naming, 2. The arrival of European naming patterns, 3. The intensive Europeanisation of the Ambo naming system, 4. The re-Africanisation of the personal nomenclature of the Ambo people, and 5. The post-independence naming of the Ambo people.[452]

The Period of Traditional Ambo Naming (–1883). This period was characterised by a single name system: a person received one real name, beside which several kinds of nicknames were used. People were also differentiated from one another with the use of patronyms. The real name was bestowed at a naming ceremony, before which the child carried a temporary name which may have referred to any of the various circumstances at the time of birth. The real name was given by the father, the main name-giving motive being the namesake relationship. All these names were Ambo names, and usually they were semantically transparent.

During this period, the Ambo people lived according to their traditional lifestyle. In the late 19th century, European influence arrived in the area in the form of traders, explorers and missionaries. In 1870, the first Finnish missionaries settled in the Ambo area.

The Arrival of European Naming Patterns (1883–1920). In 1883, the first Ambo converts were baptised by the Finns, and they received European and biblical names at baptism. During this period, people bearing foreign names formed a small minority in the Ambo communities, and they were often ridiculed because of their names. The majority of baptisms at this time were adult baptisms. Some Ambo kings and members of royal families were baptised at the beginning of the 20th century, which gave impetus to the spread of new names in the Ambo area.

The work of the Finnish and German missionaries started to change the traditional Ambo culture. The migrant labour system also transmitted European cultural influence to the Ambo area since the early 20th century.

The Intensive Europeanisation of the Ambo Naming System (1920–1950). During this period, European and biblical names became an important part of Ambo personal nomenclature. Beginning in the 1920s, these names spread rapidly through the Ambo area, together with the spread of Christianity. The mission stations, which were founded all over the Ambo region, served as centres for the geographical distribution of this innovation. The Ambos who were educated in mission schools and were baptised adopted foreign names first. These names also became fashionable, and many unbaptised people adopted them as well. Consequently, the status of traditional Ambo names declined.

The names given at baptisms were almost exclusively adopted from the Bible or taken from the Europeans who were working in the Ambo area, which led to the increasing popularity of a limited number of names. Gradually, the patronyms of the Ambo people also became European and biblical, which led to considerable difficulties in identifying people, as too many people carried similar names. In 1937, the Finnish missionaries decided to promote the use of African baptismal names, but this did not have any significant influence on baptismal name-giving. At this time, traditional name-giving ceremonies also started to become rare.

Culturally, this was a period of intensive missionary work and acculturation. All spheres of traditional Ambo culture were affected by European and Christian influence, and many old customs disappeared at this time. The migrant labour system continued to Europeanise the Ambo way of life as well.

The Re-Africanisation of the Personal Nomenclature of the Ambo People (1950–1990). Starting in the 1950s, Ambo names started to become popular as baptismal names. They were typically given as second or third names, whereas the first baptismal names remained European and biblical. Many people chose to use their Ambo names in official contexts too. Since the late 1950s, the Ambos began to adopt hereditary surnames that were based on traditional Ambo personal names (patronyms). Gradually, women also started to adopt their husbands' surnames when they got married. However, the surname system also faced criticism among the Ambo people, as it was seen to be unsuitable in a matrilineal society.

This period was characterised by the strengthening of the apartheid policy of the South African government and by the struggle for independence which intensified in 1966 and turned the Ambo area into a battlefield. Because of the war, thousands of Ambo people left the country and lived in exile until independence in 1990.

The Post-independence Naming of the Ambo People (1990–2000). During the first ten years of Namibian independence, the personal naming of the Ambo people was influenced by two major trends: Africanisation and Westernisation. African names continued to be fashionable, and especially among the Ambos living in Windhoek, names were increasingly borrowed from other ethnic groups too. As English was chosen as the only official language of the new republic, English names became popular as well. The role of the father as the name-giver started to weaken, as many parents decided to choose names for their children together. Many Ambo women also chose to use hyphenated surnames instead of their husbands' surnames.

317

This period was characterised by the new independence of the country. After the end of apartheid, the ethnic groups in Namibia started to be in more frequent contact with each other. Thousands of Ambos moved to Windhoek, and urbanisation was rapid. Africanisation was a major cultural trend, but the Western lifestyle also continued to attract the Ambo people.

Changes in European and Ambo Naming Systems

The changes in the 20th century Ambo naming system resemble greatly the onomastic changes in Medieval Europe, which were analysed at the beginning of this study.[453] The reasons for these changes were also largely similar, the primary motives being the adoption of Christianity and the demands of administration in a developing society. Let us review these changes more carefully.

Earlier, we pointed out that the traditional European naming systems resembled the traditional African ones in many respects. In the traditional Germanic and Proto-Finnic naming systems, as well as in the Ambo system, personal names were originally meaningful, and the connection between the name and the person was regarded as close. Thus, names were used for various ritual purposes. In European naming systems, personal names seem to have been unique in the beginning, but later naming after other people, especially after family members, became a common practice. This meant that the original meaning of the name lost its significance. It is possible that a similar development took place in the traditional Ambo naming system too, at some stage of its early history, even if there are no documents on this development. All these traditional naming systems were also based on a system of a single real name, beside which miscellaneous bynames were used.

In all these systems, the adoption of Christianity led to the adoption of biblical names and names of important religious characters. In Medieval Europe, naming after canonised saints, e.g. early martyrs and fathers of the church, became the prevalent custom. In Ambo society, as well as in many other African societies, names of European missionaries were adopted along with biblical names, apparently because these people were the first Christians that the Ambo people came to know, and their names were thus regarded as Christian. In a sense, these European names were given according to similar principles as saints' names in Medieval Europe: the Ambos hoped that the missionaries could serve as model Christians for their children and take care of them in various ways. This practice was also supported by the traditional Ambo namesake custom.

In this process, traditional names were largely replaced by new foreign names which were not understood by the people. In Europe, these new names were often of Hebrew, Greek or Latin origin; some local saints also had indigenous names. In Ambo society, the new names were not only biblical, e.g. Hebrew and Greek names, but also names of Finnish, German and Afrikaans origin. Hence, it is clear that the new "Christian" names were equally foreign to the Finns, the Germans and the Ambos at the time when they were adopted. In all these societies, these new names were not given because of their meanings, however, but because of their reference to particular biblical or other religious characters. Everywhere, these names also became domesticated, as they were adapted phonologically to their new environment.

It is interesting to note that contrary to many European naming systems, the spread of new foreign names ran parallel to the spread of Christianity in the Ambo area. The Ambo people assumed these names from the time of the first baptisms, whereas in Europe it generally took several centuries after the advent of Christianity before biblical names and names of saints became popular among the people. In Europe, the adoption of foreign names and the custom of naming children after saints has been explained by the fact that the traditional naming system had been impoverished while many names had lost their semantic transparency. Hence, there seems to have been a latent need for a new type of names. The new naming principle also stressed individual name choice, contrary to naming children after family members, and thus it reflected the new individualistic trends of the time. It is difficult to judge if the Ambo naming system was also impoverished in some sense in the late 19th century. However, it is clear that the new names filled a need that the traditional names could not fill. First of all, they served to show that the person in question had become a Christian. These names were also needed when dealing with the European employers in the south, for whom African names were often difficult to pronounce.

In Medieval Europe, as well as in the Ambo communities, foreign names started to spread rapidly also because they became fashionable. This innovation was spread both geographically and in the social hierarchy of these communities. The fact that royal families also assumed foreign names also gave impetus to the process. Both in Medieval Europe and in Ambo society, the adoption of new foreign names led to the decline in the name stock and to the growing frequency of a limited number of names, such as *Johannes, Petrus, Anna* and *Elisabet*. It also became clear that the old single name system could not serve to individualise people in the developing society. Gradually, this led to the adoption of hereditary surnames in all these naming systems. The main source for surnames in these societies has been traditional bynames, which are typically indigenous names. Surnames also became a status symbol, and this innovation was first adopted among the upper classes of the society; in the Ambo area, it was first adopted by the educated people. Both in Ambo society and Medieval Europe, surnames were needed for various administrative purposes, e.g. to exercise juridical rights. In addition, they served to emphasise the role of the nuclear family in the society. Multiple first names, as well as hyphenated first names, also became adopted as a fashion in these naming systems.

The developments in the Ambo naming system also share common characteristics with the onomastic developments in Europe after the Middle Ages. Both in the Ambo area and the Protestant areas in Europe, indigenous names became popular again later. These names often had Christian meanings too (e.g. *Gottlieb* in Germany and *Natangwe* in the Ambo area). In Finland and in Ambo society, this development was also attached to the national awakening of the people. Kiviniemi (1998, p. 212) describes the developments in the Finnish personal naming in the 19th century, which indeed resemble the developments in the Ambo personal naming in the latter half of the 20th century:

> The 1840s marked the beginning of a strong national awakening in Finland, and this was reflected, for example, in the fact that Finns wanted to give their children names that were Finnish. Because Finnish names did not exist in the first names that were officially in use at the time, they had to be created. This happened surprisingly quickly. In just over fifty years, hundreds of new names came into use and spread in the same way as innovations generally spread. ... New names of Finnish origin began to appear on calendars as early as at the end of the 19th century, but this did not have a significant influence on the spread of these names. More significant for the spread of these new names was Finnish nationalism and the fact that they became fashionable. (Kiviniemi 1998, p. 212–213.)

In recent times, the influence of literature, films, television and other popular culture on personal names has been significant in these naming systems as well. Similarly, the religious motives which explained the adoption of the first biblical and other foreign names, are not as important as they used to be. Today, these names are often adopted for secular reasons. However, there are also differences in the recent name-giving trends. In Europe, the euphony of names has become a central motive in name-giving, whereas in the Ambo culture, name meaningfulness continues to be an important aspect when choosing an Ambo name for the child; many of these names also continue to reflect the Christian worldview of the name-giver.

The biggest difference between the onomastic changes in Europe and the Ambo area is the rate of this process. In Europe, these changes generally took several centuries, whereas in Ambo society the whole process took place within a little more than a hundred years. This is not surprising, as in general, the Westernisation and modernisation of African societies has been an extremely rapid process.

Conclusion

The main aim of this study was to investigate the changes in the anthroponymic system of the Ambo people in Namibia caused by the Christianisation and Europeanisation of the traditional Ambo culture. The most significant of these changes are the adoption of biblical and European names, the practice of giving more than one "real" name to a person, the replacement of traditional name-giving ceremonies with the ceremony of baptism, and the adoption of surnames. In this process, many tendencies have been at work simultaneously. On the one hand, there has been a strong tendency towards the Europeanisation of the naming system, and on the other hand, this development has been resisted. The result of this process, however, is a naming system which consists of both African and European elements, and in which these elements have specific and separate functions. Hence, the encounter between African and European naming systems in the Ambo area has not only led to the adoption of new names into the personal nomenclature of the Ambo people, but to a formation of a new "African-European" naming system.

As is the case with all cultural change, this process has been a dynamic one, and its consequences have not been totally predictable. Thus, this process proves what V. Kohlheim (1998, p. 177) has stated: that the perturbations which the extralinguistic environment exerts upon the naming system cannot determine any changes within it, it can only set them in motion. Indeed, what Malinowski (1945, p. 25) said about cultural change in general can be said about this particular onomastic change as well:

> The nature of culture change is determined by factors and circumstances which cannot be assessed by the study of either culture alone, or of both of them as lumber rooms of elements. The clash and interplay of the two cultures produce new things.

This change in the Ambo naming system also shows that personal names are a mirror of the culture of the people, as Essien (1986, p. 87) has remarked. The various changes in the Ambo naming system have reflected clearly the various sociocultural changes in Ambo society. For example, this study reveals how the adoption of Christian beliefs and later the struggle for Namibian independence caused significant changes in the personal naming of the Ambo people. Thus, this research, together with many others, proves that personal names are situated on the level of language which is most susceptible to variations and innovations (Raper 1983, p. 4). In Ambo society, as in other societies, personal names can be seen as "products and reflections of the intimate links between language and sociocultural organization" (Herbert 1998, p. 187).

One of the main findings of this study was that the changes in the Ambo naming system in the 20th century greatly resemble the changes in European naming systems in the Middle Ages. As was pointed out, there have been similar changes in many other African naming systems too. Therefore, one may claim that basically the same process has taken place in these African and European societies, even if they are far away from each other both geographically and historically. These similarities seem to support the idea that after all, personal naming follows more or less similar patterns in all human cultures. Hence, there are no fundamental differences between personal naming in Africa and Europe. As Kiviniemi (1982b, p. 30) points out, similar sociocultural developments tend to cause similar changes in personal naming in different societies.

The main factor in the onomastic changes in the 20th century Ambo area and in Medieval Europe was the adoption of Christianity. Undoubtedly, Christianity has been one of the major forces in the globalisation of personal names all over the world. This analysis of the Christianisation of personal names in the Ambo culture has also revealed the usefulness of African church registers in such research. In fact, Ambo society turned out to be an ideal context for a study on the influence of Christianity on personal naming. Firstly, this process has been precisely documented in the parish records of the Lutheran church, starting from the early years of Christian influence in the area. Secondly, compared to many other societies, the Ambo area was highly uniform with regard to its population, as the people living in this area were almost exclusively Ambo-speaking. Thirdly, the European influence in the Ambo area was restricted to a few major factors only, the most important of them being the Finnish missionary work. Thus, the onomastic change in the Ambo area was much less complicated to analyse than the corresponding changes in many other societies were.

This study also aimed to show the usefulness of the anthropological acculturation theories in the analysis of onomastic change. In this research, the general theories of cultural change were thus connected to the linguistic theories of onomastic change. Nevertheless, it is obvious that a lot of work remains to be done in this field. The theories of the influence of culture contact and language contact on personal names need to be further developed and analysed from different viewpoints.

In the introduction of this thesis, it was pointed out that this study should not be understood to represent Ambo linguistics in the first place. Clearly, the analysis of the Ambo personal names in this study was not as systematic as it could have been, had it been carried out by an Ambo linguistic specialist. The general approach of this study was also historical, the main focus being on the late 19th and early 20th centuries. It is also obvious that the general point of view of this research was European, and in particular Finnish. Therefore, one can only hope that in the years to come, Namibian scholars will study the more recent trends in Ambo personal naming – from a Namibian viewpoint.

NOTES

452   These stages, not surprisingly, resemble the ones presented by Dickens (1985, p. 4) for the development of the Zulu anthroponymic system.

453   Morgan (1995, p. 123–124) has presented four periods for the development of the Welsh naming system: 1. Pre-conquest period of Welsh naming (an indigenous system of Welsh names), 2. Bilingual situation (Welsh names survive in regular use, but Anglo-French and biblical names become increasingly popular), 3. Period of almost total assimilation (indigenous Welsh names are scarcely used in formal contexts), and 4. Period of renaissance, of a new awareness of Welsh identity (the revival of traditional Welsh names and the coining of new Welsh names).

BIBLIOGRAPHY

Published Sources Concerning the Ambo area and Namibia

Aarni, Teddy, 1982: The Kalunga Concept in Ovambo Religion from 1870 onwards. Acta Universitas Stockholmiensis. Stockholm Studies in Comparative Religion, 22. Almqvist & Wicksell International, Stockholm.

Aho, Hilja, 1933: Ihmisten hylkäämä – Herran korjaama. Suomen Lähetysseura, Helsinki.

Aho, Hilja, 1941: Noidan tytär: Noituuden kiroista kristityn vapauteen. Suomen Lähetysseura, Helsinki.

"Allerlei aus den Rheinischen Missionsgebieten: Ovamboland." In: Berichte der Rheinischen Missionsgesellschaft 1897 (11), Barmen, p. 341–343.

Andersson, Charles John, 1967: Lake Ngami or Explorations and Discovery during Four Years of Wanderings in Wilds of South-Western Africa. Facsimile Reprint. Africana Collectanea Volume XXIV. C. Struik (Pty.) Ltd., Cape Town.

Auala, Leonard, 1975: Kerron elämästäni. Suomen Lähetysseura, Helsinki.

"Aus dem Norden Deutsch-Südwest-Afrikas." In: Deutsche Kolonialzeitung, 1.9.1904.

Aus den Anfangstagen der Ovambomission: Nach den Aufzeichnungen des Missionars Wulfhorst. 1904. Verlag des Missionshauses, Barmen.

Boulanger, Jean-Claude (ed.), 1990: Proceedings of the XVIth International Congress of Onomastic Sciences: Québec, Université Laval, 16–22 August, 1987. Les Presses de l'Université Laval, Québec.

Brenzinger, Matthias, 1999: Personal Names of the Kxoe: the Example of Tcoo-names. In: Khoisan Forum working paper, Köln, vol. 10, p. 5–18.

Brincker, Peter H., 1894: Zur etymologischen Deutung des Namens "Ov-ámbo". In: Globus. Illustrierte Zeitschrift für Länder- und Völkerkunde, Bd. 66, 10/1894, p. 207–208.

Brincker, P.H., 1900: Unsere Ovambo-Mission sowie Land, Leute, Religion, Sitten, Gebräuche, Sprache usw. der Ovakuánjama-Ovámbo, nach Mitteilungen unserer Ovambo-Missionare zusammengestellt. Rheinisches Missionshaus, Barmen.

Bruwer, J.P. van S., 1966: South West Africa: The Disputed Land. Nasionale Boekhandel, Beperk.

Budack, K.F.R., 1979: Byname in Basterland. In: Namibiana 1(1) 1979, p. 7–19.

Budack, K.F.R., 1988: Inter-Ethnic Names for White Men in South-West Africa. In: Nomina Africana 2(2) 1988, p. 171–186.

Büttner, Friedrich, o.J. [without year]: Die Mission unter den Owambo. Neue Missionsschriften 7. Buchhandlung der Berliner evangelischen Missionsgesellschaft, Berlin.

The Constitution of the Republic of Namibia. 1990. The Ministry of Information and Broadcasting, Windhoek.

Dammann, Ernst, 1972/73: Alte Berichte aus dem Ovamboland von Martti Rautanen. In: Journal XXVII. S.W.A. Wissenschaftliche Gesellschaft 1972/73, p. 31–47.

Dammann, Ernst, 1981: Zur Erinnerung an Toivo Emil Tirronen. In: Namibiana 3(2) 1981, p. 7–15.

Dammann, Ernst, 1984: Der deutsche Anteil an der Erforschung Südwestafrikanischer Sprachen. In: Namibiana 5(1) 1984, p. 69–91.

Dammann, Ernst & Tirronen, Toivo E., 1975: Ndonga-Anthologie. Folge der Beihefte zur Zeitschrift für Eingeborenen-Sprachen, Beiheft 29. Verlag von Dietrich Reimer, Berlin.

Dierks, Klaus, 1999: Chronology of Namibian History from Pre-historical Times to Independent Namibia. Namibia Scientific Society, Windhoek.

Duggal, N.K. (ed.), 1981: Toward a Language Policy for Namibia: English as the Official Language: Perspectives and Strategies. Based on the work of R. Chamberlain, A. Diallo and E. John. Namibia Studies Series 4. United Nations Institute for Namibia, Lusaka.

Eirola, Martti, 1985: Namibiana in Finland I: Opas suomalaisiin Namibiaa ennen vuotta 1938 koskeviin arkistolähteisiin – Guide to the Finnish Archival Sources Concerning Namibia before 1938. Historian tutkimuksia – Studies in History 2. Joensuun yliopisto, Humanistinen tiedekunta, Joensuu.

Eirola, Martti, 1992: The Ovambogefahr: The Ovamboland Reservation in the Making. Pohjois-Suomen historiallinen yhdistys, Jyväskylä.

Eirola, Martti & Rytkönen, Seppo & Siiskonen, Harri & Sivonen, Seppo, 1983: The Cultural and Social Change in Ovamboland 1870–1915. Historian, maantieteen ja muiden aluetieteiden osaston julkaisuja 39. Joensuun korkeakoulu, Joensuu.

Erstlinge von den Arbeitsgebieten der rheinischen Mission. 1899. Rheinische Missions-Traktate 94. Verlag des Missionshauses, Barmen.

Estermann, Carlos, 1976: The Ethnography of Southwestern Angola. I: The Non-Bantu Peoples, The Ambo Ethnic Group. Edited by Gordon D. Gibson. Africana Publishing Company, New York.

First, Ruth, 1963: South West Africa. Penguin African Library, Penguin Books Ltd, Harmondsworth, Middlesex.

Fisch, Maria, 1979: Personennamen und Namensgebung: Eine ethnologisch-etymologische Studie bei den Kavangostämmen. In: Journal XXXIV/XXXV – SWA Wissenschaftliche Gesellschaft Windhoek, 1979/80 – 1980/81, p. 27–42.

Fivaz, Derek, 1986: A Reference Grammar of Oshindonga (Wambo). African Studies of the Academy, Volume No 1 of the Department of African Languages, Windhoek.

Fourie, D.J., 1992: Oshiwambo: Past, Present and Future. Discourse 4. University of Namibia, Windhoek.

Galton, Francis, 1853: The Narrative of an Explorer in Tropical South Africa, London.

Gordon, Robert J., 1992: The Bushman Myth: The Making of a Namibian Underclass. Westview Press, Boulder.

Green, Reginald H. & Kiljunen, Kimmo & Kiljunen, Marja-Liisa (ed.), 1981: Namibia: The Last Colony. Longman Group Ltd, Burnt Mill.

Green, Reginald H. & Kiljunen, Kimmo, 1981: Unto what End? The Crisis of Colonialism in Namibia. In: Green, Reginald H. & Kiljunen, Kimmo & Kiljunen, Marja-Liisa (ed.), Namibia: The Last Colony, p. 1–22.

Grotpeter, John J., 1994: Historical Dictionary of Namibia. African Historical Dictionaries, No. 57. The Scarecrow Press, Inc., London.

Haahti, Hannu, 1913: Mustien maassa: Muistelmia tarkastusmatkalta Ambomaalle. Suomen Lähetysseura, Helsinki.

Hahn, C.H.L., 1928: The Ovambo. In: The Native Tribes of South West Africa, p. 1–36.

Hamutumua, Raakel, 1955: Raakelin kirja. Suomen Lähetysseura, Helsinki.

Hänninen, Aug., 1924: Lähetystyömme Uukuanjamassa 1918–1923. Suomen Lähetysseura, Helsinki.

Harling-Kranck, Gunilla (ed.), 2001: Namn i en föränderlig värld. Rapport från den tolfte nordiska namnforskarkongressen, Tavastehus 13–17 juni 1998. Studier i nordisk filologi 78. Svenska litteratursällskapet i Finland, Helsingfors.

Hartmann, Georg, 1903: Das Amboland. In: Deutsche Kolonialzeitung 21.5.1903, p. 201–203.

Haussleiter, G., 1906: Zur Eingeborenen-Frage in Deutsch-Südwest-Afrika: Erwägungen und Vorschläge. Verlag von Martin Warneck, Berlin.

Helenius, Linda 1930: Jumalan puutarha. Vaikutelmia työajaltani Ambomaalla. Suomen Lähetysseura, Helsinki.

Hillebrecht, Werner, 1985: Namibia in Theses and Dissertations: A Bibliography on All Aspects of Namibian Concern Including German Colonial Policy and International Law 1851–1984; Namibia in Hochschulschriften. Eine Bibliographie zu namibischen Angelegenheiten aus allen Wissensgebieten, unter Einschluss deutscher Kolonialpolitik und internationalen Rechts 1851–1984. Basler Afrika Bibliographien, Basel.

Hiltunen, Maija, 1986: Witchcraft and Sorcery in Ovambo. Transactions 17. Finnish Anthropological Society, Helsinki.

Hiltunen, Maija, 1993: Good Magic in Ovambo. Transactions 33. Finnish Anthropological Society, Helsinki.

Himmelreich, F.H., 1900: Ovamboland. Zweites Heft. Geschichte der Mission unter den Ovambo. Verlag des Missionshauses, Barmen.

Hishongwa, Ndeutala, 1992: The Contract Labour System and its Effects on Family and Social Life in Namibia: A Historical Perspective. Gamsberg Macmillan, Windhoek.

Holopainen, Raimo, 1993: Rakentajana Afrikassa. Kirjaneliö, Helsinki.

Hopeasalmi, Jalmari 1946: Pakanain "paratiisi": Ambolaisten uskontoa ja tapoja. Suomen Lähetysseura, Helsinki.

Hynönen, Erkki, 1963: Olupandu – Suuren kiitoksen leiri. Suomen Lähetysseura, Helsinki.

Hynönen, Erkki, 1981: Bushmannit viimeisellä hiekkadyynillään. Werner Söderström Osakeyhtiö, Porvoo.

Ihamäki, Kirsti 1985: Leonard Auala, Namibian musta paimen. Kirjaneliö, Pieksämäki.

Iyambo, Nickey, 1970: Namibia. In: Tuomioja, Erkki (ed.), Valkoisen vallan Afrikka, p. 67–92.

Kane-Berman, John, 1972: Contract Labour in South West Africa. South African Institute of Race Relations (Inc.), Johannesburg.

Katjavivi, Peter H., 1989: A History of Resistance in Namibia. 2nd edition. Unesco Press, Paris.

Kemppainen, Kati, 1998: Suomalaisen lähetyksen suhteet anglikaaneihin ja katolilaisiin Lounais-Afrikassa 1919–1937. Suomen kirkkohistoriallisen seuran toimituksia 180, Helsinki.

Kena, Kirsti, 2000: Eevat apostolien askelissa: Lähettinaiset Suomen Lähetysseuran työssä 1870–1945. Suomen Lähetysseura, Helsinki.

Kiljunen, Kimmo & Kiljunen, Marja-Liisa (ed.), 1980: Namibia – viimeinen siirtomaa. Kustannusosakeyhtiö Tammi, Helsinki.

Kiljunen, Marja-Liisa, 1980: Lounais-Afrikasta Namibiaksi. In: Kiljunen, Kimmo & Kiljunen, Marja-Liisa (ed.), Namibia – viimeinen siirtomaa, p. 13–54.

Kiljunen, Marja-Liisa, 1981: The Land and its People. In: Green, Reginald H. & Kiljunen, Kimmo & Kiljunen, Marja-Liisa (ed.), Namibia: The Last Colony, p. 23–29.

Kivelä, Laina, 1991: Elämän saatossa: Afrikassa koettua 1949–1986. Author's edition, Ylivieska.

Kiviniemi, Eero & Mustakallio, Sari (ed.), 1996: Nimet, aatteet, mielikuvat: Kolme näkökulmaa etunimiin. Kieli 11. Helsingin yliopiston suomen kielen laitos, Helsinki.

Kuusi, Matti, 1970: Ovambo Proverbs with African Parallels. FF Communications 208. Suomalainen tiedeakatemia, Helsinki.

Laamanen, Markku, 1994: Suomen kehitysyhteistyöhankkeet Namibiassa. In: Namibia. Suomi–Namibia-Seuran tiedote 3/94, p. 12–13.

Legère, Karsten, 1998a: Oshikwanyama in Namibia. In: Legère, Karsten (ed.), Cross-Border Languages: Reports and Studies, p. 40–73.

Legère, Karsten (ed.), 1998b: Cross-Border Languages: Reports and Studies. Regional Workshop on Cross-Border Languages. National Institute for Educational Development (NIED). Okahandja, 23–27 September 1996. Gamsberg Macmillan Publ., Windhoek.

Lehtonen, Lahja, 1999: Schools in Ovamboland from 1870 to 1970. The Finnish Evangelical Lutheran Mission, Helsinki.

Levänen, Lyyli, 1935: Simbuela: Henkilökuvia Ambomaalta. Suomen Lähetysseura, Helsinki.

Levänen, Lyyli, 1963: Siihen aikaan. Suomen Lähetysseura, Helsinki.

Levänen, Lyyli, 1964: Heimo herää. Suomen Lähetysseura, Helsinki.

Maho, J. F., 1998: Few People, Many Tongues: The Languages of Namibia. Gamsberg Macmillan Publishers, Windhoek.

Malan, J.S., 1978: Social Evolution among the Ovambo. In: Cimbebasia (B) 2(12), p. 259–266.

Malan, J.S., 1990: Aspekte van identiteitsvorming en -verandering onder die Wambo. In: South African Journal of Ethnology 13(1), p. 1–10.

Malan, J.S., 1995: Peoples of Namibia. Rhino Publishers, Wingate Park.

Martti Rautasen Ambomaan kokoelma Suomen kansallismuseossa – Martti Rautanen's Ambo Collection at the National Museum of Finland. 1983. Museovirasto, Helsinki.

Meinecke, Gustav (ed.): Koloniales Jahrbuch. Das Jahr 1890. Carl Heymanns Verlag, Berlin.

Melander, Anni & Tamminen, Rauha & Helenius, Linda, 1942: Terveisiä Ambomaalta. Werner Söderström Osakeyhtiö, Porvoo.

Möller, L.A., 1986: Duitse plekname in Suidwes-Afrika. In: Raper, P.E. (ed.), Names 1983: Proceedings of the Second Southern African Names Congress, p. 193–208.

Möller, Lucie A., 1990: The Influence of Indigenous Languages on German Toponyms in Namibia. In: Boulanger, Jean-Claude (ed.), Proceedings of the XVIth International Congress of Onomastic Sciences, p. 407–415.

Moritz, W., 1983: Einige Ortsnamen in Namaland. In: Namibiana 4(2) 1983, p. 75–77.

Mustakallio, Joos., 1903: Pienoiskuva Ondongasta. Suomen Lähetysseura, Helsinki.

Nambala, Shekutaamba V.V., 1994: History of the Church in Namibia. Edited by Oliver K. Olson. Lutheran Quartely, United States of America.

Nambala, Shekutaamba V.V., 1995: Ondjokonona yaasita naateolohi mu ELCIN 1925–1992. Oshinyanyangidho shOngeleki ELCIN, Oniipa.

Nampala, Lovisa, 2000: "Thousands of Needy Heathens": Christianisation and Cultural Change – a Case Study from Oniipa. "Public History: Forgotten History". University of Namibia, 22–25 August, 2000.

Namuhuja, H.D., 1996: Ezimo lyaawa yaNdonga. Out of Africa Publishers (Pty) Ltd, Windhoek.

Närhi, O.E., 1929: Taikasauva ja risti: Mustan kansan tapoja, taikoja ja uskomuksia. Suomen Lähetysseura, Helsinki.

The Native Tribes of South West Africa. 1928. Cape Times Limited, Cape Town.

Nienaber, G.S. & Raper, P.E., 1977, 1980: Toponymica Hottentotica A & B. 3 vols. Human Sciences Research Centre, Pretoria.

"Nochmals zur Namensgebung in den deutschen Schutzgebieten." In: Deutsche Kolonialzeitung 31 (1914) Nr. 1, Berlin, p. 4–5.

Notkola, Veijo & Siiskonen, Harri, 2000: Fertility, Mortality and Migration in SubSaharan Africa: The Case of Ovamboland in North Namibia, 1925–90. Macmillan Press Ltd, London.

Otto, A., 1985: Herero-naamgewing. In: Logos 5 (1/2) 1985, p. 126–132.

"Pakanalasten kaste Valaskalalahdella." In: Suomen Lähetyssanomia 1891, Lisälehti p. 61–63.

Peltola, Matti, 1958: Suomen Lähetysseuran Afrikan työn historia. Sata vuotta suomalaista lähetystyötä 1859–1959 2. Suomen Lähetysseura, Helsinki.

Peltola, Matti, 1994: Martti Rautanen: Mies ja kaksi isänmaata. Kirjapaja, Helsinki.

Pentti, Elias J. (ed.), 1959: Ambomaa. 2nd edition. Suomen Lähetysseura, Helsinki.

Perheentupa, Antti, 1923: Uusi ajanjakso ambolähetystyössä. Suomen Lähetysseura, Helsinki.

Perheentupa, Antti, 1935: Muistelmia Afrikasta: Lähetyssaarnaajan elämyksiä ja kokemuksia. Suomen Lähetysseura, Helsinki.

Pütz, Martin, 1991: "Südwesterdeutsch" in Namibia: Sprachpolitik, Sprachplanung und Spracherhalt. In: Linguistische Berichte 136, 1991, p. 455–476.

Ranttila, Hilma, 1935: Äitinsä kiroama: Kuvauksia lähetystyöstä Ambomaalla. Suomen Lähetyseura, Helsinki.

Raper, P.E., 1978: Place Names in South West Africa: Problems and Difficulties Encountered in Field Research into Khoekhoen (Hottentot) Place Names in South West Africa. In: Onoma 22, 1978, p. 225– 233.

Reijonen, Tobias, 1883: "Vuosikertomus Omulongan Lähetyspaikalta, vuodelta 1882." In: Suomen Lähetyssanomia n:o 5 1883, p. 69–72.

Von Rohden, Ludwig, 1874: Die Mission in Ovamboland. In: Allgemeine Missions-Zeitschrift: Monatshefte für geschichtliche und theoretische Missionskunde. Druck und Verlag von C. Bertelsmann, Gütersloh.

Saarelma-Maunumaa, Minna, 1996a: Kun Nangulasta tuli Aino Johanna: Eurooppalaistumisen vaikutus Namibian Ambomaan henkilönnimistöön 1883–1993. In: Kiviniemi, Eero & Mustakallio, Sari (ed.), Nimet, aatteet, mielikuvat, p. 99–238.

Saarelma-Maunumaa, Minna, 1996b: The Influence of Westernization on Ovambo Personal Names in Namibia. In: Nomina Africana 10(1–2) 1996, p. 20–29.

Saarelma-Maunumaa, Minna, 1997a: Finnish Personal Names in Ovamboland, Namibia. In: Pitkänen, Ritva Liisa & Mallat, Kaija (ed.), You Name it, p. 274–282.

Saarelma-Maunumaa, Minna, 1999a: Albelitina, Esitela and Vilihema: European and Biblical Names in an African Context. In: Studia anthroponymica Scandinavica. Årgång 17, p. 51–66.

Saarelma-Maunumaa, Minna, 1999b: Name Sharing in the Naming System of the Ovambos in Namibia. In: Nomina Africana 13(1–2) 1999, p. 35–45.

Saarelma-Maunumaa, Minna, 2001: Personnamn och kulturförändring i Namibia. In: Harling-Kranck, Gunilla (ed.): Namn i en föränderlig värld, p. 283–289.

Saari, Heikki, 1952: Luotilanka. Suomen Lähetysseura, Helsinki.

Savola, Alb., 1903: Ensimmäiset kristityt ruhtinaat Ondongassa eli Albin j'Iitope ja Martin hänen veljensä. Pakanalähetyksen kirjasia 16. 2nd edition. Suomen Lähetysseura, Helsinki.

Savola, Albin, 1907: Jokaisellako uskolla autuaaksi? Piirteitä ambolaisten uskonnosta. Suomen Lähetysseura, Helsinki.

Savola, Albin, 1908: Ošindongan kielioppi. Suomen Lähetysseura, Helsinki.

Savola, Albin, 1924: Ambomaa ja sen kansa. 2nd, revised edition. Suomen Lähetysseura, Helsinki.

Schlipköter, August (ed.), 1925: Der heiden Licht: Bilder aus der Heidenmission. Chr. Belser A.G., Verlagsbuchhandlung, Stuttgart.

Seidel, A., 1891: Die Sprachverhältnisse in den deutschen Schutzgebieten. In: Meinecke, Gustav (ed.), Koloniales Jahrbuch. Das Jahr 1890, p. 26–45.

Shejavali, Abisai, 1970: Ongerki Yomowambokavango – Ambo-Kavangon kirkko – The Ovambo-Kavango Church. Suomen Lähetysseura, Helsinki.

Siiskonen, Harri, 1990: Trade and Socioeconomic Change in Ovamboland 1850–1906. Studia Historica 35. Suomen Historiallinen Seura, Helsinki.

Siiskonen, Harri, 1994: Ambomaan kirkonkirjojen pelastustyö hyvällä alulla. In: Namibia. Suomi–Namibia-Seura ry:n tiedote 3/94, p. 25–26.

Soggot, David, 1986: Namibia – The Violent Heritage. Rex Collings, London.

Suomalaista raivaustyötä Afrikan erämaassa. 1945. Suomen Lähetysseura, Helsinki.

Suomen kehitysyhteistyö 2000: Ulkoasiainministeriön kehitysyhteistyökertomus eduskunnalle vuodelta 2000. 2001. Ulkoasiainministeriö, Porvoo.

Suomen Lähetysseuran vuosikirja 2000: Kertomus vuoden 1999 toiminnasta. – Finska Missionssällskapets årsbok 2000: Verksamhetsberättelse för år 1999. 2000. Suomen Lähetysseura, Helsinki.

Suomen Lähetysseuran vuosikirja 2001: Kertomus vuoden 2000 toiminnasta. – Finska Missionssällskapets årsbok 2001: Verksamhetsberättelse för år 2000. 2001. Suomen Lähetysseura, Helsinki.

"Tärkeä kaste Hereromaalla." In: Suomen Lähetyssanomia 12/1891, p. 180–182.

Tarkkanen, Matti, 1927: Ambolähetyksemme ennen ja nyt. Suomen Lähetysseura, Helsinki.

Tirronen, Toivo, 1960: Praktiese Ndonga. Suomen Lähetysseura, Oniipa.

327

Tirronen, Toivo, 1976: Kirja Ambomaalla. In: Vastauksemme: lähetys, p. 47–56.

Tirronen, Toivo E., 1977: Ndongan kielen oppikirja. Suomen Lähetysseura, Helsinki.

Tönjes, Hermann, 1996: Ovamboland: Country People Mission: With Particular Reference to the Largest Tribe, The Kwanyama. (German edition first published in 1911.) Namibia Scientific Society, Windhoek.

Tötemeyer, Gerhard, 1978: Namibia Old and New: Traditional and Modern Leaders in Ovamboland. C. Hurst & Company, London.

Tuomioja, Erkki (ed.), 1970: Valkoisen vallan Afrikka. 2nd edition. Tammi, Helsinki.

Tuupainen, Maija, 1970: Marriage in a Matrilineal African Tribe: A Social Anthropological Study of Marriage in the Ondonga Tribe in Ovamboland. Transactions of the Westermarck Society XVIII, Helsinki.

Väänänen, Nestori, 1935: Kuinka mustasta tulee kristitty? Suomen Lähetysseura, Helsinki.

Väisälä, Marja, 1980: Suomalainen lähetystyö. In: Kiljunen, Kimmo & Kiljunen, Marja-Liisa (ed.), Namibia – viimeinen siirtomaa, p. 230–249.

Vastauksemme: lähetys. Suomen Lähetysseuran vuosikirja 1976. Suomen Lähetysseura, Helsinki.

Vedder, Heinrich, 1973: Das alte Südwestafrika: Südwestafrikas Geschichte bis zum Tode Mahareros 1890. S.W.A. Wissenschaftliche Gesellschaft, Windhoek. (Erstausgabe 1934 im Martin Warneck Verlag, Berlin.)

Weikkolin, Ida, 1888: Swarta Sara från Owambolandet. Helsingfors.

Welsch, H., 1923: Petrus ja Schamena: Ein Lebensbild aus der Ovambomission. Rheinische Missionsschriften 192. Verlag des Missionshauses, Barmen.

Welsch, Heinrich, 1925: Ein Stück Missionsarbeit aus dem Ovamboland. In: Schlipköter, August (ed.), Der heiden Licht: Bilder aus der Heidenmission, p. 114–129.

Williams, Frieda-Nela, 1994: Precolonial Communities of Southwestern Africa: A History of Owambo Kingdoms 1600–1920. Archeia No. 16. 2nd edition. National Archives of Namibia, Windhoek.

Wulfhorst, Aug. 1912: Schiwesa, ein Simeon aus den Ovambochristen. Verlag des Missionshauses, Barmen.

Other Research Literature

Abell, S. Opunabo, 1992: African Names and their Meanings. Vantage Press, New York.

Aceves, Joseph B., (ed.) 1972: Aspects of Cultural Change. Southern Anthropological Society, Proceedings, No. 6. The University of Georgia Press, Athens.

Aguessy, Honorat, 1979: Traditional African Views and Apperceptions. In: Introduction to African Culture, p. 83–123.

Ainiala, Terhi, 1997: Muuttuva paikannimistö. Suomalaisen Kirjallisuuden Seuran Toimituksia 667. Suomalaisen Kirjallisuuden Seura, Helsinki.

Akinnaso, F. Niyi, 1980: The Sociolinguistic Basis of Yoruba Personal Names. In: Anthropological Linguistics 22(6) 1980, p. 275–304.

Akinnaso, F. Niyi, 1983: Yoruba Traditional Names and the Transmission of Cultural Knowledge. In: Names 31 (3) 1983, p. 139–158.

Alford, Richard D., 1988: Naming and Identity: A Cross-Cultural Study of Personal Naming Practices. HRAF Press, New Haven.

Algeo, John, 1973: On Defining the Proper Name. University of Florida Humanities Monograph 41. University of Florida Press, Gainesville.

Allan, Keith, 1986: Linguistic Meaning. Volume 2. Routledge & Kegan Paul, London.

Amin, N.O., 1993: Names as a Factor in Cultural Identity among the Akan, Ga and Ewe Tribes of Ghana. Part II: Given names. Forum 12. Centre for Development Analysis, Pretoria.

Andersson, Thorsten & Brylla, Eva & Jacobson-Widding, Anita (ed.), 1998: Personnamn och social identitet: Handlingar från ett Natur och Kultur -symposium i Sigtuna 19–22 september 1996. Konferenser 42. Kungl. Vitterhets Historie och Antikvitets Akademien, Stockholm.

Applebaum, Herbert (ed.), 1987: Perspectives in Cultural Anthropology. State University of New York Press, Albany.

Asante, Molefi Kete & Asante, Kariamu Welsh (ed.), 1985: African Culture: The Rhythms of Unity. Contributions in Afro-American and African Studies, Number 81. Greenwood Press, Westport, Connecticut.

Asante, Molefi Kete, 1985: Afrocentricity and Culture. In: Asante, Molefi Kete & Asante, Kariamu Welsh (ed.), African Culture: The Rhythms of Unity, p. 3–12.

Asante, Molefi Kete, 1991: The Book of African Names. Africa World Press, Trenton, New Jersey.

Ashley, Leonard, 1996: Middle Names. In: Eichler, Ernst & Hilty, Gerold & Löffler, Heinrich & Steger, Hugo & Zgusta, Ladislav (ed.), Namenforschung. Volume 2, p. 1218–1221.

Austin, J.L., 1962: How to do Things with Words. Harvard University Press, Cambridge.

Ayandele, E.A., 1979: The Missionary Impact on Modern Nigeria 1842–1914: A Political and Social Analysis. 4th edition. Longman Group Ltd, London.

Ayisi, Eric O., 1988: An Introduction to the Study of African Culture. 2nd edition. James Currey Ltd, London.

Bach, Adolf, 1953: Deutsche Namenkunde I. Die deutschen Personennamen 2. Die deutschen Personennamen in geschichtlicher, geographischer, soziologischer und psychologischer Betrachtung. Carl Winter Universitätsverlag, Heidelberg.

Bank, Andrew & Heese, Hans & Loff, Chris (ed.), 1998: The Proceedings of the Khoisan Identities and Cultural Heritage Conference, organised by the Institute for Historical Research, University of the Western Cape, held at the South African Museum, Cape Town, 12–16 July 1997. The Institute for Historical Research and Infosource CC, Cape Town.

Bean, Susan S., 1980: Ethnology and the Study of Proper Names. In: Anthropological Linguistics 22(7) 1980, p. 305–316.

Beidelman, T.O., 1974: Kaguru Names and Naming. In: Journal of Anthropological Research 30/1974, p. 281–293.

Benson, Sven, 1990: Variations in the Swedish Forename System. In: Närhi, Eeva Maria (ed.), ICOS 1990 Helsinki, Volume 1, p. 194–201.

Bernardi, Bernardo (ed.), 1977: The Concept and Dynamics of Culture. Mouton Publishers, the Hague.

Bitterli, Urs, 1989: Cultures in Conflict: Encounters between European and Non-European Cultures, 1492–1800. Stanford University Press, Stanford, California.

Blakely, Thomas D. & Van Beek, Walter E.A. & Thomson, Dennis L. 1994: Religion in Africa: Experience & Expression. James Currey Ltd, London.

Blanár, Vincent 1996: Das anthroponymische System und sein Funktionieren. In: Eichler, Ernst & Hilty, Gerold & Löffler, Heinrich & Steger, Hugo & Zgusta, Ladislav (ed.), Namenforschung. Volume 2, p. 1179–1182.

Blomqvist, Marianne, 1988: Från tillnamn till släktnamn i österbottnisk allmogemiljö. Skrifter utgivna av Svensk-österbottniska Samfundet 44. Arkiv för Svenska Österbotten 18. Vasa.

Blomqvist, Marianne, 1993: Personnamnsboken. Finn Lectura, Loimaa.

Blomqvist, Marianne, 1998: Names in Almanacs of Finland. In: Nicolaisen, W.F.H. (ed.), Proceedings of the XIXth International Congress of Onomastic Sciences, Volume 3, p. 58–64.

Blount, Ben G. & Sanches, Mary, 1977a: Introduction: Sociocultural Dimensions of Language Change. In: Blount, Ben G. & Sanches, Mary (ed.), Sociocultural Dimensions of Language Change, p. 1–20.

Blount, Ben G. & Sanches, Mary (ed.), 1977b: Sociocultural Dimensions of Language Change. Academic Press, New York.

Boahen, A. Adu, 1990: Africa under Colonial Domination 1880–1935. General History of Africa VII. Abridged edition. The United Nations Educational, Scientific and Cultural Organization, California, U.S.A.

Boas, Franz, 1963: The Mind of Primitive Man. Revised edition. The Free Press, New York.

Bodley, John H., 1994: Cultural Anthropology: Tribes, States, and the Global System. Mayfield Publishing Company, Mountain View, California.

Brady, Ivan A. & Isaac, Barry L. (ed.) 1975: A Reader in Culture Change. Volume I: Theories. Schenkman Publishing Company, Cambridge.

Brandström, Per, 1998: Lolandi – se jag är! En historia om det berättande namnet hos sukuma-nyamwezi i Tanzania. In: Andersson, Thorsten & Brylla, Eva & Jacobson-Widding, Anita (ed.), Personnamn och social identitet, p. 139–155.

Brandt, Elizabeth A., 1972: Language, Linguistics, and Social Change: Retrospect and Prospect. In: Aceves, Joseph. B. (ed.), Aspects of Cultural Change, p. 49–62.

Braun, Friederike, 1988: Terms of Address: Problems of Patterns and Usage in Various Languages and Cultures. Contributions to the Sociology of Language 50. Mouton de Gruyter, Berlin.

Busia, K.A., 1970: The Ashanti of the Gold Coast. In: Forde, Daryll (ed.), African Worlds: Studies in the Cosmological Ideas and Social Values of African Peoples, p. 190–209.

Cajot, José & Kremer, Ludger & Niebaum, Hermann (ed.), 1995: Lingua Theodisca: Beiträge zur Sprach- und Literaturwissenschaft: Jan Goossens zum 65. Geburtstag. Lit Verlag, Münster.

Christensen, Torben & Göransson, Sven, 1974: Kirkkohistoria 2: Paavin jumalanvaltiosta uskonnonvapauteen. Gaudeamus, Helsinki.

Chuks-Orji, Ogonna, 1972: Names from Africa. Johnson, Chicago.

Chupungco, Anscar J., 1998: Baptism, Marriage, Healing, and Funerals: Principles and Criteria for Inculturation. In: Stauffer, S. Anita (ed.), Baptism, Rites of Passage, and Culture, p. 47–69.

Coetser, A., 1996: Afrikaans se Bydrae tot Familiename in Xhosa. In: Nomina Africana 10 (1–2) 1996, p. 43–53.

Cox, H.L. & Vanacker, V.F. & Verhofstadt, E. (ed.) 1986: Wortes Anst – Verbi gratia. Donum natalicium Gilbert A.R. de Smet. Acco, Leuven.

Daeleman, Jan, 1977: Proper Names used with 'Twins' and Children succeeding them in Sub-Saharan Languages. In: Onoma XXI (1–2) 1977, p. 189–195.

Dahl, Gudrun, 1998: Naming a Boraana. In: Andersson, Thorsten & Brylla, Eva & Jacobson-Widding, Anita (ed.), Personnamn och social identitet, p. 311–336.

Debus, Friedhelm & Seibicke, Wilfried (ed.), 1989: Reader zur Namenkunde I: Namentheorie. Germanistische Linguistik 98–100. Georg Olms Verlag, Hildesheim.

Debus, Friedhelm & Seibicke, Wilfried (ed.), 1993: Reader zur Namenkunde II: Anthroponymie. Germanistische Linguistik 115–118. Georg Olms Verlag, Hildesheim.

Downs, James F., 1971: Cultures in Crisis. Glencoe Press, Beverly Hills, California.

Dunkling, Leslie Alan, 1977: First Names First. Gale Research Company, Book Tower, Detroit, Michigan, U.S.A.

Ebeogu, Afam, 1993: Onomastics and the Igbo Tradition of Politics. In: African Languages and Cultures 6(2) 1993, p. 133–146.

Edlund, Lars-Erik (ed.), 1994: Kulturgränser – myt eller verklighet? Diabas 4. Den dialektgeografiska databasen inom Institutionen för nordiska språk vid Umeå universitet, Umeå.

Edwards, John, 1985: Language, Society and Identity. Basil Blackwell Ltd, Oxford.

Ehlich, Konrad, 1994: Communication Disruptions: On Benefits and Disadvantages of Language Contact. In: Pütz, Martin (ed.), Language Contact and Language Conflict, p. 103–122.

Eichler, Ernst & Fleischer, Wolfgang & Große, Rudolf & Neubert, Albrecht & Walther, Hans (ed.), 1973: Der Name in Sprache und Gesellschaft: Beiträge zur Theorie der Onomastik. Akademie-Verlag, Berlin.

Eichler, Ernst, 1989: Sprachkontakte im Lichte der Onomastik. In: Debus, Friedhelm & Seibicke, Wilfried (ed.), Reader zur Namenkunde I, p. 377–389.

Eichler, Ernst & Hilty, Gerold & Löffler, Heinrich & Steger, Hugo & Zgusta, Ladislav (ed.), 1995: Namenforschung – Name Studies – Les noms propres: Ein internationales Handbuch zur Onomastik – An International Handbook of Onomastics – Manuel international d'onomastique. Volume 1. Walter de Gruyter, Berlin.

Eichler, Ernst & Hilty, Gerold & Löffler, Heinrich & Steger, Hugo & Zgusta, Ladislav (ed.), 1996: Namenforschung – Name Studies – Les noms propres: Ein internationales Handbuch zur Onomastik – An International Handbook of Onomastics – Manuel international d'onomastique. Volume 2. Walter de Gruyter, Berlin.

Ekpo, Monday U., 1978: Structure in Ibibio Names. In: Names 26, 1978, p. 271–284.

Ennis, Elisabeth Logan, 1945: Women's Names among the Ovimbundu of Angola. In: African Studies 4(1) 1945, p. 1–8.

Essien, Okon E., 1986: Ibibio Names: Their Structure and their Meanings. Daystar Press, Ibadan.

Evans-Pritchard, E.E., 1948: Nuer Modes of Address. In: Uganda Journal, Vol. 12, 1948, p. 166–171.

Fedders, Wolfgang, 1995: Aspekte der Vornamengebung in Lippe zwischen 1500 und 1800. In: Cajot, José & Kremer, Ludger & Niebaum, Hermann (ed.), Lingua Theodisca, p. 755–767.

Fellows-Jensen, Gillian & Holmberg, Bente (ed.), 1994: Vikingetidens sted- og personnavne. Rapport fra NORNAs 22. symposium i Kœbenhavn 14.–16. januari 1993. Norna-rapporter 54. Norna-förlaget, Uppsala.

Finlayson, Rosalie, 1984: The Changing Nature of Isihlonipho Sabafazi. In: African Studies 43(2) 1984, p. 137–146.

Finlayson, Rosalie, 1987: Southern-Bantu Origins. In: South African Journal of African Languages 7(2) 1987, p. 50–57.

Flannery, Austin, O.P. (ed.), 1980: Vatican Council II: The Conciliar and Post Conciliar Documents. 5th printing. Liturgical Press, Collegeville, Minnesota.

Fleischer, Wolfgang, 1968: Die deutschen Personennamen. 2nd, revised edition. Wissenschaftliche Taschenbücher Band 20. Akademie-Verlag, Berlin.

Forde, Daryll (ed.), 1970: African Worlds: Studies in the Cosmological Ideas and Social Values of African Peoples. 7th impression. 1st edition 1954. Oxford University Press, London.

Forsman, A.V., 1894: Pakanuudenaikainen nimistö. Tutkimuksia Suomen kansan persoonallisen nimistön alalla. I. Suomi. Kirjoituksia isänmaallisista aineista. Suomalaisen Kirjallisuuden Seura, Helsinki.

Friedl, John, 1976: Cultural Anthropology. Harper's College Press, New York.

Fritze, Georg, 1930: Der neue Name: Das neue Leben der Dschaggachristen im Lichte ihrer Taufnamen. Verlag der Evangelisch-lutherischen Mission, Leipzig.

Galton, Francis, 1853: The Narrative of an Explorer in Tropical South Africa, London.

Gerritzen, Doreen, 1998: First Name Choices in the Netherlands 1992–1995. In: Nicolaisen, W.F.H. (ed.), Proceedings of the XIXth International Congress of Onomastic Sciences, Volume 3, p. 140–147.

Golele, N.C.P., 1991: Compounding as a Process of Naming in Xitsonga. In: Nomina Africana 5(2) 1991, p. 32–38.

Gregersen, Edgar A., 1977: Language in Africa: An Introductory Survey. Gordon and Breach Science Publishers Inc., New York.

Greschat, Hans-Jürgen & Jungraithmayr, Herrmann (ed.), 1969: Wort und Religion: Kalima na dini. Studien zur Afrikanistik, Missionswissenschaft, Religionswissenschaft. Ernst Dammann zum 65. Geburtstag. Evangelischer Missionsverlag GmbH, Stuttgart.

Gulliver, P.H., 1952: Bell-Oxen and Ox-Names among the Jie. In: Uganda Journal, Vol. 16, 1952, p. 72–75.

Gunner, Liz & Gwala, Mafika, 1994a: Introduction: Izibongo, Power and the Popular Voice. In: Gunner, Liz & Gwala, Mafika (ed.), 1994b: Musho: Zulu Popular Praises, p. 1–52.

Gunner, Liz & Gwala, Mafika (ed.), 1994b: Musho: Zulu Popular Praises. Witwatersrand University Press, Johannesburg.

Haarmann, Harald, 1983: Die Rolle von Eigennamen und Familiennamen im Sprachkontakt. In: Beiträge zur Namenforschung. Neue Folge. Band 18 (1983), Heft 2, p. 154–170.

Hallgren, Roland, 1988: The Good Things in Life: A Study of the Traditional Religious Culture of the Yoruba People. Plus Ultra, Löberöd.

Hammond, Peter B. (ed.), 1969: Cultural and Social Anthropology: Selected Readings. 10th printing. Collier-Macmillan Limited, London.

Hanks, Patrick & Hodges, Flavia, 1990: A Dictionary of First Names. Oxford University Press, Oxford.

Haslett, Beth, 1989: Communication and Language Acquisition Within a Cultural Context. In: Ting-Toomey, Stella & Korzenny, Felipe (ed.), Language, Communication, and Culture, p. 19–34.

Hastings, Adrian, 1976: African Christianity: An Essay in Interpretation. Geoffrey Chapman, London.

Henle, Paul, 1969: Language, Thought, and Culture. In: Hammond, Peter B. (ed.), Cultural and Social Anthropology: Selected Readings, p. 378–392.

Herbert, R.K., 1995: The Sociolinguistics of Personal Names: Two South African Case Studies. In: South African Journal of African Languages 15(1) 1995, p. 1–8.

Herbert, R.K., 1996: The Dynamics of Personal Names and Naming Practices in Africa. In: Eichler, Ernst & Hilty, Gerold & Löffler, Heinrich & Steger, Hugo & Zgusta, Ladislav (ed.), Namenforschung. Volume 2, p. 1222–1227.

Herbert, Robert K., 1997: The Politics of Personal Naming in South Africa. In: Names 45(1) 1997, p. 3–17.

Herbert, Robert K., 1998: Personal Naming and Social Organization: The Comparative Anthroponymy of Southern Africa. In: Nicolaisen, W.F.H. (ed.), Proceedings of the XIXth International Congress of Onomastic Sciences, Volume 3, p. 187–194.

Herbert, Robert K., 1999a: Anthroponymy and Culture Change in Southern Africa. In: Onoma 34, 1999, p. 215–227.

Herbert, Robert K., 1999b: Personal Names as Social Protest: The Status of African Political Names. In: Names 47(2) 1999, p. 109–124.

Herbert, R.K. & Bogatsu, Senna, 1990: Changes in Northern Sotho and Tswana Personal Naming Patterns. In: Nomina Africana 4(2) 1990, p. 1–14.

Herskovits, Melville J., 1958: Acculturation: The Study of Culture Contact. Peter Smith, Cloucester, Mass.

Herskovits, Melville J., 1967: The Human Factor in Changing Africa. Alfred A. Knopf, New York.

Hiebert, Paul G., 1983: Cultural Anthropology. 2nd edition. Baker Book House, Grand Rapids, Michigan.

Hoebel, E. Adamson, 1972: Anthropology: The Study of Man. 4th edition. McGraw-Hill Book Company, New York.

Hurskainen, Arvi & Siiriäinen, Ari, 1995: Afrikan kulttuurien juuret. Tietolipas 134. Suomalaisen Kirjallisuuden Seura, Helsinki.

Ikenga-Metuh, Emefie, 1987: The Shattered Microcosm: A Critical Survey of Explanations of Conversion in Africa. In: Petersen, Kristen Holst (ed.), Religion, Development and African Identity, p. 11–27.

Introduction to African Culture: General Aspects. 1979. United Nations Educational, Scientific and Cultural Organization, Paris.

Iso Raamatun tietosanakirja 1973. Toinen osa. Illustrert Bibelleksikon A/S Oslo, Kuopio.

Iwundu, Mataebere, 1973: Igbo Anthroponyms: Linguistic Evidence for Reviewing the Ibo Culture. In: Names 21, 1973, p. 46–49.

Jenni, Ernst, 1996: Biblische Namen. In: Eichler, Ernst & Hilty, Gerold & Löffler, Heinrich & Steger, Hugo & Zgusta, Ladislav (ed.), Namenforschung. Volume 2, p. 1853–1856.

Jespersen, Otto, 1924: The Philosophy of Grammar. Allen & Unwin, London.

Kaleta, Zofia, 1990: On the Stabilization of Slavic Surnames. In: Närhi, Eeva Maria (ed.), ICOS 1990 Helsinki, Volume 1, p. 53–68.

Kangas, Urpo, 1991: Ihmisen nimi: Nimenmääräytymisen oikeudelliset rajat. Lakimiesliiton kustannus, Helsinki.

Kasanko, A. (ed.), 1982: Nimi ja usko: Ortodoksinen ristimänimiopas. 2nd edition. Ortodoksinen veljestö, Joensuu.

Kepsu, Saulo, 1991: Forna finska förnamn. In: Studia anthroponymica Scandinavica 9, 1991, p. 33–59.

Kidd, Dudley, 1906: Savage Childhood: A Study of Kafir Children. Adam and Charles Black, London.

Kimenyi, Alexandre, 1989: Kinyarwanda and Kirundi Names: A Semiolinguistic Analysis of Bantu Onomastics. African Studies. Volume 7. The Edwin Mellen Press, Lewiston.

Kirby, Jon B., 1994: Cultural Change & Religious Conversion in West Africa. In: Blakely, Thomas D. & Van Beek, Walter E.A. & Thomson, Dennis L. 1994, Religion in Africa, p. 57–71.

Kiviniemi, Eero, 1982a: Rakkaan lapsen monet nimet: Suomalaisten etunimet ja nimenvalinta. Weilin+Göös, Espoo.

Kiviniemi, Eero, 1982b: Suomen varhaisiin henkilönnimisysteemeihin liittyviä ongelmia. In: Suku ja tieto: Sukututkimuspäivien esitelmiä 1979–1980, p. 29–43.

Kiviniemi, Eero, 1990: Perustietoa paikannimistä. Suomalaisen Kirjallisuuden Seuran Toimituksia 516. Suomalaisen Kirjallisuuden Seura, Helsinki.

Kiviniemi, Eero, 1993: Iita Linta Maria: Etunimiopas vuosituhannen vaihteeseen. Suomalaisen Kirjallisuuden Seura, Helsinki.

Kiviniemi, Eero, 1998: History of First Names of Finnish Origin. In: Nicolaisen, W.F.H. (ed.), Proceedings of the XIXth International Congress of Onomastic Sciences. Volume 3, p. 212–217.

Kleinöder, Rudolf, 1996: Konfessionelle Namengebung in der Oberpfalz von der Reformation bis zur Gegenwart. Europäische Hochschulschriften, Reihe XXI: Linguistik, Bd. 165. Peter Lang, Frankfurt am Main.

De Klerk, Vivian & Bosch, Barbara, 1995: Naming in Two Cultures: English and Xhosa Practices. In: Nomina Africana 9(1) 1995, p. 68–85.

De Klerk, Vivian & Bosch, Barbara, 1996: Naming Practices in the Eastern Cape Province of South Africa. In: Names 44(3) 1996, p. 167–188.

Kohlheim, Rosa, 1996a: Entstehung und geschichtliche Entwicklung der Familiennamen in Deutschland. In: Eichler, Ernst & Hilty, Gerold & Löffler, Heinrich & Steger, Hugo & Zgusta, Ladislav (ed.), Namenforschung. Volume 2, p. 1280–1284.

Kohlheim, Rosa, 1996b: Typologie und Benennungssysteme bei Familiennamen: prinzipiell und kulturvergleichend. In: Eichler, Ernst & Hilty, Gerold & Löffler, Heinrich & Steger, Hugo & Zgusta, Ladislav (ed.), Namenforschung. Volume 2, p. 1247–1259.

Kohlheim, Volker, 1977a: Regensburger Rufnamen des 13. und. 14. Jahrhunderts: Linguistische und sozio-onomastische Untersuchungen zu Struktur und Motivik spätmittelalterlicher Anthroponymie. Zeitschrift für Dialektologie und Linguistik. Herausgegeben von Joachim Göschel & Werner H. Veith. Beihefte. Neue Folge Nr. 19. Der Zeitschrift für Mundartforschung. Franz Steiner Verlag GmbH, Wiesbaden.

Kohlheim, Volker, 1977b: Zur Erforschung der Diffusion onomastischer Innovationen. In: Beiträge zur Namenforschung. Neue Folge. Band 12 (1977), p. 1–34.

Kohlheim, Volker, 1996a: Die christliche Namengebung. In: Eichler, Ernst & Hilty, Gerold & Löffler, Heinrich & Steger, Hugo & Zgusta, Ladislav (ed.), Namenforschung. Volume 2, p. 1048–1057.

Kohlheim, Volker, 1996b: Fremde Rufnamen. In: Eichler, Ernst & Hilty, Gerold & Löffler, Heinrich & Steger, Hugo & Zgusta, Ladislav (ed.), Namenforschung. Volume 2, p. 1203–1207.

Kohlheim, Volker, 1998: Towards a Definition of the Onymic System. In: Nicolaisen, W.F.H. (ed.), Proceedings of the XIXth International Congress of Onomastic Sciences, Volume 1, p. 173–178.

Koopman, Adrian, 1979a: The Linguistic Difference between Nouns and Names in Zulu. In: African Studies 38(1) 1979, p. 67–80.

Koopman, Adrian, 1979b: Male and Female Names in Zulu. In: African Studies 38(2) 1979, p. 153–166.

Koopman, Adrian, 1987a: The Praises of Young Zulu Men. In: Theoria Vol. 70, 1987, p. 41–54.

Koopman, Adrian, 1987b: Zulu Names and Other Modes of Address. In: Nomina Africana 1(1) 1987, p. 136–164.

Koopman, Adrian, 1989: The Aetiology of Zulu Personal Names. In: Nomina Africana 3(2) 1989, p. 31–48.

Koopman, Adrian, 1992: The Socio-Cultural Aspects of Zulu Ox- and Dog-Names. In: Nomina Africana 6(1) 1992, p. 1–13.

Kremer, Ludger, 1986: Vornamenwandel zwischen 1400 und 1800: Die Bürgerbücher von Ahaus (1400–1811) und Ottenstein (1476–1664) als namenkundliche Quelle. In: Cox, H.L. & Vanacker, V.F. & Verhofstadt, E. (ed.), Wortes Anst – Verbi gratia, p. 277–286.

Krige, Eileen Jensen, 1988: The Social System of the Zulus. [Originally published in Great Britain by Longmans Green & Co. Ltd (1936).] Tenth impression. Shuter & Shooter, Pietermaritzburg.

Kripke, Saul, 1980: Naming and Necessity. Basil Blackwell, Oxford.

Kroeber, A.L., 1948: Anthropology. New revised edition. Harcourt, Brace and Company, New York.

Kroeber, Alfred L., 1987: The Nature of Culture. In: Applebaum, Herbert (ed.), Perspectives in Cultural Anthropology, p. 80–84.

Kroeber, A.L. & Kluckhohn, C., 1952: Culture: A Critical Review of Concepts and Definitions. Vintage Books, New York.

Kruken, Kristoffer (ed.), 1995: Slektsnamn i Norden. Rapport frå NORNAs tjueførste symposium i Oslo 17.–20. september 1992. Norna-rapporter 58. Norna-förlaget, Uppsala.

Landar, Herbert, 1966: Language and Culture. Oxford University Press, New York.

Langacker, Ronald W., 1994: Culture, Cognition, and Grammar. In: Pütz, Martin (ed.), Language Contact and Language Conflict, p. 25–53.

Van Langendonck, Willy, 1990: On the Combination of Forename and Surname, with Special Reference to Flemish Dialects. In: Närhi, Eeva Maria (ed.), ICOS 1990 Helsinki, Volume 2, p. 436–443.

Van Langendonck, Willy, 1995: Name Systems and Name Strata. In: Eichler, Ernst & Hilty, Gerold & Löffler, Heinrich & Steger, Hugo & Zgusta, Ladislav (ed.), Namenforschung. Volume 1, p. 485–489.

Van Langendonck, Willy, 1996: Bynames. In: Eichler, Ernst & Hilty, Gerold & Löffler, Heinrich & Steger, Hugo & Zgusta, Ladislav (ed.), Namenforschung. Volume 2, p. 1228–1232.

Van Langendonck, Willy, 1997: Proper Names and their Categorical Presupposition. In: Pitkänen, Ritva Liisa & Mallat, Kaija (ed.), You Name it: Perspectives on Onomastic Research, p. 37–46.

Langness, L.L., 1985: The Study of Culture. 7th printing (1st printing 1974). Chandler & Sharp Publishers, Inc., Los Angeles.

Laur, Wolfgang, 1989: Der Name: Beiträge zur allgemeinen Namenkunde und ihrer Grundlegung. In: Beiträge zur Namenforschung, Neue Folge, Beiheft 28. Carl Winter, Heidelberg.

Lehmann, Arno, 1969: Der neue Name. In: Greschat, Hans-Jürgen & Jungraithmayr, Herrmann (ed.), Wort und Religion, p. 172–181.

Lempiäinen, Pentti, 1965: Kastekäytäntö Suomen kirkossa 1500- ja 1600-luvulla. Suomen kirkkohistoriallinen seura, Helsinki.

Lindgren, Björn, 1998: Ndebele Identity as a Practice of Naming: Negotiation of Social Position in Umzingwane, Zimbabwe. In: Andersson, Thorsten & Brylla, Eva & Jacobson-Widding, Anita (ed.), Personnamn och social identitet, p. 53–71.

Lucas, W.V., 1950: Christianity and Native Rites. Central Affica House Press, London.

Luther, Martti, 1983a–b: Valitut teokset I–II. Edited by Lennart Pinomaa. 2nd edition. Werner Söderström Osakeyhtiö, Porvoo.

Madubuike, Ihechukwu, 1976: A Handbook of African Names. Three Continents Press, Washington, D.C.

Magesa, Laurenti, 1998: African Religion: The Moral Traditions of Abundant Life. Paulines Publications Africa, Nairobi.

Maliniemi, Aarno, 1947: Henkilönnimet esihistoriallisena ja katolisena aikana. In: Teppo, Hannes & Vilkuna, Kustaa (ed.), Etunimikirja, p. 40–57.

Malinowski, Bronislaw, 1945: The Dynamics of Culture Change: An Inquiry into Race Relations in Africa. Yale University Press, New Haven.

Mbiti, John S., 1969: African Religions & Philosophy. Heinemann, London.

Mbiti, John S., 1991: Introduction to African Religion. 2nd revised edition. Heinemann International Literature and Textbooks, Oxford.

Meldgaard, Eva Villarsen 1994: De kristne personnavne kommer. In: Fellows-Jensen, Gillian & Holmberg, Bente (ed.), Vikingetidens sted- og personnavne, p. 201–217.

Menzel, Gustav, 1978: Die Rheinische Mission: Aus 150 Jahren Missionsgeschichte. Verlag der Vereinigten Evangelischen Mission, Wuppertal.

Mikkonen, Pirjo & Paikkala, Sirkka, 1992: Sukunimet. 3rd printing. Kustannusosakeyhtiö Otava, Helsinki.

Mill, John Stuart, 1906: A System of Logic: Ratiocinative and Inductive. 8th edition. Longmans, Green, and Co., London.

Mirbt, Carl, 1905: Die evangelische Mission als Kulturmacht. Beiträge zur Missionskunde, 9. Heft. Buchhandlung der Berliner evangelischen Missionsgesellschaft, Berlin.

Mohome, Paulus M., 1972: Naming in Sesotho: Its Sociocultural and Linguistic Basis. In: Names 20, 1972, p. 171–185.

Morgan, Gerald, 1995: Naming Welsh Women. In: Nomina, Journal of the Society for Name Studies in Britain and Ireland 18/1995, p. 119–139.

Moyo, Themba, 1996: Personal Names and Naming Practices in Northern Malawi. In: Nomina Africana 10 (1–2) 1996, p. 10–19.

Mtuze, P.T., 1994: Towards Decolonizing African Culture. In: Nordic Journal of African Studies 3(2) 1994, p. 92–100.

Mugambi, J.N.K., 1995: From Liberation to Reconstruction: African Christian Theology After the Cold War. East African Educational Publishers, Nairobi.

Murphy, Robert F., 1989: Cultural and Social Anthropology: An Overture. 3rd edition. Prentice Hall, Englewood Cliffs, New Jersey.

Musere, Jonathan, 1998: Proverbial Names of the Baganda. Research report. In: Names 46 (1) 1998, p. 73–79.

Nanda, Serena, 1987: Cultural Anthropology. 3rd edition. Wadsworth Publishing Company, Belmont, California.

Närhi, Eeva Maria (ed.), 1990: ICOS 1990 Helsinki. Proceedings of the XVIIth International Congress of Onomastic Sciences. Volumes 1 & 2. The University of Helsinki and the Finnish Research Centre for Domestic Languages, Helsinki.

Nau, Tim, 1993: The Names of the Popes. In: Onomastica Canadiana 75(2) 1993, p. 59–66.

Ndimande, Nobuhle, 1998: A Semantic Analysis of Zulu Surnames. In: Nomina Africana 12(2) 1998, p. 88–98.

Ndoma, Ungina, 1977: Kongo Personal Names Today: a Sketch. In: Names 25, 1977, p. 88–98.

Neethling, S.J., 1988: Voorname in Xhosa. In: Nomina Africana 2(2) 1988, p. 223–238.

Neethling, S.J., 1990: Iziteketiso in Xhosa. In: Nomina Africana 4(1) 1990, p. 11–34.

Neethling, S.J., 1994: Xhosa Nicknames. In: South African Journal of African Languages 14(2) 1994, p. 88–92.

Neethling, Siebert J., 1995: Names and Naming in Xhosa. In: Eichler, Ernst & Hilty, Gerold & Löffler, Heinrich & Steger, Hugo & Zgusta, Ladislav (ed.), Namenforschung. Volume 1, p. 956–959.

Neethling, S.J., 1996: Exploring Xhosa Surnames. In: Nomina Africana 10(1–2) 1996, p. 30–42.

Neumann, Isolde, 1973: Zur Herausbildung des anthroponymischen Prinzips der Doppelnamigkeit. In: Eichler, Ernst & Fleischer, Wolfgang & Große, Rudolf & Neubert, Albrecht & Walther, Hans (ed.), Der Name in Sprache und Gesellschaft: Beiträge zur Theorie der Onomastik, p. 192–202.

Nicolaisen, Wilhelm F.H., 1995: Name and Appellative. In: Eichler, Ernst & Hilty, Gerold & Löffler, Heinrich & Steger, Hugo & Zgusta, Ladislav (ed.), Namenforschung. Volume 1, p. 384–393.

Nicolaisen, W.F.H. (ed.), 1998: Proceedings of the XIXth International Congress of Onomastic Sciences Aberdeen, August 4–11, 1996. Scope, Perspectives and Methods of Onomastics. Volumes 1 & 3. Department of English, University of Aberdeen, Aberdeen.

Nissilä, Viljo, 1965: Tutkimus itämerensuomalaisesta henkilönnimistöstä. In: Virittäjä 1965/1, p. 78–89.

Njock, Pierre Emmanuel, 2001: Die Bàsàa-Sprache im Kontakt mit den europäischen Sprachen: Entlehnungen aus dem Deutschen. In: IDS Sprachreport. Informationen und Meinungen zur deutschen Sprache. Herausgegeben vom Institut für Deutsche Sprache, Mannheim. Heft 1/2001. 17. Jahrgang, p. 11–13.

Nsimbi, N.B., 1950: Baganda Traditional Personal Names. In: Uganda Journal, Vol. 14, 1950, p. 204–214.

Nyaga, Daniel Fr., 1997: Customs and Traditions of the Meru. East African Educational Publishers, Nairobi.

Obeng, Samuel Gyasi, 1998: Akan Death-Prevention Names: A Pragmatic and Structural Analysis. In: Names 46 (3) 1998, p. 163–187.

Ojoade, J. Olowo, 1980: African Proverbial Names: 101 Ilaje Examples. In: Names 28, 1980, p. 195–214.

Okere, Theophilus, 1996a: Names as Building Blocks of an African Philosophy. In: Okere, Theophilus (ed.), Identity and Change, p. 133–149.

Okere, Theophilus (ed.), 1996b: Identity and Change. Nigerian Philosophical Studies, I. Published with the support of CIPSH/UNESCO by Paideia Publishers. The Council for Research in Values and Philosophy. Washington DC.

Omari, C.K., 1970: Personal Names in Socio-cultural Context. In: Kiswahili 40(2) 1970, p. 65–71.

Osuntoki, Chief, 1970: The Book of African Names. Drum and Spear, Washington D.C.

Paikkala, Sirkka, 1988: Finnische Familiennamen auf -(i)nen. In: Studia anthroponymica Scandinavica. Årgång 6, p. 27–69.

Paikkala, Sirkka, 1995: Från olika namnsystem till ett enhetligt släktnamnssystem i Finland. In: Kruken, Kristoffer (ed.), Slektsnamn i Norden, p. 109–127.

Palva, Heikki, 1974: Raamatun tietosanasto. Werner Söderström Osakeyhtiö, Porvoo.

Parrinder, Geoffrey, 1969: Religion in Africa. Penguin African Library, AP 26. Penguin Books Ltd, Harmondsworth, Middlesex, England.

Parrinder, Geoffrey, 1981: African Traditional Religion. 3rd edition, 4th impression. Sheldon Press, London.

Peil, Margaret & Oyeneye, Olatunji, 1998: Consensus, Conflict and Change: A Sociological Introduction to African Societies. East African Educational Publishers, Nairobi.

Petersen, Kristen Holst (ed.), 1987: Religion, Development and African Identity. Seminar Proceedings No 17. Scandinavian Institute of African Studies, Uppsala.

Pitkänen, Ritva Liisa & Mallat, Kaija (ed.), 1997: You Name it: Perspectives on Onomastic Research. Studia Fennica. Linguistica 7. Finnish Literature Society, Helsinki.

Pollock, John L., 1982: Language and Thought. Princeton University Press, Princeton.

Pulgram, Ernst, 1993: Historisch-soziologische Betrachtung des modernen Familiennamens. In: Debus, Friedhelm & Seibicke, Wilfried (ed.), Reader zur Namenkunde II: Anthroponymie, p. 319–350.

Pütz, Martin (ed.), 1994: Language Contact and Language Conflict. John Benjamins Publishing Company, Amsterdam.

Raper, P.E., 1983: Sociology and the Study of Names. Occasional paper 5. Human Sciences Research Council, Pretoria.

Raper, P.E., (ed.), 1986: Names 1983: Proceedings of the Second Southern African Names Congress, Pretoria, 13–15 September 1983. Human Sciences Research Council, Pretoria.

Raper, P.E., 1995: South African Onomastics. In: Eichler, Ernst & Hilty, Gerold & Löffler, Heinrich & Steger, Hugo & Zgusta, Ladislav (ed.), Namenforschung. Volume 1, p. 256–264.

Ryan, Pauline M., 1981: An Introduction to Hausa Personal Nomenclature. In: Names 29, 1981, p. 139–164.

Saunders, George R., 1988a: Transformations of Christianity: Some General Observations. In: Saunders, George R. (ed.), Culture and Christianity, p. 179–193.

Saunders, George R. (ed.), 1988b: Culture and Christianity: The Dialectics of Transformation. Greenwood Press, New York.

Schneider, Edgar, 1994: Eigennamen. Eine sprachphilosophische Untersuchung. Königshausen & Neumann GmbH, Würtzburg.

Schwarz, Ernst 1949: Deutsche Namenforschung. 1. Ruf- und Familiennamen. Vandenhoeck & Ruprecht, Göttingen.

Seibicke, Wilfried, 1982: Die Personennamen im Deutschen. Sammlung Göschen 2218. Walter de Gruyter, Berlin.

Seibicke, Wilfried, 1996: Typologie und Benennungssysteme. In: Eichler, Ernst & Hilty, Gerold & Löffler, Heinrich & Steger, Hugo & Zgusta, Ladislav (ed.), Namenforschung. Volume 2, p. 1176–1178.

Service, Elman R., 1975: The Prime-Mover of Cultural Evolution. In: Brady, Ivan A. & Isaac, Barry L. (ed.), A Reader in Culture Change, p. 85–98.

Siebs, Benno Eide, 1970: Die Personennamen der Germanen. Dr. Martin Sändig oHG., Wiesbaden.

Siiriäinen, Ari, 1995: Ihmisen ja talousmuotojen kehitys Afrikassa. In: Hurskainen, Arvi & Siiriäinen, Ari, Afrikan kulttuurien juuret, p. 17–147.

Von Staden, Paul M.S. 1987: Persoonsname in Zulu. In: South African Journal of Linguistics 5(1) 1987, p. 171–189.

De Stadler, L.G., 1990: Proper Names in South Africa: A Sociological Perspective. In: Närhi, Eeva Maria (ed.), ICOS 1990 Helsinki, Volume 2, p. 377–384.

Stauffer, S. Anita (ed.), 1998: Baptism, Rites of Passage, and Culture. LWF Studies 1/1999. The Lutheran World Federation, Department for Theology and Studies, Geneva.

Steward, Julian H., 1963: Theory of Culture Change: The Methodology of Multilinear Evolution. University of Illinois Press, Urbana.

Stoebke, Detlef-Eckhard, 1964: Die alten ostseefinnischen Personennamen im Rahmen eines urfinnischen Namensystems. Nord- und osteuropäische Geschichtsstudien. Band IV. Leibniz-Verlag, Hamburg.

Suku ja tieto: Sukututkimuspäivien esitelmiä 1979–1980. 1982. Suomen sukututkimusseuran julkaisuja 34. Suomen sukututkimusseura, Helsinki.

Sumbwa, Nyambe, 1997: Some Zambian Names as Sources of Diversified Knowledge: The Barotse and Other Examples. In: Nomina Africana 11(2) 1997, p. 47–66.

Summerell, Orrin F., 1995: Philosophy of Proper Names. In: Eichler, Ernst & Hilty, Gerold & Löffler, Heinrich & Steger, Hugo & Zgusta, Ladislav (ed.), Namenforschung. Volume 1, p. 368–372.

Suzman, Susan M., 1994: Names as Pointers: Zulu Personal Naming Practices. In: Language in Society 23(2) 1994, p. 253–272.

Šrámek, Rudolf, 1978: Zu den theoretischen Problemen der Namenforschung im Sprachkontakt. In: Onoma XXII, 1978, p. 388–401.

Tengan, Alexis B., 1994: European Languages in African Society and Culture: A View on Cultural Authenticity. In: Pütz, Martin (ed.), Language Contact and Language Conflict, p. 125–138.

Teppo, Hannes & Vilkuna, Kustaa (ed.), 1947: Etunimikirja. Tietolipas 5. Suomalaisen Kirjallisuuden Seura, Helsinki.

Thipa, H.M., 1986: By their Names you shall Know them. In: Raper, Peter (ed.), Names 1983, p. 286–291.

Thonus, Terese, 1991: The Influence of English on Female Names in Brazil. In: Names 39(1) 1991, p. 27–38.

Ting-Toomey, Stella & Korzenny, Felipe (ed.), 1989: Language, Communication, and Culture: Current Directions. International and Intercultural Communication. Annual Volume XIII, 1989. SAGE Publications, Newbury Park.

Titiev, Mischa, 1959: Introduction to Cultural Anthropology. Holt, Rinehart and Winston, New York.

Trigg, Jonathan D., 1994: Baptism in the Theology of Martin Luther. E.J. Brill, Leiden.

Turnbull, Colin M., 1966: Tradition and Change in African Tribal Life. The World Publishing Company, Cleveland.

Turnbull, Colin M., 1976: Man in Africa. Penguin Books Ltd, Harmondsworth, Middlesex, England.

Turner, Noleen S., 1992: Zulu Names as Echoes of Censure, Discontent and Disapproval within the Domestic Environment. In: Nomina Africana 6(2) 1992, p. 42–56.

Turner, Noleen S., 1997: Onomastic Caricatures: Names Given to Employers and Co-workers by Black Employees. In: Nomina Africana 11(1) 1997, p. 50–66.

Tylor, Edward B., 1974: Primitive Culture: Researches into the Development of Mythology, Philosophy, Religion, Art, and Custom. Vol. I. Gordon Press, New York.

Utterström, Gudrun, 1994: Personnamn – gränsöverskridande och begränsning. In: Edlund, Lars-Erik (ed.), Kulturgränser – myt eller verklighet?, p. 287–296.

Vandebosch, Heidi 1998: The Influence of Media on Given Names. In: Names 46(4) 1998, p. 243–262.

Vermeersch, Etienne, 1977: An Analysis of the Concept of Culture. In: Bernardi, Bernardo (ed.), The Concept and Dynamics of Culture, p. 9–73.

Vilkuna, Kustaa, 1947: Uudempien suomalaisten etunimien historiaa. In: Teppo, Hannes & Vilkuna, Kustaa (ed.), Etunimikirja, p. 58–92.

Visser, Hessel & Visser, Cobi, 1998: Analysis of Naro Names. In: Bank, Andrew & Heese, Hans & Loff, Chris (ed.), The Proceedings of the Khoisan Identities and Cultural Heritage Conference, p. 225–231.

Wardhaugh, Ronald, 1992: An Introduction to Sociolinguistics. 2nd edition. Blackwell, Oxford.

Warneck, G., 1900: Evangelische Missionslehre: Ein missionstheoretischer Versuch. Friedrich Andreas Perthes, Gotha.

Weinreich, Uriel, 1968: Languages in Contact: Findings and Problems. 6th edition. Mouton, The Hague.

White, Leslie A., 1969: The Evolution of Culture. In: Hammond, Peter B. (ed.), Cultural and Social Anthropology: Selected Readings, p. 406–426.

Wieschhoff, H.A., 1941: The Social Significance of Names among the Ibo of Nigeria. In: American Anthropologist. Vol. 43, 1941.

Wilson, Stephen, 1998: The Means of Naming: A Social and Cultural History of Personal Naming in Western Europe. UCL Press Limited, London.

Wittgenstein, Ludwig, 1922: Tractatus Logico-Philosophicus. German/English. Kegan Paul, Trench, Trubner & Co., London.

World Bank Atlas 2000. The World Bank, Washington, DC, USA.

Books of Reference
(Name books, dictionaries etc. used for the analysis of the name data)

Afrikaanse Voorname. 196X. Opgestel deur die Taalkomissie van die Suid-Afrikaanse Akademie vir Wetenskap en Kuns. Heer Drukkers (EDMS) BPK, Pretoria.

Bahlow, Hans, 1967: Deutsches Namenlexikon. Familien- und Vornamen nach Ursprung und Sinn erklärt. Keysersche Verlagsbuchhandlung, München.

Bosman, D.B. & Van der Merwe, I.W. & Hiemstra, L.W., 1962: Tweetalige Woordeboek Afrikaans – Engels. 4th edition. Nasionale Boekhandel Bpk, Johannesburg.

Bosman, D.B. & Van der Merwe, I.W. & Barnes, A.S.V., 1997: Tweetalige Sakwoordeboek Afrikaans–Engels Engels–Afrikaans. Pharos Woordeboeke, Nasionale Boekhandel Beperk, Kaapstad.

Burkart, Walter, 1993: Neues Lexikon der Vornamen. Bastei–Lübbe-Taschenbuch. Naumann & Göbel Verlagsgesellschaft, Köln.

Drosdowski, Günther, 1968: Lexikon der Vornamen: Herkunft, Bedeutung und Gebrauch von mehr als 3000 Vornamen. Duden-Taschenbücher. Bibliographisches Institut, Mannheim.

Dunkling, Leslie & Gosling, William, 1983: Everyman's Dictionary of First Names. J.M. Dent & Sons Ltd., London.

English–Ndonga Dictionary 1996. Compiled by ELCIN Church Council Special Committees. Resolution 292/92. ELCIN Printing Press, Oniipa.

Farmer, David, 1996: The Oxford Dictionary of Saints. 3rd edition. Oxford University Press, Oxford.

Hanks, Patrick & Hodges, Flavia, 1990: A Dictionary of First Names. Oxford University Press, Oxford.

Huizinga, A., 1957: Encyclopedie van voornamen. Een vraagbaak over de afkomst en betekenis van onze Nederlandse en Vlaamse voornamen. A.J.G. Strengholt's Uitgeversmaatschappij N.V., Amsterdam.

Internationales Handbuch der Vornamen – International Handbook of Forenames – Manuel international des prénoms. 1986. Herausgegeben von der Gesellschaft für deutsche Sprache e.V., Wiesbaden, und dem Bundesverband der deutschen Standesbeamten e.V., Bad Salzschlirf. Verlag für Standesamtswesen, Frankfurt am Main.

Johansson, Karin, 1991: Namnboken. Läsförlaget ab, Trondhjem.

Lempiäinen, Pentti, 1983: Nimipäiväsanat. Kirjapaja, Helsinki.

Mackensen, Lutz, 1987: Das große Buch der Vornamen. Herkunft, Ableitungen und Verbreitung, Koseformen, berühmte Namensträger, Gedenk- und Namenstage, verklungene Vornamen. Ullstein-Buch Nr. 34425. Ullstein-Sachbuch, Frankfurt/M.

Magnusson, Magnus (ed.), 1990: Chambers Biographical Dictionary. 5th edition. W & R Chambers Ltd, Cambridge.

Malmsten, Anders, 1993: Nittiotalets namnbok: Med 3000 namnförslag. Bokförlaget Prisma, Stockholm.

Nienaber, G.S., 1955: Afrikaanse familiename: 'n geselsie vir belangstellende leke oor die betekenis van ouer Afrikaanse vanne. A.A. Balkema, Kaapstad.

Omaimbilo gOngerki Onkwaevangeli pa Luther yOwambokavango. I. Ndonga & Kwanyama. 1967. Enyanyangidho lyoopalekululwa, lya ziminwa kOshigongingerki shomumvo 1966. Finnish Mission Press, Oniipa.

Ombibeli Ondjapuki moshindonga 1954. (The Holy Bible in Ndonga). Bibelihangeno lja Britania no ljiilongo, London.

Ombimbeli Ondjapuki 1977. (The Bible in Ndonga). First edition 1954, second edition (standard orthography) 1977. Bible Society of South Africa, Cape Town.

Ombimbeli Ondjapuki 1986. (The Bible in Ndonga). First edition. Bible Society of South Africa, Cape Town.

Ondjalulamasiku Jomumvo 1938. 1938. Suomen Lähetysseura, Oniipa.

Pyhä Raamattu 1951. Raamatunkäännöskomitean tekemä yleisen kirkolliskokouksen v. 1938 hyväksymä uusi suomennos. Werner Söderström Osakeyhtiö, Porvoo.

Raamattu. 1992. Suomen evankelis-luterilaisen kirkon kirkolliskokouksen vuonna 1992 käyttöön ottama suomennos. Kirjapaja, Suomen Kirkon Sisälähetysseura, Helsinki.

Van Rooyen, Annelize, 1994: Die Afrikaanse Naamboek. Queillerie-Uitgewers (Edms.) Bpk., Kaapstad.

Rosenthal, Eric, 1965: South African Surnames. Howard Timmins, Cape Town.

Salmi, J.W. & Linkomies, Edwin, 1976: Latinalais-suomalainen sanakirja. 9th printing. Otava, Helsinki.

Van der Schaar, J., 1992: Woordenboek van voornamen. Prisma Woordenboeken. Het Spectrum BV, Utrecht.

Schill, Ines, 1990: 4000 Vornamen aus aller Welt: Von Adrian bis Zarah. Niederhausen/ Ts., Basserman.

Schwegel, Janet, 1990: The Baby Name Countdown: Meanings and Popularity Ratings for over 50.000 Names. Paragon House, New York.

Seibicke, Wilfried, 1996: Historisches deutsches Vornamenbuch. Band 1, A–E. Walter de Gruyter, Berlin.

Teinonen, Seppo A., 1999: Teologian sanakirja: 7400 termiä. Kirjapaja, Helsinki.

Telecom Namibia 92/93. Telephone and Telex Directory. Telecom Namibia Limited, Windhoek.

Tirronen, T.E., 1986: Ndonga–English Dictionary. ELOC Printing Press, Oniipa.

Tirronen, Toivo E., 1980: Ndongan kielen sanakirja. Suomen Lähetysseura, Helsinki.

Vilkuna, Kustaa, 1993: Etunimet. 3rd edition. Kustannusosakeyhtiö Otava, Helsinki.

Vuorela, Vilho (ed.), 1951: Raamatun hakusanakirja I: Vanha testamentti. Werner Söderström Osakeyhtiö, Helsinki.

Vuorela, Vilho (ed.), 1954: Raamatun hakusanakirja II: Uusi testamentti. Werner Söderström Osakeyhtiö, Helsinki.

Wasserzieher, Ernst, 1964: Hans und Grete: Zweitausend Vornamen erklärt. Fried. Dümmlers Verlag, Bonn.

Withycombe E.G., 1977: The Oxford Dictionary of English Christian Names. 3rd edition. Oxford University Press, Oxford.

Yliopiston Nimipäiväalmanakka – Universitetets namndagsalmanacka – Universitehta nammabeaivealmmenáhkki. Vuodeksi – För året – Jahkái 2000. 1999. Viides vuosikerta. Helsingin yliopisto. Otava, Keuruu.

Unpublished Theses and Manuscripts

Dickens, Sybil Maureen, 1985: Western Influences on the Zulu System of Personal Naming. M.A. thesis in English language, Rhodes University.

Haakana, Martta, 1960: Kristinusko ja kansantavat Ambomaalla. M.Th. thesis in theological ethics, University of Helsinki.

Halme, Riikka, 1998: Tone in Kwanyama Nouns. M.A. thesis in African studies, University of Helsinki.

Hjort af Ornäs, Tiia Riitta, 1987: Efundula: Tyttöjen aikuistumisrituaali Ambokuanjamakulttuurin kokonaisuudessa. M.A. thesis in comparative religion, University of Helsinki.

Høy, Arvid, 1995: The Namibian Churches and the Liberation Struggle in the 1960s and 1970s: With an Emphasis on the Role of the Black Lutheran Churches. Postgraduate thesis in history, University of Bergen.

Hukka, Alpo, 1954: Uskonnollisen elämän piiriin kuuluvien käsitteiden ilmaisuvaikeuksista varhaiskantaisessa sielunelämässä. M.A. thesis in psychology, University of Helsinki.

Janse van Vuuren, W.J.H.J., 1966: Die ortografie en klankstelsel van Kwanyama en Ndonga. M.A. Thesis, Potchefstroom University for Christian Higher Education.

Koopman, Adrian, 1986: The Social and Literary Aspects of Zulu Personal Names. M.A. thesis in Zulu language and literature, University of Natal.

Kouvalainen, Marja Liisa, 1980: Ambomaan siirtotyöläisyyden synty. M.A. thesis in economic and social history, University of Helsinki.

Mbenzi, Petrus: Manuscript on Oshiwambo Praise Poetry. Unpublished and undated manuscript, received from the writer at the University of Namibia in October 2000.

Möller, L.A., 1987: A Toponymic-Linguistic Investigation into German Place Names of South West Africa. Ph.D. thesis, University of Natal, Durban.

Nambala, Shekutaamba V.V., 1987: To Remember, to Remind: A Contextual History of the Church in Namibia 1484–1986. M.Th. thesis in church history, Luther Northwestern Theological Seminary, Saint Paul, Minnesota.

Saarelma-Maunumaa, Minna, 1995: Kun Nangulasta tuli Aino: Namibian Ambomaan henkilönnimistö 1883–1993. M.A. thesis in Finnish/onomastics, University of Helsinki.

Saarelma-Maunumaa, Minna, 1997b: Henkilönnimet kulttuurimurroksessa: Kristinuskon ja eurooppalaistumisen vaikutus Namibian Ambomaan henkilönnimistöön. Licentiate thesis in Finnish/onomastics, University of Helsinki.

Salokoski, Märta, 1992: Symbolic Power of Kings in Precolonial Ovambo Societies. Licentiate thesis in sociology / social anthropology, University of Helsinki.

Varis, Tuula, 1988: Kun mustasta Saarasta tehtiin valkoista: Analyysi pastoraalisesta vallasta Suomen Lähetysseuran Ambomaan työssä vuosina 1870–1925. Licentiate thesis in international politics, University of Tampere.

Viljoen, J.J., 1972: Die Konjugasie van die Werkwoord in Ndonga. M.A. thesis, University of South Africa, Pretoria.

Viljoen, J.J., 1979: Die Kopulatief in Ndonga en Kwanyama. Ph.D. thesis, University of South Africa, Pretoria.

Zimmermann, W., 1971: Die selfstandige naamwoord in Kwanyama. M.A. thesis, University of South Africa, Pretoria.

Archive Sources

Valtionarkisto (National Archives of Finland, Helsinki)

Suomen Lähetysseuran arkisto (Archives of the Finnish Missionary Society, FMSA)

Daa:30 Lähetysjohtajan kirjekonseptit ja -jäljennökset (Drafts and Copies of the Letters by the Mission Director)

Dea:4 Afrikan lähetyskenttien tarkastuskertomukset (Inspection Reports on the Mission Fields in Africa)

Eac:3–38 Lähetysjohtajalle lähetyskentiltä saapuneet kirjeet (Letters Received by the Mission Director from the Mission Fields)

Hha:4–15 Afrikan lähettien kokousten pöytäkirjat (Minutes of the Missionary Conferences in Africa)

Hhb:2 Ambolähetystä koskevat kertomukset ja raportit (Reports Concerning the Ovambo Mission)

Hk:2 Muut lähetystyötä koskevat asiakirjat (Other Records Concerning Mission Work)

Hp:10 Julia ja August Hännisen kokoelma (The Julia and August Hänninen Collection)

Hp:34 Kalle Koivun kokoelma (The Kalle Koivu Collection)

Hp:91 Anna ja August Pettisen kokoelma (The Anna and August Pettinen Collection)

Hp:110, 122 Martti Rautasen kokoelma (The Martti Rautanen Collection)

Hp:125 Albin Savolan kokoelma (The Albin Savola Collection)

Hp:XXXIX Nestori Väänäsen kokoelma (The Nestori Väänänen Collection)

Suomen Lähetysseuran henkilöarkisto (Personnel archives of the Finnish Evangelical Lutheran Mission, Helsinki)

Helsingin yliopiston kirjasto (Helsinki University Library, Helsinki)
Coll. 344 Emil Liljebladin kokoelma (The Emil Liljeblad Collection). Afrikan
amboheimojen kansantietoutta. [Collected in Ovamboland by Rev. K. E. Liljeblad
1930–1932.] (ELC)

Joensuun yliopiston historian laitos
(Department of History, University of Joensuu)
Hilma Koivun kokoelma (The Hilma Koivu Collection, HKC) (photo copies of origi-
nal manuscripts)

Baptismal registers of the Evangelical Lutheran Church in Namibia (ELCIN)
(microfilms). Elim, Okahao and Oshigambo congregations.

Archiv der Vereinten Evangelischen Mission
(United Evangelical Mission Archives, Wuppertal-Barmen) (UEMA)

B Personalakten
B/cII:32 G. Viehe
C–H Feldakten
C/h:52 Namakunde, 1899–1914
C/i:20 Rückblick auf 25 Jahre Ovambomission 1917; 1966. (Aug. Wulfhorst: 25 Jahre
unserer Ovambo-Arbeit.)
C/k:22 Vorträge und Aufsätze zur Ovambo-Mission von A. Wulfhorst 1910–1933
Sckär, Karl Ovamboland: Historisches, Ethnographisches, Animismus, Varia. 1932.
(unpublished manuscript)

Bundesarchiv, Berlin (ehem. Zentrales Staatsarchiv der DDR, Potsdam)
(Federal Archives, Berlin) (former Central State Archives of the GDR, Potsdam)

10.01 Reichskolonialamt (RKA)
Nr. 2159 Die Ovambos 1896–1904
Nr. 2235 Verwaltungsmaßnahmen gegenüber der einheimischen Bevölkerung in D-
SWA

Interviews

Amaambo 3.4.1997. Interview with Rev. Eino Amaambo, lecturer of theological studies
at the United Lutheran Theological Seminary Paulinum in Windhoek. Windhoek,
Namibia, 3.4.1997.
Amakali 10.10.2000. Interview with Mr. Petrus Amakali, manager of Gamsberg
Macmillan publishing company and book shop in Oshakati. Oshakati, Namibia,
10.10.2000.
Amkongo 14.4.1997. Interview with Mr. Moses Amkongo, managing director of the
ELCIN Printing Press. Oniipa, Namibia, 14.4.1997.
Amushila 11.10.2000. Interview with father Stefanus Amushila, deacon of the Roman
Catholic Mission in Oshikuku. Oshikuku, Namibia, 11.10.2000.
A. Enkono 18.10.2000. Interview with Rev. Alpo Enkono. Windhoek, Namibia,
18.10.2000.
E. Enkono 14.10.2000. Interview with Ms. Ester Enkono, midwife at the Onandjokwe
Lutheran Hospital. Onandjokwe, Namibia, 14.10.2000.
Hukka 2.3.2000. Interview with Rev. Alpo Hukka, missionary of the Finnish Evangeli-
cal Lutheran Mission in Ovamboland 1947–63, moderator of the Lutheran
Ovambo-Kavango Church 1958–63. Helsinki, Finland, 2.3.2000.
Ihambo 7.10.2000. Interview with Rev. Jefta Ihambo, pastor of the Windhoek City
Congregation of ELCIN. Windhoek, Namibia, 7.10.2000.

Kanana 19.9.2000. Interview with Rev. Aron Kanana. Pietermaritzburg, South Africa, 19.9.2000.

Lehtonen 17.11.1994. Interview with M.A. Lahja Lehtonen, English teacher of Oshigambo High School 1954–1991. Helsinki, Finland, 17.11.1994.

Lehtonen 2.4.1997. Interview with M.A. Lahja Lehtonen. Oniipa, Namibia, 2.4.1997.

Malua 19.9.2000. Interview with Rev. Abraham Hatuiikulipi Malua. Pietermaritzburg, South Africa, 19.9.2000.

Mbenzi 24.3.1997. Interview with B.A. (Hons) Petrus Mbenzi, junior lecturer (Oshiwambo) at the Department of African languages, University of Namibia. Windhoek, Namibia, 24.3.1997.

Munyika 16.10.2000. Interview with Th.D. Veikko Munyika. Oniipa, Namibia, 16.10.2000.

Mwaetako 14.10.2000. Interview with Rev. Radius Mwaetako, vicar of the St. Thomas Anglican parish in Oshakati. Oshakati, Namibia, 14.10.2000.

Nambala 14.4.1997. Interview with Th.D., M.A. Shekutaamba V.V. Nambala. Oniipa, Namibia, 14.4.1997.

Namuhuja 14.4.1997. Interview with school inspector and author, B.A. (Hons) Hans Namuhuja. Oniipa, Namibia, 14.4.1997.

Nashihanga 18.4.1997. Interview with Rev. Halolye Nashihanga, pastor of the Lutheran Oniipa congregation. Oniipa, Namibia, 18.4.1997.

Säynevirta 12.4.1997. Interview with Ms. Päivi Säynevirta, physiotherapist at the Onandjokwe Lutheran Hospital. Oniipa, Namibia, 12.4.1997.

Voipio-Vaalas 15.8.1995. Interview with sacr.min.kand. Rauha Voipio-Vaalas, lecturer of theological studies in Lutheran theological seminaries Namibia 1946–74. Helsinki, Finland, 15.8.1995.

Appendix 1

The Surname Data

(Surnames of Ambo theologians, source: Nambala 1995)

Abraham	Haipinge	Kanguma
Ailonga	Haipinge	Kankondi
Aludhilu	Haitula	Kantalelo
Alugongo	Haixuxwa	Kapewangolo
Alugongo	Hambia	Kapofi
Alweendo	Hameva	Kapofi
Amaambo	Hamukwaya	Kapolo
Amadhila	Hamulungu	Kashihakumwa
Amadhila	Hamunyela	Kashokulu
Amagola	Hamutenya	Katjimba
Amakali	Hangula	Katoma
Amakutuwa	Hanyango	Kaukungwa
Ambinga	Hasheela	Kaulinge
Ambunda	Hashikutuva	Kaulinge
Ampweya	Haufiku	Kondjila
Amukoto	Haufiku	Kuungumene
Amukugo	Haufiku	Leonard
Amunyela	Haulofu	Malwa
Amupolo	Haunini	Manya
Amupolo	Hauwanga	Mbadhi
Amushila	Heita	Mbango
Amuaalwa	Heita	Moonde
Amwaama	Heita	Mtuleni
Andreas	Henok	Mufeti
Angula	Ihambo	Mufeti
Angula	Iihuhwa	Munalye
Ashipala	Iihuhwa	Munashimwe
Ashipala	Iihuhwa	Mundjele
Auala	Iileka	Mungungu
Avia	Iilonga	Mungungu
Dama	Iimene	Munyika
David	Iimene	Musheko
Dengeinge	Iipito	Mvula
Dumeni	Iita	Mvula
Egumbo	Iitope	Mwafufya
Ekandjo	Iitula	Mweutota
Ekandjo	Iitula	Nafine
Ekandjo	Iiyambo	Nailenge
Elago	Iiyambo	Nakamhela
Endjala	Iiyambo	Nakanwe
Enkono	Iiyambo	Nakanyala
Gweendama	Ikumba	Nambala
Haikokola	Imalwa	Nambili
Haileka	Imalwa	Nambundunga
Haileka	Kaapanda	Nampala
Haimbili	Kalenga	Namunyekwa
Haindongo	Kambonde	Namunyekwa
Hainghumbi	Kamho	Namunyekwa
Haipinge	Kanana	Nangolo

Nangolo	Ngodji	Shipena
Nanhapo	Ngula	Shipingana
Nantanga	Nhinda	Shipunda
Nantinda	Niinkoti	Shituwa
Nashidengo	Niitshinda	Shivolo
Nashidengo	Ntinda	Shivolo
Nashihanga	Ntinda	Shivute
Nashongo	Shaanika	Shivute
Ndamanomhata	Shaduka	Shivute
Ndatipo	Shakaalela	Shivute
Ndeikwila	Shanghala	Shiwagala
Ndemuweda	Shangheta	Shiwana
Ndeutapo	Shangheta	Shiyagaya
Ndevahoma	Shanyengange	Shiyoma
Ndinoshiho	Shejavali	Shomagwe
Ndiwakalunga	Shidute	Shongolo
Ndjoba	Shifiona	Shongolo
Ndume	Shifula	Shoombe
Nelumbu	Shihepo	Shuukwanyama
Nelumbu	Shiimi	Shuuveni
Nengola	Shikesho	Shuuya
Nepela	Shikomba	Taanyanda
Nepembe	Shikongo	Taapopi
Ngaikukwete	Shikongo	Tuutaleni
Nghatanga	Shilongo	Uugulu
Nghatanga	Shilongo	Uugwanga
Nghihalwa	Shimakeleni	Uushona
Nghikembwa	Shinana	Uushona
Nghipandulua	Shindongo	Uusiku
Nghole	Shininge	Uusizi
Ngipandulua	Shipanga	Wahengo

Appendix 2

Ambo Names of Women and Men in the Name Data

(Baptismal names of Elim, Okahao and Oshigambo congregations 1913–1993)

Ambo names of women

Aanemunandje + 1	Angaleni + 2	Dhiginina 1 + 10
Afutala + 1	Ashikongo + 1	Dhiladhileni + 1
Ageshe + 2	Asino + 1	Dhimbulukweni + 3
Ambonde + 1	Atupupo + 1	Diginina + 2
Ambondo + 4	Atutala + 1	Dinelago + 1
Amukwaya + 1	Ayeshaantu + 1	
Amunjela + 1	Ayihe + 1	Eeno + 1
Amupaja + 1		Efaishe + 1
Amupunda + 1	Dagamakune + 1	Elago + 1
Amushe + 1	Dahumala + 1	Elindi + 1
Andija + 1	Dapewa 1	Eluhole + 2
Andmeise + 1	Deya + 1	Endeleleni 1
Andoone + 1	Dhaanda + 1	Etuhole 1 + 11

345

Fiindje + 3
Fileni + 1
Fudheni + 2

Gamena 1 + 3
Gandjomuenjo + 12
Gandjomuenyo + 1
Gandjomwenjo + 3
Gongaleni + 5
Gundjileni + 5
Gundyileni + 2
Gwashamba + 1

Hafeleinge + 1
Hafeni 1 + 2
Haloiye + 1
Hambelela + 7
Hambeleleni 1+ 20
Hambeleni 1 + 1
Hanganen + 1
Hanganeni + 8
Hekelekwa + 1
Hiinani + 1
Hinanas·o + 1
Hinandjoleti + 1
Hinasha + 1

Ifinahonde + 1
Igandjeleni + 1
Iijaloo + 1
Iileni 1 + 1
Iilonga + 1
Iisitile + 1
Iivuleni + 1
Ijabo + 1
Ilenikelago + 1
Ilenimo 1 + 2
Imene + 1
Inamuluma + 1
Inamumvulua + 1
Inamushidhimbwa + 1
Inamutila + 1
Inamuuluma + 1
Inamuvulua 1 + 1
Inamuvulwa 1 + 1
Inamwulwa + 1
Indileni 1 + 1
Ineekela + 3
Inekela + 7
Inene + 1
Ingayomwena 1
Iningishiua + 1
Inotila + 1
Ipuleni + 1
Itatunengua + 1
Iyaloo + 4
Iyambo + 1

Jakundeni + 2
Jaloo + 1
Jataleni + 2
Joleni + 1
Jolenimo + 1
Jolokeni + 1
Joolokeni + 1

Kaagwana + 1
Kaanante + 1
Kaanda + 1
Kaaningilamo + 1
Kaavulu + 1
Kaaziwapo + 1
Kafo + 1
Kaiinekelua + 1
Kakuneni + 1
Kalaneinekelo + 1
Kalaputse + 1
Kalenanas·o + 1
Kalihulu + 1
Kaliipo + 1
Kalonge + 1
Kamana + 3
Kamati + 1
Kambweshe + 1
Kaminina + 1
Kamulilo + 1
Kamutjusha + 1
Kamwene + 1
Kanaiti 1
Kandali + 12
Kandalindishiwo 1
Kandalipo + 1
Kandishi + 1
Kandishiwo + 1
Kandiuapa + 1
Kandiwapa + 6
Kanime + 1
Kanjama + 1
Kapena + 1
Kapenambili + 3
Kapongo + 1
Kashiimonika + 1
Kashimupenga + 1
Kashinasha + 2
Kashinini + 1
Kashipo + 1
Kashipu + 1
Kashivulika + 1
Kashuupulua + 1
Katiikuthwa + 1
Katulimondjila + 3
Katunashili + 1
Katuulwete + 1
Kauko + 4

Kaukowe 1
Kauliikuthwa + 1
Kaulikufwa + 1
Kaulinaua + 1
Kauna 1 + 3
Kaunahafo + 2
Kaunalenga + 1
Kaunambili + 1
Kaunapaua + 1
Kaunapawa + 10
Kaupo + 1
Kaushiuetu + 2
Kaushiwetu + 2
Kaushiweye + 1
Kaušiuetu 1
Kauthimbulua + 1
Kautondokwa + 1
Kavaikwa + 1
Kawiikwa + 1
Kawipopilua + 1
Kaydamwenyo + 1
Kayeo + 1
Kayikoshwa + 1
Kehetuljeni + 1
Kelago + 1
Kelaino + 1
Kenemunandje + 1
Keshikeni + 1
Ketsawe + 1
Keulukuwa + 1
Kombala + 1
Kombanda + 1
Komesho 1
Kondja 1 + 3
Kondjashili 1 + 1
Kondjela + 2
Kondjeleni + 1
Kondjelomuenjo + 1
Kondjelomwenjo + 1
Kondjeni + 6
Kongeni + 2
Kongondunge + 1
Kuasha + 1
Kuejuupe + 1
Kuku + 2
Kulipikuwa + 1
Kundweni 1
Kunekulilo + 1
Kunonele + 1
Kuutondokwa 1
Kuwa + 1

Lago + 1
Landuleni + 1
Landulimo + 1
Lendina + 1

Leshanomuenjo + 1
Ligola + 1
Ligoleni + 7
Lihapa + 1
Lineekela + 2
Linekela + 2
Lipitwa + 1
Livule + 1
Ljaanjuka + 1
Ljapuapo + 3
Ljashulapo + 1
LjOmuwa + 1
Longeni + 1
Loteni + 2
Lugambo + 5
Lugodhi + 1
Luwa + 1

Madhigila + 3
Magano 10 + 187
Makadhona + 1
Mayenge + 1
Mbushandje + 1
Mbute + 3
Mbutte + 1
Megameno 1 + 20
Mejo + 1
Meke + 1
Mekondjo + 2
Melago + 1
Metine + 1
Metumo + 1
Mggano + 2
Minikila + 1
Mondjila + 1
Mpingana 1 + 27
Muaalua + 2
Muadina + 1
Muajonandje + 1
Muakondja + 1
Mualele + 2
Mualua + 2
Muatantandje + 1
Muazina + 2
Mueetandi + 1
Muegatja + 1
Mueja + 1
Muejapo + 2
Muejatila + 1
Mueneni +1
Mueneuna + 1
Mueshitjandje + 1
Muetulundila + 1
Muisaneni + 1
Mukuilongo + 2
Mulenga + 1

Mulipo + 1
Mumbala + 4
Munageni + 2
Munondjene + 1
Mupaja + 1
Mupandeni + 1
Mupolo + 2
Mupongolitha + 1
Musheetha + 1
Mutaleni + 9
Mutaleninohenda 1 + 3
Mutigueendama + 1
Mutuvule + 1
Muyenda + 1
Mvute + 1
Mwaahua + 1
Mwaalele + 1
Mwaalwa + 3
Mwadhina + 3
Mwadhinandye + 1
Mwahafa 1
Mwajolandje + 1
Mwaluka + 1
Mwapopie + 1
Mweenda + 1
Mwegeendeka + 1
Mweneni + 1
Mweshilongo + 1
Mweshitja + 1
Mwetugwedha + 1
Mwetulamba + 1
Mweya + 1
Mwiilumba + 1
Mwiithaneni + 1

Naakalako + 1
Naambo 1 + 16
Naango 1 + 15
Naapopje + 1
Naapopye + 2
Naashuwe + 2
Naatoolewe + 1
Naatye + 1
Nadhipite + 1
Nagalote + 1
Nahambelelue + 1
Nahambelelwe + 1
Nahambo + 2
Nahango + 1
Nahenda 1 + 1
Nailoke 1 + 4
Nailonga + 1
Naitsuwe + 1
Nakadhilu + 1
Nakakale + 1
Nakambale + 4

Nakapele + 1
Nakashua + 3
Nakashwa + 1
Nakashupi 1 + 1
Nakashwa + 4
Nakasigona + 1
Nakulilua + 1
Nakulwa + 1
Nakushe + 2
Nakuti + 1
Nakwenje + 1
Nalijele + 1
Nalitaandele + 1
Nalitje + 1
Nalitunge + 4
Nalondje + 1
Nalooliwa + 1
Naluendo + 2
Nalukale + 2
Naluko + 1
Nalumutange + 1
Nalweendo + 1
Nalwendo + 1
Nalwoondje + 1
Namadhila + 7
Namalwa + 1
Namatanga + 1
Namatsi + 3
Nambahu + 2
Nambali + 1
Nambalu + 1
Nambashu + 4
Nambat + 1
Nambili + 1
Nambudhi + 2
Nambula + 5
Namendji + 1
Namene + 4
Nameya + 1
Namhahu + 1
Namilue + 1
Namolyona + 1
Nampweya + 1
Namuapo 1
Namuenjo + 3
Namuhua + 1
Namukua + 1
Namukuwa + 2
Namunjela + 1
Namunyela + 1
Namupa + 9
Namupala + 18
Namupasita + 7
Namupunda + 1
Namutena + 4
Namutenja 1 + 33

347

Namutenya + 10
Namvula + 3
Namwenjo + 4
Nandigolo + 11
Nandjala + 2
Nandjamba 1
Nandjambi + 2
Nandjela + 1
Nandjelo + 1
Nandjila + 3
Nandjungu + 1
Nanewo + 1
Nangeni + 1
Nangolo + 4
Nangombe 1 + 34
Nangula 1 + 54
Nankali + 2
Nankelo + 6
Nantinda + 1
Nantongo + 1
Napandulwe + 1
Napopje + 1
Napopye + 1
Našiningue + 1
Nasaantu + 1
Nashilongo + 7
Nashipolo + 2
Nashiye + 1
Natango + 1
Natangue + 15
Natangwe 1 + 20
Nathinge + 1
Natongue + 1
Natumutange + 2
Natwiuthile + 1
Nayiloke + 3
Nayitsuwe + 3
Ndaambelela + 1
Ndadilepo + 1
Ndaetelwa + 1
Ndafapawa + 1
Ndafimina + 1
Ndafudha + 1
Ndaguedha + 2
Ndaguenapo + 1
Ndagwedha + 2
Ndahafa + 10
Ndahalako + 1
Ndahalavali + 1
Ndahambelela 1 + 53
Ndahekelekua + 3
Ndahekelekwa + 5
Ndahekumuna + 1
Ndahempuluka + 1
Ndahepa + 1
Ndahepuluka + 1

Ndaithanua + 1
Ndajambekua + 2
Ndajuulukua + 1
Ndakalako + 1
Ndakila + 1
Ndakoko + 1
Ndakola + 2
Ndakondja + 10
Ndakondjele + 1
Ndakoneka + 1
Ndakulilua + 40
Ndakulilwa + 27
Ndakumua + 1
Ndakumwa + 1
NDakumwa 1
Ndakundana + 2
Ndalakolako + 1
Ndalalele + 1
Ndalekelekwa + 1
Ndalelua + 1
Ndalikokule + 2
Ndalila + 1
Ndalimbililua + 1
Ndalipondjo + 1
Ndalulilua + 1
Ndamanguluka + 7
Ndamanguluki + 1
Ndamona + 3
Ndamonako + 1
Ndamonekuatho + 1
Ndamongehenda + 1
Ndamono + 6
Ndamonohamba + 1
Ndamonohenda 1 + 9
Ndamonongenda 1 + 1
Ndamononghend + 1
Ndananuku + 1
Ndananukua + 3
Ndanengua + 1
Ndangengua + 1
Ndangi + 3
Ndanjanjukua + 6
Ndanjanjukwa + 1
Ndanjengua + 1
Ndanyanyukua + 1
Ndanyanyukwa + 4
Ndapanda + 59
Ndapandula 3 + 41
Ndapendukapo + 1
Ndapeua 4 + 56
Ndapeuapeke + 1
Ndapeuashange + 1
Ndapeululwa + 1
Ndapeuomagano + 2
Ndapeuoshali + 1
Ndapeuoshilonga + 2

Ndapewa 7 + 82
Ndapewashali + 1
Ndapewomagano + 6
Ndapewoshali 1 + 6
Ndapiita + 1
Ndapohoni + 1
Ndapoulya + 1
Ndapua + 2
Ndapuomagano + 1
Ndapwa + 5
Ndašilua + 1
Ndashulilua + 1
Ndashunje + 1
Ndasilohenda + 1
Ndasiluohenda + 21
Ndasilwohenda 1 + 16
Ndataambua + 3
Ndatala + 2
Ndatalako + 1
Ndateelela + 2
Ndateetela + 1
Ndatega + 1
Ndategako 2 + 11
Ndategelel + 1
Ndategelela + 10
Ndategetela + 1
Ndatelela + 1
Ndathigilua + 1
NDathigwapo + 1
Ndatila + 3
Ndatilangi + 1
Ndatinda + 1
Ndatindangi + 1
Ndatitangi + 4
Ndatoleue + 1
Ndatolewe + 2
Ndatooleue 2 + 3
Ndatoolewe 1
Ndatoolomba + 1
Ndatuminwa + 1
Ndauapeka + 1
Ndauedapo + 1
Ndaupanjokua + 1
Ndavulwa + 1
Ndawana + 1
Ndayaalukua + 1
Ndayambekwa + 1
Ndayela + 1
Ndayelekwa + 1
Ndayooloka + 1
Ndeapo + 2
Ndeenda + 1
Ndeendelago 1 + 2
Ndeetapo + 1
Ndegapewa + 1
Ndegathetwa + 2

Ndeilenga + 1
Ndeiluka + 1
Ndeitaneka + 1
Ndejamo + 1
Ndejapewa + 1
Ndejapo 1 + 13
Ndekutega + 1
Ndelinika + 1
Ndemušikula + 1
Ndemutega 1 + 2
Ndemuvula + 1
Ndenyanyukwa + 1
Ndeshaala + 1
Ndesheetelwa + 1
Ndeshihafela 1 + 11
Ndeshihala + 4
Ndeshihaluka + 2
Ndeshimona + 6
Ndeshimupandela + 1
Ndeshiningilua + 3
Ndeshiningilwa + 1
Ndeshipanda 2 + 11
Ndeshipewa + 4
Ndeshitala + 1
Ndeshithigilwa + 1
Ndeshitiwa + 1
Ndeshuva + 1
Ndeuhala + 1
Ndeuhepela + 3
Ndeuhulilwa + 1
Ndeukumua + 1
Ndeukumuua + 1
Ndeukumwa + 3
Ndeumona + 7
Ndeunyema + 1
Ndeushuwa + 1
Ndeutala + 14
Ndeutalala + 1
Ndeutenge + 2
Ndeuthigilwa + 2
Ndewenda + 1
Ndeyamo + 1
Ndeyamono + 1
Ndeyapewa + 1
Ndeyapo + 28
Ndhimbulukweni 1
Ndiehanua + 1
Ndihimeke + 1
Ndiholetate + 1
Ndiiguedha + 1
Ndiili + 3
Ndiiluka + 1
Ndiinekela + 3
Ndiinguanena + 1
Ndiiuanena + 1
Ndikuhole + 1

Ndilimeke 3 + 44
Ndilimekondjo + 1
Ndilimevava + 1
Ndilinasho + 1
Ndilinaua + 1
Ndilipawa + 1
Ndilipeke + 2
Ndilipo + 2
Ndilipune 1 + 3
Ndilipunye + 1
Ndina 1 + 1
Ndinaetegameno + 1
Ndinake + 1
Ndinehafo 1 + 8
Ndinekela + 1
Ndinelaago + 1
Ndinelago 5 + 157
Ndinombili + 1
Ndinomuami + 2
Ndinomugameni + 7
Ndinomukualhi +1
Ndinomukuathi + 5
NdinOmukulili + 1
Ndinomukwathi 1 + 3
Ndinomuua + 1
NdinoOmvula + 1
Ndishishi + 1
Ndiweni + 1
Ndiwoye + 1
Ndiyana + 1
Ndjambeha + 1
Ndjamo + 1
Ndjelipa + 1
Ndjunie + 1
Nduuviteko + 1
Nduuwundi + 1
Nduvundi + 1
Neelu + 2
Nefundja + 3
Negumbo + 1
Nehale + 1
Nehoja 1 + 2
Neje + 1
Nekandje + 1
Nekandjo + 1
Nekondjelo + 1
Nekondo + 1
Nekulilo 3 + 13
Nekulu + 6
Nekuru + 2
Nelaago + 3
Nelago 6 + 110
Nelombo + 1
Nemushi + 2
Nemwati + 1
Nena + 1

Nenayishula + 1
Neneuo + 1
Nengegeni + 1
Nenjanju + 1
Nenyanyu + 1
Ngaamwene + 1
Ngaje 1
Ngavule + 1
Ngeetuna + 1
Ngetuna + 1
Ngeno 1
Ngetokondjo 1
Nghiimovali + 1
Nginanajo + 1
Ngiitokondjo 1
Ngomashendjo + 1
Ngondjodhi + 1
Ngueenandje + 1
Ngutati + 1
Ngwedha + 1
Ngweenandje + 1
Niilonga 2 + 15
Niimbondi + 1
Niimpungu + 2
Niinjandu + 1
Niintambo + 1
Niipindi + 7
Niipopja + 1
Niishiyo + 1
Niita 1 + 38
Niitembo + 1
Niitembu + 8
Niitula + 6
Niiwa + 2
Niiye + 2
Nije + 1
Ningeni 1
Niye + 1
Njandeleniko + 1
Njanjukueni + 17
Njanjukweni + 10
Njanyukweni + 2
Njowa + 2
Nndapeua + 1
Nohenda + 1
Nombili 1
Nongekueni + 1
Nuudano + 1
Nuuguanga + 3
Nuugulu + 1
Nuugwanga 2 + 10
Nuukelo + 2
Nuukesho + 1
Nuukongo + 3
Nuukwawo + 1
Nuušekete + 1

Nuusiku 2 + 21
Nuuta + 1
Nyambali + 1
Nyanjukweni + 6
Nyanyukueni + 4
Nyanyukwa + 1
Nyanyukweni 1 + 17
Nyowa + 3

Omagano 1 + 12
Omondili + 1
Omuwetuna + 2
Omwaalwa + 1
Ondahala 1
Ondemutega 1
Opondili + 2
Osiike + 4
Osiiketulipo 1
Otseniyamwe 1
Oyandje + 1

Paahukeni + 1
Pandapeua + 1
Pandeni + 2
Panduleni 1 + 38
Pandulo + 2
Pashukeni + 2
Peethi + 1
Peingondjambi + 1
Peleni 1
Pembili 1
Pena + 2
Pendukapo + 1
Pendukeni + 8
Penehaf 1
Penehafo 1 + 14
Penejambeko 1 + 11
Penekondjo + 1
Penekwatho + 1
Penelao + 1
Peneyambeko 2 + 8
Penihe 1
Penomukuathi + 2
Penomukwathi + 1
Penondjila + 1
Penoshinge + 1
Penouike + 1
Pewa + 1
Peyavali + 4
Piingedina + 1
POmbili + 1
Popjeni + 3
Punango + 1
Putuda + 1
Pwayendohamba + 1

Sakongo 1
Senane + 1
Shaanika + 1
Shaguanepandulo + 1
Shagwana + 3
Shagwane + 1
Shagwanepandulo + 1
Shagwanithwa + 1
Shambekela + 1
Shambekeleni + 1
Shandje + 1
Shanjenga + 1
Shanyenge + 1
Shasimana + 1
Shatika + 1
Shatsakana + 1
Sheeya + 2
Shekupe 2 + 12
Shekupo + 1
Shemunyenge + 1
Shetunyenga + 1
Sheya + 2
Shikongo + 1
Shikuuvu + 1
Shikwambi + 1
Shikwete + 1
Shile + 1
Shilokwa + 1
Shimanya + 2
Shindondola + 1
Shishshuame + 1
Shishuweni + 1
Shitenga + 1
Shiwomwenyo + 1
Shoololo + 1
Shoopala + 2
Shooshawo 1
Sigoonena + 1
Simaneka 1 + 12
Simanekohamba + 1
Simanekwa + 1
Siveli + 1
Sondaha 2 + 3
Šetulimba + 1
Šikongo + 1
Šimana + 1
Šoopala +1

Taakondjo + 1
Taamba + 1
Taambeni + 1
Taambeyambeko + 1
Taati 1 + 6
Taatsu + 1
Tagayena + 1
Takatsu + 5

Talahole + 1
Talamondjila + 1
Talapombanda + 1
Taleni + 2
Taleniko + 1
Taliiko + 1
Talipiti + 1
Talishi + 1
Talohole + 20
Tambuleni + 1
Tanga + 1
Tangani + 1
Tangeni + 14
Tangi + 9
Tangomona + 1
TangOmuwa + 1
Tashija + 1
Tashiya + 1
Tashiyo + 1
Tatutale + 1
Taunyengendje + 1
Tautungenge + 1
Tegamena + 1
Tegandje + 1
Tegelela 1 + 24
Tegelele + 1
Tegeleleni + 2
Tegetela + 1
Tegomukuathi + 1
Temapo + 1
Teuthigilwa + 1
Thigipo + 1
Thikamena + 1
Thikameni + 2
Tileni + 1
Tilenuuyuni + 1
Tilomalenga + 1
Timomukuathi + 1
Tjuuljandjo + 1
Tolata + 1
Tonata + 7
Tonateni 1 + 10
Toti + 1
Tsenaje + 1
Tsenaye + 1
Tshapwa 1
Tuakulilua + 1
Tualukula + 1
Tudheni + 1
Tuegathetua + 1
Tuejuupe + 1
Tueufiilua + 1
Tueufilua + 1
Tueumona + 1
Tueuthigilua + 2
Tueuthigilwa + 2

Tugakula + 1
Tuhafeni + 5
Tuhulu + 1
Tuihaleni + 2
Tuilika + 4
Tuipuleni + 1
Tujambula + 1
Tujelenjomutima + 1
Tujenikelago + 2
Tujoleni + 2
Tukaleni + 3
Tukondjele + 1
Tukondjeni + 2
Tulela + 2
Tuleni + 1
Tulikemanya + 1
Tulimegameno + 1
Tulimeuaua + 1
Tulimiita + 1
Tulinane + 1
Tulonga + 14
Tumueneni + 1
Tunekwatho + 1
Tunelago + 2
Tunohoole + 1
Tunomukuathi + 3
Tunomukwathi + 4
Tunomuwiliki + 2
Tunowiino + 1
Tunuuyelele + 1
Tunyanyukweni + 1
Tupawo + 1

Tutala + 2
Tutale + 1
Tutaleni + 1
Tuti + 1
Tuuhulu + 2
Tuuilika + 3
Tuukondjele + 1
Tuunikelago + 1
Tuuthigilua + 1
Tuwilika + 12
Tuyakula + 3
Tuyambeka + 1
Tuyeni + 1
Tuyenikelago + 9
Tuyenikelao 1 + 1
Tuyenikemanya + 1
Tuykondjele + 1
Tuyoleni + 4
Twafikashimwe + 1
Twanmena + 1
Twayile 1
Twegathetwa + 2
Tweoolama + 1
Tweufilwa + 2
Tweufulwa + 1
Tweuhanga + 1
Tweuthigilwa + 5
Twewaadha + 1
Tweyamuwo + 1
Twilongeni + 1
Tyeni + 1

Uilika 30 + 1
Uilka 1
Uillika 1 + 1
Upulauo + 1
Ušindje + 1
Uujuni + 1
Uulumbu + 1
Uupindi + 1
Uusiku + 1
Uveni + 1

Vangi + 1
Vatilange + 1
Vulika + 1
Vulikeni + 3
Vululukueni + 3
Vululukwa + 1
Vululukweni + 1

Watjapuwo + 2
Watyakokehulilo + 1
Wayele + 1
Wetupa 1
Wetutala + 1
Weyakelago + 1
Wilika 7 + 2

Yadhiminapo + 1
Yalukeni + 1

Ziginina + 2
Zilazila + 1
Zimbuka + 1
Zimolimwe + 1

Ambo names of men

Aantu +1
Aantuyoye + 1
Adhiindje + 1
Ageshe + 1
Agesheogandje + 1
Akuenye + 1
Aludhilu+ 1
Aludilu + 1
Alueendo + 1
Aluendo + 4
Alugodhi 1
Alugongo + 1
Aluzilu + 1
Alveta 1
Alweendo + 3
Amaambo + 1
Amadhila 2 + 7

Amakali 1 + 4
Amalovu + 2
Amalua + 3
Amalwa + 3
Amaskoa 1
Ambambi + 1
Ambata + 1
Ambili + 1
Ambuga + 1
Ambunda + 1
Ampindo + 1
Amuaalua 1
Amuaama + 1
Amuama + 2
Amukušu + 1
Amukwaja + 1
Amukwaya + 2

Amunela 1
Amunjela + 6
Amunyela 1 + 3
Amupadi + 1
Amupala + 1
Amupembe + 1
Amupolo + 3
Amupunda + 1
Amushembe + 1
Amushila + 1
Amutako + 1
Amutenja + 11
Amutenya + 6
Amuthenu + 1
Amvula + 1
Amwanyena + 2
Anaula + 1

351

Andoone + 1

Andili 2

Angala + 7

Angaleni + 1

Angolo + 1

Angombe + 1

Angula 1 + 17

Anguwo + 1

Ankama + 1

Ankonga + 1

Antsimo + 1

Asheela + 1

Asheendo + 1

Ashikoto + 3

Ashilungu + 1

Ashipala + 3

Atshipala + 1

Atukeuka + 1

Atuti + 1

Atuukakuni + 1

Atuukapeni + 1

Aufilisa 1

Awene + 1

Cikameni + 1

Dapanda + 1

Dhameni 1

Dhiginina + 4

Dhiladhileni + 2

Dhimbulukueni + 2

Dhimbulukweni + 4

Edhiga + 1

Eeno + 1

Egameno + 1

Egumbo + 1

Einekelo + 1

Ekandjo + 12

Ekelyombili + 1

Ekondo + 1

Elago 4 + 44

Elhiindje + 1

Elombo + 1

Eloolo + 1

Embula + 1

Emvula 1 + 5

Endelela + 1

Endeleleni + 1

Endjala + 1

Enkali + 1

Eposhe + 1

Etuna 2 + 6

Findje + 1

Gaali + 1

Galukeni + 1

Galukiindye + 1

Gamona + 1

Gandjajihe + 1

Gongaleni 1

Gošizimbua + 1

Gshidimbua + 1

Gundjileni + 1

Hafeni 4 + 19

Halolye + 1

Halolyoye + 1

Hambelela + 1

Hambeleleni + 1

Hanganeni + 1

Hango + 13

Hashondali 1

Hashondalindishi + 1

Hatutale + 1

Haufiku + 2

Haukongo + 1

Hauwanga + 1

Heita + 1

Hekeleka + 1

Helao + 1

Hilifa + 2

Hilifavali + 3

Hilifawe + 1

Hilifilua + 1

Hilifiluawali + 1

Hilisilua + 1

Hishidmbwa + 1

Hishiwo 1

Homata + 1

Homaten + 1

Homateni + 9

Hupitho + 1

Ifewa + 1

Iigonda + 1

Iijaloo + 1

Iijambo + 8

Iilatuye + 1

Iileka + 7

Iilende + 3

Iilonga + 5

Iilongela + 1

Iimbondi + 1

Iimene + 1

Iimongwa + 1

Iinamutila + 1

Iindongo + 1

Iingo + 2

Iingonda + 1

Iipinge 2 + 16

Iipuleni + 2

Iipumbu 2 + 1

Iisete + 2

Iishidhimbua + 1

Iishiposha + 1

Iita + 20

Iitalukua + 1

Iitembu 1 + 5

Iithelenga + 1

Iitika + 1

Iitope 1

Iitula + 1

Iiyambo 2 + 10

Ijambo + 1

Ijlungu + 1

IlakOmwene + 1

Ileni + 4

Ilifa + 2

Ilifavali + 2

Ilonga + 1

Imene + 1

Inamutila + 1

Indila + 1

Indileni + 3

Indjimba + 1

Inedhimbwa + 1

Ineekela 1 + 3

Inekela 1 + 4

Inekeleni + 1

Ingandipula + 1

Ingashifika + 1

Ingashipwa + 1

Ingingemwutile + 1

Inodhimbwandje + 1

Inodhimua + 1

Inotila + 1

Ipangelwa + 1

Ipuleni + 1

Ishidhimbua + 1

Ishidhimbwa + 2

Ishidimbwa + 1

Ishiposha + 1

Ishiwa + 1

Itaala 1

Itandutumuwe + 1

Itembu + 1

Itula + 1

Iyaloo + 1

Iyambo + 2

Jafeni + 1

Jandje + 2

Jataleni + 1

Jatileni + 1

Jelukeni + 1

Jolokeni 1

Kaagwana 1
Kaali 2
Kaamhulua + 1
Kaapanda + 3
Kaashinawa + 1
Kaashiyo + 1
Kaatoole + 1
Kaayone + 1
Kadhikwa + 1
Kafula 1
Kagadhinua + 2
Kagadhinwa + 1
Kagandhinua + 1
Kagasheka + 1
Kaindi + 1
Kakandeni + 1
Kakololo + 1
Kakunde + 1
Kakutu + 1
Kakuua + 1
Kalangula + 1
Kalaputse + 1
Kalenga + 1
Kaleni + 1
Kalimbo + 2
Kalitek + 1
Kalola + 1
Kalumbi + 1
Kalumbu + 1
Kamati + 6
Kambala + 1
Kambonde + 3
Kamene + 1
Kamenye + 1
Kampelo + 1
Kamunantoehe + 1
Kamusheetha + 1
Kamutwe + 1
Kandali + 2
Kandalindishi + 1
Kandalindishishi + 1
Kandinshi + 1
Kandiuapa + 2
Kandiuapanditumbule + 1
Kandiwapa + 6
Kandiwapakutumbula + 1
Kandushe + 1
Kangunde + 1
Kangundo + 1
Kanime + 1
Kankono + 1
Kanume + 1
Kapalwa + 1
Kapapu + 1
Kapawanwa + 1
Kapenambili + 1

Kapinda + 1
Kapueja + 1
Kapueya + 1
Kapulwa + 1
Kapukulu 1
Kasheeta + 1
Kashele + 1
Kashikulwa + 1
Kashina + 1
Kashinambudhi + 1
Kashinjenga + 1
Kashipondolosha + 1
Kasiimbindjola + 1
Kasondaha + 1
Katangolo + 1
Katili 1
Katusiuo + 1
Katuwushi + 1
Katuzamo + 1
Kauiha + 1
Kauko 1 + 6
Kaukowe + 1
Kaulinaua + 1
Kauna + 2
Kaunapaua + 1
Kaunapawa + 1
Kaunawoye + 1
Kaunda + 1
Kaupo + 2
Kaushiueni + 1
Kaushiuetu + 1
Kaushiweni + 1
Kaushiwetu + 6
Kaušiuetu + 1
Kautondokua + 1
Kautondokwa + 1
Kaveto + 1
Kawela + 1
Kayamba + 1
Keenatuka + 1
Kekwetha + 1
Kenaatuka + 2
Kene + 1
Kiinge + 1
Kinekela + 1
Kola + 1
Kombandjajevi + 1
Kondja + 1
Kondjashili + 3
Kondjela + 2
Kondjeni + 16
Kondjila + 1
Kondyeni + 1
Konga + 1
Kongenielago + 1
Kotokeni + 12

Kuedi + 1
Kume + 1
Kumwe + 1
Kuna + 1
Kunenga 1
Kunwa + 1
Kuume 1 + 7
Kuumekashe + 1
Kuumeketu + 1
Kuutondokua + 1
Kuutondokwa + 1
Kwatha + 1
Kwatuutati + 1
Kwedhi + 1

Landuleni + 8
Lindombo + 1
Lineekela + 1
Linekela + 3
Lipuleni + 1
Ljangongo + 1
Ljapuapo + 1
Ljashula + 1
Londoloka + 1
Lotitha + 1
Lukamba + 1
Lukongo + 1
Lungameni + 1
Lyapwapo + 1
Luzinyu 1

Magano + 5
Mahalevo + 1
Malenga + 1
Matukeni + 1
Mbago + 1
Mbandeka + 1
Mbilinatse + 1
Mbula + 1
Mbushandje + 2
Mbusheyetu + 1
Mbwalala + 2
Megameno + 15
Meitaalo + 1
Meke + 2
Mekeliwa + 1
Mekololo + 1
Mekondjo + 25
Menongelo + 1
Mesaha 1
Metumo + 1
Mewawa + 1
Mohole + 1
Movingi + 1
Muala + 1
Muatala + 1

Muatile 1
Muatotelandje + 1
Mueenda + 1
Mueneeshindje + 1
Mueneni + 2
Mueshikolela + 1
Muetako + 1
Muetupopila + 1
Mukushu + 1
Mulanduleni + 2
Mulilitha + 1
Mulipo + 1
Mumbala + 1
Munomuenjo + 1
Mushaandja + 1
Mushiki + 1
Musigona + 1
Musoko + 1
Mutaleni + 1
Mutileni + 1
Mvula + 1
Mwaafa + 1
Mwaala + 6
Mwadhina 2 + 1
Mwahangashapwa + 1
Mwayeka + 1
Mweendeleli + 1
Mweneni 1 + 3
Mweshikolela + 2
Mweuli + 1
Mweutapo + 1

Naatangwe + 1
Nade + 1
Nadhipite + 6
Nadhitope + 1
Nahenda + 1
Nakambale + 1
Nakapanda + 1
Nakashona + 1
Nalangwe + 1
Nalimanguluke + 4
Nalipite + 1
Nalitandele + 1
Naluwe + 1
Nalue 1
Namalunga + 1
Namashana + 1
Nambahu + 1
Nambala + 3
Nambili + 2
Nambinga + 1
Namgongo + 1
Nampala + 1
Nampueja + 1
Nampweja + 1

Namukuambi + 1
Namule + 1
Namulo + 1
Namupala 1 + 3
Namupembe + 1
Namupolo + 1
Namutenja 1
Namwaapo + 1
Namwele + 1
Nande + 1
Nandeinotya + 1
Nandjele + 1
Nanewo + 1
Nangolo + 11
Nangombe 1 + 2
Nanguti + 1
Nankalu + 1
Napandulwe + 1
Nashilongo + 1
Nashilongweshipwe + 1
Nashima + 2
Našilongo + 1
Našima + 1
Nasimone + 1
Natango + 1
Natangue + 34
Natangwe 5 + 99
Nathipite + 1
Natongue + 2
Nayiloke + 1
Nayitsikile + 1
Ndaalulilua + 1
Ndafudha + 1
Ndagwedha + 1
Ndahafa + 2
Ndahambelela + 1
Ndaindila 1
Ndajulukua + 1
Ndakalako + 2
Ndakola + 2
Ndakondja + 2
Ndakondje + 1
Ndakuathua + 1
Ndakulilwa + 2
Ndakutamo + 1
Ndakwathwa 1 + 1
Ndalemana + 1
Ndalengelwe + 1
Ndali 1
Ndalikokule + 3
Ndalikupopya + 1
Ndalikutala + 1
Ndalilwa + 1
Ndalulilua + 2
Ndamono + 3
Ndamonohenda + 2

Ndamononawene + 1
Ndangi + 13
Ndapamekwa + 1
Ndapanda + 5
Ndapandula + 10
Ndapenda + 1
Ndapeua + 5
Ndapeuomano + 1
Ndapewa + 1
Ndapewamo + 1
Ndapewoshali + 2
Ndapopi + 1
Ndapua + 1
Ndara + 1
Ndasilwohenda 1 + 1
Ndatega + 2
Ndategelela + 1
Ndati + 1
Ndatipo + 1
Ndatitangi 2 + 4
Ndatjatangi + 1
Ndatoleue + 2
Ndatoolewe + 2
Ndatuminua + 1
Ndauedapo + 1
Ndayaamena + 1
Ndeipanda + 1
Ndeitodhino + 1
Ndejanale + 2
Ndejapo 1 + 2
Ndejapuno + 1
Ndelyompata + 1
Ndemufajo + 2
Ndemufayo + 2
Ndemugueda + 1
Ndemugueza 1
Ndemugwedha + 1
Ndemulunde + 1
Ndemutila + 1
Ndemuweda + 1
Ndeshihala 1 + 2
Ndeshiningilwa + 1
Ndeshipand + 1
Ndeshipanda + 43
Ndeshipewa + 1
Ndeshipona + 1
Ndeshithigilwa + 1
Ndešalanala + 1
Ndešipeua + 1
Ndešitila + 1
Ndeukumwa + 1
Ndeumono + 1
Ndeutala + 1
Ndeutapo + 1
Ndeutenge + 1
Ndeutondoka + 1

Ndeweetelua + 1
Ndeyamo + 1
Ndeyamona + 2
Ndeyanale + 4
Ndeyapo 1 + 2
Ndeyapunye + 1
Ndiholike + 1
Ndiinekela + 1
Ndijana + 2
Ndikuhole + 1
Ndilimegameno + 1
Ndilimeke + 4
Ndilinawa + 1
Ndilipo 1
Ndilipune + 1
Ndina + 2
Ndinehafo + 1
Ndinenyanyu + 1
Ndinomukuathi + 1
Ndinoshiho + 1
Ndinovanhu + 1
Ndipašimue + 1
Ndishaantu + 1
Ndishishi + 2
Nditumbako + 1
Ndiyana + 1
Ndizilemo + 1
Ndjalo + 1
Ndjekela + 1
Ndjelli + 1
Ndjodhi + 1
Ndjundo + 1
Ndoondji + 1
Ndumbo + 1
Nduuvuli + 1
Nduuvundi + 1
Ndyene + 1
Negoli + 1
Negonga + 1
Negongo + 1
Negumbo 1 + 8
Nehale + 2
Nekamato + 1
Neke + 1
Nekongo + 1
Nekua + 1
Nekuaja + 2
Nekuaya + 1
Nekwa + 1
Nelenge + 1
Neleutenge 1
Nelulu + 1
Nema + 1
Nemuno + 1
Nemushi + 1
Nendongo + 1

Nenouili + 1
Ngame + 1
Ngaikukuete 1
Ngedipohamba + 1
Ngeteje + 1
Nghidengua + 1
Nghidimbwa + 1
Nghidinua + 1
Nghidinwa + 1
Nghidinwavali + 1
Nghidipo + 1
Nghidishange + 1
Nghiimovali + 1
Nghilifa + 2
Nghilifavali 1 + 3
Nghilifilua + 1
Nghilifilwa + 1
Nghilimbililua + 1
Nghimondono + 1
Nghinaunje + 1
Nghinaunye 1
Nghindinimuntu + 1
Nghinyekwahamba + 1
Nghipandulwa + 2
Nghishidhimbua + 1
Nghishidimbwa + 1
Nghishiningwa + 1
Nghitenanye + 1
Nghituminwa + 1
Ngilifa + 1
Ngula + 1
Ngunga + 1
Niiho + 1
Niilenge 1 + 5
Njanjukueni + 1
Nkandi + 3
NKoshi + 1
Nokadhidhi + 1
Nondumbo + 1
Ntsilu + 2
Nunjango + 1
Nuujoma + 2
Nuujuni + 1
Nuukongo + 1
Nuundjomba + 1
Nuunjango + 2
Nuunyango + 2
Nuuta + 4
Nuuyoma 1 + 3
Nyanyukueni + 3
Nyanyukuwen + 1
Nyanyukwa + 2
Nyanyukweni 1 + 5

Ohiike 1
Omagano 1 + 1

Omalovu + 1
Omuenjo + 1
Omuna + 1
Omusamane + 1
Omuwa + 1
Omuwene + 1
Opeipawa + 1
Opondili + 1
Oshaguanaepandulo + 1
Oshiuanawa 1
Osiike + 1
Otsenalje + 1
Otulimegameno + 1
Otulina + 1

Pahalo + 1
Pamwenatse + 1
Pandeni + 5
Pandu + 2
Pandulen + 3
Panduleni 3 + 51
Pandulo + 1
Panduteni + 1
Pashukeni + 1
Pašukeni + 1
Peingelao + 1
Pelema + 2
Penda + 3
Pendapala 1 + 17
Pendapaleni 1
Pendjewo + 1
Pendukapo + 2
Pendukeni + 6
Pendulen + 1
Penekondjo + 1
Penethimbo + 1
Penohamba + 1
Penombili + 1
Penomukuathi + 1
Pethimbo + 1
Peyavali + 1
Pitimo 1
Piitimo + 1
POmbili + 1
Pongo + 1
Popepi + 1
Potseni + 1
Pukulukeni + 1
Pweja + 1

Sali + 1
Sampaališi + 1
Sasimana + 1
Senale + 1
Shaanika + 25
Shaanjekwa + 1

Shaatu 1
Shageya + 1
Shali 2 + 4
Shambekela + 1
Shandje + 2
Shange 1
Shangula + 2
Shaningua + 1
Shaningwa + 4
Shanyenga +1
Shapaka + 1
Shapiishuna + 1
Shapumba + 2
Shatika + 1
Shatimuene + 1
Shatimwene + 1
Shatipamba + 2
Shatjohamba 1
Shatumbu + 2
Shavuka + 1
Shawapola + 1
Shayilemo + 1
Sheefa + 1
Sheefeni + 1
Sheeham + 1
Sheehama + 3
Sheeja + 2
Sheelekandje + 1
Sheetela + 1
Shekutamba 1 + 3
Shekuza + 2
Shelekeni + 1
Shembekela + 1
Shetheni + 1
Shetunjenga + 2
Shetunyenga + 1
Shetwaadha + 2
Sheya + 2
Shigueda + 1
Shiguedha + 3
Shigwedha 1 + 4
Shihafeleni + 1
Shihumbu + 1
Shiimi + 4
Shiinda + 1
Shikesho + 1
Shikokola + 1
Shikongeni + 3
Shikongo + 16
Shikoyeni + 1
Shikutamba + 1
Shikuvule + 1
Shikwambi + 2
Shilompoka + 1
Shilongo + 11
Shilumbu + 1

Shimbili + 1
Shimbilinga + 1
Shimbundu + 1
Shimwelago + 1
Shimwetheleni + 1
Shingenge + 1
Shinjenu + 1
Shinyenu + 1
Shipandeni + 4
Shipanga + 1
Shipingana + 3
Shiponga + 1
Shipopjeni + 3
Shipulakeni + 1
Shipulua + 1
Shishaki + 1
Shishiweni + 1
Shitalen + 1
Shitaleni + 1
Shitatala + 2
Shithigona + 2
Shitshuueni 1
Shityani + 1
Shivute + 6
Shiwa + 1
Shiwanda + 1
Shiwomwenyo + 2
Shiwoomuenjo + 1
Shiyagaya + 1
Shonena + 1
Shoololo + 1
Shoombe + 3
Shoopala 1 + 9
Shukifeni 1
Shulitha 1
Shuuja + 1
Shuutheni + 2
Shuuveni + 5
Siguezu + 1
Silunga + 1
Simaneka + 10
Sondaha 1 + 4
Soopala + 1
Šaanika + 1
Šalukeni + 1
Šapumba 2
Šatumbu 1
Šigueza + 1
Šiimi 1 + 3
Šikambi + 1
Šikeukeni + 1
Šikongo + 2
Šikuambi + 1
Šilongo + 1
Šilumbu 1
Šilume + 1

Šisigona + 1
Šitatala + 1
Šivute + 2
Šoopala 1 + 1
Šuuseni + 1

Taamba 2
Taanjanda + 2
Taapi + 1
Taapopi 1 + 5
Taati + 1
Talamondjila + 1
Taleinge + 1
Taleni + 1
Taleninawa + 1
Talohole + 2
Talomapelo + 1
Tamukondjo + 1
Tanganatango + 1
Tangeni + 47
Tangenindje + 1
Tangeyambeko + 1
Tangi + 11
Tango + 1
Tapopi + 1
Tataati + 1
Tate + 5
Tatekulu + 1
Taukondjele + 1
Tautungu + 1
Tegameno + 1
Tegelela + 5
Tetekela + 1
Tetonga + 1
Thiginina + 1
Thikama + 1
Thikameni + 9
Thikaneni + 1
Tileni + 1
Tiloveta + 1
Tohafeni + 1
Tonata 2 + 8
Tonateni 1 + 5
Tongeni + 1
Tsenaye + 1
Tseniongolo + 1
Tshavuka + 1
Tshigwedha + 1
Tshitshuweni + 1
Tshivute + 1
Tuajambekua + 1
Tualikokule + 1
Tuamanguluka + 1
Tuamoneni + 1
Tuaningilua + 1
Tudheni + 2

Tuegathetua + 2
Tuegathetwa + 1
Tuejapewa + 1
Tuenikumue + 1
Tueshiningilua + 1
Tueusika + 1
Tuhafeni 2 + 9
Tuhaleni + 1
Tuiindileni + 1
Tujenjondapo + 1
Tujoleni + 1
Tukaleningwa + 1
Tukondjeni + 2
Tukondjenimeitaalo + 1
Tulimekondjo + 4
Tulimeutholjondjaji + 1
Tulimevitjetu + 1
Tulinane + 1
Tulipohamba + 1
Tulipomwene + 1
Tulonga + 2
Tumweneni + 1
Tuna + 2
Tunaemonathano + 1
Tunakuku + 1
Tunamukwathi + 1
Tunatate + 1
Tunejambeko + 1
Tunemanya + 1
Tunenyanyu + 1
Tuningeninawa + 1

Tunokwathi + 1
Tunomugatheni + 1
Tunomukuathi + 1
Tunyanyukweni + 1
Tutaleni + 6
Tutanateni 1
Tutegeni + 1
Tutolokeni + 1
Tuukeni + 1
Tuukenikumwe + 1
Tuutaleni + 9
Tuwilika + 2
Tuyekelago + 1
Tuyeni + 2
Tuyenikelago + 2
Tuyoleni + 7
Twakondjeni + 2
Twapewa + 1
Twegathetwa + 2
Tweshiihaluka + 1
Tweshiningilwa + 1
Tweshipanda + 1
Tweushiga 1
Tweuthigilwa + 1

Utengeni 1
Uugala + 1
Uuguanga + 3
Uugwanga + 7
Uujage + 1
Uujague + 1

Uujuni + 1
Uukaku + 1
Uulenga + 1
Uulumbu + 1
Uunguwanga + 1
Uunona + 2
Uupapa + 1
Uupindi + 4
Uushini + 1
Uushona + 15
Uusiga + 1
Uusija + 1
Uusiku 2 + 8
Uutapale + 1
Uutoni + 1
Uuyuni + 1

Vakengameka + 1
Vulikeni + 2

Watjapuwo + 1
Watutale + 1
Weshitile 1
Wulikeni 1
Wulikuni + 1

Yaaligatala + 1
Yalukeni + 1
Yambukeni + 1

Zimbulukueni + 2
Zimina + 1
Zimolimue + 1

INDEX OF NAMES

This list contains names of people, places, institutions, ethnic groups and languages that appear in this study. The most common names, such as *Africa*, *Europe* and *Ambo/Ovambo/Owambo/Oshiwambo*, were not included in this index. The names appearing in the name data of this study, as well as their possible origins, which are all given in chapter "Analysis of the Name Data", were not included in this list either.